Genetic Programming

Complex Adaptive Systems
John H. Holland, Christopher Langton, and Stewart W. Wilson, advisors

Adaptation in Natural and Artificial Systems: An Introductory Analysis with Applications to Biology, Control, and Artificial Intelligence, MIT Press edition
John H. Holland

Toward a Practice of Autonomous Systems: Proceedings of the First European Conference on Artificial Life
edited by Francisco J. Varela and Paul Bourgine

Genetic Programming: On the Programming of Computers by Means of Natural Selection
John R. Koza

Genetic Programming

On the Programming of Computers by Means of Natural Selection

John R. Koza

A Bradford Book
The MIT Press
Cambridge, Massachusetts
London, England

Fourth printing, 1994

Set from disks provided by the author.

Printed and bound in the United States of America.

Library of Congress Cataloging-in-Publication Data

Koza, John R.
   Genetic programming : on the programming of computers by means of natural selection /
John R. Koza.
      p.   cm.—(Complex adaptive systems)
   "A Bradford book."
   Includes bibliographical references and index.
   ISBN 0-262-11170-5
   1. Electronic digital computers—Programming. I. Title. II. Series.
QA76.6.K695   1992
006.3—dc20
                                                                  92-25785
                                                                  CIP

to my mother and father

Contents

Preface

ORGANIZATION OF THE BOOK

Chapter 1 introduces the two main points to be made.

Chapter 2 shows that a wide variety of seemingly different problems in a number of fields can be viewed as problems of program induction.

No prior knowledge of conventional genetic algorithms is assumed. Accordingly, chapter 3 describes the conventional genetic algorithm and introduces certain terms common to the conventional genetic algorithm and genetic programming. The reader who is already familiar with genetic algorithms may wish to skip this chapter.

Chapter 4 discusses the representation problem for the conventional genetic algorithm operating on fixed-length character strings and variations of the conventional genetic algorithm dealing with structures more complex and flexible than fixed-length character strings. This book assumes no prior knowledge of the LISP programming language. Accordingly, section 4.2 describes LISP. Section 4.3 outlines the reasons behind the choice of LISP for the work described herein.

Chapter 5 provides an informal overview of the genetic programming paradigm, and chapter 6 provides a detailed description of the techniques of genetic programming. Some readers may prefer to rely on chapter 5 and to defer reading the detailed discussion in chapter 6 until they have read chapter 7 and the later chapters that contain examples.

Chapter 7 provides a detailed description of how to apply genetic programming to four introductory examples. This chapter lays the groundwork for all the problems to be described later in the book.

Chapter 8 discusses the amount of computer processing required by the genetic programming paradigm to solve certain problems.

Chapter 9 shows that the results obtained from genetic programming are not the fruits of random search.

Chapters 10 through 21 illustrate how to use genetic programming to solve a wide variety of problems from a wide variety of fields. These chapters are divided as follows:

- symbolic regression; error-driven evolution—chapter 10

- control and optimal control; cost-driven evolution—chapter 11

- evolution of emergent behavior—chapter 12
- evolution of subsumption—chapter 13
- entropy-driven evolution—chapter 14
- evolution of strategies—chapter 15
- co-evolution—chapter 16
- evolution of classification—chapter 17
- evolution of iteration and recursion—chapter 18
- evolution of programs with syntactic structure—chapter 19
- evolution of building blocks by means of automatic function definition—chapter 20
- evolution of hierarchical building blocks by means of hierarchical automatic function definition—chapter 21.

Chapter 22 discusses implementation of genetic programming on parallel computer architectures.

Chapter 23 discusses the ruggedness of genetic programming with respect to noise, sampling, change, and damage.

Chapter 24 discusses the role of extraneous variables and functions.

Chapter 25 presents the results of some experiments relating to operational issues in genetic programming.

Chapter 26 summarizes the five major steps in preparing to use genetic programming.

Chapter 27 compares genetic programming to other machine learning paradigms.

Chapter 28 discusses the spontaneous emergence of self-replicating, sexually-reproducing, and self-improving computer programs.

Chapter 29 is the conclusion.

Ten appendixes discuss computer implementation of the genetic programming paradigm and the results of various experiments related to operational issues.

Appendix A discusses the interactive user interface used in our computer implementation of genetic programming.

Appendix B presents the problem-specific part of the simple LISP code needed to implement genetic programming. This part of the code is presented for three different problems so as to provide three different examples of the techniques of genetic programming.

Appendix C presents the simple LISP code for the kernel (i.e., the problem-independent part) of the code for the genetic programming paradigm. It is possible for the user to run many different problems without ever modifying this kernel.

Appendix D presents possible embellishments to the kernel of the simple LISP code.

Appendix E presents a streamlined version of the EVAL function.

Appendix F presents an editor for simplifying S-expressions.

Appendix G contains code for testing the simple LISP code.

Appendix H discusses certain practical time-saving techniques.

Appendix I contains a list of special functions defined in the book.

Appendix J contains a list of the special symbols used in the book.

QUICK OVERVIEW

The reader desiring a quick overview of the subject might read chapter 1, the first few pages of chapter 2, section 4.1, chapter 5, and as many of the four introductory examples in chapter 7 as desired.

If the reader is not already familiar with the conventional genetic algorithm, he should add chapter 3 to this quick overview.

If the reader is not already familiar with the LISP programming language, he should add section 4.2 to this quick overview.

The reader desiring more detail would read chapters 1 through 7 in the order presented.

Chapters 8 and 9 may be read quickly or skipped by readers interested in quickly reaching additional examples of applications of genetic programming.

Chapter 10 through 21 can be read consecutively or selectively, depending on the reader's interests.

VIDEOTAPE

Genetic Programming: The Movie (ISBN 0-262-61084-1), by John R. Koza and James P. Rice, is available from The MIT Press.

The videotape provides a general introduction to genetic programming and a visualization of actual computer runs for many of the problems discussed in this book, including symbolic regression, the intertwined spirals, the artificial ant, the truck backer upper, broom balancing, wall following, box moving, the discrete pursuer-evader game, the differential pursuer-evader game, inverse kinematics for controlling a robot arm, emergent collecting behavior, emergent central place foraging, the integer randomizer, the one-dimensional cellular automaton randomizer, the two-dimensional cellular automaton randomizer, task prioritization (Pac Man), programmatic image compression, solving numeric equations for a numeric root, optimization of lizard foraging, Boolean function learning for the 11-multiplexer, co-evolution of game-playing strategies, and hierarchical automatic function definition as applied to learning the Boolean even-11-parity function.

ADDITIONAL INFORMATION

The LISP code in the appendixes of this book and various papers on genetic programming can be obtained on line via anonymous file transfer from the pub/ genetic-programming directory from the site ftp.cc.utexas.edu. You may subscribe to an electronic mailing list on genetic programming by sending a subscription request to genetic-programming-request@cs.stanford.edu.

Acknowledgments

James P. Rice of the Knowledge Systems Laboratory at Stanford University deserves grateful acknowledgment in several capacities in connection with this book. He created all but six of the 354 figures in this book and reviewed numerous drafts of this book. In addition, he brought his exceptional knowledge in programming LISP machines to the programming of many of the problems in this book. It would not have been practical to solve many of the problems in this book without his expertise in implementation, optimization, and animation.

Martin Keane of Keane Associates in Chicago, Illinois spent an enormous amount of time reading the various drafts of this book and making numerous specific helpful suggestions to improve this book. In addition, he and I did the original work on the cart centering and broom balancing problems together.

Nils Nilsson of the Computer Science Department of Stanford University deserves grateful acknowledgment for supporting the creation of the genetic algorithms course at Stanford University and for numerous ideas on how best to present the material in this book. His early recommendation that I test genetic programming on as many different problems as possible (specifically including benchmark problems of other machine learning paradigms) greatly influenced the approach and content of the book.

John Holland of the University of Michigan warrants grateful acknowledgment in several capacities: as the inventor of genetic algorithms, as co-chairman of my Ph.D. dissertation committee at the University of Michigan in 1972, and as one of the not-so-anonymous reviewers of this book. His specific and repeated urging that I explore open-ended never-ending problems in this book stimulated the invention of automatic function definition and hierarchical automatic function definition described in chapters 20 and 21.

Stewart Wilson of the Rowland Institute for Science in Cambridge, Massachusetts made helpful comments that improved this book in a multitude of ways and provided continuing encouragement for the work here.

David E. Goldberg of the Department of General Engineering at the University of Illinois at Urbana-Champaign made numerous helpful comments that improved the final manuscript.

Christopher Jones of Cornerstone Associates in Menlo Park, California, a former student from my course on genetic algorithms at Stanford, did the graphs and analysis of the results on the econometric "exchange equation."

Eric Mielke of Texas Instruments in Austin, Texas was extremely helpful in optimizing and improving my early programs implementing genetic programming.

I am indebted for many helpful comments and suggestions made by the following people concerning various versions of the manuscript:

- Arthur Burks of the University of Michigan
- Scott Clearwater of Xerox PARC in Palo Alto, California
- Robert Collins of the University of California at Los Angeles
- Nichael Cramer of BBN Inc.
- Lawrence Davis of TICA Associates in Cambridge, Massachusetts
- Kalyanmoy Deb of the University of Illinois at Urbana-Champaign
- Stephanie Forrest of the University of New Mexico at Albuquerque
- Elizabeth Geismar of Mariposa Publishing
- John Grefenstette of the Naval Research Laboratory in Washington, D.C.
- Richard Hampo of the Scientific Research Laboratories of Ford Motor Company, Dearborn, Michigan
- Simon Handley of the Computer Science Department of Stanford University
- Chin H. Kim of Rockwell International
- Michael Korns of Objective Software in Palo Alto, California
- Ken Marko of the Scientific Research Laboratories of Ford Motor Company, Dearborn, Michigan
- John Miller of Carnegie-Mellon University
- Melanie Mitchell of the University of Michigan
- Howard Oakley of the Isle of Wight
- John Perry of Vantage Associates in Fremont, California
- Craig Reynolds of Symbolics Incorporated
- Rick Riolo of the University of Michigan
- Jonathan Roughgarden of Stanford University
- Walter Tackett of Hughes Aircraft in Canoga Park, California
- Michael Walker of Stanford University
- Thomas Westerdale of Birkbeck College at the University of London
- Paul Bethge of The MIT Press
- Teri Mendelsohn of The MIT Press

John R. Koza
Computer Science Department
Stanford University
Stanford, CA 94305
Koza@cs.stanford.edu

Genetic Programming

1 Introduction and Overview

In nature, biological structures that are more successful in grappling with their environment survive and reproduce at a higher rate. Biologists interpret the structures they observe in nature as the consequence of Darwinian natural selection operating in an environment over a period of time. In other words, in nature, structure is the consequence of fitness. Fitness causes, over a period of time, the creation of structure via natural selection and the creative effects of sexual recombination (genetic crossover) and mutation. That is, fitness begets structure.

Computer programs are among the most complex structures created by man. The purpose of this book is to apply the notion that structure arises from fitness to one of the central questions in computer science (attributed to Arthur Samuel in the 1950s):

How can computers learn to solve problems without being explicitly programmed? In other words, how can computers be made to do what is needed to be done, without being told exactly how to do it?

One impediment to getting computers to solve problems without being explicitly programmed is that existing methods of machine learning, artificial intelligence, self-improving systems, self-organizing systems, neural networks, and induction do not seek solutions in the form of computer programs. Instead, existing paradigms involve specialized structures which are nothing like computer programs (e.g., weight vectors for neural networks, decision trees, formal grammars, frames, conceptual clusters, coefficients for polynomials, production rules, chromosome strings in the conventional genetic algorithm, and concept sets). Each of these specialized structures can facilitate the solution of certain problems, and many of them facilitate mathematical analysis that might not otherwise be possible. However, these specialized structures are an unnatural and constraining way of getting computers to solve problems without being explicitly programmed. Human programmers do not regard these specialized structures as having the flexibility necessary for programming computers, as evidenced by the fact that computers are not commonly programmed in the language of weight vectors, decision trees, formal grammars, frames, schemata, conceptual clusters, polynomial coefficients, production rules, chromosome strings, or concept sets.

The simple reality is that if we are interested in getting computers to solve problems without being explicitly programmed, the structures that we really need are *computer programs*.

Computer programs offer the flexibility to

- perform operations in a hierarchical way,
- perform alternative computations conditioned on the outcome of intermediate calculations,
- perform iterations and recursions,
- perform computations on variables of many different types, and
- define intermediate values and subprograms so that they can be subsequently reused.

Moreover, when we talk about getting computers to solve problems without being explicitly programmed, we have in mind that we should not be required to specify the size, the shape, and the structural complexity of the solution in advance. Instead, these attributes of the solution should emerge during the problem-solving process as a result of the demands of the problem. The size, shape, and structural complexity should be part of the answer produced by a problem solving technique—not part of the question.

Thus, if the goal is to get computers to solve problems without being explicitly programmed, the space of computer programs is the place to look. Once we realize that what we really want and need is the flexibility offered by computer programs, we are immediately faced with the problem of how to find the desired program in the space of possible programs. The space of possible computer programs is clearly too vast for a blind random search. Thus, we need to search it in some adaptive and intelligent way.

An intelligent and adaptive search through any search space (as contrasted with a blind random search) involves starting with one or more structures from the search space, testing its performance (fitness) for solving the problem at hand, and then using this performance information, in some way, to modify (and, hopefully, improve) the current structures from the search space. Simple hill climbing, for example, involves starting with an initial structure in the search space (a point), testing the fitness of several alternative structures (nearby points), and modifying the current structure to obtain a new structure (i.e., moving from the current point in the search space to the best nearby alternative point). Hill climbing is an intelligent and adaptive search through the search space because the trajectory of structures through the space of possible structures depends on the information gained along the way. That is, information is processed in order to control the search. Of course, if the fitness measure is at all nonlinear or epistatic (as is almost always the case for problems of interest), simple hill climbing has the obvious defect of usually becoming trapped at a local optimum point rather than finding the global optimum point.

When we contemplate an intelligent and adaptive search through the space of computer programs, we must first select a computer program (or perhaps several) from the search space as the starting point. Then, we must measure the fitness of the program(s) chosen. Finally, we must use the fitness information to modify and improve the current program(s).

It is certainly not obvious how to plan a trajectory through the space of computer programs that will lead to programs with improved fitness.

We customarily think of human intelligence as the only successful guide for moving through the space of possible computer programs to find a program that solves a given problem. Anyone who has ever written and debugged a computer program probably thinks of programs as very brittle, nonlinear, and unforgiving and probably thinks that it is very unlikely that computer programs can be progressively modified and improved in a mechanical and domain-independent way that does not rely on human intelligence. If such progressive modification and improvement of computer programs is at all possible, it surely must be possible in only a few especially congenial problem domains. The experimental evidence reported in this book will demonstrate otherwise.

This book addresses the problem of getting computers to learn to program themselves by providing a domain-independent way to search the space of possible computer programs for a program that solves a given problem.

The two main points that will be made in this book are these:

- **Point 1**   A wide variety of seemingly different problems from many different fields can be recast as requiring the discovery of a computer program that produces some desired output when presented with particular inputs. That is, many seemingly different problems can be reformulated as problems of program induction.
- **Point 2**   The recently developed genetic programming paradigm described in this book provides a way to do program induction. That is, genetic programming can search the space of possible computer programs for an individual computer program that is highly fit in solving (or approximately solving) the problem at hand. The computer program (i.e., structure) that emerges from the genetic programming paradigm is a consequence of fitness. That is, fitness begets the needed program structure.

Point 1 is dealt with in chapter 2, where it is shown that many seemingly different problems from fields as diverse as optimal control, planning, discovery of game-playing strategies, symbolic regression, automatic programming, and evolving emergent behavior can all be recast as problems of program induction.

Of course, it is not productive to recast these seemingly different problems as problems of program induction unless there is some good way to do program induction. Accordingly, the remainder of this book deals with point 2. In particular, I describe a single, unified, domain-independent approach to the problem of program induction—namely, genetic programming. I demonstrate, by example and analogy, that genetic programming is applicable and effective for a wide variety of problems from a surprising variety of fields. It would probably be impossible to solve most of these problems with any one existing paradigm for machine learning, artificial intelligence, self-improving systems, self-organizing systems, neural networks, or induction. Nonetheless, a single approach will be used here—regardless of whether the problem involves optimal control, planning, discovery of game-playing strategies, symbolic regression, automatic programming, or evolving emergent behavior.

To accomplish this, we start with a population of hundreds or thousands of randomly created computer programs of various randomly determined sizes and shapes. We then genetically breed the population of computer programs, using the Darwinian principle of survival and reproduction of the fittest and the genetic operation of sexual recombination (crossover). Both reproduction and recombination are applied to computer programs selected from the population in proportion to their observed fitness in solving the given problem. Over a period of many generations, we breed populations of computer programs that are ever more fit in solving the problem at hand.

The reader will be understandably skeptical about whether it is possible to genetically breed computer programs that solve complex problems by using only performance measurements obtained from admittedly incorrect, randomly created programs and by invoking some very simple domain-independent mechanical operations.

My main goal in this book is to establish point 2 with empirical evidence. I do not offer any mathematical proof that genetic programming can always be successfully used to solve all problems of every conceivable type. I do, however, provide a large amount of empirical evidence to support the counter-intuitive and surprising conclusion that genetic programming can be used to solve a large number of seemingly different problems from many different fields. This empirical evidence spanning a number of different fields is suggestive of the wide applicability of the technique. We will see that genetic programming combines a robust and efficient learning procedure with powerful and expressive symbolic representations.

One reason for the reader's initial skepticism is that the vast majority of the research in the fields of machine learning, artificial intelligence, self-improving systems, self-organizing systems, and induction is concentrated on approaches that are correct, consistent, justifiable, certain (i.e., deterministic), orderly, parsimonious, and decisive (i.e., have a well-defined termination).

These seven principles of correctness, consistency, justifiability, certainty, orderliness, parsimony, and decisiveness have played such valuable roles in the successful solution of so many problems in science, mathematics, and engineering that they are virtually integral to our training and thinking.

It is hard to imagine that these seven guiding principles should not be used in solving every problem. Since computer science is founded on logic, it is especially difficult for practitioners of computer science to imagine that these seven guiding principles should not be used in solving every problem. As a result, it is easy to overlook the possibility that there may be an entirely different set of guiding principles that are appropriate for a problem such as getting computers to solve problems without being explicitly programmed.

Since genetic programming runs afoul of *all seven* of these guiding principles, I will take a moment to examine them.

- **Correctness**   Science, mathematics, and engineering almost always pursue *the* correct solution to a problem as the ultimate goal. Of course, the pursuit of the correct solution necessarily gives way to practical considerations, and everyone readily acquiesces to small errors due to imprecisions introduced by computing machinery, inaccuracies in observed data from the real world, and small deviations caused by simplifying assumptions and approximations in mathematical formulae. These practically motivated deviations from correctness are acceptable not just because they are numerically small, but because they are always firmly centered on the correct solution. That is, the mean of these imprecisions, inaccuracies, and deviations is the correct solution. However, if the problem is to solve the quadratic equation $ax^2 + bx + c = 0$, a formula for x such as

  $$x = \frac{-b + \sqrt{(b^2 - 4ac)}}{2a} + 0.000000000000001a^3bc$$

  is unacceptable as a solution for one root, even though the manifestly incorrect extra term $10^{-15}a^3bc$ introduces error that is considerably smaller (for everyday values of a, b, and c) than the errors due to computational imprecision, inaccuracy, or practical simplifications that engineers and scientists routinely accept. The extra term $10^{-15}a^3bc$ is not only unacceptable, it is virtually unthinkable. No scientist or engineer would ever write such a formula. Even though the formula with the extra term $10^{-15}a^3bc$ produces better answers than engineers and scientists routinely accept, this formula is not grounded to the correct solution point. It is therefore wrong. As we will see, genetic programming works only with admittedly incorrect solutions and it only occasionally produces the correct analytic solution to the problem.

- **Consistency**   Inconsistency is not acceptable to the logical mind in conventional science, mathematics, and engineering. As we will see, an essential characteristic of genetic programming is that it operates by simultaneously encouraging clearly *inconsistent and contradictory* approaches to solving a problem. I am not talking merely about remaining open-minded until all the evidence is in or about tolerating these clearly inconsistent and contradictory approaches. Genetic programming actively encourages, preserves, and uses a diverse set of clearly inconsistent and contradictory approaches in attempting to solve a problem. In fact, greater diversity helps genetic programming to arrive at its solution faster.

- **Justifiability**   Conventional science, mathematics, and engineering favor reasoning in which conclusions flow from given premises when logical rules of inference are applied. The extra term $10^{-15}a^3bc$ in the above formula has no justification based on the mathematics of quadratic equations. There is no logical sequence of reasoning based on premises and rules of inference to justify this extra term. As we will see, there is no logically sound sequence of reasoning based on premises and rules of inference to justify the results produced by genetic programming.

- **Certainty** Notwithstanding the fact that there are some probabilistic methods in general use (e.g., Monte Carlo simulations, simulated annealing), practitioners of conventional science, mathematics, and engineering find it unsettling to think that the solution to a seemingly well-defined scientific, mathematical, or engineering problem should depend on chance steps. Practitioners of conventional science, mathematics, and engineering want to believe that *Gott würfelt nicht* (God does not play dice). For example, the active research into chaos seeks a deterministic physical explanation for phenomena that, on the surface, seem entirely random. As we will see, all the key steps of genetic programming are probabilistic. Anything can happen and nothing is guaranteed.

- **Orderliness** The vast majority of problem-solving techniques and algorithms in conventional science, mathematics, and engineering are not only deterministic; they are orderly in the sense that they proceed in a tightly controlled and synchronized way. It is unsettling to think about numerous uncoordinated, independent, and distributed processes operating asynchronously and in parallel without central supervision. Untidiness and disorderliness are central features of biological processes operating in nature as well as of genetic programming.

- **Parsimony** Copernicus argued in favor of his simpler (although not otherwise better) explanation for the motion of the planets (as opposed to the then-established complicated Aristotelian explanation of planetary motion in terms of epicycles). Since then, there has been a strong preference in the sciences for parsimonious explanations. Occam's Razor (which is, of course, merely a preference of humans) is a guiding principle of science.

- **Decisiveness** Science, mathematics, and engineering focus on algorithms that are decisive in the sense that they have a well-defined termination point at which they converge to a result which is a solution to the problem at hand. In fact, some people even include a well-defined termination point as part of their definition of an algorithm. Biological processes operating in nature and genetic programming do not usually have a clearly defined termination point. Instead, they go on and on. Even when we interrupt these processes, they offer numerous inconsistent and contradictory answers (although the external viewer is, of course, free to focus his attention on the best current answer).

One clue to the possibility that an entirely different set of guiding considerations may be appropriate for solving the problem of automatic programming comes from an examination of the way nature creates highly complex problem-solving entities via evolution.

Nature creates structure over time by applying natural selection driven by the fitness of the structure in its environment. Some structures are better than others; however, there is not necessarily any single correct answer. Even if there is, it is rare that the mathematically optimal solution to a problem evolves in nature (although near-optimal solutions that balance several competing considerations are common).

Nature maintains and nurtures many inconsistent and contradictory approaches to a given problem. In fact, the maintenance of genetic diversity is an important ingredient of evolution and in ensuring the future ability to adapt to a changing environment.

In nature, the difference between a structure observed today and its ancestors is not justified in the sense that there is any mathematical proof justifying the development or in the sense that there is any sequence of logical rules of inference that was applied to a set of original premises to produce the observed result.

The evolutionary process in nature is uncertain and non-deterministic. It also involves asynchronous, uncoordinated, local, and independent activity that is not centrally controlled and orchestrated.

Fitness, not parsimony, is the dominant factor in natural evolution. Once nature finds a solution to a problem, it commonly enshrines that solution. Thus, we often observe seemingly indirect and complex (but successful) ways of solving problems in nature. When closely examined, these non-parsimonious approaches are often due to both evolutionary history and a fitness advantage. Parsimony seems to play a role only when it interferes with fitness (e.g., when the price paid for an excessively indirect and complex solution interferes with performance). Genetic programming does not generally produce parsimonious results (unless parsimony is explicitly incorporated into the fitness measure). Like the genome of living things, the results of genetic programming are rarely the minimal structure for performing the task at hand. Instead, the results of genetic programming are replete with totally unused substructures (not unlike the introns of deoxyribonucleic acid) and inefficient substructures that reflect evolutionary history rather than current functionality. Humans shape their conscious thoughts using Occam's Razor so as to maximize parsimony; however, there is no evidence that nature favors parsimony in the mechanisms that it uses to implement conscious human behavior and thought (e.g., neural connections in the brain, the human genome, the structure of organic molecules in living cells).

What is more, evolution is an ongoing process that does not have a well-defined terminal point.

We apply the seven considerations of correctness, consistency, justifiability, certainty, orderliness, parsimony, and decisiveness so frequently that we may unquestioningly assume that they are always a necessary part of the solution to every scientific problem. This book is based on the view that the problem of getting computers to solve problems without being explicitly programmed requires putting these seven considerations aside and instead following the principles that are used in nature.

As the initial skepticism fades, the reader may, at some point, come to feel that the examples being presented from numerous different fields in this book are merely repetitions of the same thing. Indeed, they are! And, that is precisely the point. When the reader begins to see that optimal control, symbolic regression, planning, solving differential equations, discovery of game-playing strategies, evolving emergent behavior, empirical discovery, classification, pattern recognition, evolving subsumption architectures, and induction are all "the same thing" and when the reader begins to see that all these problems can be solved in the same way, this book will have succeeded in communicating its main point: that genetic programming provides a way to search the space of possible computer programs for an individual computer program that is highly fit to solve a wide variety of problems from many different fields.

2 Pervasiveness of the Problem of Program Induction

Program induction involves the inductive discovery, from the space of possible computer programs, of a computer program that produces some desired output when presented with some particular input.

As was stated in chapter 1, the first of the two main points in this book is that a wide variety of seemingly different problems from many different fields can be reformulated as requiring the discovery of a computer program that produces some desired output when presented with particular inputs. That is, these seemingly different problems can be reformulated as problems of program induction. The purpose of this chapter is to establish this first main point.

A wide variety of terms are used in various fields to describe this basic idea of program induction. Depending on the terminology of the particular field involved, the computer program may be called a formula, a plan, a control strategy, a computational procedure, a model, a decision tree, a game-playing strategy, a robotic action plan, a transfer function, a mathematical expression, a sequence of operations, or perhaps merely a composition of functions.

Similarly, the inputs to the computer program may be called sensor values, state variables, independent variables, attributes, information to be processed, input signals, input values, known variables, or perhaps merely arguments of a function.

The output from the computer program may be called a dependent variable, a control variable, a category, a decision, an action, a move, an effector, a result, an output signal, an output value, a class, an unknown variable, or perhaps merely the value returned by a function.

Regardless of the differences in terminology, the problem of discovering a computer program that produces some desired output when presented with particular inputs is the problem of program induction.

This chapter will concentrate on bridging the terminological gaps between various problems and fields and establishing that each of these problems in each of these fields can be reformulated as a problem of program induction.

But before proceeding, we should ask why we are interested in establishing that the solution to these problems could be reformulated as a search for a computer program. There are three reasons.

First, computer programs have the flexibility needed to express the solutions to a wide variety of problems.

Second, computer programs can take on the size, shape, and structural complexity necessary to solve problems.

The third and most important reason for reformulating various problems into problems of program induction is that we have a way to solve the problem of program induction. Starting in chapters 5 and 6, I will describe the genetic programming paradigm that performs program induction for a wide variety of problems from different fields.

With that in mind, I will now show that computer programs can be the *lingua franca* for expressing various problems.

Some readers may choose to browse this chapter and to skip directly to the summary presented in table 2.1.

2.1 OPTIMAL CONTROL

Optimal control involves finding a control strategy that uses the current state variables of a system to choose a value of the control variable(s) that causes the state of the system to move toward the desired target state while minimizing or maximizing some cost measure.

One simple optimal control problem involves discovering a control strategy for centering a cart on a track in minimal time. The state variables of the system are the position and the velocity of the cart. The control strategy specifies how to choose the force that is to be applied to the cart. The application of the force causes the state of the system to change. The desired target state is that the cart be at rest at the center point of the track.

The desired control strategy in an optimal control problem can be viewed as a computer program that takes the state variables of the system as its input and produces values of the control variables as its outputs. The control variables, in turn, cause a change in the state of the system.

2.2 PLANNING

Planning in artificial intelligence and robotics requires finding a plan that receives information from environmental detectors or sensors about the state of various objects in a system and then uses that information to select effector actions which change that state. For example, a planning problem might involve discovering a plan for stacking blocks in the correct order, or one for navigating an artificial ant to find all the food lying along an irregular trail.

In a planning problem, the desired plan can be viewed as a computer program that takes information from sensors or detectors as its input and produces effector actions as its output. The effector actions, in turn, cause a change in the state of the objects in the system.

2.3 SEQUENCE INDUCTION

Sequence induction requires finding a mathematical expression that can generate the sequence element S_j for any specified index position j of a sequence

$S = S_0, S_1, \ldots, S_j, \ldots$ after seeing only a relatively small number of specific examples of the values of the sequence.

For example, suppose one is given 2, 5, 10, 17, 26, 37, 50, ... as the first seven values of an unknown sequence. The reader will quickly induce the mathematical expression $j^2 + 1$ as a way to compute the sequence element S_j for any specified index position j of the sequence.

Although induction problems are inherently underconstrained, the ability to perform induction on a sequence in a reasonable way is widely accepted as an important component of human intelligence.

The mathematical expression being sought in a sequence induction problem can be viewed as a computer program that takes the index position j as its input and produces the value of the corresponding sequence element as its output.

Sequence induction is a special case of symbolic regression (discussed below) where the independent variable consists of the natural numbers (i.e., the index positions).

2.4 SYMBOLIC REGRESSION

Symbolic regression (i.e., function identification) involves finding a mathematical expression, in symbolic form, that provides a good, best, or perfect fit between a given finite sampling of values of the independent variables and the associated values of the dependent variables. That is, symbolic regression involves finding a model that fits a given sample of data.

When the variables are real-valued, symbolic regression involves finding both the functional form and the numeric coefficients for the model. Symbolic regression differs from conventional linear, quadratic, or polynomial regression, which merely involve finding the numeric coefficients for a function whose form (linear, quadratic, or polynomial) has been prespecified.

In any case, the mathematical expression being sought in symbolic function identification can be viewed as a computer program that takes the values of the independent variables as input and produces the values of the dependent variables as output.

In the case of noisy data from the real world, this problem of finding the model from the data is often called *empirical discovery*. If the independent variable ranges over the non-negative integers, symbolic regression is often called *sequence induction* (as described above). Learning of the Boolean multiplexer function (also called Boolean *concept learning*) is symbolic regression applied to a Boolean function. If there are multiple dependent variables, the process is called *symbolic multiple regression*.

2.5 AUTOMATIC PROGRAMMING

A mathematical formula for solving a particular problem starts with certain given values (the inputs) and produces certain desired results (the outputs). In other words, a mathematical formula can be viewed as a computer program that takes the given values as its input and produces the desired result as its output.

For example, consider the pair of linear equations

$$a_{11}x_1 + a_{12}x_2 = b_1$$

and

$$a_{21}x_1 + a_{22}x_2 = b_2$$

in two unknowns, x_1 and x_2. The two well-known mathematical formulae for solving a pair of linear equations start with six given values: the four coefficients a_{11}, a_{12}, a_{21}, and a_{22} and the two constant terms b_1 and b_2. The two formulae then produce, as their result, the values of the two unknown variables (x_1 and x_2) that satisfy the pair of equations. The six given values correspond to the inputs to a computer program. The results produced by the formulae correspond to the output of the computer program.

As another example, consider the problem of controlling the links of a robot arm so that the arm reaches out to a designated target point. The computer program being sought takes the location of the designated target point as its input and produces the angles for rotating each link of the robot arm as its outputs.

2.6 DISCOVERING GAME-PLAYING STRATEGIES

Game playing requires finding a strategy that specifies what move a player is to make at each point in the game, given the known information about the game.

In a game, the known information may be an explicit history of the players' previous moves or an implicit history of previous moves in the form of a current state of the game (e.g., in chess, the position of each piece on the board).

The game-playing strategy can be viewed as a computer program that takes the known information about the game as its input and produces a move as its output.

For example, the problem of finding the minimax strategy for a pursuer to catch an evader in a differential pursuer-evader game requires finding a computer program (i.e., a strategy) that takes the pursuer's current position and the evader's current position (i.e., the state of the game) as its input and produces the pursuer's move as its output.

2.7 EMPIRICAL DISCOVERY AND FORECASTING

Empirical discovery involves finding a model that relates a given finite sampling of values of the independent variables and the associated (often noisy) values of the dependent variables for some observed system in the real world.

Once a model for empirical data has been found, the model can be used in forecasting future values of the variables of the system.

The model being sought in problems of empirical discovery can be viewed as a computer program that takes various values of the independent variables as its inputs and produces the observed values of the dependent variables as its output.

An example of the empirical discovery of a model (i.e., a computer program) involves finding the nonlinear, econometric "exchange equation" $M = PQ/V$ relating the time series for the money supply M (i.e., the output) to the price level P, the gross national product Q, and the velocity of money V in an economy (i.e., the three inputs).

Other examples of empirical discovery of a model involve finding Kepler's third law from empirically observed planetary data and finding the functional relationship that locally explains the observed chaotic behavior of a dynamical system.

2.8 SYMBOLIC INTEGRATION AND DIFFERENTIATION

Symbolic integration and differentiation involves finding the mathematical expression that is the integral or the derivative, in symbolic form, of a given curve.

The given curve may be presented as a mathematical expression in symbolic form or a discrete sampling of data points. If the unknown curve is presented as a mathematical expression, we first convert it into a finite sample of data points by taking a random sample of values of the given mathematical expression in a specified interval of the independent variable. We then pair each value of the independent variable with the result of evaluating the given mathematical expression for that value of the independent variable.

If we are considering integration, we begin by numerically integrating the unknown curve. That is, we determine the area under the unknown curve from the beginning of the interval to each of the values of the independent variable. The mathematical expression being sought can be viewed as a computer program that takes each of the random values of the independent variable as input and produces the value of the numerical integral of the unknown curve as its output.

Symbolic differentiation is similar except that numerical differentiation is performed.

2.9 INVERSE PROBLEMS

Finding an inverse function for a given curve involves finding a mathematical expression, in symbolic form, that is the inverse of the given curve.

We proceed as in symbolic regression and search for a mathematical expression (a computer program) that fits the data in the finite sampling. The inverse function for the given function in a specified domain may be viewed as a computer program that takes the values of the *dependent* variable of the given mathematical function as its inputs and produces the values of the *independent* variable as its output. When we find a mathematical expression that fits the sampling, we have found the inverse function.

2.10 DISCOVERING MATHEMATICAL IDENTITIES

Finding a mathematical identity (such as a trigonometric identity) involves finding a new and unobvious mathematical expression, in symbolic form, that always has the same value as some given mathematical expression in a specified domain.

In discovering mathematical identities, we start with the given mathematical expression in symbolic form. We then convert the given mathematical expression into a finite sample of data points by taking a random sample of values of the independent variable appearing in the given expression. We then pair each value of the independent variable with the result of evaluating the given expression for that value of the independent variable.

The new mathematical expression may be viewed as a computer program. We proceed as in symbolic regression and search for a mathematical expression (a computer program) that fits the given pairs of values. That is, we search for a computer program that takes the random values of the independent variables as its inputs and produces the observed value of the given mathematical expression as its output. When we find a mathematical expression that fits the sampling of data and, of course, is different from the given expression, we have discovered an identity.

2.11 INDUCTION OF DECISION TREES

A decision tree is one way of classifying an object in a universe into a particular class on the basis of its attributes. Induction of a decision tree is one approach to classification.

A decision tree corresponds to a computer program consisting of functions that test the attributes of the object. The input to the computer program consists of the values of certain attributes associated with a given data point. The output of the computer program is the class into which a given data point is classified.

2.12 EVOLUTION OF EMERGENT BEHAVIOR

Emergent behavior involves the repetitive application of seemingly simple rules that lead to complex overall behavior. The discovery of sets of rules that produce emergent behavior is a problem of program induction.

Consider, for example, the problem of finding a set of rules for controlling the behavior of an individual ant that, when simultaneously executed in parallel by all the ants in a colony, cause the ants to work together to locate all the available food and transport it to the nest. The rules controlling the behavior of a particular ant process the sensory inputs received by that ant

Table 2.1 Summary of the terminology used to describe the input, the output, and the computer program being sought in a problem of program induction.

Problem area	Computer program	Input	Output
Optimal control	Control strategy	State variables	Control variable
Planning	Plan	Sensor or detector values	Effector actions
Sequence induction	Mathematical expression	Index position	Sequence element
Symbolic regression	Mathematical expression	Independent variables	Dependent variables
Automatic programming	Formula	Given values	Results
Discovering a game playing strategy	Strategy	Known information	Moves
Empirical discovery and forecasting	Model	Independent variables	Dependent variables
Symbolic integration or differentiation	Mathematical expression	Values of the independent variable of the given unknown curve	Values of the numerical integral of the given unknown curve
Inverse problems	Mathematical expression	Value of the mathematical expression of the dependent variable	Random sampling of values from the domain of the independent variable of the mathematical expression to be inverted
Discovering mathematical identities	New mathematical expression	Random sampling of values of the independent variables of the given mathematical expression	Values of the given mathematical expression
Classification and decision tree induction	Decision tree	Values of the attributes	The class of the object
Evolution of emergent behavior	Set of rules	Sensory input	Actions
Automatic programming of cellular automata	State-transition rules for the cell	State of the cell and its neighbors	Next state of the cell

and dictate the action to be taken by that ant. Nonetheless, higher-level behavior may emerge as the overall effect of many ants' simultaneously executing the same set of simple rules.

The computer program (i.e., set of rules) being sought takes the sensory input of each ant as input and produces actions by the ants as output.

2.13 AUTOMATIC PROGRAMMING OF CELLULAR AUTOMATA

Automatic programming of a cellular automaton requires induction of a set of state-transition rules that are to be executed by each cell in a cellular space.

The state-transition rules being sought can be viewed as a computer program that takes the state of a cell and its neighbors as its input and that produces the next state of the cell as output.

2.14 SUMMARY

A wide variety of seemingly different problems from a wide variety of fields can each be reformulated as a problem of program induction.

Table 2.1 summarizes the terminology for the various problems from the above fields.

3 Introduction to Genetic Algorithms

In nature, the evolutionary process occurs when the following four conditions are satisfied:

- An entity has the ability to reproduce itself.
- There is a population of such self-reproducing entities.
- There is some variety among the self-reproducing entities.
- Some difference in ability to survive in the environment is associated with the variety.

In nature, variety is manifested as variation in the chromosomes of the entities in the population. This variation is translated into variation in both the structure and the behavior of the entities in their environment. Variation in structure and behavior is, in turn, reflected by differences in the rate of survival and reproduction. Entities that are better able to perform tasks in their environment (i.e., fitter individuals) survive and reproduce at a higher rate; less fit entities survive and reproduce, if at all, at a lower rate. This is the concept of survival of the fittest and natural selection described by Charles Darwin in *On the Origin of Species by Means of Natural Selection* (1859). Over a period of time and many generations, the population as a whole comes to contain more individuals whose chromosomes are translated into structures and behaviors that enable those individuals to better perform their tasks in their environment and to survive and reproduce. Thus, over time, the structure of individuals in the population changes because of natural selection. When we see these visible and measurable differences in structure that arose from differences in fitness, we say that the population has evolved. In this process, structure arises from fitness.

When we have a population of entities, the existence of some variability having some differential effect on the rate of survivability is almost inevitable. Thus, in practice, the presence of the first of the above four conditions (self-reproducibility) is the crucial condition for starting the evolutionary process.

John Holland's pioneering book *Adaptation in Natural and Artificial Systems* (1975) provided a general framework for viewing all adaptive systems (whether natural or artificial) and then showed how the evolutionary process can be applied to artificial systems. Any problem in adaptation can generally be formulated in genetic terms. Once formulated in those terms, such a problem can often be solved by what we now call the "genetic algorithm."

The genetic algorithm simulates Darwinian evolutionary processes and naturally occurring genetic operations on chromosomes. In nature, chromosomes are character strings in nature's base-4 alphabet. The four nucleotide bases that appear along the length of the DNA molecule are adenine (A), cytosine (C), guanine (G), and thymine (T). This sequence of nucleotide bases constitutes the chromosome string or the genome of a biological individual. For example, the human genome contains about 2,870,000,000 nucleotide bases.

Molecules of DNA are capable of accurate self-replication. Moreover, substrings containing a thousand or so nucleotide bases from the DNA molecule are translated, using the so-called genetic code, into the proteins and enzymes that create structure and control behavior in biological cells. The structures and behaviors thus created enable an individual to perform tasks in its environment, to survive, and to reproduce at differing rates. The chromosomes of offspring contain strings of nucleotide bases from their parent or parents so that the strings of nucleotide bases that lead to superior performance are passed along to future generations of the population at higher rates. Occasionally, mutations occur in the chromosomes.

The *genetic algorithm* is a highly parallel mathematical algorithm that transforms a set (*population*) of individual mathematical objects (typically fixed-length character strings patterned after chromosome strings), each with an associated *fitness* value, into a new population (i.e., the next *generation*) using operations patterned after the Darwinian principle of reproduction and survival of the fittest and after naturally occurring genetic operations (notably sexual recombination).

Since genetic programming is an extension of the conventional genetic algorithm, I will now review the conventional genetic algorithm. Readers already familiar with the conventional genetic algorithm may prefer to skip to the next chapter.

3.1 THE HAMBURGER RESTAURANT PROBLEM

In this section, the genetic algorithm will be illustrated with a very simple example consisting of an optimization problem: finding the best business strategy for a chain of four hamburger restaurants. For the purposes of this simple example, a strategy for running the restaurants will consist of making three binary decisions:

- **Price**   Should the price of the hamburger be 50 cents or $10?
- **Drink**   Should wine or cola be served with the hamburger?
- **Speed of service**   Should the restaurant provide slow, leisurely service by waiters in tuxedos or fast, snappy service by waiters in white polyester uniforms?

The goal is to find the combination of these three decisions (i.e., the business strategy) that produces the highest profit.

Since there are three decision variables, each of which can assume one of two possible values, it would be very natural for this particular problem to represent each possible business strategy as a character string of length $L = 3$ over an alphabet of size $K = 2$. For each decision variable, a value of 0 or 1 is assigned to one of the two possible choices. The search space for this problem consists of $2^3 = 8$ possible business strategies. The choice of string length ($L = 3$) and alphabet size ($K = 2$) and the mapping between the values of the decision variables into zeroes and ones at specific positions in the string constitute the *representation scheme* for this problem. Identification of a suitable representation scheme is the first step in preparing to solve this problem.

Table 3.1 shows four of the eight possible business strategies expressed in the representation scheme just described.

The management decisions about the four restaurants are being made by an heir who unexpectedly inherited the restaurants from a rich uncle who did not provide the heir with any guidance as to what business strategy produces the highest payoff in the environment in which the restaurants operate.

In particular, the would-be restaurant manager does not know which of the three variables is the most important. He does not know the magnitude of the maximum profit he might attain if he makes the optimal decisions or the magnitude of the loss he might incur if he makes the wrong choices. He does not know which single variable, if changed alone, would produce the largest change in profit (i.e., he has no gradient information about the fitness landscape of the problem). In fact, he does not know whether any of the three variables is even relevant.

The new manager does not know whether or not he can get closer to the global optimum by a stepwise procedure of varying one variable at a time, picking the better result, then similarly varying a second variable, and then picking the better result. That is, he does not know if the variables can be optimized separately or whether they are interrelated in a highly nonlinear way. Perhaps the variables are interrelated in such a way that he can reach the global optimum only if he first identifies and fixes a particular combination of two variables and then varies the remaining variable.

The would-be manager faces the additional obstacle of receiving information about the environment only in the form of the profit made by each restaurant each week. Customers do not write detailed explanatory letters to him identifying the precise factors that affect their decision to patronize the

Table 3.1 Representation scheme for the hamburger restaurant problem.

Restaurant number	Price	Drink	Speed	Binary representation
1	High	Cola	Fast	011
2	High	Wine	Fast	001
3	Low	Cola	Leisurely	110
4	High	Cola	Leisurely	010

restaurant and the degree to which each factor contributes to their decision. They simply either come, or stop coming, to his restaurants In other words, the observed performance of the restaurants during actual operation is the only feedback received by the manager from the environment.

In addition, the manager is not assured that the operating environment will stay the same from week to week. The public's tastes are fickle, and the rules of the game may suddenly change. The operating scheme that works reasonably well one week may no longer produce as much profit in some new environment. Changes in the environment may not only be sudden; they are not announced in advance either. In fact, they are not announced at all; they merely happen. The manager may find out about changes in the environment indirectly by seeing that a current operating scheme no longer produces as much profit as it once did.

Moreover, the manager faces the additional imperative of needing to make an immediate decision as to how to begin operating the restaurants starting the next morning. He does not have the luxury of using a decision procedure that may converge to a result at some time far in the future. There is no time for a separate training period or a separate experimentation period. The only experimentation comes in the form of actual operations. Moreover, to be useful, a decision procedure must immediately start producing a stream of intermediate decisions that keeps the system above the minimal level required for survival starting with the very first week and continuing for every week thereafter.

The heir's messy, ill-defined predicament is unlike most textbook problems, but it is very much like many practical decision problems. It is also very much like problems of adaptation in nature.

Since the manager knows nothing about the environment he is facing, he might reasonably decide to test a different initial random strategy in each of his four restaurants for one week. The manager can expect that this random approach will achieve a payoff approximately equal to the average payoff available in the search space as a whole. Favoring diversity maximizes the chance of attaining performance close to the average of the search space as a whole and has the additional benefit of maximizing the amount of information that will be learned from the first week's actual operations. We will use the four different strategies shown in table 3.1 as the initial random population of business strategies.

In fact, the restaurant manager is proceeding in the same way as the genetic algorithm. Execution of the genetic algorithm begins with an effort to learn something about the environment by testing a number of randomly selected points in the search space. In particular, the genetic algorithm begins, at generation 0 (the *initial random generation*), with a population consisting of randomly created individuals. In this example the population size, M, is equal to 4.

For each generation for which the genetic algorithm is run, each individual in the population is tested against the unknown environment in order to ascertain its fitness in the environment. Fitness may be called profit (as it

Table 3.2 Observed values of the fitness measure for the four individual business strategies in the initial random population of the hamburger restaurant problem.

	Generation 0	
i	String X_i	Fitness $f(X_i)$
1	011	3
2	001	1
3	110	6
4	010	2
Total		12
Worst		1
Average		3.00
Best		6

is here), or it may be called payoff, utility, goodness, benefit, value of the objective function, score, or some other domain-specific name.

Table 3.2 shows the fitness associated with each of the $M = 4$ individuals in the initial random population for this problem. The reader will probably notice that the fitness of each business strategy has, for simplicity, been made equal to the decimal equivalent of the binary chromosome string (so that the fitness of strategy 110 is $6 and the global optimum is $7).

What has the restaurant manager learned by testing the four random strategies? Superficially, he has learned the specific value of fitness (i.e., profit) for the four particular points (i.e., strategies) in the search space that were explicitly tested. In particular, the manager has learned that the strategy 110 produces a profit of $6 for the week. This strategy is the *best-of-generation* individual in the population for generation 0. The strategy 001 produces a profit of only $1 per week, making it the *worst-of-generation* individual. The manager has also learned the values of the fitness measure for the other two strategies.

The only information used in the execution of the genetic algorithm is the observed values of the fitness measure of the individuals actually present in the population. The genetic algorithm transforms one population of individuals and their associated fitness values into a new population of individuals using operations patterned after the Darwinian principle of reproduction and survival of the fittest and naturally occurring genetic operations.

We begin by performing the Darwinian operation of *reproduction*. We perform the operation of fitness-proportionate reproduction by copying individuals in the current population into the next generation with a probability proportional to their fitness.

The sum of the fitness values for all four individuals in the population is 12. The best-of-generation individual in the current population (i.e., 110) has fitness 6. Therefore, the fraction of the fitness of the population attributed to individual 110 is 1/2. In fitness-proportionate selection, individual 110 is given a probability of 1/2 of being selected for each of the four positions in the new population. Thus, we expect that string 110 will occupy two of the four positions in the new population. Since the genetic algorithm is probabilistic, there is a possibility that string 110 will appear three times or one time in the new population; there is even a small possibility that it will appear four times or not at all. Goldberg (1989) presents the above value of 1/2 in terms of a useful analogy to a roulette wheel. Each individual in the population occupies a sector of the wheel whose size is proportional to the fitness of the individual, so the best-of-generation individual here would occupy a 180° sector of the wheel. The spinning of this wheel permits fitness proportionate selection.

Similarly, individual 011 has a probability of 1/4 of being selected for each of the four positions in the new population. Thus, we expect 011 to appear in one of the four positions in the new population. The strategy 010 has probability of 1/6 of being selected for each of the four positions in the new population, whereas the strategy 001 has only a probability 1/12 of being so selected. Thus, we expect 010 to appear once in the new population, and we expect 001 to be absent from the new population.

If the four strings happen to be copied into the next generation precisely in accordance with these expected values, they will appear 2, 1, 1, and 0 times, respectively, in the new population. Table 3.3 shows this particular possible outcome of applying the Darwinian operation of fitness-proportionate reproduction to generation 0 of this particular initial random population. We call the resulting population the *mating pool* created after reproduction.

Table 3.3 One possible mating pool resulting from applying the operation of fitness-proportionate reproduction to the initial random population.

	Generation 0			Mating pool created after reproduction	
i	String X_i	Fitness $f(X_i)$	$\dfrac{f(X_i)}{\sum f(X_i)}$	Mating pool	$f(X_i)$
1	011	3	.25	011	3
2	001	1	.08	110	6
3	110	6	.50	110	6
4	010	2	.17	010	2
Total		12			17
Worst		1			2
Average		3.00			4.25
Best		6			6

The effect of the operation of fitness-proportionate reproduction is to improve the average fitness of the population. The average fitness of the population is now 4.25, whereas it started at only 3.00. Also, the worst single individual in the mating pool scores 2, whereas the worst single individual in the original population scored only 1. These improvements in the population are typical of the reproduction operation, because low-fitness individuals tend to be eliminated from the population and high-fitness individuals tend to be duplicated. Note that both of these improvements in the population come at the expense of the genetic diversity of the population. The strategy 001 became extinct. Of course, the fitness associated with the best-of-generation individual could not improve as the result of the operation of fitness-proportionate reproduction, since nothing new is created by this operation. The best-of-generation individual after the fitness-proportionate reproduction in generation 0 is, at best, the best randomly created individual.

The genetic operation of *crossover* (sexual *recombination*) allows new individuals to be created. It allows new points in the search space to be tested. Whereas the operation of reproduction acted on only one individual at a time, the operation of crossover starts with two parents. As with the reproduction operation, the individuals participating in the crossover operation are selected proportionate to fitness. The crossover operation produces two offspring. The two offspring are usually different from their two parents and different from each other. Each offspring contains some genetic material from each of its parents.

To illustrate the crossover (sexual recombination) operation, consider the first two individuals from the mating pool (table 3.4).

The crossover operation begins by randomly selecting a number between 1 and $L - 1$ using a uniform probability distribution. There are $L - 1 = 2$ interstitial locations lying between the positions of a string of length $L = 3$. Suppose that the interstitial location 2 is selected. This location becomes the crossover point. Each parent is then split at this crossover point into a crossover fragment and a remainder.

The *crossover fragments* of parents 1 and 2 are shown in table 3.5.

After the crossover fragment is identified, something remains of each parent. The *remainders* of parents 1 and 2 are shown in table 3.6.

Table 3.4 Two parents selected proportionate to fitness.

Parent 1	Parent 2
011	110

Table 3.5 Crossover fragments from the two parents.

Crossover fragment 1	Crossover fragment 2
01—	11—

Table 3.6 Remainders from the two parents.

Remainder 1	Remainder 2
$--1$	$--0$

Table 3.7 Two offspring produced by crossover.

Offspring 1	Offspring 2
111	010

Table 3.8 One possible outcome of applying the reproduction and crossover operations to generation 0 to create generation 1.

	Generation 0			Mating pool created after reproduction		After crossover (generation 1)		
i	String X_i	Fitness $f(X_i)$	$\dfrac{f(X_i)}{\sum f(X_i)}$	Mating pool	Pool $f(X_i)$	Crossover point	X_i	$f(X_i)$
1	011	3	.25	011	3	2	111	7
2	001	1	.08	110	6	2	010	2
3	110	6	.50	110	6	—	110	6
4	010	2	.17	010	2	—	010	2
Total	12				17			17
Worst	1				2			2
Average	3.00				4.25			4.25
Best	6				6			7

We then combine remainder 1 (i.e., $--1$) with crossover fragment 2 (i.e., $11-$) to create offspring 1 (i.e., 111). We similarly combine remainder 2 (i.e., $--0$) with crossover fragment 1 (i.e., $01-$) to create offspring 2 (i.e., 010). The two offspring are shown in table 3.7.

Both the reproduction operation and the crossover operation require the step of selecting individuals proportionately to fitness. We can simplify the process if we first apply the operation of fitness-proportionate reproduction to the entire population to create a mating pool. This mating pool is shown under the heading "mating pool created after reproduction" in table 3.3 and table 3.8. The mating pool is an intermediate step in transforming the population from the current generation (generation 0) to the next generation (generation 1).

We then apply the crossover operation to a specified percentage of the mating pool. Suppose that, for this example, the *crossover probability* p_c is 50%. This means that 50% of the population (a total of two individuals) will participate in crossover as part of the process of creating the next generation (i.e., generation 1) from the current generation (i.e., generation 0). The remaining 50% of the population participates only in the reproduction operation used to create the mating pool, so the *reproduction probability* p_r is 50% (i.e., 100% − 50%) for this particular example.

Table 3.8 shows the crossover operation acting on the mating pool. The two individuals that will participate in crossover are selected in proportion to fitness. By making the mating pool proportionate to fitness, we make it possible to select the two individuals from the mating pool merely by using a uniform random distribution (with reselection allowed). The two offspring that were randomly selected to participate in the crossover operation happen to be the individuals 011 and 110 (found on rows 1 and 2 under the heading "Mating pool created after reproduction"). The crossover point was chosen between 1 and $L − 1 = 2$ using a uniform random distribution. In this table, the number 2 was chosen and the crossover point for this particular crossover operation occurs between position 2 and position 3 of the two parents. The two offspring resulting from the crossover operation are shown in rows 1 and 2 under the heading "After crossover." Since p_c was only 50%, the two individuals on rows 3 and 4 do not participate in crossover and are merely transferred to rows 3 and 4 under the heading "After crossover."

The four individuals in the last column of table 3.8 are the new population created as a result of the operations of reproduction and crossover. These four individuals are generation 1 of this run of the genetic algorithm.

We then evaluate this new population of individuals for fitness. The best-of-generation individual in the population in generation 1 has a fitness value of 7, whereas the best-of-generation individual from generation 0 had a fitness of only 6. Crossover created something new, and, in this example, the new individual had a higher fitness value than either of its two parents.

When we compare the new population of generation 1 as a whole against the old population of generation 0, we find the following:

- The average fitness of the population has improved from 3 to 4.25.
- The best-of-generation individual has improved from 6 to 7.
- The worst-of-generation individual has improved from 1 to 2.

A genealogical audit trail can provide further insight into why the genetic algorithm works. In this example, the best individual (i.e., 111) of the new generation was the offspring of 110 and 011. The first parent (110) happened to be the best-of-generation individual from generation 0. The second parent (011) was an individual of exactly average fitness from the initial random generation. These two parents were selected to be in the mating pool in a probabilistic manner on the basis of their fitness. Neither was below average. They then came together to participate in crossover. Each of the offspring produced contained chromosomal material from both parents. In this instance, one of the offspring was fitter than either of its two parents.

This example illustrates how the genetic algorithm, using the two operations of fitness-proportionate reproduction and crossover, can create a population with improved average fitness and improved individuals.

The genetic algorithm then iteratively performs the operations on each generation of individuals to produce new generations of individuals until some *termination criterion* is satisfied.

For each generation, the genetic algorithm first evaluates each individual in the population for fitness. Then, using this fitness information, the genetic algorithm performs the operations of reproduction, crossover, and mutation with the frequencies specified by the respective probability parameters p_r, p_c, and p_m. This creates the new population.

The termination criterion is sometimes stated in terms of a maximum number of generations to be run. For problems where a perfect solution can be recognized when it is encountered, the algorithm can terminate when such an individual is found.

In this example, the best business strategy in the new generation (i.e., generation 1) is the following:

- sell the hamburgers at 50 cents (rather than $10),
- provide cola (rather than wine) as the drink, and
- offer fast service (rather than leisurely service).

As it happens, this business strategy (i.e., 111), which produces $7 in profits for the week, is the optimum strategy. If we happened to know that $7 is the global maximum for profitability, we could terminate the genetic algorithm at generation 1 for this example.

One method of *result designation* for a run of the genetic algorithm is to designate the best individual in the current generation of the population (i.e., the best-of-generation individual) at the time of termination as the result of the genetic algorithm. Of course, a typical run of the genetic algorithm would not terminate on the first generation as it does in this simple example. Instead, typical runs go on for tens, hundreds, or thousands of generations.

A *mutation* operation is also usually used in the conventional genetic algorithm operating on fixed-length strings. The frequency of applying the mutation operation is controlled by a parameter called the *mutation probability*, p_m. Mutation is used very sparingly in genetic algorithm work. The mutation operation is an asexual operation in that it operates on only one individual. It begins by randomly selecting a string from the mating pool and then randomly selecting a number between 1 and L as the mutation point. Then, the single character at the selected mutation point is changed. If the alphabet is binary, the character is merely complemented. No mutation was shown in the above example; however, if individual 4 (i.e., 010) had been selected for mutation and if position 2 had been selected as the mutation point, the result would have been the string 000. Note that the mutation operation had the effect of increasing the genetic diversity of the population by creating the new individual 000.

It is important to note that the genetic algorithm does not operate by converting a random string from the initial population into a globally optimal string via a single mutation any more than Darwinian evolution consists of converting free carbon, nitrogen, oxygen, and hydrogen into a frog in a single flash. Instead, mutation is a secondary operation that is potentially useful in restoring lost diversity in a population. For example, in the early generations of a run of the genetic algorithm, a value of 1 in a particular position of the string may be strongly associated with better performance. That is, starting from typical initial random points in the search space, the value of 1 in that position may consistently produce a better value of the fitness measure. Because of the higher fitness associated with the value of 1 in that particular position of the string, the exploitative effect of the reproduction operation may eliminate genetic diversity to the extent that the value 0 disappears from that position for the entire population. However, the global optimum may have a 0 in that position of the string. Once the search becomes narrowed to the part of the search space that actually contains the global optimum, a value of 0 in that position may be precisely what is required to reach the global optimum. This is merely a way of saying that the search space is nonlinear. This situation is not hypothetical since virtually all problems in which we are interested are nonlinear. Mutation provides a way to restore the genetic diversity lost because of previous exploitation.

Indeed, one of the key insights in *Adaptation in Natural and Artificial Systems* concerns the relative unimportance of mutation in the evolutionary process in nature as well as its relative unimportance in solving artificial problems of adaptation using the genetic algorithm. The genetic algorithm relies primarily on the creative effects of sexual genetic recombination (crossover) and the exploitative effects of the Darwinian principle of survival and reproduction of the fittest. Mutation is a decidedly secondary operation in genetic algorithms.

Holland's view of the crucial importance of recombination and the relative unimportance of mutation contrasts sharply with the popular misconception of the role of mutation in evolution in nature and with the recurrent efforts to solve adaptive systems problems by merely "mutating and saving the best." In particular, Holland's view stands in sharp contrast to *Artificial Intelligence through Simulated Evolution* (Fogel, Owens, and Walsh 1966) and other similar efforts at solving adaptive systems problems involving only asexual mutation and preservation of the best (Hicklin 1986; Dawkins 1987).

The four major steps in preparing to use the conventional genetic algorithm on fixed-length character strings to solve a problem involve

(1) determining the representation scheme,

(2) determining the fitness measure,

(3) determining the parameters and variables for controlling the algorithm, and

(4) determining the way of designating the result and the criterion for terminating a run.

The representation scheme in the conventional genetic algorithm is a mapping that expresses each possible point in the search space of the problem as a fixed-length character string. Specification of the representation scheme requires selecting the string length L and the alphabet size K. Often the alphabet is binary. Selecting the mapping between the chromosome and the points in the search space of the problem is sometimes straightforward and sometimes very difficult. Selecting a representation that facilitates solution of the problem by means of the genetic algorithm often requires considerable insight into the problem and good judgment.

The fitness measure assigns a fitness value to each possible fixed-length character string in the population. The fitness measure is often inherent in the problem. The fitness measure must be capable of evaluating every fixed-length character string it encounters.

The primary parameters for controlling the genetic algorithm are the population size (M) and the maximum number of generations to be run (G). Secondary parameters, such as p_r, p_c, and p_m, control the frequencies of reproduction, crossover, and mutation, respectively. In addition, several other quantitative control parameters and qualitative control variables must be specified in order to completely specify how to execute the genetic algorithm (chapter 27).

The methods of designating a result and terminating a run have been discussed above.

Once these steps for setting up the genetic algorithm have been completed, the genetic algorithm can be run.

The three steps in executing the genetic algorithm operating on fixed-length character strings can be summarized as follows:

(1) Randomly create an initial population of individual fixed-length character strings.

(2) Iteratively perform the following substeps on the population of strings until the termination criterion has been satisfied:
   (a) Evaluate the fitness of each individual in the population.
   (b) Create a new population of strings by applying at least the first two of the following three operations. The operations are applied to individual string(s) in the population chosen with a probability based on fitness.
      (i) Copy existing individual strings to the new population.
      (ii) Create two new strings by genetically recombining randomly chosen substrings from two existing strings.
      (iii) Create a new string from an existing string by randomly mutating the character at one position in the string.

(3) The best individual string that appeared in any generation (i.e., the best-so-far individual) is designated as the result of the genetic algorithm for the run. This result may represent a solution (or an approximate solution) to the problem.

Figure 3.1 is a flowchart of these steps for the conventional genetic algorithm operating on strings. The index i refers to an individual in a population of size M. The variable GEN is the current generation number.

There are numerous minor variations on the basic genetic algorithm; this flowchart is merely one version. For example, mutation is often treated as an

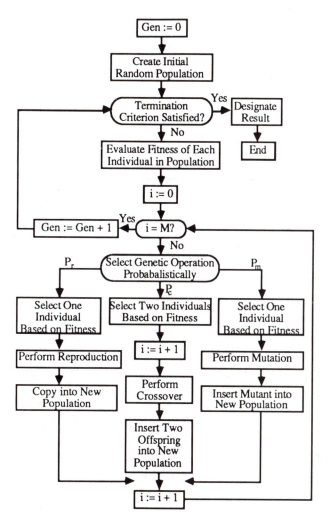

Figure 3.1 Flowchart of the conventional genetic algorithm.

operation that can occur in sequence with either reproduction or crossover, so that a given individual might be mutated and reproduced or mutated and crossed within a single generation. Also, the number of times a genetic operation is performed during one generation is often set to an explicit number for each generation (as we do later in this book), rather than determined probabilistically as shown in this flowchart.

Note also that this flowchart does not explicitly show the creation of a mating pool (as we did above to simplify the presentation). Instead, one or two individuals are selected to participate in each operation on the basis of fitness and the operation is then performed on the selected individuals.

It is important to note that the genetic algorithm works in a *domain-independent* way on the fixed-length character strings in the population. For this reason, it is a "weak method." The genetic algorithm searches the space of possible character strings in an attempt to find high-fitness strings. To guide this search, it uses only the numerical fitness values associated with the explicitly tested points in the search space. Regardless of the particular problem domain, the genetic algorithm carries out its search by performing the same amazingly simple operations of copying, slicing and dicing, and occasionally randomly mutating strings.

In practice, genetic algorithms are surprisingly rapid in effectively searching complex, highly nonlinear, multidimensional search spaces. This is all the more surprising because the genetic algorithm does not know anything about the problem domain or the fitness measure.

The user may employ domain-specific knowledge in choosing the representation scheme and the fitness measure and also may exercise additional judgment in choosing the population size, the number of generations, the parameters controlling the probability of performing the various operations, the criterion for terminating a run, and the method for designating the result. All of these choices may influence how well the genetic algorithm performs in a particular problem domain or whether it works at all. However, the main point is that the genetic algorithm is, broadly speaking, a domain-independent way of rapidly searching an unknown search space for high-fitness points.

3.2 WHY THE GENETIC ALGORITHM WORKS

Let us return to the example of the four hamburger restaurants to see how Darwinian reproduction and genetic recombination allow the genetic algorithm to effectively search complex spaces when nothing is known about the fitness measure.

As previously mentioned, the genetic algorithm's creation of its initial random population corresponds to the restaurant manager's decision to start his search by testing four different random business strategies.

It would superficially appear that testing the four random strings does nothing more than provide values of fitness for those four explicitly tested points.

One additional thing that the manager learned is that $3 is the average fitness of the population. It is an estimate of the average fitness of the search space. This estimate has a statistical variance associated with it, since it is not the average of all K^L points in the search space but merely a calculation based on the four explicitly tested points.

Once the manager has this estimate of the average fitness of the unknown search space, he has an entirely different way of looking at the fitness he observed for the four explicitly tested points in the population. In particular, he now sees that

- 110 is 200% as good as the estimated average for the search space,
- 001 is 33% as good as the estimated average for the search space,
- 011 is 100% as good as the estimated average for the search space, and
- 010 is 67% as good as the estimated average for the search space.

We return to the key question: What is the manager going to do during the second week of operation of the restaurants?

One option the manager might consider for week 2 is to continue to randomly select new points from the search space and test them. A blind random search strategy is nonadaptive and nonintelligent in the sense that it does not use information that has already been learned about the environment to influence the subsequent direction of the search. For any problem with a nontrivial search space, it will not be possible to test more than a tiny fraction of the total number of points in the search space using blind random search. There are K^L points in the search space for a problem represented by a string of length L over an alphabet of size K. For example, even if it were possible to test a billion (10^9) points per second and if the blind random search had been going on since the beginning of the universe (i.e., about 15 billion years), it would be possible to have searched only about 10^{27} points with blind random search. A search space of $10^{27} \approx 2^{90}$ points corresponds to a binary string with the relatively modest length $L = 90$.

Another option the manager might consider for the second week of operation of his restaurants is to greedily exploit the best result from his testing of the initial random population. The greedy exploitation strategy involves employing the 110 business strategy for all four restaurants for every week in the future and not testing any additional points in the search space. Greedy exploitation is, unlike blind random search, an adaptive strategy (i.e., an intelligent strategy), because it uses information learned at one stage of the search to influence the direction of the search at the next stage. Greedy exploitation can be expected to produce a payoff of $6 per restaurant per week. On the basis of the current $3 estimate for the average fitness of points in the search space as a whole, greedy exploitation can be expected to be twice as good as blind random search.

But greedy exploitation overlooks the virtual certainty that there are better points in the search space than those accidently chosen in the necessarily tiny initial random sampling of points. In any interesting search space of meaningful size, it is unlikely that the best-of-generation point found in a small initial random sample would be the global optimum of the search space, and it is similarly unlikely that the best-of-generation point in an early generation would be the global optimum. The goal is to maximize the profits over time, and greedy exploitation is highly premature at this stage.

While acknowledging that greedy exploitation of the currently observed best-of-generation point in the population (110) to the exclusion of everything else is not advisable, we nonetheless must give considerable weight to the fact that 110 performs at twice the estimated average of the search space as a whole. Indeed, because of this one fact alone, all future exploration of random points in the search space now carries a known and rather hefty cost of exploration. In particular, the estimated cost of testing a new random point in the search space is now $6 − $3 = $3 per test. That is, for each new random point we test, we must forgo the now-known and available payoff of $6.

But if we do not test any new points, we are left only with the already-rejected option of greedily exploiting forever the currently observed best point from the small initial random sampling. There is also a rather hefty cost of *not* testing a new random point in the search space. This cost is $f_{max} - \$6$, where f_{max} is the as-yet-unknown fitness of the global maximum of the search space. Since we are not likely to have stumbled into anything like the global maximum of the search space on our tiny test of initial random points, this unknown cost is likely to be very much larger than the $\$6 - \$3 = \$3$ estimated cost of testing a new random point. Moreover, if we continue this greedy exploitation of this almost certainly suboptimal point, we will suffer the cost of failing to find a better point for all future time periods.

Thus, we have the following costs associated with two competing, alternative courses of action:

- Associated with exploration is an estimated $3 cost of allocating future trials to new random points in the search space.
- Associated with exploration is an unknown (but probably very large) cost of *not* allocating future trials to new points.

An optimally adaptive (intelligent) system should process currently available information about payoff from the unknown environment so as to find the optimal tradeoff between the cost of exploration of new points in the search space and the cost of exploitation of already-evaluated points in the search space. This tradeoff must also reflect the statistical variance inherently associated with costs that are merely estimated costs.

Moreover, as we proceed, we will want to consider the even more interesting tradeoff between exploration of new points from a *portion of the search space which we believe may have above-average payoff* and the cost of exploitation of already-evaluated points in the search space.

But what information are we going to process to find this optimal tradeoff between further exploration and exploitation of the search space? It would appear that we have already extracted everything there is to learn from our initial testing of the $M = 4$ initial random points.

An important point of Holland's *Adaptation in Natural and Artificial Systems* is that there is a wealth of hidden information in the seemingly small population size of $M = 4$ random points from the search space.

We can begin to discern some of this hidden information if we enumerate the possible explanations (conjectures, hypotheses) as to why the 110 strategy pays off at twice the average fitness of the population. Table 3.9 shows seven possible explanations as to why the business strategy 110 performs at 200% of the population average.

Each string shown in the right column of table 3.9 is called a *schema* (plural: *schemata*). Each schema is a string over an extended alphabet consisting of the original alphabet (the 0 and 1 of the binary alphabet, in this example) and an asterisk (the *"don't care" symbol*).

Row 1 of table 3.9 shows the schema 1**. This schema refers to the conjecture (hypothesis, explanation) that the reason why 110 is so good is the

Table 3.9 Seven possible explanations as to why strategy 110 performs at 200% of the population average fitness.

It's the low price.	1**
It's the cola.	*1*
It's the leisurely service.	**0
It's the low price in combination with the cola.	11*
It's the low price in combination with the leisurely service.	1*0
It's the cola in combination with leisurely service.	*10
It's the precise combination of the low price, the cola, and the leisurely service.	110

low price of the hamburger (the specific bit 1 in the leftmost bit position). This conjecture does not care about the drink (the * in the middle bit position) or the speed of service (the * in the rightmost bit position). It refers to a single variable (the price of the hamburger). Therefore, the schema 1** is said to have a *specificity* (*order*) of 1 (i.e., there is one specified symbol in the schema 1**).

On the second-to-last row of table 3.9, the schema *10 refers to the conjecture (hypothesis, explanation) that the reason why 110 is so good is the combination of cola and leisurely service (i.e., the 1 in bit position 2 and the 0 in bit position 3). This conjecture refers to two variables and therefore has specificity 2. There is an asterisk in bit position 1 of this schema because it refers to the effect of the combination of the specified values of the two specified variables (drink and service) without regard to the value of the third variable (price).

We can restate this idea as follows: A schema H describes a set of points from the search space of a problem that have certain specified similarities. In particular, if we have a population of strings of length L over an alphabet of size K, then a schema is identified by a string of length L over the extended alphabet of size $K + 1$. The additional element in the alphabet is the asterisk.

There are $(K + 1)^L$ schemata of length L. For example, when $L = 3$ and $K = 2$ there are 27 schemata.

A string from the search space belongs to a particular schema if, for all positions $j = 1, \ldots, L$, the character found in the jth position of the string matches the character found in the jth position of the schema, or if the jth position of the schema is occupied by an asterisk. Thus, for example, the strings 010 and 110 both belong to the schema *10 because the characters found in positions 2 and 3 of both strings match the characters found in the schema *10 in positions 2 and 3 and because the asterisk is found in position 1 of the schema. The string 000, for example, does not belong to the schema *10 because the schema has a 1 in position 2.

When $L = 3$, we can geometrically represent the $2^3 = 8$ possible strings (i.e., the individual points in the search space) of length $L = 3$ as the corners of a hypercube of dimensionality 3.

Figure 3.2 shows the $2^3 = 8$ possible strings in bold type at the corners of the cube.

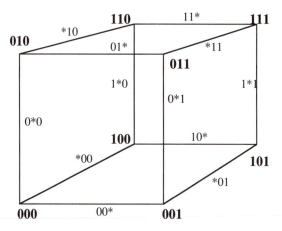

Figure 3.2 Search space for the hamburger restaurant problem.

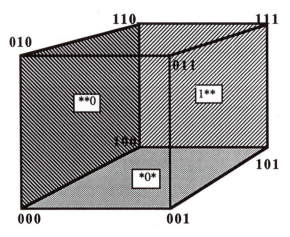

Figure 3.3 Three of the six schemata of specificity 1.

We can similarly represent the other schemata as various geometric entities associated with the cube. In particular, each of the 12 schemata with specificity 2 (i.e., two specified positions and one "don't care" position) contains two points from the search space. Each such schema corresponds to one of the 12 edges (one-dimensional hyperplanes) of this cube. Each of the edges has been labeled with the particular schema to which its two endpoints belong. For example, the schema *10 is one such edge and is found at the top left of the cube.

Figure 3.3 shows three of the six schemata with specificity 1 (i.e., one specified position and two "don't care" positions). Each such schema contains four points from the search space and corresponds to one of the six faces (two-dimensional hyperplanes) of this cube. Three of the six faces have been shaded and labeled with the particular schema to which the four corners associated with that face belong. For example, the schema *0* is the bottom face of the cube.

Table 3.10 Schema specificity, dimension of the hyperplane corresponding to that schema, geometric realization of the schema, number of points from the search space contained in the schema, and number of such schemata.

Schema specificity $O(H)$	Hyperplane dimension	Geometric realization	Individuals in the schema	Number of such schemata
3	0	Point	1	8
2	1	Line	2	12
1	2	Plane	4	6
0	3	Entire cube	8	1
			Total	27

The eight schemata with specificity 3 (i.e., three specified positions and no "don't care" positions) correspond to the actual points from the search space and to the corner points (zero-dimensional hyperplanes) of this cube.

The single schema with specificity 0 (i.e., no specified positions and three "don't care" positions) consists of the cube itself (the three-dimensional hyperplane). There is one such three-dimensional hyperplane (i.e., the cube itself). Note that, for simplicity, schema *** was omitted from table 3.9.

Table 3.10 summarizes the schema specificity, the dimension of the hyperplane corresponding to that schema, the geometric realization of the schema, the number of points from the search space contained in the schema, and the number of such schemata for the binary case (where $K = 2$). A schema of specificity $O(H)$ (column 1 of the table) corresponds to a hyperplane of-dimensionality $L - O(H)$ (column 2) which has the geometric realization shown in column 3. This schema contains $2^{L-O(H)}$ individuals (column 4) from the hypercube of dimension L. The number of schemata of specificity $O(H)$ is

$$\binom{L}{O(H)} 2^{O(H)}.$$

Table 3.11 shows which of the $2^L = 2^3 = 8$ individual strings of length $L = 3$ over an alphabet of size $K = 2$ from the search space appear in each of the $(K + 1)^L = 3^L = 27$ schemata.

An important observation is that each individual in the population belongs to 2^L schemata. The 2^L schemata associated with a given individual string in the population can be generated by creating one schema from each of the 2^L binary numbers of length L. This is done as follows: For each 0 in the binary number, insert the "don't care" symbol * in the schema being constructed. For each 1 in the binary number, insert the specific symbol from that position from the individual string in the schema being constructed. The individual string from the population belongs to each of the schemata thus created. Note that this number is independent of the number K of characters in the alphabet. For example, when $L = 3$, the $2^3 = 8$ schemata to which the string 010 belongs are the seven schemata explicitly shown in table 3.12 plus the schema *** (which, for simplicity, is not shown in the table).

Table 3.11 Individual strings belonging to each of the 27 schemata.

	Schema	Individual strings
1	000	000
2	001	001
3	00*	000, 001
4	010	010
5	011	011
6	01*	010, 011
7	0*0	000, 010
8	0*1	001, 011
9	0**	000, 001, 010, 011
10	100	100
11	101	101
12	10*	100, 101
13	110	110
14	111	111
15	11*	110, 111
16	1*0	100, 110
17	1*1	101, 111
18	1**	100, 101, 110, 111
19	*00	000, 100
20	*01	001, 101
21	*0*	000, 001, 100, 101
22	*10	010, 110
23	*11	011, 111
24	*1*	010, 011, 110, 111
25	**0	000, 010, 100, 110
26	**1	001, 011, 101, 111
27	***	000, 001, 010, 011, 100, 101, 110, 111

Let us now return to the discussion of how each of the four explicitly tested points in the population tells us something about various conjectures (explanations, hypotheses). Each conjecture corresponds to a schema.

The possible conjectures concerning the superior performance of strategy 110 were enumerated in table 3.9. Why does the strategy 010 pay off at only 2/3 the average fitness of the population? Table 3.12 shows seven of the possible conjectures for explaining why 010 performs relatively poorly.

The problem of finding the correct explanation for the observed performance is more complicated than merely enumerating the possible explanations for the observed performance because, typically, the possible explanations conflict with one another. For example, three of the possible explanations for the observed performance of the point 010 conflict with the possible explanations for the observed good performance of the point 110. In particular, *1* (cola drink), **0 (leisurely service), and *10 (cola drink and leisurely service) are potential explanations for both above-average performance and below-average performance. That should not be surprising, since we should not expect all possible explanations to be valid.

Table 3.12 Seven possible explanations as to why strategy 010 performs at only 2/3 of the population average fitness.

It's the high price.	0**
It's the cola.	*1*
It's the leisurely service.	**0
It's the high price in combination with the cola.	01*
It's the high price in combination with the leisurely service.	0*0
It's the cola in combination with leisurely service.	*10
It's the precise combination of the high price, the cola, and the leisurely service.	010

If we enumerate the possible explanations for the observed performance of the two remaining points from the search space (011 and 001), additional conflicts between the possible explanations appear.

In general, these conflicts can result from the inherent nonlinearities of a problem (i.e., the genetic linkages between various decision variables), from errors introduced by statistical sampling (e.g., the seemingly good performance of **0), from noise in the environment, or even from changes in the environment (e.g., the non-stationarity of the fitness measure over time).

How are we going to resolve these conflicts?

An important insight in Holland's *Adaptation in Natural and Artificial Systems* is that we can view these schemata as competing explanations, each of which has a fitness value associated with it. In particular, the *average fitness of a schema* is the average of the fitness values for each individual in the population that belongs to a given schema. This schema average fitness is, like most of the averages discussed throughout this book, an estimate which has a statistical variance associated with it. Some averages are based on more data points than others and therefore have lower variance. Usually, more individuals belong to a less specific schema, so the schema average fitness of a less specific schema usually has lower variance.

Only the four individuals from the population are explicitly tested for fitness, and only these four individuals appear in genetic algorithm worksheets (such as table 3.8). However, in the genetic algorithm, as in nature, the individuals actually present in the population are of secondary importance to the evolutionary process. In nature, if a particular individual survives to the age of reproduction and actually reproduces sexually, at least some of the chromosomes of that individual are preserved in the chromosomes of its offspring in the next generation of the population. With the exceptions of identical twins and asexual reproduction, one rarely sees two exact copies of any particular individual. It is the genetic profile of the population as a whole (i.e., the schemata), as contained in the chromosomes of the individuals of the population, that is of primary importance. The individuals in the population are merely the vehicles for collectively transmitting a genetic profile and the guinea pigs for testing fitness in the environment.

When a particular individual survives to the age of reproduction and reproduces in nature, we do not know which single attribute or combination of attributes is responsible for this observed achievement. Similarly, when a single individual in the population of four strategies for running a restaurant has a particular fitness value associated with it, we do not know which of the $2^3 = 8$ possible combinations of attributes is responsible for the observed performance.

Since we do not know which of the possible combinations of attributes (explanations) is actually responsible for the observed performance of the individual as a whole, we rely on averages. If a particular combination of attributes is repeatedly associated with high performance (because individuals containing this combination have high fitness), we may begin to think that that combination of attributes is the reason for the observed performance. The same is true if a particular combination of attributes is repeatedly associated with low or merely average performance. If a particular combination of attributes exhibits both high and low performance, then we begin to think that the combination has no explanatory power for the problem at hand. The genetic algorithm implements this highly intuitive approach to identifying the combination of attributes that is responsible for the observed performance of a complex nonlinear system.

The genetic algorithm implicitly allocates credit for the observed fitness of each explicitly tested individual string to *all* of the $2^L = 8$ schemata to which the particular individual string belongs. In other words, all $2^L = 8$ possible explanations are credited with the performance of each explicitly tested individual. In other words, we ascribe the successful performance (i.e., survival to the age of reproduction and reproduction) of the whole organism to every schema to which the chromosome of that individual belongs. Some of these allocations of credit are no doubt misdirected. The observed performance of one individual provides no way to distinguish among the $2^L = 8$ possible explanations.

A particular schema will usually receive allocations that contribute to its average fitness from a number of individuals in the population. Thus, an estimate of the average fitness for each schema quickly begins to build up. Of course, we never know the actual average fitness of a schema, because a statistical variance is associated with each estimate. If a large amount of generally similar evidence begins to accumulate about a given schema, the estimate of the average fitness of that schema will have a relatively small variance. We will then begin to have higher confidence in the correctness of the average fitness for that schema. If the evidence about a particular schema suggests that it is greatly superior to other schemata, we will begin to pay greater attention to that schema (perhaps overlooking the variance to some degree).

Table 3.13 shows the $2^3 = 8$ schemata to which the individual 110 belongs. The observed fitness of 6 for individual 110 (which was 200% of the population average fitness) contributes to the estimate of the average fitness of each of the eight schemata.

As it happens, for the first four schemata in table 3.13, 110 is the only individual in our tiny population of four that belongs to these schemata. Thus,

Table 3.13 The $2^L = 8$ schemata to which individual 110 belongs.

	Schema	Average fitness
1	110	6
2	11*	6
3	1*0	6
4	1**	6
5	***10**	**4**
6	***1***	**3.67**
7	**0	4
8	***	3

the estimate of average fitness (i.e., 6) for the first four schemata is merely the observed fitness of the one individual.

However, for the next four schemata in table 3.13, 110 is not the only individual contributing to the estimate of average fitness. For example, on row 5 of table 3.13, two individuals (110 and 010) belong to the schema *10. The observed fitness of individual 110 ($6) suggests that the *10 schema may be good, while the observed fitness of individual 010 ($2) suggests that *10 may be bad. The average fitness of schema *10 is $4.

Similarly, for example, on row 6 of table 3.13, three individuals (110, 010, and 011) belong to the schema *1*. The average fitness of schema *1* is thus the average of $6 from 110, $2 from 010, and $3 from 010 (that is, $3.67). Since this average is based on more data points (although still very few), it has a smaller variance than the other averages just mentioned.

For each of the other two individuals in the population, one can envision a similar table showing the eight schemata to which the individual belongs. The four individuals in the current population make a total of $M2^L = 32$ contributions to the calculation of the $3^L = 27$ values of schema average fitness. Of course, some schemata may be associated with more than one individual.

In creating generation 1, we did not know the precise explanation for the superiority of 110 from among the 2^L possible explanations for its superiority. Similarly, we did not know the precise explanation for the performance of 011 from among the 2^L possible explanations for its averageness. In creating generation 1, there were two goals. First, we wanted to continue the search in areas of the search space that were likely to produce higher levels of fitness. The only available evidence suggested continuing the search in parts of the search space that consisted of points that belonged to schemata with high observed fitness (or, at least, not low fitness). Second, we did not want merely to retest any points that had already been explicitly tested (i.e., 110 and 011). Instead, we wanted to test new points from the search space that belonged to the same schemata to which 110 and 011 belonged. That is, we wanted to test new points that were similar to 110 and 011. We wished to construct and test new and different points whose schemata had already been identified as being of relatively high fitness.

The genetic algorithm provides a way to continue the search of the search space by testing new and different points that are similar to points that have already demonstrated above-average fitness. The genetic algorithm directs the search into promising parts of the search space on the basis of the information available from the explicit testing of the particular (small) number of individuals contained in the current population.

Table 3.14 shows the number of occurrences of each of the $3^L = 27$ schemata among the $M = 4$ individuals in the population. Column 3 shows the number of occurrences $m(H, 0)$ of schema H for generation 0. This number ranges between 0 and 4 (i.e., the population size M). The sum of column 3 is $32 = M2^L$, because each individual in the population belongs to a total of $2^L = 8$ schemata and therefore contributes to 8 different calculations of schema average fitness. Some schemata receive contributions from two or more individuals in the population and some receive no contributions. The total number of schemata with a nonzero number of occurrences is 20 (as shown in the last row of the table). Column 4 shows the average fitness $f(H, 0)$ of each schema. For example, for the schema $H = {}^*1^*$ on row 24, the number of occurrences $m(H, 0)$ is 3, because strings 010, 011, and 110 belong to this schema. Because the sum of the fitness values of the three strings is 11, the schema average fitness is $f(H, t) = f({}^*1^*) = 3.67$.

Note that *there is no table displaying $3^L = 27$ schemata like table 3.14 anywhere in the genetic algorithm.* The $M2^L = 32$ contributions to the average fitnesses of the $3^L = 27$ schemata appearing in table 3.14 are all *implicitly stored* within the $M = 4$ strings of the population.

No operation is ever explicitly directly performed on the schemata by the genetic algorithm.

No calculation of schema average fitness is ever made by the genetic algorithm.

The genetic algorithm operates only on the $M = 4$ individuals in the population. Only the $M = 4$ individuals in the current population are ever explicitly tested for fitness. Then, using these $M = 4$ fitness values, the genetic algorithm performs the operations of reproduction, crossover, and mutation on the $M = 4$ individuals in the population to produce the new population.

We now begin to see that a wealth of information is produced by the explicit testing of just four strings. We can see, for example, that the estimate of average fitness of certain schemata is above average, while the estimate of average fitness of some other schemata is below average or merely average.

We would clearly like to continue the search to the portions of the search space suggested by the current above-average estimates of schema average fitness. In particular, we would like to construct a new population using the information provided by the schemata.

While constructing the new population using the available information, we must remember that this information is not perfect. There is a possibility that the schemata that are currently observed to have above-average fitness may lose their luster when more evidence accumulates. Similarly, there is a possibility that an "ugly duckling" schema that is currently observed to have below-average fitness may turn out ultimately to be associated with the optimal

Table 3.14 Number of occurrences (column 3) and schema average fitness (column 4) for each of the 27 schemata in generation 0.

#	H	Generation 0	
		$m(H, 0)$	$f(H, 0)$
1	000	0	0
2	001	1	1
3	00*	1	1
4	010	1	2
5	011	1	3
6	01*	2	2.5
7	0*0	1	2
8	0*1	2	2
9	0**	3	2
10	100	0	0
11	101	0	0
12	10*	0	0
13	110	1	6
14	111	0	0
15	11*	1	6
16	1*0	1	6
17	1*1	0	0
18	1**	1	6
19	*00	0	0
20	*01	1	1
21	*0*	1	1
22	*10	2	4
23	*11	1	3
24	*1*	3	3.67
25	**0	2	4
26	**1	2	2
27	***	4	3
Total		32	96
Mean			3.00
Nonzero items		20	20

solution. Thus, we must use the available information to guide our search, but we must also remember that the currently available evidence may be wrong.

The question, therefore, is how best to use this currently available information to guide the remainder of the search. The answer comes from the solution to a mathematical problem known as the two-armed-bandit (TAB) problem and its generalization, the multi-armed-bandit problem. The TAB problem starkly presents the fundamental tension between the benefit associated with continued *exploration* of the search space and the benefit associated with immediate greedy *exploitation* of the search space.

The two-armed-bandit problem was described as early as the 1930s in connection with the decision-making dilemma associated with testing new drugs and medical treatments in controlled experiments necessarily involving relatively small numbers of patients. There may come a time when one treatment is producing better results than another and it would seem that the better treatment should be adopted as the standard way for thereafter treating all patients. However, the observed better results have an associated statistical variance, and there is always some uncertainty as to whether the currently observed best treatment is really the best. The premature adoption of the currently observed better treatment may doom all future patients to an actually inferior treatment. See also Bellman 1961.

Consider a slot machine with two arms, one of which pays off considerably better than the other. The goal is to maximize the payoff (i.e., minimize the losses) while playing this two-armed bandit over a period of time. If one knew that one arm was better than the other with certainty, the optimal strategy would be trivial; one would play that arm 100% of the time. Absent this knowledge and certainty, one would allocate a certain number of trials to each arm in order to learn something about their relative payoffs. After just a few trials, one could quickly start computing an estimate of average payoff p_1 for arm 1 and an estimate of average payoff p_2 for arm 2. But each of these estimates of the actual payoffs has an associated statistical variance (σ^2_1 and σ^2_2, respectively).

After more thorough testing, the currently observed better arm may actually prove to be the inferior arm. Therefore, it is not prudent to allocate 100% of the future trials to the currently observed better arm. In fact, one must *forever* continue testing the currently observed poorer arm to some degree, because of the possibility (ever diminishing) that the currently observed poorer arm will ultimately prove to be the better arm. Nonetheless, one clearly must allocate more trials to the currently observed better arm than to the currently observed poorer arm.

But precisely *how many more* future trials should be allocated to the currently observed better arm, with its current variance, than the currently poorer arm, with its current variance?

The answer depends on the two payoffs and the two variances. For each additional trial one makes of the currently observed poorer arm (which will be called arm 2 hereafter), one expects to incur a cost of exploration equal to the difference between the average payoff of the currently observed better arm (arm 1 hereafter) and the average payoff of the currently observed poorer arm (arm 2). If the currently observed better arm (i.e., arm 1) ultimately proves to be inferior, one should expect to forgo the difference between the as-yet-unknown superior payoff p_{max} and p_1 for each pull on that arm. If the current payoff estimates are based on a very small random sampling from a very large search space (as is the case for the genetic algorithm and all other adaptive techniques starting at random), this forgone difference is likely to be very large.

A key insight of Holland's *Adaptation in Natural and Artificial Systems* is that we should view the schemata as being in competition with one another, much like the possible pulling strategies of a multi-armed-bandit problem. As each individual in the genetic population grapples with its environment, its fitness is determined. The average fitness of a schema is the average of the fitnesses of the specific individuals in the population belonging to that schema. As this explicit testing of the individuals in the population occurs, an estimate begins to accumulate for the average fitness of each schema represented by those individuals. Each estimate of schema average fitness has a statistical variance associated with it. As a general rule, more information is accumulated for shorter schema and therefore the variance is usually smaller for them. One clearly must allocate more future trials to the currently observed better arms. Nevertheless, one must continue *forever* to allocate some additional trials to the currently observed poorer arms, because they may ultimately turn out to be better.

Holland developed a formula for the optimal allocation of trials in terms of the two currently observed payoffs of the arms and their variances and extended the formula to the multi-armed case. He showed that the mathematical form of the optimal allocation of trials among random variables in a multi-armed-bandit problem is approximately exponential. That is, the optimal allocation of future trials is approximately an exponentially increasing number of trials to the better arm based on the ratio of the currently observed payoffs.

Specifically, consider the case of the two-armed bandit. Suppose that N trials are to be allocated between two random variables with means μ_1 and μ_2 and variances σ_1^2 and σ_2^2, respectively, where $\mu_1 > \mu_2$. Holland showed that the minimal expected loss results when the number n^* of trials allocated to the random variable with the smaller mean is

$$n^* \approx b^2 \ln\left(\frac{N^2}{8\pi b^4 \ln N^2}\right),$$

where

$$b = \frac{\sigma_1}{\mu_1 - \mu_2}.$$

Then, $N - n^*$ trials are allocated to the random variable with the larger mean.

Most remarkably, Holland shows that the approximately exponential ratio of trials that an optimal sequential algorithm should allocate to the two random variables is approximately produced by the genetic algorithm.

Note that this version of the TAB problem requires knowing which of the two random variables will have the greater observed mean at the end of the N trials. This adaptive plan therefore cannot be realized, since a plan does not know the outcome of the N trials before they occur. However, this idealization is useful because, as Holland showed, there are realizable plans that quickly approach the same expected loss as the idealization.

The above discussion of the TAB problem is based on Holland's analysis. See also DeJong 1975. Subsequently, the multi-armed-bandit problem has been definitively treated by Gittins 1989. See also Berry and Fristedt 1985. Moreover, Frantz (1991) discovered mathematical errors in Holland's solution. These errors in no way change the thrust of Holland's basic argument or Holland's important conclusion that the genetic algorithm approximately carries out the optimal allocation of trials specified by the solution to the multi-armed-bandit problem. In fact, Frantz shows that his bandit is realizable and that the genetic algorithm performs like it. The necessary corrections uncovered by Frantz's work are addressed in detail in the revised edition of Holland's 1975 book (Holland 1992).

Stated in terms of the competing schemata (explanations), the optimal way to allocate trials is to allocate an approximately exponentially increasing (or decreasing) number of future trials to a schema on the basis of the ratio (called the *fitness ratio*) of the current estimate of the average fitness of the schema to the current estimate of the population average fitness. Thus, if the current estimate of the average fitness of a schema is twice the current estimate of the population average fitness (i.e., the fitness ratio is 2), one should allocate twice as many future trials to that schema as to an average schema. If this 2-to-1 estimate of the schema average persists unchanged for a few generations, this allocation based on the fitness ratio would have the effect of allocating an exponentially increasing number of trials to this above-average schema. Similarly, one should allocate half as many future trials to a schema that has a fitness ratio of 1/2.

Moreover, we want to make an optimal allocation of future trials *simultaneously* to all $3^L = 27$ possible schemata from the current generation to determine a target number of occurrences for the 3^L possible schemata in the next generation. In the context of the present example, we want to construct a new population of $M = 4$ strings of length $L = 3$ for the next generation so that *all* $3^L = 27$ possible schemata to which these M new strings belong simultaneously receives its optimal allocation of trials. That is, we are seeking an approximately exponential increase or decrease in the number of occurrences of each schema based on its fitness ratio.

Specifically, there are $ML = 12$ binary variables to choose in constructing the new population for the next generation. After these 12 choices for the next generation have been made, each of the $M2^L = 32$ contributions to the $3^L = 27$ schemata must cause the number of occurrences of each schema to equal (or approximately equal) the optimal allocation of trials specified by Holland's solution to his version of the multi-armed-bandit problem.

It would appear impossibly complicated to make an optimal allocation of future trials for the next generation by satisfying the $3^L = 27$ constraints with the $ML = 12$ degrees of freedom. This seemingly impossible task involves starting by choosing the $M = 4$ new strings of length $L = 3$. Then, we must increment by one the number of occurrences of each of the $2^L = 8$ schemata to which each of the $M = 4$ strings belongs. That is, there are $M2^L = 32$ contributions to the $3^L = 27$ counts of the number of occurrences of the various schemata. The goal is to make the number of occurrences of each of the $3^L = 27$ schemata equal the targeted number of occurrences for that schema given by the solution to the multi-armed-bandit problem.

Holland's fundamental theorem of genetic algorithms (also called the *schema theorem*) in conjunction with his results on the optimal allocation of trials shows that the genetic algorithm creates its new population in such a way as to *simultaneously* satisfy all of these $3^L = 27$ constraints.

In particular, the schema theorem in conjunction with the multi-armed-bandit theorem shows that the straightforward Darwinian operation of fitness-proportionate reproduction causes the number of occurrences of every one of the unseen hyperplanes (schemata) to grow (and decay) from generation to generation at a rate that is mathematically near optimal. The genetic operations of crossover and mutation slightly degrade this near-optimal performance, but the degradation is small for the cases that will prove to be of greatest interest. In other words, the genetic algorithm is, approximately, a mathematically near optimal approach to adaptation in the sense that it maximizes overall expected payoff when the adaptive process is viewed as a set of multi-armed-bandit problems for allocating future trials in the search space on the basis of currently available information.

For the purposes of stating the theorem, let $f(H, t)$ be the *average fitness of a schema H*. That is, $f(H, t)$ is the average of the observed fitness values of the individual strings in the population that belong to the schema.

$$f(H, t) = \frac{\sum_{x_i \in H} f(x_i, t)}{m(H, t)},$$

where $m(H, t)$ is the number of occurrences of schema H at generation t. We used this formula in computing $f(*1*) = 3.67$ for row 24 of table 3.14. This schema average fitness has an associated variance that depends on the number of items being summed to compute the average.

The fitness ratio (FR) of a given schema H is

$$FR(H, t) = \frac{f(H, t)}{\overline{f(t)}},$$

where $\overline{f(t)}$ is the *average fitness of the population* at generation t.

The schema theorem states that, for a genetic algorithm using the Darwinian operation of fitness-proportionate reproduction and the genetic operations of crossover and mutation, the expected number $m(H, t + 1)$ of occurrences of *every* schema H in the next generation is approximately

$$m(H, t + 1) \geq \frac{f(H, t)}{\overline{f(t)}} m(H, t)(1 - \varepsilon_c)(1 - \varepsilon_m),$$

where ε_c is the probability of disruption of the schema H due to the crossover operation and ε_m is the probability of disruption of the schema H due to the mutation operation.

To the extent that ε_c and ε_m are small, the genetic algorithm produces a new population in which each of the 3^L schemata appears with approximately the near-optimal frequency. For example, if the fitness ratio

$$\frac{f(H, t)}{\overline{f(t)}}$$

of a particular schema H were to be above unity by at least a constant amount over several generations, that schema would be propagated into succeeding generations at an exponentially increasing rate.

Note that the schema theorem applies *simultaneously* to *all* 3^L schemata in the next generation. That is, the genetic algorithm performs a near-optimal allocation of trials simultaneously, in parallel, for all schemata.

Moreover, this remarkable result is *independent of the fitness measure* involved in a particular problem and is *problem-independent*.

Table 3.15 begins to illustrate the schema theorem in detail. Table 3.15 shows the effect of the reproduction operation on the 27 schemata. The first four columns of this table come from table 3.14. Column 5 shows the number of occurrences $m(H, MP)$ of schema H in the mating pool (called MP). Column 6 shows the schema average fitness $f(H, MP)$ in the mating pool.

A plus sign in column 5 of table 3.15 indicates that the operation of fitness-proportionate reproduction has caused the number of occurrences of a schema to increase as compared to the number of occurrences shown in column 3 for the initial random population. Such increases occur for the schemata numbered 13, 15, 16, 18, 22, 24, and 25. These seven schemata are shown in bold type in table 3.15. Note that the string 110 belongs to each of these seven schemata. Moreover, string 110, like all strings, belongs to the all-encompassing trivial schema *** (which counts the population). The individual 110 had a fitness of 6. Its fitness ratio is 2.0 because its fitness is twice the average fitness of the population $\overline{f} = 3$. As a result of the probabilistic operation of fitness-proportionate reproduction, individual 110 was reproduced two times for the mating pool. This copying increases the number of occurrences of all eight schemata to which 110 belongs. Each schema has grown in an exponentially increasing way based on the fitness ratio of the individual 110. Note that the number of occurrences of the all-encompassing schema *** does not change, because this particular copying operation will be counterbalanced by the failure to copy some other individual. This simultaneous growth in number of occurrences of the non-trivial schemata happens merely as a result of the Darwinian reproduction (copying) operation. In other

Table 3.15 Number of occurrences $m(H, MP)$ and the average fitness $f(H, MP)$ of the 27 schemata in the mating pool reflecting the effect of the reproduction operation.

#	H	Generation 0		Mating pool created after reproduction	
		$m(H, 0)$	$f(H, 0)$	$m(H, MP)$	$f(H, MP)$
1	000	0	0	0	0
2	001	1	1	0 −	0
3	00*	1	1	0 −	0
4	010	1	2	1	2
5	011	1	3	1	3
6	01*	2	2.5	2	2.5
7	0*0	1	2	1	2
8	0*1	2	2	1 −	3
9	0**	3	2	2 −	2.5
10	100	0	0	0	0
11	101	0	0	0	0
12	10*	0	0	0	0
13	**110**	**1**	**6**	**2 +**	**6**
14	111	0	0	0	0
15	**11***	**1**	**6**	**2 +**	**6**
16	**1*0**	**1**	**6**	**2 +**	**6**
17	1*1	0	0	0	0
18	**1****	**1**	**6**	**2 +**	**6**
19	*00	0	0	0	0
20	*01	1	1	0 −	0
21	*0*	1	1	0 −	0
22	***10**	**2**	**4**	**3 +**	**4.67**
23	*11	1	3	1	3
24	***1***	**3**	**3.67**	**4 +**	**4.25**
25	****0**	**2**	**4**	**3 +**	**4.67**
26	**1	2	2	1 −	3
27	***	4	3	4	4.25
Total		32	96	32	136
Mean			3.00		4.25
Nonzero items		20	20	16	16

words, Darwinian fitness-proportionate reproduction leads to an optimal allocation of trials on the basis of the currently available performance information. Darwinian fitness-proportionate reproduction is the reason genetic algorithms cause a mathematically near-optimal allocation of future trials of the search space.

The result of Darwinian fitness-proportionate reproduction is that the mating pool (i.e., columns 5 and 6) has a different genetic profile (i.e., histogram over the schemata) than the original population at generation 0 (i.e., columns 3 and 4).

A minus sign in column 5 of table 3.15 indicates that the operation of fitness-proportionate reproduction has caused the number of occurrences of a schema to decrease as compared to the number of occurrences shown in column 3. Such decreases occur for the schemata numbered 2, 3, 8, 9, 20, 21, and 26. The individual 001 belongs to these seven schemata (and to the all-encompassing schema ***). The individual 001 was the worst-of-generation individual in the population at generation 0. It has a fitness ratio of 1/3, because its fitness is only a third of the average fitness of the population $\bar{f}$. As a result of the probabilistic operation of fitness-proportionate reproduction, individual 001 was not copied at all into the mating pool, because its fitness ratio of 1/3 caused it to receive zero copies in the mating pool. Individual 001 became extinct.

As a result of the extinction of 001, the population became less diverse (as indicated by the drop from 20 to 16 in the number of distinct schemata contained in the population as shown in the last row of table 3.15). On the other hand, the population became fitter; the average fitness of the population increased from 3.0 to 4.25, as shown on the second-to-last row of table 3.15.

The fitness of individual 011 equals the average fitness of the population. It appeared once in generation 0. Its fitness ratio is 1.0. As a result, we expect this individual to appear once in the mating pool. There will be no change in any schema to which 011 belongs as a result of this copying.

Note that the genetic algorithm never performs any explicit bookkeeping to update the number of occurrences or the values of average fitness of the various schemata as a result of the reproduction operation used to create the mating pool. There is no explicit table such as table 3.15 for the mating pool in the genetic algorithm. All of this computation occurs implicitly. The $M = 4$ individuals in the population contain all of the information about all of the schemata.

Note that no new individuals and no new schemata are ever created as a result of the Darwinian operation of reproduction used to create the mating pool. Natural selection does not create variety. It merely selects from whatever variety is already present in the population in order to increase the average fitness of the population as a whole.

The genetic crossover operation serves the necessary function of creating promising new individuals in the search space; however, it slightly degrades the optimal allocation of trials described above. The degradation is small for a schema with tight genetic linkage.

For the conventional genetic algorithm operating on strings, the *defining length* $\delta(H)$ of a schema H is the distance between the outermost specific, non-* symbols. The number of interstitial points where crossover may occur is $L - 1$. For example, the defining length of the schema $H = 1*1$ is $\delta(1*1) = 2$, whereas $\delta(*11) = 1$. If a string of length $L = 3$ (such as 011) belongs to a schema of defining length $\delta(H) = 1$ (such as *11), then the probability is $1/2$ that the crossover point will be selected outside this schema (i.e., between the first and second position in the string). If the crossover point is between the first and the second position of the string, the schema *11 will not be disrupted by crossover. If the crossover point is selected inside the schema and the second parent participating in the crossover does not belong to the schema (as is usually the situation), the offspring will usually not belong to the schema.

In general, the probability ε_c of disruption of a schema H due to the crossover is approximately

$$\varepsilon_c = \frac{\delta(H)}{L - 1}.$$

Therefore, ε_c is small when $\delta(H)$ is small. That is, a schema with a relatively short defining length appears in future generations with nearly the targeted optimal frequency (i.e., an exponentially increasing frequency).

The genetic mutation operation serves the desirable function of introducing occasional variety into a population and of restoring lost diversity to a population; however, it slightly degrades the optimal allocation of trials described above. The degradation is small for a schema with low specificity $O(H)$ (i.e., a relatively few defined positions). For example, a random mutant of the string 011 has a greater chance of continuing to belong to the schema **1 (whose specificity is only 1) than of continuing to belong to the schema *11 (whose specificity is 2).

As to the mutation operation for the conventional genetic algorithm operating on strings, the probability of disruption of a schema H due to the mutation ε_m is given by

$$\varepsilon_m = (1 - p_m)^{O(H)} \approx 1 - p_m O(H),$$

where $O(H)$ is the specificity (order) of the schema involved. Therefore, ε_m is small when $O(H)$ is small.

The allocation of future trials is most nearly optimal when ε_c and ε_m are both small. A schema with a relatively short defining length and a relatively few defined positions is a building block which will be propagated from generation to generation at close to the near-optimal rate. The genetic algorithm processes such schema most favorably. A problem whose solution can be incrementally built up from schemata of relatively short defining length and relatively few defined positions is handled by genetic algorithms in a near-optimal way.

Table 3.16 shows the number of occurrences (column 7) of each of the 27 schemata and the average fitness of each schema (column 8) after both the operations of reproduction and crossover are performed (that is, for generation 1).

In table 3.16, a plus sign in column 7 indicates that the crossover operation has caused the number of occurrences of a schema to increase as compared to the number of occurrences shown in column 5 for the mating pool. This occurs for schemata numbered 4, 8, 14, and 17. In fact, schemata 14 and 17 were not represented in the population prior to crossover. Schema 14 (i.e., 111) represents the optimal individual business strategy being sought in the problem.

A minus sign in column 7 indicates a schema showing a decrease. This occurs for the schemata numbered 5, 7, 13, and 16.

The average fitness values are estimates based on the average of all the similar individuals constituting a schema. Even though these similar individuals are not actually present in the current population, the estimates of the schema average fitness can point the genetic algorithm into areas of the search space worthy of additional sampling and search.

Note that the genetic algorithm never performs any explicit bookkeeping to update the number of occurrences or the values of average fitness of the various schemata as a result of the crossover operation. There is no explicit table such as table 3.16 in the genetic algorithm. All of this computation occurs implicitly. The $M = 4$ individuals in the population contain all of the information about all of the schemata.

Genetic algorithms superficially seem to process only the particular individual binary character strings actually present in the current population. *Adaptation in Natural and Artificial Systems* focused attention on the fact that the genetic algorithm actually implicitly processes, in parallel, a large amount of useful information concerning unseen Boolean hyperplanes (schemata).

Thus, the genetic algorithm has the remarkable property of *implicit parallelism* (sometimes also called intrinsic parallelism), which enables it to create individual strings for the new population in such a way that the hyperplanes representing these similar other individuals can all be expected to be automatically represented in proportion to the ratio of the fitness of the hyperplane (schema) $f(H, t)$ to the average population fitness $\overline{f(t)}$.

Moreover, this implicit computation is accomplished without any explicit memory beyond the population itself and without any explicit computation beyond the simple genetic operations acting on the individual strings in the population. The only memory involved in the genetic algorithm is the state of the system itself (that is, the population containing merely $M = 4$ strings).

As Schaffer (1987) points out, "Since there are very many more than N hyperplanes represented in a population of N strings, this constitutes the only known example of the combinatorial explosion working to advantage instead of disadvantage."

Table 3.16 Number of occurrences (column 7) and the schema average fitness (column 8) of each of the 27 schemata in generation 1.

#	H	Generation 0		Mating pool created after reproduction		Generation 1 created after crossover	
		$m(H, 0)$	$f(H, 0)$	$m(H, MP)$	$f(H, MP)$	$m(H, 1)$	$f(H, 1)$
1	000	0	0	0	0	0	0
2	001	1	1	0	0	0	0
3	00*	1	1	0	0	0	0
4	**010**	**1**	**2**	**1**	**2**	**2+**	**2**
5	011	1	3	1	3	0−	0
6	01*	2	2.5	2	2.5	2	2
7	0*0	1	2	1	2	0−	0
8	**0*1**	**2**	**2**	**1**	**3**	**2+**	**2**
9	0**	3	2	2	2.5	2	2
10	100	0	0	0	0	0	0
11	101	0	0	0	0	0	0
12	10*	0	0	0	0	0	0
13	110	1	6	2	6	1−	6
14	**111**	**0**	**0**	**0**	**0**	**1+**	**7**
15	11*	1	6	2	6	2	6.5
16	1*0	1	6	2	6	1−	6
17	**1*1**	**0**	**0**	**0**	**0**	**1+**	**7**
18	1**	1	6	2	6	2	6.5
19	*00	0	0	0	0	0	0
20	*01	1	1	0	0	0	0
21	*0*	1	1	0	0	0	0
22	*10	2	4	3	4.67	3	3.3
23	*11	1	3	1	3	1	7
24	*1*	3	3.67	4	4.25	4	4.25
25	**0	2	4	3	4.67	3	3.3
26	**1	2	2	1	3	1	7
27	***	4	3	4	4.25	4	4.25
Total		32	96	32	136	32	136
Mean			3.00		4.25		4.2
Nonzero items		20	20	16	16	16	16

3.3 EXAMPLES OF REPRESENTATION SCHEMES

The genetic algorithm is a procedure that searches the space of character strings of the specified length to find strings with relatively high fitness. In preparing to apply the genetic algorithm to a particular problem, the first step involves determining the way to represent the problem in the chromosome-like language of genetic algorithms.

An immediate question arises as to whether it is possible to represent many problems in a chromosome-like way. In the simple example in the previous section, each possible business strategy for managing the hamburger restaurants involved three binary variables so that each possible business strategy was very naturally representable by a binary string of length 3.

This section presents two examples illustrating how two other problems can be represented in this chromosome-like way.

3.3.1 Optimization of an Engineering Design

The first example illustrates a "vanilla" representation scheme that is often used in practical applications of the genetic algorithm to optimization problems. The problem is an engineering optimization problem described by Goldberg and Samtani (1986).

Figure 3.4 shows a ten-member truss whose ten cross-sectional areas are identified as A_1, A_2, ..., A_{10}. The truss is supported from a wall on the left and must support two loads as shown. Moreover, the stress on each member must lie in an allowable range as expressed by a stress constraint for that member. The goal is to find the cross-sectional area for each member of this load-carrying truss so as to minimize the total weight (cost) of the material used in building it.

This problem requires a search of a ten-dimensional space of real numbers for the combination of values of A_1, A_2, ..., A_{10} that have the best fitness (i.e., least cost or weight).

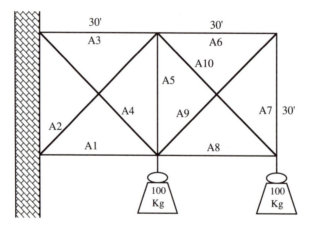

Figure 3.4 Ten-member truss.

The first major step in preparing to use the conventional genetic algorithm operating on strings is to select the representation scheme. One popular representation scheme is to represent a set of real numbers as a fixed-length binary string in which each real number is associated with part of the overall string. Goldberg and Samtani decided to represent the ten cross-sectional areas by a 40-bit string. Goldberg and Samtani then decided that a cross-sectional area equal to 0.1 square inch would be represented by the four bits 0000 and that a cross-sectional area equal to 10.0 square inches would be represented by the four bits 1111. Each of the remaining 14 bit patterns encoded suitable intermediate values for the cross-sectional area.

Figure 3.5 shows a chromosome of length 40 representing a ten-member truss. The first four bits in this 40-bit string encode the cross-sectional area A_1 of the first member of the truss. These four bits allow the first member of the truss to take on one of 16 different possible values of cross-sectional area. For example, the first cross-sectional area A_1 is encoded by 0010 and is 0.66 square inch. Each of the remaining nine cross-sectional areas is similarly represented by four bits.

In selecting the representation scheme for this problem, Goldberg and Samtani used their understanding of the particular problem to select a minimum and a maximum cross-sectional area to consider and to select the granularity of the different possible values of the cross-sectional area. Alternatively, if 16 beam sizes were commercially available, they might have chosen to encode the four-bit substrings 0000 through 1111 to correspond to the available sizes.

In summary, the representation scheme used by Goldberg and Samtani involved an alphabet of size 2 (i.e., $K = 2$), chromosomes of length 40 (i.e., $L = 40$), and the mapping between the ten real-valued cross-sectional areas and the 40-bit chromosome as described above. The selection of K, L, and the mapping constitutes the first major step in preparing to use the conventional genetic algorithm operating on fixed-length character strings.

The search space for this problem is of size 2^{40}, which is about 10^{12}.

The second major step in preparing to use the conventional genetic algorithm operating on strings is to identify the fitness measure that ascertains how well a particular ten-member truss represented by a particular 40-bit string performs in solving the problem. Goldberg and Samtani decided that the fitness of a given point in the search space (i.e., a given design for the truss) would be the total cost of the material for all ten members of the truss. If a point in the search space violates one or more of the ten stress constraints, the fitness is the total cost of the material plus a penalty for infeasibility. In this problem, fitness is a highly nonlinear function of the ten variables.

The third major step in preparing to use the conventional genetic algorithm is the selection of the parameters and variables for controlling the algorithm.

| 0010 | 1110 | 0001 | 0011 | 1011 | 0011 | 1111 | 0011 | 0011 | 1010 |

Figure 3.5 Chromosome of length 40 representing a ten-member truss.

The two most important parameters are population size (M) and the maximum number of generations to be run (G). In solving this problem, Goldberg and Samtani used a population of $M = 200$ individual bit strings of length $L = 40$ and a maximum allowed number of generations of $G = 40$.

The fourth major step in preparing to use the conventional genetic algorithm is deciding on the method of terminating a run and the method for designating the result. Goldberg and Samtani terminated their runs after the maximum allowed number of generations were run and designated the best result obtained during the run (the "best-so-far" individual) as the result of the run.

Once these four preparatory steps are done, the genetic algorithm proceeds in a *domain-independent* way to try to solve the problem. The goal of the genetic algorithm is to search this multidimensional, highly nonlinear search space for the point with globally optimal fitness (i.e., weight or cost).

In practice, Goldberg and Samtani used a population size M of 200. They performed several runs in which about 8,000 individuals were processed on each run (i.e., 40 generations of 200 individuals). In each such run, they obtained a feasible design for the ten-member truss for which the total cost of the material was within about 1% of the known best solution.

The number of individuals that must be processed to solve a given problem is often used as the measure of the computational burden associated with executing the genetic algorithm.

3.3.2   Artificial Ant

As a second illustration of a representation scheme used for the conventional genetic algorithm operating on strings, consider the task of navigating (Jefferson et al. 1991; Collins and Jefferson 1991a, 1991b) an artificial ant so as to find all the food lying along an irregular trail. The goal is to find a finite-state automaton for performing this task.

The artificial ant operates in a square 32×32 toroidal grid in the plane. It starts in the upper left cell of the grid identified by the coordinates $(0, 0)$ facing east.

The "Santa Fe trail" is an irregular winding trail consisting of 89 food pellets. The trail is not straight and continuous, but instead has single gaps, double gaps, single gaps at corners, double gaps at corners (short knight moves), and triple gaps at corners (long knight moves). The Santa Fe trail, designed by Christopher Langton, is a somewhat more difficult trail than the "John Muir trail" originally used for this problem.

Figure 3.6 shows the Santa Fe trail. Food is represented by solid black squares, while gaps in the trail are represented by gray squares. The numbers identify key features of the trail in terms of the number of pieces of food occurring along the trail between the starting point and that feature. For example, the number 3 highlights the first corner (located after three pieces of food along the trail). Similarly, the number 11 highlights the first single gap along the trail and the number 38 highlights the first short knight's move.

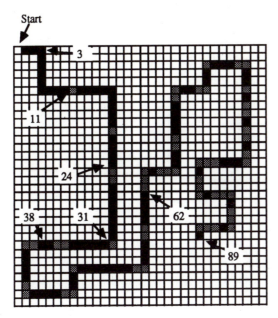

Figure 3.6 The Santa Fe trail for the artificial ant problem.

The artificial ant has a very limited view of its world. In particular, the ant has a sensor that can see only the single immediately adjacent cell in the direction the ant is currently facing. The ant can execute any of the following four primitive actions:

- RIGHT turns the ant right by 90° (without moving the ant).
- LEFT turns the ant left by 90° (without moving the ant).
- MOVE moves the ant forward in the direction it is currently facing. When an ant moves into a square, it eats the food, if there is any, in that square (thereby eliminating food from that square and erasing the trail).
- NO–OP (No Operation) does nothing.

The ant's goal is to traverse the entire trail (thereby eating all of the food) within a reasonable amount of time. This problem, with a time limit, presents a difficult and challenging planning problem. Jefferson, Collins, et al. successfully used the genetic algorithm operating on fixed-length character strings to search for and discover a finite-state automaton enabling the artificial ant to traverse the trail.

The first major step in preparing to use the conventional genetic algorithm operating on strings is to select the representation scheme. Jefferson, Collins, et al. started by deciding to represent an individual automaton in the population by a binary string representing the state-transition table of the automaton (and its initial state).

To illustrate the process of representing a finite-state automaton with a fixed-length character string, consider the four-state automaton whose state-transition diagram is shown in figure 3.7.

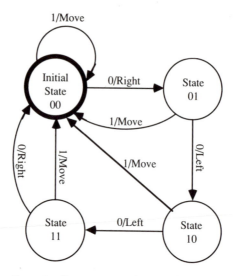

Figure 3.7 State-transition diagram of an illustrative four-state automaton.

This diagram is interpreted as follows: The automaton has four states, represented by the four circles. The automaton starts at its initial state (state 00) in the upper left corner of the figure. The input to the automaton comes from the ant's sensor and consists of a single bit indicating whether or not there is any food in the immediately adjacent square in the direction in which the ant is facing. If the ant senses food (i.e., the input is 1), the ant MOVES forward. Both the sensor input of 1 to the automaton and the output of MOVE are shown on the arc starting at state 00 at the top of the figure. This arc (labeled "1 / MOVE") represents the state transition that occurs when the automaton is in state 00 and receives the sensor input of 1. The next state associated with this arc happens to be state 00. This arc also represents the output (i.e., the action MOVE by the ant). The interpretation of this state transition is that if the ant senses food, it MOVES forward (eating the food pellet present on the trail) and then returns to state 00.

On the other hand, if the ant senses no food (i.e., the input is 0), the ant turns RIGHT and ends up at the new state 01 (in the upper right corner of the figure). This state transition is indicated by the arc labeled "0 / RIGHT."

In this new state, 01, if the ant now senses food, it MOVES forward (eating the food) and returns to state 00. But if the ant still senses no food, it turns LEFT and ends up at state 10.

State 10 is an intermediate state in a sequence of two consecutive actions. By turning LEFT, the ant has reoriented itself to its original facing direction. Since the ant has not yet moved and we know that there is no food in its original facing direction, it will necessarily turn LEFT and end up at state 11. A state transition labeled "1 / MOVE" from state 10 is shown for the sake of completeness; however, this state transition can never occur.

If the ant senses food in state 11, it MOVES forward (eating the food) and returns to state 00.

Table 3.17 State-transition table for the illustrative four-state automaton.

	Current state	Input	New state	Operation
1	00	0	01	10 = Right
2	00	1	00	11 = Move
3	01	0	10	01 = Left
4	01	1	00	11 = Move
5	10	0	11	01 = Left
6	10	1	00	11 = Move
7	11	0	00	10 = Right
8	11	1	00	11 = Move

00	0110	0011	1001	0011	1101	0011	0010	0011

Figure 3.8 Chromosome of length 34 representing the state-transition table of the four-state automaton.

Thus, if there originally is food in front of the ant, or to the right, or to the left, the ant will MOVE to that square (eating the food) and will return to state 00 so that it is ready to repeat the process at its new location. This illustrative four-state automaton is therefore capable of successfully navigating the ant along the trail provided food is present in front of the ant, or to the right, or to the left.

If there is no food to the right, or to the left, or in front of the ant, the ant goes back to state 00. This return to state 00 will lead to an infinite loop. Since the trail has many gaps and irregularities, this illustrative four-state automaton is inadequate as a solution to the artificial ant problem.

The state-transition diagram (figure 3.7) for this four-state automaton can be converted into the state-transition table shown in table 3.17 where each row represents a combination of one of the four states (shown in column 2) and the binary input (shown in column 3). State 00 is understood to be the initial state. Column 4 shows the new state to which the automaton goes given that it started in the state shown in column 2 and received the input shown in column 3. Column 5 shows the action taken by the ant.

Table 3.17 has one row for each of the eight state transitions (arcs) contained in figure 3.7.

We can then convert this table into a binary string (i.e., a chromosome, or a genome) by stringing together the four bits from the last two columns in each of the eight rows. We can designate the initial state by appending two additional bits (i.e., 00) to the beginning of the string.

Figure 3.8 shows the 34-bit chromosome (genome) that represents the state-transition table for the illustrative four-state automaton.

Any four-state automaton can be converted into a 34 bit string in this manner. Moreover, because of the presence of the No-Op operation, every 34-bit string represents a valid and executable finite-state automaton.

This representation scheme allows us to put a finite-state automaton into the chromosomal form required by the genetic algorithm. Note, however, that this 34-bit representation scheme can only represent an automaton with four or fewer states. If the solution to the problem requires more than four states, this representation scheme cannot express or represent that solution. Thus, for this problem, the selection of the representation scheme determines the maximum size and structural complexity of the eventual solution. The representation scheme is established by the user as a preparatory step that is performed before the genetic algorithm starts running. In the conventional genetic algorithm, the representation scheme is generally not changed during the run; however, it is changed during the run in some variants of the algorithm, including those of Steven F. Smith (1980, 1983), Shaefer (1987), Goldberg, Korb, and Deb (1989).

As it happens, four states are not sufficient to solve this problem, because the trail has so many different types of gaps and irregularities. Knowing this, Jefferson, Collins, et al. did not, in fact, select a 34-bit representation scheme for this problem. Instead, they allowed for up to 32 states. The state-transition table for a finite-state automaton with 32 states has 64 rows (32 states, each with two possible sensory inputs). For each row in the state-transition table, the ant's action (i.e., the output of the automaton) can still be coded as two bits (for the operations of MOVE, LEFT, and RIGHT). The next state of the automaton must be coded with five bits to accommodate a 32-state automaton. The complete behavior of a 32-state automaton can be specified by a binary string (genome) with 453 bits (64 substrings of length 7 plus 5 additional bits representing the initial state).

In summary, the representation scheme actually used by Jefferson, Collins, et al. for this problem involved an alphabet of size two (i.e., $K = 2$), chromosomes of length $L = 453$, and the mapping between automata and chromosomes as described above. The selection of K, L, and the mapping constitutes the first major step in preparing to use the conventional genetic algorithm operating on strings.

The second major step in preparing to use the conventional genetic algorithm is to identify the fitness measure that ascertains how well a particular string performs in solving the problem. The fitness of a particular 453-bit string in this problem is simply how much food the ant eats, in a reasonable amount of time, if its actions are controlled by the finite-state automaton represented by the 453-bit string. A maximum number of time steps is established both because a finite-state automaton can go into an infinite loop (as we have already seen) and because we want to exclude automata that exhaustively search all 1,024 squares on the grid using a random walk or a tessellating pattern. For this problem, this limit might be 200 time steps. If an ant "times out," its fitness is simply the amount of food eaten up to that moment. Thus, fitness ranges between 0 and 89 (i.e., the number of food pellets on the trail).

The third major step in preparing to use the conventional genetic algorithm is the selection of the parameters and variables for controlling the algorithm.

The population size M was 65,536, and the maximum number of generations G allowed to be run was 200. Generally, a larger population is required to solve a problem involving a longer bit string.

In one particular run on the massively parallel Connection Machine, a single individual attained a perfect score of 89 pieces of food after 200 generations. This particular solution happened to complete the task of finding all 89 pieces of food in precisely 200 time steps.

A finite-state automaton is only one way to control the activities of an artificial ant in carrying out a complex task. A second way is to use a neural network. A third way is to use a computer program that specifies the sequence of operations to be performed. The third way will be the main subject of this book.

We will revisit the artificial ant problem in section 7.2.

Jefferson, Collins, et al. also successfully searched for and discovered a multilayer neural net enabling the artificial ant to traverse the trail. Neural networks consist of processing elements that are connected with various weighted signal lines (Rumelhart, Hinton, and Williams 1986; Hinton 1989; Nilsson 1990). Jefferson, Collins, et al. started by assuming that the neural net necessary to solve the problem would have two linear threshold processing elements in the input layer (representing the two possible sensory inputs of the ant), five linear threshold processing elements in the hidden layer, and four linear threshold processing elements in the output layer (for the four possible operations of the ant). They also decided that the network would be fully connected between consecutive layers in the forward direction, and they decided that the output of each processing element of the hidden layer would feed back into all processing elements of that layer. Consequently, the five processing elements in the hidden layer and the four processing elements in the output layer each had seven inputs (the outputs from both processing elements of the input layer and the outputs from all five processing elements of the hidden layer).

Once the arrangement of linear processing elements and their connections is established, a neural net is defined by the values of various floating-point numbers representing the weights on various signal lines connecting the various linear processing elements, the thresholds of the linear processing elements, and the initial activation levels of the linear processing elements. The representation scheme for a neural network can therefore be a binary string of 520 bits that encodes this set of floating-point numbers. As such, it is similar to the "vanilla" representation scheme used by Goldberg and Samtani for their ten-member truss. Using a population size of 65,536, they were successful in finding a neural network to solve the artificial ant problem.

3.4 SOURCES OF ADDITIONAL INFORMATION ABOUT GENETIC ALGORITHMS

- *Adaptation in Natural and Artificial Systems* by John Holland (1975) of the University of Michigan is the pioneering monograph that established the field of genetic algorithms. A new edition was published by The MIT Press in 1992.

- *Genetic Algorithms in Search, Optimization, and Machine Learning* by David E. Goldberg (1989) of the University of Illinois at Champaign-Urbana is both a textbook and a survey of the field. This book contains an extensive bibliography which will be updated in the upcoming second edition.

- *Genetic Algorithms and Simulated Annealing* by Lawrence Davis (1987) is an edited collection of research papers that provides a broad overview of research activity in the field of genetic algorithms.

- *Handbook of Genetic Algorithms* by Lawrence Davis (1991) contains a tutorial on applying genetic algorithms to practical problems, a collection of 13 application case studies, a description of the computer program for the Object-Oriented Genetic Algorithm (OOGA) written in Common LISP and CLOS, and a description of the GENESIS genetic algorithm program in C. The software is available separately through the publisher.

- *Induction: Processes of Inference, Learning, and Discovery* by Holland et al. (1986) provides the basic description of genetic classifier systems.

- *Parallelism and Programming in Classifier Systems* by Stephanie Forrest (1991) describes work on semantic networks and classifier systems.

- Rick Riolo (1988a) describes recent research into classifier systems. Riolo (1988b) also describes domain-independent software written in C for implementing classifier systems.

- *Genetic Algorithms and Robotics* by Yuval Davidor 1991 describes applications of genetic algorithms to robotics.

- *Genetic Algorithms + Data Structures = Evolution Programs* by Zbigniew Michalewicz further describes genetic algorithms.

There are two sets of proceedings devoted entirely to genetic algorithms and related fields:

- The proceedings of the 1985, 1987, 1989, and 1991 International Conferences on Genetic Algorithms (ICGA). See Grefenstette 1985, Grefenstette 1987, Schaffer 1989, and Belew and Booker 1991.

- The proceedings of the workshop on Foundations of Genetic Algorithms (FOGA) contain numerous current research papers on the theoretical foundations of genetic algorithms. See Rawlins 1991.

The proceedings of the following regularly scheduled conferences on adaptive behavior and artificial life contain a significant number of papers on genetic algorithms.

- The proceedings of the conferences on Parallel Problem Solving from Nature (PPSN) contain numerous current research papers on genetic algorithms and the closely related *Evolutionsstrategie* ("ES") developed in Germany independently from the work in the United States on genetic algorithms. See Schwefel and Maenner 1991. A successor conference is scheduled in 1992.

- The proceedings of the 1990 conference on Simulation of Adaptive Behavior (SAB) contain numerous current research papers on genetic algorithms. See Meyer and Wilson 1991. A successor conference is scheduled in 1992.

- The proceedings of the 1987 and 1990 conferences on Artificial Life contain numerous current research papers on genetic algorithms. See Langton 1989 and Langton et al. 1991. In addition, a videotape *Artificial Life II Video Proceedings* contains visualizations of the proceedings of the 1990 conference (Langton 1991). A successor conference is scheduled in 1992.

- The proceedings of the 1991 European Conference on Artificial Life contain numerous current research papers on genetic algorithms. See Varela and Bourgine 1992.

- The proceedings of the first annual conference on evolutionary programming (Fogel and Atmar 1992) report on continuing work in the field of simulated evolution.

The journal *Complex Systems* and the new journal *Adaptive Behavior*, published by The MIT Press, contain many articles relevant to genetic algorithms.

Much of the ongoing work of the Santa Fe Institute in New Mexico, as reported in technical reports and other publications, is related to genetic algorithms.

In addition, numerous other regularly held conferences and journals on neural networks, artificial intelligence, and machine learning include some papers on genetic algorithms or have occasional special issues on genetic algorithms (Goldberg and Holland 1988; De Jong 1990).

4 The Representation Problem for Genetic Algorithms

Representation is a key issue in genetic algorithm work because genetic algorithms directly manipulate a coded representation of the problem and because the representation scheme can severely limit the window by which a system observes its world. The conventional genetic algorithm operating on fixed-length character strings is capable of solving a great many problems. The mathematical tractability of fixed-length character strings (as compared with mathematical structures which are more complex) permitted Holland and subsequent researchers to construct a significant body of theory as to why genetic algorithms work. Nonetheless, the use of fixed-length character strings leaves many issues unsettled.

For many problems, the most natural representation for a solution is a hierarchical computer program rather than a fixed-length character string. The size and the shape of the hierarchical computer program that will solve a given problem are generally not known in advance, so the program should have the potential of changing its size and shape. It is difficult, unnatural, and constraining to represent hierarchical computer programs of dynamically varying sizes and shapes with fixed-length character strings.

Representation schemes based on fixed-length character strings do not readily provide the hierarchical structure central to the organization of computer programs (into programs and subroutines) and the organization of behavior (into tasks and subtasks).

Representation schemes based on fixed-length character strings do not provide any convenient way of representing arbitrary computational procedures or of incorporating iteration or recursion when these capabilities are desirable or necessary to solve a problem.

Moreover, such representation schemes do not have dynamic variability. The initial selection of string length limits in advance the number of internal states of the system and limits what the system can learn.

The predetermination of the size and shape of solutions and the pre-identification of the particular components of solutions has been a bane of machine learning systems from the earliest times (Samuel 1959).

4.1 PREVIOUS WORK

The need for more powerful representations for genetic algorithms has been recognized for some time (De Jong 1985, 1987, 1988).

One approach to the problem of representation in genetic algorithms has been to provide greater flexibility by increasing the complexity of the structures undergoing adaptation in the genetic algorithm.

Such efforts began with early work by Cavicchio (1970) and with Holland's (1975) proposed broadcast language. The broadcast language led directly to the genetic classifier system (Holland and Reitman 1978) and to the "bucket brigade" apportionment-of-credit algorithm for classifier systems (Holland 1986; Holland et al. 1986; Holland and Burks 1987; Holland and Burks 1989; Booker, Goldberg, and Holland 1989).

The classifier system represented a considerable extension of the complexity of the structures undergoing adaptation. The genetic classifier system is a cognitive architecture that allows the adaptive modification of a set of if-then rules. The architecture of the classifier system blends important features from the contemporary paradigms of artificial intelligence, connectionism, and machine learning, including

- the power, understandability, and convenience of if-then rules from expert systems,
- a connectionist-style allocation of credit that rewards specific rules when the system as a whole takes an external action that produces a reward, and
- the creative power and efficient search capability of the conventional genetic algorithm operating on fixed-length character strings.

In the classifier system, there is a set of if-then rules. Both the condition part and the action part of each if-then rule consist of a fixed-length character string. The condition part of an if-then rule in the classifier system typically contains one or more "don't care" positions so that a rule can be fired when a subset of environmental features is detected. The "bucket brigade" algorithm then apportions credit among the if-then rules on the basis of their contribution toward making the system take an external action that produces a reward. The genetic algorithm then operates on the set of if-then rules to create new rules. The objective of the classifier system is to breed a co-adapted set of if-then rules that successfully work together to solve a problem.

Steven F. Smith (1980, 1983) argued for the flexibility provided by variable-length strings; he departed from the "Michigan" approach of emphasizing fixed-length character strings in genetic algorithms and classifier systems. In addition, in Smith's LS-1 system the individual elements of a strings are if-then rules (rather than single characters) so that a single string represents a set of rules. Smith's work is an example of the "Pitt" (Pittsburgh) approach to classifier systems.

Antonisse and Keller (1987) proposed applying genetic methods to higher-level representations. See also Antonisse 1991. Bickel and Bickel (1987) allied genetic methods to if-then expert system rules. In their system, each if-then rule had one action part while the condition part of each rule was a tree of Boolean operators (such as AND, OR, and NOT) and various Boolean relations (such as =, <, and >). In Grefenstette's (1989) SAMUEL system, the condition part of each if-then expert system rule consisted of a combination of one or more Boolean predicates involving ranges of sensor values.

Wilson (1987b) recognized the central importance of hierarchies in representing the tasks and subtasks (that is, programs and subroutines) that are needed to solve complex problems. Accordingly, Wilson extended Holland's "bucket brigade" algorithm for credit allocation in genetic classifier systems by introducing hierarchical credit allocation. Wilson's approach encourages the creation of hierarchies of rules in lieu of the exceedingly long sequences of rules that are otherwise characteristic of classifier systems.

Goldberg, Korb, and Deb (1989) introduced the messy genetic algorithm that processes populations of variable-length character strings. Messy genetic algorithms solve problems by combining relatively short, well-tested substrings that deal with part of a problem to form longer, more complex strings that will deal with more complex aspects of the problem.

In addition, domain-specific structures that are more complex than character strings have been devised and applied to various particular applications notably, combinatorial optimization problems such as the traveling salesperson problem (TSP), job shop scheduling problem, VLSI layout problems, and robotics problems (Davidor 1991). In each instance, the crossover operation has been modified in an application-specific way so as either (1) to maintain syntactic legality while preserving the building blocks relevant to the particular application, (2) to repair syntactic illegality while preserving the building blocks relevant to the application, or (3) to compensate for syntactic illegality in some manner appropriate to the application. Many of these application-specific variations on the structures undergoing adaptation are surveyed in Goldberg 1989.

Cramer (1985) approached the problem of program induction in a group of three highly innovative and creative experiments involving two-input, single-output programs consisting of zeroing, looping, and incrementing operations for multiplying two positive integers. Cramer's seminal work on programs consisting of sequences of zeroing, looping, and incrementing operations reported on the highly epistatic nature and difficulties of program induction.

Hicklin (1986) applied reproduction and mutation to the problem of generation of LISP programs. Fujiki (1986) recognized the desirability of extending this work by applying all the genetic operations to LISP programs. Subsequently, Fujiki and Dickinson (1987) implemented crossover and inversion as well as reproduction and mutation in order to manipulate the if-then clauses of a program consisting of a single LISP conditional (COND) statement specifying the strategy for playing the iterated prisoner's dilemma game.

As can be seen, the common feature of many of the foregoing efforts is that they focused on combining the power, understandability, and convenience of if-then rules with the genetic algorithm.

Early efforts at program induction not involving genetic algorithms consisted of efforts to discover automata or computer programs to solve problems using only asexual mutation or a combination of only asexual mutation and reproduction.

For example, Friedberg's early work (1958, 1959) attempted to artificially generate entire computer programs in a hypothetical assembly language on a hypothetical computer with a one-bit register. Friedberg randomly created and randomly mutated individual assembly-code instructions in a program consisting of 64 such instructions. He then executed each program to determine whether or not it performed a certain task, such as adding two bits. Friedberg did not use his all-or-nothing fitness measure to guide the creation of later programs. The search was a blind random search, because the information about fitness that was learned was not used to influence the future direction of the search. There was effectively no concept of reproduction, because programs that successfully performed some or all of the task were not carried forward in time for future modification or use. Moreover, even though millions of programs were created at various times, there was effectively no concept of population, because each program was acted on without reference to any other program. There was *a fortiori* no concept of crossover which recombined parts of two individuals to create an offspring. Moreover, there was effectively no concept of the temporal generations of populations of individuals and no concept of memory, because programs that did not perform the task were discarded. In summary, Friedberg's work contained the elements of random initialization, mutation, and fitness, but not the elements of reproduction, population, generation, memory, or crossover.

In *Artificial Intelligence through Simulated Evolution*, L. J. Fogel, Owens, and Walsh (1966) attempted to evolve small finite automata to produce certain outputs using both mutation and reproduction. Their simulated evolution (evolutionary programming) concept employed the concept of a population of individuals which was not present in Friedberg's work. Simulated evolution started with an initial random population (typically of size two). Each individual in the population was evaluated as to its fitness in performing the task at hand. The population played a role in that the better of the two individuals was saved (i.e., reproduced) for the next generation. The individual automata in the population were randomly mutated as to starting state, state transitions, outputs, or number of states. This mutation was performed on each individual automaton in the population without reference to the other automaton in the population. Since the mutation was asexual, there was no concept of crossover (sexual recombination) between individuals in the population. Thus, simulated evolution contained the elements of random initialization, mutation, fitness, reproduction, population, generation, and memory, but not the concept of crossover. Even though simulated evolution has been successfully applied to a number of different problems (D. B. Fogel 1991), complete reliance on reproduction and mutation makes it very difficult to solve many problems in any reasonable amount of time. Consequently, this early work was not favorably received.

In addition to efforts explicitly aimed at inducing programs to solve problems, there have been an enormous number of different efforts over the years in the broader field of machine learning (Carbonell, Michalski, and Mitchell 1986).

In his ground-breaking work in the field of machine learning, Samuel (1959) lamented the fact that it "is necessary to specify methods of problem solution in minute and exact detail, a time-consuming and costly procedure. Programming computers to learn from experience should eventually eliminate the need for much of this detailed programming effort."

In Samuel's original program for learning to play checkers, learning consisted of progressively adjusting numerical coefficients in an algebraic expression of a predetermined functional form (specifically, a polynomial). The polynomial assigned a value to a configuration of pieces on the checker board. By using the current polynomial to evaluate the boards that would arise if the player made various alternative moves, a best move could be selected on the basis of the current polynomial. The numerical coefficients of the polynomial were then adjusted with experience, so that the predictive quality of the value assigned to a board by the polynomial progressively improved. Samuel predetermined the polynomial functional form and its component terms. Nonetheless, Samuel recognized from the beginning the importance of allowing learning to take place without predetermining the size and shape of the solution and of "[getting] the program to generate its own parameters for the evaluation polynomial."

Similarly, Selfridge (1959), Uhr and Vassler (1966), and Newell, Shaw, and Simon (1979) recognized the importance of allowing learning to occur without being required to specify in advance the size and shape of the eventual solution.

Rosenblatt (1958) used an interconnected network of threshold processing elements situated in layers to classify patterns such as two-dimensional images. Networks with two layers of such threshold processing elements were called *perceptrons*, and those with additional layers are now called *neural networks* (Minsky and Papert 1969; Rumelhart, Hinton, and Williams 1986; Hinton 1989; Nilsson 1990). As with Samuel's checkers player, learning consisted of progressively adjusting numerical coefficients (i.e., a vector of weights) in a space of weights of predetermined size.

Amarel (1972) proposed approaching the problem of finding a computer program that represent a theory by solving a constraint satisfaction problem involving grammars.

Quinlan's (1986) ID3 algorithm provided an efficient means of inducing a decision tree for classifying objects into classes. In ID3, the exact size and shape of the resulting hierarchical tree were not predetermined but instead emerged from an incremental growth process driven by a heuristic measure involving entropy.

Lenat's well-publicized work on AM and EURISKO (Lenat 1976; Lenat 1983; Lenat and Brown 1984) generated LISP representations under the guidance of heuristic rules as will be discussed in chapter 9. See also Green et al. 1974.

Michalski (1983) developed methods for learning production rules and conceptual clustering (Michalski and Stepp 1983).

Mitchell, Utgoff, and Banerji (1983) developed the LEX system for symbolic integration.

In addition to coefficients for polynomials, weight vectors, decision trees, LISP representations, conceptual clusters, if-then rules, and production rules, other paradigms for machine learning have operated on a wide variety of structures, including formal grammars, graphs, formal logical expressions, sets for concept formation, frames, and schemata.

Excellent overviews of current research in machine learning can be found in Michalski, Carbonell, and Mitchell 1983; Michalski, Carbonell, and Mitchell 1986; Kodratoff and Michalski 1990; and Shavlik and Dietterich 1990.

In summary, in the field of genetic algorithms, efforts toward getting programs to learn to solve problems without being explicitly programmed have focused on providing greater flexibility by using increasingly complex representations (often incorporating if-then rules). In the field of program induction, work has largely focused on using mutation and reproduction. In the field of machine learning, work has involved a wide variety of structures, such as weight vectors for neural networks, decision trees for induction, formal grammars, frames, schemata, conceptual clusters, production rules, formal logical expressions, chromosome strings in the conventional genetic algorithm, coefficients for polynomials, and sets for concept formation.

4.2 INTRODUCTION TO LISP

As will be seen, the genetic programming paradigm described in this book applies many of the key ideas of the conventional genetic algorithm to structures that are more complex than character strings patterned after chromosome strings and considerably more general and expressive than the specialized structures used in past work on extending the conventional genetic algorithm. In particular, genetic programming operates with very general, hierarchical computer programs.

Virtually any programming language (e.g., PASCAL, FORTRAN, C, FORTH, LISP) is capable of expressing and executing the general, hierarchical computer programs.

For reasons that are detailed in the next section, I have chosen the LISP (LISt Processing) programming language for the work with genetic programming. In particular, I have chosen the Common LISP dialect (Steele 1990).

This section provides a brief outline of the LISP programming language. The reader already familiar with LISP may wish to skip it.

LISP has only two main types of entities: atoms and lists. The constant 7 and the variable TIME are examples of atoms in LISP. A list in LISP is written as an ordered set of items inside a pair of parentheses. Examples of lists are (A B C D) and (+ 1 2).

A symbolic expression (S-expression) is a list or an atom in LISP. The S-expression is the only syntactic form in pure versions of the LISP programming language. In particular, the programs of LISP are S-expressions.

The LISP compiler and operating system works so as to evaluate whatever it sees. When seen by LISP, constant atoms (e.g., 7) evaluate to themselves and variable atoms (e.g., TIME) evaluate to their current value. When a list is seen by LISP, the list is evaluated by treating the first element of the list (i.e., whatever is just inside the opening parenthesis) as a function and then causing the application of that function to the remaining items of the list. That is, these remaining items are themselves evaluated and then treated as arguments to the function.

For example, (+ 1 2) is a LISP S-expression. In this S-expression, the addition function + appears just inside the opening parenthesis of the S-expression. This S-expression calls for the application of the addition function + to two arguments (i.e., the atoms 1 and 2). The value returned as a result of the evaluation of the S-expression (+ 1 2) is 3. LISP S-expressions are examples of Polish notation (also called "prefix notation").

If any of the arguments in an S-expression are themselves lists (rather than atoms that can be immediately evaluated), LISP first evaluates these arguments (in a recursive, depth-first way, starting from the left, in Common LISP).

The LISP S-expression

(+ (* 2 3) 4)

illustrates the way that computer programs in LISP can be viewed as compositions of functions. This S-expression calls for the application of the addition function + to two arguments, namely the sub-S-expression (* 2 3) and the constant atom 4. In order to complete the evaluation of the entire S-expression, LISP must first evaluate the argument (* 2 3). The sub-S-expression (* 2 3) calls for the application of the multiplication function * to the two constant atoms 2 and 3. This sub-S-expression evaluates to 6, and the entire S-expression evaluates to 10.

Other programming languages apply functions to arguments in a similar manner. For example, the FORTH programming language uses reverse Polish notation; thus, the above S-expression would be written in FORTH as

2 3 * 4 +

FORTH first evaluates the subexpression 2 3 * by applying the function * to the 2 and the 3 to get 6. It then applies the function + to the 6 and the 4 to get 10.

The term "computer program," of course, carries the connotation of the ability to do more than merely perform compositions of simple arithmetic operations. Among the connotations of the term "computer program" is the ability to perform alternative computations conditioned on the outcome of intermediate calculations, to perform operations in a hierarchical way, and to perform computations on variables of many different types. LISP goes about doing all these seemingly different things in the same way: LISP treats the item

just inside the outermost left parenthesis as a function and then applies
that function to the remaining items of the list (i.e., the arguments).

For example, the LISP S-expression

```
(+ 1 2 (IF (> TIME 10) 3 4))
```

illustrates how LISP views conditional and relational elements of computer
programs as applications of functions to arguments. In the sub-S-expression
(> TIME 10), the relation > is viewed as a function and is applied to the
variable atom TIME and the constant atom 10. The subexpression (> TIME 10)
then evaluates to either T (True) or NIL (False), depending on the current value
of the variable atom TIME.

The conditional operator IF is then viewed as a function which is applied
to three arguments: the logical value (T or NIL) returned by the subexpression
(> TIME 10), the constant atom 3, and the constant atom 4. If its first argument evaluates to T (more precisely, anything other than NIL), the function IF
returns the result of evaluating its second argument (i.e., the constant atom 3),
but if its first argument evaluates to NIL, the function IF returns the result of
evaluating its third argument (i.e., the constant atom 4).

Thus, the S-expression evaluates to either 6 or 7, depending on whether the
current value of the variable atom TIME is or is not greater than 10.

Any LISP S-expression can be graphically depicted as a rooted point-labeled
tree with ordered branches. Figure 4.1 shows the tree corresponding to the
above LISP S-expression.

In this graphical depiction, the three internal points of the tree are labeled
with functions (i.e., +, IF, and >). The six external points (leaves) of the tree are
labeled with terminals (e.g., the variable atom TIME and the constant atoms 1,
2, 10, 3, and 4). The root of the tree is labeled with the function (i.e., +)
appearing just inside the leftmost opening parenthesis of the S-expression.

Note that this tree form of a LISP S-expression is equivalent to the parse
tree which many compilers construct internally to represent a given computer
program.

An important feature of LISP is that all LISP computer programs have just
one syntactic form (i.e., the S-expression). The programs of the LISP programming language are S-expressions, and an S-expression is, in effect, the parse
tree of the program.

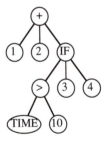

Figure 4.1 The LISP S-expression (+ 1 2 (IF (> TIME 10) 3 4)) depicted as a rooted,
point-labeled tree with ordered branches.

4.3 REASONS FOR CHOOSING LISP

It is possible to implement genetic programming using any programming language that can manipulate computer programs as data and that can then compile, link, and execute the new programs (or support an interpreter to execute the new programs). As previously mentioned, virtually any programming language (e.g., PASCAL, FORTRAN, C, FORTH, LISP) is capable of expressing and evaluating the compositions of functions and terminals necessary to implement genetic programming.

No one reason is decisive in my choice of LISP as the programming language for the work with genetic programming, but the cumulative effect of the following reasons strongly favors the choice of LISP.

First, in the LISP programming language, both programs and data have the same form (i.e., S-expressions). Thus, it is both possible and convenient to treat a computer program in the genetic population as *data* so that it can first be genetically manipulated. Then, it is both possible and convenient to immediately execute the result of the manipulation as a *program*.

Second, the above-mentioned common form for both programs and data in LISP (i.e., S-expressions) is equivalent to the parse tree for the computer program. In spite of their outwardly different appearance and syntax, most compiled programming languages internally convert, at the time of compilation, a given program into a parse tree representing the underlying composition of functions and terminals of that program. In most programming languages, this parse tree is not accessible (or at least not conveniently accessible) to the programmer. And, if it were accessible, it would have a different appearance and syntax than the programming language itself. We need access to the parse tree of the computer program because we want to genetically manipulate the parts of the programs (i.e., subtrees of the parse tree). LISP provides this access because a LISP program is, in effect, its own parse tree.

Third, the EVAL function of LISP provides an almost effortless way of executing a computer program that was just created or genetically manipulated.

Fourth, LISP facilitates the programming of structures whose size and shape change dynamically (rather than being determined in advance). Moreover, LISP's dynamic storage allocation and garbage collection provide administrative support for the programming of dynamically changing structures. The underlying philosophy of all aspects of the LISP programming language is to impose no limitation on programs beyond the limitation inherently imposed by the physical and virtual memory limitations of the computer on which the program is being run. While it is possible to handle structures whose size and shape change dynamically in many programming languages, LISP is especially well suited for this.

Fifth, LISP facilitates the convenient handling of hierarchical structures.

Sixth, the basic PRINT function of the LISP programming language provides ways to present parse trees in an understandable manner.

Seventh, software environments offering an unusually rich collection of programmer tools are commercially available for the LISP programming language.

It is important to note that I did *not* choose the LISP programming language because genetic programming makes any use of the list data structure from LISP or the list manipulation functions unique or peculiar to LISP (such as CONS, CAR, CDR, or APPEND).

5 Overview of Genetic Programming

This chapter provides an overview of the genetic programming paradigm, and the next chapter provides a considerably more detailed description of it.

The genetic programming paradigm continues the trend of dealing with the problem of representation in genetic algorithms by increasing the complexity of the structures undergoing adaptation. In particular, the structures undergoing adaptation in genetic programming are general, hierarchical computer programs of dynamically varying size and shape.

As we saw in chapter 2, many seemingly different problems in artificial intelligence, symbolic processing, and machine learning can be viewed as requiring discovery of a computer program that produces some desired output for particular inputs.

I claim that the process of solving these problems can be reformulated as a search for a highly fit individual computer program in the space of possible computer programs. When viewed in this way, the process of solving these problems becomes equivalent to searching a space of possible computer programs for the fittest individual computer program. In particular, the search space is the space of all possible computer programs composed of functions and terminals appropriate to the problem domain. Genetic programming provides a way to search for this fittest individual computer program.

In genetic programming, populations of hundreds or thousands of computer programs are genetically bred. This breeding is done using the Darwinian principle of survival and reproduction of the fittest along with a genetic recombination (crossover) operation appropriate for mating computer programs. As will be seen, a computer program that solves (or approximately solves) a given problem may emerge from this combination of Darwinian natural selection and genetic operations.

Genetic programming starts with an initial population of randomly generated computer programs composed of functions and terminals appropriate to the problem domain. The functions may be standard arithmetic operations, standard programming operations, standard mathematical functions, logical functions, or domain-specific functions. Depending on the particular problem, the computer program may be Boolean-valued, integer-valued, real-valued, complex-valued, vector-valued, symbolic-valued, or multiple-valued. The creation of this initial random population is, in effect, a blind random search of the search space of the problem.

Each individual computer program in the population is measured in terms of how well it performs in the particular problem environment. This measure is called the *fitness measure*. The nature of the fitness measure varies with the problem.

For example, in the artificial ant problem (subsection 3.3.2), the fitness was the number of pieces of food eaten by the ant. The more food, the better. In a problem involving finding the strategy for playing a game, the fitness measure would be the score (payoff) received by a player in the game. For many problems, fitness is naturally measured by the error produced by the computer program. The closer this error is to zero, the better the computer program. If one is trying to find a good randomizer, the fitness of a given computer program might be measured via entropy. The higher the entropy, the better the randomizer. If one is trying to recognize patterns or classify examples, the fitness of a particular program might be the number of examples (instances) it handles correctly. The more examples correctly handled, the better. On the other hand, in a problem of optimal control, the fitness of a computer program may be the amount of time (or fuel, or money, etc.) it takes to bring the system to a desired target state. The smaller the amount of time (or fuel, or money, etc.), the better. For some problems, fitness may be consist of a combination of factors such as correctness, parsimony, or efficiency.

Typically, each computer program in the population is run over a number of different *fitness cases* so that its fitness is measured as a sum or an average over a variety of representative different situations. These fitness cases sometimes represent a sampling of different values of an independent variable or a sampling of different initial conditions of a system. For example, the fitness of an individual computer program in the population may be measured in terms of the sum of the absolute value of the differences between the output produced by the program and the correct answer to the problem. This sum may be taken over a sampling of 50 different inputs to the program. The 50 fitness cases may be chosen at random or may be structured in some way.

Unless the problem is so small and simple that it can be easily solved by blind random search, the computer programs in generation 0 will have exceedingly poor fitness. Nonetheless, some individuals in the population will turn out to be somewhat fitter than others. These differences in performance are then exploited.

The Darwinian principle of reproduction and survival of the fittest and the genetic operation of sexual recombination (crossover) are used to create a new offspring population of individual computer programs from the current population of programs.

The reproduction operation involves selecting, in proportion to fitness, a computer program from the current population of programs, and allowing it to survive by copying it into the new population.

The genetic process of sexual reproduction between two parental computer programs is used to create new offspring computer programs from two parental programs selected in proportion to fitness. The parental programs are typically of different sizes and shapes. The offspring programs are composed of subexpressions (subtrees, subprograms, subroutines, building blocks) from their parents. These offspring programs are typically of different sizes and shapes than their parents.

Intuitively, if two computer programs are somewhat effective in solving a problem, then some of their parts probably have some merit. By recombining randomly chosen parts of somewhat effective programs, we may produce new computer programs that are even fitter in solving the problem.

After the operations of reproduction and crossover are performed on the current population, the population of offspring (i.e., the new generation) replaces the old population (i.e., the old generation).

Each individual in the new population of computer programs is then measured for fitness, and the process is repeated over many generations.

At each stage of this highly parallel, locally controlled, decentralized process, the state of the process will consist only of the current population of individuals. The force driving this process consists only of the observed fitness of the individuals in the current population in grappling with the problem environment.

As will be seen, this algorithm will produce populations of computer programs which, over many generations, tend to exhibit increasing average fitness in dealing with their environment. In addition, these populations of computer programs can rapidly and effectively adapt to changes in the environment.

Typically, the best individual that appeared in any generation of a run (i.e., the best-so-far individual) is designated as the result produced by genetic programming.

The hierarchical character of the computer programs that are produced is an important feature of genetic programming. The results of genetic programming are inherently hierarchical. In many cases the results produced by genetic programming are default hierarchies, prioritized hierarchies of tasks, or hierarchies in which one behavior subsumes or suppresses another.

The dynamic variability of the computer programs that are developed along the way to a solution is also an important feature of genetic programming. It would be difficult and unnatural to try to specify or restrict the size and shape of the eventual solution in advance. Moreover, advance specification or restriction of the size and shape of the solution to a problem narrows the window by which the system views the world and might well preclude finding the solution to the problem at all.

Another important feature of genetic programming is the absence or relatively minor role of preprocessing of inputs and postprocessing of outputs. The inputs, intermediate results, and outputs are typically expressed directly in terms of the natural terminology of the problem domain. The computer programs produced by genetic programming consist of functions that are natural for the problem domain.

Finally, the structures undergoing adaptation in genetic programming are active. They are not passive encodings of the solution to the problem. Instead, given a computer on which to run, the structures in genetic programming are active structures that are capable of being executed in their current form.

The genetic programming paradigm is a domain-independent (weak) method. It provides a single, unified approach to the problem of finding a computer program to solve a problem. In this book, I show how to reformulate a wide variety of seemingly different problems into a common form (i.e., a problem of induction of a computer program) and, then, how to apply this single, unified approach (i.e., genetic programming) to the problem of program induction. (See Koza 1988, 1989, 1990a, 1990d, 1990e, 1992g.)

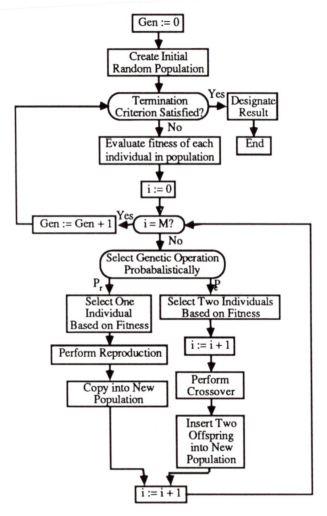

Figure 5.1 Flowchart for the genetic programming paradigm.

In summary, the genetic programming paradigm breeds computer programs to solve problems by executing the following three steps:

(1) Generate an initial population of random compositions of the functions and terminals of the problem (computer programs).

(2) Iteratively perform the following substeps until the termination criterion has been satisfied:

    (a) Execute each program in the population and assign it a fitness value according to how well it solves the problem.

    (b) Create a new population of computer programs by applying the following two primary operations. The operations are applied to computer program(s) in the population chosen with a probability based on fitness.

        (i) Copy existing computer programs to the new population.

        (ii) Create new computer programs by genetically recombining randomly chosen parts of two existing programs.

(3) The best computer program that appeared in any generation (i.e., the best-so-far individual) is designated as the result of genetic programming. This result may be a solution (or an approximate solution) to the problem.

Figure 5.1 is a flowchart for the genetic programming paradigm. The index i refers to an individual in the population of size M. The variable GEN is the number of the current generation. The box labeled "Evaluate fitness of each individual in the population" in this flowchart is explained in additional detail in figure 7.6. This flow chart is often embedded within an outer loop for controlling multiple independent runs as shown in figure 8.1.

6 Detailed Description of Genetic Programming

The previous chapter contained an overview of the genetic programming paradigm. This chapter contains a detailed description of genetic programming. Some readers may prefer to read the next chapter containing four introductory examples before reading this chapter.

Adaptation (or learning) involves the changing of some structure so that it performs better in its environment. Holland's *Adaptation in Natural and Artificial Systems* (1975) provides a general perspective on adaptation and identifies the key features common to all adaptive systems. In this chapter, we use this perspective to describe genetic programming in terms of

- the structures that undergo adaptation,
- the initial structures,
- the fitness measure which evaluates the structures,
- the operations which modify the structures,
- the state (memory) of the system at each stage,
- the method for terminating the process,
- the method for designating a result, and
- the parameters that control the process.

We end this chapter with a discussion of the schemata that are implicitly processed in genetic programming.

6.1 THE STRUCTURES UNDERGOING ADAPTATION

In every adaptive system or learning system, at least one structure is undergoing adaptation.

For the conventional genetic algorithm and genetic programming, the structures undergoing adaptation are a *population* of individual points from the search space, rather than a single point. Genetic methods differ from most other search techniques in that they simultaneously involve a parallel search involving hundreds or thousands of points in the search space.

The individual structures that undergo adaptation in genetic programming are hierarchically structured computer programs. The size, the shape, and the contents of these computer programs can dynamically change during the process.

The set of possible structures in genetic programming is the set of all possible compositions of functions that can be composed recursively from the set of N_{func} functions from $F = \{f_1, f_2, \ldots, f_{N_{func}}\}$ and the set of N_{term} terminals from $T = \{a_1, a_2, \ldots, a_{N_{term}}\}$. Each particular function f_i in the function set F takes a specified number $z(f_i)$ of arguments $z(f_1)$, $z(f_2)$, ..., $z(f_{N_{func}})$. That is, function f_i has arity $z(f_i)$.

The functions in the function set may include

- arithmetic operations (+, −, *, etc.),
- mathematical functions (such as sin, cos, exp, and log),
- Boolean operations (such as AND, OR, NOT),
- conditional operators (such as If-Then-Else),
- functions causing iteration (such as Do-Until),
- functions causing recursion, and
- any other domain-specific functions that may be defined.

The terminals are typically either variable atoms (representing, perhaps, the inputs, sensors, detectors, or state variables of some system) or constant atoms (such as the number 3 or the Boolean constant NIL). Occasionally, the terminals are functions taking no explicit arguments, the real functionality of such functions lying in their side effects on the state of the system (e.g., the artificial ant problem).

Consider the function set

```
F = {AND, OR, NOT}
```

and the terminal set

```
T = {D0, D1},
```

where D0 and D1 are Boolean variable atoms that serve as arguments for the functions.

We can combine the set of functions and terminals into a combined set C as follows:

```
C = F ∪ T = {AND, OR, NOT, D0, D1}.
```

We can then view the terminals in the combined set C as functions requiring zero arguments in order to be evaluated. That is, the five items in the set C can be viewed as taking 2, 2, 1, 0, and 0 arguments, respectively.

As an example, consider the even-2-parity function (i.e., the not-exclusive-or function, the equivalence function) with two arguments. This function returns T (True) if an even number of its arguments (i.e., D0 and D1) are T; otherwise, this function returns NIL (False). This Boolean function can be expressed in disjunctive normal form (DNF) by the following LISP

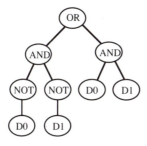

Figure 6.1 Even-2-parity function depicted as a rooted, point-labeled tree with ordered branches.

S-expression:

```
(OR (AND (NOT D0) (NOT D1)) (AND D0 D1)).
```

Figure 6.1 graphically depicts the above LISP S-expression as a rooted, point-labeled tree with ordered branches. The five internal points of the tree are labeled with functions (OR, AND, NOT, NOT, and AND). The four external points (leaves) of the tree are labeled with terminals (the Boolean variable atoms D0, D1, D0, and D1, respectively). The root of the tree is labeled with the function appearing just inside the outermost left parenthesis of the LISP S-expression (the OR). This tree is equivalent to the parse tree which most compilers construct internally to represent a given computer program.

The search space for genetic programming is the space of all possible LISP S-expressions that can be recursively created by compositions of the available functions and available terminals for the problem. This search space can, equivalently, be viewed as the space of rooted point-labeled trees with ordered branches having internal points labeled with the available functions and external points (leaves) labeled with the available terminals.

The structures that undergo adaptation in genetic programming are different from the structures that undergo adaptation in the conventional genetic algorithm operating on strings. The structures that undergo adaptation in genetic programming are hierarchical structures. The structures that undergo adaptation in the conventional genetic algorithm are one-dimensional fixed-length linear strings. In Steven F. Smith's (1980, 1983) variation of the conventional genetic algorithm, the individual structures undergoing adaptation are one-dimensional linear variable length strings.

In genetic programming, the terminal set and the function set should be selected so as to satisfy the requirements of closure and sufficiency.

6.1.1 Closure of the Function Set and Terminal Set

The *closure* property requires that each of the functions in the function set be able to accept, as its arguments, any value and data type that may possibly be returned by any function in the function set and any value and data type that may possibly be assumed by any terminal in the terminal set. That is, each function in the function set should be well defined and closed for any combination of arguments that it may encounter.

In the simple case where the function set consists of Boolean functions such as AND, OR, and NOT and the terminal set consists of Boolean variables that can assume only the values of T or NIL, this closure property is easily satisfied. However, ordinary computer programs usually contain numerical variables, conditional comparative operators, and conditional branching operators.

In ordinary programs, arithmetic operations operating on numerical variables are sometimes undefined (e.g., division by zero). Many common mathematical functions operating on numerical variables are also sometimes undefined (e.g., logarithm of zero). In addition, the value returned by many common mathematical functions operating on numerical variables is sometimes a data type that is unacceptable in a particular program (e.g., square root or logarithm of a negative number). Moreover, the Boolean value (i.e., T or NIL) typically returned by a conditional operator is generally not acceptable as the argument to an ordinary arithmetic operation.

It therefore might appear that satisfaction of this closure property is not possible for ordinary computer programs, or that if possible, it would call for a very complex and restrictive syntactic structure to be imposed on the programs. In fact, as we will see, this is not the case. Closure can be achieved in a straightforward way for the vast majority of problems merely by careful handling of a small number of situations. (Some of the other situations are discussed in chapter 19.)

If the arithmetic operation of division can encounter the numerical value of 0 as its second argument, the closure property will not be satisfied unless some arrangement is made to deal with the possibility of division by 0. One simple approach to guarantee closure is to define a protected division function. The protected division function % takes two arguments and returns one when division by 0 is attempted (including 0 divided by 0), and, otherwise, returns the normal quotient. It might be programmed as follows in LISP:

```
(defun % (numerator denominator)
  "The Protected Division Function"
  (if (= 0 denominator) 1 (/ numerator denominator))).
```

Alternatively, we could have achieved closure by defining the division function so as to return the symbolic value :undefined and then rewriting each of the ordinary arithmetic functions so as to return the symbolic value :undefined whenever they encounter :undefined as one of their arguments.

If the square root function can encounter a negative argument or if the logarithm function can encounter a nonpositive argument in a problem where the complex number that ordinarily would be returned is unacceptable, we can guarantee closure by using a protected function. For example, the protected square root function SRT takes one argument and returns the square root of the absolute value of its argument. It might be programmed as

```
(defun srt (argument)
   "The Protected Square Root Function"
   (sqrt (abs argument))),
```

where SQRT is the Common LISP square root function.

The protected natural logarithm function RLOG returns 0 if its one argument is 0 and otherwise returns the natural logarithm of the absolute value of its argument. It might be programmed as

```
(defun rlog (argument)
   "The Protected Natural Logarithm Function"
   (if (= 0 argument) 0 (log (abs argument)))),
```

where LOG is the Common LISP natural logarithm function.

The protected division function %, the protected square root function SRT, and the protected natural logarithm function RLOG will be used frequently throughout this book.

If a program contains a conditional operator in a problem where the Boolean value that would ordinarily be returned is unacceptable, then the conditional operator can be modified in any one of the following three ways:

- Numerical-valued logic can be used.
- Conditional comparative operators can be redefined.
- Conditional branching operators can be redefined.

Let us consider these three approaches in detail.

First, if numerical-valued logic is used, a numerical-valued conditional comparative operator is defined so as to return numbers (such as $+1$ and -1 or perhaps 1 and 0) instead of returning Boolean values (i.e., T and NIL). For example, the numerical-valued greater-than function GT over two arguments would be defined so as to return $+1$ if its first argument is greater than its second argument and to return -1 otherwise. Such a function does not introduce a Boolean value into the program. The numerical-valued greater-than function GT might be programmed as

```
(defun gt (first-argument second-argument)
   "The numerically-valued greater-than function"
   (if (> first-argument second-argument) 1 -1))).
```

Second, a conditional comparative operator can be defined so as to first perform the desired comparison and to then execute an alternative depending on the outcome of the comparison test. For example, the conditional comparative operator IFLTZ (If Less Than Zero) can be defined over three arguments so as to execute its second argument if its first argument is less than 0, but to execute its third argument otherwise. Such an operator returns the result of evaluating whichever of the second and third arguments is actually selected on the basis of the outcome of the comparison test. It therefore does not introduce a Boolean value into the program.

This conditional comparative operator cannot be implemented directly as an ordinary LISP function. The reason is that ordinarily, when LISP evaluates a function call, it first evaluates each of the arguments to the function and then passes the *values* to which the arguments have evaluated into the function. For example, when LISP calls the addition function in the S-expression (+ (* 3 4) 5), it passes the *values* 12 and 5 to the addition function. The value 12 was, of course, obtained by evaluating the first argument to the addition function, (* 3 4). This evaluation takes place outside the addition function. If the argument to a function happens to have a side effect (which is not the case in multiplying 3 times 4), the side effect would occur *unconditionally* at the time of the evaluation of the argument (i.e., outside the function). This early and unconditional execution of the side effect of an argument is not what is desired if the operator is intended to execute the side effect in a conditional manner based on the outcome of some test that has yet to be conducted.

As an example, consider the IFLTZ conditional comparison operator. When the IFLTZ conditional comparative operator is evaluated, we do not want its arguments to be executed before entry into the function. Instead, we want the IFLTZ conditional comparative operator to first determine if the first argument is less than 0, and we then want IFLTZ to evaluate only the one argument that is appropriate in view of the outcome of the comparison test. If the first argument is less than 0, we want the second argument to be evaluated; if it is not, we want the third argument to be evaluated. In other words, we want the conditional evaluation of one or the other argument to be performed as if the LISP evaluation function EVAL were operating inside the IFLTZ conditional comparison operator. In many problems, the primary functionality of the various functions in the problem lies in their side effects on the state of some system, and we do not want those side effects to be performed on the system unless a specified condition is satisfied. Thus, we must suppress premature evaluation of the arguments of the IFLTZ conditional operator until after the operator makes its determination about whether the first argument is less than 0. The arguments must be evaluated dynamically inside the conditional comparative operator.

Note that this problem cannot be readily remedied by introducing the LISP QUOTE special form into the function set, because that approach would result in incorrect performance whenever the argument to QUOTE happened to occur at a crossover point and became separated from its associated QUOTE.

The desired behavior is usually implemented in Common LISP by defining a macro, instead of a function, for the conditional comparative operator in question. For example, we can implement the IFLTZ conditional comparative operator using a macro in the following way:

```
1 #+TI (setf sys:inhibit-displacing-flag t)

2 (defmacro ifltz
3     (first-argument then-argument else-argument)
4   `(if (< (eval ',first-argument) 0)
5      (eval ',then-argument)
6      (eval ',else-argument))).
```

The macro definition appears on lines 2 through 6. As can be seen on line 3, there are three arguments being supplied to this macro: the first-argument, the then-argument, and the else-argument. The < Boolean function on line 4 in the if expression evaluates to T if the result of evaluating the first-argument is less than 0, and otherwise returns NIL. If T is returned, the then-argument on line 5 is evaluated, but otherwise, the else-argument on line 6 is evaluated. Either the then-argument or the else-argument is evaluated, but not both. The evaluation occurs inside the IFLTZ conditional comparative operator. Additional details on macros can be found in any textbook on Common LISP. Line 1 is explained in detail in appendix B.3.

The three-argument conditional comparative operator IFLTZ is used in the "truck backer upper" problem (section 11.2).

The four-argument conditional comparative operator IFLTE (similarly defined with a macro) is used in the wall following problem (section 13.1), the box moving problem (section 13.2), and the task prioritization problem (section 12.3). It is similarly implemented with a macro. In addition, macros are used to implement the iterative DU ("Do-Until") operator (section 18.1) and the iterative SIGMA summation operator (section 18.2).

Third, a conditional branching operator can be defined so as to access some state or condition external to the program and then execute an alternative depending on that external state or condition. Such an operator returns the result of evaluating whichever argument is actually selected on the basis of the outcome of the test and does not introduce a Boolean value into the program.

For example, suppose we wanted to define a conditional branching operator to sense for food directly in front of the ant as required in the artificial ant problem (subsection 3.3.2). We would want this IF-FOOD-AHEAD operator to first determine if food is present at the location on the grid toward which the ant is currently facing; then we would want this operator to evaluate only the one argument that is appropriate in view of the presence or absence of food. For example, we would want the S-expression

```
(IF-FOOD-AHEAD (MOVE) (TURN-RIGHT))
```

to cause the ant to move forward if food is directly in front of the ant, but to turn the ant to the right if food is not there. We would not want this S-expression to both move the ant forward and turn it. We can implement the desired IF-FOOD-AHEAD conditional branching operator using a macro in the following way:

```
1 #+TI (setf sys:inhibit-displacing-flag t)

2 (defmacro if-food-ahead (then-argument else-argument)

3   `(if *food-directly-in-front-of-ant-p*

4       (eval ',then-argument)

5       (eval ',else-argument))).
```

As can be seen on line 2 of this macro definition, there are two arguments being supplied to this macro: the then-argument and the else-argument.

The first argument of the `if` operator on line 3 is the predicate `*food-directly-in-front-of-ant-p*`, which evaluates to `T` if food is present directly in front of the ant, but which otherwise evaluates to `NIL`. The `*food-directly-in-front-of-ant-p*` predicate acquires its value elsewhere after a calculation involving the ant's current `facing-direction` and the current food status of the two-dimensional grid. If food is present, the `if` operator causes the evaluation of the `then-argument` on line 4, using the LISP evaluation function `eval`. If food is not present, the `if` operator causes the evaluation of the `else-argument` on line 5, also using the LISP evaluation function `eval`.

Macros are similarly used to implement the conditional branching operators in the emergent central place food foraging problem (section 12.1), the emergent collecting problem (section 12.2), the task prioritization problem (section 12.3), the grammar induction problem (section 17.2), and the non-hamstrung squad car problem (appendix B).

The closure property is desirable, but it is not absolutely required. If this closure property does not prevail, we must then address alternatives such as discarding individuals that do not evaluate to an acceptable result or assigning some penalty to such infeasible individuals. The issue of how to handle infeasible points is not unique to genetic methods and has been extensively (and inconclusively) debated in connection with numerous other algorithmic methods. There is no entirely satisfactory general resolution of this issue, so all the examples in this book will satisfy the closure property and we do not address this issue further.

LISP programmers are well aware that unrestricted S-expressions are sufficient for writing a vast variety of different programs (although this may not be intuitively obvious to programmers unfamiliar with this particular programming style). If one selects a function set and a terminal set having the closure property, the vast majority of problems in this book can be handled using only unrestricted S-expressions. Some problems do, in fact, require constraining syntactic structure, and this additional structure can readily be handled in the manner described in chapter 19.

Note that the closure property is required only for terminals and functions that may actually be encountered. If the structures undergoing adaptation are known to comply with some constraining syntactic rules of construction, closure is required only over the values of terminals and values returned by functions that will actually be encountered.

6.1.2 Sufficiency of the Function Set and the Terminal Set

The *sufficiency* property requires that the set of terminals and the set of primitive functions be capable of expressing a solution to the problem. The user of genetic programming should know or believe that some composition of the functions and terminals he supplies can yield a solution to the problem.

The step of identifying the variables that have sufficient explanatory power to solve a particular problem is common to virtually every problem in science.

Depending on the problem, this identification step may be obvious or may require considerable insight.

For example, Kepler's Third Law, discovered in 1618, states that the cube of a planet's distance from the sun is proportional to the square of the period of the planet around the sun. If one were trying to predict the period of a planet traveling around the sun, considerable insight would required (in the early seventeenth century anyway) to see that the distance of the planet from the sun is *the one* variable that has explanatory power for this problem. If one had access only to data about the diameter, the number of moons, and the surface coloration of each planet, one would be unable to express or discover the Third Law because these variables have no explanatory power whatsoever for the problem at hand.

In some domains, the task of identifying the variables having sufficient explanatory power to solve the problem may be virtually impossible (e.g., predicting interest rates or the results of elections).

This book provides numerous illustrative examples of how to select a terminal set containing variables with sufficient explanatory power to solve a problem. The tables in chapter 26 may also be helpful. However, it is ultimately the user who must supply a terminal set appropriate for his problem.

Similarly, the step of identifying a set of functions that is sufficient to solve a particular problem may be obvious or may require considerable insight.

In some domains, the requirements for sufficiency in the set of primitive functions are well known. For example, in the domain of Boolean functions, the function set

F={AND,OR,NOT}

is known to be sufficient for realizing any Boolean function. If the function OR is removed from this function set, it is also well known that the remaining function set is still sufficient for realizing any Boolean function. However, if the function NOT is removed, the remaining function set is no longer sufficient for expressing all Boolean functions. For example, the exclusive-or (odd-parity) function cannot be expressed. The remaining function set is nonetheless sufficient to realize some Boolean functions.

On the other hand, for many domains the requirements for sufficiency in the set of primitive functions are not clear. For example, if one were given only the functions of addition and subtraction (instead of multiplication and division), one cannot express or discover Kepler's Third Law; however, some knowledge and understanding of celestial mechanics is required to know that the function set {+, −} is insufficient for solving the problem.

If one were given only the primitive functions RIGHT and LEFT (but not MOVE), one could not possibly solve the artificial ant problem (subsection 3.3.2). Similarly, if one were given only the primitive function MOVE (but not RIGHT or LEFT), one could not possibly solve that problem. Before Jefferson, Collins, et al. could begin their search for a finite-state automaton or a neural network to solve their problem, they had to ascertain, using their knowledge and insight of what it takes for an ant to find food, that the minimum requirements for successful navigation of their ant along their trail were primitive functions such as MOVE and either RIGHT or LEFT. Nothing from the theory of automata, neural networks, genetic algorithms, machine learning, or artificial intelligence provided any assistance to them in selecting the primitive functions for their problem or in establishing that any particular set of primitive functions would prove to be sufficient.

Although this book provides numerous illustrative examples of how to select a sufficient set of primitive functions for a problem, it is ultimately the user who must supply a function set appropriate for his problem.

6.1.3   Universality of Selecting Primitive Functions and Terminals

The steps (performed by the user) of determining the repertoire of primitive functions and terminals in genetic programming are equivalent to similar required steps in other machine learning paradigms. These two steps (which often go under other names) are often not explicitly identified, discussed, or recognized by researchers describing other paradigms. The reason for this omission may be that the researcher involved considers the choice of primitive functions and terminals to be inherent in the statement of the problem. This view is especially understandable if the researcher is focusing on only one specific type of problem from one specific field. If this book contained only one problem from only one field (e.g., only the artificial ant problem), it probably would not occur to the reader to think about the source of the primitive functions being used by the machine learning paradigm.

The two steps of determining the primitive functions and terminals are necessary preparatory steps for solving a problem using algorithms for inducing decision trees (such as ID3), an algorithm for empirical discovery (such as BACON), a neural network, a finite-state automaton, a genetic classifier system, a conventional planning algorithm from the domain of symbolic artificial intelligence, and other paradigms. In each instance, the user must identify and supply the primitive functions and terminals to be used in solving the problem.

Let us consider a few examples.

The two steps of determining the primitive functions and terminals are necessary preparatory steps to the induction of decision trees using the ID3 algorithm and its variants. The ID3 algorithm (Quinlan 1986) produces a decision tree that can classify an object into a class. Each object has several attributes. A certain value of each attribute is associated with each object. The ID3 algorithm constructs a decision tree that, if presented with a particular object, classifies the object into a particular class. The internal points of the decision tree consist of attribute-testing functions, which test the given object for a particular attribute. Before one can use ID3, the user must select the set of attribute-testing functions that can appear at the internal points of the decision tree. ID3 does not make this selection for the user.

For example, if the problem is to classify national flags, consisting of precisely three stripes, the objects are flags. Each flag might have four attributes, namely the direction of the stripes, the color of the first stripe, the color of the second stripe, and the color of the third stripe. If the user selects a set of attribute-testing functions that is insufficient to solve the problem, it will not be possible to solve the problem using ID3. For example, failing to include a primitive function for testing the direction of stripes would make it impossible to distinguish the Italian flag from the Iranian flag.

If the user selects a function set that contains irrelevant and extraneous attribute-testing functions, ID3 will usually be able to find a solution; however, ID3's performance will probably be degraded to some degree. For example, if a user of ID3 includes an attribute-testing function for the kind of cloth used in the flag, ID3 will quickly discover that this particular function is not helpful in discriminating among the flags.

This same determination of primitive functions and terminals occurs in heuristic systems for the induction of scientific laws from empirical data, such as BACON (Langley et al. 1987). BACON requires the user to supply a repertoire of heuristic rules (i.e., the function set) and to identify the independent variables of the problem (i.e., the terminal set). Before one can use BACON, the user must select the set of heuristic rules and the independent variables of the problem. BACON does not make these selections for the user. For example, BACON cannot induce Kepler's Third Law from the empirical data if the user selects a repertoire of heuristic rules involving only the functions of addition and subtraction (but not the functions of multiplication or division). Similarly, it will not be possible to induce Kepler's Third Law using BACON if the empirical data provided to BACON includes the diameter of the planet, but not the distance from the sun. If the set of heuristic rules chosen by the user includes numerous irrelevant and extraneous heuristic rules that never apply to the data, BACON will usually be able to find a solution; however, BACON's performance may be somewhat degraded.

Before Jefferson, Collins, et al. could begin their search for a neural network to solve the artificial ant problem (subsection 3.3.2), they selected MOVE, RIGHT, and LEFT as the set of primitive functions for their problem. They decided that the output of the neural network at each time step would activate one of those three primitive functions. Similarly, they decided that a signal representing the presence or absence of food on the grid in the position directly in front of the ant would constitute the input to the neural network. In the field of neural networks, these steps are referred to as the process of identifying the inputs and outputs of a network. Having made these decisions, they could proceed to the problem of finding the weights that would enable the neural network to solve the problem. Neural nets do not move or turn; they look at inputs and emit certain signals for certain combinations of inputs. If Jefferson, Collins, et al. had neglected to feed the signal from the food sensor into the neural network, the neural net could not possibly have solved their problem. If they had forgotten to connect some output signal from the neural network to the primitive function MOVE, no amount of neural network technology would have moved the ant along the food trail.

Similarly, before Jefferson et al. could begin their search for a finite-state automaton to solve the artificial ant problem, they again had to select their set of primitive functions. They again chose MOVE, RIGHT, and LEFT as their set of primitive functions. They decided that the output of the finite-state automaton at each time step would activate one of those three primitive functions. Similarly, they decided that a signal representing the presence or absence of food on the grid in the position directly in front of the ant would constitute the input to the automaton. Having made these decisions, they could proceed to the problem of finding the behavior that would enable the automaton to solve the problem.

If we were using a genetic classifier system to solve the artificial ant problem, we would first have to select a set of primitive functions and a set of terminals. The output interface of the classifier system would interpret certain messages posted to the message list of the classifier to cause the activation of the external actions of MOVE, RIGHT, and LEFT. The signal representing the presence or absence of food on the grid in the position directly in front of the ant would be fed into the environmental interface (input) of the classifier system as a particular message on the message list.

Before using a planning tool from the field of symbolic artificial intelligence, we would have to identify the primitive functions (i.e., MOVE, RIGHT, and LEFT) that could be invoked by the planning algorithm. The planning algorithm would also refer to the signal representing the presence or absence of food on the grid in the position directly in front of the ant.

The choice of the set of available functions and terminals, of course, directly affects the character and appearance of the solutions. The available functions and terminals form the basis for generating potential solutions.

For example, the function sets {AND, OR, NOT}, {IF, AND, OR, NOT}, {NAND}, and {NOR} are all sufficient for realizing any Boolean function; however, the solutions produced by using them are very different in appearance and character. For example, if one is working with semiconductor layouts, the function set {NAND} may be appealing. On the other hand, the inclusion of the function IF often makes solutions more understandable to humans.

Similarly, if the function set for the artificial ant included a diagonal move and a knight's move (instead of the simple function for moving forward), the function set would still be sufficient for solving the problem, but the solutions produced would be very different.

For most of the problems in this book, the function set is not only minimally sufficient to solve the problem at hand, but contains extraneous functions. The effect on performance of extraneous functions in the function set of genetic programming is complex. In general, numerous extraneous functions in a function set degrade performance to some degree; however, a particular additional function in a function set may dramatically improve performance for a particular problem. For example, the addition of the extraneous function IF to the computationally complete Boolean function set {OR, NOT} improves performance for certain Boolean learning problems described in this book.

Section 24.3 presents several experiments showing the effect of adding extraneous functions to the function set.

Since many of the problems in this book were originated by others in connection with their work involving other paradigms of machine learning, artificial intelligence, and neural networks, we often rely, as a practical matter, on their choices of the primitive function and terminals.

Of course, in some problems it is not at all clear in advance what set of functions is minimally sufficient to solve the problem. In those cases, it is generally better to include potentially extraneous functions than to miss a solution altogether.

The effect on performance of extraneous terminals is clearer than the effect of extraneous functions. Usually, extraneous terminals reduce performance. Sections 24.1 and 24.2 present experiments showing the degradation associated with adding extraneous terminals to the terminal set.

6.2 THE INITIAL STRUCTURES

The initial structures in genetic programming consist of the individuals in the initial population of individual S-expressions for the problem.

The generation of each individual S-expression in the initial population is done by randomly generating a rooted, point-labeled tree with ordered branches representing the S-expression.

We begin by selecting one of the functions from the set F at random (using a uniform random probability distribution) to be the label for the root of the tree. We restrict the selection of the label for the root of the tree to the function set F because we want to generate a hierarchical structure, not a degenerate structure consisting of a single terminal.

Figure 6.2 shows the beginning of the creation of a random program tree. The function + (taking two arguments) was selected from a function set F as the label for the root of the tree.

Whenever a point of the tree is labeled with a function f from F, then $z(f)$ lines, where $z(f)$ is the number of arguments taken by the function f, are created to radiate out from that point. Then, for each such radiating line, an element from the combined set $C = F \cup T$ of functions and terminals is randomly selected to be the label for the endpoint of that radiating line.

If a function is chosen to be the label for any such endpoint, the generating process then continues recursively as just described above. For example, in figure 6.3, the function ∗ from the combined set $C = F \cup T$ of functions and terminals was selected as the label of the internal nonroot point (point 2) at

Figure 6.2 Beginning of the creation of a random program tree, with the function + with two arguments chosen for the root of the tree.

Figure 6.3 Continuation of the creation of a random program tree, with the function * with two arguments chosen for point 2.

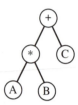

Figure 6.4 Completion of the creation of a random program tree, with the terminals A, B, and C chosen.

the end of the first (leftmost) line radiating from the point with the function + (point 1). Since a function was selected for point 2, it will be an internal, nonroot point of the tree that will eventually be created. The function * takes two arguments, so the figure shows two lines radiating out from point 2.

If a terminal is chosen to be the label for any point, that point becomes an endpoint of the tree and the generating process is terminated for that point. For example, in figure 6.4, the terminal A from the terminal set T was selected to be the label of the first line radiating from the point labeled with the function *. Similarly, the terminals B and C were selected to be the labels of the two other radiating lines in figure 6.3. This process continues recursively from left to right until a completely labeled tree has been created, as shown in figure 6.4.

This generative process can be implemented in several different ways resulting in initial random trees of different sizes and shapes. Two of the basic ways are called the "full" method and the "grow" method. The depth of a tree is defined as the length of the longest nonbacktracking path from the root to an endpoint.

The "full" method of generating the initial random population involves creating trees for which the length of every nonbacktracking path between an endpoint and the root is equal to the specified maximum depth. This is accomplished by restricting the selection of the label for points at depths less than the maximum to the function set F, and then restricting the selection of the label for points at the maximum depth to the terminal set T.

The "grow" method of generating the initial random population involves growing trees that are variably shaped. The length of a path between an endpoint and the root is no greater than the specified maximum depth. This is accomplished by making the random selection of the label for points at depths less than the maximum from the combined set $C = F \cup T$ consisting of the union of the function set F and the terminal set T, while restricting the random selection of the label for points at the maximum depth to the terminal set T. The relative number of functions in the function set F and the number of terminals in the terminal set T determine the expected length of paths between the root and the endpoints of the tree.

The generative method that I believe does best over a broad range of problems is a method I call "ramped half-and-half." In genetic programming, we usually do not know (or do not wish to specify) the size and shape of the solution in advance. The ramped half-and-half generative method produces a wide variety of trees of various sizes and shapes.

The "ramped half-and-half" generative method is a mixed method that incorporates both the full method and the grow method. I have now adopted this method for all new problems and it is used for most problems in this book. The exceptions are the special analysis of Boolean functions in chapter 9 and a few runs made before my adoption of this method. The ramped half-and-half generative method involves creating an equal number of trees using a depth parameter that ranges between 2 and the maximum specified depth. For example, if the maximum specified depth is 6 (the default value in this book), 20% of the trees will have depth 2, 20% will have depth 3, and so forth up to depth 6. Then, for each value of depth, 50% of the trees are created via the full method and 50% of the trees are produced via the grow method.

Note that, for the trees created with the full method for a given depth, all paths from the root of the tree to an endpoint are the same length and therefore have the same shape. In contrast, for the trees created via the grow method for a given value of depth, no path from the root of the tree to an endpoint has a depth greater than the given value of depth. Therefore, for a given value of depth, these trees vary considerably in shape from one another.

Thus, the ramped half-and-half method creates trees having a wide variety of sizes and shapes. I prefer this method for this reason.

Several experiments comparing generative methods are briefly presented in section 25.1.

Duplicate individuals in the initial random generation are unproductive deadwood; they waste computational resources and undesirably reduce the genetic diversity of the population. Thus, it is desirable, but not necessary, to avoid duplicates in the initial random population. In genetic programming, duplicate random individuals are especially likely to be created in the initial random generation when the trees are small (as it is for a certain percentage of population in the ramped half-and-half and grow methods). Thus, each newly created S-expression is checked for uniqueness before it is inserted into the initial population. If a new S-expression is a duplicate, the generating process is repeated until a unique S-expression is created. Occasionally (e.g., for small trees), we must substitute a larger tree during the generative process when we have exhausted the set of possible trees of a given size.

The *variety* of a population is the percentage of individuals for which no exact duplicate exists elsewhere in the population. If duplicate checking is done, the variety of the initial random population is 100%. In later generations, the creation of duplicate individuals via the genetic operation of reproduction is an inherent part of genetic processes.

In contrast, in the conventional genetic algorithm operating on fixed-length character strings, each of the characters in a string in the initial random population is typically created by calling a binary randomizer. For example, the binary strings of length 453 used by Jefferson et al. (1991) in the artificial ant problem are created by a binary randomizer and come from a search space of size 2^{453} (i.e., about 10^{137}). It would be most unusual to have any duplicates among the mere 65,536 individual strings in the population when the search space is of size 10^{137}. Thus, in conventional genetic algorithms, no effort is usually expended to ensure against duplicates. However, duplicate checking is sometimes done (Davis 1991).

In this book, particular individuals are not primed (seeded) into the initial population. If such priming is attempted, it should be remembered that inserting relatively high-fitness individuals into an initial population of random (and necessarily low-fitness) individuals will after one generation, result in almost total dominance of the population by copies and offspring of the primed individuals. In terms of genetic diversity, the result will be, after only one generation, very similar to starting with a population of size equal to the relatively tiny number of primed individuals. If such priming is attempted, 100% of the initial population should be primed with individuals of a generally similar level of fitness.

6.3 FITNESS

Fitness is the driving force of Darwinian natural selection and, likewise, of both conventional genetic algorithms and genetic programming.

In nature, the fitness of an individual is the probability that it survives to the age of reproduction and reproduces. This measure may be weighted to consider the number of offspring. In the artificial world of mathematical algorithms, we measure fitness in some way and then use this measurement to control the application of the operations that modify the structures in our artificial population.

Fitness may be measured in many different ways, some explicit and some implicit.

The most common approach to measuring fitness is to create an explicit fitness measure for each individual in the population. This approach is used in the vast majority of applications of the conventional genetic algorithm and for the vast majority of examples in this book. Each individual in a population is assigned a scalar fitness value by means of some well-defined explicit evaluative procedure.

Fitness may also be computed in a co-evolutionary way as when the fitness of a game playing strategy is determined by playing that strategy against an entire population (or sampling) of opposing strategies.

The fact that individuals exist and survive in the population and successfully reproduce may be indicative of their fitness (as is the case in nature). This implicit definition of fitness is often used in research in artificial life (Ray 1990, 1991a, 1991b, 1991c; Holland 1990, 1992; chapter 28 below). However, for the moment, we will focus on the more common situation where fitness is explicitly computed. I will now describe the four measures of fitness that are used in this book:

- raw fitness,
- standardized fitness,
- adjusted fitness, and
- normalized fitness.

6.3.1 Raw Fitness

Raw fitness is the measurement of fitness that is stated in the natural terminology of the problem itself. For example, raw fitness in the artificial ant problem was the number of pieces of food eaten by the ant. The more food, the better. Raw fitness ranged from 0 (i.e., the least food and therefore the worst value) to 89.

Fitness is usually, but not always, evaluated over a set of *fitness cases*. These fitness cases provide a basis for evaluating the fitness of the S-expressions in the population over a number of different representative situations sufficiently large that a range of different numerical raw fitness values can be obtained. The fitness cases are typically only a small finite sample of the entire domain space (which is usually very large or infinite). For Boolean functions with a few arguments, it is practical to use all possible combinations of values of the arguments as the fitness cases. The fitness cases must be representative of the domain space as a whole, because they form the basis for generalizing the results obtained to the entire domain space.

One can minimize the effect of selecting a particular selection of fitness cases by computing fitness using a different set of fitness cases in each generation. Because the potential benefit of this approach is offset by the inconvenience associated with noncomparability of performance of a particular individual across generations, we do not use this approach in this book. Instead, the fitness cases are chosen at the beginning of each run and not varied from generation to generation.

The most common definition of raw fitness used in this book is that raw fitness is error. That is, the raw fitness of an individual S-expression is the sum of the distances, taken over all the fitness cases, between the point in the range space returned by the S-expression for the set of arguments associated with the particular fitness case and the correct point in the range space associated with the particular fitness case. The S-expression may be Boolean-valued, integer-valued, floating-point-valued, complex-valued, vector-valued, multiple-valued, or symbolic-valued.

If the S-expression is integer-valued or floating-point-valued, the sum of distances is the sum of the absolute values of the differences between the numbers involved. When raw fitness is error, the raw fitness $r(i, t)$ of an individual S-expression i in the population of size M at any generational time step t is

$$r(i,t) = \sum_{j=1}^{N_e} |S(i,j) - C(j)|,$$

where $S(i,j)$ is the value returned by S-expression i for fitness case j (of N_e cases) and where $C(j)$ is the correct value for fitness case j.

If the S-expression is Boolean-valued or symbolic-valued, the sum of distances is equivalent to the number of mismatches. If the S-expression is complex-valued, or vector-valued, or multiple-valued, the sum of the distances is the sum of the distances separately obtained from each component of the structure involved.

If the S-expression (or each component of a vector or list) is real-valued or integer-valued, the square root of the sum of the squares of the distances can, alternatively, be used to measure fitness (thereby increasing the influence of more distant points).

Because raw fitness is stated in the natural terminology of the problem, the better value may be either smaller (as when raw fitness is error) or larger (as when raw fitness is food eaten, benefit achieved, etc.).

6.3.2 Standardized Fitness

The *standardized fitness* $s(i,t)$ restates the raw fitness so that a lower numerical value is always a better value. For example, in an optimal control problem, one may be trying to minimize some cost measure, so a lesser value of raw fitness is better. Similarly, if, in a particular problem, one is trying to minimize error, a lesser value of raw fitness is better (and a raw fitness of 0 is best).

If, for a particular problem, a lesser value of raw fitness is better, standardized fitness equals the raw fitness for that problem. That is,

$$s(i,t) = r(i,t).$$

It is convenient and desirable to make the best value of standardized fitness equal 0. If this is not already the case, it can be made so by subtracting (or adding) a constant.

If, for a particular problem, a greater value of raw fitness is better, standardized fitness must be computed from raw fitness. For example, in the artificial ant problem we were trying to maximize the amount of food discovered along the trail; thus, a bigger value of raw fitness was better. In that situation, standardized fitness equals the maximum possible value of raw fitness (denoted by r_{max}) minus the observed raw fitness. That is, we require a reversal,

$$s(i,t) = r_{max} - r(i,t).$$

If the artificial ant finds 5 of the 89 pieces of food using a given computer program, the raw fitness is 5 and the standardized fitness is 84.

If no upper bound r_{max} is known and a bigger value of raw fitness is better, the adjusted fitness and the normalized fitness (both described below) can be computed directly from the raw fitness. If a smaller value of raw fitness is better and no lower bound is known, the sign can be reversed and the adjusted fitness and the normalized fitness can be computed directly from the raw fitness.

6.3.3 Adjusted Fitness

In addition, for all problems in this book involving an explicit calculation of fitness, we apply an optional adjustment to fitness. The *adjusted fitness* measure $a(i, t)$ is computed from the standardized fitness $s(i, t)$ as follows:

$$a(i, t) = \frac{1}{1 + s(i, t)},$$

where $s(i, t)$ is the standardized fitness for individual i at time t.

The adjusted fitness lies between 0 and 1. The adjusted fitness is bigger for better individuals in the population.

It is not necessary to use the adjusted fitness in genetic programming; however, I believe it is generally helpful, and I use it consistently throughout this book. The adjusted fitness has the benefit of exaggerating the importance of small differences in the value of the standardized fitness as the standardized fitness approaches 0 (as often occurs on later generations of a run). Thus, as the population improves, greater emphasis is placed on the small differences that make the difference between a good individual and a very good one. This exaggeration is especially potent if the standardized fitness actually reaches 0 when a perfect solution to the problem is found (as is the case for many problems in this book). For example, if the standardized fitness can range between 0 (the best) and 64 (the worst), the adjusted fitnesses of two poor individuals scoring 64 and 63 are 0.0154 and 0.0159, respectively; however, the adjusted fitnesses of two good individuals scoring 4 and 3 are 0.20 and 0.25, respectively. This effect is less potent (but still valuable) when the best value of the standardized fitness cannot be defined so as to reach 0 for the best individual (e.g., in optimization problems where the nonzero best minimal value is not known in advance).

Note that for certain methods of selection other than fitness proportionate selection (e.g., tournament selection and rank selection), adjusted fitness is not relevant and not used.

6.3.4 Normalized Fitness

If the method of selection employed is fitness proportionate (as is the case for all problems in this book except for the experiments with tournament selection found in section 25.7), the concept of normalized fitness is also needed.

The *normalized fitness* $n(i, t)$ is computed from the adjusted fitness value $a(i, t)$ as follows:

$$n(i, t) = \frac{a(i, t)}{\sum\limits_{k=1}^{M} a(k, t)}.$$

The normalized fitness has three desirable characteristics:

- It ranges between 0 and 1.
- It is larger for better individuals in the population.
- The sum of the normalized fitness values is 1.

The phrases "proportional to fitness" or "fitness proportionate" in this book refer to the normalized fitness.

Note that for certain methods of selection other than fitness proportionate selection (e.g., tournament selection and rank selection), normalized fitness is not relevant and not used.

As will be seen, it is also possible for the fitness function to give some weight to secondary or tertiary factors. Examples of such additional factors are parsimony of the S-expression (sections 18.1 and 25.13), efficiency of the S-expression (section 18.1), and compliance with the initial conditions of a differential equation (section 10.7).

6.3.5 Greedy Over-Selection

The population size M of 500 is sufficient for solving about two-thirds of the problems described in this book. More complex problems generally require larger population sizes to solve. These more complex problems are usually the problems which entail exceedingly time-consuming fitness calculations. Thus, the problem of limited computer resources becomes especially acute for these problems because both the population size and the amount of time required to evaluate fitness are large.

It is possible to considerably enhance the performance of genetic programming (and the conventional genetic algorithm) for many problems by greedily over-selecting the fitter individuals in the population. That is, when individuals are selected from the population to participate in the various operations (e.g., reproduction and crossover), the fitter individuals are given an even better chance of selection than is already the case with normalized fitness. This greedy *over-selection* amounts to a further adjustment to the fitness measure.

It is not necessary to use over-selection in genetic programming for any problem. We do not ever use over-selection on problems where the population size is 500 or below. However, unless otherwise indicated, we use over-selection in order to improve performance on the minority of problems where the population size is 1,000 or larger.

We implement over-selection by envisioning the individuals in the population being sorted in order of their normalized fitness $n(i, t)$, with the fittest individual appearing first. For a population size of 1,000, the fittest individuals together accounting for $c = 32\%$ of the normalized fitness are placed in group I, whereas the remaining less fit individuals are placed in group II. Then 80% of the time, an individual is selected from group I in proportion to its normalized fitness, whereas 20% of the time, an individual is selected from group II in proportion to its normalized fitness. The procedure is the same for a population of 2,000, 4,000, and 8,000, except that the cumulative percentage c is 16%, 8%, and 4%, respectively.

The progression 32%, 16%, 8%, and 4% and the 80%-20% split has no particular justification; it merely provides a convenient way of causing the greedy over-selection of the fittest.

For the sake of illustration, suppose the the best 10 individuals each have normalized fitness 0.024, the next 100 individuals each have normalized fitness of 0.0008, and the worst 890 individuals each have normalized fitness of $0.68/890 = 0.000764$. The best 110 individuals together account for $c = 32\%$ of the population (i.e., 10×0.024 plus 100×0.0008). The worst 890 individuals cumulatively account for $1 - c = 68\%$ of the population (i.e., 890×0.000764).

80% of the time, we will select from the group of 110 best individuals. The best 10 individuals of this 110 will each have a probability of being selected of 0.06 (i.e., $0.024 \times 0.80/0.32$) and a cumulative probability of being chosen of 0.6. The next 100 individuals of this 110 will each have a net probability of being selected of 0.002 (i.e., $0.0008 \times 0.80/0.32$) and a cumulative probability of being selected of 0.2.

20% of the time, we will select from the group of 890. The worst 890 individuals will each have a net probability of being selected of 0.00002247 (i.e., $0.000764 \times 0.20/0.68$) and a cumulative probability of being selected of 0.2.

6.4 PRIMARY OPERATIONS FOR MODIFYING STRUCTURES

This section describes the two primary operations used to modify the structures undergoing adaptation in genetic programming:

- Darwinian reproduction
- crossover (sexual recombination).

The secondary operations that are sometimes used in genetic programming are described in the next section.

6.4.1 Reproduction

The *reproduction* operation for genetic programming is the basic engine of Darwinian natural selection and survival of the fittest. The reproduction operation is asexual in that it operates on only one parental S-expression and produces only one offspring S-expression on each occasion when it is performed.

The operation of reproduction consists of two steps. First, a single S-expression is selected from the population according to some selection method based on fitness. Second, the selected individual is copied, without alteration, from the current population into the new population (i.e., the new generation).

There are many different selection methods based on fitness. The most popular is fitness-proportionate selection. This method, described in Holland's

Adaptation in Natural and Artificial Systems (1975), underpins many of Holland's theoretical results. It is the method used throughout this book.

If $f(s_i(t))$ is the fitness of individual s_i in the population at generation t, then, under fitness-proportionate selection, the probability that individual s_i will be copied into the next generation of the population as a result of any one reproduction operation is

$$\frac{f(s_i(t))}{\sum_{j=1}^{M} f(s_j(t))}.$$

Typically, $f(s_i(t))$ is the normalized fitness $n(s_i(t))$ computed in the manner described above, so that the probability that individual s_i will be copied into the next generation of the population as a result of any one reproduction operation is simply its normalized fitness $n(s_i(t))$. If over-selection is invoked, $f(s_i(t))$ is the result of applying over-selection to the values of normalized fitness $n(s_i(t))$.

When the reproduction operation is performed by means of the fitness-proportionate selection method, it is called *fitness-proportionate reproduction*.

Among the alternative selection methods are tournament selection and rank selection (Goldberg and Deb 1990). In *rank selection*, selection is based on the rank (not the numerical value) of the fitness values of the individuals in the population (Baker 1985). Rank selection reduces the potentially dominating effects of comparatively high-fitness individuals in the population by establishing a predictable, limited amount of selection pressure in favor of such individuals. At the same time, rank selection exaggerates the difference between closely clustered fitness values so that the better ones can be sampled more. See also Whitley 1989.

In *tournament selection*, a specified group of individuals (typically two) are chosen at random from the population and the one with the better fitness (i.e., the lower standardized fitness) is then selected. When two bulls fight over the right to mate with a given cow, tournament selection is occurring.

Note that the parent remains in the population while selection is performed during the current generation. That is, the selection is done with replacement (i.e., reselection) allowed. Parents can be selected *and, in general, are selected* more than once for reproduction during the current generation. Indeed, the differential rate of survival and reproduction for fitter individuals is an essential part of genetic algorithms.

A considerable amount of computer time can be saved by not computing the fitness for any individual that appears in the present generation as a result of reproduction from the previous generation. The fitness of such a copied individual will be unchanged and therefore need not be recomputed (unless the fitness cases vary from generation to generation). If the reproduction operation is being applied to, say, 10% of the population on each generation, this technique alone results in 10% fewer calculations of fitness on every generation. Since the calculation of fitness consumes the vast majority of computer time for any non-trivial problem, this simple technique produces an immediate overall saving of close to 10% on every run.

6.4.2 Crossover

The *crossover* (sexual recombination) operation for genetic programming creates variation in the population by producing new offspring that consist of parts taken from each parent. The crossover operation starts with two parental S-expressions and produces two offspring S-expressions. That is, it is a sexual operation.

The first parent is chosen from the population by the same fitness-based selection method used for selection for the reproduction operation (which, in this book, means that the first parent is chosen with a probability equal to its normalized fitness). Moreover, in this book, the second parent is chosen by means of the same selection method (that is, with a probability equal to its normalized fitness).

The operation begins by independently selecting, using a uniform probability distribution, one random point in each parent to be the crossover point for that parent. Note that the two parents typically are of unequal size.

The crossover fragment for a particular parent is the rooted subtree which has as its root the crossover point for that parent and which consists of the entire subtree lying below the crossover point (i.e., more distant from the root of the original tree). Viewed in terms of lists in a LISP S-expression, the crossover fragment is the sublist starting at the crossover point. This subtree (sublist) sometimes consists of one terminal.

The first offspring S-expression is produced by deleting the crossover fragment of the first parent from the first parent and then inserting the crossover fragment of the second parent at the crossover point of the first parent. The second offspring is produced in a symmetric manner.

For example, consider the two parental LISP S-expressions in figure 6.5. The functions appearing in these two S-expressions are the Boolean AND, OR, and NOT functions. The terminals appearing in the figure are the Boolean arguments D0 and D1.

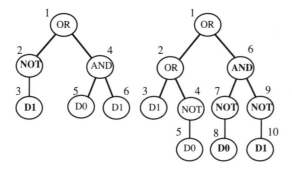

Figure 6.5 Two parental computer programs.

Equivalently, in terms of LISP S-expressions, the two parents are

```
(OR (NOT D1) (AND D0 D1)),
```

and

```
(OR (OR D1 (NOT D0)) (AND (NOT D0) (NOT D1))).
```

Assume that the points of both trees above are numbered in a depth-first, left-to-right way. Suppose that the second point (out of the six points of the first parent) is randomly selected as the *crossover point* for the first parent. The crossover point of the first parent is therefore the NOT function. Suppose also that the sixth point (out of the ten points of the second parent) is selected as the crossover point of the second parent. The crossover point of the second parent is therefore the AND function. The portions of the two parental S-expressions in boldface in figure 6.5 are the *crossover fragments*. The remaining portions of the two parental S-expressions in figure 6.5 are called the *remainders*.

Figure 6.6 depicts these two crossover fragments and figure 6.7 shows the two offspring resulting from crossover.

Note that the first offspring S-expression in figure 6.7,

```
(OR (AND (NOT D0) (NOT D1)) (AND D0 D1)),
```

happens to be the even-2-parity function (i.e., the equivalence function). The second offspring is

```
(OR (OR D1 (NOT D0)) (NOT D1)).
```

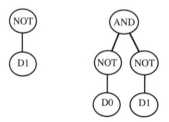

Figure 6.6 The crossover fragments resulting from selection of point 2 of the first parent and point 6 of the second parent as crossover points.

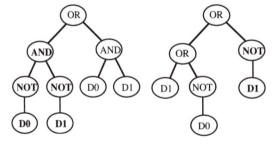

Figure 6.7 The two offspring produced by crossover.

Because entire subtrees are swapped, and because of the closure property of the functions themselves, this genetic crossover (recombination) operation *always* produces syntactically legal LISP S-expressions as offspring regardless of the selection of parents or crossover points.

If a terminal is located at the crossover point in precisely one parent, then the subtree from the second parent is inserted at the location of the terminal in the first parent (thereby introducing a subtree in lieu of a single terminal point) and the terminal from the first parent is inserted at the location of the subtree in the second parent. This will often have the effect of producing an offspring with considerable depth.

If terminals are located at both crossover points selected, the crossover operation merely swaps these terminals from tree to tree. The effect of crossover, in this event, is akin to a point mutation. Thus, occasional point mutation is an inherent part of the crossover operation.

If the root of one parental S-expression happens to be selected as the crossover point, the crossover operation will insert the entire first parent into the second parent at the crossover point of the second parent. In this event, the entire first parent will become a subtree (i.e., a subroutine) within the second parent. This will often have the effect of producing an offspring with considerable depth. In addition, the crossover fragment of the second parent will then become the other offspring.

In the rare situation where the root of one parental S-expression happens to be selected as the crossover point and the crossover fragment from the second parent happens to be a single terminal, the first parent becomes one offspring and the other offspring will be a LISP S-expression consisting of the single terminal.

If the roots of two parents both happen to be chosen as crossover points, the crossover operation simply degenerates to an instance of reproduction of those two parents.

When an individual incestuously mates with itself or when two identical individuals mate the two resulting offspring will generally be different (because the crossover points selected are, in general, different for the two parents). This is in contrast to the case of the conventional genetic algorithm operating on fixed-length character strings where the one selected crossover point applies to both parents.

There is an important consequence of the way incestuous mating operates in genetic programming, as compared to the conventional genetic algorithm operating on fixed-length character strings. For both genetic methods, if a particular individual in the population has extraordinarily good fitness relative to the other individuals currently in the population, the Darwinian reproduction operation will cause many copies of that one individual to be produced. This will be the case even if this extraordinary individual is mediocre in the search space as a whole. If, for example, reproduction is performed on 10% of the population selected probabilistically proportionate to fitness, as much as 10% of the next generation may be copies of this one individual. This fact creates a tendency toward *convergence* of the population (i.e., all the individuals in the population becoming identical). In addition, the extraordinary individual (and its copies) will be selected frequently to participate in crossover, so many crossovers will be incestuous.

In the conventional genetic algorithm, when an individual incestuously mates with itself (or copies of itself), the two resulting offspring will be identical. This fact strengthens the tendency toward *convergence* in the conventional genetic algorithm. Convergence is called *premature convergence* if the population converges to a globally suboptimal result. Premature convergence can occur when a mediocre suboptimal individual happens to have extraordinarily good fitness relative to the other individuals in the population at the time. In this situation (sometimes called "survival of the mediocre"), the conventional genetic algorithm fails to find the global optimum. Of course, if a global optimum is discovered in the conventional genetic algorithm, there is also very likely to be convergence of the entire population to that globally optimal individual. Once the population converges in conventional genetic algorithm, the only way to change the population is mutation. Mutation can, in principle, lead anywhere; however, in practice, the population often quickly reconverges.

In contrast, in genetic programming, when an individual incestuously mates with itself (or copies of itself), the two resulting offspring will, in general, be different (except in the relatively infrequent case when the crossover points are the same). As before, the Darwinian reproduction operation creates a tendency toward convergence; however, in genetic programming, the crossover operation exerts a counterbalancing pressure away from convergence. Thus, convergence of the population is unlikely in genetic programming.

A maximum permissible size (measured via the depth of the tree) is established for offspring created by the crossover operation. This limit prevents the expenditure of large amounts of computer time on a few extremely large individual S-expressions. If a crossover between two parents would create an offspring of impermissible size, the contemplated crossover operation is aborted for that one offspring and the first of its parents is arbitrarily chosen to be reproduced into the new population. Note that the other offspring produced by the crossover may be of permissible size. If the crossover is aborted because both offspring are too large, both parents are reproduced into the new population. Of course, if we could execute all the individual S-expressions in the population in parallel (as nature does) in a manner such that the infeasibility of one individual in the population does not disproportionately jeopardize the resources needed by the population as a whole, we would not need such a size limitation.

A default value of 17 for this maximum permissible depth, established in section 6.9 for all problems in this book, permits potentially enormous programs. For example, the largest permissible LISP program consisting of entirely diadic functions would contain $2^{17} = 131,072$ functions and terminals. If four LISP functions and terminals are roughly equivalent to one line of a program written in some conventional programming language, then the largest permissible program consisting of entirely diadic functions is about 33,000 lines. Many of the larger LISP S-expressions created to solve problems in this book contain somewhere about 500 functions and terminals, corresponding to about 125 lines in a conventional programming language. Thus, this limit on the maximum permissible depth has no practical importance in terms of constraining solutions to the problems described in this book.

Simple LISP computer code for the crossover operation is presented in appendix C.

6.5 SECONDARY OPERATIONS

In addition to the two primary genetic operations of reproduction and crossover in genetic programming, there are five optional secondary operations worth mentioning:

- mutation
- permutation
- editing
- encapsulation, and
- decimation.

These operations are used only for occasional runs described in this book.

6.5.1 Mutation

The mutation operation introduces random changes in structures in the population.

In conventional genetic algorithms operating on strings, the mutation operation can be beneficial in reintroducing diversity in a population that may be tending to converge prematurely. In the conventional genetic algorithm, it is common for a particular symbol (i.e., an allele) appearing at a particular position on a chromosome string to disappear at an early stage of a run because that particular allele is associated with inferior performance, given the alleles prevailing at other positions of the chromosome string at that stage of the run. Then, because of the nonlinearities of the problem, the now-extinct allele may be precisely what is needed to achieve optimal performance at a later stage of the run, since a different and better combination of alleles is now prevailing at the other positions of the chromosome string. The situation just described is not conjectural but is, in fact, very typical. Genetic methods are normally applied to problems with highly nonlinear search spaces, and this situation is the essence of what is involved in nonlinear search spaces.

In this situation, the mutation operation may occasionally have beneficial results. Nonetheless, it is important to recognize that the mutation operation is a relatively unimportant secondary operation in the conventional genetic algorithm (Holland 1975; Goldberg 1989).

Mutation is asexual and operates on only one parental S-expression. The individual is selected with a probability proportional to the normalized fitness. The result of this operation is one offspring S-expression.

The mutation operation begins by selecting a point at random within the S-expression. This *mutation point* can be an internal (i.e., function) point or an external (i.e., terminal) point of the tree. The mutation operation then removes whatever is currently at the selected point and whatever is below the selected point and inserts a randomly generated subtree at that point.

This operation is controlled by a parameter that specifies the maximum size (measured by depth) for the newly created subtree that is to be inserted. This parameter typically has the same value as the parameter for the maximum initial size of S-expressions in the initial random population.

A special case of the mutation operation involves inserting a single terminal at a randomly selected point of the tree. This point mutation occurs occasionally in the crossover operation when the two selected crossover points are both terminals.

For example, in the "before" diagram in figure 6.8, point 3 (i.e., D0) of the S-expression was selected as the mutation point. The subexpression (NOT D1) was randomly generated and inserted at that point to produce the S-expression shown in the "after" diagram.

The above argument in favor of the occasional usefulness of mutation in the conventional genetic algorithm operating on strings is largely inapplicable to genetic programming.

First, in genetic programming, particular functions and terminals are not associated with fixed positions in a fixed structure. Moreover, when genetic programming is used, there are usually considerably fewer functions and terminals for a given problem than there are positions in the chromosome in the conventional genetic algorithm. Thus, it is relatively rare for a particular function or terminal ever to disappear entirely from a population in genetic programming. Therefore, to the extent that mutation serves the potentially important role of restoring lost diversity in a population for the conventional genetic algorithm, it is simply not needed in genetic programming.

Second, in genetic programming, whenever the two crossover points in the two parents happen to both be endpoints of trees, the crossover operation

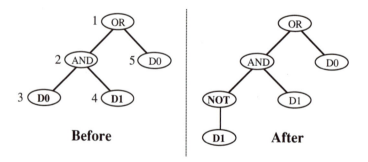

Figure 6.8 A computer program before and after the mutation operation is performed at point 3.

operates in a manner very similar to point mutation. Thus, to the extent that point mutation may be useful, the crossover operation already provides it.

The effect of the mutation operation is briefly considered in sections 25.6 and 25.7; however, none of the other runs described in this book use it.

Simple LISP code for the mutation operation is found in appendix C.

6.5.2 Permutation

The *permutation* operation is a generalization of the inversion operation for the conventional genetic algorithm operating on strings.

The inversion operation for the conventional genetic algorithm reorders characters found between two selected points of a single individual by reversing the order of all the characters between the two selected points. The inversion operation brings certain alleles closer together (while moving others farther apart). When applied to individuals with relatively high fitness, the inversion operation may aid in the establishment of a close genetic linkage between combinations of alleles that perform well together within a chromosome. These co-adapted sets of alleles are more likely to be preserved for the future, because they will be less subject to disruptive effects of crossover operating on the string. In the conventional genetic algorithm, alleles have meaning because they occupy particular positions in the chromosome string. Therefore, when the inversion operation is performed on a chromosome string the alleles must be accompanied by markers, so that when the chromosome string is decoded at the end of the run, the alleles are given their intended meaning.

Permutation is asexual in that it operates on only one parental S-expression. The individual is selected in the same way as for reproduction and crossover (i.e., in this book, with a probability proportional to the normalized fitness). The result of this operation is one offspring S-expression.

The permutation operation begins by selecting a function (internal) point of the LISP S-expression at random. If the function at the selected point has k arguments, a permutation is selected at random from the set of $k!$ possible permutations. Then the arguments of the function at the selected point are permuted in accordance with the random permutation. If the function at the selected point happens to be commutative, there is no immediate effect on the value returned by the S-expression as a result of the permutation operation.

The "before" diagram in figure 6.9 shows an S-expression with the function % (i.e., the protected division function) at point 4 operating on the argument B (at point 5) and the argument C (at point 6). If point 4 is chosen as the permutation point, the order of the two arguments (i.e., B and C) will be permuted. The "after" diagram shows the result of permuting the order of the two arguments. The argument C now appears at point 5 and the argument B now appears at point 6.

The permutation operation described here differs from the inversion operation for the conventional genetic algorithm in that it allows any one of $k!$ possible permutations to occur, whereas the inversion operation for the con-

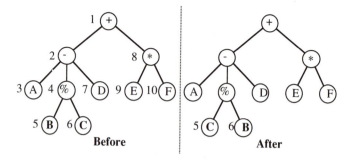

Before   **After**

Figure 6.9 An S-expression before and after the permutation operation is performed at point 4 containing the protected division function %.

ventional genetic algorithm merely allows a particular one of $k!$ possible permutations (i.e., the simple reversal).

The usefulness of the inversion operation has not been conclusively demonstrated in genetic algorithm work (Goldberg 1989).

The effect of the permutation operation is briefly considered in section 25.3; however, no other runs described in this book use it.

6.5.3   Editing

The *editing* operation provides a means to edit and simplify S-expressions as genetic programming is running.

Editing is asexual in that it operates on only one parental S-expression. The result of this operation is one offspring S-expression.

The editing operation recursively applies a pre-established set of domain-independent and domain-specific *editing rules* to each S-expression in the population.

The universal domain-independent editing rule is the following: If any function that has no side effects and is not context dependent has only constant atoms as arguments, the editing operation will evaluate that function and replace it with the value obtained from the evaluation. For example, the numeric expression (+ 1 2) will be replaced by 3 and the Boolean expression (AND T T) will be replaced by T (True).

In addition, the editing operation applies a pre-established set of domain-specific editing rules. For numeric problem domains, there might be an editing rule that inserts 0 whenever a subexpression is subtracted from itself. In Boolean domains, one might use editing rules such as the following:

(AND X X) → X

(OR X X) → X

(NOT (NOT X)) → X.

In addition, one might use an an editing rule to apply one of De Morgan's laws to S-expressions.

The recursive application of editing rules makes the editing operation very time consuming.

There is no equivalent of the editing operation for the conventional genetic algorithm operating on fixed-length character strings, since the individuals are already encoded and are of uniform structural complexity.

The editing operation can be used in the following two distinct ways in genetic programming:

First, the editing operation may be used *cosmetically* (i.e., entirely external to the run) to make the output of displayed individuals more readable. I routinely use the editing operation in this way for every run of every problem. The computer program implementing genetic programming always displays all individuals in the output files in both unedited and edited form.

Second, the editing operation may be used during the run in an attempt either to produce simplified output (without sacrificing the attainment of results) or to improve the overall performance of genetic programming.

When used with either of these two motivations, the editing operation is applied to each individual in the population at the time.

The editing operation is controlled by a frequency parameter specifying whether the editing operation is to be applied to every generation, to no generation, or with a certain frequency. For example, if the frequency of editing f_{ed} is 1, the editing operation is applied to all generations; if it is 0, it is applied to no generations; and if it is an integer greater than 1, it is applied to every generation number which is 0 modulo the specified integer.

There is an arguable position that the editing operation can improve performance by reducing the vulnerability of nonparsimonious, collapsible sub-S-expressions to disruption by the crossover operation. For example, when the editing operation simplifies a nonparsimonious S-expression such as

```
(NOT (NOT (NOT (NOT X))))
```

to the more parsimonious S-expression x, the S-expression becomes less vulnerable to a crossover that might exactly reverse the Boolean value of the expression as a whole. A more parsimonious S-expression might be less vulnerable to such value-changing disruption due to crossover.

On the other hand, there is an argument that the editing operation can degrade performance by prematurely reducing the variety of structures available for recombination.

The effect of the editing operation during a run is very unclear and is related to the unsettled and difficult question of whether breeding for parsimony is potentially helpful or deleterious to finding the solution to problems with genetic programming. The effect of the editing operation is briefly considered in section 25.5; however, except for the routine cosmetic editing mentioned above, no other runs described in this book use this operation.

Simple LISP computer code for the editing operation is presented in appendix F.

6.5.4 Encapsulation

The encapsulation operation is a means for automatically identifying a potentially useful subtree and giving it a name so that it can be referenced and used later.

A key issue in artificial intelligence and in machine learning is how to scale up promising techniques that succeed in solving subproblems so as to solve larger problems. One way to solve a large problem is to decompose it into a hierarchy of smaller subproblems. Identifying smaller subproblems that usefully decompose the problem is the key step. An important goal of artificial intelligence and machine learning is to make this identification in an automated way.

Encapsulation is asexual in that it operates on only one parental S-expression. The individual is selected in the same way as for reproduction and crossover (i.e., in this book, with a probability proportional to the normalized fitness). This operation results in one offspring S-expression.

The encapsulation operation begins by selecting a function (internal) point of the LISP S-expression at random. The result of this operation is one offspring S-expression and one new subtree definition.

The encapsulation operation removes the subtree located at the selected point and defines a new function to permit references to the deleted tree. The new encapsulated function has no arguments. The body of the new *encapsulated function* is the subtree originally located at the selected point. These new encapsulated functions are named E0, E1, E2, E3, ..., as they are created. Each new encapsulated function is, for efficiency, then compiled using LISP's incremental compilation facility.

A call to the newly created function is then inserted at the selected point in the LISP S-expression.

The function set of the problem is then augmented to include the new function so that, if the mutation operation is being used in the run, the new subtree being grown at the selected mutation point can incorporate the new encapsulated function.

For example, consider the LISP S-expression

(+ A (* B C)).

In figure 6.10, point 3 (the multiplication) was selected as the point for applying the encapsulation operation.

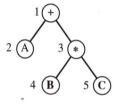

Figure 6.10 A computer program with point 3 designated as the point for applying the encapsulation operation.

The encapsulated function E0 taking no arguments is created as follows:

```
(defun E0 ()
   (* B C)
).
```

A copy of the original individual is made using the COPY-TREE function, and the subtree (* B C) is replaced in the copy by a call to the new encapsulated function E0 with no arguments. This produces the new S-expression

```
(+ A (E0))
```

in lieu of the original S-expression.

Figure 6.11 depicts this new S-expression. This new tree has the call (E0) in lieu of the subtree (* B C). In effect, the call (E0) has become a new indivisible atom (terminal) in the tree.

In implementing this operation on the computer, the subtree calling for the multiplication of B and C is first copied and then compiled during the execution of the overall run. The LISP programming language facilitates this encapsulation operation in two ways. First, the data and the program have the same form in LISP, and therefore one can alter a program by merely performing operations on it as if it were data. Second, it is possible to compile a new function "on the fly" during the execution of an overall run and then execute the new function.

The effect of the encapsulation operation is that the selected subtree in the newly created individual is no longer subject to the potentially disruptive effects of crossover, because it is now an indivisible single point. In effect, the newly encapsulated function is a potential building block for future generations. Note that it may proliferate in the population in later generations.

The original parent S-expression is not changed by the operation. Moreover, since the selection of the parental S-expression is in proportion to fitness (with reselection allowed), the original unaltered parental S-expression may participate in additional genetic operations (including reproduction, crossover, or even another encapsulation operation) during the current generation.

In earlier work (Koza 1990a; Koza and Rice 1991b), the encapsulation operation was called the "define building block" operation and the encapsulated function was called the "defined function." I now use the term "automatically defined function" (ADF) for a different concept described in chapters 20 and 21.

The encapsulation operation is used in designing neural networks in section 19.9 in order to achieve connectivity within the network. The effect of the

Figure 6.11 Result of the encapsulation operation.

encapsulation operation is briefly considered in section 25.4; however, no other runs described in this book use it.

6.5.5 Decimation

For some complex problems, the distribution of fitness values over the initial random population may be skewed so that a very large percentage of the individuals have very poor fitness (e.g., a raw fitness of 0). This skewing may occur in problems where individuals in the population are assigned some penalty value of fitness because they would otherwise consume an infinite amount of time (as in time optimal control problems or problems involving iterative loops). In such problems, enormous amounts of computer time may be expended and wasted in early generations on very poor individuals. Moreover, when a highly skewed distribution of fitness values occurs, the few individuals with marginally better fitness values immediately begin to dominate the population and the variety of the population quickly begins to drop. In genetic programming, the crossover operation is usually capable of quickly reintroducing variety into the population. However, because the selection of parents to participate in crossover is based on fitness, the crossover operation concentrates on the few individuals in the population with the marginally better fitness values.

The *decimation* operation offers a faster way to deal with this situation. The decimation operation is controlled by two parameters: a percentage and a condition specifying when the operation is to be invoked. For example, the percentage may be 10% and the operation may be invoked on generation 0. In that event, immediately after the fitness calculation for generation 0, all but 10% of the population is deleted. If decimation were being performed on generation 0, one would start the run with 10 times the population desired for the remainder of the run. The selection of the individuals in the decimation operation is done probabilistically on the basis of fitness. In the decimation operation, reselection is disallowed so as to maximize diversity in the remaining population. Thus, if there initially were no duplicates in generation 0 of the population and decimation is applied after the fitness calculation for generation 0, the population will still have no duplicates as it goes into generation 1.

6.6 STATE OF THE ADAPTIVE SYSTEM

In genetic programming, the state of the adaptive system at any point during the process consists *only* of the current population of individuals. No additional memory or centralized bookkeeping is necessary.

In a computer implementation of the genetic programming paradigm, it is also necessary to cache the control parameters for the run, the terminal set and the function set (if mutation is being used), and the best-so-far individual (section 6.8 below) if it is being used as part of the process of result designation for the run.

6.7 TERMINATION CRITERION

The genetic programming paradigm parallels nature in that it is a never-ending process. However, as a practical matter, a run of the genetic programming paradigm terminates when the *termination criterion* is satisfied.

The termination criterion for genetic programming used throughout this book is that the run terminates when either a prespecified maximum number G of generations have been run (the *generational predicate*) or some additional problem-specific *success predicate* has been satisfied.

The success predicate often involves finding a 100%-correct solution to the problem (e.g., some individual in the population has attained a standardized fitness of 0). For problems where we may not recognize a solution even when we see it (e.g., optimization problems) or problems where we do not ever expect an exact solution (e.g., creating a mathematical model for noisy empirical data), we usually adopt some appropriate lower criterion for success for purposes of terminating a run. For some problems, there is no success predicate; we merely analyze the results after running for G generations.

6.8 RESULT DESIGNATION

The method of *result designation* for genetic programming used throughout this book is to designate the best individual that ever appeared in any generation of the population (i.e., the *best-so-far* individual) as the result of a run of genetic programming. Note that we do not guarantee a berth for the best-so-far individual in all subsequent generations (i.e., we do not follow the so-called *elitist strategy*). We merely cache the best-so-far individual and report it as the result of the entire run when the run eventually terminates according to the termination criterion. When this method of result designation is used, the state of the system consists of the current population of individuals and the one cached best-so-far individual.

An alternative method of result designation is to designate the best-of-generation individual in the population at the time of termination as the result of a run. No caching is required when this method is used. This alternative method usually produces the same result as the best-so-far method because the best-so-far individual is usually in the population at the time of termination (i.e., it is usually also the best-of-generation individual of the last generation). The reasons for this are either (1) it was created in an earlier generation and, because of its high fitness, copied into the current generation by the reproduction operation or (2) the run was terminated at the current generation by virtue of the creation of this very individual (i.e., it satisfied the termination criterion).

In some problems, the population as a whole or a subpopulation selected proportionate to fitness is designated as the result. In that event, the set of individuals acts as a set of alternative solutions to the problem (i.e., a mixed strategy).

6.9 CONTROL PARAMETERS

The genetic programming paradigm is controlled by 19 control parameters, including two major numerical parameters, 11 minor numerical parameters, and six qualitative variables that select among various alternative ways of executing a run.

Except as otherwise specifically indicated, the values of all of these control parameters are fixed at the default values described below for all problems in this book.

The two major numerical parameters are the population size (M) and the maximum number of generations to be run (G).

- The population size M is 500.

- The maximum number G of generations is 51 (an initial random generation, called generation 0, plus 50 subsequent generations).

The eleven minor numerical parameters used to control the process are described below:

- The probability of crossover, p_c, is 0.90. That is, crossover is performed on 90% of the population for each generation. For example, if the population size is 500, then 450 individuals (225 pairs) from each generation are selected (with reselection allowed) to participate in crossover.

- The probability of reproduction, p_r, is 0.10. For example, if the population size is 500, 50 individuals from each generation are selected for reproduction (with reselection allowed).

- In selecting crossover points, we use a probability distribution that allocates $p_{ip} = 90\%$ of the crossover points equally among the internal (function) points of each tree and 10% of the crossover points equally among the external (terminal) points of each tree. This distribution promotes the recombining of larger structures whereas a uniform probability distribution over all points would do an inordinate amount of mere swapping of terminals from tree to tree in a manner more akin to point mutation than to recombining of small substructures or building blocks.

- A maximum size (measured by depth), $D_{created}$, is established as 17 for S-expressions created by the crossover operation (or any secondary genetic operations that may be used in a given run).

- A maximum size (measured by depth), $D_{initial}$, is established as 6 for the random individuals generated for the initial population.

- The probability of mutation, p_m, specifying the frequency of performing mutation is 0.

- The probability of permutation, p_p, specifying the frequency of performing permutation is 0.

- The parameter specifying the frequency, f_{ed}, of applying the operation of editing is 0.

- The probability of encapsulation, p_{en}, specifying the frequency of performing encapsulation is 0.

- The condition for invoking the decimation operation is set to NIL.

- The decimation percentage, p_d, is irrelevant if the condition for invoking the decimation operation is NIL, and is arbitrarily set to 0.

The following six qualitative variables select among different ways of executing the runs:

- The generative method for the initial random population is ramped half-and-half.

- The method of selection for reproduction and for the first parent in crossover is fitness-proportionate reproduction (except for the optimization problem in section 11.3).

- The method of selecting the second parent for a crossover is the same as the method for selecting the first parent (as opposed, say, to spousal selection wherein the second parent is chosen with a uniform random probability distribution). See Schaffer 1987.

- The optional adjusted fitness measure is used.

- Over-selection is not used for populations of 500 and below and is used for populations of 1,000 and above.

- The elitist strategy is not used.

The major parameters of population size M and number of generations G depend on the difficulty of the problem involved. The choices for $D_{initial}$ and $D_{created}$ above depend on the difficulty of the problem involved. Larger values may be required where the structure of the solution is thought to be complex or in problems where the syntax of the individuals in the population is restricted by complex additional syntactic rules of construction (as discussed in chapter 19).

Table 6.1 summarizes the default values used in this book for the numerical parameters and qualitative variables for controlling the genetic programming paradigm.

Many problems described in this book undoubtedly could be solved better or faster by means of different choices of these parameters and variables. I have not undertaken any detailed studies of the optimal choice for the numerical parameters or the qualitative variables that control genetic programming runs (although several experiments in this area are described below in chapter 25).

My omission of a detailed consideration of the optimal choice for these parameters and variables and my failure to use better values of them on certain problems is *intentional*. The focus in this first book on genetic programming is on demonstrating the two main points cited in chapter 1. The first point was established in chapter 2. The main focus of the remainder of this book is on establishing the second point by means of numerous successful examples covering a wide variety of problems from a wide variety of fields. In my view,

Table 6.1 Default values of the 19 control parameters for genetic programming.

Two major numerical parameters
Population size $M = 500$.
Maximum number G of generations to be run $= 51$.
Eleven minor numerical parameters
Probability p_c of crossover $= 90\%$.
Probability p_r of reproduction $= 10\%$.
Probability p_{ip} of choosing internal points for crossover $= 90\%$.
Maximum size D_c for S-expressions created during the run $= 17$.
Maximum size D_i for initial random S-expressions $= 6$.
Probability p_m of mutation $= 0.0\%$.
Probability p_p of permutation $= 0.0\%$.
Frequency f_{ed} of editing $= 0$.
Probability p_{en} of encapsulation $= 0.0\%$.
Condition for decimation $=$ NIL.
Decimation target percentage $p_d = 0.0\%$.
Six qualitative variables
Generative method for initial random population is ramped half-and-half.
Basic selection method is fitness proportionate.
Spousal selection method is fitness proportionate.
Adjusted fitness is used.
Over-selection is not used for populations of 500 and below and is used for populations of 1,000 and above.
Elitist strategy is not used.

the optimal choices for the control parameters become relevant only after one has been persuaded of the basic usefulness of genetic programming. In the present volume, this process of persuasion would be undermined if I were to frequently vary the many numerical parameters and qualitative variables that control the runs; the reader might come to attribute the results to fortuitous selection of the parameters. Since studying performance is not a main purpose of this book, I have generally made more or less the same choices for the control parameters from chapter to chapter. Of course, I do change occasionally parameters for illustrative purposes, or when necessary (e.g., certain complex problems clearly do require a larger population size), or for certain specific reasons that are stated in connection with particular problems.

6.10   THE SCHEMATA

In the conventional genetic algorithm (and genetic programming) the number of individuals actually contained in the current genetic population is usually infinitesimal in comparison to the search space of the problem.

One of the key insights in Holland's *Adaptation in Natural and Artificial Systems* (1975) was that the genetic algorithm operating on fixed-length character strings implicitly processes, in parallel, information about an enormous number of unseen schemata (hyperplanes). In particular, the genetic algorithm implicitly recomputes, for each generation, an estimate of the value of the average fitness for each of these unseen schemata. Thus, although the genetic operations of fitness-proportionate reproduction and crossover explicitly operate only on the M individuals actually present in the population, implicit computation is operating on a much larger number of schemata.

For a string of length L over an alphabet of size K, a schema is identified by a string of length L over an extended alphabet consisting of the K alphabet symbols and the metasymbol * ("don't care"). A schema consists of the set of individual strings from the population whose symbols match the symbols of the identifier for all specific positions (i.e., all positions except where the identifier has the * symbol). There are $(K + 1)^L$ such schemata. Each individual string occurs in 2^L such schemata, regardless of K. Therefore, a population of only M individual strings appears in up to $M2^L$ schemata (depending on the diversity of the population).

Holland showed that for genetic algorithms using fitness-proportionate reproduction and crossover, the expected number of occurrences of every schema H in the next generation is approximately

$$m(H, t + 1) \geq \frac{f(H, t)}{\overline{f(t)}} m(H, t)(1 - \varepsilon),$$

where $\overline{f(t)}$ is the average fitness of the population and ε is small.

When

$$\frac{f(H, t)}{\overline{f(t)}}$$

remains above unity by at least a constant amount over several generations, this means that a schema with above-average fitness appears in the next generation at an approximately exponentially increasing rate over those generations. Holland also showed that the mathematical form of the optimal allocation of trials among random variables in a problem involving a multi-armed-bandit (involving minimizing losses while exploring new or seemingly nonoptimal schemata, while also exploiting seemingly optimal schemata) is similarly approximately exponential. Consequently, the processing of schemata by genetic algorithms using fitness-proportionate reproduction and crossover is mathematically near optimal. In particular, this allocation of trials is most nearly optimal when ε is small. For strings, ε is computed by dividing the defining length $\delta(H)$ of the schema involved (i.e., the distance between the outermost specific, non-* symbols) by $L - 1$ (i.e., the number of interstitial points where crossover may occur). Therefore, ε is small when $\delta(H)$ is short (i.e., the schema is a small, short, compact building block). Thus, genetic algorithms process short-defining-length schemata most favorably. More important, as a result, problems whose solutions can be incrementally built up from such small building blocks are most optimally handled by genetic algorithms.

In genetic programming, the individuals in the population are LISP S-expressions (i.e., rooted, point-labeled trees with ordered branches) rather than linear character strings. A *schema in genetic programming* is the set of all individual trees from the population that contain, as subtrees, one or more specified subtrees. That is, a schema is a set of LISP S-expressions (i.e., a set of rooted, point-labeled trees with ordered branches) sharing common features.

Suppose the common feature is a single subtree consisting of s specified points. That is, there are no unspecified ("don't care") points within the schema. The set of individuals sharing the common feature is the set consisting of all trees containing the designated subtree with s points as a subtree. This set of such trees is infinite. However, in genetic programming, we always, in practice, limit both the size of initial random trees and the size to which a tree can grow as a result of crossover. This maximum size, W, can be defined in terms of the total number of points in the tree.

Once W is specified, the set consisting of all trees with W or fewer points that contain the specified subtree with s points as a subtree is a finite set. Moreover, the *average fitness of the schema in genetic programming*, $f(H)$, is simply the average of the fitness values of all the individual trees belonging to that schema.

Holland's results concerning the growth (or decay) of the number of occurrences of schemata as a result of fitness-proportionate reproduction and concerning the optimal allocation of trials do not depend on the character of the individual objects in the population. Fitness-proportionate reproduction causes growth (or decay) in the number of occurrences of a particular schema in the new population in accordance with the ratio of the fitness of the schema to the average fitness of the population in precisely the same way as it does for conventional genetic algorithms operating on strings. Specifically, if the fitness of a particular individual in the population is twice the average fitness of the population (i.e., the individual has a fitness ratio of 2.0), we can expect that fitness-proportionate reproduction will make two copies of that individual. The two copies of the original individual now each participate two times in the calculation of the value of fitness of each schema to which that individuals belongs. The number of occurrences $m(H, t)$ in the population of each schema to which the individual belongs is increased. If there was only one occurrence of a particular schema before the copying, there would now be two occurrences as a consequence of the reproduction operation. Thus, the number of occurrences of each schema grows (or decays) as a result of fitness-proportionate reproduction in genetic programming in the same exponential way as for genetic algorithms. If the schemata are viewed as being in competition with one another, the allocation of future trials among the schemata gives an exponentially increasing (or decreasing) number of trials to the schemata in accordance with the fitness ratio of each schema.

Deviations from the near-optimal exponential rate of growth (or decay) of a schema are caused by the crossover operation.

For strings, the disruptive effect of crossover is relatively small when the maximum distance between the positions in the string involved in the definition of the schema (i.e., the defining length) is relatively small. To the extent that the disruptive effect of crossover is small, the growth (or decay) of the number of occurrences of the schemata will be close to the optimal allocation of trials.

For genetic programming, disruption is smallest and the deviation from the optimal allocation of trials among the schemata is smallest when the schema is defined in terms of a single compact subtree. If W is 50, then a schema defined as containing a single specified subtree with three points is less likely to be disrupted than a schema defined as containing a single specified subtree with six points. Thus, for the case where the schema is defined as containing a single specified subtree, the overall effect of fitness-proportionate reproduction and crossover is that subprograms (i.e., subtrees, sublists) from relatively high-fitness programs are used as building blocks for constructing new individuals in an approximately near-optimal way. Over a period of time, this concentrates the search of the solution space into subspaces of LISP S-expressions of ever-decreasing dimensionality and ever-increasing fitness.

This argument also applies to schemata defined as containing more than one specified subtree. The deviation from optimality is relatively small to the extent that both the total number of points in the subtrees defining the schema is relatively small and to the extent that the minimal tree encompassing all the disjoint subtrees defining the schema is relatively small. Thus, the overall effect is that subprograms (i.e., subtrees) from relatively compact high-fitness individuals are used as building blocks for constructing new individuals.

Genetic programming is similar to the conventional genetic algorithm operating on strings in another way. Genetic algorithms, in general, are mathematical algorithms which are based on Darwinian principles of reproduction and survival of the fittest. In this view, a character found at a particular position in a mathematical character string in a conventional genetic algorithm is considered analogous to one of the four nucleotide bases (adenine, cytosine, guanine, or thymine) found in molecules of DNA. The observed fitness in the environment of the entire biological individual created using the information in a particular linear string of DNA is used in the computation of average schema fitness for each schema represented by that individual.

The computational procedure carried out by a LISP S-expression in genetic programming can be viewed as analogous to the work performed by a protein in a living cell. The observed fitness in the environment of the entire biological individual created as a result of the action of the LISP S-expressions contributes, in the same way as with conventional genetic algorithms, directly to the computation of average schema fitness for each schema to which that individual belongs. That is, genetic programming employs the same automatic allocation of credit inherent in the conventional genetic algorithm described by Holland (1975) and inherent in Darwinian reproduction and survival of the fittest among biological populations in nature. This automatic allocation of credit contrasts with the connectionistic bucket brigade algorithm for credit allocation and reinforcement used in classifier systems, which is not founded on any observed natural mechanism involving adaptation among biological populations (Westerdale 1985).

7   Four Introductory Examples of Genetic Programming

This chapter contains examples of the genetic programming paradigm applied to four simple introductory problems. The goal here is to genetically breed a computer program to solve one illustrative example problem from each of the following four fields:

- **Optimal control**   Evolve a control strategy (i.e., a computer program) that will apply a force so as to bring a cart moving along a track to rest at a designated target point in minimal time.
- **Robotic planning**   Evolve a robotic action plan (i.e., a computer program) that will enable an artificial ant to find all the food along a trail containing various gaps and irregularities.
- **Symbolic regression**   Evolve a mathematical expression (i.e., a computer program) that closely fits a given finite sample of data.
- **Boolean 11-multiplexer**   Evolve a Boolean expression (i.e., a computer program) that performs the Boolean 11-multiplexer function.

There are five major steps in preparing to use the genetic programming paradigm to solve a problem:

- determining the set of terminals,
- determining the set of functions,
- determining the fitness measure,
- determining the parameters and variables for controlling the run, and
- determining the method of designating a result and the criterion for terminating a run.

For each of the above four problems, this chapter will detail the application of the five major preparatory steps, the generally poor performance associated with randomly produced individuals, one or more intermediate results which show the general path taken by genetic programming as it progressively approaches a solution to the problem, and the result of one successful run for each problem.

For each problem, solutions were found on numerous runs. However, since the genetic programming paradigm is a probabilistic method, different runs almost never yield precisely the same S-expression. No one particular run and no one particular result is typical or representative of all the others.

Chapters 10 through 21 will present numerous additional problems from numerous other fields. Cumulatively, the problems presented will involve functions that are real-valued, integer-valued, Boolean-valued, and symbolic-valued. Some of the problems require iteration for their solution. Some of the problems involve functions whose real functionality lies in the side effects they cause on the state of the system involved, rather than the actual value returned by the function. Many of the problems are benchmark problems that have been the subjects of previous studies in connection with machine learning, artificial intelligence, neural nets, induction, decision trees, classifier systems, and various other paradigms.

For each problem presented in this book, the author believes that sufficient information is provided herein (or in the references cited) to allow the experiment to be independently replicated so as to produce substantially similar results (within the limits inherent in any process involving stochastic operations and minor details of implementation).

Chapter 8 will revisit each of the four problems and will provide statistical information on the performance of genetic programming over a large number of runs and a method for measuring the amount of computation likely to be required to solve the problem by means of genetic programming.

7.1 CART CENTERING

The cart centering (isotropic rocket) problem involves a cart that can move to the left or the right on a frictionless one-dimensional track. The problem is to center the cart, in minimal time, by applying a force of fixed magnitude (a *bang-bang force*) so as to accelerate the cart toward the left or the right.

In figure 7.1, the cart's current position $x(t)$ at time t is negative and its velocity $v(t)$ is positive. That is, the position $x(t)$ of the cart is to the left of the origin (0.0) and the cart's current velocity $v(t)$ is toward the positive direction (i.e., toward the right). The bang-bang force F is positive. That is, the bang-bang force F is being applied by the rocket to the cart so as to accelerate it in the positive direction (i.e., toward the right).

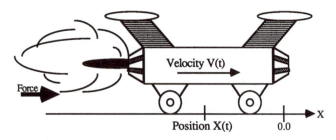

Figure 7.1 The cart centering problem.

The cart centering problem is a problem of optimal control. Such problems involve a system whose state is described by state variables. The choice of the control variable causes the state of the system to change. The goal is to choose the value of the control variable so as to cause the system to go to a specified target state with an optimal cost. The cost may be measured in, for example, time, distance, fuel, or dollars. The goal is typically stated in terms of minimizing the cost.

In reading this section, the reader uninterested in control theory should focus on the fact that this problem has a well-known solution, which we intend to evolve by means of genetic programming. The reader interested in control theory will find considerable additional details about this problem in Macki 1982 and in Bryson and Ho 1975.

There are two state variables for the system in the cart centering problem: the current position $x(t)$ of the cart along the track and the current velocity $v(t)$ of the cart.

There is one control variable for this system: the direction from which a rocket applies a bang-bang force F to the center of mass of the cart so as to accelerate the cart in either the positive or the negative direction along the track.

The target state for the system is the state for which the cart is at rest (i.e., velocity 0.0) and centered at the origin (i.e., position 0.0).

The goal in the cart centering problem is to choose a sequence of values for the control variable so as to cause the state of the system to go to the target state in minimal time.

At each time step, the choice of the control variable of the system (i.e., the bang-bang force F) causes a change in the state variables of the system (i.e., the position and the velocity of the cart). In particular, when the bang-bang force $F(t)$ is applied to the cart at time t, the cart accelerates according to Newton's Law as follows:

$$a(t) = \frac{F(t)}{m},$$

where m is the mass of the cart. Then, as a result of this acceleration $a(t)$, the velocity $v(t + 1)$ of the cart at time step $t + 1$ (which occurs a small amount of time τ after time step t) becomes

$$v(t + 1) = v(t) + \tau a(t),$$

where τ is the size of the time step.

At time step $t + 1$, the position $x(t + 1)$ of the cart becomes

$$x(t + 1) = x(t) + \tau v(t).$$

Thus, the choice of value of the control variable (i.e., the quantity $u(t)$ equal to a multiplier of either $+1$ or -1 to the magnitude $|F|$ of the force F) at time step t causes a change in the state variables of the system at time step $t + 1$.

The problem is to find a time-optimal control strategy for centering the cart that satisfies the following three conditions:

(1) The control strategy specifies how to apply the bang-bang force for any given current position $x(t)$ and current velocity $v(t)$ of the cart at each time step.

(2) The cart approximately comes to rest at the origin (i.e., the cart reaches a target state of a position of approximately 0.0 with a speed of approximately 0.0).

(3) The time required is minimal.

The exact time-optimal solution is, for any given current position $x(t)$ and current velocity $v(t)$, to apply the bang-bang force $F(t)$ to accelerate the cart in the positive direction if

$$-x(t) > \frac{v(t)^2 \operatorname{Sign} v(t)}{2|F|/m}$$

or, otherwise, to apply the bang-bang force F to accelerate the cart in the negative direction. The Sign function returns $+1$ for a positive argument and -1 otherwise.

If the mass of the cart m happens to be 2.0 kilograms and the force F is 1.0 newtons, the denominator $2|F|/m$ equals 1.0 and can be hereafter ignored for the purposes of this introductory problem.

There are many ways of presenting a control strategy, including an equation (such as the one above), a computer program (such as we are seeking by means of genetic programming), and a graph. Figure 7.2 is a graph that depicts the time-optimal solution to the cart centering problem. Each pair of values of the two state variables of this system corresponds to some point (x, v) in the position-velocity state space (i.e., the plane). If $-x(t) > v^2 \operatorname{Sign} v(t)$, then the point lies in the shaded portion of the figure and the bang-bang force will be set to $+F$ (since the control variable $u = +1$) and the bang-bang force will accelerate the cart in the positive direction. Otherwise, the point lies in the unshaded portion of the figure and the bang-bang force will be set to $-F$ (since the control variable $u = -1$) and the bang-bang force will accelerate the cart in the negative direction.

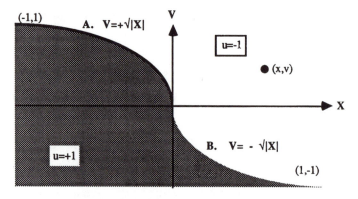

Figure 7.2 Time-optimal solution to the cart centering problem.

On the left side of figure 7.2 (where position $x < 0$), the boundary between the shaded and unshaded regions is the curve $v = +\sqrt{|x|}$ labeled A). On the right side of this figure (where position $x > 0$), the boundary is the curve $v = -\sqrt{|x|}$ (labeled B). This boundary is called the *switching curve* for this problem.

Over many time steps, every control strategy causes the state of the system to trace a trajectory through the state space. The system may start at some initial condition point in the state space. Then, at each time step, the control strategy causes the state of the system to change to a new state. The sequence of such states forms a trajectory through the state space. The time-optimal control strategy causes this trajectory to end at or near the origin in minimal time.

Note that on the right side of figure 7.2 (where position $x > 0$) the boundary is in the shaded region so that when the state of the system is a point precisely on the boundary (an event that rarely occurs with the floating-point numbers used in a computer), u will be set to $+1$. Conversely, on the left side of this figure (where position $x < 0$) the boundary is in the unshaded (white) region, so that when the state of the system is a point precisely on the boundary, u will be set to -1. In both situations, if the state of the system is precisely on the boundary, the bang-bang force is applied so as to move the state of the system toward the origin along the switching curve.

Suppose that we want to write a computer program (a control strategy) to control the application of these bang-bang forces so as to center the cart in minimal time.

A computer program is often described as a sequence of instructions that starts with certain inputs and produces certain outputs. Thus, a computer program is merely a mathematical transformation (i.e., a function) that maps certain inputs (arguments, independent variables, detectors, sensors) into certain outputs (dependent variables, effectors). In this problem, the inputs to the computer program are the two state variables of the system (i.e., x and v). The output from the computer program is interpreted as the single control variable of the system (the direction, $+1$ or -1, for the bang-bang force F).

The large variety of different types of operations, statements, and instructions found in most programming languages, along with the preoccupation with physical storage locations in the computer, obscures an important commonality underlying all computer programs: that a *computer program is simply a composition of various functions acting on various arguments*. To illustrate this important commonality, let us write a computer program to implement the time-optimal solution to the cart-centering problem in three different types of programming languages:

- PASCAL, a high-level programming language,
- MIX, a hypothetical symbolic assembly language for a hypothetical computer, and
- LISP, a functional programming language.

    Four Introductory Examples of Genetic Programming

Each of these programs will be a composition of functions acting on various arguments.

Note that, in this book, the word "function" is used to collectively describe ordinary functions, operations, operators, control structures, and any other transformation that takes certain arguments, does some processing, and returns zero, one, or more results.

7.1.1 Program in PASCAL

In PASCAL, we might write a computer program to implement the time-optimal solution to the cart centering problem as follows:

```
function controller (x,v:real):real;
begin
if (-1.0*x > v*ABS(v)) then controller :=  1.0
                        else controller := -1.0;
end;
```

This PASCAL computer program receives x and v as inputs to the function called controller. If $-x$ is greater than $v|v|$, the program assigns the value $+1.0$ to controller (which is the output of the program); otherwise, it assigns the value -1.0 to controller.

The reader familiar with a programming language such as FORTRAN, C, or BASIC should have no difficulty visualizing how to write an equivalent program in that language.

Composition (cascading) of functions occurs repeatedly in a programming language such as PASCAL. For example, in evaluating the arithmetic expression

$$x + v|v|$$

there are three levels of composition in which the value returned by one function becomes an argument to the next function. The result is obtained by applying the addition function to two arguments:

- the variable x and
- the result obtained by having previously applied the multiplication function to two arguments:
  - the variable v and
  - the result obtained by having previously applied the one-argument absolute-value function to the single argument v.

The composition (cascading) that occurs in high-level languages is often not as obvious as it is for the arithmetic expression $x + v|v|$. For example, consider the following if-then-else statement from PASCAL:

```
if (-1.0*x > v*ABS (v)) then controller :=  1.0
                        else controller := -1.0;
```

We can view this statement as being the result of applying the logical function "if" to three arguments:

- the logical predicate (-1.0*x > v*ABS (v)), which returns a logical value such as True or False,
- the assignment statement controller := 1.0, and
- the assignment statement controller := -1.0.

This function if evaluates the first argument; then, depending on whether the first argument is true or false, it evaluates either the second argument or the third.

7.1.2 Program in Symbolic Assembly Code

The fact that computer programs are compositions of functions acting on various arguments is even more apparent in assembly code than in a higher-level language such as PASCAL. In assembly code, the result obtained by applying one operation (function) usually ends up in a particular register, so that the next operation (function) can then be applied to this result. A sequence of consecutive assembly-code instructions operating on a particular register is a composition of functions. The value returned by the composition of functions is the value found in the register when the entire sequence of operations is executed.

If we were writing the computer program for cart centering using Knuth's (1981a) hypothetical symbolic assembly code for his hypothetical MIX computer, we might write something like table 7.1.

This hypothetical language program in symbolic assembly language starts at the program location labeled START on line 1 of table 7.1. The program performs the "load accumulator register A" (LDA) operation. The operand of the LDA operation on line 1 is a numerical variable (i.e., the velocity of the cart) stored in memory location v. This operation loads the variable v (from storage)

Table 7.1 MIX assembly code for optimal control strategy for the cart centering problem.

	Program location	Operation code	Operand
1	START	LDA	V
2		JAP	OK
3		LDAN	V
4	OK	MUL	V
5		ADD	X
6		JAN	RETURN1
7		LDA	-1.0
8		JMP	DONE
9	RETURN1	LDA	1.0
10	DONE	END	

into the accumulator (arithmetic) register of our hypothetical computer. Control then passes sequentially to the next program location (line 2 of the program).

On line 2, this program performs the "jump on accumulator positive" (JAP) operation. The operand of this operation is the program location labeled "OK." The JAP operation on line 2 causes control to jump down to the program location labeled OK (line 4) if the contents of the accumulator (which contains the velocity v of the cart) is positive. Otherwise, control passes sequentially to the next program location (line 3 of the program).

On line 3, the program performs the "load accumulator negative" (LDAN) on the variable v from memory. This operation loads the accumulator with the negative of the value of the variable v stored in memory. Since we can get to line 3 of this program only if we have already established that the variable v is negative, the effect of this operation is to load the accumulator with the absolute value of the variable v. Control passes sequentially to line 4 of the program.

When control has reached line 4 (either via the conditional jump operation on line 2 or via the usual sequential flow from line 3), the accumulator contains the absolute value of the velocity v of the cart. The program then performs the "multiply" (MUL) operation by multiplying the contents of the arithmetic register by the variable v. This operation multiplies the arithmetic register by the variable v (from storage). This completes the calculation of v^2 Sign v. We assume here that all numbers are floating-point numbers and all the operations we used work appropriately on such numbers.

On line 5 the program performs the "add" (ADD) operation on the variable x. This operation adds the variable x (from storage) into the accumulator. The accumulator now contains the result of the composition of functions executed so far, namely $x + v^2$ Sign v.

Then, on line 6, the "jump on accumulator negative" (JAN) operation branches to the program location labeled RETURN1 (line 9) if the arithmetic register is negative. Otherwise, control in the program proceeds in the ordinary sequential way to line 7.

On line 7, the "load accumulator register A" (LDA) operation loads the constant -1.0 from memory into the accumulator.

Then, on line 8, the program "jumps unconditionally" (JMP) to the program location labeled DONE (line 10).

On line 9 (which is reached only via the conditional jump operation from line 6), the "load accumulator register A" (LDA) operation loads the constant $+1.0$ into the arithmetic register. Control then passes sequentially to the program location labeled END (line 10), where the program ends.

Line 10 is also reachable via the unconditional branching operation from line 8.

The reader familiar with another assembly language should be able to visualize how to write an equivalent program in that language.

7.1.3 Program in LISP

The fact that a computer program is a composition of applications of functions to arguments is especially overt in a functional programming language. LISP is the most widely used language of this kind.

If we were writing the time-optimal computer program for solving the cart centering problem in LISP, we might write the parsimonious LISP S-expression

```
(GT (* -1 X) (* V (ABS V))).
```

In this S-expression, the greater-than function GT is a numerical-valued function of two arguments that returns $+1$ if its first argument is greater than its second argument and returns -1 otherwise (as described in subsection 6.1.1).

Figure 7.3 graphically depicts this S-expression as a rooted point-labeled tree with ordered branches.

The interpretation of this LISP computer program is as follows: Starting with x and v as inputs, take the absolute value of v and multiply it by v. Then, multiply x by -1. Then compare $-x$ and $v|v|$. If $-x$ is greater than $v|v|$, the S-expression evaluates to $+1$ and the bang-bang force F will be applied in the positive direction; otherwise, the S-expression evaluates to -1 and the bang-bang force F will be applied in the negative direction. Once this program has determined whether the bang-bang force is to be applied from the left or the right, the above-mentioned simulation involving Newton's equations of motion updates the state of the system for the next time step.

7.1.4 Measuring the Fitness of a Computer Program

Having now written a time-optimal computer program for centering the cart in three different computer programming languages, we naturally wonder what result these programs produce. Indeed, how long does it take to center the cart if we execute the computer program?

The time required for centering, of course, depends on the initial conditions of the cart at time 0, namely the initial position $x(0)$ and the initial velocity $v(0)$. If, by chance, the cart is already at (or very near) the origin and has zero (or very low) speed, it takes practically no time. On the other hand,

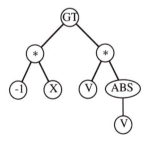

Figure 7.3 LISP S-expression for solving the cart centering problem.

Four Introductory Examples of Genetic Programming

if the cart, by chance, starts with a large position and a large velocity (either both positive or both negative), the cart is distant from the origin and heading in the wrong direction, and centering it will take a relatively long time. Thus, we can answer this question only by taking an average over a representative sampling of possible inputs to the computer program.

If we chose 1,000 points (x, v) at random in the square whose opposite corners are $(-0.75, 0.75)$ and $(0.75, -0.75)$, where the position x is in meters and the velocity v is in meters per second, we would find that it takes about 2,020 seconds to center the cart using the time-optimal control strategy for these 1,000 random fitness cases in this domain. That is, the optimal time for centering the cart averages 2.02 seconds for a random initial condition point lying in the specified domain. A computer program that correctly performs the task of centering the cart in optimal time would take an average of 2.02 seconds for a random initial condition point lying in the specified domain.

Several pages ago, when I spoke of writing a computer program to center the cart in optimal time, you probably assumed that I was talking about writing a *correct* computer program to solve this problem. Nothing could be further from the truth. In fact, this book focuses almost entirely on *incorrect* programs. In particular, I want to develop the notion that there are gradations in performance among computer programs. Some incorrect programs are very poor; some are better than others; some are approximately correct; occasionally, one may be 100% correct. Expressing this biologically, one could say that some computer programs are fitter than others in their environment. It is rare for any biological organism to be optimal.

Now consider, in the context of the cart centering problem, what makes a computer program poor rather than good and what makes a program approximately correct rather than 100% correct. Consider, for a moment, the following nonoptimal control strategy for cart centering:

$$-x(t) > \frac{v(t)^3}{2|F|/m}.$$

We could write this new, nonoptimal control strategy in PASCAL as

```
function controller(x,v:real):real;
begin
if (-1.0*x > v*v*v) then controller :=  1.0
                    else controller := -1.0;
end;
```

or in LISP as

```
(GT (* -1 X) (* V (* V V))).
```

The left half of figure 7.4 shows the optimal curve $v = +\sqrt{|x|}$ (labeled A) in the second quadrant. It also shows the new switching curve $x = v^3$ (labeled C) in the second quadrant for the new nonoptimal control strategy. The right half of the figure shows the optimal curve $v = -\sqrt{|x|}$ (labeled B) in the fourth

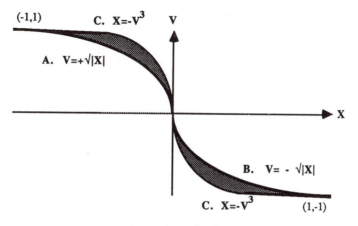

Figure 7.4 First nonoptimal control strategy for the cart centering problem.

quadrant. It also shows the continuation of the new, nonoptimal curve $x = v^3$ (labeled C) in the fourth quadrant.

But even though this new control strategy is not optimal, it is not worthless. This control strategy still produces the same direction for the bang-bang force, except for points in the relatively small shaded region lying between the curves in figure 7.4. This shaded region represents only 5% of the area lying in the domain for this problem, namely the square whose opposite corners are $(-0.75, 0.75)$ and $(0.75, -0.75)$.

If we again chose 1,000 points at random in the specified domain, we find that this new, nonoptimal control strategy (like the optimal strategy) is successful in centering the cart for all 1,000 fitness cases. That is, it never "times out." However, this new, nonoptimal control strategy takes an average of 3.42 seconds to center the cart, whereas the optimal strategy takes an average of 2.02 seconds. In other words, the nonoptimal control strategy takes 69% more time.

Now consider a second nonoptimal control strategy:

$$-x(t) > \frac{v(t)^2}{2|F|/m}.$$

We could write this strategy in LISP as

```
(GT (* -1 X) (* V V)).
```

This second nonoptimal control strategy is considerably different from both the optimal strategy and the first nonoptimal strategy.

The left half of figure 7.5 shows the optimal curve, $v = +\sqrt{|x|}$ (labeled A), in the second quadrant. The right half of the figure shows the second nonoptimal curve, $v = +\sqrt{|x|}$, in the first quadrant (labeled C). The optimal curve for the right half of the figure is the curve $v = -\sqrt{|x|}$ in the fourth quadrant (labeled B).

This second nonoptimal control strategy, $v = +\sqrt{|x|}$, is not entirely worthless. In particular, it is still produces the same direction for the bang-bang

Four Introductory Examples of Genetic Programming

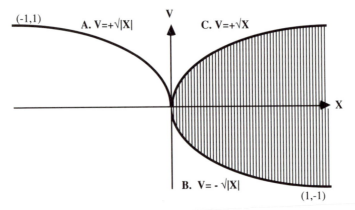

Figure 7.5 Second nonoptimal control strategy for the cart centering problem.

force for points lying in the second quadrant, points lying in the third quadrant, points lying below the curve labeled B in the fourth quadrant, and points lying above the curve labeled C in the first quadrant. However, this second nonoptimal control strategy is nonoptimal in the points in the striped area in figure 7.5. This striped area represents about 37% of the area in the domain for this problem.

The deficiency of this second nonoptimal strategy, $v = -\sqrt{|x|}$, is not just a matter of additional time being required, as was the case with the first nonoptimal strategy. This second nonoptimal control strategy *never* succeeds in bringing the cart to rest once the state of the system enters the shaded region (either because the system initially started there or because some trajectory of the strategy brought it there).

In particular, if the state of the system is in the upper half of the striped region (i.e., in the first quadrant), the position and the velocity of the cart are already positive and the incorrect positive bang-bang force is now applied so as to increase the velocity in the positive direction still more. In other words, the cart's position relentlessly becomes greater and greater in the positive direction and the cart goes flying off to positive infinity.

The result is just as dire if the state of the system is in the lower half of the striped region (i.e., in the fourth quadrant). In the lower half of the striped region, the position is already positive but the velocity of the cart is slightly negative. But because the state of the system is represented by a point above the curve $v = -\sqrt{|x|}$ (labeled B), the velocity of the cart is not sufficiently negative to counteract the effect of the force being applied so as to accelerate the cart in the positive direction. As a result, the cart again goes flying off to positive infinity.

The fitness of a control strategy is determined by evaluating it over a set of fitness cases consisting of the initial conditions of the state variables of the system (i.e., position x and velocity v). Because this set is necessarily finite, the set of fitness cases must be representative of the problem as a whole. One way that would be likely to produce the desired representativeness is to select a reasonably large number of initial condition points at random within some appropriate domain. Another way would be to select a reasonably large number of fitness cases in some regular and structured way. In any event, the goal is that the control strategy learned using the finite set of fitness cases be able to correctly handle new, previously unseen initial conditions. In other words, the fitness cases must be sufficiently representative of the problem as a whole to allow correct generalization.

For this problem, the set of fitness cases consists of 20 points (x, v) chosen at random from the square whose opposite corners are $(-0.75, 0.75)$ and $(0.75, -0.75)$. Twenty such randomly chosen points appear to be sufficiently representative of the points in this square domain to allow genetic programming to find a general solution to the cart centering problem in this domain.

The reader may find it helpful to think of these 20 representative (random) fitness cases as the environment to which the genetic population of computer programs must adapt.

We need a method for measuring time that accounts for control strategies that succeed in centering the cart for a given fitness case as well as for those that fail. This is accomplished in the following way: Time is discretized into time steps of $\tau = 0.02$ seconds. At each time step, the distance between the state of the system and the desired target state (position 0.0 and velocity 0.0) is computed. This distance is the standard Euclidean distance in the state space. That is, this distance is the square root of the sum, taken over the two state variables, of the square of the difference between the value of a state variable and the target value of that state variable. If, at any time step, this distance becomes less than a pre-established capture radius, the system is considered to have arrived at the desired target state for that fitness case. In that event, the time consumed by the control strategy for that fitness case is simply the time expended (in seconds).

A maximum number of time steps is established (e.g., 500), so that if a given control strategy fails to bring the system to a state whose distance to the target state is less than the capture radius within that amount of time (e.g., 10 seconds) for a particular fitness case, the system "times out." If the system times out, the time associated with that fitness case is a penalty value equal to the maximum time (i.e., 10 seconds).

There will be numerous additional occasions throughout this book to establish time-out conditions. Time-out conditions are required, as a practical matter, when one is working on a serial computer with finite capabilities. In nature, everything occurs in parallel on such a vast scale that the entire process is never brought to a halt if one individual is highly inefficient. The inefficient individual simply executes its inappropriate behavior and quickly dies off, with minimal effect on the overall process.

If we again choose 1,000 points at random in the specified domain, we find that this second nonoptimal control strategy (unlike the optimal strategy and the first nonoptimal strategy) is successful in centering the cart for only 429 out of the 1,000 fitness cases. The time for this second nonoptimal control strategy, as measured with the penalty for timing out described above, is 6,520 seconds for the 1,000 cases (i.e., an average of 6.52 seconds per fitness case).

The total of 6,520 seconds is about 322% of the 2,020 seconds associated with the optimal control strategy.

The three control strategies just described illustrate how we can numerically rank the performances of different programs in solving a given problem so that we can say that some programs are better than others. The raw fitnesses of these three computer programs are the three total times (in seconds) of 2,020, 3,420, and 6,520. We would certainly prefer the optimal computer program to the first nonoptimal program, and we would prefer the first optimal program to the second nonoptimal program.

Before we write too many more incorrect computer programs for centering the cart, we should make certain that the output of every computer program unambiguously specifies how to apply the bang-bang force to the cart. A bang-bang force represents a binary choice; however, all the inputs and outputs of the programs are floating-point values. We solve this problem by wrapping the computer program in an output interface (called a *wrapper*). For this problem, the wrapper specifies that any positive numerical output will be interpreted so as to apply the bang-bang force F to accelerate the cart in the positive direction. Any other output (of whatever type) will be interpreted so as to apply the bang-bang force F to accelerate the cart in the negative direction. The function GT serves as the wrapper for this problem.

An input interface (i.e., preprocessing) is rarely necessary since genetic programming permits the problem to be expressed in terms of the natural terminology of the problem. No preprocessing was required to solve any of the problems in this book.

The goal now is to find a high-fitness computer program capable of centering the cart.

The first major step in preparing to use the genetic programming paradigm is to identify the set of terminals to be used in the individual computer programs in the population.

The terminals can be viewed as the input to the computer program being sought by genetic programming. In turn, the output of the computer program consists of the value(s) returned by the program.

In problems involving a system whose state variables are controlled by one or more control variables, one natural approach is to think of the computer program as taking the state variables of the system as input and producing the control variable(s) as output. The state variables of the system are those variables which have explanatory power for solving the system at hand and which must be processed in some way to produce an action of some kind. If one adopts this approach for the cart centering problem, the physics of the problem dictate that the variables having explanatory power for the problem are the position x of the cart along the track and the velocity v of the cart. Thus, the terminal set for the cart centering problem is

T = {X, V, -1},

where X represents the position x and where V represents the velocity v.

Note that the numerical constant -1 was included in the terminal set above because we thought it might be useful. We defer discussion of the general method for automatically creating needed numerical constants to sections 10.1 and 10.2.

The second major step in preparing to use genetic programming is to identify a set of functions. The terminals and the functions are the ingredients from which the individual computer programs in the population are composed.

The identification of the function set for a given problem may be simple and straightforward or it may require considerable thought. For problems involving real-valued domains, it seems natural to include the four ordinary arithmetic operations (addition, subtraction, multiplication, and division) in the function set. The four ordinary arithmetic operations allow the creation of polynomials in the state variables of the system as well as quotients of such polynomials. One or more of the arithmetic operations may prove to be extraneous for a particular problem (as they are for this problem). For a problem involving making a decision, it also seems natural to include some conditional operation for allowing decisions to be made. This particular function set is adequate for solving this problem. We might well have chosen other function sets for this problem.

In selecting the function set for a given problem, the closure principle should be observed. Each function in the function set should be well defined for every combination that might be encountered of elements from the terminal set and elements from the range of every function in the function set. For example, if division is to be used, the division function should be modified so that the result of a division by zero is acceptable to every function in the function set. One way to do this is to use the protected division function % (described in subsection 6.1.1) instead of the usual mathematical division function.

A second application of this closure principle is required in the cart centering problem. In writing the LISP program

```
(GT (* -1 X) (* V (ABS V)))
```

above, we used the "greater than" function GT rather than the LISP's counterpart to the logical predicate > (used in the PASCAL program above). The function GT is a numerically valued logical function whose range consists of the numeric value $+1$ (for True) and -1 (for False or NIL). In contrast, the range of the ordinary logical predicate > found in Common LISP (and PASCAL) consists of the logical values T (True) and NIL (False). The arithmetic functions (such as +, −, *, and %) are not well defined for logical values such as T and NIL, but they are well defined for the numeric values -1 and $+1$. Thus, we achieve closure in the function set by using real-valued logic (via the GT function) rather than ordinary Boolean-valued logic.

Thus, the function set F for this problem will consist of

```
F = {+, -, *, %, GT, ABS},
```

taking two, two, two, two, two and one argument, respectively.

The third major step in preparing to use genetic programming is identifying a way of evaluating how good a given computer program is at solving the problem at hand.

In the case of the cart centering problem, we have already seen that some computer programs are better than others at solving the problem. The fitness measure is the total time required to center the cart after starting at a representative sampling of random initial condition points (x, v) in the domain specified for this problem. Computing this total time requires testing a given computer program over the fitness cases. The fitness cases are randomly chosen values for the initial conditions of the state variables within the specified domain. In particular, we might randomly choose 20 pairs of values for the initial position $x(0)$ and the initial velocity $v(0)$ from the specified domain, and then test the performance of the given computer program on each of those 20 fitness cases and compute the total time.

Figure 7.6 is a flowchart for computing fitness over a number $N_{fc} = 20$ of fitness cases for one individual in the population. This flowchart expands the single box contained in the flowchart in figure 5.1 for evaluating the fitness of a single individual in the population. As this flowchart shows, we initialize the

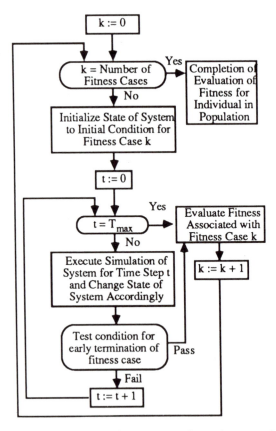

Figure 7.6 Flowchart for computing fitness for one individual over N_{fc} fitness cases, each involving a simulation over T_{max} time steps.

state of the simulated system to the particular initial conditions associated with fitness case k. Then, starting with time $t = 0$, we execute the simulation of the system for time t. We increment time and continue this process until t exceeds some maximum $T_{\max}$. At that point, we have completed the evaluation of fitness for fitness case k. We then increment k and continue this process until k exceeds the maximum N_{fc}. At that moment, we have completed the evaluation of the fitness of one individual in the population.

It is useful to define an auxiliary measure, *hits*, for monitoring runs of the genetic programming paradigm. For this problem and other optimal control problems, the number of fitness cases that do not time out is a useful subgoal to monitor during a run.

Hits should not be confused with fitness. Fitness is the numerical measure that drives the Darwinian selection process that lies at the heart of genetic methods. The hits measure is an auxiliary monitoring and descriptive device which is usually entirely external to genetic programming. If it is used internally at all, it is only used as part of the termination predicate to terminate a run. For example, if the subgoal represented by hits is especially salient and indicative of attainment of a solution, we sometimes include attainment of a hit on 100% of the fitness cases as part of the termination predicate for a problem. Of course, for this particular problem, the attainment of a hit is a very modest and unimpressive subgoal that is entirely unsuitable for the purpose of termination.

The fourth major step in preparing to use genetic programming involves selecting the values of certain parameters to control the runs. For this problem (and most of the problems in this book), the population size (M) has been chosen as 500 and the maximum number of generations to be run (G) has been chosen as 51 (i.e., generation 0 and 50 additional generations). In addition to these two major parameters for controlling runs, there are several minor parameters whose default values were identified in section 6.9.

The fifth major step in preparing to use genetic programming involves specifying the criterion for designating a result and the criterion for terminating a run. For this problem, we will terminate a given run after running a maximum number G of 51 generations. We designate the best-so-far individual as the result of the genetic programming paradigm.

Table 7.2 summarizes the key features of the cart centering (isotropic rocket) problem.

Thirty-nine other tables similar to table 7.2 will appear throughout this book. We call each such table the *tableau* for the problem. Each tableau summarizes the main choices made while applying the five major preparatory steps of genetic programming to the problem at hand.

The second and third rows of each tableau correspond to the first and second major preparatory steps for genetic programming and summarize the choices for the terminal set and function set, respectively, for the problem. The choice of the terminal set and function set determines whether a wrapper is needed. The eighth row specifies the wrapper, if any, for the problem.

Table 7.2 Tableau for the cart centering problem.

Objective:	Find a time-optimal bang-bang control strategy to center a cart on a one-dimensional frictionless track.
Terminal set:	The state variables of the system: x (positive X of the cart) and v (velocity V of the cart).
Function set:	+, −, *, %, ABS, GT.
Fitness cases:	20 initial condition points (x, v) for position and velocity chosen randomly from the square in position-velocity space whose opposite corners are $(-0.75, 0.75)$ and $(0.75, -0.75)$.
Raw fitness:	Sum of the time, over the 20 fitness cases, taken to center the cart. When a fitness case times out, the contribution is 10.0 seconds.
Standardized fitness:	Same as raw fitness for this problem.
Hits:	Number of fitness cases that did not time out.
Wrapper:	Converts any positive value returned by an S-expression to $+1$ and converts all other values (negative or zero) to -1.
Parameters:	$M = 500.$ $G = 51.$
Success predicate:	None.

The fourth through seventh rows of each tableau correspond to the third major preparatory step and present the choices made concerning the fitness measure for the problem.

The ninth row corresponds to the fourth major preparatory step and presents the control parameters for the problem. This row always includes the two major parameters, namely the population size M and the number of generations to be run G. The other numerical and qualitative control parameters are not specifically mentioned unless they differ from the default values established in section 6.9.

The tenth row corresponds to the fifth major preparatory step. Since the method of result designation for genetic programming is always the best-so-far method (section 6.8) and the termination criterion is always the disjunction of a generational predicate (based on G) and a problem-specific success predicate (section 6.7), only the success predicate is mentioned here. As it happens, there is no success predicate for this particular problem. We chose not to use available knowledge about the optimal amount of time for centering the cart to terminate runs of this problem.

Now that we have completed the five major steps for preparing to use genetic programming, we will review an actual run of genetic programming. The process starts with the generation of a population of 500 random control strategies, each recursively composed from the available functions (+, −, *, %, ABS, GT) from the function set and the available terminals (x and v) from the terminal set.

Predictably, this initial population of random control strategies includes a wide variety of highly unfit control strategies. In fact, this will always be the case unless the problem is so simple that it can be solved with a blind random search or unless one is extraordinarily lucky in creating the initial random population.

Some of the control strategies from this initial population unconditionally apply the force in only one direction. For example, the S-expression

```
(* (* V X) (* V X))
```

relentlessly accelerates the cart in the positive direction and causes it to fly off to infinity.

Some of the random strategies are partially blind in that they ignore one or more state variables necessary to solve the problem. An example is the S-expression

```
(+ V V).
```

Without paying attention to the position of the cart, this partially blind strategy calls for the bang-bang force to be applied so as to accelerate the cart in a direction equal to the current velocity of the cart.

The above two highly unfit random strategies are among the 14% of the 500 initial random strategies that time out for all 20 fitness cases. Each is assigned the penalty value of 10.0 seconds for each fitness case, and therefore each has a total raw fitness of 200.0 seconds. None of these individuals score any hits.

In addition, another 44% of these 500 highly unfit initial random strategies time out for all but one of the 20 initial condition points. Each of these scores one hit. One example of this group is the control strategy whose switching curve consists of the straight line with slope $+45°$. This individual consumes 196.4 seconds to center the cart over the 20 fitness cases (for an average of 9.82 seconds per fitness case).

Because so many of the control strategies in the initial random population time out, the average fitness of the entire initial random population of 500 individuals is 187.4 seconds. This population average fitness is equivalent to 9.37 seconds per fitness case. This means that most of the fitness cases receive the penalty value of fitness of 10.0 seconds. Even in this highly unfit initial random population, some control strategies are somewhat better than others.

The third-best control strategy is equivalent, when simplified, to the S-expression

```
(- X (+ V (* 2 V X))).
```

This control strategy is one of only four strategies out of the 500 that centers the cart in less than 10 seconds for all 20 fitness cases. This third-best strategy is equivalent to

Sign $(x - v - 2vx)$.

This third-best control strategy is rather slow in that it takes 178.6 seconds (an

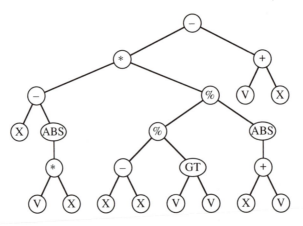

Figure 7.7 Best-of-generation individual for generation 0 of the cart centering problem.

average of 8.93 seconds per fitness case) to center the cart. However, slow is fast when compared to never!

The second-best control strategy is even better. It takes 130.0 seconds (an average of 6.05 seconds per fitness case).

The best individual control strategy in the population for generation 0 takes only 48.6 seconds (an average of 2.43 seconds per fitness case). The *structural complexity* of this individual S-expression is 23 since it consists of 23 *points* (i.e., functions and terminals). This best-of-generation individual is

```
(-  (*  (-  X  (ABS  (*  V  X)))
        (%  (%  (-  X  X)  (GT  V  V))
            (ABS  (+  X  V))))
    (+  V  X)).
```

Figure 7.7 graphically depicts this best-of-generation individual for generation 0 of this run of this problem as a rooted, point-labeled tree with ordered branches.

Since the entire left branch of this S-expression (containing 19 points) evaluates to the constant value of 0, this best-of-generation individual is numerically equivalent to the following S-expression involving only five points:

```
(-  0  (+  V  X)).
```

Figure 7.8 shows that the switching curve corresponding to this best-of-generation individual is a straight line with slope $-45°$. That is, this computer program returns -1 for all points in the two-dimensional position-velocity state space above the straight line with slope $-45°$ and $+1$ for all points on the line or below it.

Although this straight line with slope $-45°$ is not the solution to this clearly nonlinear problem, it has reasonably good performance. For example, the bang-bang force is applied correctly for every point in the unshaded portion of the figure, but incorrectly in the shaded portion.

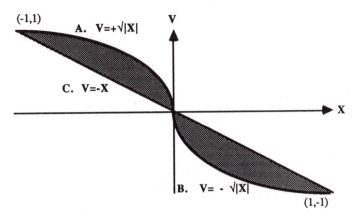

Figure 7.8 Switching curve for best-of-generation individual from generation 0 of one run of the cart centering problem.

In the valley of the blind, the one-eyed man is king. This individual is the best of its generation and has the best value of fitness.

The Darwinian reproduction operation and the genetic crossover operation are then applied to parents selected from the current population with probabilities proportionate to fitness to breed a new population of control strategies. The numerical fitness value (i.e., total time) associated with each control strategy in the population is used to drive this evolutionary process.

The vast majority of the offspring in this newly created generation 1 are, like their parents from generation 0, highly unfit. However, some of these individuals tend to be somewhat fitter than others. Moreover, some of them are slightly fitter than their parents.

In generation 3, the best-of-generation individual handled the 20 fitness cases for this problem in an average of 2.24 seconds per fitness case. This individual, which had 18 points, is shown below:

```
(- (- (* (+ (GT (GT X X) (ABS X))
             (* (ABS V) -1)))
        V)
      X)
   X).
```

Figure 7.9 graphically depicts this best-of-generation individual for generation 3 as a rooted, point-labeled tree with ordered branches. This expression is equivalent, for the range of x being used here, to

$$-v[1 + |v|] - 2x.$$

This individual is far from perfect, but it is about 10% better than the best-of-generation individual of generation 0.

Figure 7.10 contains the *fitness* curves for this run. It is the first of 19 similar curves found in this book. This figure shows, by generation, the progress of one run of the cart centering problem between generations 0 and 33, using three plots: the standardized fitness of the best-of-generation individual in

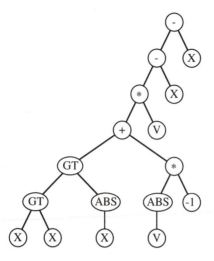

Figure 7.9 Best-of-generation individual for generation 3 of the cart centering problem.

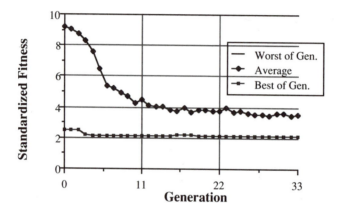

Figure 7.10 Fitness curves for the cart centering problem (measured per fitness case).

the population, the standardized fitness of the worst-of-generation individual in the population, and the average value of standardized fitness for all the individuals in the population. These fitnesses are stated per fitness case for this particular problem. As can be seen, the standardized fitness of the best-of-generation individual started at 2.43 seconds per fitness case in generation 0 and improved (i.e., decreased) to 2.13 seconds per fitness case in generation 33. The improvement in fitness from generation to generation was steady, but not perfectly monotonic; there was no great leap in performance. The average standardized fitness of the population also improved between generations 0 and 33. Again, there was no great leap in performance. The plot of the worst-of-generation individual runs across the top of the figure since, for every generation, there was at least one individual in the population that timed out for every fitness case and was therefore assigned the penalty value of 10.0 seconds for each fitness case. A figure showing these three plots appears as

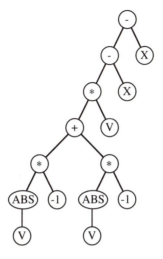

Figure 7.11 Best-of-run individual for the cart centering problem.

part of the discussion of numerous problems throughout this book and is labeled the graph of "standardized fitness" for the problem.

In generation 33, the best-of-generation S-expression in the population performs the cart centering task faster than any individual from any previous generation. This best-of-generation individual had 15 points as shown below:

```
(- (- (* (+ (* (ABS V) -1) (* (ABS V) -1))
           V)
      X)
    X).
```

As it happens, this best-of-generation individual from generation 33 is a 100%-correct solution to the problem because it is mathematically equivalent to the known time-optimal solution, namely

```
(GT (* -1 X) (* V (ABS V))).
```

We can therefore identify this individual as the best-of-run individual for this run of the cart centering problem.

Figure 7.11 graphically depicts this best-of-run individual as a rooted, point-labeled tree with ordered branches. Note that this particular individual did not incorporate the GT function provided in the function set.

Note that in applying genetic programming to this problem we made no assumption in advance about the size, the shape, or the structural complexity of the eventual solution. The solution found in generation 33 of this run happens to have a total of 15 points; however, we did not specify this in advance. We did not specify the eventual shape of the S-expression in advance. We did not specify the particular functions and terminals that would appear at particular points of the S-expression. The size, shape, and contents of the S-expression that solves this problem evolved in response to the selective pressure exerted by the fitness measure (i.e., time). This problem illustrates how structure arises from fitness.

Since genetic programming is a probabilistic algorithm, we rarely get a solution in precisely the form we contemplated. For example, the solution produced in generation 33 above has 15 points whereas the more compact S-expression in figure 7.3 has only 8 points.

Moreover, genetic programming rarely produces exactly the same result twice. Anything can happen and nothing is guaranteed. Examples of other superficially different results that are equivalent to the known time-optimal solution include

```
(GT (% V (% -1 (ABS V))) X),
```

and

```
(GT (* (GT (* -1 X) X) (ABS X))
    (* (ABS V) V)),
```

and the rather mystifying, but still equivalent,

```
(GT -1 (% (+ (GT (- V -1) (- -1 V)) (ABS (GT (% (+ (GT (-
V -1) (- -1 V)) (ABS (+ (+ V (+ X V)) (% X X)))) (GT V (%
(% (* X -1) (% (- -1 V) (GT V (* X -1)))) (* -1 -1)))) -1)))
(GT V (% (* X -1) (ABS V))))).
```

We do not always obtain a time-optimal solution on a particular run within the pre-established arbitrary maximum number G of generations to be run. On those runs, we usually obtain a near-optimal control strategy of some kind. One example is the near-optimal control strategy below, which requires 100.45% of the optimal time:

```
(+ (GT (* (+ (GT (* (ABS (GT V (GT V V))) (* X -1)) (GT
(+ V (* V V)) (ABS V))) X) (* V V)) X) (- (+ (GT (GT (*
(+ (* (* X X) (+ -1 X)) (GT V V)) (+ V X)) X) X) (* (* X
V) V)) V)).
```

Another run yielded the near-optimal control strategy below, which requires 100.5% of the optimal time:

```
(GT (* (+ (+ (GT -1 V) (- -1 X)) (* (+ (+ (+ (% (- X (GT
V (- -1 X))) (* -1 (GT V (ABS X)))) (GT X (* (ABS X) V)))
(- -1 X)) (* X (* (% (+ -1 X) (GT (GT (GT V (% X -1)) X)
(* (% X -1) V))) V))) V)) X) V).
```

Yet another example is the near-optimal control strategy below, which requires 101.1% of the optimal time:

```
(- (* -1 X) (% (GT (GT (- (ABS (* (ABS V) (+ X (GT (* X
X) X)))) (% (GT (GT (GT (* X -1) (+ V X)) X) (+ V V))
-1)) X) (+ X X)) -1)).
```

You no doubt approached this book with an understandable skepticism about whether it is possible to genetically breed computer programs that solve complex problems using only performance measurements obtained from admittedly incorrect, randomly created programs to control the invocation of some very simple domain-independent mechanical operations. This skepticism was probably fortified by some personal experience in writing and debugging computer programs that did not work the first time. To humans, computer programs seem very rigid in their grammatical and structural requirements. The experience of most programmers is that if everything is not perfect, the program does not work at all. In any event, the goal of most programmers is to write a program that is 100% correct.

One can begin to see why the genetic breeding of computer programs works by thinking of the space of all possible computer programs that might solve the cart centering problem and then thinking about the trajectory through the space of computer programs that a human programmer would likely take to find the 100%-correct program.

The human programmer, using human intelligence and knowledge of control theory and mathematics, might begin by deriving the formula

$$-x(t) > \frac{v(t)^2 \operatorname{Sign} v(t)}{2|F|/m}$$

to specify when to apply the bang-bang force to accelerate the cart in the positive direction. Then he might draw on his intelligence and his knowledge of computer programming to write a program to implement this mathematical formula. He would then type his program into the computer. The human programmer might make an error in deriving the formula, in writing the program, or in typing the program into his computer.

In most cases, the program written by the human programmer would not work the first time. Instead, there would be several cycles of attempting to run the program, examining the results, and correcting the program. For example, when the program was run the first time, the output might be some symbolic string such as "INCORRECT SYNTAX" (perhaps because of a missing semicolon in a PASCAL program, a missing operand in assembly code, or a mismatched parenthesis in a LISP program).

After correction of the syntax error, the output on the next run might be the symbolic string "FUNCTION ASB NOT FOUND."

After correcting the typing mistake in the name of the absolute-value function ABS, the human programmer might find that his program produced the correct output only some of the time. After studying the output, the programmer might realize that the mass m is in the denominator of the denominator of the fraction on the right whereas he had placed it elsewhere in his formula or program.

After correction of that mistake, the program might still be producing correct outputs only some of the time. Again, after studying the output, the programmer might realize that he had entered the constant 0.2 instead of 2.0.

With that problem fixed, the output might now be $+1$ when it should be -1, but -1 when it should be $+1$. This error might be due to the programmer's having confused the order of comparison in coding the formula. After correction of this mistake, the human programmer's program might be 100% correct.

Each of the five programs in the human programmer's trajectory through the space of computer programs was obtained by testing the performance of the current program and by modifying it using the performance information obtained. That is, the human programmer conducted an adaptive and intelligent search of the space of possible computer programs. However, the human programmer used the performance information in a highly sophisticated, highly information-rich, highly problem-dependent, and intelligent way. He applied his knowledge of mathematics, his knowledge about writing computer programs, and his heuristic knowledge and experience about debugging computer programs.

The intelligence that a human programmer brings to bear often produces a great leap in performance. For example, the human programmer's second-to-last program was wrong on 100% of the cases on which the program was tested and produced output which was very distant from the correct answer. The human programmer used his intelligence to identify the cause as a reversal of the order of comparison of two variables in the program.

It is difficult to generalize about the nature of the historical sequence of incorrect programs that human programmers typically write before arriving at the final correct program versus the sequence of intermediate programs produced by genetic programming. Nonetheless, it is frequently true that successive programs written by a human differ by only one or a few characters. Moreover, the results produced by the two successive programs written by a human are often much farther from one another (when measured via the natural metric of the space in which the results are stated) than the results of two successive programs produced by genetic programming. The second-to-last program described above for the human programmer would almost never be the second-to-last program in the trajectory of programs produced by genetic programming.

Now let us compare the trajectory through the space of possible computer programs taken by genetic programming with the trajectory taken by human programmer. The third best program from generation 1 of the run of genetic programming described above was

Sign $(x - v - 2vx)$,

and the best-of-generation program from generation 3 obtained through genetic programming was

$-v[1 + |v|] - 2x.$

These programs are nothing like the intermediate programs along the human programmer's trajectory through the space of possible computer programs. There is virtually no conceivable sequence of mistakes in mathematical derivation, programming, or typing by which a human programmer could ever have produced such programs. However, these two incorrect programs from the trajectory of computer programs produced by genetic programming are typical of the early and intermediate results produced by genetic programming in three important ways.

First, the admittedly poor performance in the actual problem domain of early programs produced by genetic programming is better than the completely nonworking early programs produced by the human.

Second, the performance of the best-of-generation program from generation 3 is slightly better in the actual problem domain than the performance of the best-of-generation program from generation 1. It, in turn, was better than the best of generation 0. There was no great leap in performance in genetic programming as there was between the human programmer's second-to-last program and his final program. Instead, genetic programming generally works by making small evolutionary changes that produce relatively small incremental improvements when measured via the natural metric of the space in which the results are stated.

Third, while the control strategy from generation 3 is admittedly suboptimal, one might conceivably use it to center a cart. The intermediate results produced by genetic programming do not work for all combinations of inputs and are certainly not time-optimal; however, they are often somewhat good at the task at hand. Similarly, the intermediate results of the evolutionary process in nature all possess the minimal level of performance required for survival, even if some fitter organism is yet to evolve. The intermediate results produced by human programmers are usually not usable at all.

Human programmers employ an entirely different style of programming (arising from their use of human intelligence and their knowledge of the problem) and make entirely different kinds of mistakes. When considering programs that do not work the first time, the trajectory of programs produced by a human programmer through the space of computer programs is very different from the trajectory produced by genetic programming.

The cart centering problem was previously studied in the field of genetic algorithms in connection with classifier systems by Goldberg (1983) and in the field of genetic programming by Koza and Keane (1990a).

7.2 Artificial Ant

As a second illustration of genetic programming, consider the task of navigating an artificial ant attempting to find all the food lying along an irregular trail as described in subsection 3.3.2 (Jefferson et al. 1991; Collins and Jefferson 1991a, 1991b). The problem involves primitive operations enabling the ant to move forward, turn right, turn left, and sense food along the irregular Santa Fe trail (figure 3.6).

When Jefferson, Collins, et al. used the conventional genetic algorithm operating on strings to find the finite-state automaton to solve this problem, it was first necessary to develop a representation scheme that converted the potential automaton into binary strings of length 453. In genetic programming, the problem can be approached and solved in a far more direct way using the natural terminology of the problem.

The first major step in preparing to use genetic programming is to identify the set of terminals; the second is to identify the set of functions.

In the cart centering problem, the computer program processed information about the current state of the system in order to generate a control variable to drive the future state of the system toward a specified target state. In this problem, we are not primarily concerned with the values of the three overt state variables of the ant (i.e., the numerical values, between 1 and 32, of the vertical and horizontal position of the ant on the grid and the direction the ant is facing). Instead, we are primarily concerned with finding food. And to find food, we must make use of the very limited amount of information about food coming from the ant's sensor.

In this problem, the information we want to process is the information coming in from the outside world via the ant's very limited sensor. Thus, one reasonable approach to this problem is to place the conditional branching operator IF-FOOD-AHEAD into the function set. The IF-FOOD-AHEAD conditional branching operator takes two arguments and executes the first argument if (and only if) the ant senses food directly in front of it, but executes the second argument if (and only if) the ant does not sense any food directly in front of it. The IF-FOOD-AHEAD conditional branching operator is implemented as a macro as described in subsection 6.1.1.

If the function set for this problem contains an operator that processes information, the terminal set for this problem should then contain the actions which the ant should execute based on the outcome of this information processing. Thus, the terminal set for this problem is

```
T = {(MOVE), (RIGHT), (LEFT)}.
```

These three terminals correspond directly to the three primitive functions defined and used by Jefferson, Collins, et al. to change the state of the ant. Since these three terminals are actually functions taking no arguments, their names are enclosed in parentheses. These three primitive functions operate via their side effects on the ant's state (i.e., the ant's horizontal and vertical position on the grid and the ant's facing direction). These three terminals evaluate to 1; however, their numeric return values are not relevant for this problem.

Recall that in the state-transition diagram for the finite-state automaton (figure 3.7), there were two lines emanating from each circle. The two lines represented the two alternative state transitions associated with the two possible sensor inputs of the ant. The IF-FOOD-AHEAD conditional branching operator implements these same two alternatives here. Recall also that there was one unconditional state transition in the state-transition diagram of the finite-state automaton. The Common LISP connective PROGN provides a connective glue for implementing such an unconditional sequence of steps. For example, the two-argument PROGN connective (also often called PROGN2 in this book) in the S-expression

```
(PROGN (RIGHT) (LEFT))
```

causes the ant to unconditionally perform the sequence of turning to the right and then turning to the left.

Therefore, the function set for this problem is

```
F = {IF-FOOD-AHEAD, PROGN2, PROGN3},
```

taking two, two and three arguments, respectively. Note that we include the PROGN connective in the function set twice (once for two arguments and once for three arguments).

The third major step in preparing to use genetic programming is to identify the fitness measure. The natural measure of the fitness of a given computer program in this problem is the amount of food eaten within some reasonable amount of time by an ant executing the given program. Each move operation and each turn operation takes one step. In our version of this problem, we limited the ant to 400 time steps. This time-out limit is sufficiently small in relation to 1,024 to prevent a random walk or a tessellating movement from covering all 1,024 squares of the grid before timing out.

Thus, the raw fitness of a computer program for this problem is the amount of food (ranging from 0 to 89) that the ant has eaten within the maximum allowed amount of time. If a program times out, its raw fitness is the amount of food eaten up to that time.

Time was computed here in the same way as in the work of Jefferson, Collins, et al. That is, the three primitive functions RIGHT, LEFT, and MOVE each take one time step to execute, whereas the IF-FOOD-AHEAD conditional branching operator and the unconditional connectives PROGN2 and PROGN3 each take no time steps to execute.

For the cart centering problem, a smaller raw fitness (time) was better. For this problem, a bigger raw fitness (food eaten) is better. Standardized fitness is a measure of fitness for which a smaller value is better than a larger value. Thus, for this problem, the standardized fitness is the maximum attainable value of raw fitness (i.e., 89) minus the actual raw fitness. A standardized fitness of 0 corresponds to a perfect solution for this problem (and many problems). For the cart centering problem, standardized fitness was identical to raw fitness.

For this problem, the auxiliary hits measure was defined to be the same as raw fitness. The hits measure was then used as part of the termination criterion. A run of this problem is terminated if any S-expression attains 89 hits or when the maximum allowed number of generations ($G = 51$) have been run.

Potentially, the fitness cases for this problem consist of all the possible combinations of initial conditions for the ant (i.e., the initial starting positions and the initial facing directions) along with all reasonable generalizations of the Santa Fe trail (i.e., trails with single gaps, double gaps, single gaps at corners, double gaps at corners, and triple gaps at corners appearing in any order). Note, however, that we do not explicitly create a multiplicity of fitness cases for this problem, as we did for the cart centering problem. Instead, we have just one fitness case, wherein the ant starts at position $(0, 0)$ while facing east and tries to navigate just one trail. We rely on the various states of the ant that actually arise along the ant's actual trajectory to be sufficiently representative of the generalized trail following problem. As we will see, this one fitness case is sufficiently representative for this particular problem to allow the ant to learn to navigate this trail and reasonable generalizations of this trail.

It should be emphasized that genetic programming genetically breeds computer programs that have high fitness in grappling with the environment (i.e., they score a high fitness for the explicit fitness cases on which they are run). The programs produced by genetic programming will generalize in the sense that they are useful in solving other problems which a human, in his mind, may envision only if the fitness cases that are chosen are sufficiently representative of the generalization envisioned by the human.

Table 7.3 summarizes the key features of the artificial ant problem for the Santa Fe trail.

The run starts with the generation of 500 random computer programs recursively composed from the available functions and terminals. Predictably, this initial population of random computer programs includes a wide variety of highly unfit computer programs. The random computer programs in generation 0 of this problem (as well as the random programs in generation 0 of the preceding cart centering problem and all later problems in this book) correspond to the computer programs that might be typed out at random by the proverbial monkeys. These random computer programs provide a baseline for comparing the more satisfactory performance achieved by genetic programming in later generations against random performance.

The most common type of individual in the initial random population for this problem fails to move at all. For example, the computer program

Table 7.3 Tableau for the artificial ant problem for the Santa Fe trail.

Objective:	Find a computer program to control an artificial ant so that it can find all 89 pieces of food located on the Santa Fe trail.
Terminal set:	(LEFT), (RIGHT), (MOVE).
Function set:	IF-FOOD-AHEAD, PROGN2, PROGN3.
Fitness cases:	One fitness case.
Raw fitness:	Number of pieces of food picked up before the ant times out with 400 operations.
Standardized fitness:	Total number of pieces of food (i.e., 89) minus raw fitness.
Hits:	Same as raw fitness for this problem.
Wrapper:	None.
Parameters:	$M = 500$. $G = 51$.
Success predicate:	An S-expression scores 89 hits.

```
(PROGN2 (RIGHT) (LEFT))
```

turns without looking. It unconditionally turns the ant right and left while not moving the ant anywhere.

Similarly, the program

```
(IF-FOOD-AHEAD (RIGHT) (LEFT))
```

looks without moving. It examines the outside world and then turns the ant different ways on the basis of what it saw; however, it does not move the ant anywhere.

Neither of these highly unfit individuals eats any of the 89 pieces of food. They are mercifully terminated by the expiration of the maximum allowed time.

Some randomly generated computer programs move without turning. For example, the program

```
(PROGN2 (MOVE) (MOVE))
```

shoots across the grid from west to east without either looking or turning. This vigorous undirected behavior accidently finds the three pieces of food located on the top row of the grid.

One randomly generated computer program (which will be called the "quilter" because it traces a quilt-like tessellating pattern across the toroidal grid) moves and turns without looking. It consists of nine points:

```
(PROGN3 (RIGHT)
        (PROGN3 (MOVE) (MOVE) (MOVE))
        (PROGN2 (LEFT) (MOVE))).
```

Note that, in this problem, the entire S-expression is executed as fully as possible and then re-executed until the maximum allowed amount of time is consumed.

Figure 7.12 shows the first part of the quilter's path. This part of the quilter's path is marked by X's. The quilter accidentally finds four pieces of food in the portion of its path shown.

One randomly generated computer program (the "looper") finds the first 11 pieces of food on the trail and then goes into an infinite loop when it encounters the first gap in the trail. In figure 7.13, the looper's path is marked by X's. The raw fitness of the looper is 11.

One randomly generated computer program (the "avoider") actually correctly takes note of the portion of food along the trail before finding the first gap in the trail, then actively avoids this food by carefully moving around it until it returns to its starting point. It continues with this unrewarding behavior until the time runs out, and never eats any food.

The S-expression for the avoider has seven points:

```
(IF-FOOD-AHEAD (RIGHT)
               (IF-FOOD-AHEAD (RIGHT)
                              (PROGN2 (MOVE) (LEFT))))).
```

Start

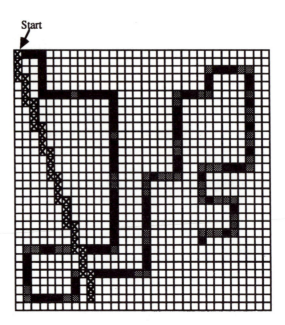

Figure 7.12 Path of the quilter from generation 0 of the artificial ant problem.

Start

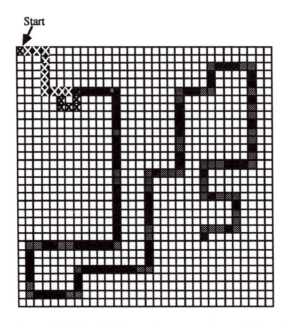

Figure 7.13 Path of the looper from generation 0 of the artificial ant problem.

Start

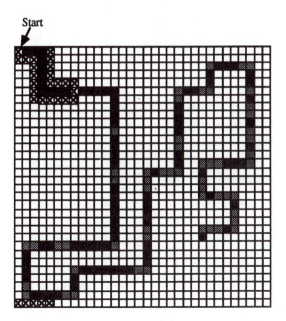

Figure 7.14 Path of the avoider from generation 0 of the artificial ant problem.

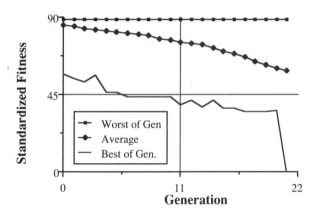

Figure 7.15 Fitness curves for the artificial ant problem.

In figure 7.14, the avoider's path is marked by X's.

In one run, the average amount of food found by the 500 individuals in the initial random population was about 3.5 pieces. The best-of-generation individual in generation 0 was able to find 32 of the 89 pieces of food; the worst individuals in the population found no food.

The Darwinian reproduction operation and the genetic crossover operation were then applied to parents selected from the current population with probabilities proportionate to fitness to breed a new population of offspring computer programs.

Figure 7.15 shows, by generation, the standardized fitness of the best-of-generation individual and the worst-of-generation individual for one run of the artificial ant problem. It also shows the average value of standardized fitness for all the individuals in the population. As can be seen, the standardized fitness of the best-of-generation individual generally improves (i.e., trends toward zero) from generation to generation, although this improvement is not monotonic. The average value of standardized fitness starts at about 85.5 (i.e., 3.5 pieces of food) and then generally improves from generation to generation. The plot of the worst-of-generation individual runs horizontally across the top of the figure because there is at least one individual in the population at every generation that finds no food at all (i.e., has a standardized fitness value of 89).

On generation 21, a computer program scoring 89 out of 89 emerged for the first time on this run. This S-expression has 18 points and is shown below:

```
(IF-FOOD-AHEAD (MOVE)
          (PROGN3 (LEFT)
                  (PROGN2 (IF-FOOD-AHEAD (MOVE)
                                         (RIGHT))
                          (PROGN2 (RIGHT)
                                  (PROGN2 (LEFT)
                                          (RIGHT))))
                  (PROGN2 (IF-FOOD-AHEAD (MOVE)
                                         (LEFT))
                          (MOVE))))).
```

Figure 7.16 graphically depicts the 100%-correct best-of-run individual that emerged on generation 21 of this run of this problem.

The interpretation of the 100%-correct S-expression in figure 7.16 is as follows: The test IF-FOOD-AHEAD senses whether there is any food in the square that the ant is currently facing. If food is present, the left branch of the IF-FOOD-AHEAD test is executed and the ant MOVEs forward. When the ant moves onto a place on the grid with food, the food is eaten and the ant receives credit for the food.

If the IF-FOOD-AHEAD test at the beginning of the S-expression senses no food, the ant enters the three-step PROGN3 sequence immediately below the

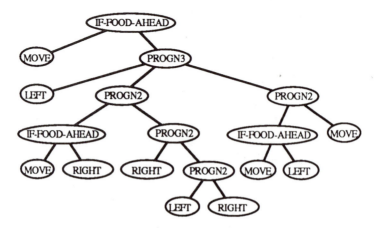

Figure 7.16 Best-of-run individual for the artificial ant problem.

IF-FOOD-AHEAD test. The ant first turns LEFT. Then, a two-step PROGN2 sequence begins with the test IF-FOOD-AHEAD. If food is present, the ant MOVEs forward. If not, the ant turns RIGHT. Then, the ant turns RIGHT again. Then, the ant pointlessly turns LEFT and RIGHT in another two-step PROGN2 sequence. The net effect is that the ant is now facing right relative to its original facing direction (i.e., its direction at the beginning of the execution of this S-expression). The ant next executes the final two-step PROGN2 subtree at the far right of the figure. If the ant now senses food via the IF-FOOD-AHEAD test, it MOVEs forward. Otherwise, it turns LEFT. The ant has now returned to its original facing direction. The ant now executes an unconditional MOVE, thereby advancing forward in its original facing direction if it has not found any food to the immediate right or left.

For any given evaluation of the S-expression, only those subtrees that are accessible by virtue of satisfaction of the conditional part of the IF-FOOD-AHEAD test are actually evaluated (i.e., executed). After the S-expression is evaluated, if there is additional time available, the S-expression is evaluated anew. Because the state of the ant changes over time as the ant moves and eats food, different parts of the S-expression are often executed on each evaluation. The repeated application of the above 100%-correct program allows the ant to negotiate all the gaps and irregularities of the trail and to eat all the food in the allotted time.

Note that there is no testing of the backward directions. See also Koza 1990c.

The pointless two-step PROGN2 subtree at the bottom of figure 7.16, where the ant unconditionally turns LEFT and RIGHT, does not harm the ant's performance; the ant is able to find 100% of the available food within the allowed maximum amount of time. Fitness in this problem was defined to be the amount of food eaten within the allowed time. The best-of-run individual from generation 21 was genetically bred with this fitness measure as the driving force. This fitness measure did not incorporate anything about minimizing the size of the S-expression or minimizing the total number of steps, except in the indirect sense that a highly inefficient individual could not find 100% of the food within the available time. Among individuals that can find 100% of the food within the available time, there is no selective pressure whatsoever in favor of efficiency or parsimony.

Humans prefer to organize their conscious thinking in a parsimonious way; however, fitness, not parsimony, is the dominant factor in natural evolution. For example, only about 1% of the sequences of nucleotide bases that occur naturally along DNA are actually expressed into the sequences of amino acids that make up the proteins that perform the work of living organisms. In addition, after a sequence of DNA is actually expressed (via messenger ribonucleic acid, mRNA) into a string of amino acids, the resulting protein structure is rarely maximally parsimonious. The human hemoglobin molecule, for example, weighs about 60,000 daltons (i.e., equivalent hydrogen atoms), yet its primary role is to transport only eight oxygen molecules from the lungs to the body cells. There is almost certainly some variation on the design of this molecule that is at least slightly smaller than 60,000 daltons. However, if this molecule successfully performs its task, there may no fitness advantage, and hence no selective pressure, in favor of attaining the most parsimonious possible design.

Secondary factors, such as efficiency and parsimony, can be incorporated into fitness measures (sections 18.1 and 25.14), but this was not done here.

Note again that in applying genetic programming to this problem we made no assumption in advance about the size, the shape, or the structural complexity of the eventual solution. The solution found above in generation 21 had 18 points. We did not specify that the solution would have 18 points, nor did we specify the shape or the contents of this 18-point S-expression. The size, shape, and contents of the 100%-correct S-expression for this problem evolved in response to the selective pressure provided by the fitness measure (i.e., the amount of food eaten). The required structure emerged from a process driven by the selective pressure exerted by the fitness measure. For this problem, structure flowed from fitness, just as it does in nature.

It is also interesting to consider the artificial ant problem with a more difficult trail.

The new "Los Altos Hills" trail begins with the same irregularities (i.e., single gaps, double gaps, single gaps at corners, double gaps at corners, and triple gaps at corners), in the same order, as the Santa Fe trail. However, the new trail has two new kinds of irregularity, which appear toward its end. Because of these added features, this new trail is embedded in a larger 100 × 100 grid and spacing has been added between the branches of the trail.

Figure 7.17 shows the Los Altos Hills trail for the artificial ant problem situated in the upper left 50 × 70 portion of the 100 × 100 grid. In this new trail, food pellet 105 corresponds to food pellet 89 (i.e., the end) of the Santa Fe trail.

The simpler of the two new irregularities in the Los Altos Hills trail requires a search of locations two steps to the left or two steps to the right of an existing piece of food. This first new irregularity appears for the first time at food pellet 116 in figure 7.17. The previously evolved program that successfully navigates the Santa Fe trail cannot handle this irregularity, since it does not regard a location that is two steps off the trail as being part of the trail. If the artificial ant masters this new irregularity, it can find 136 pieces of food.

The more difficult of the two new irregularities in the Los Altos Hills trail requires moving one step ahead and then searching locations two steps to the left or two steps to the right of an existing piece of food. The second new irregularity appears for the first time at food pellet 136 in the figure. If the artificial ant masters both of these two new irregularities, it can find 157 pieces of food.

We approach this upwardly scaled version of the problem in the same way as we approached the simpler version. In particular, we use the same terminal set, the same basic function set, and the same fitness measure. We increase the available time steps to 3,000. This number is sufficiently small in relation to 10,000 to prevent a random walk or any simple tessellating movement from

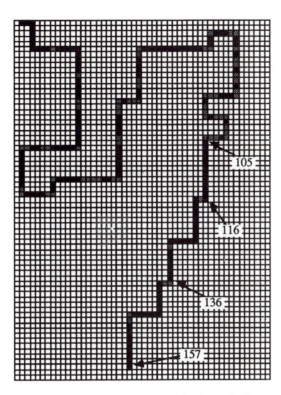

Figure 7.17 The Los Altos Hills trail for the artificial ant.

finding all the food merely by visiting all 10,000 squares of the grid. We added PROGN4 to the basic function set. We increased the population size to 2,000.

Figure 7.18 shows, by generation, the average of the standardized fitness for the population as a whole and the standardized fitness of the best-of-generation and worst-of-generation individuals for one run of the artificial ant problem with the Los Altos Hills trail.

In one run (in fact, our first run of this scaled-up version of the problem), the following S-expression was obtained on generation 19. This best-of-run individual is capable of finding all 157 pieces of food on this new Los Altos Hills trail within 1,808 time steps.

```
(PROGN4 (IF-FOOD-AHEAD (PROGN2 (PROGN3 (MOVE) (PROGN2
(MOVE) (MOVE)) (RIGHT)) (IF-FOOD-AHEAD (MOVE)
(IF-FOOD-AHEAD (IF-FOOD-AHEAD (LEFT) (LEFT))
(PROGN4 (PROGN2 (IF-FOOD-AHEAD (MOVE) (RIGHT))
(MOVE)) (RIGHT) (MOVE) (MOVE))))) (PROGN4 (PROGN2
(IF-FOOD-AHEAD (MOVE) (RIGHT)) (MOVE)) (RIGHT)
(MOVE) (MOVE))) (IF-FOOD-AHEAD (IF-FOOD-AHEAD (MOVE)
(IF-FOOD-AHEAD (IF-FOOD-AHEAD (MOVE) (LEFT))
(IF-FOOD-AHEAD (LEFT) (RIGHT)))) (IF-FOOD-AHEAD
(LEFT) (RIGHT))) (PROGN2 (PROGN3 (MOVE) (MOVE)
(RIGHT)) (IF-FOOD-AHEAD (PROGN2 (PROGN3 (MOVE)
```

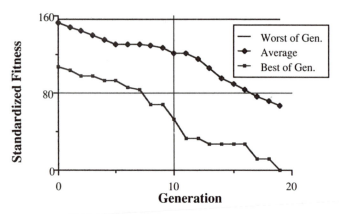

Figure 7.18 Fitness curves for the artificial ant problem with the Los Altos Hills trail.

```
(PROGN2 (MOVE) (MOVE)) (RIGHT)) (IF-FOOD-AHEAD
(IF-FOOD-AHEAD (MOVE) (MOVE)) (MOVE))) (MOVE))) (MOVE)).
```

The above best-of-run S-expression contains 66 points. Not surprisingly, solving the more difficult Los Altos Hills trail required an S-expression with more internal and external points than the solution for the original Santa Fe trail. This individual can be simplified to the following:

```
(PROGN7 (IF-FOOD-AHEAD
          (PROGN5 (MOVE) (MOVE) (MOVE) (RIGHT)
                  (IF-FOOD-AHEAD
                    (MOVE)
                    (PROGN5 (RIGHT) (MOVE)
                            (RIGHT)
                            (MOVE) (MOVE))))
          (PROGN5 (RIGHT) (MOVE) (RIGHT)
                  (MOVE) (MOVE)))
        (IF-FOOD-AHEAD (MOVE) (RIGHT))
        (MOVE)
        (MOVE)
        (RIGHT)
        (IF-FOOD-AHEAD
          (PROGN5 (MOVE) (MOVE) (MOVE) (RIGHT)
                  (MOVE))
          (MOVE))
        (MOVE)).
```

Whenever this best-of-run individual encounters any irregularity in the trail (and occasionally when it does not), this S-expression causes the ant to make a loop that is three squares wide and two squares long. This looping action allows the ant to successfully navigate the two new kinds of irregularities. This looping action is somewhat wasteful and inefficient; however, it works. That is, this S-expression finds 100% of the food within the allowed amount of time and therefore has maximal fitness given the fitness measure we are using.

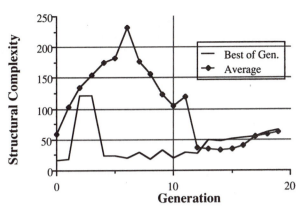

Figure 7.19 Structural complexity curves for the artificial ant problem with the Los Altos Hills trail.

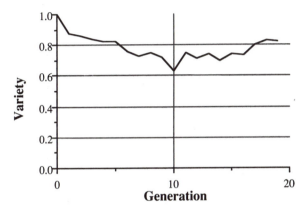

Figure 7.20 Variety curve for the artificial ant with the Los Altos Hills trail.

This problem is typical of most problems in that the structural complexity (i.e., total number of function points and terminal points) of the average S-expression in the population increases in later generations of a given run.

Figure 7.19 contains the *structural complexity curves* for this problem. It is one of 13 similar curves found in this book. It shows, by generation, the average of the structural complexity of the population as a whole and the structural complexity of the best-of-generation individual for one run of the artificial ant problem with the Los Altos Hills trail with the primitive function RIGHT deleted. As can be seen, the total number of function points and terminal points of the best-of-generation individual starts at 16 for generation 0 and rises to 66 for generation 19.

Size, of course, is not the only contributor to the complexity of an organism; however, studying gross size and complexity is a first step in studying the evolution of complex structures (Bonner 1988).

Figure 7.20 is the *variety curve* showing the variety of the population, by generation, during one run of the artificial ant problem with the Los Altos Hills trail. This variety curve is one of nine similar curves found in this book. For this

Four Introductory Examples of Genetic Programming

problem, variety starts at 100% at generation 0 because duplicate checking is done when the initial random population is created. It then fluctuates around 80% for most of this particular run. The operation of fitness-proportionate reproduction is alone responsible for reducing variety after generation 0 by the probability p_r of reproduction (10% here). It is common for variety to dip for one generation whenever a small number of individuals have distinctly better fitness than the remainder of the population. Such a dip occurs at generation 10 of this run.

The *hits histogram* is a useful monitoring tool for the population as a whole for a particular generation. The horizontal axis of the hits histogram is the number of hits; the vertical axis is the number of individuals in the population scoring that number of hits. There are 10 sets of similar histograms throughout this book.

Figure 7.21 shows the hits histograms for five selected generations of this run. The first 15 ticks in the horizontal axis of the histogram represent a range of 150 levels of fitness between 0 and 149; the last tick represents the eight levels of fitness between 150 and 157. Note, in the progression from generation to generation, the left-to-right undulating movement of both the high point and the center of mass of the histogram. This "slinky" movement reflects the improvement of the population as a whole. The arrow marks the barely visible occurrence of one 100%-correct individual scoring 157 on generation 19.

The selection of the terminal set and the selection of the function set are important steps in genetic programming because these sets provide the ingredients from which genetic programming attempts to build a solution. In general, the selection of these sets affects the appearance of the results, the ease of finding a solution, and, indeed, whether a solution can be found at all. For example, in the discussion above, we used both the RIGHT and LEFT primitive functions because that is how this problem was originally defined by Jefferson, Collins, et al. Since both the RIGHT and LEFT operations are obviously not needed, it is interesting to consider the artificial ant problem with the primitive function LEFT deleted. When the problem was rerun with this smaller set of primitive functions using the Santa Fe trail, genetic programming found the following solution in generation 19 of one run:

```
(PROGN2 (PROGN2 (IF-FOOD-AHEAD (MOVE) (RIGHT))
                (PROGN2 (MOVE) (RIGHT)))
        (PROGN2 (IF-FOOD-AHEAD
                    (PROGN3 (MOVE)
                            (PROGN2 (MOVE) (RIGHT))
                            (RIGHT))
                 (RIGHT))
                (IF-FOOD-AHEAD (RIGHT)
                               (RIGHT))))).
```

This S-expression has 20 points and is a 100%-correct solution to the problem. For this particular problem, the removal of one superfluous primitive

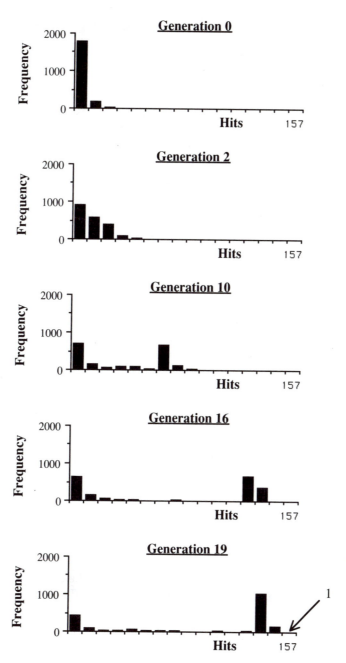

Figure 7.21 Hits histograms for generations 0, 2, 10, 16, and 19 for artificial ant problem with the Los Altos Hills trail.

Four Introductory Examples of Genetic Programming

function does not substantially affect the performance of genetic programming (subsection 24.3.3).

7.3 SIMPLE SYMBOLIC REGRESSION

As a third illustration of genetic programming, consider a simple form of the problem of symbolic regression (symbolic function identification).

In linear regression, one is given a set of values of various independent variable(s) and the corresponding values for the dependent variable(s). The goal is to discover a set of numerical coefficients for a linear combination of the independent variable(s) that minimizes some measure of error (such as the square root of the sum of the squares of the differences) between the given values and computed values of the dependent variable(s). Similarly, in quadratic regression the goal is to discover a set of numerical coefficients for a quadratic expression that minimizes error. In Fourier "regression," the goal is to discover a set of numerical coefficients for various harmonics of the sine and cosine functions that minimizes error.

Of course, it is left to the researcher to decide whether to do a linear regression, a quadratic regression, a higher-order polynomial regression, or whether to try to fit the data points to some non-polynomial family of functions. But often, *the* issue is deciding what type of function most appropriately fits the data, not merely computing the numerical coefficients after the type of function for the model has already been chosen. In other words, the real problem is often *both* the discovery of the correct functional form that fits the data and the discovery of the appropriate numeric coefficients that go with that functional form. We call the problem of finding a function, in symbolic form, that fits a given finite sample of data *symbolic regression*. It is "data-to-function" regression. The desirability of doing regression without specifying in advance the functional form of the eventual solution was recognized by Dallemand (1958), Westervelt (1960), and Collins (1968).

For example, suppose we are given a sampling of the numerical values from a target curve over 20 points in some domain, such as the real interval $[-1.0, +1.0]$. That is, we are given a sample of data in the form of 20 pairs (x_i, y_i), where x_i is a value of the independent variable in the interval $[-1.0, +1.0]$ and y_i is the associated value of the dependent variable. The 20 values of x_i were chosen at random in the interval $[-1.0, +1.0]$. For example, these 20 pairs (x_i, y_i) might include pairs such as $(-0.40, -0.2784)$, $(+0.25, +0.3320)$, ..., and $(+0.50, +0.9375)$.

These 20 pairs (x_i, y_i) are the fitness cases that will be used to evaluate the fitness of any proposed S-expression.

The goal is to find a function, in symbolic form, that is a good or a perfect fit to the 20 pairs of numerical data points. The solution to this problem of finding a function in symbolic form that fits a given sample of data can be viewed as a search for a mathematical expression (S-expression) from a space of possible S-expressions that can be composed from a set of available functions and terminals.

The first major step in preparing to use genetic programming is to identify the set of terminals. In the cart centering problem, the computer program (which was called a control strategy) processed information about the current state of the system in order to generate a control variable to drive the future state of the system to a specified target state. In the artificial ant problem, the computer program *processed information* about whether food was present immediately in front of the ant in order to move the ant around the grid. In this problem, the information which the mathematical expression must process is the value of the independent variable X. Thus, the terminal set is

```
T = {X}.
```

The second major step in preparing to use genetic programming is to identify the set of functions that are used to generate the mathematical expressions that attempt to fit the given finite sample of data. If we wanted to use our knowledge that the answer is $x^4 + x^3 + x^2 + x$, a function set consisting only of the addition and multiplication operations would be sufficient for this problem. A more general choice might be the function set consisting of the four ordinary arithmetic operations of addition, subtraction, multiplication, and the protected division function %. If we want the possibility of creating a wider variety of expressions and solving a wider variety of problems, we might also include the sine function SIN, the cosine function COS, the exponential function EXP, and the protected logarithm function RLOG (described in subsection 6.1.1). If we accept the above reasons for selecting the function set, then the function set F for this problem consists of eight functions (six of which are extraneous to the immediate problem) and is

```
F = {+, -, *, %, SIN, COS, EXP, RLOG},
```

taking two, two, two, two, one, one, one, one and one arguments, respectively.

The third major step in preparing to use genetic programming is to identify the fitness measure. The raw fitness for this problem is the sum, taken over the 20 fitness cases, of the absolute value of the difference (error) between the value in the real-valued range space produced by the S-expression for a given value of the independent variable x_i and the correct y_i in the range space. The closer this sum of errors is to 0, the better the computer program. Error-based fitness is the most common measure of fitness used in this book. Standardized fitness is equal to raw fitness for this problem.

The hits measure for this problem counts the number of fitness cases for which the numerical value returned by the S-expression comes within a small tolerance (called the *hits criterion*) of the correct value. For example, the hits criterion might be 0.01. In monitoring runs, hits is a much more intuitive measure than fitness. The fact that an S-expression in the population comes within 0.01 of the target value y_i of the dependent variable for a number of points gives an immediate picture of the progress of a run.

Table 7.4 summarizes the key features of the simple symbolic regression problem with the target function of $x^4 + x^3 + x^2 + x$.

Table 7.4 Tableau for the simple symbolic regression problem.

Objective:	Find a function of one independent variable and one dependent variable, in symbolic form, that fits a given sample of 20 (x_i, y_i) data points, where the target function is the quartic polynomial $x^4 + x^3 + x^2 + x$.
Terminal set:	X (the independent variable).
Function set:	+, −, *, %, SIN, COS, EXP, RLOG.
Fitness cases:	The given sample of 20 data points (x_i, y_i) where the x_i come from the interval $[-1, +1]$.
Raw fitness:	The sum, taken over the 20 fitness cases, of the absolute value of difference between value of the dependent variable produced by the S-expression and the target value y_i of the dependent variable.
Standardized fitness:	Equals raw fitness for this problem.
Hits:	Number of fitness cases for which the value of the dependent variable produced by the S-expression comes within 0.01 of the target value y_i of the dependent variable.
Wrapper:	None.
Parameters:	$M = 500. G = 51.$
Success predicate:	An S-expression scores 20 hits.

Predictably, the initial population of random S-expressions includes a wide variety of highly unfit S-expressions.

In one run, the worst-of-generation individual in generation 0 was the S-expression

```
(EXP (- (% X (- X (SIN X))) (RLOG (RLOG (* X X))))).
```

The sum of the absolute values of the differences between this worst-of-generation individual and the 20 data points (i.e., the raw fitness) was about 10^{38}.

The median individual in the initial random population was

```
(COS (COS (+ (- (* X X) (% X X)) X))),
```

which is equivalent to

```
Cos [Cos (x² + x - 1)].
```

The sum of the absolute values of the differences between this median individual and the 20 data points was 23.67.

Figure 7.22 shows a graph in the interval $[-1, +1]$ of this median individual from generation 0 and a graph of the target quartic curve $x^4 + x^3 + x^2 + x$). The distance between the curve for this median individual and the target curve averaged about 1.2 units over the 20 fitness cases. Although this curve is not particularly close to the target curve, its distance is considerably closer than 10^{38}.

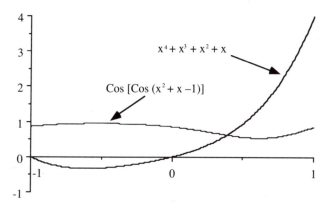

Figure 7.22 Median individual from generation 0 compared to target quartic curve $x^4 + x^3 + x^2 + x$ for the simple symbolic regression problem.

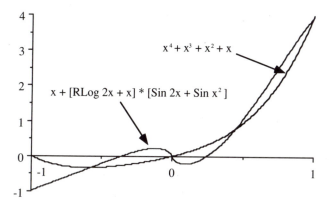

Figure 7.23 Second-best individual from generation 0 compared to target quartic curve $x^4 + x^3 + x^2 + x$ for the simple symbolic regression problem.

The second-best individual in the initial random population, when simplified, was

```
x + [RLog 2x + x] * [Sin 2x + Sin x²].
```

The sum of the absolute values of the differences between this second-best individual over the 20 fitness cases was 6.05. That is, its raw fitness was 6.05.

Figure 7.23 shows the curve for this second-best individual and the target curve. This second-best curve is considerably closer to the target curve than the median individual above. The average distance between the curve for this second-best individual and the target curve over the 20 points was about 0.3 per fitness case.

The best-of-generation individual in the population at generation 0 was the following S-expression with 19 points:

```
(* X (+ (+ (- (% X X) (% X X)) (SIN (- X X)))
        (RLOG (EXP (EXP X))))).
```

This S-expression is equivalent to xe^x.

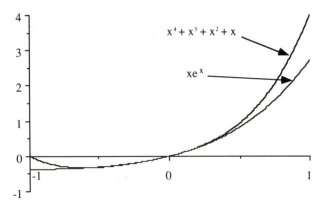

Figure 7.24 Best-of-generation individual from generation 0 compared to target quartic curve $x^4 + x^3 + x^2 + x$ for the simple symbolic regression problem.

The raw fitness for this best-of-generation individual was 4.47.

Figure 7.24 shows the curve for this best-of-generation individual and the target curve. The average distance between the curve for this best-of-generation individual and the target curve over the 20 points is about 0.22 per fitness case. As can be seen, this best-of-generation individual is considerably closer to the target curve than the second-best individual above.

The best-of-generation individual from the initial random population (namely xe^x) produced a value that came within this hits criterion (0.01 for this problem) of the correct value of the target curve for two of the 20 fitness cases. That is, it scored two hits. All the other individuals of generation 0 scored no hits or only one hit.

Although xe^x is not a particularly good fit (much less a perfect fit) to the target curve, this individual is nonetheless visibly better than the worst individual in the initial random population, the median individual, and the second-best individual. When graphed, xe^x bears some similarity to the target curve $x^4 + x^3 + x^2 + x$. First, both xe^x and $x^4 + x^3 + x^2 + x$ are zero when x is 0. The exact agreement of the two curves at the origin accounts for one of the two hits scored by xe^x and the closeness of the two curves for another value of x near 0 accounts for the second hit. Second, when x approaches $+1.0$, xe^x approaches 2.7, while $x^4 + x^3 + x^2 + x$ approaches the somewhat nearby value of 4.0. Also, when x is between 0.0 and about -0.7, xe^x and $x^4 + x^3 + x^2 + x$ are very close.

Table 7.5 contains a simplified calculation that further illustrates the above. In this simplified calculation, we use only five equally spaced x_i points in the interval $[-1, 1]$, instead of 20 randomly generated points. These five values of x_i are shown in row 1 of this table.

Row 2 shows the value of the best-of-generation individual $y = xe^x$ from generation 0 for the five values of x_i. Row 3 shows the target data T representing the target curve $x^4 + x^3 + x^2 + x$. Row 4 shows the absolute value of the difference between the target data T and the value of the best-of-generation individual $y = xe^x$ from generation 0. The sum of the five

Table 7.5 Simplified presention of the simple symbolic regression problem with only five fitness cases.

1	x_i	-1.0	-0.5	.00	$+.5$	$+1.0$
2	$y = xe^x$	$-.368$	$-.303$	.000	.824	2.718
3	T	0.0	$-.312$	.000	.938	4.0
4	$|T - y|$	.368	.009	.000	.113	1.212

items in row 4 (i.e., the raw fitness) is 1.702. If this raw fitness were zero, the function y on row 2 would be a perfect fit to the given data on row 3.

By generation 2, the best-of-generation individual in the population was the S-expression with 23 points

```
(+ (* (* (+ X (* X (* X (% (% X X) (+ X X))))))
      (+ X (* X X))) X) X),
```

which is equivalent to

```
x⁴ + 1.5x³ + 0.5x² + x.
```

The raw fitness of this best-of-generation individual improved to 2.57 for generation 2 (as compared to 4.47 from generation 0). This is an average of about 0.13 per fitness case. This best-of-generation individual from generation 2 scored five hits as compared to only two hits for the best-of-generation individual from generation 0.

This best-of-generation individual from generation 2 bears a greater similarity to the target function than any of its predecessors. It is, for example, a polynomial. Moreover, it is a polynomial of the correct order (i.e., 4). Moreover, the coefficients of two of its four terms (its quartic term and its linear term) are already correct. In addition, the incorrect coefficients (1.5 for the cubic term and 0.5 for the quadratic term) are not too different from the correct coefficients (1.0 and 1.0).

Before we proceed farther, notice that even though no numerical coefficients were explicitly provided in the terminal set, genetic programming automatically created the rational coefficient 0.5 for the quadratic term x^2 by first creating $1/2x$ (by dividing $x/x = 1$ by $x + x = 2x$) and then multiplying by x. The rational coefficient 1.5 for the cubic term x^3 was created similarly.

Figure 7.25 shows, by generation, the standardized fitness of the best-of-generation individual, the worst-of-generation individual, and the average individual in the population between generations 0 and 34 of one run of the symbolic regression problem. Because of the large magnitudes of standardized fitness for the worst-of-generation individual and the average individual in the population, a logarithmic scale is used on the vertical axis of this figure. As can be seen, the standardized fitness of the best-of-generation individual generally improves (i.e., decreases) and trends toward the horizontal line representing the near-zero value of 10^{-6}.

By generation 34, the sum of the absolute values of the differences between the best-of-generation individual and the target curve $x^4 + x^3 + x^2 + x$ over the 20 fitness cases reached 0.0 for the first time in this run. This individual, of

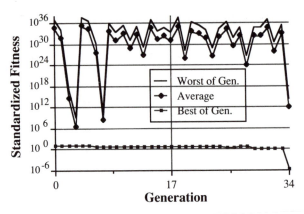

Figure 7.25 Fitness curves for the simple symbolic regression problem.

course, also scored 20 hits. This best-of-generation individual for generation 34 was the following S-expression containing 20 points:

```
(+ X (* (+ X (* (* (+ X (- (COS (- X X)) (- X X))) X)
        X)) X)).
```

Note that the cosine term (COS (- X X)) evaluates merely to 1.0. This entire S-expression is equivalent to $x^4 + x^3 + x^2 + x$, which is, of course, the target curve.

Figure 7.26 graphically depicts this 100%-correct best-of-run individual from generation 34.

The best-of-run S-expression obtained in generation 34 has 20 points. There were varying numbers of points in the best-of-generation S-expression for the various intermediate generations (e.g., 19 points for generation 0 and 23 points for generation 2). We did not specify that the solution would have 20 points, nor did we specify the shape or the particular content of the S-expression that emerged in generation 34. The size, shape, and content of the S-expression that solves this problem evolved in response to the selective pressure exerted by the fitness (error) measure.

The function we discovered is complete in the sense that it is defined for any point in the original interval $[-1, +1]$. Thus, this discovered function can be viewed as a model of the process that produced the 20 observed data points (i.e., the 20 fitness cases). The discovered function can be used to give a value of the dependent variable (i.e., y) for any value of the independent variable (i.e., x) in the interval if one accepts this discovered model. As it happens, the discovered function is also well defined beyond the original interval $[-1, +1]$; in fact, it is well defined for any real value of x. Thus, the discovered function can be used to forecast the value of the dependent variable (i.e., y) for any real value of the independent variable (i.e., x) if one accepts this discovered model.

Although all 20 pairs of observed data (x_i, y_i) for this particular example were consistent and noncontradictory, the symbolic regression problem would have proceeded in an identical fashion even if two different values of the

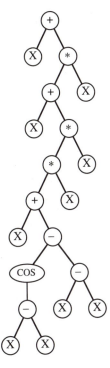

Figure 7.26 100%-correct best-of-run individual for the simple symbolic regression problem.

dependent variable (i.e., *y*) happened to be associated with one particular value of the dependent variable. In such a case of noisy data, one would not expect the error (i.e., raw fitness) ever to reach 0 and would not expect 20 hits.

The best-of-run individual shown above employed the functions +, −, *, and cos, but did not employ %, SIN, EXP, and RLOG. That is, four of the eight primitive functions in the function set were extraneous for the actual best-of-run individual. In other runs of this problem, we have obtained a solution using only the functions + and *, thus rendering six of the eight primitive functions extraneous.

Constant creation in connection with symbolic regression will be discussed in sections 10.1 and 10.2.

7.4 BOOLEAN MULTIPLEXER

As a fourth illustration of genetic programming, consider the problem of Boolean concept learning (i.e., discovering a composition of Boolean functions that can return the correct value of a Boolean function after seeing a certain number of examples consisting of the correct value of the function associated with a particular combination of arguments). This problem may be viewed as similar to the problem of symbolic regression of a polynomial except that Boolean functions and arguments are involved. It may also be viewed as a problem of electronic circuit design.

Four Introductory Examples of Genetic Programming

Boolean functions provide a useful test bed for machine learning for several reasons.

First, it is intuitively easy to see how the structural components of the S-expression for a Boolean function contribute to the overall performance of the Boolean expression. This direct connection between structure and performance is much harder to comprehend for most other problems presented in this book.

Second, there are fewer practical obstacles to computer implementation for Boolean functions than for most other types of problems described in this book. There are no overflows or underflows generated by arbitrary compositions of Boolean functions, and there is no time-consuming simulation to write as there is with the artificial ant problem and the cart centering problem. Thus, the reader will find it particularly easy to work with Boolean problems and to replicate the results of this section.

Third, Boolean problems have an easily quantifiable search space. This is not the case for most other problems presented herein.

Fourth, for Boolean functions, the number of fitness cases is finite; thus, it is possible and practical to test 100% of the possible fitness cases for some Boolean problems. Testing of 100% of the fitness cases for a given problem sidesteps the question of whether the set of fitness cases is sufficiently representative of the problem domain to allow proper generalization. As will be shown in section 23.2, even when the number of fitness cases is finite, it is often considerably more efficient to measure fitness by a statistical sampling of the fitness cases.

7.4.1   11-multiplexer

Consider the problem of learning the Boolean 11-multiplexer function.

The solution of this problem (which has a search space of size approximately 10^{616}) will serve to show the interplay, in genetic programming, of

- the genetic variation inevitably created in the initial random generation,
- the small improvements for some individuals in the population via localized hill climbing from generation to generation,
- the way particular individuals become specialized so as to be able to correctly handle certain subcases of the problem (case splitting),
- the creative role of crossover in recombining valuable parts of fitter parents to produce new individuals with new capabilities, and
- how the nurturing of a large population of alternative solutions to the problem (rather than a single point in the solution space) helps avoid false peaks in the search for a solution to the problem.

This problem will also serve to illustrate the importance of hierarchies in solving problems and making the ultimate solution understandable. Moreover, the progressively changing size and shape of the various individuals in the population in various generations shows the importance of not determining in advance the size and shape of the ultimate solution or the intermediate results that may contribute to the solution.

The input to the Boolean N-multiplexer function consists of k address bits a_i and 2^k data bits d_i, where $N = k + 2^k$. That is, the input to the Boolean multiplexer function consists of the $k + 2k$ bits

$$a_{k-1}, \ldots, a_1, a_0, d_{2k-1}, \ldots, d_1, d_0.$$

The value of the Boolean multiplexer function is the Boolean value (0 or 1) of the particular data bit that is singled out by the k address bits of the multiplexer.

For example, figure 7.27 shows a Boolean 11-multiplexer (i.e., $k = 3$) in which the three address bits $a_2 a_1 a_0$ are currently 110. The multiplexer singles out data bit 6 (i.e., d_6) to be the output of the multiplexer. Specifically, for an input of **11001000000**, the output of the multiplexer is **1**.

The first major step in preparing to use genetic programming is to select the set of terminals that will be available for constructing the computer programs (S-expressions) that will try to solve the problem. The terminal set for a problem generally consists of the information that the computer program being discovered by genetic programming must process in order to solve the problem. In this problem, the information that must be processed by a computer program corresponds to the 11 inputs to the Boolean 11-multiplexer. That is, the terminal set contains the 11 arguments as shown below:

```
T = {A0, A1, A2, D0, D1, ..., D7}.
```

Note that these terminals are not distinguished (to genetic programming) as being address lines versus data lines.

The second major step in preparing to use genetic programming is to select the set of functions that will be available for constructing the computer programs (S-expressions) that will try to solve the problem. There are many possible choices of sufficient function sets for this problem. The AND, OR, NOT, and IF functions often produce easily understood S-expressions. Thus, the function set for this problem is

```
F = {AND, OR, NOT, IF},
```

having two, two, one, and three arguments, respectively.

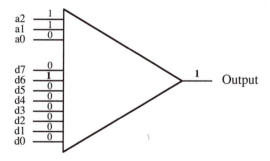

Figure 7.27 Boolean 11-multiplexer with input of 11001000000 and output of 1.

Four Introductory Examples of Genetic Programming

The IF function is the Common LISP function that performs the IF-THEN-ELSE operation. That is, the IF function returns the results of evaluating its third argument (the "else" clause) if its first argument is NIL (False) and otherwise returns the results of evaluating its second argument (the "then" clause).

The search space for this problem is the set of all LISP S-expressions that can be recursively composed of functions from the function set and terminals from the terminal set. Another way to look at the search space is that the Boolean multiplexer function with $k + 2^k$ arguments is a particular one of $2^{2^{k+2^k}}$ possible Boolean functions of $k + 2^k$ arguments. For example, when $k = 3$, then $k + 2^k = 11$ and this search space is of size $2^{2^{11}}$. That is, the search space is of size 2^{2048}, which is approximately 10^{616}. One can appreciate the infeasibility of blind random search for searching spaces of this magnitude by noting that a search conducted at the rate of a billion (i.e., 10^9) points per second since the estimated beginning of the universe (i.e., 1.5×10^9 years ago) would by now have searched only about 10^{27} points.

Every possible Boolean function of $k + 2^k$ arguments can be realized by at least one LISP S-expression composed from the functions and terminals above (for example, disjunctive normal form).

The third major step in preparing to use genetic programming is to identify the fitness measure for the problem.

There are $2^{11} = 2{,}048$ possible combinations of the 11 arguments $a_0 a_1 a_2 d_0 d_1 d_2 d_3 d_4 d_5 d_6 d_7$ along with the associated correct value of the 11-multiplexer function. For this particular problem, we use the entire set of 2,048 combinations of arguments as the fitness cases for evaluating fitness. That is, we do not use sampling.

We begin by defining raw fitness in the simplest way that comes to mind using the natural terminology of the problem. The raw fitness of a LISP S-expression in this problem is simply the number of fitness cases (taken over all 2,048 fitness cases) where the Boolean value returned by the S-expression for a given combination of arguments is the correct Boolean value. Thus, the raw fitness of an S-expression can range over 2049 different values between 0 and 2,048. A raw fitness of 2,048 denotes a 100%-correct S-expression.

After defining raw fitness for the problem, we proceed to define standardized fitness. Since a bigger value of raw fitness is better, standardized fitness is different from raw fitness for this problem. In particular, standardized fitness equals the maximum possible value of raw fitness r_{max} (i.e., 2,048) minus the observed raw fitness. The standardized fitness can also be viewed as the sum, taken over all 2,048 fitness cases, of the Hamming distances between the Boolean value returned by the S-expression for a given combination of arguments and the correct Boolean value. The Hamming distance is 0 if the Boolean value returned by the S-expression agrees with the correct Boolean value and is 1 if it disagrees. Thus, the sum of the Hamming distances is equivalent to the number of mismatches.

We define the auxiliary hits measure for this problem to be equal to the raw fitness.

The fourth major step in preparing to use genetic programming involves selecting the values of certain parameters. A population of size 4,000 was chosen for this problem in order to produce an 100%-correct solution by an early generation and to thereby facilitate production of a genealogical audit trail for the run.

Finally, the fifth major step in preparing to use genetic programming involves specifying the criterion for designating a result and the criterion for terminating a run. In this problem, we have a way to recognize a solution when we find it. The termination criterion for this problem is to terminate a run after a specified maximum number of generations G (e.g., 51) or earlier if we find an individual with a standardized fitness of 0 (i.e., the raw fitness and the number of hits equals 2,048).

Table 7.6 summarizes the key features of the Boolean 11-multiplexer problem.

We now discuss in detail one particular run of the problem of learning the Boolean 11-multiplexer function.

As usual, generation 0 includes a variety of highly unfit individuals. Many individual S-expressions in this initial random population are merely constants, such as the contradictory (AND A0 (NOT A0)). Other individuals, such as (NOT (NOT A1)), are passive and merely pass a single input through as the output without much computation. Other individuals are inefficient, such as (OR D7 D7).

Some of these initial random individuals base their decisions on precisely the wrong arguments, such as (IF D0 A0 A2). This individual uses a data bit

Table 7.6 Tableau for the Boolean 11-multiplexer problem.

Objective:	Find a Boolean S-expression whose output is the same as the Boolean 11-multiplexer function.
Terminal set:	A0, A1, A2, D0, D1, D2, D3, D4, D5, D6, D7.
Function set:	AND, OR, NOT, IF.
Fitness cases:	The $2^{11} = 2,048$ combinations of the 11 Boolean arguments.
Raw fitness:	Number of fitness cases for which the S-expression matches correct output.
Standardized fitness:	Sum, taken over the $2^{11} = 2,048$ fitness cases, of the Hamming distances (i.e., number of mismatches). Standardized fitness equals 2,048 minus raw fitness for this problem.
Hits:	Equivalent to raw fitness for this problem.
Wrapper:	None.
Parameters:	$M = 4,000$ (with over-selection). $G = 51$.
Success predicate:	An S-expression scores 2,048 hits.

(i.e., D0) to decide what output to take. Many of the initial random individuals are partially blind in that they do not incorporate all 11 arguments that are manifestly necessary to solve the problem. Some S-expressions are just nonsense, such as

```
(IF (IF (IF D2 D2 D2) D2 D2) D2 D2).
```

Nonetheless, even in this highly unfit initial random population, some individuals are somewhat fitter than others. For this particular run, the individuals in the initial random population had values of standardized fitness ranging from 768 mismatches (i.e., 1,280 matches or hits) to 1,280 mismatches (i.e., 768 matches).

The worst-of-generation individual for generation 0 was

```
(OR (NOT A1) (NOT (IF (AND A2 A0) D7 D3))).
```

This individual had a standardized fitness of 1,280 (i.e., a raw fitness of only 768). Its performance was worse than merely always guessing T (i.e., True or 1) for all 2,048 combinations of the 11 terminals.

As it happens, 23 individuals in this initial random population tied with the highest score of 1,280 matches (i.e., hits) on generation 0. One of these 23 high scoring individuals was the S-expression

```
(IF A0 D1 D2),
```

which achieves a score of 1,280 matches by getting 512 matches for the one-fourth (i.e., 512) of the 2,048 fitness cases for which A2 and A1 were both NIL (i.e., False or 0) and by scoring an additional 768 matches on 50% of the remaining three-fourths (i.e., 1,536) of the fitness cases.

This individual has obvious shortcomings. Notably, it is partially blind in that it uses only three of the 11 terminals necessary to correctly solve the problem. As a consequence of this fact alone, this individual cannot be a correct solution to the problem. This individual nonetheless does some things right. For example, it uses one of the three address bits (A0) as the basis for its action. It could easily have done this wrong and used one of the eight data bits. In addition, it uses only data bits (D1 and D2) as its output. It could have done this wrong and used address bits. Moreover, if A0 (which is the low order binary bit of the three-bit address) is T, this individual selects one of the four odd-numbered data bits (D1) as its output. Moreover, if A0 is NIL, this individual selects one of the four even-numbered data bits (D2) as its output. In other words, this individual correctly links the parity of the low-order address bit A0 with the parity of the data bit it selects as its output. This individual is far from perfect, but it is far from being without merit. It is fitter than 3,977 of the 4,000 individuals in the population.

Figure 7.28 shows a scoreboard in which each of the 2,048 cells represents one of the 2,048 combinations of the 11 inputs to the multiplexer. There is a black square for each of the 1,280 combinations of inputs for which the best-of-generation individual from generation 0 produces the correct Boolean output, and an open square for each of the 768 combinations of inputs for

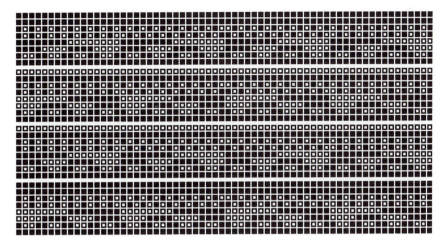

Figure 7.28 Scoreboard for best-of-generation individual for generation 0 of Boolean 11-multiplexer problem.

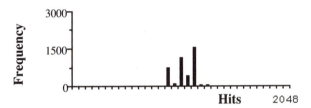

Figure 7.29 Hits histogram for generation 0 of the 11-multiplexer problem.

which this individual produces the wrong output. If the scoreboard were showing a perfect solution to the problem, there would be 2,048 black squares and no open squares.

The average standardized fitness for all 4,000 individuals in the population for generation 0 is 985.4. This value of average standardized fitness for the initial random population forms the baseline and serves as a useful benchmark for monitoring later improvements in the average standardized fitness of the population as a whole.

Figure 7.29 shows the hits histogram of the population for generation 0 of this run of this problem. Each tick on the horizontal axis represents a range of 64 hits values. The mode (high point) of this histogram occurs at 1,152 hits; there are 1,490 individuals scoring 1,152 hits. There are 1,553 individuals out of 4,000 (i.e., about 39%) scoring between 1,152 and 1,215 hits.

A new population is then created from the current population using the operations of Darwinian fitness-proportionate reproduction and crossover. When these operations are completed, the new population (i.e., the new generation) replaces the old population.

In going from generation 0 to generation 1, genetic programming works with the inevitable genetic variation existing in an initial random population. The initial random generation is an exercise in blind random search. The search is a parallel search of the search space because there are 4,000 individual points involved.

The average standardized fitness of the population immediately begins improving (i.e., decreasing) from the baseline value of 985.4 for generation 0 to about 891.9 for generation 1. This kind of general improvement in average standardized fitness from generation to generation is typical. As it happens, in this particular run of this particular problem, the average standardized fitness improves (i.e., decreases) monotonically between generations 2 and 9 and assumes values of 845, 823, 763, 731, 651, 558, 459, and 382, respectively. We usually see a general improvement in average standardized fitness from generation to generation, but not necessarily a monotonic improvement.

Similarly, we usually see a general improvement trend in the standardized fitness of the best-of-generation individual in the population from generation to generation. As it happens, in this particular run of this particular problem the standardized fitness of the best-of-generation individual in the population improves (i.e., decreases) monotonically between generation 2 and generation 9. In particular, it assumes progressively the values of 640, 576, 384, 384, 256, 256, 128, and 0 (i.e., a perfect score).

In this run, the standardized fitness of the worst-of-generation individual starts at 1,280, fluctuates a little between generations 1 and 9, and ends up at 1,792 by generation 9 (i.e., worse than where it started). The lack of a trend in this particular statistic of the run is typical, since it measures a single deviant individual that is, by definition, an accidental by-product of the process.

Figure 7.30 shows the standardized fitness (i.e., mismatches) for generations 0 through 9 of this run for the worst-of-generation individual, the average for the population, and the best-of-generation individual in the population. Raw fitness (i.e., number of hits or matches) is shown on the right axis. Standardized fitness is 2,048 minus raw fitness for this problem.

In generation 1, the raw fitness of the best-of-generation individual in the population rose to 1,408 (i.e., a standardized fitness of 640). Only one individual in the population attained this high score of 1,408 in generation 1, namely

```
(IF A0 (IF A2 D7 D3) D0).
```

Note that this individual performs better than the best-of-generation individual from generation 0 for two reasons. First, it considers two of the three address bits (A0 and A2) in deciding which data bit to choose as output, whereas the best individual in generation 0 considered only one of the three address bits (A0). Second, this best individual from generation 1 incorporates three of the eight data bits as its output, whereas the best individual in generation 0 incorporated only two of the eight potential data bits as output. Although still far from perfect, the best individual from generation 1 is less blind and more complex than the best individual of the previous generation. This best-of-generation individual consists of seven points, whereas the best-of-generation individual from generation 0 consisted of only four points. Although the number of points in the individual S-expression is not directly related to its fitness, this increase in the structural complexity of the S-

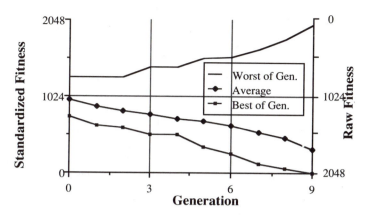

Figure 7.30 Fitness curves for the 11-multiplexer problem.

expression is indicative of the dynamic way in which structures adaptively develop in genetic programming to address various problem environments.

This best-of-generation individual from generation 1 differs in size and shape from the best-of-generation individual from generation 0. The progressive change in size and shape of the individuals in the population is a characteristic of genetic programming.

In generation 2, no new ground was broken in terms of the fitness of the best-of-generation individual; however, the population as a whole improved. Although the best raw fitness remained at 1,408, the number of individuals in the population scoring 1,408 rose from 1 to 21. The population became richer in a second way. The high point of the hits histogram of the population advanced from 1,152 for generation 0 to 1,280 for generation 2. There were 1,620 individuals with 1,280 hits.

In generation 3, one individual in the population attained a new high score of 1,472 hits (i.e., a standardized fitness of 576). This individual, which had 16 points, is

```
(IF A2 (IF A0 D7 D4)
        (AND (IF (IF A2 (NOT D5) A0) D3 D2) D2)).
```

Generation 3 showed further advances in fitness for the population as a whole. The number of individuals with 1,280 hits (the high point for generation 2) rose to 2,158 for generation 3. Moreover, the center of gravity of the hits histogram shifted significantly from left to right. In particular, the number of individuals with 1,280 hits or better rose from 1,679 in generation 2 to 2,719 in generation 3. Note that the best S-expression for generation 3 contains both AND and NOT functions. Although good performance (and even a perfect solution) can be obtained using these functions, the IF function seems more useful for solving this problem and will eventually dominate.

In generations 4 and 5, the best-of-generation individual had 1,664 hits. This new high score was attained by only one individual in generation 4, but was attained by 13 individuals in generation 5. One of these 13 individuals

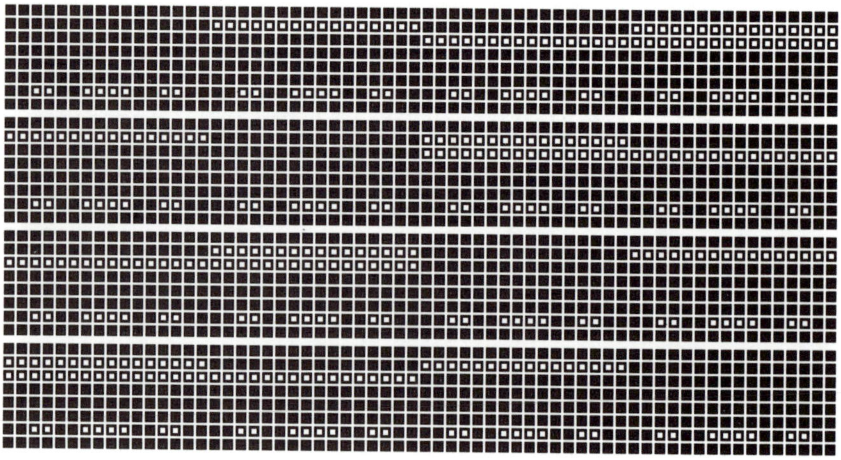

Figure 7.31 Scoreboard for best-of-generation individual for generation 4 of the 11-multiplexer problem.

was

```
(IF A0 (IF A2 D7 D3)
       (IF A2 D4 (IF A1 D2 (IF A2 D7 D0)))).
```

This individual used all three address bits (A2, A1, and A0) in deciding upon the output. Moreover, it had only data bits as the second and third arguments of the IF functions. Moreover, this S-expression also used five of the eight data bits. By generation 4, the high point of the hits histogram had moved to 1,408 with 1,559 individuals.

The scoreboard in figure 7.31 shows, using black squares, the 1,644 combinations of inputs (out of 2,048) for which a best-of-generation individual from generation 4 produces the correct Boolean output. The 404 of the 2,048 combinations for which this individual is incorrect are shown as open squares.

In generation 6, each of four individuals attained a score of 1,792 hits. The high point of the histogram moved to 1,536 hits.

In generation 7, each of 70 individuals attained this score of 1,792 hits.

In generation 8, there were four best-of-generation individuals. Each attained a score of 1,920 hits. The mode (high point) of the histogram moved to 1,664. 1,672 individuals shared this value. Moreover, an additional 887 individuals scored 1,792 each.

The scoreboard in figure 7.32 shows, using black squares, the 1,920 combinations of inputs for which one of the several best-of-generation individuals from generation 8 produced the correct Boolean output. The 128 combinations for which this individual was incorrect are shown as open squares. Considerable regularity is now apparent in the pattern of the errors.

The best-of-generation individual emerging in generation 9,

```
(IF A0 (IF A2 (IF A1 D7 (IF A0 D5 D0))
              (IF A0 (IF A1 (IF A2 D7 D3) D1) D0))
```

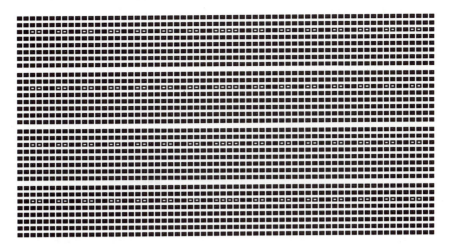

Figure 7.32 Scoreboard for one of the best-of-generation individuals for generation 8 of the 11-multiplexer problem.

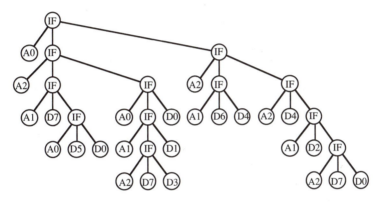

Figure 7.33 The best-of-run individual from generation 9 solves the 11-multiplexer problem.

```
(IF A2 (IF A1 D6 D4)
       (IF A2 D4 (IF A1 D2 (IF A2 D7 D0)))))),
```

had a perfect score of 2,048 hits.

Figure 7.33 graphically depicts this 100%-correct best-of-run individual from generation 9. This hierarchical structure consists of 37 points (i.e., 12 functions and 25 terminals).

Note that the size and the shape of this solution emerged from genetic programming. The particular size, shape, and content of this hierarchical structure were not specified in advance. Instead, this structure evolved as a result of the relentless pressure exerted by the fitness (error) measure. The number of points in the best-of-generation individual in the population then varied from generation to generation. It was 4, 7, 7, 16, 16, 16, 25, 25, 22, and 37 for generations 0 through 9, respectively. In this particular problem, the increasing number of points, among other things, overcame the partial blindness of the early structures. This problem, like the other problems in this book, illustrates how structure arises from fitness via genetic programming.

This 100%-correct individual can be simplified (either manually or via the editing operation) to

```
(IF A0 (IF A2 (IF A1 D7 D5) (IF A1 D3 D1))
       (IF A2 (IF A1 D6 D4) (IF A1 D2 D0))),
```

which makes it easier to see that this individual correctly performs the 11-multiplexer function by first examining address bits A0, A2, and A1 and then choosing the appropriate one of the eight possible data bits.

Figure 7.34 shows the hits histograms for generations 0, 2, 6, 8, and 9 of this run. Progressing from generation to generation, note the left-to-right undulating movement of the center of mass of the histogram and the high point of the histogram. The single 100%-correct individual with 2,048 hits at generation 9 is invisible because of the scale of the vertical axis.

A genealogical audit trail can provide further insight into how genetic programming works. This audit trail consists of a complete record of the ancestors of a given individual and of each genetic operation that was performed on the ancestor in producing the current individual. For the crossover operation, the details include the particular points chosen within both ancestors.

Construction of the audit trail starts with the individuals of the initial random generation. Certain additional information, such as the individual's standardized fitness and its rank location in the population (found by sorting by standardized fitness), is also carried along as a convenience in interpreting the genealogy. Then, as each operation is performed to create a new individual for the next generation, a list is recursively formed consisting of the type of the operation performed, the individual(s) participating in the operation, the details of that operation (e.g., crossover point selected), and, finally, a pointer to the audit trail previously assembled for the individual(s) participating in that operation.

An individual occurring at generation h has up to 2^{h+1} ancestors. The number of ancestors is less than 2^{h+1} to the extent that operations other than crossover are involved and to the extent that an individual crosses over with itself. For example, an individual occurring at generation 9 has up to 1,024 ancestors. Note that a particular ancestor often appears more than once in this genealogy, because all selections of individuals to participate in the basic genetic operations are skewed in proportion to fitness, with reselection allowed. However, even for a small value of h, 2^{h+1} will typically be greater than the population size (although it is not for this particular run of this problem). The repeated occurrence of a particular ancestor in the genealogical tree, of course, does nothing to reduce the size of the tree. Even with the use of pointers from descendants back to ancestors, construction of a complete genealogical audit trail is exponentially expensive in both computer time and memory space. The audit trail must be constructed for each individual of each

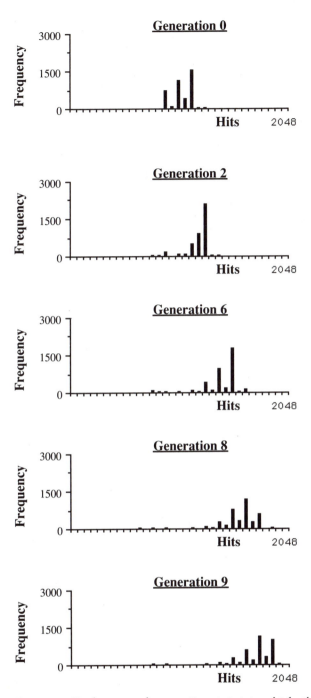

Figure 7.34 Hits histograms for generations 0, 2, 6, 8, and 9 for the 11-multiplexer problem.

generation, because the identity of the 100%-correct individual(s) eventually solving the problem is not known in advance. Thus, there are 4,000 audit trails. By generation 9, each of these 4,000 audit trails recursively incorporates information about operations involving up to 1,024 ancestors. The audit trail for the single 100%-correct individual of interest in generation 9 alone occupies about 27 densely printed pages.

The creative role of crossover and case splitting is illustrated by an examination of the genealogical audit trail for the 100%-correct individual emerging at generation 9.

The 100%-correct individual emerging at generation 9 is the child resulting from a crossover of two parents from generation 8. The first parent from generation 8 was the 58th best individual (out of 4,000) in the population and scored 1,792 hits (out of 2,048). The second parent was one of the several best-of-generation individuals from generation 8 and scored 1,920 hits. Note that it is entirely typical that the individuals selected to participate in crossover have relatively high ranks in the population, since crossover is performed among individuals in a mating pool created proportionate to fitness.

The first parent from generation 8 (scoring 1,792) was

```
(IF A0 (IF A2 D7 D3)
        (IF A2 (IF A1 D6 D4)
               (IF A2 D4 (IF A1 D2 (IF A2 D7 D0)))))).
```

Figure 7.35 graphically depicts the first parent from generation 8.

This imperfect first parent starts by examining address bit A0. When A0 is T, this first parent is not 100% correct. The incorrect portion of this S-expression in boldface applies. Address bit A2 is examined, and the output is set to D7 or D3 without any consideration of address bit A1. This incorrect portion is partially blind and does not even contain data bits D1 and D5.

When A0 is NIL, this first parent is 100% correct. It examines A2. If A2 is T, it then examines A1 and makes the output equal to D6 or D4 according to

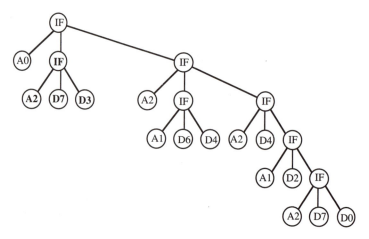

Figure 7.35 First parent (58th best individual) from generation 8 of the 11-multiplexer problem.

whether A1 is T or NIL. But if A2 is NIL, it unnecessarily (but harmlessly) retests A2 and then correctly makes the output equal to (IF A1 D2 D0). Note that the 100%-correct portion of this first parent, namely the subexpression

```
(IF A2 (IF A1 D6 D4)
       (IF A2 D4 (IF A1 D2 (IF A2 D7 D0)))),
```

is itself a 6-multiplexer. This embedded 6-multiplexer tests A2 and A1 and correctly selects among D6, D4, D2, and D0. This fact becomes clearer if we simplify this subexpression by removing the two extraneous tests and the unreachable portion containing D7. This subexpression then simplifies to

```
(IF A2 (IF A1 D6 D4)
       (IF A1 D2 D0)).
```

In other words, this imperfect first parent handles part of its environment correctly and part of its environment incorrectly. In particular, this first parent handles the even-numbered data bits correctly but is only partially correct in handling the odd-numbered data bits.

The tree representing this first parent has 22 points. The crossover point chosen at random at the end of generation 8 was point 3, which corresponds to the second occurrence of the function IF. That is, the crossover fragment consists of the incorrect subexpression

```
(IF A2 D7 D3).
```

Figure 7.36 is a scoreboard for the first parent (the 58th-best individual) from generation 8. There are black squares for the 1,792 out of 2,048 fitness cases that are correctly handled by the first parent. There are open squares for the 256 fitness cases that are incorrectly handled. The open squares (indicating errors) appear in rows 3, 7, 11, 15, 19, 23, 27, and 31. These open squares are disjoint from the open squares of the second parent shown in figure 7.38.

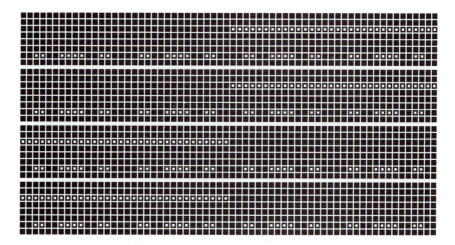

Figure 7.36 Scoreboard for the first parent (58th-best individual) from generation 8.

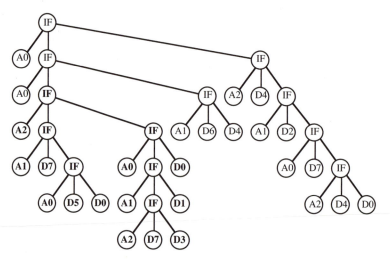

Figure 7.37 Second parent (best-of-generation individual) from generation 8 of the 11-multiplexer problem.

The second parent from generation 8 (scoring 1,920 hits) was

```
(IF A0 (IF A0 (IF A2 (IF A1 D7 (IF A0 D5 D0))
                     (IF A0 (IF A1 (IF A2 D7 D3)
                                    D1)
                             D0))
              (IF A1 D6 D4))
       (IF A2 D4
              (IF A1 D2 (IF A0 D7 (IF A2 D4 D0)))))).
```

Figure 7.37 graphically depicts the second parent from generation 8.

The tree representing this second parent has 40 points. The crossover point chosen at random for this second parent was point 5. This point corresponds to the third occurrence of the function IF. That is, the crossover fragment consists of the subexpression of the second parent in boldface.

This subexpression of the second parent correctly handles the case when A0 is T (i.e., the odd-numbered addresses). This subexpression makes the output equal to D7 when the address bits are 111; it makes the output equal to D5 when the address bits are 101; it makes the output equal to D3 when the address bits are 011; and it makes the output equal to D1 when the address bits are 001.

Note that the 100%-correct portion of this second parent, namely the subexpression

```
(IF A2 (IF A1 D7 (IF A0 D5 D0))
       (IF A0 (IF A1 (IF A2 D7 D3)
                      D1)
               D0)),
```

is itself a 6-multiplexer.

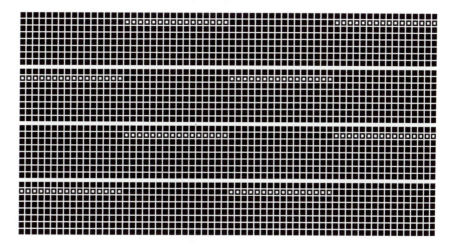

Figure 7.38 Scoreboard for second parent (best-of-generation individual) from generation 8 of the 11-multiplexer problem.

This embedded 6-multiplexer in the second parent tests A2 and A1 and correctly selects among D7, D5, D3, and D1 (i.e., the odd-numbered data bits). This fact becomes clearer if we simplify this subexpression to

```
(IF A2 (IF A1 D7 D5)
       (IF A1 D3 D1)).
```

Figure 7.38 is a scoreboard for the second parent (the best-of-generation individual) from generation 8. There are black squares for the 1,920 out of 2,048 fitness cases that are handled correctly by the second parent. There are open squares for the 128 fitness cases that are handled incorrectly. The open squares appear in rows 2, 10, 18, and 26 for the second parent, whereas the open squares appeared in rows 3, 7, 11,15, 19, 23, 27, and 31 for the first parent as shown in figure 7.36. When compared, these two figures show that the sets of fitness cases that are incorrectly handled by the two parents are disjoint.

This imperfect second parent handles part of its environment correctly and part of its environment incorrectly. It correctly handles the odd-numbered data bits, but is only partially correct when A0 is NIL (i.e., the even-numbered data bits).

Even though neither parent is perfect, these two imperfect parents contain complementary, co-adapted portions which, when mated, produce a 100%-correct offspring individual. In effect, the crossover operation blends the two cases into which the environment has been split into a single 100%-correct solution. There are, of course, many other combinations of individuals that are capable of solving this problem.

Figure 7.39 shows this case splitting by restating the 100%-correct offspring from generation 9 as an IF function that tests A0 and then conditionally selects between two 6-multiplexers. The first 6-multiplexer comes from the second parent from generation 8 and uses A2 and A1 to select among the

Four Introductory Examples of Genetic Programming

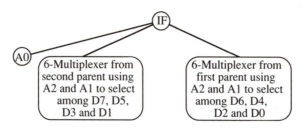

Figure 7.39 The solution to the 11-multiplexer problem is a hierarchical conditional composition of two 6-multiplexers.

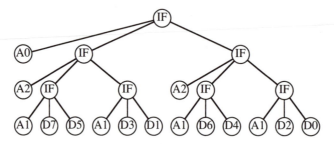

Figure 7.40 The solution to the 11-multiplexer problem is a hierarchical conditional composition of 3-multiplexers (i.e., IF–THEN–ELSE functions).

odd-numbered data lines (i.e., D7, D5, D3, and D1). The second 6-multiplexer comes from the first parent and uses A2 and A1 to select among the even-numbered data lines (i.e., D6, D4, D2, and D0). The 100%-correct solution to the 11-multiplexer problem is thus a conditional composition of two 6-multiplexers.

Figure 7.40 shows both 6-multiplexers from figure 7.39 as a conditional composition of two 3-multiplexers (i.e., IF–THEN–ELSE functions). The 100%-correct solution to the 11-multiplexer problem is thus a hierarchical conditional composition of 3-multiplexers.

Of course, not all crossovers between individuals are useful and productive. In fact, many individuals produced by the genetic operations are useless here, as they are in nature. The existence of a population of alternative solutions to a problem provides the ingredients with which genetic recombination (crossover) can produce some improved individuals. The relentless pressure of natural selection based on fitness then causes these improved individuals to be fruitful and multiply. Moreover, genetic variation and the existence of a population of alternative solutions to a problem make it unlikely that the entire population will become trapped in a local maximum.

Interestingly, the same crossover that produced the 100%-correct individual also produced a runt scoring only 256 hits. In this particular crossover, the two crossover fragments not used in the 100%-correct individual combined to produce an unusually unfit individual. This is one of the reasons why there is considerable variability from generation to generation in the worst-of-generation individual.

If we trace the ancestry of the 100%-correct individual created in generation 9 deeper back into the genealogical audit tree (i.e., toward earlier generations), we encounter parents scoring generally fewer and fewer hits. That is, we encounter more S-expressions that perform irrelevant, counterproductive, partially blind, and incorrect work. But if we look at the sequence of hits in the forward direction, we see localized hill climbing in the search space occurring in parallel throughout the population as the creative operation of crossover recombines complementary, co-adapted portions of parents to produce improved offspring. See also Koza 1991d.

7.4.2   Hierarchies

The result of the genetic programming paradigm is always hierarchical. This almost obvious yet very important characteristic is inherent in genetic programming. The hierarchical structure is a direct result of the way the individuals in the initial random population are created and the way the genetic operations are defined.

Hierarchies are an efficient and often highly understandable way of presenting the steps and substeps (tasks and subtasks, routines and subroutines) that constitute the solution to a problem. Moreover, hierarchical structures are amenable to scaling up to larger problems.

In many cases, the hierarchies produced can be very informative. As we just saw in the previous subsection, the solution to the 11-multiplexer problem found by genetic programming was a hierarchy of 6-multiplexers. Moreover, genetic programming used the IF function from the function set. The IF function is the 3-multiplexer (i.e., if-then-else). Thus, the solution produced for the Boolean 11-multiplexer was a hierarchy of 6-multiplexers, each consisting of a hierarchy of 3-multiplexers.

7.4.3   6-multiplexer

Genetic programming has also been applied to the simpler Boolean 6-multiplexer using a population size of 500. Because this 6-multiplexer problem requires so much less computer time to run than the 11-multiplexer, it is used frequently in this book for statistical experiments requiring large numbers of runs.

In one run, the following 100%-correct solution of the Boolean 6-multiplexer problem was obtained:

```
(IF A1 (IF A0 D3 D2) (IF A0 D1 D0)).
```

Figure 7.41 graphically depicts this S-expression, which contains 10 points.

Since the IF function is the 3-multiplexer (i.e., if-then-else), the solution to the 6-multiplexer problem is itself a hierarchy of 3-multiplexers.

Figure 7.42 shows the solution to the 6-multiplexer problem as a conditional composition of 3-multiplexers.

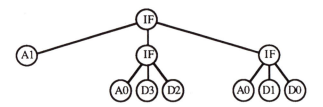

Figure 7.41 The solution to 6-multiplexer is a hierarchy of conditional compositions of 3-multiplexers.

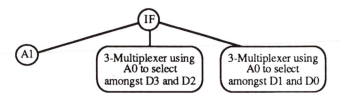

Figure 7.42 The solution to 6-multiplexer is a hierarchical conditional composition of two 3-multiplexers.

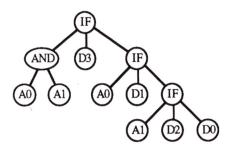

Figure 7.43 A solution to the 6-multiplexer problem containing a default hierarchy.

7.4.4 Default Hierarchies

A *default hierarchy* is a set of rules covering a variety of situations in which one subrule (called the *default rule*) handles a majority of the situations and one or more specific subrules handle various exceptional specific situations. A familiar example of a default hierarchy is the spelling rule "I before E, except after C."

Default hierarchies are considered desirable in induction problems (Holland et al. 1986, Holland 1986) because they are often a parsimonious and human-like way of dealing with situations.

Default hierarchies are often produced by genetic programming.

In one run of the Boolean 6-multiplexer problem, the following 100%-correct S-expression containing 12 points emerged:

```
(IF (AND A0 A1) D3 (IF A0 D1 (IF A1 D2 D0))).
```

Figure 7.43 graphically depicts this S-expression.

This S-expression is a default hierarchy. Specifically, this default hierarchy provides one way of correctly handling a certain minority of the 64 fitness cases of this problem, namely the 16 fitness cases for which (AND A0 A1) is true. For these 16 fitness cases, the output is D3. The default hierarchy then provides a default way of correctly handling the majority of the 64 fitness cases, namely the 48 fitness cases for which (AND A0 A1) is false. For these 48 fitness cases, the output defaults to

```
(IF A0 D1 (IF A1 D2 D0)).
```

Wilson's noteworthy BOOLE experiments (1987a) originally found a set of eight if-then classifier system rules for the Boolean 6-multiplexer that correctly (but tediously) handled each particular subcase of the problem. Subsequently, Wilson (1988) modified the credit allocation scheme in Holland's classifier system and successfully produced a default hierarchy that solved the problem correctly and parsimoniously.

7.4.5   3-multiplexer

Finally, the 3-multiplexer function, which is equivalent to the simple IF function (i.e., the if-then-else function) was run with the function set

```
F = {AND, OR, NOT}.
```

In one run, the following 100%-correct solution was obtained:

```
(OR (AND (AND D0 D0) (NOT A0))
    (AND D1 (AND D1 (OR D0 A0)))),
```

which in disjunctive normal form is equivalent to

```
(OR (AND (NOT A0) D0)
    (AND A0 D1)))).
```

The Boolean 3-multiplexer problem will be discussed again in chapter 8, where we investigate the amount of processing required by genetic programming.

7.5   RECAPITULATION

We started this chapter by showing that every computer program (regardless of whether the programming language is assembly code, PASCAL, or LISP) is a composition of functions operating on various arguments.

We then developed the notion, using the cart centering problem, that there is a spectrum of computer programs that are less or more fit at solving a given problem. We demonstrated that genetic programming can find the time optimal program to solve the cart centering problem. In so doing, genetic programming produced a trajectory of computer programs through the space of possible programs that was very different from the programs a human programmer would produce in dealing with this problem. The trajectory of programs produced by genetic programming started with highly unfit programs, proceeded to programs that were partially competent at solving the problem, and ended with a 100% effective program. We repeatedly witnessed a progressive improvement in results from generation to generation as opposed to one great leap in fitness.

We then demonstrated that genetic programming could be applied to other problems from very different problem domains. The artificial ant problem was a planning problem involving robotic actions.

In the symbolic regression problem, the trajectory of programs produced by genetic programming started with highly unfit mathematical expressions, proceeded to approximately correct polynomials of the correct order, and ended with a 100%-correct polynomial.

The genealogical audit trail of the 100%-correct solution of the Boolean 11-multiplexer problem showed how crossover combined a portion of each parent that was capable of perfectly handling part of the problem into an offspring that was capable of perfectly handling the entire problem.

For each of these four problems from the four different problem domains, we applied genetic programming in the same, domain independent, way. We started with the five major steps for preparing to use genetic programming, namely determination of the terminals, the functions, the fitness measure, the control parameters, and the termination criterion and method of result designation.

After this preparation, we then executed a run of genetic programming in the same, domain independent, way. We first created an initial population of random computer programs composed of the available functions and terminals and then iteratively proceeded through the generations. For each generation, we computed the fitness of each individual computer program in the population in terms of its ability to solve the problem at hand. We then used the fitness measure to select individual programs to participate in the Darwinian operation of fitness-proportionate reproduction and the genetic operation of crossover.

For each of the four introductory problems, the initial random generation consisted of highly unfit individuals; the intermediate generations contained a few somewhat fit individuals; and the final generation of each run contained at least one individual that was 100% effective in solving the problem at hand.

8 Amount of Processing Required to Solve a Problem

This chapter describes a method for measuring the performance of the genetic programming paradigm in terms of the amount of computer processing necessary to solve a particular problem. Specifically, we measure the number of individuals that must be processed in order to satisfy the success predicate of the problem with a certain specified probability (e.g., 99%). This number provides a measure of the difficulty of a problem.

Both the conventional genetic algorithm operating on fixed-length character strings and genetic programming involve probabilistic steps at three points in the algorithm, namely

- creating the initial population,
- selecting individuals from the population on which to perform each operation (e.g., reproduction, crossover), and
- selecting a point (e.g., the crossover point) within the selected individual at which to perform the genetic operation.

There is often additional randomness involved in the creation of the fitness cases used to measure fitness. Moreover, in some versions of the conventional genetic algorithm, the number of genetic operations that are actually executed varies probabilistically.

Because of these probabilistic steps, anything can happen and nothing is guaranteed for any given run of either the conventional genetic algorithm or genetic programming. In particular, there is no guarantee that a given run will yield an individual that satisfies the success predicate of the problem after being run for a particular number of generations.

As a given run progresses, the population may converge (i.e., become identical) or fail to converge. Premature convergence (i.e., convergence to a globally suboptimal result) is a major concern with the conventional genetic algorithm (Booker 1987). The exponentially increasing allocation of future trials resulting from Darwinian fitness-proportionate selection is both a strength and a weakness of genetic methods. This Darwinian allocation is a weakness of genetic methods because it may result in premature convergence; it is a strength because it is the fundamental reason why genetic methods work in the first place.

Non-convergence and premature convergence should be viewed as inherent features of both the conventional genetic algorithm and genetic programming, rather than as problems to be cured by altering the fundamental Darwinian nature of the methods. Nature can be the guide here. The analogue of premature convergence in genetic methods manifests itself in nature as the so-called niche preemption principle. According to this principle, a biological niche in nature tends to become dominated by a single species (Magurran 1988). Each independent run of a genetic algorithm or genetic programming can be viewed as a separate niche which may become dominated by a particular individual species (which may or may not be globally optimal). Nature carries out its genetic experiments in parallel in numerous niches, some of them virtually identical. The species that ultimately dominates any given niche may be decided by the unique initial conditions of that niche and the subsequent unique history of probabilistic events in that niche. The best individual arising from a group of separate niches is then available to proliferate and become dominant in the future.

Therefore, one way to minimize the effect of niche preemption, premature convergence, initial conditions, and other random events when using genetic methods is to make multiple independent runs of a problem. The best-of-run individual from all such multiple independent runs can then be designated as the result of the group of runs. These multiple independent runs are entirely separate runs with entirely separate populations—in contrast to the so-called distributed genetic algorithm (Tanese 1989), in which there are subpopulations linked via periodic emigration and immigration (chapter 22). The groups of multiple independent runs yield virtually linear speedup when implemented on parallel computer architectures, but their amenability to efficient parallelization is not the point here.

The flowchart in figure 8.1 contains a loop executing multiple independent runs of genetic programming. The result of the best run is designated as the overall result for the group of runs. The box labeled "Execute run" refers to all the steps contained in the basic flowchart for genetic programming in figure 5.1.

One way to measure the amount of computational resources required by genetic programming (or the conventional genetic algorithm) is to determine the number of independent runs (i.e., niches) needed to yield a success with a

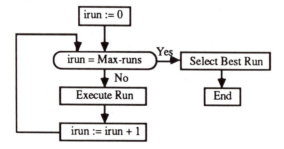

Figure 8.1 Flowchart for multiple independent runs.

certain probability (say 99%). Once we determine the likely number of independent runs required, we can then multiply by the amount of processing required for each run to get the total amount of processing.

The amount of processing required for each run depends primarily on the product of

- the number of individuals M in the population,
- the number of generations executed in that run, and
- the amount of processing required to measure the fitness of an individual over all the applicable fitness cases.

Contrary to what one might initially think, the third factor above is often not uniform during a run; it may, in fact, vary in complex and unobvious ways. For example, the structural complexity of the S-expressions in the population often increases as the run progresses and the population becomes fitter, thereby increasing the amount of processing required in later generations of a run. In addition, there are some problems (notably those involving simulations of behavior, such as the cart centering problem) where measuring the fitness of the highly unfit individuals typically encountered in the early generations of a run takes much more time than measuring the fitter individuals encountered in later generations. This is due to the fact that many individuals from early generations consume the maximum amount of time allowed by the simulation (i.e., time out) and the fact that individuals from later generations have become better at solving the problem. On the other hand, the reverse may be true for simulation problems where there is a means to recognize certain highly unfit individuals and quickly truncate the simulation for them. These unfit individuals may be absent in later generations.

In the remainder of this chapter, we will avoid this issue of nonuniformity and assume that the processing time to measure the fitness of an individual is uniform over all individuals and over all generations. Consequently, we can focus on the population size M and on the number of generations G in the run as the major factors in determining the amount of processing.

We start the process of measuring the amount of processing required by experimentally obtaining an estimate for the probability $Y(M, i)$ that a particular run with a population of size M yields, for the first time, on a specified generation i, an individual satisfying the success predicate for the problem. The experimental measurement of $Y(M, i)$ usually requires a substantial number of runs.

In any event, once we have obtained the instantaneous probability $Y(M, i)$ for each generation i, we compute the cumulative *probability of success* $P(M, i)$ for all the generations between generation 0 and generation i.

The probability of satisfying the success predicate by generation i at least once in R runs is then $1 - [1 - P(M, i)]^R$. If we want to satisfy the success predicate with a probability of, say, $z = 1 - \varepsilon = 99\%$, then it must be that

$$z = 1 - [1 - P(M, i)]^R.$$

The number $R(z)$ of independent runs (niches) required to satisfy the success

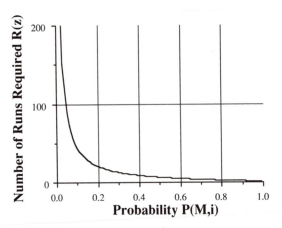

Figure 8.2 Number of independent runs $R(z)$ required as a function of the cumulative probability of success $P(M, i)$ for $z = 99\%$.

predicate by generation i with a probability of, say, $z = 1 - \varepsilon = 99\%$, depends on both z and $P(M, i)$. After taking logarithms, we find

$$R(z) = \left\lceil \frac{\log(1 - z)}{\log(1 - P(M, i))} \right\rceil = \left\lceil \frac{\log \varepsilon}{\log(1 - P(M, i))} \right\rceil,$$

where $\varepsilon = 1 - z = 0.01$ and where the square brackets indicates the so-called ceiling function for rounding up to the next highest integer. Note that $P(M, i)$ depends on the population size M and the generation number i.

Figure 8.2 shows a graph of the number of independent runs $R(z)$ required to yield a success with probability $z = 99\%$ as a function of the cumulative probability of success $P(M, i)$. For example, if the cumulative probability of success $P(M, i)$ is a mere 0.09, then 48 independent runs are required to yield a success with a 99% probability. If $P(M, i)$ is 0.68, only four independent runs are required; if $P(M, i)$ is 0.78, then only three independent runs are required; and if $P(M, i)$ is 0.90, only two independent runs are required. Of course, if $P(M, i)$ is 0.99, only one run is required. The three values of $P(M, i)$ of 68% (i.e., about two-thirds), 78% (i.e., about three-quarters), and 90% are important thresholds since they are the smallest percentages of success for which only four, three, or two independent runs, respectively, will yield a success with a probability of $z = 99\%$.

8.1 EFFECT OF NUMBER OF GENERATIONS

As previously mentioned, the population size M and the maximum number G of generations to be run on any one run are the primary control parameters for genetic programming (as well as the conventional genetic algorithm).

For a fixed population size M, the cumulative probability $P(M, i)$ of satisfying the success predicate of a problem inevitably increases (or, at least, does not decrease) if a particular run is continued for additional generations. In principle, any point in the space of possible outcomes can eventually be

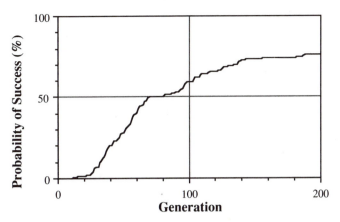

Figure 8.3 Cumulative probability of success $P(M, i)$ for the 6-multiplexer problem with a population size $M = 500$ for generations 0 through 200.

Table 8.1 Total number of individuals that must be processed by generations 25, 50, 100, 150, and 200 of the 6-multiplexer problem with a population size $M = 500$.

Generation number	Cumulative probability of success $P(M, i)$	Number of independent runs $R(z)$ required	Total number of individuals that must be processed $I(M, i, z)$
25	3%	171	2,223,000
50	28%	15	382,500
100	59%	6	303,000
150	73%	4	302,000
200	76%	4	402,000

reached by any genetic method if mutation is available and the run continues for a sufficiently large number of generations. However, there is a point after which the cost of extending a given run exceeds the benefit obtained from the increase in the cumulative probability of success $P(M, i)$.

Figure 8.3 shows, for the 6-multiplexer problem (subsection 7.4.3), a graph between generations 0 and 200 of the cumulative probability of success $P(M, i)$ that at least one S-expression in the population yields a success (i.e., the correct Boolean output for all 64 fitness cases). The graph is based on 150 runs of the problem for a population size of $M = 500$. The function set is $F_1 = \{\text{AND, OR, IF, NOT}\}$.

Table 8.1 shows the total number of individuals that must be processed in order to yield a solution to this problem with 99% probability by generation 25, 50, 100, 150, or 200. As will be seen, this table will show that there is a point after which the cost of extending a given run exceeds the benefit obtained from the increase in the cumulative probability of success $P(M, i)$.

Specifically, if this particular problem is run from generation 0 through generation 25 (i.e., a total of 26 generations) with a population size $M = 500$, the cumulative probability of success $P(M, i)$ is found by measurement to be about 3% (as shown in column 2 of row 1). Column 3 of row 1 shows that yielding a probability of $z = 99\%$ for solving this problem by generation 25 requires making $R(z) = 171$ independent runs (as shown in figure 8.2). Column 4 of row 1 shows that these 171 runs require processing of 2,223,000 individuals (i.e., 500 × 171 runs × 26 generations). Note that the number in column 4 is somewhat overstated because it is possible that more than one run may yield a solution and it is also possible that a solution may appear before generation 25. Nonetheless, processing 2,223,000 individuals will yield a solution with 99% probability by generation 25.

If this particular problem is run from generation 0 through generation 50, the cumulative probability of success $P(M, i)$ is found by measurement to be 28% (as shown in column 2 of row 2). Column 3 shows that yielding a probability of $z = 99\%$ for solving this problem requires making $R(z) = 15$ independent runs. Column 4 shows that these five runs require processing of 382,500 individuals (i.e., 500 × 15 runs × 51 generations).

Rows 3, 4, and 5 show that if the run is extended out to generation 100, 150, or 200, the cumulative probability of success $P(M, i)$ increases to 59%, 73%, or 76%, respectively. These higher values of $P(M, i)$ mean that only 6, 4, or 4 independent runs are sufficient to solve this problem with 99% probability. However, extending the run to generation 100, 150, and 200 requires processing 303,000, 302,000, and 402,000 individuals, respectively.

As can be seen, the cumulative probability of success is highest at generation 200; however, the computational effort required to yield a solution to this problem with 99% probability is higher at generation 200 than at at least three earlier generations (i.e., 50, 100, and 150) having lower values of $P(M, i)$.

Figure 8.4 contains two overlaid graphs which together show, by generation, the relationship between the choice of the number of generations to be run and the total *number of individuals that need be processed, $I(M, i, z)$,* in order to yield a solution to the 6-multiplexer problem with 99% probability for a

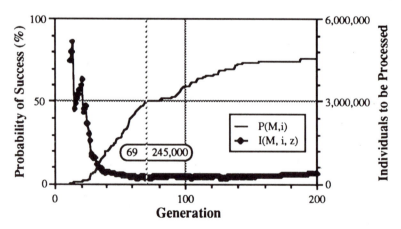

Figure 8.4 Performance curves for the 6-multiplexer problem with a population size $M = 500$ for generations 0 through 200.

population of size 500. The horizontal axis applies to both of these overlaid graphs and runs between 0 and 200 generations. The rising curve is the cumulative probability $P(M, i)$ of success and is scaled by the left vertical axis running between 0% and 100%. This rising curve is the same graph as in figure 8.3 and is based on the same 150 runs. The falling curve shows, by generation, the total number of individuals $I(M, i, z)$ that must be processed in order to solve the problem with $z = 99\%$ probability, and is scaled by the right vertical axis running between 0 and 6,000,000 individuals.

Until a nonzero cumulative probability $P(M, i)$ is achieved (as is the case at generation 12), the total number of individuals $I(M, i, z)$ that must be processed is undefined. If $P(M, i)$ had been measured over a sufficiently large number of runs or with a sufficiently large population, there would have been a small nonzero probability of solving the problem for every generation, including even generation 0 (representing probability of solving the problem by blind random search).

Only one of 150 runs was successful at solving the 6-multiplexer problem by generation 12, so the cumulative probability of success $P(M, i)$ was a mere 0.0067. With this low cumulative probability of success, $R(z) = 689$ independent runs are required to yield a solution to this problem by generation 12 with a 99% probability. This requires processing 4,478,500 individuals (500 × 13 generations × 689 runs).

Between generations 12 and 69 the $P(M, i)$ curve has a rather steep slope. The curve rises rapidly from generation to generation, causing the required number of independent runs $R(z)$ to drop rapidly from generation to generation. Meanwhile, the product of $M \times i$ increases only linearly from generation to generation. Thus, between generations 12 and 69 the total number of individuals that must be processed $I(M, i, z)$ drops steadily until it reaches a minimum. The minimum occurs at generation 69.

At generation 69 the cumulative probability of success is 49%, so the number of independent runs $R(z)$ is 7. Thus, processing only 245,000 individuals (i.e., 500 × 70 generations × 7 runs) is sufficient to yield a solution of this problem with a 99% probability. Generation 69 is highlighted with a light vertical line on figure 8.4. Both the generation number (i.e., 69) and the number of individuals that need to be processed (i.e., 245,000) are shown in the oval in the figure.

After generation 69, the increase in the cumulative probability of success $P(M, i)$ from 69% is slower from generation to generation. Consequently, the decrease in $R(z)$ occurs very slowly. It takes so many additional generations to increase $P(M, i)$ so that $R(z)$ can be reduced that there is a net increase, after generation 69, in the total number of individuals that must be processed in order to solve the problem with 99% probability. Between generations 69 and 92, the total amount of computation relentlessly increases by 500 individuals for each additional generation; however, $R(z)$ remains at 7. It is not until generation 93 that the cumulative probability of success $P(M, i)$ reaches 54%, thereby reducing the required number of independent runs $R(z)$ from 7 to 6. At generation 93, the number of individuals that must be processed $I(M, i, z)$ is

282,000 (i.e., 500 × 94 generations × 6 runs). This 282,500 is greater than the 245,000 individuals required by generation 69.

By generation 200, the probability of success $P(M, i)$ has reached 76% and the number of independent runs $R(z)$ has dropped to 4, so the number of individuals that must be processed is 402,000 (i.e., 500 × 201 generations × 4 runs). This 402,000 is considerably greater than the 245,000 individuals required by generation 69.

Note that increasing the number of generations beyond 69 definitely does increase the cumulative probability of success; however, the cost of this increased probability, as measured by the total amount of computation, outweighs the benefit. It is not that a particular run of genetic programming is incapable of solving the problem if it is continued for a sufficiently large number of generations. The point is that it is inefficient to continue a particular run for a large number of generations. The cost of solving the problem in genetic programming is minimized by making numerous shorter runs, rather than one long run.

Forty-two *performance curves* similar to figure 8.4 will appear throughout this book. Each such figure will contain two overlaid graphs showing, by generation, the probability of success, $P(M, i)$, and the number of individuals that must be processed $I(M, i, z)$. Each such figure will also contain an oval containing two numbers: the minimum number of individuals that must be processed to solve the problem with $z = 99\%$ probability for the stated choice of population size M and the generation number where the minimum is achieved. The minimum number of individuals that must be processed is an indication of the difficulty of the problem for the particular choice of population size M. Note that the sawtooth in the $I(M, i, z)$ curve peaking at generation 21 is an anomaly created because of the approximate nature of the values of the $P(M, i)$ curve.

8.2 ROLE OF POPULATION SIZE

The above discussion concerned only the choice of the number of generations to be run, given a population size M of 500. We now consider the choice of the population size M. Our experience is that a larger population size M increases the cumulative probability $P(M, i)$ of satisfying the success predicate of a problem for genetic programming. In the extreme case, if the population is large enough, a solution to the problem can be found at generation 0 by blind random search. However, there is a point after which the cost of a larger population (in terms of individuals to be processed) begins to exceed the benefit obtained from the increase in the cumulative probability of success $P(M, i)$. We proceed by considering the 6-multiplexer problem with a population size of 1,000, 2,000, and 4,000. To simplify the discussion, we do not employ over-selection here; however, we do revisit these same three population sizes with over-selection in section 25.6.

Figure 8.5 shows the performance curves for a population size of 1,000 (without over-selection) for the 6-multiplexer problem and with the function set $F_1 = \{$AND, OR, IF, NOT$\}$. The figure is based on 38 runs. The cumulative probability $P(M, i)$ of success is 50% at generation 48 and 53% at generation 50. The numbers 48 and 343,000 in the oval indicate that, if this problem is run through to generation 48, processing a total of 343,000 individuals (i.e., $1,000 \times 49$ generations $\times 7$ runs) is sufficient to yield a solution of this problem with 99% probability.

Figure 8.6 shows the performance curves for a population size of 2,000 (without over-selection) for the 6-multiplexer problem and with the function set $F_1 = \{$AND, OR, IF, NOT$\}$. The figure is based on 148 runs. The cumulative probability $P(M, i)$ of success is 91% at generation 50. The numbers 49 and 200,000 in the oval indicate that if this problem is run through to generation 49, processing a total of 200,000 individuals (i.e., $2,000 \times 50$ generations $\times$ 2 runs) is sufficient to yield a solution of this problem with 99% probability by generation 49.

The cumulative probability of success $P(M, i)$ at generation 49 is 91%. In contrast, just one generation earlier (i.e., at generation 48), $P(M, i)$ is 86%,

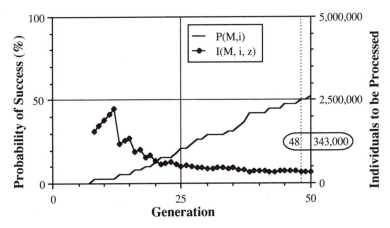

Figure 8.5 Performance curves for population size $M = 1,000$ for the 6-multiplexer problem.

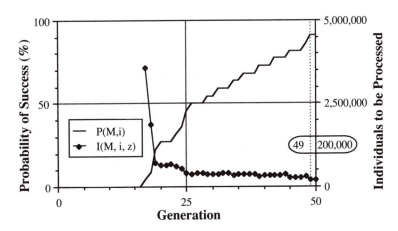

Figure 8.6 Performance curves for population size $M = 2,000$ for the 6-multiplexer problem.

Amount of Processing Required to Solve a Problem

so the number of independent runs $R(z)$ is 3 and 294,000 individuals (i.e., $2,000 \times 49$ generations $\times$ 3 runs) are required. That is, the slopes of the $P(M, i)$ curve and the $R(z)$ function are such that, as $P(M, i)$ rises past the threshold percentage of 89%, $R(z)$ drops from 3 to 2. Thus, by continuing the run for one additional generation, the total number of individuals that must be processed is cut by approximately one-third.

Figure 8.7 shows the performance curves for a population size of 4,000 (without over-selection) for the 6-multiplexer problem and with the function set $F_1 = \{\text{AND, OR, IF, NOT}\}$. The cumulative probability of success $P(M, i)$ at generation 39 is 100%. The figure is based on 15 runs. The numbers 39 and 160,000 in the oval indicate that if this problem is run through to generation 39, processing a total of 160,000 (i.e., $4,000 \times 40$ generations $\times$ 1 run) individuals is sufficient to yield a solution of this problem with 99% probability by generation 39.

In contrast, just one generation earlier (i.e., at generation 38), $P(M, i)$ is 93%, so the number of independent runs $R(z)$ is 2 and 312,000 individuals (i.e., $4,000 \times 39$ generations $\times$ 2 runs) are required. That is, the slopes of the $P(M, i)$ curve and the $R(z)$ function are such that, as $P(M, i)$ rises past 99%, $R(z)$ drops from 2 to 1. Thus, by continuing the run for one additional generation, the total number of individuals that must be processed is cut approximately in half.

In summary, a choice of population size of $M = 4,000$ yields a solution after processing only 160,000 individuals for the 6-multiplexer problem with the function set $F_1 = \{\text{AND, OR, IF, NOT}\}$. This total of 160,000 is better than the total of 245,000 required for a population size $M = 500$, the 343,000 for $M = 1,000$, and the 294,000 for $M = 2,000$.

Note that the size of the search space ($2^{64} \approx 10^{19}$) for the 6-multiplexer problem is very large in relation to the 160,000 individuals that need be processed using genetic programming for a population size of $M = 4,000$. Even if we used a less efficient population size, such as 500, 1,000, or 2,000,

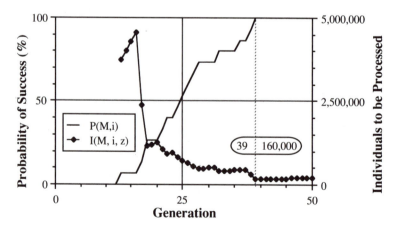

Figure 8.7 Performance curves for population size $M = 4,000$ for the 6-multiplexer problem.

the number of individuals that need be processed (i.e., between 245,000 and 343,000) is still very small in relation to the size of the search space.

All of the analysis in this chapter is, of course, retrospective. That is, we started by making numerous runs (successful and unsuccessful) of the problem in order to obtain the instantaneous probabilities of success $Y(M, i)$ by generation. We then computed the cumulative probabilities $P(M, i)$ of success by generation. We then used the cumulative probabilities to determine the number of independent runs R required to yield at least one successful run of the problem with a 99% probability. Finally, we computed the computational effort $I(M, i, z)$ required from the number of independent runs. Computational effort provides a basis for measuring the difficulty of solving a particular problem and a basis for comparing the relative difficulty of solving different problems. This retrospective analysis may be useful in planning future runs if one believes that some new problem is similar in difficulty to a problem for which the performance curves have already been established. In that event, the performance curves may provide some general guidance on the choice of the population size M and the maximum number G of generations to be run for the new problem. The guidance will be especially useful if one believes that the choice of the population size was optimal or near-optimal for the previous problem.

8.3 PERFORMANCE CURVES

All of the above statistics, of course, depend strongly on the particular problem being solved. Accordingly, performance curves for the cart centering, artificial ant, and simple symbolic regression problems from chapter 7 will now be presented.

8.3.1 Cart Centering

Figure 8.8 shows, for a population size M of 500 and for generations 0 through 50, the performance curves showing $P(M, i)$ and $I(M, i, z)$ for the cart centering problem (section 7.1). The graph is based on 18 runs. $P(M, i)$ is the cumulative probability that, by generation i, at least one individual control strategy in the population causes the cart to come to rest and become centered (within the allowed amount of time). For example, 11 of the 18 runs are successful by generation 23, so the cumulative probability of success $P(500, 23)$ is 61%, whereas 15 of the 18 runs are successful by generation 50, so the cumulative probability of success $P(500, 50)$ is 83%. The numbers 13 and 35,000 in the oval indicate that if this problem is run through to generation 13, processing a total of $I(M, i, z) = I(500, 13, 0.99) = 35,000$ individuals (i.e., 500×14 generations $\times 5$ runs) is sufficient to yield a solution of this problem with 99% probability.

Note that this performance curve could, as an alternative, have been made on the basis of a control strategy causing the cart to come to rest and become centered within an amount of time that is within, say, 5% of the known optimal time.

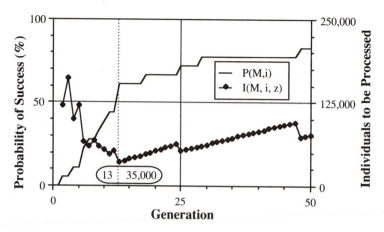

Figure 8.8 Performance curves for the cart centering problem.

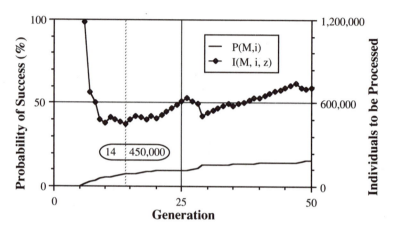

Figure 8.9 Performance curves for population size $M = 500$ for the artificial ant problem with the Santa Fe trail.

8.3.2 Artificial Ant

Figure 8.9 shows, for generations 0 through 50, the performance curves showing $P(M, i)$ and $I(M, i, z)$ for the artificial ant problem for the Santa Fe trail (section 7.2). The graph is based on 148 runs and a population size of 500. $P(M, i)$ is the cumulative probability that by generation i at least one computer program in the population causes the ant to collect all 89 pieces of food along the Santa Fe trail within the allowed time (i.e., scores 89 hits). For example, the cumulative probability of success $P(500, 14)$ is 7%, whereas the cumulative probability of success $P(500, 50)$ is 16%. The numbers 14 and 450,000 in the oval indicate that if this problem is run through to generation 14, processing a total of $I(M, i, z) = I(500, 14, 0.99) = 450,000$ individuals (i.e., 500×15 generations $\times 60$ runs) is sufficient to yield a solution of this problem with 99% probability by generation 14.

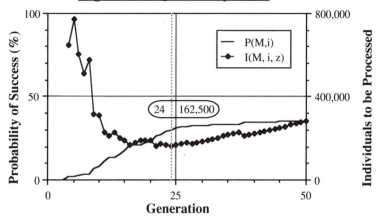

Figure 8.10 Performance curves for population size $M = 500$ for the simple symbolic regression problem.

8.3.3 Simple Symbolic Regression

Figure 8.10 shows, for a population size M of 500 and for generations 0 through 50, the performance curves showing $P(M, i)$ and $I(M, i, z)$ for the simple symbolic regression problem with $x^4 + x^3 + x^2 + x$ as the target curve (section 7.3). The graph is based on 113 runs. The cumulative probability that by generation i at least one individual mathematical expression in the population comes within 0.01 of the target function for all 20 fitness cases (i.e., scores 20 hits) is given by $P(M, i)$. For example, the cumulative probability of success $P(M, i)$ by generation 24 is 30%, whereas the cumulative probability of success $P(M, i)$ by generation 50 is 35%. The numbers 24 and 162,500 in the oval indicate that if this problem is run through to generation 24, processing a total of 162,500 individuals (i.e., 500 × 25 generations × 13 runs) is sufficient to yield a solution of this problem with 99% probability.

9   Nonrandomness of Genetic Programming

This chapter discusses the question of whether the results produced by genetic programming might be the fruits of blind random search. It provides several different arguments and partial evidence to support a negative answer to this question.

As will be seen, comparing the performance of genetic programming and blind random search is far more difficult than it appears. The difficulty arises, in part, when one tries to numerically evaluate what the deceptively simple phrase "random search" means when applied to the space of possible computer programs.

The solution to the typical problem described in this book is usually only one isolated point (or, at most, a relatively small number of points) in an enormous space of possibilities. Both the size of the search space of the problem and the size of the space of possible computer programs that can be composed using the available terminals and functions are enormous. Both of these spaces are much larger than the mere 10^4 or 10^5 individuals processed in a typical single run of genetic programming described in this book. In addition, both of these spaces are much larger than the mere 10^5 or 10^6 individuals that must be processed to yield a solution with a 99% probability over multiple independent runs (calculated in the manner described in chapter 8).

The number of different computer programs (i.e., LISP S-expressions) that may be created from a set of available functions and a set of available terminals is, of course, the same as the number of possible compositions of the available functions and terminals. This number, in turn, is the same as the number of rooted, point-labeled trees with ordered branches where the internal points of the trees are labeled with functions from the function set and the external points of the tree (leaves) are labeled with terminals from the terminal set. The number of such trees increases surprisingly rapidly as a function of the number of points in the tree. This growth is so rapid because the number of such trees is the product of three factors, each of which increases with the number of points in the tree. These three factors are the substantial number of different tree structures, the enormous number of permutations in labeling the internal and external points of a particular tree structure with the available functions and terminals, and the number of ways of designating one of the internal points of a particular tree structure as the root.

The fact that we do not encounter solutions to the problems described in this book on the initial random generation reinforces the vastness of the search spaces involved. For most of the problems described in this book, I explicitly present the fitness level of the initial random generation and provide at least one example of a randomly created individual. I intentionally include this discussion to focus the reader's attention on what constitutes random performance for the problem involved. The typical randomly created individual and even the best-of-generation individual from generation 0 is consistently highly unfit. We have observed the manifest unfitness of randomly created individuals in the dozens, hundreds, and sometimes thousands of runs that we have made of each problem. In addition, we have explicitly tested between 100,000 and 20,000,000 additional initial random individuals for most of the problems described in this book. With the obvious exception of certain designated trivial problems (some of which appear later in this chapter for analytic purposes), we have never encountered a solution to any problem in our tests involving these additional 100,000 and 20,000,000 initial random individuals.

The fact that we do not solve a problem on generation 0, but do solve the problem before generation 50 on a high percentage of the runs, alone suggests that genetic programming is not a blind random search.

The above arguments alone are sufficient to strongly suggest that the success of genetic programming in solving the wide variety of problems described in this book is not the fruit of blind random search.

While the solution to a given problem may be only one isolated point (or a relatively small region) in a very large search space, there is nonetheless an arguable possibility that the probability of solving a problem with blind random search might be significantly higher in the space of randomly generated compositions of functions and terminals than the probability of finding a solution point in the original search space of the problem. In other words, there might be something about the space of compositions of functions and terminals that facilitates the discovery of solutions to problems. If this facilitation were slight, it would be, of course, a very good reason to consider problems in terms of the space of compositions of functions and terminals. However, if this facilitation were great enough, it might mean that the solutions being found were really just the results of random search.

There is no *a priori* reason to believe that compositions of functions and terminals that solve the problems described in this book are denser in the space of randomly generated compositions of functions than solutions to the problem in the original search space of the problem.

To make the discussion specific, consider the problem of finding the LISP S-expression for the Boolean 11-multiplexer function (subsection 7.4.1). The probability of randomly choosing zeros and ones for the 2^{11} rows of a truth table for a particular Boolean function of 11 Boolean arguments is 1 in $2^{2^{11}}$. Specifically, the Boolean 11-multiplexer function is a unique function out of the $2^{2^{11}} = 2^{2048} \approx 10^{616}$ possible Boolean functions of 11 arguments and one

Boolean output. The solution to the Boolean multiplexer problem is the one and only point in an enormous search space of size 2^{2048} that solves the problem. The size of the search space (10^{616}) for the 11-multiplexer problem is very large in relation to the number of individuals involved in the one run of genetic programming described in subsection 7.4.1 (i.e., only 4,000 × 10 generations = 40,000).

We want to explore the possibility that the probability of generating a random composition of the Boolean functions AND, OR, NOT, and IF that realizes the 11-multiplexer function is significantly better than 1 in 2^{2048}.

To test against this possibility, we performed a control experiment for the Boolean 11-multiplexer problem consisting of a blind random search. In particular, we generated 5,000,000 random S-expressions to check if we could randomly generate a composition of functions and terminals that realized the 11-multiplexer function. Five million is 125 times the 40,000 individuals in the one run of genetic programming described in subsection 7.4.1. For this control experiment, we used the same algorithm and parameters used to generate the initial random population in the normal runs of the problem. No 100%-correct individual was found in this blind random search.

In addition, on the first 1,000,000 of these 5,000,000 random S-expressions, we computed an entire hits histogram of raw fitness values. The best-of-generation score in this histogram involving 1,000,000 individuals was only 1,408 hits (out of a possible 2,048) and the low score was 704 hits. Moreover, only ten individuals achieved this best score of 1,408. The mode (i.e., high point) of the hits histogram came at 1,152 hits; the second-highest point came at 896 hits; and the third-highest point came at 1,024 hits. In other words, not only was no 100%-correct solution found, but nothing even close to an individual scoring 2,048 hits was found. Instead, the number of hits clustered around the 50% level (i.e., 1024), as one would expect.

We performed a similar control experiment for the Boolean 6-multiplexer problem involving 10,000,000 randomly generated individual S-expressions. Ten million is about 62 times the 160,000 individuals that must be processed in order to yield a solution to the 6-multiplexer problem with 99% probability with a population size of 4,000 as shown in figure 8.8. The search space for the Boolean 6-multiplexer problem is of size $2^{2^6} = 2^{64} \approx 10^{19}$. As before, no 100%-correct individual was found in this blind random search. In fact, no individual had more than 52 (of 64 possible) hits. The size of the search space for the 6-multiplexer (i.e., 10^{19}) is very large in relation to the 160,000 individuals that need to be processed in order to solve the 6-multiplexer problem with 99% probability.

In this section, we will conclude that solutions to these problems are not denser in the space of randomly generated compositions of functions and terminals than solutions in the original search space of the problem. Therefore, we will conclude that the results are not the fruits of a blind random search.

As a matter of fact, we have evidence from simpler Boolean problem domains suggesting that the solutions to nontrivial problems of Boolean function learning are appreciably sparser in the space of randomly generated compositions of functions and terminals than solutions in the original search space of the problem. This evidence comes from the domains of Boolean functions with two arguments and Boolean functions with three arguments, where it is possible to perform certain exhaustive comparative experiments.

Consider first the domain of Boolean functions with two Boolean arguments and one Boolean output. There are only $2^{2^2} = 2^4 = 16$ possible Boolean functions with two Boolean arguments and one Boolean output. Thus, in the search space of truth tables for Boolean functions, the probability of randomly choosing T's and NIL's for the four rows of a truth table that realizes this particular Boolean function is only 1 in 16. Fourteen of these 16 functions involving only two arguments are very simple. Let us therefore focus on one of the two remaining functions, namely the odd-2-parity-function with two Boolean arguments (i.e., the exclusive-or function). The odd-k-parity function of k Boolean arguments returns T (True) if the number of non-NIL arguments is odd and returns NIL (False) otherwise.

As one experiment involving Boolean functions of two arguments, we generated 100,000 random individuals using a function set consisting of the three Boolean functions

```
F = {AND, OR, NOT}.
```

If randomly generated compositions of the basic Boolean functions that realize the exclusive-or function were as dense as solutions are in the original search space of the problem (i.e., the space of truth tables for Boolean functions of two arguments), we would expect about 6,250 in 100,000 (i.e., 1 in 16) random compositions of functions to realize the exclusive-or function. Instead, we found that only 110 out of 100,000 randomly generated compositions realized the exclusive-or function. This is a frequency of only 1 in 909. In other words, randomly generated compositions of functions realizing the exclusive-or function are about 57 times sparser than solutions in the original search space of truth tables for Boolean functions.

As a second experiment involving Boolean functions of two arguments, we changed the function set to

```
F = {AND, OR, NOT, IF}
```

and generated an additional 100,000 random individuals using this function set. We found that only 116 out of 100,000 randomly generated compositions realized the exclusive-or function (i.e., a frequency of 1 in 862). That is, with this second function set, randomly generated compositions of functions realizing the exclusive-or function are still about 54 times sparser than solutions in the original search space of truth tables for Boolean functions.

As a third experiment involving Boolean functions of two arguments, we changed the function set to

```
F = {AND, OR, NAND, NOR}
```

and generated an additional 100,000 random individuals using this function set. We found that only 118 out of 100,000 randomly generated compositions realized the exclusive-or function (i.e., a frequency of 1 in 846). That is, with this third function set, randomly generated compositions of functions realizing the exclusive-or function are about 53 times sparser than solutions in the original search space of truth tables for Boolean functions.

As can be seen, the choice of the function set has only a minor effect on this observation.

Thus, solutions to the odd parity (exclusive-or) function with two arguments appear to be 53, 54, or 57 times sparser in the space of randomly generated compositions of functions than solutions in the original search space of the problem.

We then considered the domain of Boolean functions with three arguments. There are only $2^{2^3} = 2^8 = 256$ Boolean functions with three Boolean arguments and one output. The probability of randomly choosing a particular combination of T (True) and NIL (False) values for the eight rows of a truth table is 1 in 256.

We then performed similar experiments on two Boolean functions with three Boolean arguments and one Boolean output, namely the odd-3-parity function and the 3-multiplexer function (commonly called the "If-Then-Else" function). We performed these experiments on 10,000,000 individuals. If the probability that a randomly generated composition of functions and terminals realizes a particular Boolean function with three arguments equaled 1 in 256, we would expect about 39,063 random compositions per 10,000,000 to realize that particular Boolean function.

After randomly generating 10,000,000 compositions of the functions AND, OR, and NOT, we found only 730 3-multiplexers and no odd-3-parity functions. That is, these randomly generated compositions of functions and terminals realizing the 3-multiplexer function are about 54 times sparser than solutions in the original search space of Boolean functions. We cannot make the numerical comparison for the odd-3-parity function, because we did not find even one after 10,000,000 tries; but this probability is probably hundreds of thousands of times scarcer than one in 256.

In summary, as to these Boolean functions, compositions of functions and terminals realizing these functions are substantially *less dense* than solutions are in the search space of the original problem (i.e., the truth table).

9.1 BOOLEAN FUNCTIONS WITH THREE ARGUMENTS

The above discussion about the nonrandomness of the results obtained from genetic programming is, of course, far from complete. In particular, it involved only comparisons among a few functions. Moreover, the comparisons used a yardstick based on the same random method of creation of individual S-expressions as used by genetic programming itself. The method of random creation used by genetic programming is reasonable, but it is not the only possible method. Moreover, the method used by genetic programming is not necessarily an ideal yardstick against which to measure the performance of genetic programming.

The purposes of this section are to offer a yardstick for this comparison which is not so closely tied to genetic programming itself and to expand the comparison to cover 100% of the functions in two particular classes of functions. The goal will be to compare the number of individuals that must be processed by genetic programming to the number of individuals that must be processed in a specified blind random search. We will first focus on the functions of three Boolean arguments and one Boolean output, because the total number of such functions is small enough to permit exhaustive examination with the available computational resources. We then repeat the process for the functions of two Boolean arguments.

We will reach the following conclusions for both classes of functions:

- Genetic programming can produce a solution for 100% of the functions in the class of functions.

- Genetic programming finds a solution after processing fewer individuals than a blind random search, except for the degenerate functions and manifestly simple functions in the class of functions under consideration. For these degenerate functions and these simple functions, genetic programming finds a solution after processing the same number of individuals or slightly more individuals (owing to its overhead) than a blind random search.

- The advantage of genetic programming over blind random search generally increases as the functions become *more complex*. In other words, genetic programming does better on the harder functions of each class.

We first consider the Boolean functions with three arguments.

A function with three Boolean arguments and one Boolean output is uniquely specified by the value of the function (T or NIL) for each of the $2^3 = 8$ possible combinations of its three Boolean arguments (D2, D1, and D0).

Table 9.1 is the truth table giving the value of one particular Boolean function for each of the $2^3 = 8$ possible combinations of its three arguments. This particular function (which one might call "Exactly Two Off") is T (1 or

Table 9.1 Truth table for Boolean function of three arguments known as "Rule 022" or "Exactly Two Off."

	D2	D1	D0	**Rule 022**
0	NIL	NIL	NIL	NIL
1	NIL	NIL	T	T
2	NIL	T	NIL	T
3	NIL	T	T	NIL
4	T	NIL	NIL	T
5	T	NIL	T	NIL
6	T	T	NIL	NIL
7	T	T	T	NIL

True) if exactly two of its arguments are NIL (0 or False) and NIL otherwise. If we think of the binary values of this function in the eight rows of this truth table as the bits of an 8-bit binary number, reading from the bottom up (i.e., 00010110), the decimal equivalent of this 8-bit binary number is 22. This particular Boolean function is called "rule 022" using the numbering scheme used by Wolfram (1986) for naming the Boolean functions in connection with three arguments associated with one-dimensional cellular automata. If we call the high-order bit of this 8-bit binary number "bit 7," then bit 7 is the value appearing in row 7 of the table. Moreover, the 0 in bit 7 of this 8-bit binary representation of 22 is the value of the Boolean function if its three arguments are the binary equivalent of decimal 7 (i.e., D2 = 1, D1 = 1, and D0 = 1). Similarly, the 0 in bit 6 of this 8-bit binary representation of 22 is the value of the Boolean function if its three arguments are the binary equivalent of decimal 6 (i.e., D2 = 1, D1 = 1, and D0 = 0).

Since each of the eight positions in the last column of this truth table can be either NIL or T, there are $2^{2^3} = 2^8 = 256$ different Boolean functions with three Boolean arguments and one output. They range from rule 000 (whose truth table consists of eight NIL's) to rule 255 (whose truth table consists of eight T's).

If we were to fill in each of the eight values (T or NIL) for the eight positions in this truth table independently and randomly with probability $\frac{1}{2}$ for NIL and $\frac{1}{2}$ for T, then the probability of creating a particular Boolean function in this manner would be $\frac{1}{256}$. If we were searching the space of Boolean functions at random by randomly filling in the eight positions in the truth table, then each of the 256 Boolean functions would be have an equal probability of $\frac{1}{256}$ of being discovered.

A perfect yardstick for comparing performance of genetic programming to random search would be to select a sufficiently large sample of random S-expressions so that we could get a statistically meaningful probability of finding an S-expression at random that solves the problem.

The process of selecting a composition of the available functions and available terminals (i.e., a LISP S-expression) at random from the space of all possible compositions presents greater difficulties than would first appear. This space is, of course, infinite. We can overcome the infiniteness of the space by partitioning the space according to some parameter (e.g., number of internal or external points in the S-expression, maximum depth of the S-expression, etc). More specifically, suppose we partition the space of S-expressions according to the number of internal points. Then, for a given number of internal points (say 20), we would like to have both (1) an enumerative count on the total number of S-expressions of 20 points and (2) a constructive algorithm for generating just a particular single designated S-expression out of the total set of S-expressions. The emphasis here is on a "single designated" S-expression since we want to be able to generate this one S-expression without having to generate an enormous number of unwanted S-expressions along the way (as would be the case with a simple recursive generating program). If we had this enumerative count and this constructive algorithm, we could then select a random number between 1 and the total count and then (ignoring commutativity) generate the single designated S-expression at random from the total set of S-expressions.

We would then repeat this procedure for many values other than 20 of the partitioning parameter (i.e., number of internal points). In particular, we would repeat this procedure for values of the parameter from 1 to some large number. For each value of the parameter, we would then select a sufficiently large sample of random S-expressions so that we could get a statistically meaningful probability of finding an S-expression at random that solves the problem. If that probability stabilized (or, preferably, tended to a single limit as the value of the parameter increased from 1 toward infinity), we would have the probability of solving the problem via random search. We could then compare that probability with the ratio of the number of times genetic programming (run with certain values for its major and minor parameters) produced a solution after processing a given number of individuals. If this ratio (i.e., probability that genetic programming produces a solution) were greater than the probability of solving the problem via random search, then we would have shown that genetic programming is performing better than random search.

Unfortunately, the reality is that we do not know of either an enumerative count or a constructive algorithm for the LISP S-expressions in general. See Chaitin 1987. We cannot, therefore, perform the above experiment. Moreover, even if we could, the computational time needed to find the desired stabilized probability would be enormous.

We can, however, perform a restricted version of the above experiment. There are three main restrictions.

First, we can develop both an enumerative count and a constructive algorithm for the LISP S-expressions if we limit ourselves to functions in the function set that take an equal number of arguments. This produces trees with sufficient symmetry to allow us to find both the desired enumerative count and the desired constructive algorithm.

Second, if we fix the number of internal points to some reasonable number (e.g., 20) and are willing to accept a limited comparison of the effect of the choice of the number of internal points with a few other nearby numbers (e.g., 10, 15, and 25), we can address the question of stability of the probabilities within a reasonable amount of computer time.

Third, if we limit ourselves to the Boolean functions of three (or two) arguments, the total number of different functions is sufficiently small that we can exhaustively study 100% of the functions and perform statistically valid experiments involving multiple runs of each function (including the most difficult functions with a given number of arguments). Since there are $2^{2^4} = 2^{16} = 65,536$ different Boolean functions with four Boolean inputs and one output, we do not expect to be able to expand these experiments to cover 100% of the four argument functions. The limitation to three arguments means that all of the functions can be discovered using a blind random process of filling in the rows of the truth table with the value of the Boolean function. That is, the truth table for a given Boolean function with three arguments can be discovered at random with a probability of only 1 in 256. For most of the 256 possible Boolean functions of three arguments, a rate of 1 in 256 is considerably better performance than we will see by generating S-expressions at random. Of course, the method of randomly filling in the truth table will not work in any reasonable amount of time for even a slightly larger number of arguments. For example, the truth table for any particular six-argument Boolean function with one output (e.g., the 6-multiplexer) is one of $2^{2^6} = 2^{64} \approx 10^{19}$ possible truth tables. In contrast, genetic programming learns the 6-multiplexer problem with 99% probability after processing only 160,000, 245,000, 294,000 or 393,000 individuals (depending on the population size).

The function set

F_1 = {AND, OR, NOT}

is unsuitable, because the AND and OR functions take two arguments each while the NOT function takes only one argument. However, the function set

F_2 = {AND, OR, NAND, NOR}

is suitable, because each of these four functions take two arguments and because F_2 is computationally complete (as is F_1).

Suppose we randomly create compositions of these four diadic functions and terminals from the terminal set

T = {D2, D1, D0}

containing exactly 20 internal points. This implies that there are 41 points altogether in each tree.

We now illustrate the process of selecting an S-expression at random. There are 6,564,120,420 unlabeled trees having 21 external points, 20 internal points (i.e., the root and 19 other internal points) with one internal point having two lines connected to it, and 19 internal points with three lines connected to it.

Each of these unlabeled trees can then be labeled in one of $3^{21}4^{19}4^1 = 11,501,279,977,342,425,366,528$ different ways with one of the four diadic functions from the function set F_2 above and one of the three terminals from the terminal set T above.

In total, there are 75,495,786,755,410,551,680,752,429,301,760 (i.e., about 7.55×10^{31}) possible trees of this type (i.e., S-expressions).

Given an integer between 1 and this total number of trees, we can algorithmically construct any desired tree directly from its number (without having to generate its predecessors). Suppose we select that integer at random using a uniform probability distribution, say, the integer 40,961,048,323,394,175,800,693,951,046,016. The constructive algorithm allows us to construct the particular S-expression (i.e., composition of 20 diadic functions from F_2 and 21 terminals from T) corresponding to this integer (without having to generate its predecessors). It is as follows:

```
(NOR (NAND (OR D2 (AND D2 D2)) D1)
    (OR (AND D2 D0)
        (NOR (NAND D0 (OR (NOR D0 (NOR D0 D0)) D2))
            (NOR D0
            (NAND D2
             (NOR (OR (NAND D1 (NOR (OR D1 D2)
                                        (AND D2 D1)))
                     D2)
             (AND D1 D1)))))))).
```

Figure 9.1 graphically depicts this S-expression as a rooted, point-labeled tree with ordered branches. As we would expect of a tree whose size, shape, and labeling are randomly selected, its appearance is irregular. Of course, whenever this constructive process is used, the result must always be equivalent to one of the 256 possible Boolean functions of three arguments. This particular S-expression is functionally equivalent to rule 64 (01000000 in binary), which corresponds to

```
(AND D2 D1 (NOT D0)).
```

There are, of course, numerous other compositions of functions and terminals that are also functionally equivalent to the rule 64.

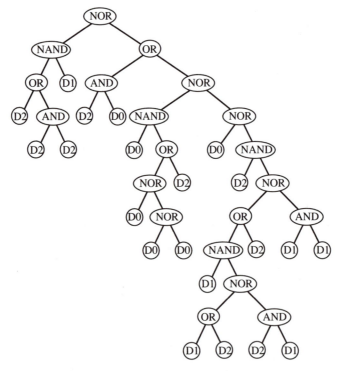

Figure 9.1 Illustrative tree with 20 internal points and 21 external points consisting of the functions AND, OR, NAND, and NOR and the terminals D2, D1, and D0.

In order to conduct the restricted experiment described above, we generated 10,000,000 random integers, each between 1 and 75,495,786,755,410,551,680,752,429,301,760. For each of the resulting 10,000,000 selected integers, we constructed the corresponding rooted, point-labeled tree with ordered branches for that integer. Each such tree had 20 internal points (labeled with the functions AND, OR, NAND, NOR) and 21 external points (labeled with the terminals D2, D1, and D0). We then constructed the truth table for each such tree and then classified the tree according to its rule number (which was, of course, always between 000 and 255). The result was a histogram showing the frequency of each of the 256 possible Boolean functions of three arguments and one output. As one would expect, some rules were more frequent than others.

In addition to the frequencies of the 256 rules, there are symmetries among the 256 rules that should be considered. For example, rule 247 (11110111 in binary) might be called "Not Three" because it returns T unless the three inputs D2, D1, and D0 are precisely the binary representation of three (i.e., 0, 1, and 1, respectively). Rule 247 can be written as

(NOT (AND (NOT D2) D1 D0).

There are two rules that are closely related to rule 247. Rule 223 (11011111 in binary) might be called "Not Five" and can be written

(NOT (AND D2 (NOT D1) D0)).

Rule 191 (10111111 in binary) might be called "Not Six" and can be written

(NOT (AND D2 D1 (NOT D0))).

These three distinct rules are related in that their structures are equivalent for our purposes here. The common structure consists of a NOT function at the root and a triadic AND function at the next level. Exactly two of the arguments to the AND function are differing terminals. The third argument to the AND function is a NOT function operating on the remaining terminal. If we consider the six permutations (mappings) of the terminals D2, D1, and D0, a total of six rules can be obtained by starting from any one rule. However, if we start with a rule such as rule 247, only three of these six mappings are functionally different for our purposes here, because of the commutativity of the functions in the function set. The three different rules (i.e., rules 247, 223, and 191) form a group of three related rules. These rules have the same tree structure. They are equally difficult to obtain in this random generation process.

In addition, there are groups of rules of size 6 and size 1. For example, if one considers the six permutations of the terminals for rule 105 (the even-3-parity function), one gets the same rule. Rule 105 is not related to any other rule and stands alone in a group of size 1. Similarly, rule 150 (the odd-3-parity function) is alone in a group of size 1.

If we partition the 256 Boolean rules according to this equivalence relation, we find that there are 80 such equivalence classes. Thus, we need not consider the 256 seemingly different Boolean rules, but can focus on the 80 equivalence classes (each of which will be represented by one of its member rules).

Table 9.2 The 80 equivalence classes of Boolean functions with three arguments

	Rule	Equivalent rules
1	**000**	**None**
2	255	None
4	085	015, 051
5	240	170, 204
6	119	063, 095
3	192	160, 136
7	017	003, 005
8	252	238, 250
9	001	None
10	128	None
11	127	None
12	245	175, 187, 207, 221, 243
13	254	None
14	080	010, 012, 034, 048, 068
15	016	002, 004
16	253	239, 251
17	064	008, 032
18	**247**	**191, 223**
19	200	168, 224
20	087	031, 055
21	021	007, 019
22	236	234, 248
23	213	143, 179
24	205	171, 241
25	084	014, 050
26	112	042, 076
27	081	011, 013, 035, 049, 069
28	117	047, 059, 079, 093, 115
29	244	174, 186, 206, 220, 242
30	162	138, 140, 176, 196, 208
31	**058**	**046, 078, 092, 114, 116**
32	197	139, 141, 163, 177, 209
33	053	027, 029, 039, 071, 083
34	216	172, 184, 202, 226, 228
35	023	None
36	**232**	**None**
37	102	060, 090
38	153	165, 195
39	020	006, 018
40	235	237, 249
41	159	183, 215
42	096	040, 072
43	009	033, 065
44	212	142, 178
45	193	137, 161
46	190	222, 246
47	077	043, 113

	Rule	Equivalent rules
48	111	123, 125
49	144	130, 132
50	122	110, 124
51	133	131, 145
52	118	062, 094
53	164	152, 194
54	067	025, 037
55	091	061, 103
56	230	188, 218
57	229	173, 185, 203, 217, 227
58	098	044, 056, 074, 088, 100
59	026	028, 038, 052, 070, 082
60	157	155, 167, 181, 199, 211
61	126	None
62	129	None
63	189	219, 231
64	024	036, 066
65	149	135, 147
66	030	054, 086
67	106	108, 120
68	169	201, 225
69	101	045, 057, 075, 089, 099
70	154	56, 166, 180, 198, 210
71	022	None
72	233	None
73	**104**	**None**
74	151	None
75	146	134, 148
76	**097**	**041, 073**
77	107	109, 121
78	158	182, 214
79	**150**	**None**
80	**105**	**None**

Table 9.2 shows the 80 equivalence classes. Column 2 of this table shows a representative of the equivalence class. Column 3 shows the five, two, or zero rules that are equivalent to the representative rule. The equivalence classes are presented in this table in what will prove to be the order of difficulty in generating them in a random search. Eight of the 80 rules will be referred to later; these are set in bold face type.

Table 9.3 reports on the difficulty of blind random search for the 80 representative rules of the Boolean functions with three arguments.

Column 2 of this table gives the rule number (from decimal number 000 to 255).

Table 9.3 Processing required by blind random search for the equivalence classes 1 through 80 of Boolean rules with three arguments.

	Rule	Truth table	Number of successes	Expected number	Log	$I(M, i, z)$
1	**000**	**00000000**	**1478478**	**6.76**	**0.83**	29
2	255	11111111	1478086	6.76	0.83	29
3	085	01010101	318217	31.4	1.50	143
4	240	11110000	314173	31.8	1.50	145
5	119	01110111	119067	84.0	1.92	385
6	192	11000000	117560	85.1	1.93	390
7	017	00010001	117411	85.2	1.93	390
8	252	11111100	116563	85.8	1.93	393
9	001	00000001	94999	105.3	2.02	483
10	128	10000000	94964	105.3	2.02	483
11	127	01111111	94914	105.4	2.02	483
12	245	11110101	94814	105.5	2.02	484
13	254	11111110	94485	105.8	2.03	486
14	080	01010000	93897	106.5	2.03	489
15	016	00010000	78269	127.8	2.11	587
16	253	11111101	77875	128.4	2.11	590
17	064	01000000	77488	129.1	2.11	593
18	**247**	**11110111**	**77264**	**129.4**	**2.11**	**594**
19	200	11001000	27360	365.5	2.56	1681
20	087	01010111	27184	367.9	2.57	1692
21	021	00010101	27116	368.8	2.57	1697
22	236	11101100	26996	370.4	2.57	1704
23	213	11010101	25179	397.2	2.60	1827
24	205	11001101	24533	407.6	2.61	1875
25	084	01010100	24512	408.0	2.61	1877
26	112	01110000	24267	412.1	2.62	1896
27	081	01010001	19709	507.4	2.71	2335
28	117	01110101	19667	508.5	2.71	2340
29	244	11110100	19615	509.8	2.71	2346
30	162	10100010	19543	511.7	2.71	2355
31	**058**	**00111010**	**3144**	**3180.7**	**3.50**	**14646**
32	197	11000101	3136	3188.8	3.50	14683
33	053	00110101	2947	3393.3	3.53	15625
34	216	11011000	2933	3409.5	3.53	15699
35	023	00010111	2469	4050.2	3.61	18650
36	**232**	**11101000**	**2443**	**4093.3**	**3.61**	**18849**
37	102	01100110	2253	4438.5	3.65	20438
38	153	10011001	2201	4543.4	3.66	20921
39	020	00010100	1887	5299.4	3.72	24403
40	235	11101011	1882	5313.5	3.73	24468
41	159	10011111	1878	5324.8	3.73	24520
42	096	01100000	1846	5417.1	3.73	24945
43	009	00001001	1558	6418.5	3.81	29556
44	212	11010100	1375	7272.7	3.86	33490
45	193	11000001	1364	7331.4	3.87	33760

	Rule	Truth table	Number of successes	Expected number	Log	$I(M, i, z)$
46	190	10111110	1331	7513.1	3.88	34598
47	077	01001101	1303	7674.6	3.89	35341
48	111	01101111	1301	7686.4	3.89	35395
49	144	10010000	1296	7716.0	3.89	35532
50	122	01111010	1272	7861.6	3.90	36202
51	133	10000101	1240	8064.5	3.91	37137
52	118	01110110	1217	8216.9	3.92	37839
53	164	10100100	1014	9861.9	3.99	45414
54	067	01000011	947	10559.7	4.02	48627
55	091	01011011	94	10570.8	4.02	48679
56	230	11100110	939	10649.6	4.03	49042
57	229	11100101	881	11350.7	4.06	52270
58	098	01100010	852	11737.1	4.07	54049
59	026	00011010	834	11990.4	4.08	55216
60	157	10011101	830	12048.2	4.08	55482
61	126	01111110	619	16155.1	4.21	74395
62	129	10000001	585	17094.0	4.23	78719
63	189	10111101	495	20202.0	4.31	93032
64	024	00011000	491	20366.6	4.31	93790
65	149	10010101	282	35461.0	4.55	163302
66	030	01111000	281	35587.2	4.55	163883
67	106	01101010	244	40983.6	4.61	188735
68	169	10010101	233	42918.5	4.63	197645
69	101	01100101	161	62111.8	4.79	286034
70	154	10011010	119	84033.6	4.92	386987
71	022	00010110	52	192307.7	5.28	885608
72	233	11101001	48	208333.3	5.32	959409
73	**104**	**01101000**	**35**	**285714.3**	**5.46**	**1315761**
74	151	10010111	31	322580.6	5.51	1485537
75	146	10010010	24	416666.7	5.62	1918819
76	**097**	**01100001**	**22**	**454545.5**	**5.66**	**2093257**
77	107	01101011	16	625000.0	5.80	2878230
78	158	10011110	13	769230.8	5.89	3542437
79	**150**	**10010110**	**2**	**5000000.0**	**6.70**	**23025849**
80	**105**	**01101001**	**0**	**NA**	**NA**	**NA**

Column 3 gives the eight-bit binary equivalence for the decimal number in column 2 and, as previously explained, shows the bit values of the Boolean function.

Column 4 shows the number of solution individuals found in the random search out of 10,000,000.

Column 5 is the *expected number* (i.e., average) of individuals that must be processed in order to find a solution individual. That is, column 5 is 10,000,000 divided by column 4. The reciprocal of column 5 (which is not shown in the table) is the probability of finding the Boolean function in a blind random search.

Column 6 is the logarithm of column 5.

Column 7 is not used in this chapter, but is provided to permit comparison with the results in chapter 8. Column 7 contains the number of individuals that must be processed in order to find a solution individual with 99% probability (computed in the manner described in chapter 8). In other words, we envision runs using a population size $M = 1$ and number of generations to be run $G = 1$ (i.e., the run consists only of generation 0) and we then compute the number of individuals $I(M, i, z) = I(1, 0, 0.99)$ that must be processed (i.e., the number of such runs) where the probability of success is the reciprocal of column 5.

In order to make table 9.3, we made 43,589 runs of genetic programming involving 33,628,600 individuals for the 80 representatives of the equivalence classes.

In what follows, references will be repeatedly made to eight particular rules, namely, in order of increasing difficulty, rules 000, 247, 058, 232, 104, 097, 150, and 105. Rule 000 (00000000 in binary) might be called "Always Off" and is a trivial Boolean function. Rule 000 is the most frequent rule generated among the 10,000,000 random trees. Accordingly, it appears on row 1 of table 9.3. Rule 000 appears 1,478,478 times in 10,000,000 random trees. In other words, the average number of individuals that must be processed by the random search in order to find an S-expression that realizes rule 000 is 6.76 individuals. The logarithm of the number of individuals that must be processed is about 0.83. Rule 000 is alone in its equivalence class. Note that there is an almost identical number (i.e., 1,478,086) of appearances (on row 2) of rule 255 ("Always On") among the 10,000,000.

Rule 247 (11110111 in binary) might be called "Not Three" because it returns T unless the three inputs D2, D1, and D0 are precisely the binary representation of three (i.e., 0 ,1, and 1, respectively). Rule 247 is the 18th most frequent rule (out of 80) and so appears on row 18 of this table. Rule 247 appears 77,264 times in 10,000,000 random trees, so that the average number of individuals that must be processed by the random search is 129 individuals. The logarithm of 129 is 2.11. The next most frequent rule (on row 19) has about one in 366 odds of appearing. Thus, rule 247 is on the boundary of those rules that are more frequent versus less frequent than 1 in 256. As previously mentioned, rule 247 is one of three rules in its equivalence class.

The other two rules in this equivalence class (i.e., rules 223 and 191) appear with about the same frequency as rule 247.

Rule 058 (00111010 in binary) might be called "If / Not-Then / Else" because it can be written as

```
(IF D2 (NOT D1) D0).
```

Rule 058 is the 31st most frequent rule. It appears 3,144 times in 10,000,000 random trees so that the average number of individuals that must be processed by the random search is 3,181 (whose logarithm is 3.50). Rule 058 is one of six rules in its equivalence class. The other five rules appeared 3,242, 3,203, 3,145, 3,015, and 3,041 times in 10,000,000, respectively.

Rule 232 (11101000 in binary) might be called "Majority On" because it returns T if two or three of its three inputs are on. Rule 232 is a fairly difficult function to find via blind random search. Rule 232 is the 36th most frequent rule (out of 80). Rule 232 appears 2,443 times in 10,000,000 random trees so that the average number of individuals is 4,093 (whose logarithm is 3.61). Rule 232 is alone in its equivalence class.

Rule 104 (01101000 in binary) might be called "Exactly Two On." It is a difficult function to find via blind random search. It is the 73rd most frequent equivalence class (i.e., 7th least frequent). Rule 104 appears 35 times in 10,000,000 random trees so that the average number of individuals is 285,714 (whose logarithm is 5.46). Rule 104 is alone in its equivalence class.

Rule 097 (01100001 in binary) might be called "Three Quarters of Even-3-Parity." This name is appropriate since if we restate this function in disjunctive normal form, rule 097 consists of a disjunction of three of the four conjunctive clauses of the even-3-parity function, namely

```
(OR (AND (NOT D2) (NOT D1) (NOT D0))
    (AND      D2  (NOT D1)      D0)
    (AND      D2       D1  (NOT D0))).
```

Rule 097 is a difficult function via blind random search. It is the 76th most frequent rule (i.e., 4th least frequent rule). It appears only 22 times in 10,000,000 random trees, so the average number of individuals is 454,546 (whose logarithm is 5.66). Rule 097 is one of three rules in its equivalence class.

Rule 150 (10010110 in binary) is the "Odd-3-Parity" function. Rule 150 (on row 79) appears only two times in 10,000,000 random trees, so the average number of individuals is about 5,000,000 (whose logarithm is 6.70). Rule 150 is very difficult to find via blind random search. It is the second least frequent rule. It is the rarest of the rules appearing at least once among the 10,000,000 random trees. Rule 150 is alone in its equivalence class. In disjunctive normal form, rule 150 consists of a disjunction of four conjunctive clauses, as follows:

```
(OR (AND (NOT D2) (NOT D1)      D0)
    (AND (NOT D2)      D1  (NOT D0))
    (AND      D2  (NOT D1) (NOT D0))
    (AND      D2       D1       D0)).
```

The DNF representation of rule 105 consists of 11 functions and 12 terminals.

Rule 105 (01101001 in binary) is the "Even-3-Parity" function. Rule 105 (on row 80) is so difficult to generate via our blind random search of random S-expressions that it did not appear at all in the 10,000,000 random trees. In fact, it has *never* appeared in any of the other experiments, involving many tens of millions of individual S-expressions, that we have performed. This is yet another confirmation that random compositions of functions and terminals and the LISP programming language do not facilitate discovery of programs.

The disjunctive normal form representation of rule 105 consists of four disjuncts, as follows:

```
(OR (AND (NOT D2) (NOT D1) (NOT D0))
    (AND (NOT D2)      D1       D0)
    (AND      D2  (NOT D1)      D0)
    (AND      D2       D1  (NOT D0))).
```

The DNF representation of rule 105 consists of 11 functions and 12 terminals.

Figure 9.2 is a plot of 80 points using information from table 9.3. The horizontal axis of this graph is the logarithm of the number of individuals that must be processed to find a solution to a particular Boolean function using blind random search for each for the 80 representative rules. The vertical axis represents the logarithm of the number of individuals processed by genetic programming in learning the Boolean function for each of the 80 Boolean functions with three arguments represented on the horizontal axis.

A population of size $M = 50$ was used, and each run was continued for up to a maximum number of generations $G = 25$. If a run failed to produce a

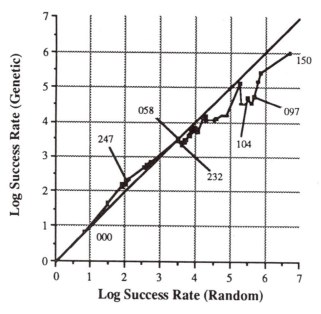

Figure 9.2 Graph on log-log scale of the number of individuals that must be processed per solution individual for blind random search (horizontal axis) versus genetic programming (vertical axis) for 80 Boolean functions with three arguments. Points below the 45° line are found more easily by genetic programming than by blind random search.

solution after 25 generations (i.e., the initial random generation plus 24 additional generations), we recorded 1,250 individuals as having been processed by genetic programming for that run. If a run produced one or more individuals that solved the problem in a given generation prior to generation 24, we immediately terminated that run and recorded $M = 50$ times the number of generations run as the number of individuals that were processed for that run. If more than one individual in the population solved the problem on the generation at which the run was terminated, this was reflected in the number of solutions reported.

After all runs were made for a given rule, we divided the total number of individuals that were processed by the number of solution individuals in the population that were produced in order to produce an average number of individuals that had to be processed for each solution individual.

Table 9.4 shows the outcome of runs of genetic programming for each of the 80 rules. Column 3 of this table shows the number of solution individuals obtained in the number of runs of genetic programming shown in column 4.

Column 5 shows the number of individuals processed by genetic programming to find the reported number of solution individuals.

Column 6 shows the average number of individuals that must be processed by genetic programming to find a solution individual (i.e., column 5 divided by column 3).

Column 7 is the logarithm of column 6.

Column 8 of this table is the difference Δ between the logarithm in column 7 and the logarithm found in column 6 of table 9.3 (representing random search). This difference is positive for Boolean functions that can be found by processing fewer individuals with genetic programming than by blind random search.

Column 9 shows the performance ratio 10^Δ (i.e., the antilog of column 8).

Column 10 is not used in this chapter, but is provided to permit comparison with the results in chapter 8. Column 10 contains the number of individuals that must be processed in order to find a solution individual with 99% probability (computed in the manner described in chapter 8). In other words, we envision runs using a population size $M = 1$ and number of generations to be run $G = 1$ (i.e., the run consists only of generation 0) and we then compute the number of individuals $I(M, i, z) = I(1, 0, 0.99)$ that must be processed (i.e., the number of such runs) where the probability of success is the reciprocal of column 6.

Rule 000 ("Always On") is so trivial that genetic programming found, in the population of size 50, multiple solution individuals for this rule on generation 0 for all 800 runs. In fact, it found a total of 5,926 solution individuals in those 800 runs. Genetic programming processed a total of 40,000 individuals (i.e., 800 runs with 50 individuals for generation 0 only), so an average of 6.75 individuals had to be processed per solution individual (row 1 of column 6 of table 9.4). This is virtually the same as the 6.76 individuals required by the random search (row 1 of column 5 of table 9.3). This near equivalence is reasonable because generation 0 of genetic programming is a blind random

Table 9.4 Processing required by genetic programming for the equivalence classes 1 through 80 of Boolean rules with three arguments.

	Rule	Number of successes	Runs	Indivs	Expected number	Log	Δ	10^Δ	$I(M, i, z)$
1	**000**	**5926**	**800**	**40000**	**6.75**	**0.83**	**0.00**	**1.00**	**29**
2	255	4459	600	30050	6.74	0.83	0.00	1.00	29
3	085	376	200	15900	42.3	1.63	−0.13	0.74	193
4	240	356	200	16050	45.1	1.65	−0.15	0.71	206
5	119	2657	2109	376250	141	2.15	−0.23	0.59	650
6	192	730	600	111900	153	2.19	−0.26	0.55	704
7	017	249	200	34400	138	2.14	−0.21	0.62	634
8	252	246	200	37000	150	2.18	−0.24	0.57	691
9	001	234	200	36500	156	2.19	−0.17	0.67	717
10	128	497	400	80550	162	2.21	−0.19	0.65	745
11	127	234	200	45150	192	2.29	−0.26	0.55	887
12	245	1383	1137	248950	180	2.26	−0.23	0.59	827
13	254	1167	1000	199550	171	2.23	−0.21	0.62	786
14	080	245	200	44000	179	2.25	−0.23	0.59	825
15	016	441	400	91250	206	2.32	−0.21	0.62	951
16	253	474	400	107850	227	2.36	−0.25	0.56	1046
17	064	684	600	144500	211	2.32	−0.21	0.61	971
18	**247**	**893**	**800**	**208650**	**233**	**2.37**	**−0.26**	**0.55**	**1074**
19	200	185	200	96650	522	2.72	−0.16	0.70	2404
20	087	187	200	96050	513	2.71	−0.14	0.72	2364
21	021	761	800	371400	488	2.69	−0.12	0.76	2246
22	236	387	400	195400	504	2.70	−0.13	0.73	2323
23	213	398	400	197000	495	2.69	−0.10	0.80	2278
24	205	691	744	372800	539	2.73	−0.12	0.76	2483
25	084	1189	1296	671400	564	2.75	−0.14	0.72	2599
26	112	374	400	215300	575	2.76	−0.15	0.72	2649
27	081	595	689	401150	674	2.83	−0.12	0.75	3103
28	117	479	548	300400	627	2.80	−0.09	0.81	2886
29	244	407	468	261100	641	2.81	−0.10	0.79	2953
30	162	171	200	113600	664	2.82	−0.11	0.77	3058
31	**058**	**141**	**400**	**415450**	**2946**	**3.47**	**0.03**	**1.08**	**13567**
32	197	570	1612	1646400	2888	3.46	0.04	1.10	13300
33	053	145	454	473350	3264	3.51	0.02	1.04	15032
34	216	223	600	612350	2746	3.44	0.09	1.24	12644
35	023	176	400	388000	2204	3.34	0.26	1.84	10151
36	**232**	**76**	**200**	**201050**	**2645**	**3.42**	**0.19**	**1.55**	**12181**
37	102	77	200	207450	2694	3.43	0.22	1.65	12405
38	153	125	300	298950	2391	3.38	0.28	1.91	11012
39	020	137	400	418000	3051	3.48	0.24	1.74	14049
40	235	224	581	602350	2689	3.43	0.30	1.98	12382
41	159	139	400	419150	3015	3.48	0.25	1.77	13885
42	096	71	200	210100	2959	3.47	0.26	1.83	13626
43	009	335	1277	1407500	4201	3.62	0.18	1.53	19347
44	212	102	400	442550	4338	3.64	0.22	1.68	19979

	Rule	Number of successes	Runs	Indivs	Expected number	Log	Δ	10^Δ	$I(M, i, z)$
45	193	148	647	715800	4836	3.68	0.18	1.52	22271
46	190	97	400	444800	4585	3.66	0.21	1.64	21116
47	077	111	400	440750	3970	3.60	0.29	1.93	18284
48	111	125	525	586800	4694	3.67	0.21	1.64	21617
49	144	115	400	436550	3796	3.58	0.31	2.03	17480
50	122	130	600	672800	5175	3.71	0.18	1.52	23832
51	133	56	259	285900	5105	3.71	0.20	1.58	23509
52	118	114	600	684700	6006	3.78	0.14	1.37	27657
53	164	60	290	328950	5482	3.74	0.25	1.80	25246
54	067	34	200	227250	6683	3.83	0.20	1.58	30778
55	091	36	200	225500	6263	3.80	0.23	1.69	28844
56	230	73	420	480450	6581	3.82	0.21	1.62	30307
57	229	41	200	229050	5586	3.75	0.31	2.03	25725
58	098	114	600	690600	6057	3.78	0.29	1.94	27896
59	026	115	600	679700	5910	3.77	0.31	2.03	27217
60	157	70	332	379400	5420	3.73	0.35	2.22	24958
61	126	63	678	811250	12877	4.11	0.10	1.25	59299
62	129	16	200	241100	15068	4.18	0.05	1.13	69392
63	189	34	400	482000	14176	4.15	0.15	1.43	65283
64	024	43	400	475700	11062	4.04	0.27	1.84	50944
65	149	42	400	480100	11431	4.06	0.49	3.10	52640
66	030	46	500	604450	13140	4.12	0.43	2.69	60511
67	106	40	400	478000	11950	4.08	0.54	3.43	55030
68	169	23	350	425750	18510	4.27	0.36	2.29	85244
69	101	26	342	416350	16013	4.20	0.59	3.88	73743
70	154	47	600	732200	15578	4.19	0.73	5.39	71741
71	022	2	200	248450	124225	5.09	0.19	1.55	572075
72	233	22	600	739000	33590	4.53	0.79	6.20	154690
73	**104**	**21**	**600**	**742050**	**35335**	**4.55**	**0.91**	**8.09**	**162725**
74	151	12	481	597900	49825	4.70	0.81	6.47	229451
75	146	15	400	493500	32900	4.52	1.10	12.66	151508
76	**097**	**9**	**400**	**496800**	**55200**	**4.74**	**0.92**	**8.23**	**254204**
77	107	5	600	747600	149520	5.17	0.62	4.18	688563
78	158	1	200	249350	249350	5.40	0.49	3.08	1148297
79	**150**	**5**	**4000**	**4998750**	**999750**	**6.00**	**0.70**	**5.00**	**4604017**
80	**105**	**2**	**1900**	**2374450**	**1187225**	**6.07**	**NA**	**NA**	**5467371**

search (although the methods of generating the initial individuals are somewhat different). The logarithm of 6.75 is 0.83. The line at 45° separates this graph into two parts. The points on the graph below the line represent Boolean functions that can be found by processing fewer individuals with genetic programming than by random search. Rule 000 appears on this 45° line.

For rule 247 ("Not Three"), a solution individual appears 893 times in 800 runs. Genetic programming processed a total of 208,650 individuals to find these 893 solution individuals (i.e., 800 runs with 50 individuals, for an average of 5.21 generations each). An average of 234 individuals had to be processed per solution individual by genetic programming (on row 18 of column 6 of table 9.4). The logarithm of 234 is 2.37. This compares to 129 individuals in the blind random search (on row 18 of column 5 of table 9.3). The logarithm of 129 is 2.11. In other words, genetic programming takes 1.81 times longer than the blind random search for this particular rule. The difference in the two logarithms is −0.26 as shown on row 18 in column 8 of table 9.4.

For rule 247 and all 28 rules between rows 3 and 30 of table 9.4, the difference in logarithms (column 8) is slightly negative and the point plotted in figure 9.2 appears slightly above the 45° line. That is, genetic programming finds a solution individual by processing more individuals than the blind random search for those rules. Many of these rules, such as (AND D2 D0), are degenerate in that they do not involve all three input arguments; the others, such as (AND D2 (AND D1 D0)), are comparatively simple Boolean rules. These 28 rules are apparently *too simple* for genetic programming to handle efficiently (because of the overhead associated with genetic programming).

For rule 058 ("If / Not-Then / Else"), a solution individual appears 141 times in 400 runs. This rule is a member of the multiplexer family. Genetic programming processed a total of 415,450 individuals to find these 141 solution individuals, for an average of 2,946 individuals processed per solution individual. In contrast, blind random search processed an average of 3,144 individuals per solution. The difference in the two logarithms is just barely positive (i.e., it is +0.03, as shown on row 31 in column 8 of table 9.4). Rule 058 is the first rule in table 9.4 for which this difference is positive. The point plotted in figure 9.2 for rule 058 appears below the 45° line. In other words, this rule is right on the 45° dividing line.

For rule 058 and all of the 49 rules that are more difficult than rule 058 to find at random, genetic programming found a solution individual by processing fewer individuals than blind random search. In other words, genetic programming works best on the harder rules. In fact, as the rules become harder to find by random search, the relative processing advantage of genetic programming generally becomes greater.

For rule 232 ("Majority On"), genetic programming processed an average of 2,645 individuals per solution individual, versus an average of 4,093 individuals for the blind random search. In other words, genetic programming is 1.55 times faster than blind random search. The difference between the two logarithms is +0.19.

For rule 104 ("Exactly Two On"), genetic programming processed an average of 35,336 individuals per solution individual, versus an average of 285,714 individuals for the blind random search. In other words, genetic programming is 8.09 times faster than blind random search. The difference between the two logarithms is $+0.91$.

For rule 097 ("Three Quarters of Even-3-Parity"), genetic programming processed an average of 55,200 individuals per solution individual, versus an average of 454,546 individuals for blind random search. In other words, genetic programming is 8.23 times faster than blind random search. The difference between the two logarithms is $+0.92$.

For rule 150 ("Odd-3-Parity"), genetic programming processed an average of 999,750 individuals per solution individual, versus an average of 5,000,000 individuals for the blind random search. In other words, genetic programming is 5 times faster than blind random search. The difference between the two logarithms is $+0.70$.

For rule 105 ("Even-3-Parity"), genetic programming processed an average of 1,187,225 individuals per solution individual. There is no direct comparison with blind random search for rule 105, since the blind random search did not find even one solution individual after processing 10,000,000 individuals.

In summary, for the Boolean functions with three arguments, as many or slightly more individuals must be processed by genetic programming than blind random search in order to find the degenerate and very simple functions, but considerably fewer individuals must be processed by genetic programming for the majority of the functions, including the harder functions (and, notably, the odd and even 3-parity functions). Moreover, the advantage of genetic programming generally increases for the harder functions.

While recognizing the compromises associated with the restricted nature of the above experiments, I believe that the focus on Boolean functions of only three arguments, the choice of $F_2 = \{\text{AND, OR, NAND, NOR}\}$ as the function set, and the choice of 20 internal points do not alter the general conclusions itemized above.

The above discussion was based on a choice of 50 as the population size for use in genetic programming. This is not the optimum population size. The conclusion that genetic programming performs better than blind random search (for all but the easy functions) is, however, established by this one choice, since it is not relevant whether there are other (better) choices of population size for which this conclusion is also true. Although we did not repeat the hundreds of runs of each of the 80 rules for other population sizes, we did do this for rule 150 (odd-3-parity) for population sizes of 100, 200, 500, and 1,000. This resulted in a total of 76,503,043 individuals being processed over 54,894 runs.

Figure 9.3 shows that the performance advantage of genetic programming over blind random search for rule 150 (the second-hardest rule) increases for the larger population sizes. Figure 9.3 is very similar to figure 9.2 except for the four additional points, reflecting the larger population sizes, on the right

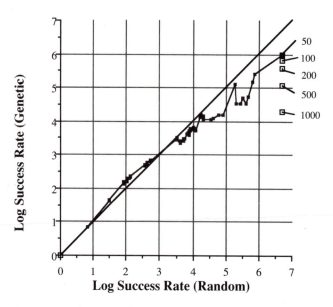

Figure 9.3 Performance advantage of genetic programming over blind random search for rule 150 for population sizes of 50, 100, 200, 500, and 1,000.

side of the figure. In particular, the number of individuals that must be processed per individual solving rule 150 decreases from 999,750 for population size 50 to 665,923, 379,876, 122,754, and 20,285 for population sizes of 100, 200, 500, and 1,000, respectively. This suggests that if we knew the optimum population size the advantage of genetic programming over blind random search would be even greater. Even though we do not know the optimum population size, it is interesting that genetic programming is at least 245 times better than blind random search for this problem.

9.2 BOOLEAN FUNCTIONS WITH TWO ARGUMENTS

The Boolean functions with two Boolean inputs and one Boolean output exhibit the same general characteristics as the Boolean functions with three arguments.

Table 9.5 reports on the difficulty of blind random search for all 16 rules of the Boolean functions with two arguments. Column 2 of this table gives the rule number (from decimal number 00 to 15). Column 3 gives the four-bit binary equivalence for the decimal number in column 2, and, as previously explained, shows the bit values of the truth table for the function. Column 4 shows the number of solution individuals found in the random search out of 1,000,000. Column 5 is the average number of individuals that must be processed in order to find a solution individual (i.e., 1,000,000 divided by column 4). Column 6 is the logarithm of column 5. Column 7 is the number of individuals that must be processed in order to find a solution individual with 99% probability (computed in the manner described in chapter 8).

Table 9.5 Amount of processing required by a blind random search for the 16 Boolean rules with two arguments.

	Rule	Truth table	Number of successes	Ratio	Log	$I(M, i, z)$
1	15	1111	208432	4.8	0.68	20
2	**00**	**0000**	**207860**	**4.8**	**0.68**	**20**
3	10	1010	127801	7.8	0.89	34
4	**05**	**0101**	**127720**	**7.8**	**0.89**	**34**
5	14	1110	34774	28.8	1.46	131
6	**08**	**1000**	**34701**	**28.8**	**1.46**	**131**
7	07	0111	34568	28.9	1.46	131
8	01	0001	34474	29.0	1.46	132
9	13	1101	31326	31.9	1.50	145
10	11	1011	31261	32.0	1.50	145
11	04	0100	31228	32.0	1.51	146
12	03	0011	31213	32.0	1.51	146
13	02	0010	31144	32.1	1.51	146
14	12	1100	31098	32.2	1.51	146
15	**09**	**1001**	**1218**	**821.0**	**2.91**	**3779**
16	**06**	**0110**	**1182**	**846.0**	**2.93**	**3894**

Rule 00 (0000 in binary) is Always Off and appears on row 2 of table 9.5. It is one of the two most frequent and most trivial Boolean functions with two arguments. Rule 00 is virtually tied with rule 15 (which appears on row 1). It appears 207,860 times in 1,000,000 random trees, so the average number of individuals that must be processed by the random search in order to find an S-expression that realizes rule 00 is 4.8 individuals. The logarithm of 4.8 is 0.68.

Rule 05 (0101 in binary) performs the function (NOT D0) and is degenerate in that its output does not functionally depend on D1. It is the fourth most frequent rule, appearing 127,720 times in 1,000,000 (i.e., an average of 7.8 random individuals must be processed).

Rule 08 (1000 in binary) is the AND function. It is the sixth most frequent rule, appearing 34,701 times in 1,000,000 (i.e., an average of about 29 individuals must be processed). Its probability of appearance is less than the 1:16 probability of appearance of a particular random truth table. The AND function is equivalent to the LISP function IF with two arguments, and, as such, is the representative of the multiplexer family among the functions with only two arguments.

Rule 09 is the even-2-parity function (also known as "Not Equal") and is the 15th most frequent (i.e., second least frequent) rule. It appears only 1,218 times per 1,000,000 (i.e., a probability of occurrence of only 1:821).

Rule 06 is the odd-2-parity function (also known as "Exclusive Or" or "XOR") and is the least frequent rule. It appears only 1,182 times per 1,000,000 (i.e., odds of occurrence of only 1:846).

Table 9.6 shows the outcome of runs of genetic programming for each of the 16 rules.

Table 9.6 Amount of processing required by genetic programming for the 16 Boolean rules with two arguments.

	Rule	Number of successes	Runs	Indivs	Ratio	Log	Δ	$10^Δ$	$I(M, i, z)$
1	15	966	100	5000	5.2	0.71	−0.03	0.93	22
2	**00**	**948**	**100**	**5000**	**5.3**	**0.72**	**−0.04**	**0.91**	**22**
3	10	284	100	5750	20.2	1.31	−0.41	0.39	91
4	**05**	**255**	**100**	**5650**	**22.2**	**1.35**	**−0.45**	**0.35**	**100**
5	14	314	100	5250	16.7	1.22	0.24	1.72	75
6	**08**	**320**	**100**	**5250**	**16.4**	**1.22**	**0.24**	**1.76**	**74**
7	07	290	100	5400	18.6	1.27	0.19	1.55	84
8	01	326	100	5300	16.3	1.21	0.25	1.78	73
9	13	207	100	5400	26.1	1.42	0.09	1.22	118
10	11	242	100	5650	23.3	1.37	0.14	1.37	106
11	04	239	100	5600	23.4	1.37	0.14	1.37	106
12	03	241	100	5450	22.6	1.35	0.15	1.42	102
13	02	231	100	6050	26.2	1.42	0.09	1.23	119
14	12	257	100	5200	20.2	1.31	0.20	1.59	91
15	**09**	**115**	**100**	**27750**	**241.3**	**2.38**	**0.53**	**3.40**	**1109**
16	**06**	**125**	**100**	**31700**	**253.6**	**2.40**	**0.52**	**3.34**	**1166**

Rule 00 ("Always Off") for the two-argument Boolean function is similar to rule 000 for the three-argument Boolean functions in that it is usually discovered on generation 0 and its performance lies very close to the 45° line.

The degenerate rule 05 (NOT DO) lies above the 45° line as do the 29 degenerate and very simple three-argument Boolean functions.

Rule 08 (AND) lies at the point where the graph goes below the 45° line. An average of 16.4 individuals had to be processed per solution individual by genetic programming (row 6 of column 6 of table 9.6). The logarithm of 16.4 is 1.22. This compares to 28.8 individuals in the blind random search (row 6 of column 5 of table 9.5). The logarithm of 28.8 is 1.46. In other words, blind random search takes 1.76 times longer than genetic programming for this particular rule. The difference between the two logarithms is +0.24, as shown in row 6 of column 8 of table 9.6. The performance ratio is shown on row 6 in column 9 of table 9.5.

Rule 09 ("even-2-parity" or "equivalence") lies well below the 45° line. Genetic programming processed an average of 241 individuals per solution individual compared to an average of 821 individuals for the blind random search. In other words, genetic programming is 3.40 times faster than blind random search. The difference in the two logarithms is +0.53.

For rule 06 ("odd-2-parity," "inequivalence," or XOR), genetic programming processed an average of 254 individuals per solution individual, versus an average of 846 individuals for the blind random search, and is therefore 3.34 times faster than blind random search. The difference between the two logarithms is +0.52.

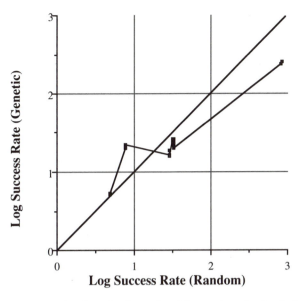

Figure 9.4 Graph on log-log scale of the number of individuals that must be processed per solution individual for blind random search (horizontal axis) versus genetic programming (vertical axis) for 16 Boolean functions with two arguments. Points below the 45° line are found more easily by genetic programming than by blind random search.

Figure 9.4 is a plot of 16 points using the information from table 9.6. The horizontal axis of this graph is the logarithm of the number of individuals that must be processed to find a solution to a particular Boolean function using blind random search for the 16 rules. The vertical axis represents the logarithm of the number of individuals processed by genetic programming in learning each of the 16 Boolean functions with two arguments represented on the horizontal axis.

A population of size $M = 50$ was used and each run was continued for up to a maximum number of generations $G = 25$.

The choice of 20 internal points has been subjected to limited comparative examination. In particular, we produced 10,000,000 S-expressions with precisely 10, 15, and 25 internal points (and 11, 16, and 26 external points) and compared the number of appearances of each of the 16 rules. The number of appearances was broadly similar between 15, 20, and 25 internal points, but was somewhat different for 10 internal points. A graph such as that appearing in figure 9.4 was created, and its appearance was broadly similar to that of figure 9.4.

In summary, the Boolean functions with two arguments are similar to the Boolean functions with three arguments in that as many or slightly more individuals must be processed by genetic programming than blind random search in order to find the degenerate and very simple functions, but considerably fewer individuals must be processed by genetic programming for the harder functions (notably, the parity functions).

9.3 AM AND EURISKO

The concern that compositions of functions and terminals solving a problem might be denser than solutions to the problem are in the search space of the original problem arises, in part, from the controversies surrounding Lenat's well-publicized work on the automated mathematician AM (Lenat 1976) and EURISKO (Lenat 1983).

In AM (Lenat 1976), mathematical concepts were generated, one by one, from a given knowledge base of about 100 initial concepts and about 230 heuristic rules. The generative process was not exhaustive, but was, instead, directed toward interesting areas of the vast space of possible concepts by the heuristics and by an "interestingness" measure (initially assigned by Lenat and then updated via formulae provided by Lenat). The end product of a run of AM was a large number of mathematical concepts, some of which might be new and interesting.

Lenat (1977) asserted "AM began its investigations with scanty knowledge of a hundred elementary concepts of finite set theory ... went off exploring elementary number theory ... [and] made rapid progress to divisibility theory. Prime pairs, Diophantine equations, the unique factorization of numbers into primes, Goldbach's conjecture—these were some of the nice discoveries by AM." EURISKO (Lenat 1983) attempted to extend the basic approach of AM to the discovery of the heuristic rules themselves.

The mathematical concepts and heuristic rules in AM were stated, in many cases, directly in terms of lists. The list is, of course, *the* primitive data type of the LISP programming language. For example, in some of the mathematical concepts, an integer was represented as a list of T's, where T denotes "true," so that an integer such as 5 was represented as the list (T T T T T).

In addition, the lists in AM were manipulated by functions that are unique or peculiar to LISP. For example, some concepts were expressed in terms of the CAR function (which returns the first element of a list), the CDR function (which returns the tail of a list), and the APPEND function (which concatenates two lists). When an integer such as 5 is represented as (T T T T T), the LISP list-manipulation function CDR has the effect of subtracting 1. When two integers are to be added, the LISP list-manipulation function APPEND has the effect of adding the two integers.

The impression has been created in some quarters that AM and EURISKO have something to do with biology, evolution, simulated evolution, or genetic algorithms. This impression may have originated because Lenat, in describing and speculating about AM and EURISKO, often used biological metaphors, referred to DNA, and sometimes likened transformations via logical rules to biological mutation. This impression may have been strengthened because certain terms such as offspring, parent, initial generation, generation, population, and fitness can be applied to AM and EURISKO. For example, when a rule of inference generates a new mathematical concept from one or more existing concepts, logicians often invoke the biological metaphor and refer to the new concept as an "offspring" or "child" and the original concept(s) as the "parents." The 100 initial concepts in AM can be thought of as belonging to an "initial generation" or a "generation 0." The set of all new concepts that are generated from generation n can be called "generation $n + 1$." The set of concepts present in any particular generation can be likened to a "population." The evaluative measures of "interestingness" and "worth" in AM can be viewed as a fitness measure (Lenat himself being, in effect, the fitness measure guiding the process).

AM and EURISKO, in fact, have virtually nothing in common with the field of genetic algorithms or simulated evolution. The starting point of the genetic algorithm and simulated evolution is random, whereas the starting point of AM and EURISKO is a large knowledge base of concepts and heuristic rules. The evaluative measures of "interestingness" and "worth" used in the genetic algorithm and simulated evolution are mechanical, algorithmic, and replicable, whereas the "interestingness" measure of AM and EURISKO is personal and externally provided. An even more important difference between AM and EURISKO and the genetic algorithm and simulated evolution becomes clear if we focus our attention on the heart of any adaptive system, namely the way the adaptive system transforms the structures (objects) from the current generation of the process into new structures. For AM and EURISKO, the key transformational operation was not biological, genetic, evolutionary, or Darwinian, but logical. That is, the structures in AM and EURISKO were transformed by the application of logical rules. These transformations in AM and EURISKO are nothing like the transformations used in the simulated evolution algorithm of Fogel, Owens, and Walsh (1966) (which uses reproduction and mutation) or the transformations used in Holland's genetic algorithm (which uses reproduction, mutation, and crossover).

AM and EURISKO have almost nothing in common with genetic programming. The basic creative engine of AM and EURISKO (i.e., its logical transformations) are nothing like the basic operations used in genetic programming (i.e., crossover, reproduction, and possibly mutation). The starting point of genetic programming is random, not a knowledge base of axioms and rules of inference. The end product of AM and EURISKO is a large number of mathematical concepts whereas the end product of genetic programming are computer programs for solving a particular problem. The evaluative measures of "interestingness" and "worth" used in genetic programming is mechanical, algorithmic, and replicable, whereas the "interestingness" measure of AM and EURISKO is personal and externally provided.

Moreover, unlike AM and EURISKO, genetic programming does not rely on LISP. The problems in this book are neither stated in terms of LISP objects (i.e., lists) nor solved using list-manipulation functions unique or peculiar to LISP. For example, the solution to the Boolean multiplexer problem is expressed in terms of ordinary Boolean functions (such as AND, OR, NOT, and IF) operating on ordinary Boolean variables; there are no lists and there are no list-manipulation functions. The cart centering, symbolic regression, and other numerical problems in this book are expressed and solved in terms of the ordinary arithmetic operations (such as addition, subtraction, multiplication, and division) operating on ordinary real-valued variables; there are no lists and there are no list-manipulation functions. The artificial ant and other planning problems in this book are expressed and solved in terms of ordinary primitive robotic functions (such as moving, turning, and looking), rather than lists and list-manipulation functions. The primitive functions and terminals for each of these problems come from the nature of the specific problem; they do not come from LISP.

None of the solutions to the above problems use lists or list-manipulation functions or depend in any way on the fact that genetic programming happened to be implemented with the LISP programming language. Indeed, virtually any programming language could be used to express the solutions to these problems and virtually any programming language could be used to implement genetic programming. As detailed in section 4.3, we chose the LISP programming language primarily because data and programs have the same form in LISP, because this common form corresponds to the parse tree of a computer program, and because of LISP's many convenient features and tools. The LISP programming language was *not* chosen because of the presence in LISP of the list as a primitive data type or because of LISP's particular functions for manipulating lists (e.g., CAR, CDR, and APPEND).

In fact, neither lists nor list-manipulation functions are involved in any of the problems described in this book (except in the irrelevant and indirect sense that, unseen by the user, the LISP programming language internally uses lists to do things that other programming languages do in different ways). The parse tree that LISP makes conveniently available to us for manipulation is the same sort of parse tree that other programming languages construct internally at the time of compilation. This parse tree is nothing more than a direct mapping of the given composition of functions and terminals (i.e., the given computer program) into a tree structure that is widely (indeed, almost universally) used by compilers to represent computer programs. We need access to this parse tree in order to do crossover in the way we want to do it (namely, on subparts of computer programs). The LISP programming language gives us this convenient access to the parse tree, the ability to conveniently manipulate this program as if it were data, and the convenient ability to immediately execute a newly created parse tree. However, we could achieve any of these effects with virtually any other programming language (albeit less conveniently).

The asserted performance of AM in generating new and interesting mathematical concepts from the vast space of possible concepts was a consequence of the given set of axioms, the given set of heuristics, the values of "interestingness" assigned to concepts by Lenat, and possibly by the fact that the entities being manipulated and the tools for manipulation were unique and peculiar to LISP. None of these four factors are in any way relevant to genetic algorithms, simulated evolution, or genetic programming.

Moreover, the performance of the genetic algorithm, simulated evolution, or genetic programming are replicable (within the limits associated any probabilistic algorithm). The entire control structure of each of these methods has been published.

What then is the origin of the concern that compositions of functions and terminals solving a problem might be denser than solutions to the problem are in the search space of the original problem?

In the article "AM: A Case Study in AI Methodology," Ritchie and Hanna (1984) raised questions about Lenat's well-publicized claim that AM was an artificially intelligent process. In addition, Ritchie and Hanna raised a series of questions about Lenat's methodology, including whether Lenat's reported results were replicable, whether the reported results were possibly produced via steps that were not included in Lenat's published descriptions, and whether personal intervention contributed more to the reported results than the automated process. In particular, Ritchie and Hanna stated, "Close inspection of the written accounts of AM suggests that there are some worrying discrepancies between the theoretical claims and the implemented program ..." and "What we wish to argue is that the written accounts ... give a misleading view of how the program worked...." In addition, Ritchie and Hanna stated, "[T]he principle claim being advanced for the AM program was [that] a simple, uniform control structure does in fact produce the impressive output.... Closer inspection ... reveals that the AM program did not actually function in this way."

The *mea culpa* article "Why AM and EURISKO appear to work" (Lenat and Brown 1984) admitted various methodological errors, but did not directly answer all the major questions raised in Ritchie and Hanna 1984. Instead, the response raised an entirely new issue and then admitted error in connection with that new issue. The new issue consisted of the assertion that AM's discovery of various mathematical concepts was greatly facilitated because AM's concepts and heuristic rules were stated in terms of LISP's primitive object (i.e., the list) and then manipulated using list-manipulation functions peculiar and unique to LISP. That is, this new issue asserted that the "interesting" mathematical concepts were denser (and hence more easily found) in the LISP space than they might be in some other unspecified space. The error that was admitted in the response article amounted to the "error" of using LISP.

It is impossible to determine the correctness of the assertion in the response article concerning the facilitating role of LISP. The response article did not provide any experiments or proof to support its argument about LISP. The response article, like the original work being criticized by Ritchie and Hanna, contained no claims that could be independently validated. As Ritchie and Hanna observed in 1984, there had been no published replication of Lenat's work in the period between 1976 and 1984 in spite of the considerable publicity surrounding this work. There has been no published replication since 1984 (see Shen 1989). Thus, there is no independent experimental evidence to support the original results of AM and EURISKO. There is also no experimental evidence or proof to support the position taken on the new issue involving LISP raised in the response article.

It is now generally recognized that the asserted performance of AM and EURISKO as an artificially intelligent process or as a simulated evolutionary process was inextricably intertwined with Lenat's personal involvement in the process. Lenat's involvement made the process unreplicable by others. In any event, AM and EURISKO had virtually nothing in common with genetic algorithms, simulated evolution, or genetic programming.

I know of no *a priori* reason or evidence (nor have I discovered any evidence) to think that there is anything about the syntax of the programs generated by genetic programming or about the syntax of the programming language used to implement genetic programming (i.e., LISP) that makes it easier to discover solutions to problems involving ordinary (i.e., nonlist) objects and ordinary (i.e., nonlist) functions. In fact, as already shown in previous sections of this chapter, we have some evidence of the opposite. However, if we had evidence that LISP actually facilitated discovery of solutions to problems, we would have a strong reason to want to use LISP (rather than the mere preference for LISP discussed in section 4.3).

10 Symbolic Regression—Error-Driven Evolution

Problems of symbolic regression require finding a function, in symbolic form, that fits a given finite sampling of data points. Symbolic regression provides a means for function identification. Symbolic regression is error-driven evolution.

In this chapter, we will show how the techniques of symbolic regression can be used to solve a wide variety of different problems, including

- discovery of trigonometric identities,
- symbolic regression involving creation of arbitrary constants,
- econometric modeling and forecasting,
- empirical discovery of scientific laws, such as Kepler's Third Law,
- symbolic integration yielding a function in symbolic form,
- symbolic differentiation yielding a function in symbolic form,
- solution of differential equations yielding a function in symbolic form,
- solution of integral equations yielding a function in symbolic form,
- solution of inverse problems yielding a function in symbolic form,
- solution of general functional equations yielding a function in symbolic form,
- solution of equations for numeric roots,
- sequence induction, and
- programmatic image compression.

We have already seen how genetic programming can be used to do symbolic regression in the introductory example of symbolic regression, where the target curve was $x^4 + x^3 + x^2 + x$ (section 7.3).

However, neither the target curve nor the terminal set for that introductory example contained any numerical constants, nor was there any explicit facility for them. The process of symbolic regression requires, in general, a method for discovering the appropriate numerical constants and coefficients. We could, of course, insert a particular constant (e.g., π, ε, or -1) into the terminal set of a problem if we happened to believe that it might be useful (as we did in section 7.1); however, in general, we have no way of knowing in advance what constant is needed for a given problem. Interestingly, in spite of the fact that we did not explicitly provide any numerical constants in section 7.3, genetic programming created several numerical constants on its own. For example, the constant 1.0 was indirectly created on two occasions via the expressions (% X X) and (COS (- X X)). In addition, several other simple rational constants, such as 0.5 and 1.5, were indirectly created in a similar way.

The first two sections in this chapter will show how to solve the problem of constant creation in symbolic regression in a general way. I start by showing how my work on the problem of discovering trigonometric identities led to my discovery of the general solution to the problem of constant creation for symbolic regression.

10.1   DISCOVERY OF TRIGONOMETRIC IDENTITIES

Finding a mathematical identity (such as a trigonometric identity) involves finding a new and unobvious mathematical expression, in symbolic form, that always has the same value as some given mathematical expression.

Symbolic methods of automated deduction and artificial intelligence approach this problem by repeatedly applying logically sound transformation rules to the given mathematical expression in order to produce a new expression.

We can use genetic programming to discover mathematical identities, such as trigonometric identities.

Consider a given mathematical expression, in symbolic form, such as

Cos $2x$.

If we can discover a new mathematical expression, in symbolic form, that equals Cos $2x$ for all values of x, we will have succeeded in finding an identity. In other words, we are seeking a new mathematical expression, in symbolic form, such as

$1 - 2 \operatorname{Sin}^2 x$.

In this process, we start with the given mathematical expression in symbolic form. We then convert the given mathematical expression into a finite sample of data points. We do this by selecting a random sample of values of the independent variables appearing in the given expression. We then evaluate the given expression over this random sampling of values of its independent variables. We pair the random domain values with the result of this evaluation. Finally, we proceed as in symbolic regression and search for a mathematical expression that fits the given pairs of values.

The first major step in preparing to use genetic programming is to identify the set of terminals. Since the trigonometric identities we are considering are expressed in terms of one independent variable, that variable x must be in the terminal set. At the time that we ran this problem we had not yet discovered the general way to create numerical constants needed in symbolic regression, so we put the constant 1.0 in the terminal set because we thought that it might be needed. Thus, the terminal set is

```
T = {X, 1.0}.
```

The second major step in preparing to use genetic programming is to identify the set of functions. The function set should contain functions we would like to see as part of the identity that is eventually to be discovered. For this problem, these functions might include one or more trigonometric functions. However, when the goal is to discover identities, it is usually inadvisable to include the original function in the function set. For example, if the COS function is included in the function set for this problem, genetic programming will usually discover only simple identities such as

$$\text{Cos } 2x = (\text{COS } (+ \text{ X X})) = \text{Cos } (x + x),$$

or

$$\text{Cos } 2x = (\text{COS } (- (- 1 1) (+ \text{ X X}))) = \text{Cos } (-2x),$$

since the COS function is inordinately useful in doing regression on a cosine curve.

Therefore, we exclude the cosine function from the function set. We include the sine function and the four arithmetic functions, so the function set for this problem is

```
F = {+, -, *, %, SIN},
```

having two, two, two, two, and one arguments, respectively.

Note that the exclusion of COS from the function set precludes the possibility of finding an identity such as

$$\text{Cos } 2x = 2 \text{ Cos}^2 x - 1.$$

The third major step in preparing to use genetic programming is identification of the fitness function for evaluating how good a given computer program is at solving the problem at hand.

We begin by choosing 20 values x_i of the variable x at random over an appropriate domain, such as the interval between 0 and 2π radians. Then, for each of the 20 values x_i, the left-hand side of the identity (i.e., Cos $2x_i$) is computed and designated as y_i. The 20 pairs (x_i, y_i) thus become the 20 fitness cases for a symbolic regression problem.

Some judgment must, of course, be exercised in creating the fitness cases for a problem. Genetic programming operates with only the particular fitness cases it is given. Therefore, if the person employing genetic programming desires that the result produced by genetic programming work correctly on fitness cases that the genetic programming paradigm has not seen, then the fitness cases must be selected so as to be representative of those unseen cases. The domain of this particular problem is the infinity of values that may be assumed by the real-valued independent variable x. Therefore, some sampling must necessarily occur in creating the fitness cases. The sampling inherently involves limitations in two different dimensions, namely the choice of the interval in which the sampling is to take place and the density of the sampling within that interval. In this problem, the selection of an interval such as $[0, 2\pi]$ radians is advisable since trigonometric functions are involved. In fact, a multiple of that interval, such as $[-6\pi, 6\pi]$ radians, might be considered. In contrast, an interval such as $[0, 1]$ radians or $[-1, +1]$ radians would be an inadvisable selection for this particular problem because the behavior of a trigonometric function over these smaller intervals would almost certainly be unrepresentative of the overall behavior of the function. The selection of the density of sampling must be considered in light of the fact that the average distance between two values of the independent variable will be $18°$ if 20 points are selected from the interval $[0, 2\pi]$ radians.

The raw fitness of a given S-expression is the sum, taken over the 20 fitness cases, of the absolute value of the difference between y_i and the value returned by the S-expression when the independent variable x takes on the value x_i. In other words, the evolutionary process will be guided by an error measure for this problem. Since a smaller error is better for error-driven evolution, standardized fitness equals raw fitness for this problem.

Table 10.1 summarizes the key features of the problem of discovery of trigonometric identities.

We illustrate this process by starting with the mathematical expression Cos $2x$. The goal is to find another mathematical expression which equals Cos $2x$ over in the interval $[0, 2\pi]$.

On generation 13 of one run, we obtained the S-expression

```
(- (- 1 (* (SIN X) (SIN X))) (* (SIN X) (SIN X))).
```

Table 10.1 Tableau for the trigonometric identity problem.

Objective:	Find a new mathematical expression, in symbolic form, that equals a given mathematical expression, for all values of its independent variables.
Terminal set:	X, the constant 1.0.
Function set:	+, −, *, %, SIN.
Fitness cases:	The 20 pairs (x_i, y_i) where the x_i are random points in the interval $[0, 2\pi]$ radians and where the y_i are the values of the given mathematical expression (i.e., Cos $2x_i$).
Raw fitness:	The sum, taken over the 20 fitness cases, of the absolute value of the difference between y_i and the value produced by the S-expression for x_i.
Standardized fitness:	Same as raw fitness for this problem.
Hits:	Number of points where S-expression comes within 0.01 of the desired value.
Wrapper:	None.
Parameters:	$M = 500$. $G = 51$.
Success predicate:	An S-expression scores 20 hits.

On another run, we obtained the S-expression

```
(- 1 (* (* (SIN X) (SIN X)) 2)).
```

Since each of the above S-expressions are equivalent to

$1 - 2 \sin^2 x,$

we just rediscovered the well-known trigonometric identity

$\cos 2x = 1 - 2 \sin^2 x.$

The most interesting run in our work with the identity for Cos $2x$ inspired the constant creation process described in greater detail in the next section.

On generation 30 of another run of this same problem, we obtained the opaque and incomprehensible S-expression as the best-of-run individual:

```
(SIN (- (- 2 (* X 2))
     (SIN (SIN (SIN (SIN (SIN (SIN (* (SIN (SIN 1))
                                      (SIN (SIN 1))
                                      )))))))))).
```

Our instrumentation reported that this mysterious best-of-run S-expression from generation 30 had nearly perfect (i.e., nearly zero) raw fitness. Suspecting an error in our program, we used the Mathematica™ software package (Wolfram 1988) to make a graph of this mysterious S-expression. Figure 10.1 shows the graph of the alleged identity for Cos $2x$. As can be seen from the graph, the mysterious S-expression was not erroneous, but did indeed closely fit the Cos $2x$ curve.

Upon examination, it became clear that genetic programming exploited the available function SIN in the function set and the available constant 1.0 in the terminal set to create a needed constant on its own. First, genetic programming computed (SIN 1)—which, since the sine function works in radians, happens to equal 0.841. Then, genetic programming created, via crossover, the subexpression (SIN (SIN 1)) which evaluates to a still smaller number, namely 0.746. The overall S-expression containing the 0.746 yielded better fitness than the overall S-expression containing 0.841.

On a later generation, (SIN (SIN 1)) was squared to yield an even smaller number, namely 0.556.

Even these steps were not sufficient to create the numerical constant that maximized fitness in this problem. Over a series of additional generations,

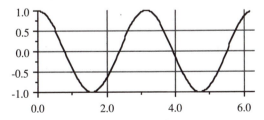

Figure 10.1 Graph of opaque best-of-run individual for Cos $2x$.

genetic programming then successively applied the SIN function six more times to obtain the following decreasing sequence of six numbers:

```
0.528, 0.504, 0.483, 0.464, 0.448, 0.433.
```

The overall result was the composition

```
(SIN (SIN (SIN (SIN (SIN (SIN (* (SIN (SIN 1))
                              (SIN (SIN 1)))))))))),
```

which evaluates to 0.433.

Then

```
2 - Sin[Sin[Sin[Sin[Sin[Sin[Sin[Sin[1]]*Sin[Sin[1]]]]]]]]
```

was computed. This equals 1.57. Note that $\pi/2$ is about 1.57.

Each successive S-expression in this 12-step process produced a constant closer to what was needed, namely $\pi/2$. Each successive S-expression that evolved had slightly better fitness in solving the problem at hand than its predecessor. In other words, genetic programming, left to its own devices, evolved the needed constant numerical value $\pi/2$ from the available ingredients. It evolved the needed constant in response to the relentless pressure applied by the fitness function and the Darwinian process of natural selection.

The result of this particular run is that we rediscovered the well-known trigonometric identity involving a phase shift, namely

$\text{Cos } 2x = \text{Sin}(\pi/2 - 2x)$.

And, more important, this particular run led to the general solution to the problem of constant creation for symbolic regression, described in greater detail in the next section.

10.2 SYMBOLIC REGRESSION WITH CONSTANT CREATION

We now illustrate the general solution to the problem of constant creation in symbolic regression.

Suppose we are given a sampling of the numerical values from the given curve

$2.718x^2 + 3.1416x$

over 20 randomly chosen points in some domain, such as the interval $[-1, +1]$.

Because of the presence of the coefficients 2.718 and 3.1416 in the target expression above, it is unlikely that we could genetically discover an S-expression that closely fits the 20 sample points using only the techniques described for symbolic regression in section 7.3. Clearly, in order to do symbolic regression in general, we need the ability to create arbitrary floating-point constants to appear in the S-expressions produced by genetic programming.

The problem of constant creation can be solved by expanding the terminal set by adding one special new terminal called the *ephemeral random constant* and denoted $\Re$. Thus, the terminal set for a symbolic regression problem with one independent variable x is expanded to

```
T = {X, R}.
```

Whenever the ephemeral random constant $\Re$ is chosen for any endpoint of the tree during the creation of the initial random population in generation 0, a random number of a specified data type in a specified range is generated and attached to the tree at that point.

For example, in the real-valued symbolic regression problem at hand, it would be natural for the ephemeral random constant to be of the floating-point type and to yield a number in some convenient range, say between -1.000 and $+1.000$. In a problem involving integers (e.g., induction of a sequence of integers), $\Re$ might yield a random integer over some convenient range (such as -5 to $+5$). In a problem involving modular numbers (say, 0, 1, 2, 3, and 4 for a problem involving modulo-5 numbers), the ephemeral random constant $\Re$ would yield a random modulo 5 integer. In a Boolean problem, the ephemeral random constant $\Re$ would necessarily yield one of the two Boolean constants, namely T (True) or NIL (False).

Note that this random generation is done anew each time an ephemeral terminal $\Re$ is encountered, so the initial random population contains a variety of different random constants. Once generated and inserted into an initial random S-expression, these constants remain fixed.

When we create floating-point random constants, we use a granularity of 0.001 in selecting floating-point numbers within the specified range.

Figure 10.2 shows an initial random individual containing two random constants, $+0.1297$ and -0.3478.

After the initial random generation, the numerous different random constants arising from the ephemeral $\Re$ terminals will then be moved around from tree to tree by the crossover operation. These random constants will become embedded in various subtrees, which then carry out various operations on them.

This moving around of the random constants is not at all haphazard; it is driven by the overall goal of achieving ever-higher fitness. For example, a symbolic expression that is a reasonably good fit to a target function may become a better fit if a particular constant is decreased slightly. A slight decrease can be achieved in several different ways. For example, there may be a multiplication by 0.90, a division by 1.11, a subtraction of 0.008, or an addition

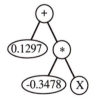

Figure 10.2 Initial random S-expression containing two random constants, $+0.1297$ and -0.3478.

of -0.0004. If a decrease of precisely 0.09 in a particular constant would produce a perfect fit, a decrease of 0.07 is usually fitter than a decrease of only 0.05. The creation of the value $\pi/2$, after a long sequence of intermediate steps, as described in the previous section, is another example.

Thus, the relentless pressure of the fitness function in the process of natural selection determines both the directions and the magnitudes of the adjustments in numerical constants.

In one run of the problem of symbolic regression for the target function $2.718x^2 + 3.1416x$, the best-of-generation S-expression in generation 41 was

```
(+ (- (+ (* -0.50677 X)
         (+ (* -0.50677 X) (* -0.76526 X)))).)
   (* (+ 0.11737) (+ (- X (* -0.76526 X)) X))).
```

This best-of-run S-expression is equivalent to

$2.76x^2 + 3.15x$.

The numerical constants -0.50677, -0.76256, and $+0.011737$ appearing in the above S-expression were originally created at random for some individuals in generation 0. These constants survived to generation 41 because they were carried from generation to generation as part of some individual in the population. If the individual carrying a particular constant is selected to participate in crossover or reproduction more than once on a particular generation, the constant would then appear in an increasing number of individuals. If no individual carrying a particular constant is selected to participate in crossover or reproduction in a particular generation, that constant would disappear from the population. As previously mentioned, crossover can combine expressions containing one or more existing constants to create new constant values.

The run producing the above S-expression was terminated at generation 41 because the S-expression came within 0.01 of the value of the target function for all 20 randomly chosen values of the independent variable x in the domain $[-1, +1]$. That is, this individual scored 20 hits. Scoring 20 hits is one of the termination criteria for this problem (the other being that the run has reached the maximum specified generation number, i.e., 50). Unlike the S-expression produced in section 7.3 for the symbolic regression problem involving the quartic polynomial $x^4 + x^3 + x^2 + x$, the S-expression above is not an exact solution to the problem. The coefficient 2.76 is near 2.718 and the coefficient 3.15 is near 3.1416, so this S-expression produces a value that is close to the given target expression for the 20 fitness cases.

The above genetically produced best-of-run S-expression is, with certainty, an approximately correct solution to the problem only for the particular 20 randomly chosen values of the independent variable x that were available to the genetic programming paradigm. If the best-of-run S-expression were a polynomial of order 19, we would wonder whether it was merely a polynomial that happened to pass through the particular 20 given x-y points. This particular suspicion does not arise here, since the best-of-run polynomial is

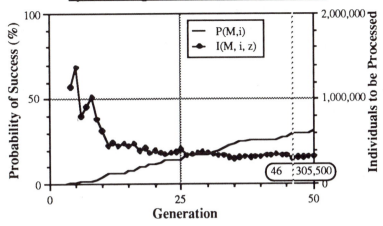

Figure 10.3 Performance curves for the symbolic regression problem with $2.718x^2 + 3.1416x$ as the target function.

only quadratic. However, the question remains as to how well this approximately correct quadratic expression discovered by genetic programming generalizes over the entire domain $[-1, +1]$.

We can begin to address this question concerning the generality of an S-expression discovered from only a limited number of fitness cases by retesting the S-expression against a much larger number of fitness cases. For example, when we retest this S-expression over 1,000 randomly chosen values of the independent variable x in the domain $[-1, +1]$, we find that the S-expression returns a value that comes within 0.01 of the target function for all 1,000 of the new fitness cases. That is, this S-expression scores 1,000 hits on the retest. This success increases our confidence that the genetically produced S-expression is a good fit for the given target function over the entire domain $[-1, +1]$.

Figure 10.3 presents the performance curves showing, by generation, the cumulative probability of success $P(M, i)$ and the number of individuals that must be processed $I(M, i, z)$ to guarantee, with 99% probability, that at least one S-expression comes within 0.01 of the target function for all 20 fitness cases for the symbolic regression problem with $2.718x^2 + 3.1416x$ as the target function. The graph is based on 100 runs and a population size of 500. The cumulative probability of success $P(M, i)$ is 30% by generation 46 and 31% by generation 50. The numbers in the oval indicate that, if this problem is run through to generation 46, processing a total of 305,500 (i.e., 500×47 generations $\times 13$ runs) individuals is sufficient to guarantee solution of this problem with 99% probability.

10.3 ECONOMETRIC MODELING AND FORECASTING

An important problem area in virtually every area of science is finding the relationship underlying empirically observed values of the variables measuring a system (Langley and Zytkow 1989; Shrager and Langley 1990). In practice, the observed data may be noisy and there may be no way to express the relationships in any precise way. Some of the data may be missing.

In this section, we demonstrate how to discover empirical relationships from actual observed data using the well-known nonlinear econometric exchange equation

$$P = \frac{MV}{Q}.$$

This equation states the relationship between the gross national product Q of an economy, the price level P, the money supply M, and the velocity of money V in the economy.

Suppose that the goal is to find the econometric model expressing the relationship between quarterly values of the price level P and the quarterly values of the three other quantities appearing in the equation. That is, the goal is to rediscover that $P = MV/Q$ from the actual observed noisy time series data. Many economists believe that inflation (which is the change in the price level) can be controlled by the central bank via adjustments in the money supply M.

In particular, suppose we are given the 120 actual quarterly values (from 1959:1 to 1988:4) of the following four econometric time series:

- the annual rate for the United States' gross national product in billions of 1982 dollars (conventionally called GNP82),
- the gross national product deflator (normalized to 1.0 for 1982) (called GD),
- the monthly values of the seasonally adjusted money stock M2 in billions of dollars, averaged for each quarter (called M2), and
- the monthly interest rate yields of 3-month Treasury bills, averaged for each quarter (called FYGM3).

The four time series used here were obtained from the CITIBASE™ database of machine-readable econometric time series (Citibank 1989) with an Apple Macintosh II™ computer using software provided by VAR Econometrics Inc. (Doan 1989).

Figure 10.4 shows the actual price level in the United States as represented by the gross national product deflator GD (normalized to 1.0 for 1982) over the 30-year, 120-quarter period from 1959:1 to 1988:4.

The actual long-term observed postwar value of the M2 velocity of money in the United States is 1.6527 (Hallman, Porter, and Small 1989; Humphrey 1989). Thus, the correct exchange equation for the United States in the postwar period is the nonlinear relationship

$$GD = \frac{(1.6527 * M2)}{GNP82}.$$

Figure 10.5 shows the fitted GD series (that is, the time series calculated from the above model) for the 120 quarters from 1959:1 to 1988:4.

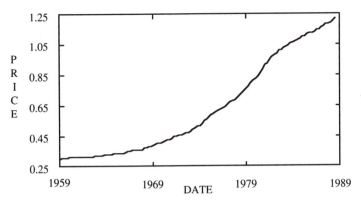

Figure 10.4 Gross national product deflator (GD) from 1959:1 to 1988:4.

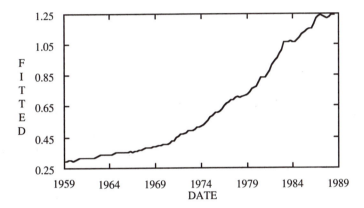

Figure 10.5 Fitted GD time series.

Figure 10.6 shows both the actual GD from 1959:1 to 1988:4 and the fitted GD series calculated from the above model for 1959:1 to 1988:4. The actual GD series is shown by the dotted points. The fitted GD series calculated from the above model is shown as a continuous path between the points.

The sum of the squared errors over the entire 30-year period (1959:1 to 1988:4) was 0.077193. The correlation R^2 was 0.993320.

Figure 10.7 shows a plot of the corresponding residuals (errors) from the fitted GD series calculated from the above model for 1959:1 to 1988:4.

10.3.1 Model Derived from the First Two-Thirds of the Data

We first divide the 30-year, 120-quarter period into a 20-year, 80-quarter in-sample period running from 1959:1 to 1978:4 and a 10-year, 40-quarter out-of-sample period running from 1979:1 to 1988:4. This allows us to use the first two-thirds of the data to create the model and to then use the last third of the data to test the model.

The terminal set for this problem is

```
T = {GNP82, FM2, FYGM3, ℜ}.
```

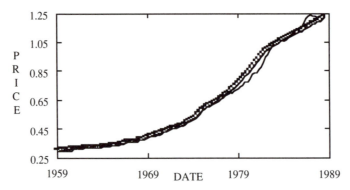

Figure 10.6 Gross national product deflator GD overlaid with fitted time series.

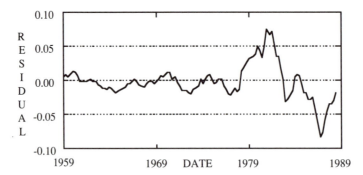

Figure 10.7 Residuals between gross national product deflator GD and the fitted time series.

The terminals GNP82, FM2, and FYGM3 correspond to the independent variables of the model and provide access to the values of the time series. The $\Re$ is the ephemeral random constant that causes random floating-point constants to be inserted into the S-expressions of generation 0. In effect, the terminals for this problem are functions of the unstated, implicit time variable that ranges over the various quarters.

Notice that we are not told *a priori* whether the unknown functional relationship between the given observed data (the three independent variables) and the target function (the dependent variable, GD) is linear, multiplicative, polynomial, exponential, logarithmic, or otherwise. The unknown functional relationship could involve a combination of these functions or could involve entirely different functions. If we do not know the nature of the relationship between the dependent variable and the independent variables of a problem, we can include functions in the function set that we suspect might express the relationship between the variables. For economic data, it is reasonable to include functions relating to growth (e.g., exponential and logarithmic functions) in addition to the usual four arithmetic operations. For example, the function set for this problem might be

```
F = {+, -, *, %, EXP, RLOG},
```

taking two, two, two, two, one, and one arguments, respectively.

Notice also that we are not given the known constant value V for the velocity of money. It is produced as part of the solution to the problem.

We are not told that the addition, subtraction, exponential, and logarithm function contained in the function set and the 3-month Treasury Bill yields (FYGM3) contained in the terminal set are all irrelevant to finding the econometric model for the dependent variable GD of this problem.

In problems of empirical discovery, the fitness cases for the problem must be the available given data points (or, perhaps, a subset of them). The fitness of an S-expression is the sum of the squares of the differences, taken over the 80 in-sample quarters, between the value of the price level produced by S-expression and the target value of the price level given by the GD time series.

There is an unusually large range in the magnitudes of the values of independent variables that will be encountered in the actual data for this problem. For example, typical values of gross national product GNP82 are in the trillions of dollars, and typical values of the money supply M2 are in the hundreds of billions of dollars. The price level GD is typically quoted as an indexed number (i.e., where the value in the base year is expressed as 100). Interest rates are fractions less than 1.00 (e.g., 0.08). Moreover, our usual range of ephemeral floating-point random constants $\Re$ is between -1.000 and $+1.000$. It seemed advisable to reduce this range of magnitudes by stating GNP82 and M2 in billions of dollars (so that they are in the neighborhood between 10^2 to 10^4) and converting the index 100 into the number 1.00. This reduces the overall range in magnitudes of the values that are assumed by the variables of the problem to about five orders of magnitude.

Table 10.2 summarizes the key features of the empirical discovery problem for the econometric exchange equation $P = MV/Q$.

The initial random population was, predictably, highly unfit. In one run, the sum of squared errors between the best-of-generation individual and the actual GD time series was 1.55. The correlation R^2 was 0.49.

In generation 1, the sum of the squared errors for the new best-of-generation individual in the population improved to 0.50.

In generation 3, the sum of the squared errors for the new best-of-generation individual in the population improved to 0.05. This is approximately a 31-to-1 improvement over the initial random generation. The value of R^2 improved to 0.98. In addition, by generation 3 the best-of-generation individual in the population scored 44 hits.

In generation 6, the sum of the squared errors for the new best-of-generation individual in the population improved to 0.027. This is approximately a 2-to-1 improvement over generation 3. The value of R^2 improved to 0.99.

In generation 7, the sum of the squared errors for the new best-of-generation individual in the population improved to 0.013. This is approximately a 2-to-1 improvement over generation 6.

In generation 15, the sum of the squared errors for the new best-of-generation individual improved to 0.011. This is an additional improvement over generation 7 and represents approximately a 141-to-1 improvement over

Table 10.2 Tableau for empirical discovery of econometric exchange equation.

Objective:	Find an econometric model for the price level, in symbolic form, that fits a given sample of 80 actual quarterly data points.
Terminal set:	GNP82, FM2, FYGM3, $\Re$, where the ephemeral random floating-point constant $\Re$ ranges over the interval $[-1.000, +1.000]$.
Function set:	+, −, *, %, EXP, RLOG.
Fitness cases:	The given sample of 80 quarterly data points.
Raw fitness:	The sum, taken over 80 quarters, of the squares of differences between the S-expression for the price level expressed in terms of the three independent variables and the actual GD time series.
Standardized fitness:	Equals raw fitness for this problem.
Hits:	Number of fitness cases for which the S-expression comes within 1% of the actual value of the GD time series.
Wrapper:	None.
Parameters:	$M = 500$. $G = 51$.
Success predicate:	An S-expression scores 80 hits.

the best-of-generation individual from generation 0. The correlation R^2 was 0.99.

The best-of-run individual,

```
(% (+ (* (+ (* -0.402 -0.583)
            (% FM2
               (- GNP82
                  (- 0.126
                     (+ (+ -0.83 0.832)
                        (% (% GNP82
                              (* (- 0.005 GNP82)
                                 (% GNP82 GNP82)))
                           0.47))))))
         FM2)
      FM2)
   GNP82),
```

had a sum of squared errors of 0.009272 over the in-sample period.

This individual is equivalent to

$$GD = \frac{(1.634 * M2)}{GNP82}.$$

Figure 10.8 graphically depicts the above best-of-run individual as a rooted, point-labeled tree with ordered branches.

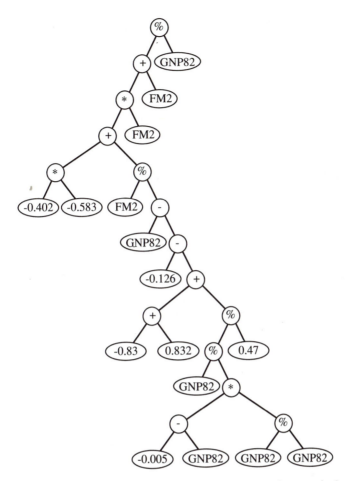

Figure 10.8 Best-of-run S-expression for price level using first two-thirds of data.

We now compare the in-sample period consisting of the first two-thirds of the data with the out-of-sample period.

Figure 10.9 shows the fitted values from this genetically produced model (derived from the 80-quarter in-sample period) over all 120 quarters. The solid vertical line divides the 20-year, 80-quarter in-sample period (1959:1 to 1978:4) from the 10-year, 40-quarter out-of-sample period (1979:1 to 1988:4).

Table 10.3 shows the sum of the squared errors and R^2 for the entire 120-quarter period, the 80-quarter in-sample period, and the 40-quarter out-of-sample period.

Figure 10.10 shows both the gross national product deflator GD and the fitted time series calculated from the above model for 1959:1 to 1988:4. The actual GD series is shown by the dotted points. The fitted GD series calculated from the above model is shown as a continuous path.

Figure 10.11 shows a plot of the residuals from the fitted GD series calculated from the above model for 1959:1 to 1988:4.

Since the out-of-sample period is chronologically later than the in-sample period, this model is a forecast.

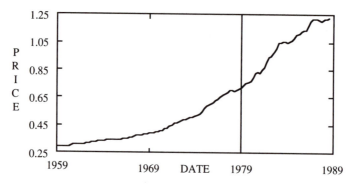

Figure 10.9 Graph of best-of-run S-expression for the price level using the first two-thirds of the data.

Table 10.3 Squared errors and correlations using the first two-thirds of the data.

Data range	1–120	1–80	81–120
R^2	0.993480	0.997949	0.990614
Sum of squared errors	0.075388	0.009272	0.066116

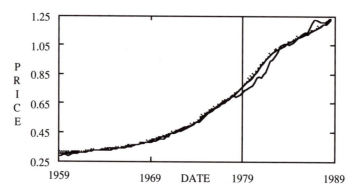

Figure 10.10 Gross national product deflator GD and the fitted time series using the first two-thirds of the data.

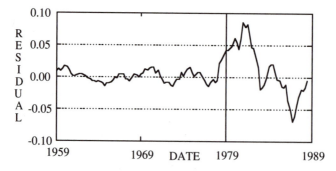

Figure 10.11 Residuals between the gross national product deflator GD and the fitted time series using the first two-thirds of the data.

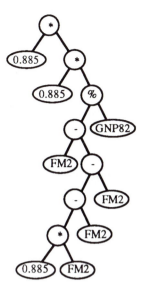

Figure 10.12 Best-of-run S-expression for price level using the last two-thirds of the data.

10.3.2 Model Derived from the Last Two-Thirds of the Data

We now divide the 30-year, 120-quarter period into a 10-year, 40-quarter out-of-sample period running from 1959:1 to 1968:4 and a 20-year, 80-quarter in-sample period running from 1969:1 to 1988:4.

The following typical best-of-run individual had a sum of squared errors of 0.076247 over the in-sample period:

```
(* 0.885 (* 0.885 (% (- FM2
                      (- (- (* 0.885 FM2) FM2) FM2))
                    GNP82))).
```

This individual is equivalent to

$$GD = \frac{(1.6565 * M2)}{GNP82}.$$

Figure 10.12 graphically depicts this best-of-run individual as a rooted, point-labeled tree with ordered branches.

Figure 10.13 shows the fitted values from this model (derived from the 80-quarter in-sample period) over all 120 quarters. The solid vertical line divides the 40-quarter out-of-sample period from the 80-quarter in-sample period.

We now compare the in-sample period consisting of the last two-thirds of the data and the out-of-sample period.

Table 10.4 shows the sum of the squared errors and R^2 for the entire 120-quarter period, the 40-quarter out-of-sample period, and the 80-quarter in-sample period.

Figure 10.14 shows both the gross national product deflator GD from 1959:1 to 1988:4 and the fitted GD series calculated from the above model for

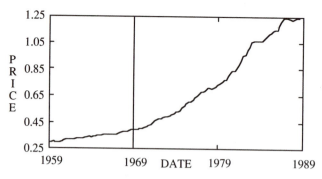

Figure 10.13 Graph of genetically produced price level using the last two-thirds of the data.

Table 10.4 Squared errors and correlations using the last two-thirds of the data.

Data range	1–120	1–40	41–120
R^2	0.993130	0.999136	0.990262
Sum of squared errors	0.079473	0.003225	0.076247

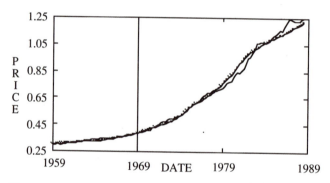

Figure 10.14 Gross national product deflator GD and fitted time series using the last two-thirds of the data.

1959:1 to 1988:4. The actual GD series is shown as a line with dotted points. The fitted GD series calculated from the above model is shown as a continuous path.

Figure 10.15 shows a plot of the residuals from the fitted GD series calculated from the above model for 1959:1.

Other Runs The same process can be carried out with a different designation of dependent and independent variables. For example, the money supply M2 can be designated as the dependent variable.

In generation 9 of one such run, the following S-expression for M2 emerged:

```
(* GD (% GNP82 (% (% -0.587 0.681) (RLOG -0.587)))).
```

Figure 10.16 graphically depicts this S-expression.

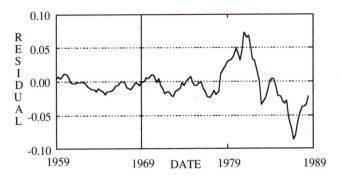

Figure 10.15   Residuals between the gross national product deflator GD and fitted time series using the last two-thirds of the data.

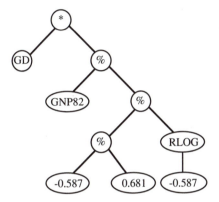

Figure 10.16 Genetically produced S-expression for money supply.

This S-expression for M2 is equivalent to

(% (* GD GNP82) 1.618),

which is equivalent to the more familiar

$$M2 = \frac{GD * GNP82}{1.618}.$$

See also Koza 1990b and Koza 1990f.

10.4   EMPIRICAL DISCOVERY OF KEPLER'S THIRD LAW

Langley et al. (1987) describe the BACON family of heuristic techniques for inducing scientific laws from empirical data. BACON starts with a set of values of an independent variable and the associated value of the dependent variable and produces a mathematical expression relating the dependent variable to the independent variable. BACON has successfully rediscovered such scientific laws as Boyle's Law, Ohm's Law, and Coulomb's Law from given finite samples of data.

One of the more complicated scientific laws reported by Langley et al. to have been rediscovered by BACON is Kepler's Third Law of Planetary Motion, which states that the cube of a planet's distance from the sun is proportional to the square of its period. That is,

$$\frac{D^3}{p^2} = c.$$

Although BACON uses different terminology than genetic programming, the steps that the user must perform prior to using the two approaches are similar. First, BACON requires the user to identify the set of independent variables that are to be used to explain the relationship. This selection corresponds to selecting the set of terminals in genetic programming. Second, BACON requires the user to supply a set of heuristics that might be used to express the unknown relationship. For example, the user might supply the following two heuristics to BACON:

- If the values of one numerical variable increase while those of another variable decrease, then consider multiplication to be the explanation.
- If the values of two numerical variables increase together, then consider division to be the explanation.

The selection of heuristics in BACON corresponds to the selection of the set of functions in genetic programming. The two functions here are multiplication and division. Third, BACON requires the user to select a sampling of pairs of values for a representative sampling of combinations of the independent and dependent variables. This selection corresponds to the selecting of the fitness cases in genetic programming. BACON applies an error measure to the differences between the values of the dependent variable produced by BACON and the values of the dependent variable associated with each fitness case. This error measure corresponds to the fitness measure in genetic programming.

BACON works by testing whether any of the user supplied heuristics are applicable to the given sampling of data. If a heuristic is applicable, then BACON considers that the two variables are related via the function identified by the heuristic. It then adjusts the sampling of data (i.e., the fitness cases) using the function identified by the heuristic so as to create an adjusted sampling (in effect, a new set of fitness cases). BACON then retests whether any of the user-supplied heuristics are applicable to the adjusted sampling. For example, if the condition of the first heuristic above is applicable to the given data, BACON considers that the two variables are related via the function of multiplication. BACON then adjusts the fitness cases by applying the function thus identified. The adjusted version of the fitness cases is then tested anew to see if any heuristic is applicable. Thus, relationships involving multiple applications of the functions in BACON's function set can be discovered. That is, BACON discovers a composition of functions from its available function set. If and when the adjusted sampling of data produces an identity between the independent variable and the adjusted version of the dependent variable, BACON is considered successful and the run terminates. In that event, BACON has produced a sequence of applications of functions (i.e., a composition of functions) relating the independent variable and the dependent variable. Because empirical data are usually involved, attainment of a perfect identity is not required.

We now use genetic programming to rediscover Kepler's Third Law. The goal is to look at the empirically observed astronomical data and find an S-expression for the period of a planet in terms of its distance from the sun. The terminal set for this problem is therefore

```
T = {DIST},
```

where DIST is the distance (in astronomical units) of a planet from the sun.

The function set for this problem is

```
F = {+, -, *, %, SRT, SIN, COS},
```

taking two, two, two, two, one, one, and one arguments, respectively. The protected square root function SRT is the square root of the absolute value (subsection 6.1.1).

Each of the nine planets provides one pair of data relating the period P of the planet (in earth years) to the distance DIST of a planet from the sun. These nine pairs of available empirical data are the nine fitness cases for this problem. The fitness of an S-expression is the sum, taken over the nine fitness cases, of

Table 10.5 Tableau for empirical discovery of Kepler's Third Law.

Objective:	Find a scientific law that fits a given sample of empirical data points.
Terminal set:	DIST.
Function set:	+, -, *, %, SRT, SIN, COS.
Fitness cases:	The given sample of nine data points for the nine planets.
Raw fitness:	The sum, over the nine fitness cases, of the absolute value of the differences between the value of the period P produced by the S-expression and the target value of P associated with that planet.
Standardized fitness:	Same as raw fitness for this problem.
Hits:	Number of fitness cases for which the value of the period P produced by the S-expression is within 1% of the target value of P.
Wrapper:	None.
Population size:	500.
Termination:	Maximum number of generations $G = 51$. Also terminate if an S-expression scores nine hits.

the absolute value of the difference between the value of the period P produced by the S-expression and the target value of the period P.

Table 10.5 summarizes the key features of the empirical discovery problem for Kepler's Third Law.

In many runs, the S-expression

```
(* DIST DIST)
```

appeared in either the initial random generation or one of the early generations. This incorrect law fits the data reasonably well, although not, of course, as well as the correct law. Interestingly, in 1608—ten years before he published the correct version of his Third Law—Kepler published this incorrect version.

After a few more generations, genetic programming produced the correct version of Kepler's Third Law in the following two forms:

```
(SRT (* DIST (* DIST DIST)))
```

and

```
(* DIST (SRT DIST)).
```

Less parsimonious forms of the correct solution included the following two S-expressions:

```
(- (* DIST (SRT DIST)) (SIN 0.0))
```

and

```
(* DIST
   (+ (- DIST DIST) (+ (- DIST DIST) (SRT DIST)))).
```

10.5 SYMBOLIC INTEGRATION

Symbolic integration involves finding a mathematical expression that is the integral, in symbolic form, of a given curve. The LEX system developed by Mitchell, Utgoff, and Banerji (1983) is a well-known approach to symbolic integration. Mills (1987) reviews various approaches to the problem of symbolic integration.

Genetic programming can be used to perform a kind of symbolic integration via a direct extension of the symbolic regression process described earlier in this chapter. The result of symbolic integration by means of genetic programming is a *function* expressed as a symbolic mathematical expression. The resulting function may be a perfect solution to the problem or it may be a function that approximates the correct integral.

The given curve may be presented either as a mathematical expression in symbolic form or a discrete sampling of data points (i.e., the symbolic form of the given curve is not explicitly specified).

If the given curve is presented as a mathematical expression, we first convert it into a finite sample of data points. We do this by taking a random sample of values $\{x_i\}$ of the independent variable appearing in the given mathematical expression over some appropriate domain. We then pair each value of the independent variable x_i with the result y_i of evaluating the given mathematical expression for that value of the independent variable.

Thus, we begin the process of symbolic integration with a given finite sampling of pairs of numerical values (x_i, y_i). If there are, say, 50 (x_i, y_i) pairs (for i between 0 and 49), then, for convenience, we assume that the values of x_i have been sorted so that $x_i < x_{i+1}$ for i between 0 and 48. The domain values x_i lie in some appropriate interval.

The goal is to find, in symbolic form, a mathematical expression that is a perfect fit (or a good fit) to the integral of the given curve using only the given 50 pairs of numerical points.

For example, if the given curve happened to be

$$Cos\, x + 2x + 1,$$

the goal would be to find its integral in symbolic form, namely

$$Sin\, x + x^2 + x,$$

given the 50 pairs (x_i, y_i). The domain appropriate to this example might be the interval $[0, 2\pi]$.

Symbolic integration is, in fact, merely symbolic regression with an additional preliminary step of numerical integration. Specifically, we numerically integrate the curve defined by the given set of 50 points (x_i, y_i) over the interval starting at x_0 and running to x_i. The integral $I(x_i)$ is a function of x_i. The value of this integral $I(x_0)$ for the first point x_0 is 0. For any other point x_i, where i is between 1 and 49, we perform a numerical integration by adding up the areas of the i trapezoids lying between the point x_0 and the point x_i. We thereby obtain an approximation to the value for the integral $I(x_i)$ of the given curve for each point x_i. We therefore obtain 50 new pairs $(x_i, I(x_i))$ for i between 0 and 49. These 50 pairs are the fitness cases for this problem.

We then perform symbolic regression to find the mathematical expression for the curve defined by the 50 new pairs $(x_i, I(x_i))$. This mathematical expression is the integral, in symbolic form, of the curve defined by the original 50 given points (x_i, y_i).

Table 10.6 illustrates the process described above using only five points, instead of 50 points. Row 1 shows five values of x_i spaced equally in the interval $[0, 2\pi]$. Row 2 shows, for each of the five values of x_i from row 1, the value of the given curve $Cos\, x + 2x + 1$. Row 3 contains the numerical

Table 10.6 Finding an integral in symbolic form.

1	x_i	0.00	1.57	3.14	4.71	6.28
2	$y = Cos\, x_i + 2x_i + 1$	2.00	4.14	6.28	10.42	14.57
3	$\int_{x=0}^{x_i} Cos\, x + 2x + 1\, dx$	0.00	4.82	13.01	26.13	45.76
4	$Sin\, x + x^2 + x$	0.00	5.04	13.01	25.92	45.76
5	Absolute error	0.00	0.21	1.78	0.21	0.00

integral of the given curve $\text{Cos}\, x + 2x + 1$ from the beginning of the interval (i.e., 0.0) to x_i. This numerical integral is computed by adding up the trapezoids lying under the unknown curve given by row 2. Symbolic regression is then applied to rows 1 and 3. Specifically, row 1 is considered to be the independent variable of the unknown function, while row 3 is considered to be the value of the dependent variable. After running for several generations, genetic programming may produce $\text{Sin}\, x + x^2 + x$, in symbolic form, as the integral of the unknown curve. Row 4 shows the value of $\text{Sin}\, x + x^2 + x$ for all five values of x_i. Row 5 shows the error between rows 3 and 4. Since the error is relatively small for all five values of x_i, the curve $\text{Sin}\, x + x^2 + x$ can be considered to be the integral of the unknown curve. One could, of course, add a constant of integration, if one so desired.

When genetic programming is applied to this problem, the terminal set should contain the independent variable(s) of the problem, so

T = {X}.

The function set should contain functions that might be needed to express the solution to the problem. Of course, the functions needed to express the integral of a given function are not, in general, known *a priori*. In this situation, we must make some kind of reasonable choice for the function set. It is probably better to include a few possibly extraneous functions in the function set than to omit a needed function. Of course, if a needed function is not in the function set, genetic programming will perform the symbolic regression as best as it can using the available functions. The following function set is a

Table 10.7 Tableau for symbolic integration.

Objective:	Find a function, in symbolic form, that is the integral of a curve presented either as a mathematical expression or as a given finite sample of points (x_i, y_i).
Terminal set:	X.
Function set:	+, −, *, %, SIN, COS, EXP, RLOG.
Fitness cases:	Sample of 50 data points (x_i, y_i).
Raw fitness:	The sum, taken over the 50 fitness cases, of the absolute value of the difference between the individual genetically produced function $f_j(x_i)$ at domain point x_i and the value of the numerical integral $I(x_i)$.
Standardized fitness:	Same as standardized fitness for this problem.
Hits:	Number of fitness cases coming within 0.01 of the target value $I(x_i)$.
Wrapper:	None.
Parameters:	$M = 500.\ G = 51.$
Success predicate:	An S-expression scores 50 hits.

reasonable choice for this problem:

```
F = {+, -, *, %, SIN, COS, EXP, RLOG},
```

taking two, two, two, two, one, one, one, and one argument, respectively.

As each individual genetically produced function f_j is generated, we evaluate $f_j(x_i)$ so as to obtain 50 pairs $(x_i, f_j(x_i))$. The raw fitness of an individual genetically produced function is the sum of the absolute value of difference between the value $f_j(x_i)$ of the individual genetically produced function f_j at domain point x_i and the value of the numerical integral $I(x_i)$. A hit for this problem occurs when $f_j(x_i)$ comes within 0.01 of the target value $I(x_i)$.

In creating the fitness cases for symbolic integration, it will usually be desirable to have a larger number of fitness cases (e.g., 50) than for an ordinary problem of symbolic regression, because of the error inherent in the extra step of numerical integration.

Table 10.7 summarizes the key features of the symbolic integration problem.

In one run, the best-of-generation S-expression in generation 4 was

```
(+ (+ (- (SIN X) (- X X)) X) (* X X)).
```

This S-expression scored 50 hits and had a standardized fitness of virtually 0. The standardized fitness (error) does not reach 0 exactly, because the integral is merely a numerical approximation and because of the small errors inherent in floating-point calculations.

This best-of-run S-expression is equivalent to

$Sin\ x + x^2 + x,$

which is, in fact, the symbolic integral of

$Cos\ x + 2x + 1.$

Figure 10.17 presents the performance curves showing, by generation, the cumulative probability of success $P(M, i)$ and the number of individuals that must be processed $I(M, i, z)$ to guarantee, with 99% probability, that at least

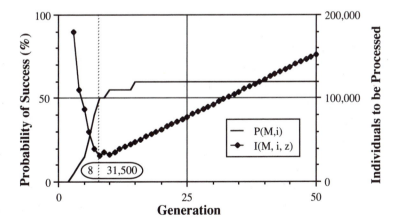

Figure 10.17 Performance curves for the symbolic integration problem.

one S-expression comes within 0.01 of the target value function for all 50 fitness cases. The graph is based on 20 runs and a population size of 500. The cumulative probability of success $P(M, i)$ is 50% by generation 8 and 60% by generation 50. The numbers in the oval indicate that, if this problem is run through to generation 8, processing a total of 31,500 (i.e., 500 × 9 generations × 7 runs) individuals is sufficient to guarantee solution of this problem with 99% probability.

In another symbolic integration run, $x^4 + x^3 + x^2 + x$ was obtained as the symbolic integral of $4x^3 + 3x^2 + 2x + 1$.

The step of numerical integration could, if desired, be replaced by symbolic integration for any S-expression that one happens to be able to integrate symbolically.

10.6 SYMBOLIC DIFFERENTIATION

Symbolic differentiation involves finding a mathematical expression that is the derivative, in symbolic form, of a given curve.

We proceed much as in the symbolic integration problem described in the previous section, since symbolic differentiation can be implemented as symbolic regression with an additional preliminary step of numerical differentiation.

The goal is to find, in symbolic form, a mathematical expression that is a perfect fit (or a good fit) to the derivative of the given curve using only the given 200 pairs of numerical points. For example, if the given curve happened to be

$$xe^x + \operatorname{Sin} x + x,$$

the goal is to find its derivative in symbolic form, namely

$$xe^x + e^x + \operatorname{Cos} x + 1,$$

given the 200 pairs (x_i, y_i). The domain appropriate to this example might be the interval $[0, 2\pi.]$.

Specifically, we numerically differentiate the curve defined by the given set of 200 points (x_i, y_i) over the interval starting at x_0 and running to x_{199}. The derivative $\mathbf{D}(x_i)$ is a function of x_i. For any point x_i other than the endpoints x_0 and x_{199}, the derivative is the average of the slope of the curve between point x_{i-1} and x_i and the slope of the curve between point x_i and x_{i+1}. For the two endpoints x_0 and x_{199} of the domain, the derivative is the unaveraged slope of the curve. We thereby obtain a value for the derivative $\mathbf{D}(x_i)$ of the given curve for each point x_i. We therefore obtain 200 new pairs $(x_i, \mathbf{D}(x_i))$ for i between 0 and 199. These 200 pairs are the fitness cases for this problem.

In creating the fitness cases for symbolic differentiation, it will usually be desirable to have a larger number of points for the numerical differentiation (e.g., 200) than for the numerical integration (i.e., 50) because numerical differentiation is less accurate than numerical integration. The definition of a

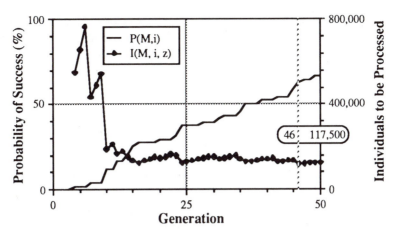

Figure 10.18 Performance curves for symbolic differentiation.

hit might be similarly loosened so that a hit occurs when $f_i(x_i)$ comes within 0.03 of the target value $\mathbf{D}(x_i)$.

We then perform symbolic regression to find the mathematical expression defined by the 200 new pairs $(x_i, \mathbf{D}(x_i))$. This mathematical expression is the derivative, in symbolic form, of the curve outlined by the original 200 given points (x_i, y_i).

In one run, the best-of-generation S-expression in generation 22 consisted of 41 points and was

```
(+ (+ (+ (REXP X) (* (REXP X) X)) (RCOS (% (* (* (% (- X
X) X) X) X) X) (+ (+ (REXP X) (* (+ X X) X)) (* (+ (- X X)
(REXP X)) (RLOG (REXP X))))))))) (RCOS X)).
```

This S-expression scored 199 hits and had a standardized fitness of 2.52 (an average of 0.0126 per fitness case). This best-of-run S-expression is equivalent to

$$xe^x + e^x + \mathrm{Cos}\, x + 1.$$

Figure 10.18 presents the performance curves showing, by generation, the cumulative probability of success $P(M, i)$ and the number of individuals that must be processed $I(M, i, z)$ to guarantee, with 99% probability, that at least one S-expression comes within 0.03 of the target value function for all 200 fitness cases. The graph is based on 68 runs and a population size of 500. The cumulative probability of success $P(M, i)$ is 62% by generation 46 and 67% by generation 50. The numbers in the oval indicate that, if this problem is run through to generation 46, processing a total of 117,500 (i.e., 500 × 47 generations × 5 runs) individuals is sufficient to guarantee solution of this problem with 99% probability.

In other runs of symbolic differentiation, $4x^3 + 3x^2 + 2x + 1$ was obtained as the symbolic derivative of $x^4 + x^3 + x^2 + x$ and $\mathrm{Cos}\, x + 2x + 1$ was obtained as the symbolic derivative of $\mathrm{Sin}\, x + x^2 + x$.

If desired, the step of numerical differentiation can be replaced by symbolic differentiation for any S-expression that one happens to be able to differentiate symbolically.

10.7 DIFFERENTIAL EQUATIONS

Genetic programming can be used to solve an equation whose solution consists of a function that satisfies the given equation. In particular, genetic programming can be used to solve differential equations (with given initial conditions), integral equations, general functional equations, and inverse problems. In each case, the result produced by genetic programming is a mathematical expression in symbolic form.

A differential equation is an equation involving one or more derivatives (of some order) of an unknown function. The solution to a differential equation is a function that, when substituted into the given equation, satisfies the equation and any given initial conditions. Differential equations are the most familiar functional equations.

It is possible, using exact analytic methods, to find the exact function that solves some differential equations. However, for most differential equations, only numerical approximations are available.

The problem of solving a differential equation may be viewed as the search in a space of compositions of functions and terminals for a particular composition that satisfies the equation and its initial conditions. Once the problem of solving differential equations is reformulated in this way, the problem is an immediate candidate for solution by genetic programming.

The approach involves an extension of the already-described techniques for symbolic integration and differentiation (which are, of course, based on symbolic regression).

Without loss of generality, we will assume that every equation in the remainder of this chapter has been transformed so that its right-hand side is 0.

10.7.1 Example 1

Consider the simple differential equation

$$\frac{dy}{dx} + y \operatorname{Cos} x = 0,$$

where $y_{\text{initial}} = 1.0$ for x_{initial} of 0.0.

The goal is to find a function that satisfies this equation and its initial condition, namely the function $e^{-\operatorname{Sin} x}$.

The terminal set and the function set for this problem are chosen in the same way as for symbolic integration.

We start by generating 200 random values of the independent variable x_i over some appropriate domain, such as the unit interval [0, 1]. We then sort these values into ascending order.

We are seeking a function $f(x)$ such that, for every one of the 200 values x_i of the variable x, we get 0 when we perform the following computation: For each i, add the derivative $f'(x_i)$ at the point x_i (i.e., dy/dx) to the product of $f(x_i)$ at point x_i (i.e., y) and the cosine of x_i. This rewording of the problem immediately suggests an orderly general procedure for genetically finding the function $f(x)$ that satisfies the given differential equation.

Given the set of 200 ascending values of x_i, we define a "curve resulting from applying the function g" to be the 200 pairs $(x_i, g(x_i))$, where g is some function.

When the jth genetically produced function f_j in the population (i.e., S-expression) is generated by genetic programming, we apply this function (i.e., S-expression) f_j to generate a curve. Specifically, we obtain 200 values of $f_j(x_i)$ corresponding to the 200 values of x_i. We call these 200 pairs $(x_i, f_j(x_i))$ the "curve resulting from applying the genetically produced function f_j" or "the f_j curve."

We then numerically differentiate this curve $(x_i, f_j(x_i))$ with respect to the independent variable x_i. That is, we apply the function of differentiation to obtain a new curve. Specifically, we obtain a new set of 200 pairs $(x_i, f_j'(x_i))$ which we call the "curve resulting from applying the differentiation function" or "the derivative curve."

We then apply the cosine function to obtain yet another curve. Specifically, we take the cosine of the 200 random values of x_i to obtain a new set of 200 pairs $(x_i, \text{Cos } x_i)$, which we call the "curve resulting from applying the cosine function" or "the cosine curve."

We then apply the multiplication function to the cosine curve and the f_j curve to obtain still another curve which we call "the product curve." In particular, we multiply the curve consisting of the set of 200 pairs $(x_i, \text{Cos } x_i)$ by $f_j(x_i)$ so as to obtain a new curve, called "the product curve," consisting of the set of 200 pairs $(x_i, f_j(x_i)^* \text{Cos } x_i)$.

We then apply the addition function to the derivative curve and the product curve to obtain a curve consisting of the set of 200 pairs $(x_i, f_j'(x_i) + f_j(x_i)^* \text{Cos } x_i)$, which we call "the sum curve."

To the extent that the sum curve is close to the "zero curve" consisting of the 200 pairs $(x_i, 0)$ (i.e., the right-hand side of the differential equation) for the 200 values of x_i, the genetically produced function f_j is a good approximation to the solution of the given differential equation.

The problem of solving the given differential equation is now equivalent, except for the matter of initial conditions, to a symbolic regression problem over the set of points $(x_i, f_j'(x_i) + f_j(x_i)^* \text{Cos } x_i)$.

In solving differential equations, the fitness of a particular genetically produced function should be expressed in terms of two components. The first component is how well the function satisfies the differential equation as just described above. The second component is how well the function satisfies the initial condition of the differential equation.

Since a mere linear function passing through the initial condition point will maximize this second component, it seems reasonable that the first component should receive the majority of the weight in calculating fitness. Therefore, we arbitrarily assign it 75% of the weight in the examples below. Specifically, the raw fitness of a genetically produced function f_j is 75% of the first component plus 25% of the second component. The closer this overall sum is to 0, the better. This division of weights creates a tension between the two factors that can be fully satisfied only by a correct solution to the differential equation that also satisfies the initial condition. One can view the initial condition as a constraint with $25/75 \times 200$ as the penalty coefficient for the penalty function used to handle the constraint.

The first component used in computing the raw fitness of a genetically produced function f_j is the sum, for i between 0 and 199, of the absolute values of the differences between the zero function (i.e., the right-hand side of the equation) and $f_j'(x_i) + f_j(x_i)^* \text{Cos} \, x_i$, namely

$$\sum_{i=0}^{199} |f_j'(x_i) + f_j(x_i)^* \text{Cos} \, x_i|.$$

Since the difference is taken with respect to the zero function, this sum of differences is merely the sum of the absolute values of the left-hand side of the equation. The closer this sum is to 0, the better.

The second component used in computing the raw fitness of a genetically produced function f_j is based on the absolute value of the difference between the given value y_{initial} for the initial condition and the value of the genetically produced function $f_j(x_{\text{initial}})$ for the particular given initial condition point x_{initial}. Since this difference is constant over all 200 points, we can simply multiply any one of these uniform differences by 200 to obtain this second component. The closer this value is to 0, the better.

Note that the initial condition should be chosen so that the zero function does not satisfy the differential equation and the initial condition; otherwise, the zero function will likely be produced as the solution by genetic programming.

A hit is defined as a fitness case for which the standardized fitness is less than 0.01. Since numerical differentiation is relatively inaccurate for the endpoints of an interval, attainment of a hit for 198 of the 200 fitness cases is one of the termination criteria for this problem.

Table 10.8 summarizes the key features of example 1 of the differential equations problem.

We now apply the above method to solving the given differential equation. In one run, the best-of-generation individual in the initial random population (generation 0) was, when simplified, equivalent to

e^{1-e^x}.

Its raw fitness was 58.09. Only 3 of the 200 points were hits.

By generation 2, the best-of-generation S-expression in the population was, when simplified, equivalent to

$e^{1-e^{\text{Sin} \, x}}$.

Its raw fitness was 44.23. Only 6 of the 200 points were hits.

Table 10.8 Tableau for differential equations.

Objective:	Find a function, in symbolic form, which, when substituted into the given differential equation, satisfies the differential equation and which also satisfies the initial conditions.
Terminal set:	X.
Function set:	+, −, *, %, SIN, COS, EXP, RLOG.
Fitness cases:	Randomly selected sample of 200 values of the independent variable x_i in some interval of interest.
Raw fitness:	The sum, taken over the 200 fitness cases, of 75% of the absolute value of the value assumed by the genetically produced function $f_j(x_i)$ at domain point x_i plus 25% of 200 times of the absolute value of the difference between $f_j(x_{\text{initial}})$ and the given value y_{initial}.
Standardized fitness:	Same as raw fitness for this problem.
Hits:	Number of fitness cases for which the standardized fitness is less than 0.01.
Wrapper:	None.
Parameters:	$M = 500.\ G = 51.$
Success predicate:	An S-expression scores 198 or more hits.

By generation 6, the best-of-generation S-expression in the population was, when simplified, equivalent to

$e^{-\operatorname{Sin} x}$.

The raw fitness of this best-of-generation individual is a mere 0.057. As it happens, this individual scores 199 hits, thus terminating the run. This best-of-run individual is, in fact, the exact solution to the differential equation.

The following three abbreviated tabulations of intermediate values for the best-of-generation individuals from generations 0, 2, and 6 will further clarify the above process.

In each simplified calculation, we use only five equally spaced x_i points in the interval [0, 1], instead of 200 randomly generated points. These five values of x_i are shown in row 1.

Table 10.9 shows this simplified calculation as applied to the best-of-generation individual from generation 0, namely

e^{1-e^x}.

Row 2 shows the value of this best-of-generation individual from generation 0 for the five values of x_i. Row 3 shows the cosine of each of the five values of x_i. Row 4 is the product of row 2 and row 3 and equals $y^* \operatorname{Cos} x_i$ for each of the five values of x_i.

Table 10.9 Simplified calculation for the best-of-generation individual from generation 0 for example 1 of the differential equations problem.

1	x_i	0.0	0.25	0.50	0.75	1.0
2	$y = e^{1-e^x}$	1.00	0.753	0.523	0.327	0.179
3	$Cos\ x_i$	1.00	0.969	0.876	0.732	0.540
4	$y^*\ Cos\ x_i$	1.00	0.729	0.459	0.239	0.097
5	$\dfrac{dy}{dx}$	−0.989	−0.955	−0.851	−0.687	−0.592
6	$\dfrac{dy}{dx} + y^*\ Cos\ x$	0.011	**−0.225**	**0.392**	**−0.447**	−0.495

Table 10.10 Simplified calculation for the best-of-generation individual from generation 2 for example 1 of the differential equations problem.

1	x_i	0.0	0.25	0.50	0.75	1.0
2	$y = e^{1-e^{Sin\ x}}$	1.00	0.755	0.541	0.376	0.267
3	$Cos\ x_i$	1.00	0.969	0.878	0.732	0.540
4	$y^*\ Cos\ x_i$	1.00	0.732	0.474	0.275	0.144
5	$\dfrac{dy}{dx}$	−0.979	−0.919	−0.758	−0.547	−0.437
6	$\dfrac{dy}{dx} + y^*\ Cos\ x$	0.021	**−0.187**	**−0.283**	**−0.271**	−0.292

Row 5 shows the numerical approximation to the derivative

$$\frac{dy}{dx}$$

for each of the five values of x_i. For the three x_i points that are not endpoints of the interval [0, 1], this numerical approximation to the derivative is the average of the slope to the left of the point x_i and the slope to the right of the point x_i. For the two endpoints of the interval [0, 1], the derivative is the slope to the nearest point.

Row 6 is the sum of row 4 and row 5 and is an approximation to the value of the left-hand side of the differential equation for the five values of x_i. Recall that if the S-expression were a solution to the differential equation, every entry in row 6 would be 0 or approximately 0 (to match the right-hand side of the equation). Of course, this best-of-generation individual from generation 0 is not a solution to the differential equation, and therefore the entries in row 6 are all nonzero.

Table 10.10 shows this simplified calculation as applied to the best-of-generation individual from generation 2, namely

$$e^{1-e^{Sin\ x}}.$$

Rows 1 through 5 are calculated using this best-of-generation individual from generation 2 in the same manner as above. Again, row 6 is an approxima-

Table 10.11 Simplified calculation for the best-of-generation individual from generation 6 for example 1 of the differential equations problem.

1	x_i	0.0	0.25	0.50	0.75	1.0
2	$y = e^{-\operatorname{Sin} x}$	1.0	0.781	0.619	0.506	0.431
3	$\operatorname{Cos} x_i$	1.0	0.969	0.878	0.732	0.540
4	$y^* \operatorname{Cos} x_i$	1.0	0.757	0.543	0.370	0.233
5	$\dfrac{dy}{dx}$	-0.877	-0.762	-0.550	-0.376	-0.299
6	$\dfrac{dy}{dx} + y^* \operatorname{Cos} x$	0.123	**−0.005**	**−0.007**	**−0.006**	−0.067

tion to the value of the left-hand side of the differential equation for the five values of x_i. The sum of the absolute values of the three non-endpoint values of row 6 is 0.74. Their average magnitude is 0.247. If we multiply this number by 200, we get 49.4. This value is close to the more accurate raw fitness of 44.23 obtained above with 200 points even though we are using only five x_i points here (instead of 200) and the Δx here is 0.25 (instead of an average of only 0.005). Of course, this best-of-generation individual from generation 2 is not a solution to the differential equation and therefore the entries in row 6 of this table are not close to 0.

Table 10.11 shows this simplified calculation as applied to the best-of-generation individual from generation 6, namely

$e^{-\operatorname{Sin} x}$.

Row 6 is an approximation to the value of the left-hand side of the differential equation for the five values of x_i. The three non-endpoint values in row 6 (shown in bold) are -0.005, -0.007, and -0.006, respectively (i.e., these three non-endpoint values are each very close to 0). The appearance of these three near-zero numbers for the non-endpoint entries in row 6 indicates that the function y on row 2 of of table 10.11 is a good approximation to a solution to the differential equation. When we use the full 200 points (instead of just five), the 200 values on row 6 average a mere 0.0003 for generation 6.

Note that the three non-endpoint values of row 6 for tables 10.9 and 10.10 were not close to 0 because the functions y shown on row 2 of those two tabulations were not solutions to the differential equation.

10.7.2 Example 2

A second example of a differential equation is

$$\frac{dy}{dx} - 2y + 4x = 0$$

with an initial condition such that $y_{\text{initial}} = 4$ when $x_{\text{initial}} = 1$.

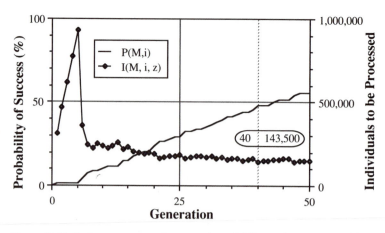

Figure 10.19 Performance curves for example 2 of differential equations problem.

In generation 28 of one run, the S-expression,

```
(+ (* (EXP (- X 1)) (EXP (- X 1))) (+ (+ X X) 1)),
```

emerged. This individual is equivalent to

$e^{-2}e^{2x} + 2x + 1,$

which is the exact solution to the differential equation.

Figure 10.19 presents the performance curves showing, by generation, the cumulative probability of success $P(M, i)$ and the number of individuals that must be processed $I(M, i, z)$ to guarantee, with 99% probability, that the left-hand side of the equation has an absolute value of less than 0.03 for all 200 fitness cases for some S-expression. The graph is based on 68 runs and a population size of 500. The cumulative probability of success $P(M, i)$ is 48% by generation 40 and 56% by generation 50. The numbers in the oval indicate that, if this problem is run through to generation 40, processing a total of 143,500 (i.e., 500 × 41 generations × 7 runs) individuals is sufficient to guarantee solution of this problem with 99% probability.

10.7.3   Example 3

A third example of a differential equation is

$$\frac{dy}{dx} = \frac{2 + \operatorname{Sin} x}{3(y - 1)^2},$$

with an initial condition such that $y_{initial} = 2$ when $x_{initial} = 0$.

This problem was run with a function set that included the cube root function CUBRT.

In generation 13 of one run, the S-expression

```
(- (CUBRT (CUBRT 1))
    (CUBRT (- (- (- (COS X) (+ 1 (CUBRT 1))) X) x)))
```

emerged. This individual is equivalent to

$$1 + (2 + 2x - \text{Cos}\, x)^{1/3},$$

which is the exact solution to the differential equation.

When the initial condition of the differential equation involves only a value of the function itself (as is typically the case when the differential equation involves only a first derivative), any point in the domain of the independent variable x may be used for the initial condition. On the other hand, when the initial condition involves a value of a derivative of the function (as may be the case when the differential equation involves second derivatives or higher derivatives), it is necessary that the value of the independent variable x involved in the initial condition be one of the points in the random set of points x_i so that the first derivative (and any required higher derivative) of the genetically produced function is evaluated for the initial condition point. In addition, it is preferable that the point x_{initial} be an internal point, rather than an endpoint of the domain since numerical differentiation is usually more accurate for the internal points of an interval.

10.8   INTEGRAL EQUATIONS

A integral equation is an equation involving the integral of an unknown function. The solution to an integral equation is a function which, when substituted into the given equation, satisfies the equation.

Integral equations can be solved by means of genetic programming by applying the same general approach described above for differential equations, the difference being that, for integral equations, we take the integral of the genetically produced function, instead of its derivative.

An example of an integral equation is

$$y(t) - 1 + 2 \int_{r=0}^{r=t} \text{Cos}(t - r) y(r)\, dr = 0.$$

In one run, we found the solution to this integral equation, namely

$$y(t) = 1 - 2te^{-t}.$$

The process of integration creates a variable (r, in this case), which is similar to the indexing variable of an iterative loop (described in section 18.1 in connection with the DU iterative operator).

10.9   INVERSE FUNCTIONS

Inverse problems involve finding the inverse function for a given function (or sample of data representing the given function). The finding of inverse functions is an important problem in many fields. Such inverse functions can be discovered by genetic programming.

Suppose we have a set of data consisting of various pairs (x_i, y_i) such as

$$\{(9, 6), (16, 8), (25, 10), (36, 12), (2.25, 3.0), \ldots\}.$$

In each of these pairs, the dependent variable y_i is twice the square root of the independent variable x_i. That is,

$$y_i = 2\sqrt{x_i}.$$

The problem of finding the inverse function is simply a problem of symbolic regression wherein the values of the original independent variable are interchanged with the values of the original dependent variable in each fitness case. Thus, we would use a set of pairs such as

$$\{(6, 9), (8, 16), (10, 25), (12, 36), (3.0, 2.25), \ldots\}$$

as the fitness cases in a symbolic regression aimed at finding the inverse function for $y_i = 2\sqrt{x_i}$.

In one run, we found an S-expression that stated that the dependent variable y_i is the square of half of the independent variable x_i. That is,

$$y_i = \left(\frac{x_i}{2}\right)^2.$$

Another example of an inverse problem is to find the inverse of the Gudermannian function

$$2\,\mathrm{Tan}^{-1}(e^x) - \frac{\pi}{2}.$$

The inverse Gudermannian function is

$$\ln(\mathrm{Sec}\,x + \mathrm{Tan}\,x) = \ln\left(\frac{1}{\mathrm{Cos}\,x} + \frac{\mathrm{Sin}\,x}{\mathrm{Cos}\,x}\right).$$

In applying genetic programming to this problem, the terminal set should contain the independent variable of the problem and the ephemeral random constant $\Re$, so

```
T = {X, ℜ}.
```

The function set should contain functions that might be needed to express the solution to the problem. As with symbolic integration, symbolic differentiation, and differential equations, the functions needed to express the inverse of a given function are not, in general, known *a priori*. For example, in this problem, it is not obvious that the secant and tangent functions are just what is needed in the function set. In this situation, we must make some kind of reasonable choice for the function set. We might, for example, try the same function set we have previously used in this chapter for solving the problems of symbolic integration, symbolic differentiation, and differential equations. That is,

```
F = {+, -, *, %, SIN, COS, EXP, RLOG},
```

taking two, two, two, two, one, one, one, and one arguments, respectively.

The fitness cases for the problem of inverting the Gudermannian function are 50 randomly chosen values of the independent variable over the range $[-4.0, +4.0]$.

In one run, we obtained the following approximately correct inverse on generation 32:

```
(+ (- (% (RLOG (COS X)) (* (RLOG 0.48800004)
                           (* (+ (- X X) (COS -0.8))
                              X)))
      (- (COS -0.8) (COS -0.8)))
   (* (COS (- (COS (COS (+ (RLOG X)
                           (RLOG (COS X)))))
              (RLOG X)))
      (* (COS (- (COS -0.8) (RLOG X)))
         (* (- (% (RLOG (COS X))
                  (* (RLOG 0.48800004)
                     (* (+ (- X X) (COS -0.8)) X)))
               (SIN X))
            (RLOG (COS (RLOG X))))))).
```

The sum, taken over the fitness cases, of the absolute value of the discrepancies between this S-expression and the actual inverse function is less than 0.01 for each of the 50 fitness cases, so this S-expression scores 50 hits. In fact, the error averages less than 0.005 per fitness case. Note that this best-of-run S-expression is neither an exact inverse nor close to the most parsimonious form for the inverse Gudermannian function. This S-expression is an approximately correct inverse Gudermannian function composed of the available functions from the function set.

The question arises as to whether this approximately correct inverse Gudermannian function generalizes over the entire range $[-4, +4]$. When we retested it using 1,000 randomly selected values of the independent variable over this range, we scored 1,000 hits.

We could, of course, facilitate the inversion of the Gudermannian function by adding both the tangent function RTAN (which is the quotient of sine and cosine functions using the protected division function %) and the secant function RSEC (which is reciprocal of the cosine function using the protected division function %) to the function set. When we used this helpful function set, we obtained, in generation 4 of one run, the S-expression

```
(- (RTAN (- X X)) (RLOG (- (RTAN X) (RSEC X)))).
```

This is a 100%-correct S-expression for the inverse Gudermannian function.

10.10 GENERAL FUNCTIONAL EQUATIONS

Functional equations, in general, are equations whose unknown is a function. The solution to a functional equation is the function that, when substituted into the given equation, satisfies the given equation.

General functional equations can be solved by means of genetic programming by applying the same general approach as for differential equations.

Consider the functional equation

$$f(2x) - 1 + 2 \operatorname{Sin}^2 x = 0.$$

The goal is to solve this functional equation for the function f that, when substituted into the equation, satisfies the equation.

As before, we begin by selecting a set of random points in a suitable domain. In particular, we select 50 points x_i in the domain of floating-point numbers between $-\pi$ and $+\pi$. We store these 50 values in a vector. We then compute a vector of 50 values corresponding to the sine of each x_i. We then compute another vector of 50 values corresponding to the square of the sine of each x_i, and we then compute yet another vector corresponding to twice the square of the sine of each x_i. Each of these computed vectors can also be viewed as a curve. Similarly, we set up a vector constant of 50 occurrences of the constant 1 (the "constant curve"). We then subtract this constant curve from the curve just computed for $2 \operatorname{Sin}^2 x$. Finally, we consider each of the S-expressions f_j in the current population of individuals.

Since the argument for the unknown function in the first term of this equation is $2x$ (instead of just x), we must first perform the step of multiplying the 50 x_i values by 2 before evaluating the function f_j. We then compute the curve for $f(2x)$ using the S-expression f_j.

If we happen to have a function f that exactly satisfies the equation, the new curve computed will consist of all zeros. In any event, raw fitness is the sum of the absolute values of the left-hand side,

$$f(2x_i) - 1 + 2 \operatorname{Sin}^2 x_i.$$

In one run, the S-expression

```
(* 1 (COS (+ X X)))
```

emerged on generation 7 with a raw fitness of zero. This best-of-run S-expression is equivalent to $\operatorname{Cos} 2x$, which is an exact solution to the given functional equation. That is, when $\operatorname{Cos} 2x$ is substituted into

$$f(2x) - 1 + 2 \operatorname{Sin}^2 x = 0,$$

the equation is satisfied (i.e., the left-hand side evaluates to 0 for each x_i).

10.11 NUMERIC ROOTS OF EQUATIONS

An important special case of the process of solving functional equations occurs when the terminal set is degenerate and consists only of numeric constants. This special case permits solution of a mathematical equation for its numeric roots.

We are not interested in solving equations for their roots *per se*. Numerous approximation methods (e.g., Newton's method) are available for finding the roots of an equation by either bifurcating intervals to locate the zero crossing or using the derivative (if it is known). This special case is important because it illustrates how genetic programming dynamically and adaptively changes the representation scheme to achieve ever-better solutions to the given problem. This special case also illustrates how genetic programming differs from the conventional genetic algorithm operating on fixed-length character strings. The conventional genetic algorithm cannot dynamically change the representation scheme during the course of solving the problem.

For this problem, the terminal set will consist only of numeric constants, so the S-expressions will consist only of numeric constants. That is,

```
T = {ℜ},
```

where $\mathfrak{R}$ is the ephemeral random floating-point constant ranging from -1.000 to $+1.000$. There are no variables (such as x) in the terminal set.

Suppose that the function set for this problem consists of four arithmetic operations,

```
F = {+, -, *, %},
```

taking two arguments each.

Consider the cubic equation

$$x^3 - 2 = 0.$$

This equation has only one real root, namely

$$x = 2^{1/3} = 1.2599211.$$

For present purposes, we replace the unknown variable x in this ordinary equation with the unknown function $f(x)$ and rewrite the ordinary cubic equation as the functional equation

$$f^3(x) - 2 = 0.$$

The problem of finding the numeric root of the ordinary cubic equation has now been converted to a problem of finding a particular function that satisfies the functional equation.

Each S-expression in the genetic population of this problem will be a composition of functions from the function set F and terminals from the terminal set T. Because no variables appear in the terminal set, the S-expressions consist only of compositions of random constants. Examples of typical S-expressions for the initial random population are

```
(+ 0.234 (* -0.685 0.478))
```

and

```
(* (* 0.537 -1.234) (+ 1.467 0.899)).
```

Because no variables appear in the function set, each S-expression f_j in this problem has a constant numeric value.

The fitness of each S-expression f_j in the population is evaluated as follows. There are 50 fitness cases, consisting of 50 random values of x_i selected from a suitable domain (such as -2.0 to $+2.0$).

A curve is then built up by cubing each x_i and then subtracting the constant value 2.0.

Each S-expression f_j in the problem has a particular numeric value, because the initial population of S-expressions contained only constants. The value of the S-expression does not depend on x_i. Thus, for this particular problem, there is no need to evaluate each S-expression f_j over all 50 fitness cases, because its value is independent of x_i. We could simply multiply any one of these identical values by 50 to obtain the fitness of the S-expression (i.e., function) f_j, or we could even skip this step altogether. The process is presented in this way to emphasize the continuity in methodology between this problem (which is degenerate) and the other problems in this chapter.

If the S-expression f_j causes the left-hand side of the equation to be 0, that S-expression (which is, in fact, a numeric constant value) satisfies the equation.

In one run, the best-of-generation S-expression of the initial random population (generation 0) was

```
(- (% (% (* (% -0.119999945 0.9670001) 0.34300005) (% (*
-0.788 0.99100006) (% -0.23699999 0.33200002)))
0.45500004) (* (% (- (- -0.30699998 0.76300013) (+
0.5810001 0.85600007)) 0.9390001) (- (* (* 0.6450001
0.82200015) 0.086000085) (- (* 0.549 0.9460001)
0.97300005))))).
```

This S-expression consists of 37 points (i.e., 37 terminals and functions) and evaluates to the constant 1.2473918.

The best-of-generation individual for generation 2 has a constant value of 1.2602566 and is

```
(+ (- 0.50600004 (+ -0.045999944 (- (- -0.23699999
0.61100006) (% -0.059999943 -0.26699996))))) (+ (* (- (-
0.8160001 -0.972) (% -0.83 -0.811)) (- (* -0.09799993
0.42700005) (% -0.269 -0.822))) (* (+ (* 0.411
-0.049999952) 0.4310001) (- (% -0.40199995 0.69500005)
-0.37799996))))).
```

The best-of-generation individual for generation 4 has a constant value of 1.2598813 and is

```
(- (+ (* (+ (% 0.15100002 (- (+ -0.045999944 (- (-
-0.23699999 0.61100006) (% -0.059999943 -0.26699996)))) (-
(% (% (* (% -0.119999945 0.9670001) 0.34300005) (% (*
-0.788 0.99100006) (% -0.23699999 0.33200002)))
0.45500004) (* (% (- (- -0.30699998 0.76300013) (+
0.5810001 0.85600007)) 0.9390001) (- (* (% (+ 0.2570001
-0.706) (* 0.9130001 -0.847)) 0.086000085) (- (* 0.549
0.9460001) 0.97300005)))))) 0.59800005) (+ (- 0.80200005
0.60800004) (+ 0.36800003 -0.559))) -0.44799995) (+ (+ (-
(* -0.861 0.9920001) 0.80700004) (* -0.09799993
0.42700005)) (* (* (* 0.10500002 0.314) (- -0.74399996
0.12400007)) (+ -0.69299996 (- 0.99600005
0.18700004)))))).
```

The best-of-generation individual for generation 6 has a constant value of 1.2599242 and is

```
(- (+ (* (+ (% 0.15100002 (- (+ -0.045999944 (- (-
-0.23699999 0.61100006) (% -0.059999943 -0.26699996)))) (-
(% (% (* (- (* (% (+ 0.2570001 -0.706) (* 0.9130001
-0.847)) 0.086000085) (- (* 0.549 0.9460001) 0.97300005))
0.34300005) (% (+ (* (% -0.119999945 0.9670001) (+ (-
0.80200005 0.60800004) (+ 0.36800003 -0.559)))
-0.44799995) (% -0.23699999 0.33200002))) 0.45500004) (*
(% (- (- -0.30699998 0.76300013) (+ 0.5810001
0.85600007)) 0.9390001) (- (* (% (+ 0.2570001 -0.706) (*
0.9130001 -0.847)) 0.086000085) (- (* 0.549 0.9460001)
0.97300005)))))) 0.59800005) (+ (- 0.80200005 0.60800004)
(+ 0.36800003 -0.559))) -0.44799995) (+ (+ (- (* -0.861
0.9920001) 0.80700004) (* -0.09799993 0.42700005)) (* (*
(* 0.10500002 0.314) (- -0.74399996 0.12400007)) (+
-0.69299996 (- 0.99600005 0.18700004)))))).
```

The best-of-generation individual for generation 14 has a constant value of 1.2599211 and is

```
(- (+ (* (+ (% 0.15100002 (- (+ -0.045999944 (- (* (* (*
0.10500002 0.314) (- -0.74399996 0.12400007)) (+
-0.69299996 (- 0.99600005 0.18700004))) -0.23699999)) (-
(% (% (* (- (* (% (+ 0.2570001 -0.706) (* 0.9130001
-0.847)) 0.086000085) (- (* 0.549 0.9460001) 0.97300005))
0.34300005) (% (+ (* (% -0.119999945 0.9670001) (+ (-
0.80200005 0.60800004) (+ 0.36800003 -0.559)))
-0.44799995) (% -0.23699999 0.33200002))) 0.45500004) (*
(% (- (- -0.30699998 0.76300013) (+ 0.5810001
0.85600007)) 0.9390001) (- (+ (+ (- (* -0.861 0.9920001)
0.80700004) (* -0.09799993 0.42700005)) (* (* (*
0.10500002 0.314) (- -0.74399996 0.12400007)) (+
-0.69299996 (- 0.99600005 0.18700004)))) (- (+ (- (*
-0.861 0.9920001) 0.80700004) (* -0.09799993 0.42700005))
0.97300005)))))) 0.59800005) (+ (- 0.80200005 0.60800004)
(+ 0.36800003 -0.559))) -0.44799995) (+ (+ (- (* -0.861
0.9920001) 0.80700004) (* -0.09799993 0.42700005)) (* (*
(* 0.10500002 0.314) (- -0.74399996 0.12400007)) (+
-0.69299996 (- 0.99600005 0.18700004)))))).
```

The above S-expression from generation 14 has value 1.2599211, and the cube root of 2 is indeed 1.2599211 (to eight significant figures). That is, genetic programming has converged onto the desired root in generation 14 to within the resolution of the floating-point numbers used for these computations.

Even a cursory glance at the above sequence of five S-expressions will indicate that they became progressively more complicated as genetic programming progressed from generation 0 to generations 2, 4, 6, and 14.

Table 10.12 Summary of fitness and structural complexity.

Generation	Value of individual S-expression	Difference from root of 1.2599211	Structural complexity of S-expression
0	1.2473918	−0.0125293	**37**
2	1.2602566	+0.0003355	**39**
4	1.2598813	−0.00000398	**89**
6	1.2599242	+0.0000031	**111**
14	1.2599211	**0.0000000**	**139**

In table 10.12, column 2 shows the value of these S-expressions from generations 0, 2, 4, 6, and 14 as they approach 1.2599211. Column 3 shows the decreasing difference from the actual root (i.e., 1.2599211). Column 4 shows the structural complexity (i.e., total number of function points and terminal points) of the S-expression. In fact, the structural complexities of these S-expressions were 37, 39, 89, 111, and 139 points, respectively.

In other words, genetic programming created ever-more-complicated S-expressions in order to obtain an ever-better approximation to the cube root of 2. The representation changed, adaptively, from generation to generation as a result of the relentless pressure of fitness.

Suppose we had attempted to find the root of this equation by means of the conventional genetic algorithm using fixed-length character strings over an alphabet of a fixed number of characters. In that event, we would have first selected the representation scheme. That is, we would have selected the length of the string and the size of the alphabet. For example, we might have chosen a binary alphabet (i.e., $K = 2$) and a length of 11 (i.e., $L = 11$), where it would be understood that one bit is to the left of the binary point and ten bits are to the right of the binary point. Such a representation scheme would allow us to represent any number greater than -2.0 (in decimal) to any number less than $+2.0$ with a granularity of about 0.001 (i.e., one part in 2^{-10} to the right of the binary point). Once we made that selection, the length of the string would have been fixed for the entire run of the algorithm. The conventional genetic algorithm would then have searched the search space of 2^{11} points and probably rapidly found the cube root of two to within one binary place (i.e., one part in 2^{-10}).

Had we instead chosen a string length of, say, 15 (i.e., 14 binary bits to the right of the binary point), we would have been able to represent numbers with a granularity of about 0.0001 (i.e., one part in 2^{-14} to the right of the binary point). If we had made that selection, the conventional genetic algorithm would have searched the search space of 2^{14} points and probably rapidly found the cube root of 2 to within one or two binary places.

However, for any particular choice of the length L and any choice of size K of alphabet, the initial choice of the representation scheme in the conventional genetic algorithm would have limited the precision of the solution, in advance, to the specified granularity of the representation scheme. Once maximal precision is obtained in the representation scheme involved, the genetic algorithm can do no more. There is no evolution of complexity.

The limiting effect of the initial selection of the representation scheme in the conventional genetic algorithm operating on fixed-length strings is one of the sources of the widespread view that the conventional genetic algorithm is very effective for rapidly finding the general neighborhood of the correct answer in a large search space, but not particularly effective at converging to a highly precise final answer. The very representation scheme that usually produces a rapid search at the beginning of the run can prevent the algorithm from converging to a highly precise answer later in the run. The impediment is that the representation scheme was pre-determined at the beginning of the run and that the conventional genetic algorithm cannot dynamically change its representation scheme during the course of the run.

In contrast, in genetic programming, the size and the shape of the solution varies dynamically as the problem is being solved. Thus, it is possible to search a large search space for the correct general neighborhood of the solution and then, by adaptively changing the representation scheme, to converge to the correct answer with an ever-higher degree of precision. If, after arriving in the correct general neighborhood of a solution, an additional small increment in fitness can still be achieved by changing the size or the shape of the S-expression, genetic programming makes the change.

Note that the initial choice of the representation scheme in the conventional genetic algorithm can, in some situations, do more than merely limit precision. If the solution to the above problem were the number 10.2599211, instead of 1.2599211, and we had chosen the representation scheme to be a binary string of length 16 representing numbers with one binary digit to the left of the binary point and 15 to the right, then we could never express or find a solution to this problem.

Shaefer (1987) discusses adaptive representation schemes for genetic algorithms. If an alphabet consisting of floating-point numbers is used at each position of the string in a conventional genetic algorithm ("real encodings"), then genetic algorithms are able to find a precise solution point with considerably greater flexibility than usual (Deb 1991; Belew, McInerney, and Schraudolph 1991). In addition, the *Evolutionsstrategie* (ES) approach also uses such floating-point numbers.

In another run, we used double-precision arithmetic in applying genetic programming to the same equation. In generation 47, we found the following S-expression containing 159 points with a fitness of 0.0000000000000326405569239796:

```
(+ (* (* -0.5403 (+ 0.5741 -0.8861)) (% (*
0.29690000000000016 0.08089999999999997) (+ (% (% (-
-0.5962000000000001 0.3902000000000001) (- (+ (% (* (+ (*
0.23550000000000004 0.15060000000000007) (* (*
-0.10289999999999999 -0.7332) 0.7723)) (*
```

```
0.23550000000000004 0.15060000000000007)) (+ 0.6026 (+ (+
(% (- 0.37250000000000005 -0.34909999999999997) (- -0.776
-0.6013)) (- -0.5250999999999999 -0.009000000000000008))
(% (- 0.2969000000000016 -0.34909999999999997) (- -0.776
-0.6013)))))) (* (+ -0.8861 (% -0.06019999999999992
0.051100000000000145)) (% -0.06019999999999992
0.051100000000000145))) (% -0.49659999999999993 0.4475)))
(+ (% (% (* (+ -0.1943999999999999 0.4366000000000001) (*
0.23550000000000004 0.15060000000000007)) (+ 0.6026 (* (*
(+ (* -0.5403 -0.017199999999999993) (%
-0.06019999999999992 0.051100000000000145)) (% (* (+
-0.1943999999999999 0.4366000000000001) (*
0.23550000000000004 0.15060000000000007)) (% (%
0.42100000000000004 -0.4275) (- -0.48160000000000003
0.5708)))) 0.7723))) (- -0.8395 -0.1986)) (% (-
0.37250000000000005 -0.34909999999999997) (- -0.776
-0.6013)))) (% (% (+ 0.6698000000000002
0.8714000000000002) (% (- -0.829 -0.636) (-
0.763500000000001 -0.15899999999999992)))) (- (- (*
-0.5403 -0.017199999999999993) (- -0.8395 -0.1986)) (- (*
(* -0.5403 -0.017199999999999993) (- 0.6004 -0.4343)) (-
-0.951 (* (% 0.7803 0.9777) 0.31920000000000015)))))))))
(+ (* (* -0.5403 -0.017199999999999993)
-0.19240000000000002) (+ (+ -0.1333999999999996 0.7944)
0.6004))).
```

This S-expression evaluates to 1.2599210498949058, whereas the cube root of 2 is 1.2599210498948732. Thus, we have solved the equation for a value correct to 14 decimal places (about 44 binary places).

Evolution in nature is a never-ending process, and it appears that genetic programming can also be a never-ending process. If we perform numerical calculations to a sufficiently large number of digits of precision, we can apparently obtain ever-more-complex S-expressions representing ever-more-precise approximations to the irrational root of this equation. As the S-expressions become better and better at performing their task, there is an accompanying increase in the structural complexity of the S-expressions.

10.12 SEQUENCE INDUCTION

The ability to correctly perform induction is widely viewed as an important component of human intelligence.

Sequence induction involves discovering a mathematical expression (computer program, LISP S-expression) that can generate any arbitrary element in an infinite sequence

$$S = S_0, S_1, \ldots, S_j, \ldots$$

after seeing only a relatively small finite number of specific examples of the values of the unknown sequence. Sequence induction is a special case of symbolic regression, namely the case where the domain of the independent variable x consists of the non-negative integers 0, 1, 2, 3, ...

Of course, there is no one correct answer to a problem of sequence induction, there being an infinity of sequences that agree with any finite number of specific examples of the unknown sequence.

Suppose one is given the first 20 values of the following simple nonrecursive sequence of integers:

S = 1, 15, 129, 547, 1593, 3711, 7465, 13539, 22737, 35983, 54321, 78915, 111049, 152127, 203673, 267331, 344865, 438159, 549217, 680163, ...

The goal is to identify a mathematical expression that produces this sequence.

Sequence induction is symbolic regression (symbolic function identification) where the domain (i.e., independent variable) ranges over the non-negative integers 0, 1, 2, ...

The terminal set for this problem consists of the index position J (i.e., the independent variable) and the ephemeral random constant $\Re$ ranging over the small integers 0, 1, 2, and 3. That is,

T = {J, $\Re$}.

The function set should contain functions that might be needed to express the solution to the problem. In this situation, if we are thinking of a sequence of integers produced by an unknown polynomial, the following function set might be appropriate and would guarantee closure:

F = {+, -, *},

taking two arguments each.

The fitness cases for this problem consist of the first 20 elements of the given sequence. Twenty sequence positions appear to be sufficient to identify this sequence. The raw fitness is the sum, taken over the 20 fitness cases, of the absolute value of the difference between the value produced by the S-expression for sequence position J and the actual value of the sequence for position J. The auxiliary hits measure is defined so as to count an exact match as a hit. Thus, the number of hits can range between 0 and 20.

The unknown mathematical expression we are seeking is

$5j^4 + 4j^3 + 3j^2 + 2j + 1$.

Note that the values of the first 20 elements of this sequence range over more than five orders of magnitude.

Table 10.13 summarizes the key features of this problem with $5j^4 + 4j^3 + 3j^2 + 2j + 1$ as the target function.

In generation 0 of one run, the raw fitness of the worst-of-generation individual was about 3×10^{13}, the average raw fitness of the initial random generation was about 6×10^{10}, and the raw fitness of the best-of-generation individual was 143,566.

Table 10.13 Tableau for sequence induction.

Objective:	Find a mathematical expression for a given finite sample of a sequence where the target sequence is $5j^4 + 4j^3 + 3j^2 + 2j + 1$.
Terminal set:	Sequence index J and $\Re$, where the ephemeral random constant $\Re$ ranges over the integers 0, 1, 2, and 3.
Function set:	$+, -, *$.
Fitness cases:	First 20 elements of the sequence.
Raw fitness:	The sum, taken over the 20 fitness cases, of the absolute value of the difference between the value produced by the S-expression for sequence position J and the actual value of the target sequence for position J.
Standardized fitness:	Same as raw fitness for this problem.
Hits:	Number of fitness cases for which the value produced by the S-expression for sequence position J exactly matches the actual value of the target sequence for position J.
Wrapper:	None.
Parameters:	$M = 500$. $G = 51$.
Success predicate:	An S-expression scores 20 hits.

By generation 38, the raw fitness of the best-of-generation individual had improved to 2,740.

By generation 42, the raw fitness (i.e., error) of the best-of-generation individual had improved to 20. In a sequence whose largest element is 680,163, an error of only 20 is nearly perfect. This S-expression was

```
(+ (+ (- (* (* 0 1) (- (* 3 J) (+ (* 0 1) J))) 2) (* (*
(* 2 J) (+ 1 J)) (* (+ J J) (- J 2)))) (- (- (+ 2 0) (*
(* 1 J) (- (- (- (+ (- (* 2 J) (+ 2 0)) (- J 3)) (- J 1))
(* (* 3 J) (+ J 1))) (- (- (+ J J) (* (- (- (+ J (+ 0 J))
(- J 2)) (* (* 3 J) (+ J 1))) 3)) (* (- J 2) (- 2 J))))))
(* (- (+ 2 J) (* J 2)) (* (* J J) (- J 3)))))).
```

When simplified, this S-expression for generation 42 is equivalent to

$5j^4 + 4j^3 + 3j^2 + 2j \underline{+ 0}$.

Then, the following 100%-correct individual emerged on generation 43:

```
(+ (+ (- (* (* 0 1) (- (* 3 J) (+ (* 0 1) J))) 2) (* (*
(* 2 J) (+ 1 J)) (* (+ J J) (- J 2)))) (- (- (+ 3 0) (*
(* 1 J) (- (- (- (+ (- (* 2 J) (+ 2 0)) (- J 3)) (- J 1))
(* (* 3 J) (+ J 1))) (- (- (+ J J) (* (- (- (+ J (+ 0 J))
(- J 2)) (* (* 3 J) (+ J 1))) 3)) (* (- J 2) (- 2 J))))))
(* (- (+ 2 J) (* J 2)) (* (* J J) (- J 3)))))).
```

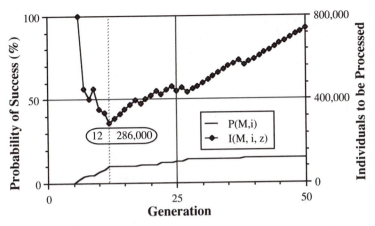

Figure 10.20 Performance curves for the sequence induction problem with $5j^4 + 4j^3 + 3j^2 + 2j + 1$ as the target function.

When simplified, this best-of-run S-expression for generation 43 is equivalent to

$$5j^4 + 4j^3 + 3j^2 + 2j \mathbf{+ 1}.$$

This is the desired mathematical expression.

Note that the only difference between the S-expressions in generation 42 and generation 43 is that the underlined sub-S-expression (+ 2 0) in boldface in generation 42 becomes (+ 3 0) in generation 43. This difference corresponds to a numerical difference of 1 which, over the 20 fitness cases, accounts for the difference of 20 in raw fitness (i.e., sum or errors). The 100%-correct individual in generation 43 is therefore slightly fitter than the almost-correct individual from generation 42. Genetic programming used crossover to convert the almost-correct individual into the 100%-correct individual.

Figure 10.20 presents the performance curves showing, by generation, the cumulative probability of success $P(M, i)$ and the number of individuals that must be processed $I(M, i, z)$ to guarantee, with 99% probability, that at least one S-expression in the population exactly matches the target function of $5j^4 + 4j^3 + 3j^2 + 2j + 1$ for the first 20 positions of the sequence for the sequence induction problem. The graph is based on 100 runs and a population size of 500. The cumulative probability of success $P(M, i)$ is 10% by generation 12 and 15% by generation 50. The numbers in the oval indicate that if this problem is run through to generation 12, processing a total of 286,000 individuals (i.e., $500 \times 13 \times 44$ runs) is sufficient to guarantee solution of this problem with 99% probability.

10.13 PROGRAMMATIC IMAGE COMPRESSION

In a series of innovative papers, Sims (1991a, 1992a, 1992b) showed that a spectacular variety of color images can be produced by hand-selecting interest-

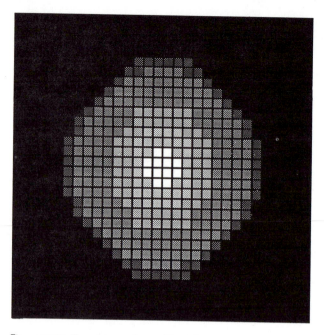

Figure 10.21 Target image for problem of programmatic image compression.

ing images from a large number of randomly produced LISP S-expressions displayed by an interactive workstation. A visualization of some related work appears as a videotape in Sims 1991b.

In this section, we perform symbolic regression on a two-dimensional array of data representing the color of the pixels of a given color image. The objective is to use symbolic regression (i.e., error-driven evolution) to discover a computer program (i.e., a LISP S-expression) that exactly or approximately represents the given color image.

Figure 10.21 is a black-and-white diagram representing an image consisting of concentric ellipses in a spectrum of different colors. In this figure, there are 30 pixels in the horizontal direction and 30 pixels in the vertical direction, for a total of 900 pixels. The center of the color image is considered the origin $(0, 0)$; the upper left corner is $(-1.0, +1.0)$; and the lower right corner is $(+1.0, -1.0)$. The color of each pixel is one of 128 different shades from a red, green, and blue (RGB) color spectrum. In our color system, each floating-point number in the interval $[-1.0, +1.0]$ corresponds to one of the 128 shades. For example, -1.0 represents 100% red; 0.0 represents 100% green; $+1.0$ represents 100% blue; and an intermediate color value, such as -0.75, has a large red component and a small green component. In the figure, the origin is colored red and the concentric ellipses surrounding it are various shades of red blended with greens. As one goes farther from the origin, one finds an elliptic area colored green. Still farther out, one finds various shades of green blended with blue. Finally, the outer areas are blue. The color videotape *Genetic Programming: The Movie*, which shows a more complex pattern being addressed, will be especially useful in connection with this section.

The pattern in the figure is produced by the expression

$$3x^2 + 2y^2 - 0.85.$$

The terminal set for this problem consists of the horizontal pixel position X, the vertical pixel position Y, and the ephemeral random floating-point constant $\Re$ ranging over the usual interval of $[-1.0, +1.0]$. That is,

```
T = {X, Y, ℜ}.
```

The function set below contains functions that might be needed to express the solution to the problem:

```
F = {+, -, *, %},
```

taking two arguments each.

The fitness cases for this problem are the 900 combinations of X and Y and the associated pixel value (from -1.0 to $+1.0$) representing one of the 128 shades of color. Fitness is the sum, taken over the 900 pixels, of the absolute value of the difference between the color value for that pixel produced by the S-expression and the correct color value for that pixel contained in the target image.

The function set is closed; however, a particular S-expression in the population may well return a numerical value outside the interval $[-1.0, +1.0]$. Therefore, we use the following wrapper to map the value produced by an S-expression into the desired range of $[-1.0, +1.0]$ and thence into the desired range of 128 color values from 0 to 127:

```
(* 64 (+ 1 (MAX -1.0 (MIN 1.0 S-EXPRESSION))))),
```

where *S-EXPRESSION* is the value of an individual S-expression from the population.

A hit is defined as a fitness case for which the value of the wrapperized S-expression comes within six color values (out of 128) of the correct value.

Since every floating-point value within an interval of size 1/128 is equated to a single color, great precision is not required in the calculations involved in this problem. Therefore, considerable computer time can be saved by using the "short float" data type. This data type is available on many implementations of LISP.

Table 10.14 summarizes the key features of this problem.

The color images produced by the randomly generated S-expressions of generation 0 bear little resemblance to the target image.

In one run, the following best-of-generation S-expression from generation 0 contains 17 points and has fitness of 260.9:

```
(* (* (- (* (% Y X) X) (% (* Y Y) (+ 0.0458984
-0.106705))) X) X).
```

Figure 10.22 is a black-and-white diagram representing the color image produced by the best-of-generation individual from generation 0. There is no red whatsoever in this image; its overall shape is diamond rather than elliptical; and it does not have many variations in shadings of color. However, there is

Table 10.14 Tableau for programmatic image compression.

Objective:	Find a LISP symbolic expression that returns the color value for each pixel in a two-dimensional image.
Terminal set:	X, Y, $\Re$, where the ephemeral random floating-point constant $\Re$ ranges over the interval $[-1.0, +1.0]$.
Function set:	+, −, *, %.
Fitness cases:	Two-dimensional array of 900 pixels.
Raw fitness:	The sum, taken over the 900 fitness cases, of the absolute value of the difference between the color value produced by the S-expression for position (X, Y) and the color value of the target image for position (X, Y).
Standardized fitness:	Same as raw fitness for this problem.
Hits:	Number of fitness cases for which the value of the wrapperized S-expression comes within 6 color values (out of 128) of the correct value.
Wrapper:	Converts arbitrary floating-point number into one of the 128 color values.
Parameters:	$M = 2{,}000$ (with over-selection). $G = 51$.
Success predicate:	An S-expression scores 900 hits.

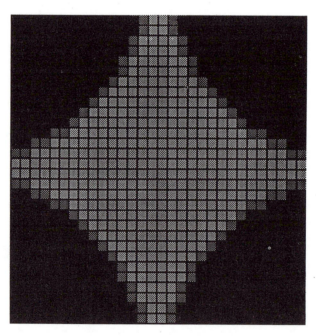

Figure 10.22 Best-of-generation individual from generation 0 for the problem of programmatic image compression.

a vague resemblance between some of the gross features of this image and the target image, notably the considerable amount of blue on the periphery and the considerable amount of green in the intermediate areas.

In generation 6, the best-of-generation individual,

```
(+ (+ (+ (* (+ (* X X) (* Y Y)) (% Y Y)) (+ (* Y Y)
-0.8116)) (+ 0.0458984-0.106705)) (* (% X 0.51979) X)),
```

contained 27 points, scored 900 hits, and had a raw fitness of 18.93. This best-of-run individual produces a color image that is virtually indistinguishable in appearance on the computer screen from the target image. Indeed, this best-of-run individual is equivalent to the expression

```
(+ (* 2.9239 X X) (* 2 Y Y) -0.8724),
```

which is, in turn, a very close approximation to the expression that was actually used to create the target image. When we retested this best-of-run individual from generation 6 using a 100 × 100 pixel version of the same problem, it scored 10,000 hits out of a possible 10,000.

In another run, the following best-of-run individual, containing 81 points and scoring 900 hits, emerged on generation 24:

```
(+ (+ (* Y Y) (* (- (- X -0.5703) (* X X)) (+ (+ -0.6077
X) (* X X)))) (- (* (- (- (- X -0.5703) (* 0.182205 X))
(* Y Y)) (+ (+ -0.6077 X) (+ (* Y Y) (* (* Y Y) (* (- (-
X -0.5703) (* X X)) (+ (+ -0.6077 X) (* X X)))))))) (+ (*
(* (- X -0.5703) -0.5445) (- -0.5342 (* X -0.7659))) (*
(* -0.683105 Y) (* (* Y Y) Y))))).
```

Interestingly, for this particular run, the above individual scoring 900 hits caused the termination of the run; however, it was not the individual in the population with the best value of fitness. The following individual containing 69 points had a superior value of 14.35 for fitness, but scored only 866 out of 900 hits:

```
(+ (+ (* Y Y) (* (- (- X -0.5703) (* X X)) (+ (+ -0.6077
X) (* X X)))) (- (* (- (- (- X -0.5703) (* 0.182205 X))
(* Y Y)) (+ (+ -0.6077 X) (+ (* Y Y) (* (+ -0.6077 X) (*
X X))))) (+ (* (* (- X -0.5703) -0.5445) (- -0.5342 (* X
-0.7659))) (* (* -0.683105 Y) (* (* Y Y) Y))))).
```

The fact that it is possible to convert a color image to a LISP S-expression demonstrates that color images involving large numbers of pixels can be represented in this compressed form and transmitted using comparatively little bandwidth. Color images can, of course, be compressed in a variety of other ways (e.g., fractal data compression) (Ali et al. 1992; Koza and Rice 1992b). The video (see p. xi) shows a more difficult example of programmatic image compression.

10.14 RECAPITULATION OF SYMBOLIC REGRESSION

In this chapter, we have seen how error-driven evolution in the form of symbolic regression can be used to solve a number of different problems.

In its simplest form, symbolic regression involves finding the function, in symbolic form, that fits (or approximately fits) data from an unknown curve. This form of symbolic regression occurs when we are seeking mathematical identities (section 10.1) and doing curve fitting (section 10.2). This form of symbolic regression is an instance of function identification or system identification.

In empirical discovery (sections 10.3 and 10.4), a model is constructed from a discrete sampling of noisy data from unknown system. The model produced can be used for forecasting future values of the system.

If an intermediate step such as numerical integration or differentiation (sections 10.5 and 10.6) is inserted into the process of symbolic regression, it is possible to find the integral in symbolic form or the derivative in symbolic form of a given function.

If we think of a sequence of differentiations, integrations, inversions, or other functional steps being performed on an unknown function, we can use symbolic regression to solve differential equations (section 10.7), integral equations (section 10.8), inverse problems (section 10.9), and general functional equations (section 10.10).

If the independent variable is removed from the terminal set, symbolic regression can be used to find the numeric roots of a mathematical equation (section 10.11).

Sequence induction is symbolic regression in which the independent variable is a sequence of non-negative integers (section 10.12).

If there are two independent variables representing the position of a pixel within a rectangular image area and the unknown function is interpreted as the color value of the pixel, then the process of symbolic regression amounts to converting a color image into a LISP S-expression (section 10.13). Thus, a color image can be expressed as a LISP S-expression capable of generating it.

11 Control—Cost-Driven Evolution

Problems of control involve a system that is described by state variables. The state of the system at a future time is controlled by the choice of certain control variables. The goal in a control problem is to choose values of the control variables so as to cause the system to move toward a specified target state. The goal of optimal control is to do this at optimal (typically minimal) cost, where the cost is measured in terms of time, distance, fuel consumed, money or some other measure.

Solutions to control problems and optimal control problems typically involve a highly nonlinear function of the state variables of the system.

The simple cart centering problem in section 7.1 is an example of an optimal control problem for which an exact mathematical solution is known; however, it is usually impossible to find an exact mathematical solution to control problems. Moreover, in practical problems, certain key elements in the statement of the problem may be available only in the form of a noisy set of empirical data points, rather than in the form of a precise mathematical formula.

Genetic programming provides a way to find an approximately correct function for problems of control and optimal control for which an exact mathematical solution is not obtainable.

This chapter demonstrates the use of genetic programming on the well-known optimal control problem of balancing a broom, the control problem of backing up a tractor-trailer truck, and an optimization problem.

11.1 BROOM BALANCING

The problem of balancing a broom in minimal time by applying a bang-bang force from either direction is a well-known optimal control problem involving an inherently unstable mechanical system. The broom balancing problem has been studied extensively in connection with neural networks (Widrow 1963, 1987; Michie 1968; Anderson 1986, 1988, 1989; Barto, Anandan, and Anderson 1983) and reviewed by Wieland (1991).

The broom balancing problem bears some similarity to the cart centering problem in that it involves a push cart with mass m_c moving on a one-dimensional frictionless track. In addition, there is a broom (an inverted pendulum) of mass m_p pivoting on the top of the cart. The broom has an angle θ

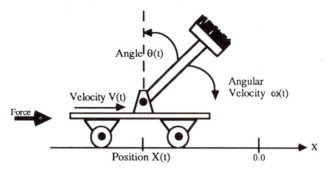

Angle θ(t)

Velocity V(t)

Angular
Velocity ω(t)

Force

Position X(t)

0.0

X

Figure 11.1 Broom balancing problem.

and an angular velocity ω. The distance from the center of mass of the broom to the pivot is λ.

There is one control variable for this system: namely a force F of fixed magnitude (i.e., a bang-bang force) which can be applied to the center of mass of the cart at each time step so as to accelerate the cart toward either the positive or the negative direction along the track.

There are four state variables of this system, namely the position x of the cart along the track, the velocity v of the cart, the angle of the broom θ (measured from the vertical), and the angular velocity ω of the broom.

Figure 11.1 shows the cart at time t with position $x(t)$, velocity $v(t)$, angle $\theta(t)$, and angular velocity $\omega(t)$ with the bang-bang force being applied so as to accelerate the cart in the positive direction (i.e., toward the right).

At each time step, the choice of value of the control variable (i.e., the quantity u equal to a multiplier of either $+1$ or -1 to the magnitude $|F|$ of the force F) at time step t causes a change in the state variables of the system at time step $t + 1$.

The state transitions of this system are expressed by nonlinear differential equations. At each discrete time step τ, the current state of the system and the force being applied at that time step determine the state of the system at the next time step.

In particular, the angular acceleration of the broom $\Phi(t)$ at time t is given by Anderson (1988) as

$$\Phi(t) = \frac{g \operatorname{Sin} \theta + \operatorname{Cos} \theta \dfrac{-F - m_p \lambda \omega \theta^2 \operatorname{Sin} \theta}{m_c + m_p}}{\lambda \left[\dfrac{4}{3} - \dfrac{m_p \operatorname{Cos}^2 \theta}{m_c + m_p} \right]}.$$

For the purposes of this problem, the constants are the mass of the cart ($m_c = 0.9$ kilogram), the mass of the broom ($m_p = 0.1$ kilogram), gravity ($g = 1.0$ meters/sec^2), the time step ($\tau = 0.02$ seconds), and the broom length ($\lambda = 0.8106$ meters).

The angular velocity $\omega(t + 1)$ of the broom at time $t + 1$ is therefore

$$\omega(t + 1) = \omega(t) + \tau \Phi(t).$$

Then, as a result of this angular acceleration $\Phi(t)$, the angle $\theta(t + 1)$ at time $t + 1$ is, using Euler approximate integration,

$$\theta(t + 1) = \theta(t) + \tau\omega(t).$$

The acceleration $a(t)$ of the cart on the track is given by

$$a(t) = \frac{F + m_p\lambda[\theta^2 \operatorname{Sin} \theta - \omega \operatorname{Cos} \theta]}{m_c + m_p}.$$

The velocity $v(t + 1)$ of the cart on the track at time $t + 1$ is therefore

$$v(t + 1) = v(t) + \tau a(t).$$

The position $x(t + 1)$ of the cart on the track at time $t + 1$ is

$$x(t + 1) = x(t) + \tau v(t).$$

The problem is to find a time optimal control strategy (i.e., a computer program) for balancing the broom that satisfies the following three conditions:

- The control strategy specifies how to apply the bang-bang force at each time step for any combination of the state variables.
- The system comes to rest with the broom balanced (i.e., reaches a target state with approximate speed 0.0, approximate angle θ of 0.0, and approximate angular velocity ω of 0.0).
- The time required is minimal.

In this section, we consider only the particular version of the broom balancing problem that controls the three state variables of velocity v, angle θ, and angular velocity ω).

The terminal set for this problem is

```
T = {VEL, ANG, AVL, ℜ},
```

where VEL represents the velocity v, ANG represents the angle θ, AVL represents the angular velocity ω, and where $\mathfrak{R}$ is the ephemeral floating-point random constant $\mathfrak{R}$ ranging from -1.000 to $+1.000$.

The exact mathematical solution to this problem is not known. Therefore, we cannot select a function set for this problem that is guaranteed to be sufficient to find an exact solution. It seems reasonable to include the usual four arithmetic functions in the function set. It also seems reasonable to include functions such as the absolute-value function ABS as well as the sign function SIG and the real-valued greater-than function GT (both defined in section 7.1) to test the sign of subexpressions that may be created (since the known exact mathematical solution to the two-dimensional cart centering problem involved such a test). In addition, the square (SQ) and cube (CUB) function are included in the function set on the speculation that they may facilitate a solution.

Thus, the function set for this problem is

```
F = {+, -, *, %, SIG, ABS, SRT, SQ, CUB, GT},
```

taking two, two, two, two, one, one, one, one, one, and two arguments, respectively.

Closure of the function set is guaranteed by the protected division function (%), the real-valued greater-than function (GT), and the function SRT (which returns the square root of the absolute value of its one argument).

The SIG, ABS, SQ, and CUB functions are all superfluous; however, the benefit of having one additional function in the function set in facilitating a rapid and parsimonious solution often outweighs its slight additional cost.

This problem is similar to the cart centering problem in that we want a binary result (i.e., a bang-bang force) whereas the state variables (terminals) and functions applied to the state variables are arbitrary floating-point numbers. We therefore need a wrapper (output interface) for this problem in order to transform the floating-point value returned by each S-expression into a binary value of -1 or $+1$. Specifically, the wrapper converts any positive numerical output into a bang-bang force F of $+1$ which, in turn, accelerates the system in the positive direction, and it converts any other output into a bang-bang force F of -1 which accelerates the system in the negative direction. In fact, the function GT serves as the wrapper for this problem.

Most problems do not require any wrapper because genetic programming allows us to use the functions and terminals in terms that are most natural for the problem. If an output interface (wrapper) is needed at all, the nature of the wrapper needed by a particular problem flows from the choice of the terminal set and the function set for the problem. If a wrapper is required, it is typically a very simple one (as is the case here).

The randomly generated initial S-expressions and the S-expressions that are produced via crossover in this problem do not, in general, neatly partition the v - θ - ω state space into two parts; however, they sometimes do.

Figure 11.2 shows a control surface that partitions the three-dimensional v - θ - ω state space into two parts. When the system is at a point (v, θ, ω) in the state space that is above the control surface, the force F is applied so as to accelerate the cart in the positive direction. Otherwise, the force is applied so as to accelerate the cart in the negative direction.

If the square root of the sum of the squares of the velocity v, the angle θ, and the angular velocity ω is less than an arbitrarily chosen small value of 0.07 (which we call the *target criterion*), the system is considered to have arrived at its target state (i.e., with the broom balanced and the cart at rest). If a particular control strategy brings the system to the target state for a particular fitness case, its fitness for that fitness case is the time required (in seconds). If a control strategy fails to bring the system to the target state before it "times out" for a particular fitness case, its fitness for that fitness case is set to that maximum amount of time. The fitness of a control strategy is the total time for the strategy over all fitness cases (identified below).

Let us now consider two examples of the broom balancing problem.

11.1.1   Example 1

The fitness cases for this version of the broom balancing problem consist of ten random initial conditions. The initial position is chosen randomly

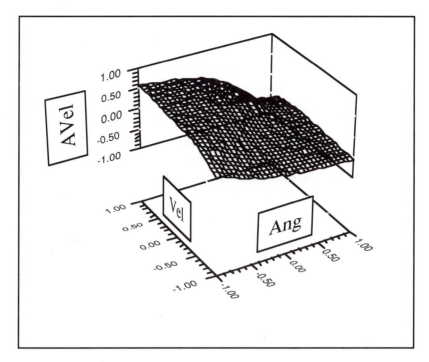

Figure 11.2 Control surface in the three-dimensional state space of the broom balancing problem.

between -0.2 and $+0.2$ meters. The initial velocity v is chosen randomly between -0.2 and $+0.2$ meters/second. The initial angle θ is chosen randomly between -0.2 radians and $+0.2$ radians (about $11.5°$). The initial angular velocity ω is chosen randomly between -0.2 and $+0.2$ radians per second. Each control strategy is executed on every time step of each fitness case. Ten is a rather small number of fitness cases; however, the time-consuming nature of the evaluation of each fitness case necessitates a compromise for this problem.

For this version of the problem, the force F is 1.0 newtons and time is discretized into 300 time steps of 0.02 second so that the time available before the system times out for a given fitness case is 6 seconds.

Raw fitness is the sum, over all ten fitness cases, of the time required to bring the system to the desired target state. As usual, if a given S-expression does not bring the system to the desired target state for a given fitness case within this maximum allowed time of 6 seconds, the contribution to raw fitness of that fitness case is set to this maximum value. Since a smaller value of raw fitness is better, standardized fitness equals raw fitness for this problem. Note that standardized fitness does not reach 0 for this problem. Since we do not know the optimal time in advance, we cannot merely subtract a constant to guarantee that the standardized fitness will reach 0.

The vast majority of the computer time will be consumed by the calculation of fitness in any run of a genetic method on a non-trivial problem. The time required to calculate fitness for this problem depends on the number of fitness cases and the maximum amount of time that the simulation of the system is allowed to run for each fitness case. In this problem, there is a tradeoff between computer resources and the likelihood of finding a solution. However, if the allowed amount of time for the simulation is decreased too much, all individuals will time out and there will be no variation of fitness among the individuals in the population. Genetic methods require such fitness among the individuals in the population. Genetic methods require such variation in fitness. Experimentation was required to select a time-out limit.

We define a hit to be a fitness case that does not time out. This definition is useful for monitoring the progress of runs, since merely bringing the broom into balance is a worthwhile subgoal to monitor in this problem.

We did not define a success predicate for this problem because we did not know the optimal value for time. Instead, we allowed each run to continue for 51 generations and studied the results afterwards. If we had started with knowledge of the optimal time, we could have defined a success predicate in terms of coming within perhaps 1% of that amount of time. Alternatively, we could have defined a success predicate in terms of doing better than the best result achieved to date.

One can envision defining more than one kind of hit for a problem such as this. For example, the first kind of hit might be defined in terms of bringing the broom into balance while the second kind of hit might be defined in terms of coming within 1% of the known optimal time. Both kinds of hits provide a useful perspective for monitoring a run. The second kind of hit might, of course, be used as a success predicate.

Table 11.1 summarizes the key features of example 1 of the broom balancing problem.

As one would expect, the initial population of random control strategies in generation 0 includes many highly unfit control strategies, including totally blind strategies that ignore all the state variables, partially blind strategies that ignore some of the state variables, strategies that repetitively apply the force from only one direction, strategies whose narrowness limits their effectiveness to a particular few parts of the state space, strategies that are totally counterproductive, and strategies that cause wild oscillations and meaningless gyrations.

In one run, the average time consumed by the initial random strategies in generation 0 was 5.3 seconds. In fact, a majority of the initial random individuals timed out at 6 seconds (and most of them would have timed out regardless of how much additional time had been available). However, even in this highly unfit initial random population, some control strategies are somewhat better than others.

The best-of-generation control strategy in generation 0 was a nonlinear strategy that was equivalent to

$$v^2 + \theta.$$

Note that this best-of-generation control strategy is partially blind in that it

Table 11.1 Tableau for broom balancing.

Objective:	Find a control strategy to balance the broom and bring the cart to rest in minimal time.
Terminal set:	VEL (velocity v), ANG (angle θ), AVL (angular velocity ω), and the ephemeral random floating-point constant $\Re$ ranging from -1.000 to $+1.000$.
Function set:	+, −, *, %, SIG, ABS, SRT, SQ, CUB, GT.
Fitness cases:	Ten initial condition points in state space of the problem (v, θ, ω).
Raw fitness:	The sum, over the fitness cases, of the times required to balance the broom and bring the cart to rest.
Standardized fitness:	Same as raw fitness for this problem.
Hits:	Number of fitness cases that do not time out.
Wrapper:	Converts any positive value returned by an S-expression to $+1$ and converts all other values (negative or zero) to -1.
Parameters:	$M = 500$. $G = 51$.
Success predicate:	None.

does not even consider the state variable ω in deciding how to apply the bang-bang force. It averaged 3.77 seconds.

The population average fitness improved to 5.27, 5.23, 5.15, 5.11, 5.04, and 4.97 seconds per fitness case in generations 1 through 6, respectively.

The best-of-generation individual of generation 4 was the simple linear strategy

```
(+ (+ ANG AVL) AVL),
```

which is equivalent to

$\theta + 2\omega$.

Figure 11.3 shows that the control surface corresponding to this S-expression for generation 4 is merely a plane. The axes here (and for the succeeding figures in this section) are the same as for figure 11.2.

In generation 6, the best-of-generation individual was the nonlinear strategy

$\theta + \sqrt{(|\omega| - \omega^2)}$.

Note that this individual considers all three state variables. This individual performed in an average of 2.66 seconds. Moreover, it succeeded in bringing in seven out of the ten fitness cases to the target state. This compares to only four such hits for the best-of-generation individual of generation 0 (where, in fact, about two-thirds of the individuals in the population scored only one hit).

By generation 10, the average population fitness had improved further to 4.8 seconds. The best-of-generation individual scored eight hits and was

$\theta + 2\omega - v^2$.

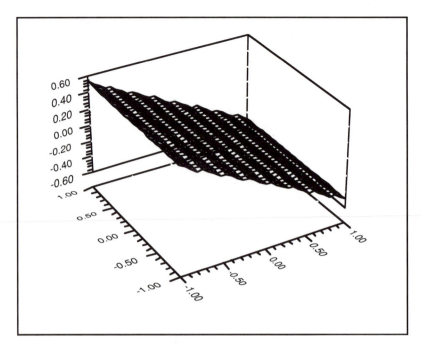

Figure 11.3 The best-of-generation individual for generation 4 of the broom balancing problem is a linear control strategy.

By generation 14, the average fitness had improved to 4.6 seconds. And, in generation 14, for the first time, the mode of the hits histogram moved from 1 (where it started at generation 0) to a higher number (4). In generation 14, 96 of the 300 individuals scored four hits.

The best-of-generation individual of generation 16 is the S-expression

```
(+ (* (SQ (+ ANG AVL)) (SRT AVL))
   (+ (- ANG (SQ VEL)) AVL)),
```

which is equivalent to

$$\sqrt{\omega(\theta + \omega)^2} + \omega + \theta - v^2.$$

Figure 11.4 shows the nonlinear control surface corresponding to this S-expression for generation 16.

In generation 24, one individual scored ten hits. The best individual in generation 24 is, when simplified, the nonlinear strategy

$$v + \theta + 2\omega + \theta^3.$$

This individual had a raw fitness of 2.63 seconds. The population average fitness improved to 4.2 seconds.

The linear control strategy below appears as a best-of-generation individual in generation 27:

$$v + 2\theta + 3\omega.$$

This individual scored ten hits and had a fitness of 2.16 seconds. This is the last

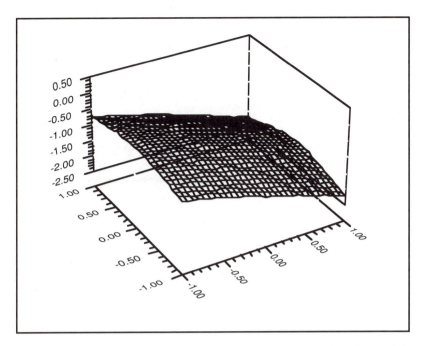

Figure 11.4 The best-of-generation individual for generation 16 of the broom balancing problem.

time that a linear strategy appears as the best individual of a generation in this run. Although there are good linear controllers for this problem, the optimal solution is nonlinear.

In generation 33, the best-of-generation individual bears a resemblance to the solution we eventually attain in generation 46. In generation 33, the best-of-generation individual is

$$8\omega^3 + v + \theta + \omega.$$

This individual has a fitness of 1.57 seconds. Moreover, 15% of the individuals in the population in generation 33 scored ten hits.

The best-of-generation individual for generation 34 was the S-expression

```
(+ (+ (+ (CUB (+ AVL AVL)) (+ VEL AVL)) ANG)
   (ABS (ABS (SQ (* (* (SRT 0.24)
                        (+ (SRT ANG) AVL))
                     (ABS VEL)))))),
```

which is equivalent to

$$(2\omega)^3 + v + \omega + \theta + |[\sqrt{0.24}(\sqrt{\theta} + \omega)|v|]^2|.$$

Figure 11.5 shows the nonlinear control surface corresponding to this S-expression for generation 34.

By generation 35, 30% of the individuals in the population scored ten hits, and the high point of the hits histogram moved from four to ten. The best-of-generation individual for generation 35 was

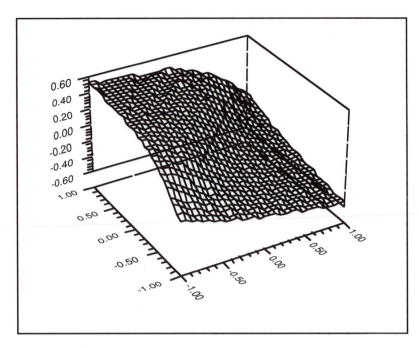

Figure 11.5 The best-of-generation individual for generation 34 of the broom balancing problem.

```
(+ (+ (+ (CUB (+ AVL AVL)) (+ VEL AVL)) ANG)
   (ABS (ABS (SQ ANG)))),
```

which is equivalent to

$$(2\omega)^3 + v + \omega + \theta + \theta^2.$$

Figure 11.6 shows the nonlinear control surface corresponding to this S-expression for generation 35.

The best-of-generation individual for generation 40 was the S-expression

```
(+ (+ (+ (CUB (+ AVL AVL)) (+ VEL AVL)) ANG)
   (+ (+ (CUB (+ (+ VEL AVL) ANG)) (+ VEL AVL)) ANG)),
```

which is equivalent to

$$(2\omega^3 + 2(v + \omega + \theta) + (v + \omega + \theta)^3.$$

Figure 11.7 shows the nonlinear control surface corresponding to this S-expression for generation 40.

The best-of-generation individual for generation 44 was the S-expression

```
(+ (+ ANG AVL) (+ (+ (+ (CUB (+ AVL AVL)) (+ VEL AVL))
                    ANG) VEL)),
```

which is equivalent to

$$2(v + \omega + \theta) + (2\omega)^3.$$

Figure 11.8 shows the nonlinear control surface corresponding to this S-expression for generation 44.

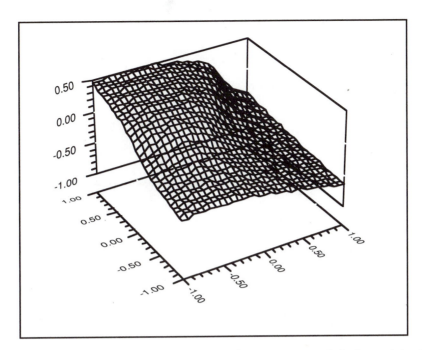

Figure 11.6 The best-of-generation individual for generation 35 of the broom balancing problem.

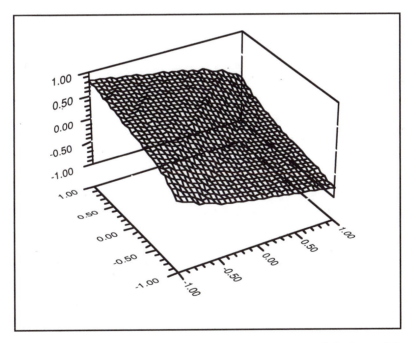

Figure 11.7 The best-of-generation individual for generation 40 of the broom balancing problem.

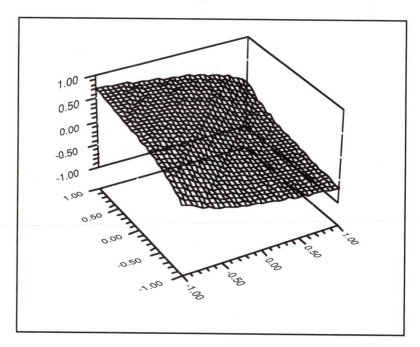

Figure 11.8 The best-of-generation individual for generation 44 of the broom balancing problem.

Finally, in generation 46, the following best-of-generation individual emerged:

```
(+ (+ (+ (CUB (+ AVL AVL)) (+ VEL AVL)) ANG)
   (+ (* (+ VEL AVL) (+ (SRT ANG) AVL)) ANG)).
```

This individual corresponds to the following eight-term nonlinear strategy:

$$v + 2\theta + \omega + 8\omega^3 + \omega^2 + v\omega + v\sqrt{\theta} + \omega\sqrt{\theta}.$$

Figure 11.9 shows the nonlinear control surface corresponding to the best-of-run individual obtained in generation 46.

As can be seen from this progression of best-of-generation control surfaces, successive surfaces often are gradual refinements of their predecessors. The solution to this problem evolves in small increments.

Figure 11.10 shows the progressive improvement (decrease) during this run of the average standardized fitness of the population and the best-of-generation individual. The raw fitness of the worst-of-generation individual is at the top of the graph for most generations of this run, indicating the presence of at least one individual in the population that timed out for all ten fitness cases. As can be seen, the standardized fitness for the best-of-generation individual appears to have plateaued.

There is no known solution for this problem, nor is there any specific test we can perform on an apparent solution that we obtain to verify that it is the optimum.

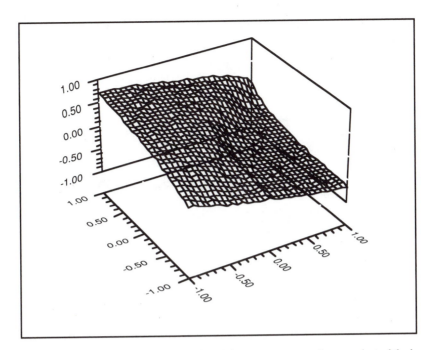

Figure 11.9 The best-of-generation individual from generation 46 for example 1 of the broom balancing problem.

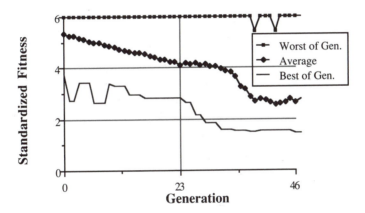

Figure 11.10 Fitness curves for example 1 of the broom balancing problem.

Control—Cost-Driven Evolution

Table 11.2 Performance of best-of-run individual for example 1 of the broom balancing problem.

Control strategy	1,000 points	Eight corners	Hardest two corners
Benchmark pseudo-optimal strategy	1.85	2.96	Infinite
$v + 2\theta + \omega + 8\omega^3 + \omega^2$ $+ v\omega + v\sqrt{\theta} + \omega\sqrt{\theta}$	1.51	2.65	4.24

Deciding when to terminate a run often presents some difficulty in optimization problems since one is seeking both the unknown optimal time and the computer program that achieves this unknown time.

After its discovery, we retested this best-of-generation control strategy found in generation 46 on 1,000 additional random fitness points. It performed in an average of 1.51 seconds.

In another test, this best-of-generation control strategy from generation 46 averaged 2.65 seconds when the initial conditions consisted of the eight corners of the three-dimensional v - θ - ω cube. In yet another test, it took 4.24 seconds when the initial conditions consisted of the hardest two corners of the cube (i.e., where the velocity, the angle, and the angular velocity have the same sign). This control strategy never timed out for any internal point or any corner point of the cube.

A pseudo-optimal strategy developed by Keane (Koza and Keane 1990a, 1990b) served as an approximate guide for verifying the possible attainment of the optimal value for time. This pseudo-optimal strategy is an approximate solution to a linear simplification of the problem.

The pseudo-optimal strategy averaged 1.85 seconds over the 1,000 random fitness cases in the retest. It averaged 2.96 seconds for the eight corners of the cube. Moreover, it was unable to handle the two hardest corners of the cube.

Table 11.2 summarizes these results as an average in seconds per fitness case.

We know of no control strategy for example 1 whose performance is as good as the genetically created nonlinear control strategy

$$v + 2\theta + \omega + 8\omega^3 + \omega^2 + v\omega + v\sqrt{\theta} + \omega\sqrt{\theta}$$

from generation 46 of the run described above. We do know that this control strategy had the best time of the many similar control strategies that we discovered, that there were numerous other control strategies that were only slightly worse (suggesting possible convergence), and that this particular control strategy is slightly better than the benchmark pseudo-optimal strategy developed by Keane.

Figure 11.11 graphically depicts the best-of-generation individual from generation 46 designated as the best-of-run individual for example 1 of the broom balancing problem.

Histograms provide a way of visualizing the progressive learning of the population as a whole.

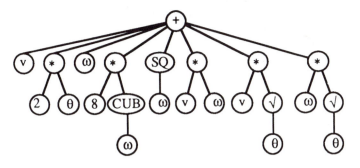

Figure 11.11 Best-of-run individual for example 1 of the broom balancing problem.

The hits histogram (seen previously in sections 7.2 and 7.4) shows the number of individuals in the population that score a particular number of hits.

The *fitness histogram* shows the number of individuals in the population whose fitness values fall into a particular decile range of values of normalized fitness.

Each of these histograms displays an undulating left-to-right "slinky-like" motion as the population as a whole progressively learns from generation to generation.

Figure 11.12 shows the hits histograms for generations 0, 8, 16, 32, and 40 of the broom balancing problem.

Figure 11.13 shows the fitness histograms for generations 0, 8, 16, 32, and 40 of the broom balancing problem.

Note that the time required by the best-of-generation individual for generation 0 is about 3 times the time of the pseudo-optimal strategy.

11.1.2 Example 2

In this version of the broom balancing problem, we enlarge the cube of possible initial values of the state variables. The fitness cases again consist of ten initial condition cases. However, the position is now chosen randomly between -0.5 and $+0.5$ meter and the velocity v is chosen randomly between -0.5 and $+0.5$ meter/second. The angle θ is chosen randomly between -0.5 radian (about 28.6°) and $+0.5$ radian. The angular velocity ω is chosen randomly between -0.5 and $+0.5$ radian/second. The force F is 4.0 newtons.

The enlarged range for the angle θ is significant because when the angle θ is limited to a domain of about $-11.5°$ to $+11.5°$ (as it was in example 1), Sin θ approximately equals θ. The enlarged range for the angle θ makes the problem clearly nonlinear.

Time was discretized into 400 time steps of 0.02 second. The total time available before the system timed out for a given control strategy was thus 8 seconds.

In one run, the average time consumed by the control strategies in the initial random population averaged 7.79 seconds. In fact, many of these 300 random

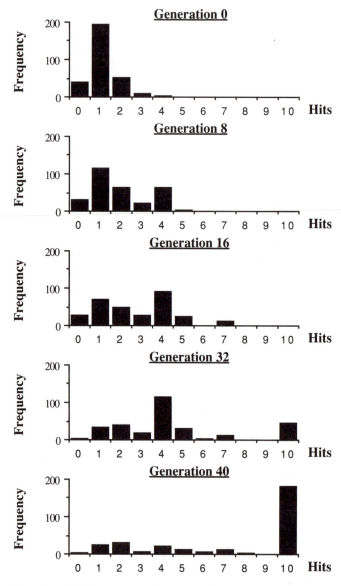

Figure 11.12 Hits histograms for generations 0, 8, 16, 32, and 40 of the broom balancing problem.

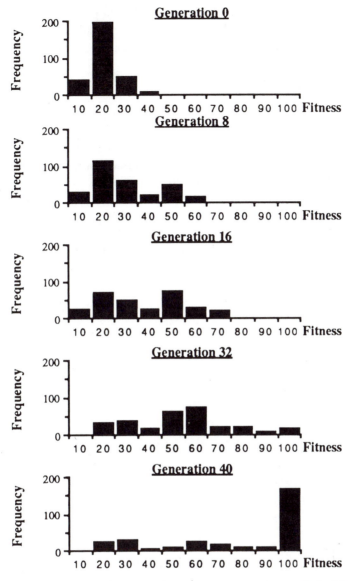

Figure 11.13 Fitness histograms for generations 0, 8, 16, 32, and 40 of the broom balancing problem.

Control—Cost-Driven Evolution

individuals timed out at 8 seconds for all ten of the fitness cases (and very likely would have timed out even if more time had been available). However, even in this highly unfit initial random population, some control strategies are somewhat better than others.

The best-of-generation control strategy for the initial random generation was the nonlinear control strategy

$v\theta$.

This strategy averaged 6.55 seconds. It handled two of the ten fitness cases correctly and timed out for eight. Notice that this control strategy is partially blind in that it does not even consider the state variable ω in specifying how to apply the bang-bang force.

The population average fitness improved in a generally monotonic progression from 7.79 to 7.78, 7.74, 7.73, 7.70, 7.69, 7.66, 7.63, 7.62 seconds per fitness case in generations 1 through 8, respectively.

In generation 6, the best-of-generation individual was the nonlinear control strategy

$\theta > v^3 |\theta + v|$.

This control strategy required an average of 6.45 seconds.

In generation 7, the best-of-generation individual in the population did not time out for four of the ten fitness cases. It required an average of 5.72 seconds.

In generation 8, the best-of-generation individual was the nonlinear control strategy

$[\theta + \omega + 2.762v + \theta^3]^3$.

This strategy required an average of only 2.56 seconds. It correctly handled all ten fitness cases.

In generation 14, the average time required by the best-of-generation individual in the population dropped below 2 seconds for the first time. In particular, the nonlinear control strategy

$\theta + \omega + v + v^2[\omega - 0.734]^2 > v\omega^2$

required an average of only 1.74 seconds. It, too, correctly handled all ten of the fitness cases.

In generation 33, the best-of-generation individual in the population was the nonlinear control strategy

$3v + 3\theta + 3\omega + v\theta^2 > v\omega^2$.

After its discovery, this control strategy was retested on 1,000 additional random fitness cases. It performed in an average of 1.76 seconds. In another test, it averaged 3.20 seconds on the eight corners of the cube but could not handle two of the eight corners.

As in example 1 above, there is no known optimal solution for this problem, nor is there any specific test we can perform on an apparent solution that we obtain to verify that it is the optimum. The pseudo-optimal strategy developed by Keane (Koza and Keane 1990a, 1990b) averaged 1.85 seconds over

Table 11.3 Performance of best-of-run individual for example 2 of the broom balancing problem.

Control strategy	1,000 points	Eight corners	Hardest two corners
Benchmark pseudo-optimal strategy	1.85	2.96	Infinite
$3v + 3\theta + 3\omega + v\theta^2 > v\omega^2$	1.76	3.20	Infinite

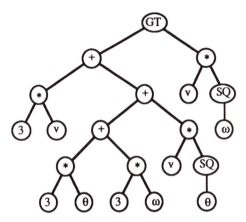

Figure 11.14 Best-of-run individual for example 2 of the broom balancing problem.

the 1,000 random fitness cases in the retest. It averaged 2.96 seconds for the eight corners of the cube. It was also unable to handle the two hardest corners of the cube. We do not know whether it is possible to solve this problem for the two hardest corners of the cube with the parameter settings used.

Table 11.3 summarizes these results as an average in seconds per fitness case.

We know of no control strategy for example 2 whose performance is as good as that of the best-of-generation control strategy,

$$3v + 3\theta + \omega + v\theta^2 > v\omega^2,$$

from generation 33 of the run described above. We do know that this control strategy had the best time of the many similar control strategies that we discovered, that there were numerous other control strategies that were only slightly worse (suggesting possible convergence), and that this particular control strategy is slightly better than the benchmark pseudo-optimal strategy developed by Keane.

Figure 11.14 shows the best-of-generation control strategy from generation 33 designated as the best-of-run individual for example 2 of the broom balancing problem.

11.2 THE TRUCK BACKER UPPER PROBLEM

Anyone who has ever tried to steer a tractor-trailer truck so as to back it up to a loading dock knows that this task presents a difficult problem of control.

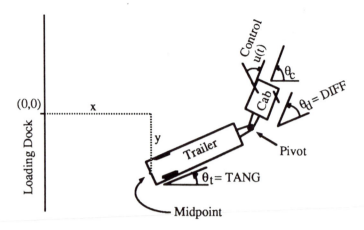

Figure 11.15 The truck backer upper problem.

Nguyen and Widrow (1990) have successfully demonstrated that a neural net can solve this difficult control problem.

Figure 11.15 shows a loading dock and a tractor-trailer. The loading dock is the y axis. The trailer and the tractor are connected at a pivot point.

The state space of the system is four-dimensional. The variable x gives the horizontal position of the midpoint of the rear of the trailer and the variable y gives the vertical position of the midpoint. The target point for the midpoint of the rear of the trailer is $(0, 0)$. The angle θ_t (also called TANG, for "trailer angle") is the angle of the trailer with respect to the loading dock (measured, in radians, from the positive x axis, counterclockwise being positive). The angle θ_d (also called DIFF, for "difference angle") is the angle of the tractor relative to the longitudinal axis of the trailer (measured, in radians, from the longitudinal axis of the trailer, counterclockwise being positive).

The truck backs up at a constant speed so that the tractor's front wheels move a fixed distance backward with each time step. Steering is accomplished by changing the angle u (i.e., the control variable) of the front tires of the tractor with respect to the current orientation of the tractor.

The goal is to guide the trailer so that it reaches the loading dock and is perpendicular to the loading dock. In particular, the midpoint of the rear of the trailer should end up at, or very close to, the target point $(0, 0)$ on the loading dock with the trailer perpendicular to the dock.

We want to find a control strategy (stated in terms of the four state variables of the system, namely x, y, θ_t, and θ_d) that specifies the angle $u(t)$ of the front tires of the tractor relative to the tractor.

The equations of motion that govern the tractor-trailer system are

$A = r \cos u[t]$,

$B = A \cos(\theta_c[t] - \theta_t[t])$,

$C = A \sin(\theta_c[t] - \theta_t[t])$,

$x[t + 1\} = x[t] - B \cos \theta_t$,

$$y[t + 1] = y[t] - B \sin \theta_t,$$

$$\theta_c[t + 1] = \tan^{-1} \left(\frac{d_c \sin \theta_c[t] - r \cos \theta_c[t] \sin u[t]}{d_c \cos \theta_c[t] + r \sin \theta_c[t] \sin u[t]} \right),$$

$$\theta_t[t + 1] = \tan^{-1} \left(\frac{d_s \sin \theta_t[t] - C \cos \theta_t[t]}{d_s \cos \theta_t[t] + C \sin \theta_t[t]} \right),$$

$$\theta_d[t] = \theta_t[t] - \theta_c[t].$$

In these equations, $\tan^{-1}(x/y)$ is the two-argument arctangent function (called ATG) delivering an angle in the range $-\pi$ to π. The length of the tractor (i.e., cab) d_c is 6 meters and the length of the trailer d_s is 14 meters. The angle θ_t is TANG. The angle of the tractor relative to the x axis is θ_c. The difference angle θ_d is DIFF.

Time is measured in steps of 0.02 second. A total of 3,000 time steps (i.e., 60 seconds) are allowed for each fitness case. As in Nguyen and Widrow 1990, the truck only moves backward. The speed of the tractor-trailer is 0.2 meter per time step. The distance moved backward in one time step is r.

The terminal set T for this problem consists of the four state variables of the problem and the ephemeral random floating-point constant $\Re$ ranging from -1.000 to $+1.000$:

T = {X, Y, TANG, DIFF, $\Re$}.

The function set F for this problem consists of the four arithmetic operations, the two-argument Arctangent function ATG, and the conditional comparative operator IFLTZ (If Less Than Zero):

F = {+, -, *, %, ATG, IFLTZ},

taking two, two, two, two, two, and three arguments, respectively.

The two-argument Arctangent function ATG is able to return an angle in the correct quadrant, since it can examine the signs of the two arguments.

The three-argument conditional function IFLTZ (If Less Than Zero) is defined in subsection 6.1.1 so as to execute its second argument if its first argument is less than 0, but to execute its third argument otherwise.

In selecting this function set, we included the two-argument Arctangent function ATG because we thought it might be useful in computing angles from the various distances involved in this problem, and we included the decision function IFLTZ so that actions could be predicated on certain conditions' being satisfied. As it developed, the Arctangent function did not appear in the best solution we found.

The fitness cases are eight sets of initial conditions for X, Y, and TANG which correspond to the corners of the initial condition space specified by Nguyen and Widrow. X is either 20 or 40 meters. Y is either -50 or 50 meters. TANG is either $-\pi/2$ or $+\pi/2$. As in Nguyen and Widrow 1990, DIFF is initially always 0 (i.e., the tractor and the trailer are coaxial). Eight is a rather small number of fitness cases; however, the time-consuming nature of the evaluation of each fitness case necessitates a compromise for this problem.

Termination of a fitness case occurs when

(1) time runs out,

(2) the trailer crashes into the loading dock (i.e., x becomes 0), or

(3) the midpoint of the rear of the trailer comes close, as defined by Nguyen and Widrow, to the target state in that the value of x is less than 0.1 meter, the absolute value of Y is less than 0.42 meter, and the absolute value of TANG is less than 0.12 radian (about 7°).

In this problem, raw fitness measures distance from the target. Raw fitness is the sum, over the fitness cases, of the sum of the squares of the difference, at the time of termination of the fitness case, between the value of x and the target value of x (i.e., 0), twice the difference between the value of Y and the target value of Y (i.e., 0), and $40/\pi$ times the difference between the value of TANG and the target value of TANG (i.e., 0). Note that we scaled the three summands so that they would have approximately equal impact on the total value of fitness.

In this problem, we used a wrapper (output interface) to convert the value returned by a given S-expression to a saturating force, rather than a bang-bang force. In particular, if the S-expression evaluates to a number between -1.0 and $+1.0$, the tractor turns its wheels to that particular angle (in radians) relative to the longitudinal axis of the tractor and backs up for one time step. If the value of the S-expression is less than -1.0 the angle saturates to -1.0 radian, but if it is greater than $+1.0$ the angle saturates $+1.0$ radian.

Table 11.4 Tableau for truck backer upper.

Objective:	Find a control strategy for backing up a tractor-trailer truck to a loading dock.
Terminal set:	X, Y, TANG, DIFF, and the ephemeral random constant $\Re$ ranging from -1.000 to $+1.000$.
Function set:	+, −, *, %, ATG, IFLTZ
Fitness cases:	8 initial condition points over the state variables X, Y, and TANG (with DIFF of 0).
Raw fitness:	The sum, taken over the 8 fitness cases, of the sum of squares of the difference between the actual values of X, Y, and TANG from their target values.
Standardized fitness:	Same as raw fitness for this problem.
Hits:	Number of fitness cases for which X is less than 0.1 meters, the absolute value of Y is less than 0.42 meters, and the absolute value of TANG is less than 0.25 radians
Wrapper:	Produces a saturated force between -1 radians and $+1$ radians.
Parameters:	$M = 1,000$ (with over-selection). $G = 51$.
Success predicate:	An S-expression scores 8 hits.

As in Nguyen and Widrow 1990, if a choice of the control variable u would cause the absolute value of the difference DIFF to exceed 90°, DIFF is constrained to 90° to prevent jack-knifing.

One can save a considerable amount of computer time in this problem by recognizing that great precision is not needed and by using the "short float" data type.

Table 11.4 summarizes the key features of the truck backer upper problem.

In one run, the best-of-generation individual in generation 0 had a raw fitness of 26,956 and was incapable of backing the tractor-trailer to the loading dock for any of the eight fitness cases. This S-expression,

```
(- (ATG (+ X Y) (ATG X Y)) (IFLTZ (- TANG X) (IFLTZ Y
TANG TANG) (* 0.3905 DIFF))),
```

has 19 points.

Figure 11.16 shows, by generation, the progressive improvement (decrease) during this run of the best-of-generation individual and the average standardized fitness of the population. As can be seen, raw fitness improves (i.e., drops) to 4,790 for generations 1 and 2, 3,131 for generation 3, and 228 for generations 4 and 5.

Moreover, for generations 4 and 5, the best-of-generation individual was successful in backing up the truck for one of the eight fitness cases.

Raw fitness improved to 202 for generation 6. By generation 11, raw fitness had improved to 38.9 and the best-of-generation individual was successful for three of the eight fitness cases. Between generations 14 and 21, raw fitness for the best-of-generation individual ranged between 9.99 and 9.08 and the best-of-generation individual was successful for five fitness cases. Between generations 22 and 25, raw fitness for the best-of-generation individual ranged between 8.52 and 8.47 and the best-of-generation individual was successful for seven fitness cases.

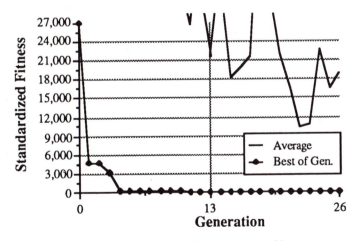

Figure 11.16 Fitness curves for the truck backer upper problem.

In generation 26, a control strategy emerged that was capable of backing up the tractor-trailer to the loading dock for all eight fitness cases. This S-expression,

```
(% (+ (+ (IFLTZ Y Y (+ (% (+ (+ (+ (+ (+ (IFLTZ DIFF Y (%
Y TANG)) (- DIFF X)) (+ (- -0.0728 Y) (% Y TANG))) (-
DIFF X)) (+ (- -0.0728 Y) (IFLTZ DIFF Y (% Y TANG)))) (%
Y TANG)) TANG) (- (% (% (+ (+ (IFLTZ Y Y (% Y TANG)) (-
TANG X)) (+ (- -0.0728 Y) (% Y TANG))) TANG) TANG) X)))
(- DIFF X)) (+ (+ (+ (+ (+ (IFLTZ DIFF Y (% Y TANG)) (-
DIFF X)) (+ (- -0.0728 Y) (% Y TANG))) (- DIFF X)) (+ (-
-0.0728 Y) (% Y TANG))) (% Y TANG))) TANG) ,
```

has a raw fitness of 7.41 and 108 points.

This best-of-run individual can be simplified by rewriting it as the following function in LISP:

```
(defun simplified-best-of-run-individual-from-gen-26 ()
  (LET* ((a (% y tang))
         (b (- -0.0728 y))
         (c (- diff x))
         (d (ifltz diff y a))
         (e (+ a b)))
    (IF (< y 0)
        (% (+ (% (* y (- 3 tang)) tang) -0.1459 d (* 3 c)) tang)
        (+ (% (+ a d (* 2 e) (* 3 c) (- x)) tang)
           (% (+ d e c) (* 0.5 tang tang))
           (% (+ a e tang (- x)) (* tang tang tang)))))).
```

As can be seen, this simplified function partitions the space into two parts according to the sign of Y.

Note that this S-expression is probably not a time-optimal solution, since it uses two different strategies for handling two cases that could, in fact, be handled in a symmetric way. Nonetheless, the S-expression does the job and scores maximal fitness with the distance-based fitness measure being used for this problem (which does not specifically call for time optimality).

Figure 11.17 shows the curved trajectory of the midpoint of the back of the trailer for one of the four fitness cases for which Y is negative for the best-of-run individual from generation 26.

Figure 11.18 shows the almost linear trajectory of the midpoint of the back of the trailer for one of the four fitness cases for which Y is positive for the best-of-run individual from generation 26.

There is no known mathematically exact solution to this problem. Interestingly, the absolute value of the number returned by the above best-of-generation S-expression from generation 26 exceeded 1 on 89.6% of the time steps. That is, the genetic solution chose to apply a bang-bang force 89.6% of the time and had discovered the virtues of a bang-bang force (as established by Pontryagin's minimization principle). See also Koza 1992c, 1992e. The

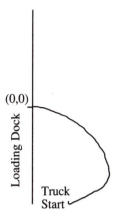

Figure 11.17 Curved trajectory of the back of trailer for a fitness cases for which Y is negative for the best-of-run individual of the truck backer upper problem.

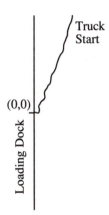

Figure 11.18 Almost linear trajectory of the back of trailer for a fitness cases for which Y is positive for the best-of-run individual of the truck backer upper problem.

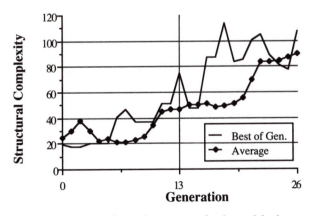

Figure 11.19 Structural complexity curves for the truck backer upper problem.

difficulty of this problem arises from Nguyen and Widrow's choice of the four states (Geva et al. 1992).

Figure 11.19 shows, by generation, the generally increasing trend of both the average structural complexity of the population as a whole and the structural complexity of the best-of-generation individual.

11.3 FINDING AN OPTIMAL FOOD FORAGING STRATEGY FOR THE CARIBBEAN *ANOLIS* LIZARD

The green, gray, and brown lizards of the genus *Anolis* in the Caribbean islands are "sit and wait" predators that typically perch head-down on tree trunks and scan the ground for desirable insects to eat (Roughgarden 1989). Figure 11.20 shows a lizard perched head-down on a tree trunk.

The optimal foraging strategy for such lizards in their environment is the behavioral rule which, when followed repetitively by a lizard, yields the maximum amount of food for the lizard.

Insects appear probabilistically within the lizard's viewing area. In this problem, the lizard sees all insects that are in a $180°$ planar area visible from the lizard's perch and always starts its chase from its perch. If insects only rarely alight within the lizard's viewing area, it would be advantageous for the lizard to unconditionally chase every insect that it sees. If insects are abundant, the lizard should certainly chase every nearby insect; however, if insects are abundant and the lizard chases a distant insect, the lizard will be away from its perch for so long that it will forgo the possibility of chasing and eating a greater number of nearby insects. This suggests ignoring distant insects. However, there is no guarantee that any insects will appear nearby during the period of time just after the lizard decides to forgo a distant insect.

The question arises as to what is the optimal tradeoff among the above competing considerations. The optimal strategy for the lizard is a function of four variables, namely the probability of appearance of the prey per square

Figure 11.20 *Anolis* lizard perched on a tree trunk. From Roughgarden 1979.

meter per second (called the abundance a), the lizard's sprint velocity v (in meters per second), and the location of the insect within the lizard's planar viewing area (expressed via two variables). The optimal strategy for the lizard optimizes the total amount of food eaten by the lizard.

The total amount of food eaten by the lizard can be maximized if the average time used to capture an insect is minimized. Time is used while the lizard waits for prey to appear and while the lizard chases the insect and returns to its perch. Determining the amount of food eaten requires a simulation of adaptive behavior.

In example 1, the lizard always finds and catches the insect if the lizard decides to chase the insect. The functional form of the optimal strategy for the lizard for example 1 is a semicircle, so the problem reduces to finding the cutoff radius r_c for the semicircle such that insects are chased if they are closer than this value and ignored if they are farther than this value.

Roughgarden (1992) has derived a closed form mathematical expression for this cutoff radius r_c using the argument that follows. The average waiting time between the appearance of insects within the semicircle of radius r is

$$\frac{1}{\int_0^{r_c} a \pi r \, dr}.$$

The average pursuit time is the integral from 0 to r_c of the product of the probability that an insect is at distance r times the pursuit time, $2r/v$, for the insect at distance r, namely

$$\int_0^{r_c} \frac{a \pi r}{\int_0^{r_c} a \pi r \, dr} \frac{2r}{v} \, dr.$$

The average waiting time w spent per insect captured is the sum of the average pursuit time and the average waiting time between the appearance of insects, namely

$$w = \frac{1}{\int_0^{r_c} a \pi r \, dr} + \int_0^{r_c} \frac{a \pi r}{\int_0^{r_c} a \pi r \, dr} \frac{2r}{v} \, dr.$$

For example 1 of this problem, Roughgarden was able to do the integration required and obtain

$$w = \frac{2}{a \pi r_c^2} + \frac{4 r_c}{3v}.$$

The optimal foraging distance r^* is the value of r_c that minimizes w. The minimum value of w occurs when the cutoff radius r_c is equal to

$$\sqrt[3]{(3v/\pi a)}.$$

The optimal control strategy for specifying when the lizard should decide to chase an insect can be expressed in terms of a function returning $+1$ for a point (x, y) in the lizard's viewing area for which it is advisable for the lizard to initiate a chase and returning -1 for points for which it is advisable to ignore the insect. Thus, if an insect appears at position (x, y) in the $180°$

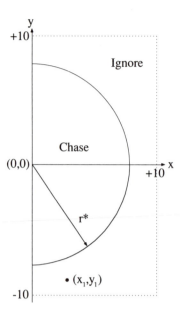

Figure 11.21 Switching curve for optimal foraging strategy.

area visible from the lizard's perch $(0, 0)$, the optimal foraging strategy as derived by Roughgarden (1993) is

$$\text{Sig}[\sqrt[3]{(3v/\pi a)} - \sqrt[2]{(x^2 + y^2)}],$$

where Sig is the sign function that returns $+1$ for a non-negative argument and -1 otherwise. That is, the lizard should chase the insect if the insect lies inside the semicircle centered at the lizard's perch of radius r^*.

Figure 11.21 shows the optimal foraging strategy derived by Roughgarden via the switching curve (i.e., semicircle) which partitions the half plane into the $+1$ (chase) region and the -1 (ignore) region. In this figure, we show an insect at position (x_1, y_1) that is in the -1 (ignore) region of the lizard's 20 meter by 10 meter viewing area.

Figure 11.22 shows the result of applying the optimal control strategy for one experiment lasting 300 seconds in the particular case where the probability of appearance of the prey (i.e., the abundance a) is 0.003 per square meter per second and where the lizard's sprint velocity v is 1.5 meters per second. Of the 180 insects shown as dots that appear in this 200 square meter area during this 300-second experiment, 91 are inside the semicircle and about 89 are outside the semicircle. Thirty-one of the 91 insects inside the semicircle are actually chased and eaten and are shown as larger dots. Sixty of the 91 insects appear in the semicircular "chase" region while the lizard is away from its perch and are shown as small dots.

Finding the above mathematical expression in closed form for the optimal strategy for example 1 of this problem depended on Roughgarden's insight that the functional form of the solution was a semicircle and his being able to perform the required integration. No such insight or integration is required with genetic programming.

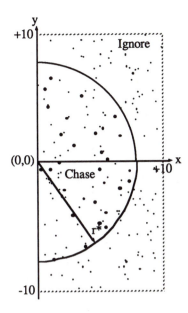

Figure 11.22 Performance of the optimal foraging strategy.

The four variables (i.e., X, Y, AB, VEL) can be viewed as inputs to the unknown computer program for optimally controlling the lizard. Here X and Y represent the position of an insect. X and Y vary each time an insect appears within a simulation. The value AB represents the abundance a and VEL represents the lizard's sprint velocity v. The values of AB and VEL are constant within any one simulation, but these parameters vary between simulations. Thus, the terminal set T for this problem is

T = {X, Y, AB, VEL, $\Re$}.

A function set F consisting of four arithmetic operations, the two-argument exponentiation function SREXPT, and the decision function IFLTE ("If Less Than or Equal") seems reasonable. That is,

F = {+, −, *, %, SREXPT, IFLTE},

taking 2, 2, 2, 2, 2, and 4 arguments, respectively.

The two-argument exponentiation function SREXPT raises the absolute value of the first argument to the power specified by its second argument. For example, (SREXPT −2.0 0.5) returns $2.0^{0.5} = \sqrt{2.0} = 1.414$.

A simulation of the lizard's behavior is required to compute the fitness of a program. Each program is tested against a simulated environment consisting of 36 combinations of values of the parameters AB and VEL. The abundance AB ranges over six values from 0.0030 to 0.0050 in steps of 0.0004. The lizard's sprint velocity VEL ranges over six values from 0.5 meters per second to 1.5 in steps of 0.2. Thirty-six combinations of values of these two parameters are used so as to provide a sufficiently varied environment to permit genetic programming to produce a solution which is likely to generalize to other combinations of values of these two parameters. Creation of the fitness cases for a problem is similar to creating a test set of data for debugging a hand-written computer program.

Since the appearance of insects is probabilistic, the simulation of the lizard's behavior should be done more than once for each of the 36 combinations of values. Computer time was conserved by performing only two experiments for each of the 36 combinations. Thus, there are 72 fitness cases (experiments) for this problem.

A total of 300 seconds of simulated time are provided for each simulation.

The raw fitness of a program in the population is the sum, over the 72 experiments, of the number of insects eaten by the lizard. A total of 17,256 insects are available in the 72 experiments, so standardized fitness is 17,256 minus raw fitness. The optimal foraging strategy derived by Roughgarden catches approximately 1,671 insects. This number is only approximate since the insects appear probabilistically in each experiment.

A hit is defined as an experiment for which the number of insects eaten is equal to or greater than one less than the number eaten using the optimal foraging strategy derived by Roughgarden. That is, a hit indicates that the program has only a small shortfall in performance for a particular experiment with respect to the optimal foraging strategy. Hits range between 0 and 72.

Table 11.5 Tableau for example 1 for the problem of finding the food foraging strategy of the Caribbean *Anolis* lizard.

Objective:	Find a control strategy enabling a lizard to maximize food by deciding whether to chase or ignore insects alighting within its territory.
Terminal set:	X, Y, AB, VEL, and the ephemeral random constant $\Re$ ranging from -1.000 to $+1.000$.
Function set:	+, -, *, %, SREXPT, IFLTE.
Fitness cases:	Two 300-second experiments for each of 36 combinations of value of abundance AB and sprint velocity VEL.
Raw fitness:	The sum, taken over the 72 fitness cases, of the number of insects eaten by the lizard when the lizard chases or ignores insects in accordance with the S-expression.
Standardized fitness:	The maximum value of raw fitness (17,256) minus the raw fitness of the S-expression.
Hits:	Number of fitness cases for which the number of insects eaten is equal to or greater than one less than the number eaten using the closed-form optimal foraging strategy.
Wrapper:	Converts any non-negative value returned by an S-expression to $+1$ and converts all other values to -1.
Parameters:	$M = 1,000$ (with tournament selection). $G = 61$.
Success predicate:	An S-expression scores 72 hits.

Since a given S-expression can return any floating-point value, a wrapper is used to convert the value returned by a given individual S-expression to a value appropriate to this problem domain. In particular, if the program evaluates to any non-negative number, the wrapper returns $+1$ (chase), but otherwise returns -1 (ignore).

Since great precision was not required by the simulations involved in this problem, a considerable saving in computer resources was achieved by using the "short float" data type for all numerical calculations.

Table 11.5 summarizes the key features of this problem.

11.3.1   Example 1

In this version of the problem, the lizard always finds and catches the insect if the lizard decides to chase the insect.

As one would expect, the performance of the random control strategies found in the initial generation (generation 0) is exceedingly poor. In one run, the worst 4% of the individual computer programs in the population of 1,000 always returned a negative value. Such programs unconditionally advise the lizard not to chase any insects and therefore have a fitness value of zero. An additional 19% of the programs enable the lizard to catch a few insects and scored no hits. 93% of these random programs score two hits or less.

The following individual from generation 0 consisted of 143 points (i.e., functions and terminals) and enables the lizard to catch 1,235 insects:

```
(+ (- (- (* (SREXPT VEL Y) (+ -0.3752 X)) (+ (* VEL
0.991) (+ -0.9522 X))) (IFLTE (+ (% AB Y) (% VEL X)) (+
(+ X 0.3201) (% AB VEL)) (IFLTE (IFLTE X AB X Y) (SREXPT
AB VEL) (+ X -0.9962) (% -0.0542984 AB)) (- (* Y Y) (* Y
VEL)))) (% (IFLTE (IFLTE (+ X Y) (+ X Y) (+ VEL AB) (* Y
Y)) (- (% 0.662094 AB) (* VEL X)) (+ (SREXPT AB X) (- X
Y)) (IFLTE (* Y Y) (SREXPT VEL VEL) (+ Y VEL) (IFLTE AB
AB X VEL))) (IFLTE (IFLTE (SREXPT X AB) (* VEL
-0.0304031) (IFLTE 0.9642 X Y AB) (SREXPT 0.0341034 AB))
(+ (- VEL 0.032898) (- X VEL)) (IFLTE (- X Y) (SREXPT VEL
0.141296) (* X AB) (SREXPT -0.6911 0.5399)) (SREXPT (+ AB
AB) (IFLTE 0.90849 VEL AB 0.9308)))))).
```

This rather unfit individual from generation 0 is in the 34th percentile of fitness (where the 99th percentile contains the most fit individuals of the population).

Figure 11.23 graphically depicts the foraging strategy of this individual as a switching curve. This figure and all subsequent figures are based on an abundance AB of 0.003 and a sprint velocity VEL of 1.5 (i.e., one of the 36 combinations of AB and VEL). A complete depiction would require showing switching curves for all the other combinations of AB and VEL. As can be seen, there are three separate "ignore" regions and one large "chase" region. This

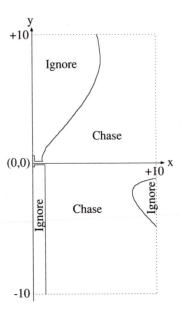

Figure 11.23 Switching curves of a program from the 34th percentile of fitness for generation 0 for example 1.

program causes the lizard to ignore about a third of the insects in the upper half of the figure, including many insects that are very close to the lizard's perch. It also causes the lizard to ignore the thin rectangular region in the lower half of the figure lying along the y axis. The main part of the "chase" region is distant from the perch, although there is a small T-shaped sliver immediately adjacent to the lizard's perch. Effective foraging behavior involves chasing insects near the perch and ignoring insects that are distant from the perch; this program usually does the opposite.

The best-of-generation individual from generation 0 enables the lizard to catch 1,460 insects. This 37-point program is shown below:

```
(- (- (+ (* 0.5605 Y) (% VEL VEL)) (* (SREXPT Y X) (* X
AB))) (* (* (+ X 0.0101929) (* -0.155502 X)) (IFLTE (+
VEL Y) (- AB X) (* X Y) (SREXPT VEL X)))).
```

Figure 11.24 shows the switching curves for this best-of-generation individual from generation 0. While this non-symmetric control strategy gives poor overall performance, it is somewhat reasonable in that many of the points for which it advises ignoring the insect are distant from the lizard's perch. In particular, all of the points in the "ignore" region at the top of the figure are reasonably distant from the lizard's perch at the origin $(0, 0)$ although the boundary is not, by any means, optimal. The "ignore" region at the bottom of the figure gives poorer performance.

However, even in this initial random population, some individuals are better than others. The gradation in performance is used by the evolutionary process to improve the population over subsequent generations. Each successive gen-

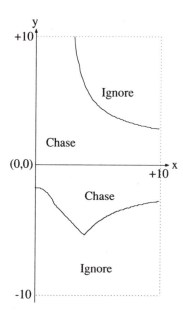

Figure 11.24 Switching curves of the best-of-generation program from generation 0 for example 1.

eration of the population is created by applying the Darwinian operation of fitness-proportionate reproduction and the genetic operation of crossover to individuals selected from the population with a probability proportional to fitness.

In generation 10, the best-of-generation individual enables the lizard to catch 1,514 insects and scores 26 hits. This 47-point program is shown below:

```
(- (- X (* (SREXPT Y X) (* X AB))) (* (* (+ X 0.0101929)
(* -0.155502 (+ AB X))) (IFLTE (+ X (+ (- (SREXPT X Y) (+
X 0.240997)) (+ 0.105392 VEL))) (% VEL 0.8255) (* (SREXPT
X VEL) (+ -0.7414 VEL)) (SREXPT VEL X)))).
```

Figure 11.25 shows the switching curves for this best-of-generation individual from generation 10. As can be seen, this program advises ignoring the insect when it appears in either of two approximately symmetric regions away from the perch.

In generation 25, the best-of-generation individual enables the lizard to catch 1,629 insects and scores 52 hits. This 81-point program is shown below:

```
(- (- (+ (- (- (- (SREXPT AB -0.9738) (SREXPT -0.443604
Y)) (* (SREXPT Y (+ (* (SREXPT (% (SREXPT Y AB) (- VEL
-0.9724)) (+ X 0.0101929)) 0.457596) (+ Y X))) (* X AB)))
(* (* (+ X 0.0101929) (% (+ Y -0.059105) (* 0.9099 Y)))
(IFLTE (+ X (SREXPT AB Y)) (% VEL 0.8255) (IFLTE Y VEL
0.282303 -0.272697) (SREXPT (* (SREXPT Y X) (* X AB))
X)))) (% AB 0.412598)) (* (SREXPT X X) (* X AB)))
0.4662).
```

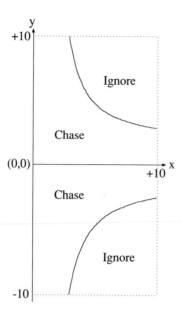

Figure 11.25 Switching curves of the best-of-generation program from generation 10 for example 1.

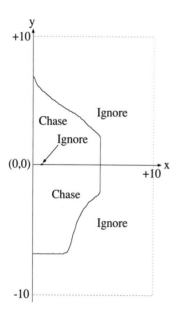

Figure 11.26 Switching curve of the best-of-generation program from generation 25 for example 1.

Figure 11.26 shows the switching curve for this best-of-generation individual from generation 25. In this figure, the control strategy advises the lizard to ignore the insect when the insect is outside an irregular region that vaguely resembles a semicircle centered at the lizard's perch. Note that there is an anomalous close-in point along the X axis where this control strategy advises the lizard to ignore any insect.

In generation 40, the best-of-generation program enables the lizard to catch 1,646 insects. This 145-point program scores 60 hits and is shown below:

```
(+ (- (+ (- (- (SREXPT AB -0.9738) (SREXPT -0.443604 Y))
(* (SREXPT X X) (* X AB))) (* (+ (+ Y -0.059105) (-
(SREXPT AB -0.9738) (+ AB X))) (% (- VEL VEL) (+ 0.7457
0.338898)))) (SREXPT Y X)) (- (- (- (SREXPT AB -0.9738)
(SREXPT -0.443604 Y)) (* (SREXPT Y X) (* X AB))) (* (* (+
X 0.0101929) (% (+ (% 0.7717 (+ Y AB)) (SREXPT (IFLTE Y
VEL X Y) (% (+ Y -0.059105) (+ VEL VEL)))) (+ (% (- Y X)
(% X AB)) VEL))) (IFLTE (- (- (- (SREXPT AB -0.9738)
(SREXPT -0.443604 Y)) (* (SREXPT X X) (* X AB))) (IFLTE X
X Y AB)) (IFLTE (SREXPT VEL VEL) (+ X 0.0101929) (% VEL
-0.407303) (+ -0.496597 AB)) (* X (SREXPT 0.838104 X))
(SREXPT VEL (+ (+ AB X) (* (% VEL VEL) (IFLTE Y VEL
0.888504 VEL))))))))).
```

In generation 60, the best-of-generation individual enables the lizard to catch 1,652 insects and scores 62 hits. This 67-point program is shown below:

```
(+ (- (+ (- (SREXPT AB -0.9738) (* (SREXPT X X) (* X
AB))) (* (+ VEL AB) (% (- VEL (% AB Y)) (+ 0.7457
0.338898)))) (SREXPT Y X)) (- (- (SREXPT AB -0.9738)
(SREXPT -0.443604 (- (- (+ (- (SREXPT AB -0.9738) (SREXPT
-0.443604 Y)) (+ AB X)) (SREXPT Y X)) (* (* (+ X
0.0101929) AB) X)))) (* (SREXPT Y Y) (* X AB)))).
```

This program is equivalent to

$$-0.44^{a+x+a^{-0.9738}} - (0.44^y + y^x + ax[x + 0.01])$$

$$+ 0.922(v + a)\left(v - \frac{a}{y}\right)$$

$$+ 2a^{-0.97} - y^x - ax(x^x + y^y).$$

Figure 11.27 shows the switching curve for this best-of-run individual from generation 60. As before, this figure is based on an abundance AB of 0.003 and a sprint velocity VEL of 1.5. As can be seen, the switching curve here is approximately symmetric and bears a reasonable resemblance to a semicircle centered at the lizard's perch. The shortfall from the known optimal strategy is one or less insects for 60 of the 72 fitness cases. Of the remaining 12 fitness cases which did not produce hits, eight had a shortfall of only two insects from the known optimal foraging strategy. The performance of this foraging

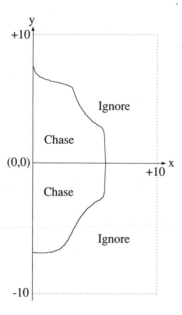

Figure 11.27 Switching curve of the best-of-run program from generation 60 for example 1.

strategy is therefore very close to the performance of the known optimal foraging strategy.

The above best-of-run control strategy is not the exact solution. It is an approximately correct computer program that emerged from a competitive genetic process that searches the space of possible programs for a satisficing result.

11.3.2   Example 2

In this version of this problem, the lizard does not necessarily find the insect at the location where it saw the insect.

In solving control problems, it is usually not possible to identify the functional form of the solution in advance and to perform integrations as Roughgarden did in the first version of this problem. However, when genetic programming is used, there is no need to have any advance insight as to the functional form of the solution and there is no need to do any integration. The solution to a problem produced by genetic programming is not just a numerical solution applicable to a single specific combination of numerical parameters, but, instead, comes in the form of a function (computer program) that maps the variables of the system into values of the control variable. There is no need to specify the exact size and shape of the computer program in advance. The needed structure is evolved in response to the selective pressures of Darwinian natural selection and genetic sexual recombination.

The lizard's 20 meter by 10 meter viewing area is divided into three regions depending on the probability that the insect will actually be present when the

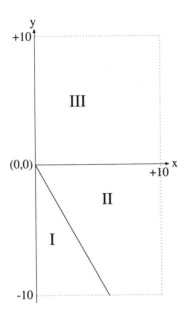

Figure 11.28 Three regions for example 2.

lizard arrives at the location where the lizard saw the insect. Figure 11.28 shows the three regions. In region I (where the angular location of points lies between $-60°$ and $-90°$), the insect is never present when the lizard arrives at the location where the lizard saw the insect. In region II (between $-60°$ and the x axis), the insect is always present. In region III, the probability that the insect is present when the lizard arrives varies with the angular location of the point within the region. Specifically, in region III, the probability is 100% along the x axis (where the angle is $0°$); the probability is 50% along the y axis (where the angle is $90°$); and the probability varies linearly as the angle varies between $0°$ and $90°$.

Although we have not attempted to derive a mathematical solution to this version of the problem, it is clear that the lizard should learn to totally ignore insects it sees in region I and that the lizard should chase insects it sees in region II that are within the same cutoff radius as in example 1. In region III, the lizard should reduce the distance it is willing to travel to catch an insect because of the uncertainty of finding the insect (the reduction being greatest for locations on the y axis).

We now proceed in the same manner as in example 1, except that the simulation of the behavior of the lizard must now incorporate the probability of actually finding an insect after the lizard decides to initiate a chase.

In one run of example 2, the best-of-generation individual from generation 0 enabled the lizard to catch 1,164 insects. This 37-point program was

```
(+ (% (* (IFLTE X VEL VEL X) (+ VEL Y)) (− (% AB X) (+ Y
Y))) (SREXPT (* (SREXPT VEL VEL) (% X Y)) (+ (IFLTE AB
VEL 0.194 X) (IFLTE VEL Y VEL VEL))))).
```

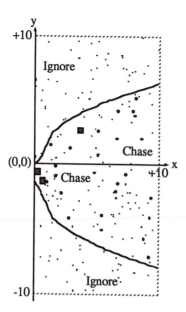

Figure 11.29 Switching curve of the best-of-generation program from generation 0 for example 2.

Figure 11.29 shows the switching curve of this best-of-generation individual from generation 0. As can be seen, the lizard ignores many locations that are near the y axis. The large gray squares indicate insects which the lizard decides to chase, but which are not present when the lizard arrives. This program is better than the others in generation 0 because it ignores an area in the bottom half of the figure that corresponds roughly to region I and because it ignores the area in the top half of this figure that corresponds roughly to the part of region III where the probability of finding an observed insect is lowest.

In generation 12, the following 107-point best-of-generation individual enables the lizard to catch 1,228 insects:

```
(IFLTE AB (* (SREXPT (* X 0.71089) (IFLTE VEL AB 0.053299
X)) (+ (- VEL Y) (IFLTE (* (IFLTE (SREXPT (% -0.175102
(SREXPT Y AB)) (SREXPT (% VEL AB) (IFLTE Y (+ 0.175598 Y)
(+ VEL (+ X (+ AB Y))) (* 0.7769 (IFLTE 0.7204 AB
0.962204 AB))))) VEL (- VEL (SREXPT (% VEL AB) (% 0.8029
0.36119))) (+ -0.157204 X)) VEL) (- X X) (+ VEL 0.8965)
(* 0.180893 AB)))) (+ (IFLTE (- VEL X) (% -0.588 Y)
(SREXPT 0.5443 -0.6836) (% X X)) (% (+ X Y) (- VEL AB)))
(- (% (SREXPT AB Y) (IFLTE Y Y X Y)) (IFLTE VEL AB X
X))).
```

Figure 11.30 shows the switching curve of this best-of-generation individual from generation 12. As can be seen, the avoidance of region I and the parts of region III are more pronounced.

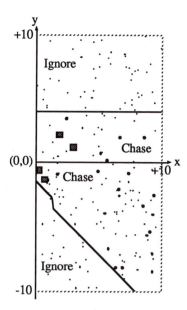

Figure 11.30 Switching curve of the best-of-generation program from generation 12 for example 2.

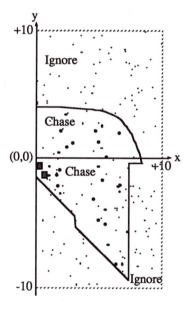

Figure 11.31 Switching curve of the best-of-run program from generation 46 for example 2.

In generation 46, the following 227-point best-of-generation program emerged:

```
(IFLTE AB (* (SREXPT (* -0.588 0.71089) (IFLTE VEL AB
0.053299 X)) (+ (- VEL Y) (IFLTE (% (SREXPT AB Y) (IFLTE
Y Y X Y)) (- VEL (IFLTE X (+ (* AB AB) (+ (IFLTE AB X AB
AB) (* VEL AB))) (* (- X X) AB) AB)) (+ VEL 0.8965) (+
0.175598 Y)))) (+ (IFLTE (+ VEL VEL) X (SREXPT 0.5443
-0.6836) (% X X)) (% (+ X Y) (- VEL AB))) (- (* (IFLTE
(SREXPT (SREXPT -0.0914 Y) (IFLTE (+ X Y) (% -0.588 Y) (*
AB 0.304092) (% X X))) X (- VEL (IFLTE Y AB X Y)) (+
-0.157204 (IFLTE (+ (- (% (% X (- VEL (IFLTE Y AB X Y)))
(- (% (SREXPT AB Y) (IFLTE Y Y X Y)) (IFLTE VEL AB X X)))
(+ (SREXPT Y Y) (- -0.172798 Y))) (IFLTE (SREXPT AB X) (-
(% AB 0.7782) 0.444794) (* (IFLTE Y (SREXPT (SREXPT X
0.299393) (+ VEL X)) 0.6398 Y) (- X -0.6541)) (IFLTE (-
(SREXPT Y 0.4991) (- (% (SREXPT AB Y) (IFLTE Y Y X Y))
(IFLTE VEL AB X X))) AB (SREXPT VEL (SREXPT (SREXPT X
0.299393) (* -0.3575 X))) (+ (% VEL AB) X)))) VEL (- VEL
(- (% (SREXPT AB Y) (+ (SREXPT Y Y) (% VEL VEL))) (IFLTE
VEL AB X X))) (+ -0.157204 X)))) VEL) (IFLTE VEL AB X
X))).
```

It enabled the lizard to catch 1,379 insects.

Figure 11.31 shows the switching curve of this best-of-run individual from generation 46. As can be seen, the lizard avoids an area that approximately corresponds to region I; chases insects in region II; and is willing to travel less far to catch an insect in region III. Moreover, the distance the lizard is willing to travel in region III is greatest when the angular location of the insect is near 0° and decreases as the angle approaches 90°.

See also Koza, Rice, and Roughgarden 1992.

12 Evolution of Emergent Behavior

The repetitive application of seemingly simple rules can lead to complex overall behavior (Steels 1990, 1991; Forrest 1991). Such emergent behavior arises in cellular automata, in dynamical systems (Devaney 1989), in fractals and chaos (Barnsley 1988), in Lindenmayer systems (Lindenmayer 1968; Lindenmayer and Rozenberg 1976; Prusinkiewicz and Lindenmayer 1990), and throughout nature. Emergent behavior is one of the main themes of research in artificial life (Langton 1989; Langton et al. 1991; Langton 1991a). Some systems of distributed artificial intelligence exhibit emergent behavior (Huhns 1987; Gasser and Huhns 1989).

In one avenue of work in emergent behavior, researchers try to conceive and then write sets of simple rules that produce complex overall behavior similar to that observed in nature. The fact that it is possible to conceive and write such sets of handwritten rules is an argument in favor of the possibility that the complex overall behavior observed in nature may be produced by similar sets of relatively simple governing rules.

If it is true that complex overall behavior can be produced from sets of relatively simple rules, it should be possible to evolve such sets of rules by means of an artificial process such as genetic programming. If such artificial evolution proves to be possible, then there is at least an argument in favor of the possibility that the evolutionary process in nature might have produced the complex overall behavior observed in nature.

In this chapter, we use genetic programming to evolve sets of seemingly simple rules (i.e., computer programs) that exhibit emergent behavior. The evolutionary process is driven only by the fitness of the rules in the problem environment. The evolved sets of rules arise from this fitness measure.

12.1 CENTRAL PLACE FOOD FORAGING BEHAVIOR

In this section, the goal is to genetically breed a common computer program that, when simultaneously executed by all the individuals in a group of independent agents (e.g., social insects such as ants or independently acting robots), causes the emergence of beneficial and interesting higher-level collective behavior. In particular, the goal is to genetically evolve a common program that causes the transportation of the available food to the nest of an ant colony.

In nature, the optimal solution to this "central place foraging" problem depends on the degree of concentration of the food (Collins and Jefferson 1991a, 1991b). When food is concentrated in large patches, it is advantageous to have workers initially search at random for food and, once food is found, to have a mechanism by which large numbers of workers can be recruited to the food source so that the large concentration of food available there can be efficiently transported to the nest. Ants initially discover food via random search; however, if food is discovered one piece at a time via random search by individual ants, only a small percentage of the available food will ever be transported to the nest. Thus, after an ant discovers food, it deposits a chemical trail of pheromones as it returns to the nest with whatever amount of food it can carry. The pheromones (which linger for a while and then dissipate) aid other ants in efficiently locating the food source. The repeated dropping of pheromones by individual ants carrying food between the food source and the nest creates a persisting pheromonal trail (Holldobler and Wilson 1990).

The problem of robots on the moon bringing rock samples back to a space ship (Steels 1991) is another version of this problem.

It is far from obvious that complex central place foraging behavior can emerge from the repetitive application of seemingly simple rules by ants. Travers and Resnick (1991) have produced a videotape showing a computer program they wrote for implementing the set of rules described above (Resnick 1991). The videotape provides a dramatic visualization of the formation, persistence, and dissipation of pheromonal clouds and the successful transportation of the food to the nest. The fact that a simple set of local rules for independent agents can produce this complex central place foraging behavior is significant evidence of the existence of emergent behavior with respect to this one problem.

Ants do not communicate with one another directly. The central place foraging problem is not solved by a coherent and synchronized set of commands being broadcast to individual ants from a central authority. Instead, each ant follows a common set of internal rules on a distributed, asynchronous, and local basis. If the environment seen by an individual ant makes one of its internal rules applicable, the ant takes the appropriate action. The internal rules are prioritized so as to resolve potential conflicts. Each ant is in direct communication with its environment. The ants communicate with one another in a very indirect way via the environment (i.e., they sense the presence or absence of pheromones and food).

In our version of the central place foraging problem for ants, there are two concentrated piles of food. A total of 144 pellets of food are piled eight deep in two 3 × 3 piles. The domain of action is a 32 × 32 grid. In deference to animal rights groups, the grid is toroidal, so that if an ant wanders off the edge it reappears on the opposite edge. The two piles of food are some distance from the nest of the colony in locations that cannot be reached by merely walking in a straight line from the nest. There are 20 ants in the colony. The state of each ant consists of its position on the grid, the direction it is facing (out of eight possible directions), and an indicator as to whether it is currently carrying food. Each ant initially starts at the nest and faces in a random direction.

Each ant in the colony is governed by a common computer program associated with the colony.

The following nine operators appear to be sufficient to solve this problem:

- MOVE-RANDOM randomly changes the direction in which an ant is facing and then moves the ant two steps in the new direction.

- MOVE-TO-NEST moves the ant one step in the direction of the nest. This implements the gyroscopic ability of many species of ants to navigate back to their nest.

- PICK-UP picks up food (if any) at the current position of the ant if the ant is not already carrying food.

- DROP-PHEROMONE drops pheromones at the current position of the ant (if the ant is carrying food). The pheromones immediately form a 3 × 3 cloud around the drop point. The cloud decays over a period of time.

- IF-FOOD-HERE is a two-argument conditional branching operator that executes its first argument if there is food at the ant's current position and that otherwise executes the second (else) argument.

- IF-CARRYING-FOOD is a similar two-argument conditional branching operator that tests whether the ant is currently carrying food.

- MOVE-TO-ADJACENT-FOOD-ELSE is a one-argument conditional branching operator that allows the ant to test for immediately adjacent food and then move one step toward it. If food is present in more than one adjacent position, the ant moves to the position requiring the least change of direction. If no food is adjacent, the "else" clause of this operator is executed.

- MOVE-TO-ADJACENT-PHEROMONE-ELSE is a conditional branching operator similar to MOVE-TO-ADJACENT-FOOD-ELSE except that is based on the adjacency of pheromones.

- PROGN is the LISP connective function that executes its arguments in sequence.

In this problem, a colony corresponds to a computer program and a computer program corresponds to an individual in the genetic population.

Each of the 20 ants in the colony executes the colony's common computer program at each time step. The action of one ant (e.g., picking up food, dropping pheromones) can, and does, alter the state of the system for the other ants. The 20 ants almost always pursue different trajectories on the grid because they initially face in random directions, they make random moves, and they encounter a changing complex pattern of food and pheromones created by the activities of other ants (and themselves). Multiple ants are allowed to occupy the same square in this problem.

In preparation for the use of genetic programming on this problem, the unconditional motion-control operators are placed in the terminal set as functions with no arguments (as in the artificial ant problem of section 7.2) and the conditional branching operators and connective operations are placed in the function set. Thus, the terminal set for this problem is

```
T = {(MOVE-RANDOM), (MOVE-TO-NEST), (PICK-UP), (DROP-
     PHEROMONE)}.
```

The function set for this problem is

```
F = {IF-FOOD-HERE, IF-CARRYING-FOOD, MOVE-TO-ADJACENT-
     FOOD-ELSE, MOVE-TO-ADJACENT-PHEROMONE-ELSE, PROGN},
```

taking two, two, one, one, and two arguments, respectively. The four conditional branching operators in this function set are implemented as macros as described in subsection 6.1.1.

The raw fitness of a computer program is measured by how many of the 144 food pellets are transported to the nest within the allotted time (i.e., 400 time steps and a maximum of 1,000 operations for each S-expression). When an ant arrives at the nest with food, the food is automatically dropped and counted.

The 20 ants (each with its own particular random initial facing direction) and the two equal piles of food in their particular off-center locations constitute the one fitness case for this problem. This one fitness case appears to be sufficiently representative to allow genetic programming to find a general solution for this particular problem.

Table 12.1 summarizes the key features of the problem of emergent central place food foraging behavior in an ant colony.

Table 12.1 Tableau for emergent central place food foraging behavior.

Objective:	Find a computer program which, when executed by a colony of 20 ants, causes emergent central place food foraging behavior in an ant colony.
Terminal set:	(MOVE-RANDOM), (MOVE-TO-NEST), (PICK-UP), (DROP-PHEROMONE).
Function set:	IF-FOOD-HERE, IF-CARRYING-FOOD, MOVE-TO-ADJACENT-FOOD-ELSE, MOVE-TO-ADJACENT-PHEROMONE-ELSE, PROGN.
Fitness cases:	One fitness case.
Raw fitness:	Number of food pellets (out of 144) transported to the nest within the allotted time.
Standardized fitness:	Total number of food pellets (144) minus raw fitness.
Hits:	Equals raw fitness for this problem.
Wrapper:	None.
Parameters:	$M = 500$. $G = 51$.
Success predicate:	An S-expression scores 144 hits.

Mere random motion by the 20 ants in a colony will not solve this problem. Random walking will bring the ants into contact with an average of only about 56 of the 144 food pellets within the allotted time. Of course, the task is substantially more complicated than ants merely coming into contact with food, since the ants must pick up the food and carry it to the nest.

Even the sequence of random contact, picking up, and carrying is not sufficient to efficiently solve the problem in any reasonable amount of time. When ants come in contact with food, they must do something that makes it easier for the other ants to find the food source. Otherwise, the other ants will be consigned to independently finding food via a time-consuming random search. To solve the problem of transporting all the food to the nest in a reasonable amount of time, ants that come into contact with food must also establish a pheromonal trail as they carry the food back to the nest. This pheromonal trail allows other ants to guide themselves to the food source without the time-consuming random search. Of course, all ants must be on the lookout for such pheromonal trails and must follow such trails to the food source (if they are not already engaged in carrying food to the nest).

In one run, 90% of the random computer programs in the initial random generation did not transport even one of the 144 food pellets to the nest within the allotted time. About 4% of these initial random programs transported only one of the 144 pellets. Even the best-of-generation computer program from the initial random generation transported only about 2.7 food pellets per ant to the nest (i.e., 53 food pellets in total).

Figure 12.1 shows, by generation, the progressive improvement in the average standardized fitness of the population as a whole and the values of standardized fitness for the best-of-generation individual and the worst-of-generation individual. For example, the best-of-generation individual for generation 2 had a standardized fitness of 71 (i.e., it collected 73 pellets), the best-of-generation individual for generation 5 had a standardized fitness of 26, and the best-of-generation individual for generation 8 had a standardized fitness of 16.

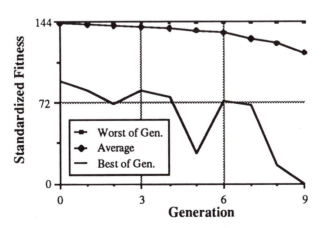

Figure 12.1 Fitness curves for problem of emergent central place foraging behavior.

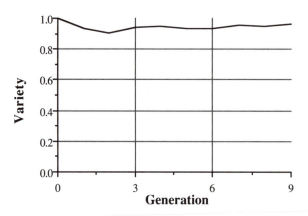

Figure 12.2 Variety curve for problem of emergent central place foraging behavior.

Figure 12.2 shows that variety remains generally stable in the neighborhood of 90% throughout the run.

Figure 12.3 shows the hits histograms for generations 0, 3, 6, 8, and 9 of this run. The first 14 ticks in the horizontal axis of the histogram each represent a range of ten levels of fitness between 0 and 139; the last tick represents the 5 levels of fitness between 140 and 144. Notice the left-to-right progression of the histogram from generation to generation. The arrow indicates the barely visible single individual scoring 144 at generation 9.

In one particular run, the following 100%-fit computer program emerged as the best-of-run individual, enabling the 20 ants to successfully transport all 144 food pellets to the nest within the allotted time:

```
(PROGN (PICK-UP) (IF-CARRYING-FOOD (PROGN (MOVE-TO-
ADJACENT-PHEROMONE-ELSE (MOVE-TO-ADJACENT-FOOD-ELSE
(MOVE-TO-ADJACENT-FOOD-ELSE (MOVE-TO-ADJACENT-FOOD-ELSE
(PICK-UP))))) (PROGN (PROGN (PROGN (PROGN (MOVE-TO-
ADJACENT-FOOD-ELSE (PICK-UP)) (PICK-UP)) (PROGN (MOVE-TO-
NEST) (DROP-PHEROMONE))) (PICK-UP)) (PROGN (MOVE-TO-NEST)
(DROP-PHEROMONE)))) (MOVE-TO-ADJACENT-FOOD-ELSE (IF-
CARRYING-FOOD (PROGN (PROGN (DROP-PHEROMONE) (MOVE-TO-
ADJACENT-PHEROMONE-ELSE (IF-CARRYING-FOOD (MOVE-TO-
ADJACENT-FOOD-ELSE (PICK-UP)) (MOVE-TO-ADJACENT-FOOD-ELSE
(PICK-UP))))) (MOVE-TO-NEST)) (IF-FOOD-HERE (PICK-UP)
(IF-CARRYING-FOOD (PROGN (IF-FOOD-HERE (MOVE-RANDOM) (IF-
CARRYING-FOOD (MOVE-RANDOM) (PICK-UP))) (DROP-PHEROMONE))
(MOVE-TO-ADJACENT-PHEROMONE-ELSE (MOVE-RANDOM))))))))).
```

An examination of this 100%-fit program shows that it is essentially equivalent to the following program:

```
1  (PROGN (PICK-UP)
2          (IF-CARRYING-FOOD
3              (PROGN (MOVE-TO-ADJACENT-PHEROMONE-ELSE
```

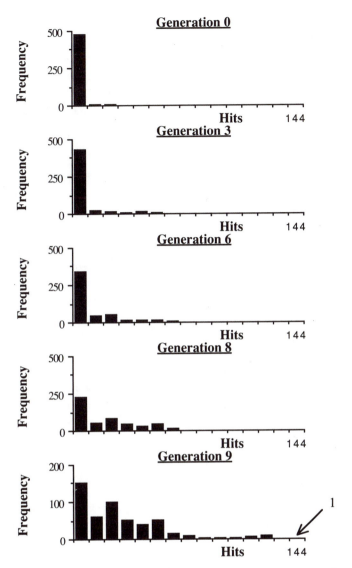

Figure 12.3 Hits histogram for generations 0, 3, 6, 8, and 9 of the problem of emergent central place foraging behavior.

```
4                        (MOVE-TO-ADJACENT-FOOD-ELSE (PICK-UP)))
5                       (MOVE-TO-ADJACENT-FOOD-ELSE (PICK-UP))
6                       (MOVE-TO-NEST)
7                       (DROP-PHEROMONE)
8                       (MOVE-TO-NEST)
9                       (DROP-PHEROMONE))
10              (MOVE-TO-ADJACENT-FOOD-ELSE
11                (IF-FOOD-HERE
12                  (PICK-UP)
13                  (MOVE-TO-ADJACENT-PHEROMONE-ELSE
14                    (MOVE-RANDOM)))))).
```

This program is a prioritized sequence of conditional behaviors that work together to solve the problem. In broad terms, this program first directs the ant to pick up any food it may encounter. If there is no food to pick up, the second priority established by this conditional sequence directs the ant to follow a previously established pheromonal trail. And, if there is no food and no pheromonal trail, the third priority directs the ant to move at random. A detailed interpretation of this program follows.

The ant begins (line 1) by picking up any food that happens to be located at the ant's current position. If the test on line 2 determines that the ant is now carrying food, then lines 3 through 9 are executed. Otherwise, lines 10 through 14 are executed.

Line 3 moves the ant to the adjacent pheromones (if any). If there is no adjacent pheromone, line 4 moves the ant to the adjacent food (if any). In view of the fact that the ant is already carrying food, these two potential moves on lines 3 and 4 generally distract the ant from a direct return to the nest and therefore somewhat reduce efficiency. Line 5 is a similar distraction, since the ant is already carrying food and cannot pick up more food. The PICK-UP operations on lines 4 and 5 are redundant, since the ant is already carrying food. Given that the ant is already carrying food, the sequence of MOVE-TO-NEST on line 6 and DROP-PHEROMONE on line 7 is the winning combination that establishes the pheromone trail as the ant moves toward the nest with the food. This move sequence in lines 8 and 9 is redundant. The establishment of the pheromone trail between the pile of food and the nest is an essential part of any efficient collective behavior for exploiting the food source.

Lines 10 through 13 apply when line 2 determines that the ant is not carrying food. Line 10 moves the ant to adjacent food (if any). If there is no adjacent food but there is food at the ant's current position (line 11), the ant picks up the food (line 12). On the other hand, if there is no food at the ant's current position (line 13), the ant moves toward any adjacent pheromones (if any). If there are no adjacent pheromones, the ant moves randomly (line 14).

When an ant moves toward adjacent pheromones, there is no guarantee that it will necessarily move in the most useful direction (i.e., toward a food pile if it is not carrying food, but toward the nest if it is carrying food). When there is a choice, the direction involving the least deflection from the current direction is chosen, so the ant is sent off in the wrong direction in many instances. Note that when a hungry ant encounters a pheromone trail, even a 50% chance of getting to the food is better than a blind random search of the grid.

The collective behavior of the ants governed by the 100%-correct program above can be visualized over a series of phases. The first phase occurs when the ants have just emerged from the nest and are randomly searching for food.

Figure 12.4 (representing evaluation step 3 of the execution of the 100%-fit program above) shows in black the two 3 × 3 piles of food in the western and northern parts of the part of the grid shown. The nest is indicated by nine +

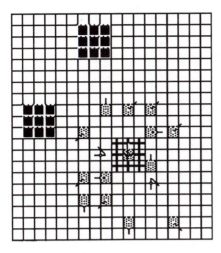

Figure 12.4 First phase: beginning of the random search for food as the 20 ants leave the nest.

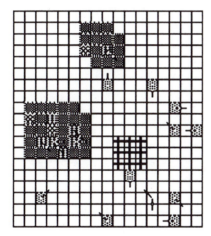

Figure 12.5 Second phase: initial contact with food and the beginning of formation of the pheromonal clouds around the two piles of food.

signs slightly southeast of the center of the grid. The ants are shown in gray, with their facing direction indicated. At this time step, all the ants are engaged in random search for food.

Figure 12.5 (representing evaluation step 12) shows the second phase. Some ants have discovered some food, have picked up the food, and have started back toward the nest, dropping pheromones as they proceed. Pheromonal clouds are just beginning to appear around the western and northern piles of food, but no pheromonal trail has yet formed linking the piles of food with the nest. As of this time step, no ant has yet brought any food to the nest.

Figure 12.6 (representing evaluation step 15) shows the third phase, which occurs when pheromonal trails have been established linking the piles of food with the nest. On this time step, the first two of the 144 food pellets have just reached the nest. This third phase persists for some time as the ants transport

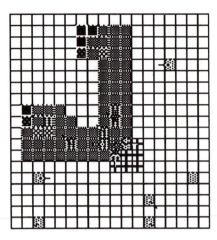

Figure 12.6 Third phase: two persistent pheromonal trails connecting the two piles of food with the nest.

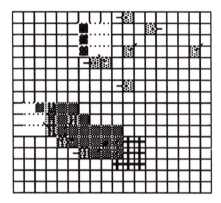

Figure 12.7 Premature disintegration of pheromonal trail to the northern pile.

the bulk of the food from the piles to the nest. At this particular time step, six of the 20 ants are still engaged in random search and have not yet been recruited into the exploitation of the two 3 × 3 piles of food; however, for most of this third phase, 100% of the 20 ants will be engaged in the exploitation of the two piles of food and none will be seen off the trails.

Figure 12.7 (representing evaluation step 129) shows the premature and temporary disintegration of the pheromonal trail connecting the northern pile of food with the nest while some food still remains in the northern pile. The pheromonal trail connecting the western pile of food with the nest is still intact. Five of the nine squares of the western pile and six of the nine squares of the northern pile are white (indicating that all of the food has been removed from those particular squares). By this time step, 118 of the 144 food pellets have already been transported to the nest.

In figure 12.8 (representing evaluation step 152), the western pile has been entirely cleared by the ants and the pheromonal trail connecting it to the nest

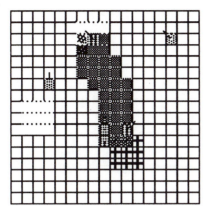

Figure 12.8 Exhaustion of the western pile and continued exploitation of the northern pile.

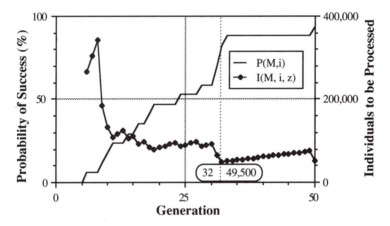

Figure 12.9 Performance curves for the problem of emergent central place foraging behavior.

is already starting to dissipate. The former location of the western pile is shown as a blank 3 × 3 area. By this time step, 136 of the 144 food pellets have been transported to the nest. The pheromonal trail connecting the nest to the northern pile (with eight food pellets remaining) has been reestablished. Exploitation of the eight food pellets still located there continues.

Shortly thereafter, the run ends with all 144 food pellets in the nest.

Figure 12.9 presents the performance curves showing, by generation, the cumulative probability of success $P(M, i)$ and the number of individuals that must be processed $I(M, i, z)$ to yield, with 99% probability, at least one S-expression scoring 144 hits on this problem. The graph is based on 17 runs and a population size of 500. The cumulative probability of success $P(M, i)$ is 82% by generation 32 and 94% by generation 50. The numbers in the oval indicate that if this problem is run through to generation 32, processing a total of 49,500 (i.e., 500 × 33 generations × 3 runs) individuals is sufficient to yield a solution to this problem with 99% probability.

12.2 EMERGENT COLLECTING BEHAVIOR

Deneubourg et al. (1986, 1991) conceived and wrote a set of rules that, when simultaneously executed by a group of independent agents (e.g., ants), can cause them to consolidate widely dispersed pellets of food into one pile. Deneubourg's stimulating work on the emergent sorting and collecting behavior of independent agents is another illustration of how complex overall patterns of behavior can emerge from a relatively simple set of rules that control the action of a distributed set of agents acting in parallel.

In this section, the goal is to evolve a computer program capable of emergent collecting behavior.

In our version of the collecting problem, there are 25 food pellets and 20 independent agents.

Figure 12.10 shows the initial configuration of food and independent agents on the 25 × 25 toroidal grid. The 25 food pellets, shown in gray, are initially isolated and dispersed in a regular rectangular pattern. Each agent, shown in black, starts at a random location and faces in a random direction, with a pointer showing the agent's initial facing direction.

All the agents are governed by a common computer program.

The PICK-UP, IF-CARRYING-FOOD, IF-FOOD-HERE, and PROGN2 functions are as defined for the central place foraging problem described in the previous section. In addition, the following four functions are also used:

- MOVE moves the agent one step in the direction it is currently facing provided there is no agent already at that location.

- MOVE-RANDOM randomly changes the direction in which an agent is facing and then executes the MOVE function twice.

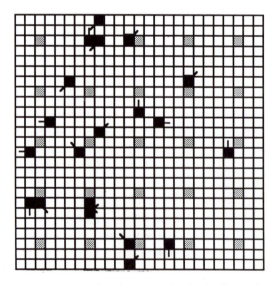

Figure 12.10 Initial configuration of 25 food pellets and 20 independent agents for the problem of emergent collecting behavior.

- DROP-FOOD drops any food that the agent is carrying provided there is no food already at that location. During the run, only one pellet of food can be on the ground at any one location on the grid.
- IF-FOOD-ADJACENT is a two-argument function that searches the positions adjacent to the agent (changing the agent's facing direction as it searches) and executes its first (then) argument if any food is discovered and, otherwise, executes the second (else) argument.

The terminal set for this problem consists of the four functions that have no arguments, namely

```
T = {(MOVE-RANDOM), (PICK-UP), (MOVE), (DROP-FOOD)}.
```

The function set for this problem consists of the three conditional branching operators and our connective function PROGN2 as shown below:

```
F = {IF-FOOD-HERE, IF-CARRYING-FOOD, IF-FOOD-ADJACENT, PROGN2},
```

each taking two arguments.

Since the goal here is to consolidate the food into one pile, raw fitness should measure compactness. In particular, raw fitness is the sum, over each of the 25 food pellets, of the distances (measured without going off the edge of the toroid) to each of the other 24 food pellets. There are 600 ways of choosing two different food pellets from 25, but by considering symmetry these 600 ways can be consolidated to 300 distinct lines connecting each pair of food pellets. For reference, the raw fitness of an individual that leaves all 25 food pellets in their original locations is 7,961. A smaller cumulative value for these 300 distances is obtained when the 25 food pellets are consolidated close together. Therefore, a smaller value of raw fitness is better, and standardized fitness equals raw fitness for this problem.

We could envision multiple fitness cases for this problem involving various different initial positions for the agents and the food pellets; however, it appears that one fitness case is sufficiently representative of the situations involved in this problem to allow a general solution to be found.

Alternatively, one could think of a signal being broadcast by each of the 25 food pellets so that the contributions to raw fitness would diminish with the signal's intensity (which would approximately reflect the distance between the pellets) (Goss and Deneubourg 1992).

At most, 1,200 evaluations of the S-expression for each agent and 3,000 individual operations are allowed. When an agent times out, any food being carried by the agent is, for purposes of computing the distances, considered to be at the location from which it was most recently picked up.

Table 12.2 summarizes the key features of the problem of emergent collecting behavior for agents.

In one run, the best-of-generation individual from generation 0 contained 31 points and had a raw fitness value of 5,353:

```
(PROGN2 (IF-CARRYING-FOOD (PROGN2 (IF-CARRYING-FOOD
(MOVE) (MOVE)) (IF-FOOD-HERE (DROP-FOOD) (DROP-FOOD)))
```

Table 12.2 Tableau for emergent collecting behavior.

Objective:	Collect the available food and consolidate it into one compact location.
Terminal set:	(MOVE-RANDOM), (PICK-UP), (MOVE), (DROP-FOOD).
Function set:	IF-FOOD-HERE, IF-CARRYING-FOOD, IF-FOOD-ADJACENT, PROGN2.
Fitness cases:	One fitness case consisting of the initial positions of the food pellets and agents.
Raw fitness:	The sum, over each of the 25 food pellets, of the distances to each of the other 24 food pellets.
Standardized fitness:	Same as raw fitness for this problem.
Hits:	Same as raw fitness for this problem.
Wrapper:	None.
Parameters:	$M = 500$. $G = 51$.
Success predicate:	None.

```
(IF-FOOD-ADJACENT (PROGN2 (DROP-FOOD) (PICK-UP)) (IF-
FOOD-ADJACENT (PICK-UP) (PICK-UP)))) (PROGN2 (IF-FOOD-
ADJACENT (IF-FOOD-ADJACENT (MOVE-RANDOM) (MOVE)) (PROGN2
(PICK-UP) (MOVE))) (IF-FOOD-ADJACENT (IF-FOOD-HERE (MOVE)
(MOVE)) (IF-CARRYING-FOOD (MOVE-RANDOM) (DROP-FOOD)))))).
```

Figure 12.11 shows the arrangement of food after execution of this best-of-generation S-expression from generation 0. As can be seen, the 25 food pellets have been moved into six rather diffuse areas.

The raw fitnesses of the best-of-generation individuals from generations 5, 10, 15, 20, 25 and 30 improved to 4,749, 3,227, 2,214, 2,250, 1,891 and 1,854, respectively.

The best-of-generation individual from generation 34 contained 111 points and is shown below:

```
(IF-FOOD-ADJACENT (IF-FOOD-ADJACENT (PROGN2 (IF-CARRYING-
FOOD (MOVE-RANDOM) (MOVE-RANDOM)) (PROGN2 (PROGN2 (IF-
FOOD-ADJACENT (PICK-UP) (MOVE-RANDOM)) (PICK-UP)) (IF-
FOOD-HERE (PROGN2 (PICK-UP) (IF-FOOD-ADJACENT (MOVE-
RANDOM) (PROGN2 (PICK-UP) (MOVE)))) (IF-FOOD-ADJACENT
(DROP-FOOD) (MOVE-RANDOM))))) (IF-FOOD-HERE (PROGN2
(PICK-UP) (MOVE)) (IF-CARRYING-FOOD (PROGN2 (DROP-FOOD)
(DROP-FOOD)) (IF-CARRYING-FOOD (PROGN2 (IF-FOOD-ADJACENT
(IF-FOOD-ADJACENT (PROGN2 (IF-CARRYING-FOOD (MOVE-RANDOM)
(MOVE-RANDOM)) (PROGN2 (PROGN2 (DROP-FOOD) (PICK-UP))
(IF-FOOD-HERE (PICK-UP) (IF-FOOD-ADJACENT (DROP-FOOD)
(MOVE-RANDOM))))) (IF-FOOD-HERE (IF-FOOD-ADJACENT (PICK-
UP) (MOVE-RANDOM)) (DROP-FOOD))) (PROGN2 (PICK-UP) (MOVE-
```

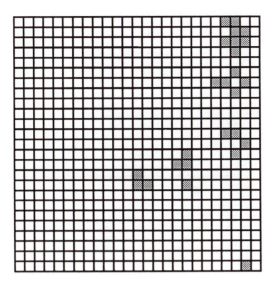

Figure 12.11 Six diffuse areas contain the 25 food pellets after execution of the best-of-generation individual from generation 0.

```
RANDOM))) (IF-FOOD-ADJACENT (DROP-FOOD) (MOVE-RANDOM)))
(MOVE-RANDOM))))) (PROGN2 (IF-FOOD-ADJACENT (IF-FOOD-
ADJACENT (MOVE) (IF-FOOD-ADJACENT (PROGN2 (IF-FOOD-
ADJACENT (IF-FOOD-ADJACENT (IF-FOOD-HERE (IF-FOOD-
ADJACENT (MOVE-RANDOM) (MOVE)) (PICK-UP)) (IF-CARRYING-
FOOD (PROGN2 (DROP-FOOD) (DROP-FOOD)) (DROP-FOOD)))
(PROGN2 (MOVE-RANDOM) (MOVE-RANDOM))) (IF-CARRYING-FOOD
(PICK-UP) (IF-CARRYING-FOOD (PROGN2 (IF-CARRYING-FOOD
(PICK-UP) (IF-FOOD-ADJACENT (MOVE-RANDOM) (IF-FOOD-HERE
(PICK-UP) (IF-FOOD-ADJACENT (DROP-FOOD) (MOVE-RANDOM)))))
(PICK-UP)) (DROP-FOOD)))) (PROGN2 (PICK-UP) (PICK-UP))))
(PROGN2 (PICK-UP) (IF-FOOD-ADJACENT (MOVE) (MOVE-
RANDOM)))) (PROGN2 (IF-FOOD-ADJACENT (MOVE) (PICK-UP))
(PROGN2 (PICK-UP) (MOVE))))).
```

This individual S-expression is highly effective in performing the task at hand. It has a fitness value of 1,667, representing an average distance between food pellets of only about 2.8 units.

When this program is executed, the agents begin by moving about at random and soon begin to locate and pick up food. Very shortly, a majority of the food is being carried around by the agents. As the random motion of agents carrying food brings them into contact with food that is still on the ground, the agents drop their food nearby, thus beginning the formation of several small islands of food. As other agents discover an island, they drop additional food in that immediate area, thus enlarging the islands. However, some food that is at islands is picked up by other agents.

Figure 12.12 shows the point at which the average number of operations per agent reached 692 (called an *epoch* for purposes of this section). At this

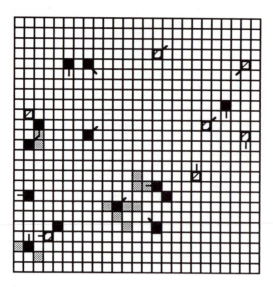

Figure 12.12 Epoch 692 of the best-of-generation individual from generation 34.

point, four main islands, containing three, five, five, and six food pellets, are present in the western and southern parts of the grid, while the other six food pellets are being carried by various agents shown as open squares. Some food pellets are invisible because an agent is present on the same square.

Figure 12.13 shows, at epoch 1,539, that all the food not being carried by agents is consolidated into one small island containing 3 food pellets and one large island containing 14 food pellets.

Figure 12.14 shows, at epoch 2,705, that all the food not being carried has been dropped into the one reasonably compact island in the bottom center part of the grid. When execution ends, 100% of the food ends up as part of this single island.

Figure 12.15 shows that variety remains generally stable in the neighborhood of 95% for this problem.

Thus, we have demonstrated the genetic breeding of a computer program, using a fitness function measuring compactness, for controlling the simultaneous actions of 25 agents in consolidating food at a single location. We did not specify in advance the size, shape, structural complexity, or content of the program that eventually evolved. The program that evolved was created as a consequence of the selective pressure exerted by the compactness measure.

12.3 TASK PRIORITIZATION

The solution to a planning problem often involves establishing priorities among tasks with differing importance and urgency. Also, when special situations suddenly arise, a radically different arrangement of priorities may be required.

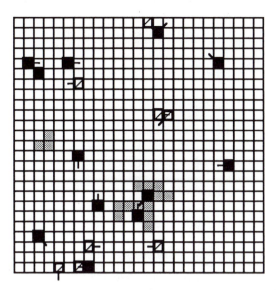

Figure 12.13 Epoch 1,539 of the best-of-generation individual from generation 34.

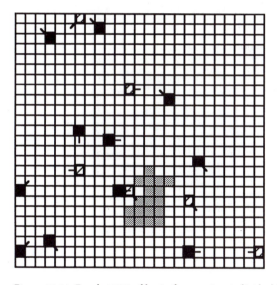

Figure 12.14 Epoch 2,705 of best-of-generation individual from generation 34.

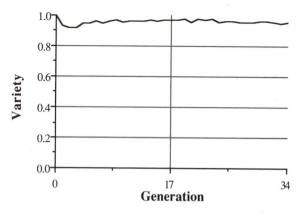

Figure 12.15 Variety curve for the problem of emergent collecting behavior.

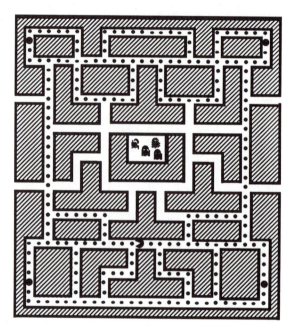

Figure 12.16 Pac Man screen.

The familiar Pac Man ® and Ms. Pac Man ® video games present a planning problem in which task prioritization is a major characteristic (Kordestani 1983).

Figure 12.16 shows the 31 × 28 toroidal grid on which the game is played. The majority of the squares are filled in, thus limiting the movement of the Pac Man to a maze of narrow corridors. There are two tunnels connecting the left side of the screen to the right side (and vice versa).

The Pac Man begins at position (13, 23) of the screen (in a coordinate system where all rows and columns are positively numbered and where the origin is in the upper left corner).

The four monsters (colored red, green, brown, and purple) begin the game in the 3 × 4 den in the center of the screen. As the game progresses, the monsters emerge at various times from their den at its doorway at position (13, 11).

We take the goal of the game to be to maximize points. Many, but not all, of the squares along the corridors contain small dots (i.e., food pellets, which are worth 10 points when encountered for the first time and eaten) by the Pac Man. Four of the squares contain energizers (flashing dots) that are worth 50 points when encountered for the first time by the Pac Man.

Shortly after the game begins at time step 0, the monsters start emerging, one at a time, from their den. Any of the four monsters will eat the Pac Man if it catches him. The monsters each have a rather limited span of attention. Out of every 25 time steps, they spend 20 time steps moving with the deliberate strategy of chasing the Pac Man whenever they see it. For five time steps out of every 25, the monsters abruptly change direction and shoot down some new corridor at random. The unpredictability of the four monsters magnifies their threat to the Pac Man.

A valuable piece of moving fruit appears at one of the entrances to the upper tunnel, namely at either position (0, 8) or position (28, 8) at time steps 25 and 125. The moving fruit moves unevasively and sluggishly around the screen for 75 time steps and then disappears. If the Pac Man catches a moving fruit, he collects 2,000 points. Thus, while the moving fruit is present on the screen, the Pac Man's priorities shift toward capturing this target of opportunity.

When the game starts, the highest priority of the Pac Man is to evade the monsters. To the extent that this first priority is being achieved, his second priority is to pursue and capture the moving fruit, if it is currently present on the screen. To the extent that this second priority is being achieved or is inapplicable, his third priority is to eat the dots.

Although the energizers (flashing dots) are worth more than ordinary dots, it is undesirable to eat the energizers merely for their 50-point value. Their significance in the game far outweighs their immediate point value. Whenever the Pac Man eats one of the energizers, all four monsters immediately turn blue and remain blue for a latency period of 40 time steps. When the monsters are blue, the roles of pursuer and evader are reversed. When the monsters are blue, the monsters try to evade the Pac Man who can eat the monsters if he catches them. The payoff for eating any one blue monster during the latency period caused by one energizer is a hefty 200 points. More important, the payoff for eating additional monsters during a single latency period increases exponentially; eating a second one is worth 400, a third 800, and a fourth 1600 points.

Thus, when the monsters are blue, the Pac Man's tasks and priorities change radically. His highest priority during the latency period is to chase the monsters (who now actively evade him). Catching even one monster during the period while they are blue is considerably more rewarding than eating ordinary dots (which are worth only 10 points). Eating an energizer (worth 50 points) during the latency period is usually a bad idea because it destroys a later opportunity to score a much larger number of points.

Since the rewards for eating monsters during the period when they are blue are so high and since the Pac Man controls the moment when the monsters turn blue (by virtue of his eating an energizer), a good tactic for the Pac Man is to actively attract the attention of several monsters and then eat the energizer when the monsters are close enough for him to catch during the relatively brief blue latency period. Of course, it is inherently very dangerous to the Pac Man to have several monsters closely chasing him prior to their being turned blue.

The human player normally controls the motion of the yellow Pac Man icon using human intelligence. In addition, the typical human player uses global knowledge of the grid to plan his play. When viewed globally, this game is a complex combination of, among other things, combinatorial optimization and distance minimization (i.e., a form of the travelling-salesperson problem), maze following, risk assessment, planning, and task prioritization. In this section, we do not attempt to find a strategy that incorporates all these complex aspects of the game. Instead, we define the functions for this problem so as to focus on an aspect of the game that emphasizes task prioritization.

There are 15 primitive operators for this problem, and they can be divided into six distinct groups.

First, two of the operators are conditional branching operators (subsection 6.1.1):

- IFB (If Blue) is a two-argument conditional branching operator that executes its first (then) argument if the monsters are currently blue and otherwise executes the second (else) argument.

- IFLTE (If-Less-Than-or-Equal) is a four-argument conditional comparative operator that executes its third argument if its first argument is less than its second argument and otherwise executes the fourth (else) argument.

Second, three of the primitive operators relate to the nearest uneaten energizer:

- APILL (Advance-to-Pill) advances the Pac Man along the shortest route to the nearest uneaten energizer. In the event of a tie between routes, this function (and all other such functions) makes an arbitrary decision to resolve the conflict. This function (and all the other functions for which a return value is not specified in its description) returns the facing direction encoded as a modulo 4 number (with 0 being north, 1 being east, etc.).

- RPILL (Retreat-from-Pill) causes the Pac Man to retreat from the nearest uneaten energizer. That is, the Pac Man moves in a direction as close to topologically opposite as possible from the direction of the shortest route to the nearest energizer.

- DISPILL (Distance-to-Pill) returns the shortest distance, measured along paths of the maze, to the nearest uneaten energizer.

Third, three of the primitive operators relate to the monster (called "Monster A") that is currently nearest as measured along paths of the maze (excluding the ghost of any monster that has been eaten by the Pac Man and whose eyes are returning to the monster den):

- AGA (Advance-to-Monster-A) advances the Pac Man along the shortest route to the nearest monster, measured along paths of the maze.

- RGA (Retreat-from-Monster-A) causes the Pac Man to retreat from the nearest monster in a manner equivalent to retreating from the energizer described above.

- DISGA (Distance-to-Monster-A) returns the shortest distance, measured along paths of the maze, to the nearest monster.

Fourth, three additional functions relate to the second nearest monster (called "Monster B"), measured along paths of the maze, and are defined in the same manner as above:

- AGB

- RGB

- DISGB.

Fifth, two primitive operators relate to uneaten dots:

- AFOOD (Advance-to-Food) advances the Pac Man along the shortest route to the nearest uneaten dot, measured along paths of the maze.

- DISU (Distance-to-Uneaten-Dot) returns the shortest distance, measured along paths of the maze, to the nearest uneaten dot.

Sixth, two functions relate to the moving fruit (if any is present on the screen at the time):

- AFRUIT (Advance-to-Fruit) advances the Pac Man along the shortest route to the moving fruit (if any is present on the screen at the time), measured along paths of the maze.

- DISF (Distance-to-Fruit) returns the shortest distance, measured along paths of the maze, to the moving fruit. If no moving fruit is present on the screen, this function (and all other functions that may, at any time, try to measure the distance to a currently nonexistent object) returns a large number.

We place the 13 primitive operators whose functionality lies primarily in their side effects on the system into the terminal set. Thus, the terminal set consists of the following 13 functions:

```
T = {(APILL), (RPILL), (DISPILL),
     (AGA), (RGA), (DISGA),
     (RGB), (AGB), (DISGB),
     (AFOOD), (DISU),
     (AFRUIT), (DISF)},
```

each taking no arguments.

The function set for this problem consists of the following two conditional operators:

```
F = {IFB, IFLTE},
```

taking two and four arguments, respectively.

Raw fitness is the number of points that the Pac Man scores before he is eaten by a monster or at the moment when all of the 222 food pellets have been eaten. One of these two outcomes is apparently inevitable given the actual dynamics of the game as we have implemented it. That is, survival is so difficult for the Pac Man that we encountered no instance where some food pellets were uneaten while he indefinitely evaded the monsters. Therefore, we did not program any other explicit success predicate for this problem.

The maximum value of raw fitness is 2,220 for the 222 food pellets, 4,000 for the two pieces of moving fruit, and 12,000 for capturing the monsters while they are blue (i.e., 4 times the sum of 200, 400, 800, and 1,600), for a grand total of 18,220.

Although we provided a facility for measuring the distance to the nearest monster (called "Monster A") and the second-nearest monster ("Monster B"), we did not provide such a facility for the other two monsters. Because of this limitation in our programming of the game, it is probably not possible to score anywhere near the potential 18,220, since attainment of the maximum score requires simultaneously maneuvering all four monsters into close proximity to an energizer and to the Pac Man and then eating all four monsters while they are blue. Thus, we did not include any termination criterion other than the maximum number of generations G to be run.

Because the execution of this problem is exceedingly slow, we used only one fitness case for the Pac Man. We did not consider differing initial positions and differing initial facing directions. Because of this limitation, the S-expression that resulted in this problem may or may not possess any generality.

Table 12.3 summarizes the key features of the problem of the task prioritization (Pac Man) problem.

As one would expect, random compositions of the above functions do not produce highly rewarding behavior for the Pac Man. For example, in one run, 29% of the 500 initial random individuals scored 0 points. These individuals did not move at all and were quickly eaten by the monsters. An additional 20% of the 500 initial random individuals scored up to 120 points while engaging in manifestly counterproductive behavior such as actively pursuing, instead of evading, the monsters.

The score achieved by the best-of-generation individual progressively increased from generation to generation.

The potential maximum score in this game is obtained if the Pac Man catches the moving fruit whenever it appears, catches all four monsters during each of the four latency periods associated with eating the four energizers, and eats all of the dots (thus terminating the game). Since the movement of the monsters (particularly the less alert monsters) is so unpredictable, it is probably not possible to achieve this maximum score in this game.

In any event, in generation 35 of one run, the following interesting S-expression scoring 9,420 points emerged:

Table 12.3 Tableau for task prioritization (Pac Man).

Objective:	Find a computer program for a Pac Man that scores the maximum number of points in the game.
Terminal set:	APILL, RPILL, DISPILL, AGA, RGA, DISGA, AGB, RGB, DISGB, AFOOD, DISU, AFRUIT, DISF.
Function set:	IFB, IFLTE.
Fitness cases:	One fitness case.
Raw fitness:	Points scored in the game.
Standardized fitness:	Standardized fitness is the maximum number of points (i.e., 18,220) minus raw fitness.
Hits:	Equals raw fitness for this problem.
Wrapper:	None.
Parameters:	$M = 500. G = 51.$
Success predicate:	None.

```
(IFB (IFB (IFLTE (AFRUIT) (AFRUIT) (IFB (IFB (IFLTE
(IFLTE (AGA) (DISGA) (IFB (IFLTE (DISF) (AGA) (DISPILL)
(IFLTE (DISU) (AGA) (AGA) (IFLTE (AFRUIT) (DISU) (AFRUIT)
(DISGA)))) (IFLTE (AFRUIT) (RGA) (IFB (DISGA) 0)
(DISGA))) (DISPILL)) (IFB (IFB (AGA) (IFLTE (IFLTE (IFLTE
(AFRUIT) (AFOOD) (DISGA) (DISGA)) (AFRUIT) 0 (IFB (AGA)
0)) (DISPILL) (IFLTE (AFRUIT) (DISPILL) (RGA) (DISF))
(AFRUIT))) 0) (AGA) (RGA)) (AFRUIT)) (IFLTE (IFLTE (RGA)
(AFRUIT) (AFOOD) (AFOOD)) (IFB (DISPILL) (IFLTE (RGA)
(APILL) (AFOOD) (DISU))) (IFLTE (IFLTE (RGA) (AFRUIT)
(AFOOD) (RPILL)) (IFB (AGA) (DISGB)) (IFB (AFOOD) 2) (IFB
(DISGB) (AFOOD))) (IFB (DISPILL) (AFOOD)))) (RPILL)) (IFB
(DISGB) (IFLTE (DISU) 0 (AFOOD) (AGA)))) (IFB (DISU)
(IFLTE (DISU) (DISU) (IFLTE (IFLTE (AFRUIT) (AFOOD)
(DISPILL) (DISGA)) (AFRUIT) 0 (IFB (AGA) 0)) (RGB))))).
```

The interpretation of this S-expression follows. When under the control of this S-expression, the Pac Man starts by heading west and then north toward the northwest energizer. When the moving fruit appears from the upper west tunnel (which connects the far west side of the screen to the east side of the screen), the Pac Man briefly sidetracks into the tunnel in order to capture the moving fruit (scoring 2,000 points). By this time, the Pac Man has also scored an additional 250 points by eating 25 food pellets.

Figure 12.17 shows the screen at time step 25, just before the Pac Man captures the moving fruit in the west entrance to the upper tunnel.

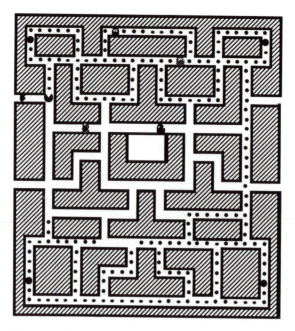

Figure 12.17 Pac Man at time step 25, just before capturing the moving fruit in west entrance to the upper tunnel.

As a result of the detour necessary to capture the moving fruit, the Pac Man now finds one monster in very close pursuit. He rushes toward the nearby northwest energizer, eats the energizer (scoring 50), and immediately doubles back and catches the pursuing monster during the blue latency period (thereby scoring 200). By this point, the Pac Man has eaten 10 more food pellets (scoring an additional 100 points). In addition, during the latency period, the Pac Man heads east, chasing the remaining three monsters.

Figure 12.18 shows the screen at time step 66, with the Pac Man pursuing the three remaining monsters in the northeast corner of the screen. The eyes of the ghost of the now-deceased first monster have just reached the doorway of the den.

The Pac Man catches two of the three blue monsters (scoring 400 and 800 points, respectively) in the northeast corner of the screen. However, while in hot pursuit of the last monster, he unnecessarily eats the northeast energizer (scoring 50) just before capturing the fourth monster. This final capture scores only 200 points, since it is the first monster the Pac Man captures after eating the northeast energizer. By this point, the Pac Man has eaten 72 food pellets. As the eyes of the ghosts of the three deceased monsters return to the monster den, the Pac Man mops up several isolated groups of food pellets in the upper part of the screen (reaching a total of 104 food pellets).

As the four monsters reemerge from the den, heading west, a second piece of moving fruit appears from the upper east tunnel. As the Pac Man catches the moving fruit (scoring an additional 2,000), two of the monsters are closely pursuing him in a dangerous pincer movement at time step 155, as shown in figure 12.19.

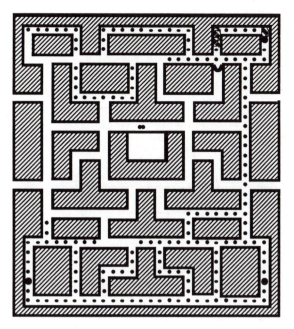

Figure 12.18 Pac Man pursuing three monsters in the northeast corner of the screen at time step 66.

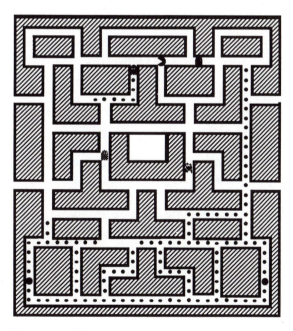

Figure 12.19 Pincer movement at time step 155.

Evolution of Emergent Behavior

Figure 12.20 Time step 301.

But the Pac Man escapes to the south. He then gets the attention of three of the four monsters and lures them into pursuing him at close range. When the monsters are close, the Pac Man eats the southwest energizer (scoring 50) and immediately turns on the three monsters (now blue). By this time, he has eaten 170 food pellets. However, the Pac Man does not overtake the three monsters during this latency period. The three monsters start to turn color as the latency period ends. Just before the three monsters actually change color, they and the Pac Man run over the southeast energizer.

Figure 12.20 shows the screen at time step 301, just as this happens.

The Pac Man now catches and consumes all three monsters (scoring 200, 400, and 800 points, respectively). Meanwhile, he heads toward the fourth monster in an attempt to catch it. This fourth monster is so far away that it turns color before he reaches it. By this point, the Pac Man has eaten 197 food pellets.

The eyes of the ghosts of the three deceased monsters return to the monster den and the three monsters quickly reemerge from the den. With all four energizers now consumed, the monsters will never again become vulnerable to the Pac Man. The Pac Man zips through the upper tunnel connecting the east side of the screen to the west side, thereby narrowly avoiding the monsters. By eating the remaining isolated food patches at the bottom of the screen (at time step 405), the Pac Man clears the screen of food, thus ending the game.

In all, the Pac Man scored 2,220 points for the 222 food pellets, 200 for the four energizers, 4,000 for the two pieces of moving fruit, and 3,000 for the monsters, for a total of 9,220 points. The Pac Man could have scored an additional 9,000 points if he had captured all four monsters on each of the four occasions when they turned blue. Thus, the genetically bred S-expression described above is not optimal.

13 Evolution of Subsumption

The conventional approach to building control systems for autonomous mobile robots is to decompose the overall problem into a series of functional units that perform functions such as perception, modeling, planning, task execution, and motor control. A central control system then executes each functional unit in this decomposition and passes the results on to the next functional unit in an orderly, closely coupled, and synchronized manner. For example, the perception unit senses the world. The results of this sensing are then passed to a modeling module which attempts to build an internal model of the perceived world. The internal model resulting from this modeling is then passed on to a planning unit which computes a plan. The plan might be devised by a consistent and logically sound technique involving, say, resolution and unification (Genesereth and Nilsson 1987), or it might be devised by one of the many heuristic techniques of symbolic artificial intelligence. In any event, the resulting plan is passed on to the task execution unit, which then executes the plan by calling on the motor control unit. The motor control unit then acts directly on the external world. In this conventional approach, typically only a few of the functional units (e.g., the perception unit and the motor control unit) are in direct communication with the world. The output of one functional unit is tightly coupled to the next functional unit.

Figure 13.1 shows five closely coupled functional units (i.e., perception, modeling, planning, task execution, and motor control) that might be found in a conventional robotic control system for an autonomous mobile robot.

An alternative to the conventional centrally controlled way of building control systems for autonomous mobile robots is to decompose the problem into a set of asynchronous task-achieving behaviors (Brooks 1986; Brooks and Connell 1986; Brooks, Connell, and Flynn 1986; Brooks 1989; Maes 1990; Maes and Brooks 1990). In this alternative approach, called the *subsumption architecture*, the overall control of the robot is achieved by the collective effect of the asynchronous local interactions of the relatively primitive task-achieving behaviors, all communicating directly with the world and among themselves (Connell 1990).

In the subsumption architecture, each task-achieving behavior typically performs some low-level function. For example, the task-achieving behaviors

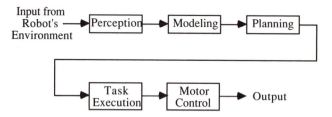

Figure 13.1 Conventional decomposition of a control system for an autonomous mobile robot into five functional units.

for an autonomous mobile robot might include wandering, exploring, identifying objects, avoiding objects, building maps, planning changes to the world, monitoring changes to the world, and reasoning about the behavior of objects. The task-achieving behaviors operate locally and asynchronously and are only loosely coupled to one another. Each of the task-achieving behaviors is typically in direct communication with the world (and with the others). The task-achieving behaviors in the subsumption architecture are typically considerably more primitive than the functional units of the conventional approach.

In the subsumption architecture, various subsets of the task-achieving behaviors typically exhibit some partial competence in solving a simpler version of the overall problem. This is important both in the initial building of the system and in the performance of the system under failure. In the subsumption architecture, the solution to a problem can be built up incrementally by adding new independent task-achieving behaviors to existing behaviors. The addition of each new behavior endows the system with more functionality. At the same time, the system may be fault tolerant in the sense that the failure of one behavior does not cause complete failure of the system but, instead, causes a graceful degradation to a lower level of performance that is possible with the still-operative behaviors. In contrast, in the conventional approach, the various functional units have no functionality when operating separately. The conventional system does not work at all until all the functional units are in place. There is a complete suspension of all performance when one functional unit fails.

Figure 13.2 shows most of the major features of the subsumption architecture. Three task-achieving behaviors are shown in the large rectangles. Within each such task-achieving behavior, there is an applicability predicate, a gate, and a behavioral action. All three task-achieving behaviors are in direct communication with the robot's environment. If the current environment satisfies the applicability predicate of a particular behavior, the gate allows the behavioral action to feed out onto the output line of that behavior. The two suppressor nodes resolve conflicts and produce the final output.

Since the task-achieving behaviors of the subsumption architecture operate independently, there is a need to resolve conflicts among behaviors. The right part of figure 13.2 shows a hierarchical arrangement of suppressor nodes used

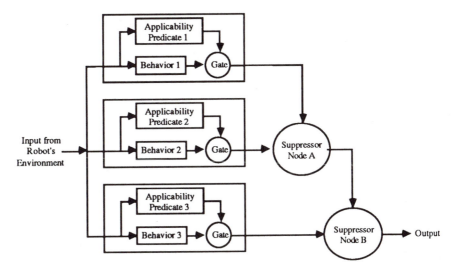

Figure 13.2 Subsumption architecture with three task-achieving behaviors.

to resolve potential conflicts among the outputs of the three task-achieving behaviors. The outputs of the task-achieving behaviors may be thought of as packets of instructions for controlling the robot. Outputs injected into the top of a suppressor node take precedence over those injected horizontally from the left. In particular, if there is any output from the first (top) behavior, it suppresses the output, if any, from the second (middle) behavior at suppressor node A. Similarly, the surviving output of suppressor node A, if any, suppresses any output of the third (bottom) behavior at suppressor node B. For example, the output from the third behavior can control the robot only if neither the first nor the second behavior is emitting an output. The particular hierarchical arrangement of suppressor nodes establishes a priority among the behaviors. The first (top) behavior has the highest priority and takes precedence over the others.

Note that figure 13.2 does not show the alarm clock timers of the augmented finite-state machines of the subsumption architecture (Brooks 1986, 1989). These timers allow a variable to be set to a certain value (i.e., state) for a prescribed period of time. Since the packets of instructions emanating from the behaviors will generally not be synchronized in an actual physical robot, the timers provide a way to allow a packet to persist for a specified amount of time. In addition, if desired, an alarm clock timer, once set, can remain in that state forever by feeding its output back to its input.

The applicability predicate of each behavior in the subsumption architecture consists of some composition (ultimately returning either T or NIL) of conditional logical functions and environmental input sensors (and perhaps states of various alarm clock timers). The action part of each behavior typically consists of some composition of functions taking some actions (typically side-effecting the environment or setting the internal state of some alarm clock timers).

The hierarchical arrangement of suppressor nodes operating on the emitted actions of the behaviors consists of some composition of logical functions (returning either an emitted action or NIL).

For example, one can reformulate the role of the three applicability predicates and the suppressor nodes shown in figure 13.2 as the following composition of ordinary if-then conditional functions:

```
(IF A-P-1 BEHAVIOR-1
        (IF A-P-2 BEHAVIOR-2
                (IF A-P-3 BEHAVIOR-3))).
```

This reformulation states that if the first applicability predicate (A-P-1) is satisfied, then BEHAVIOR-1 is executed. Otherwise, if A-P-2 is satisfied, BEHAVIOR-2 is executed. Otherwise, the lowest-priority behavior (i.e., BEHAVIOR-3) is executed.

This reformulation makes clear that the net effect of the applicability predicates and suppressor nodes of the subsumption architecture is merely that of a composition of ordinary conditional if-then-else functions. The default hierarchies presented in subsection 7.4.4 operate in the same way. Similarly, the hierarchy of alternative rules contained in the genetically evolved problem for the central place food foraging problem (section 12.1) operate in the same way. The hierarchy of prioritized rules in the task prioritization problem (section 12.3) is yet another example of such a composition of conditional if-then-else functions. In other words, applicability predicates and suppressor nodes, default hierarchies, hierarchies of alternative rules, and hierarchies of prioritized rules are, essentially, different terms for the same idea.

Considerable ingenuity and skill on the part of a human programmer are required in order to conceive and write a suitable set of task-achieving behaviors that are actually able to solve a particular problem in the style of the subsumption architecture.

The question arises as to whether it is possible to evolve a subsumption architecture to solve problems. This evolution would involve finding

- the appropriate behaviors, including the appropriate applicability predicate and the appropriate behavioral actions for each, and
- the appropriate conflict resolution hierarchy.

This chapter demonstrates the evolution by means of genetic programming of a subsumption architecture enabling an autonomous mobile robot to follow a wall in an irregular room and to find a box in the middle of an irregular room and push it to a wall.

13.1 WALL-FOLLOWING ROBOT

Mataric (1990) has implemented the subsumption architecture by conceiving and writing a set of four LISP computer programs for performing four task-achieving behaviors which together enable an autonomous mobile robot called TOTO to follow the walls in an irregular room.

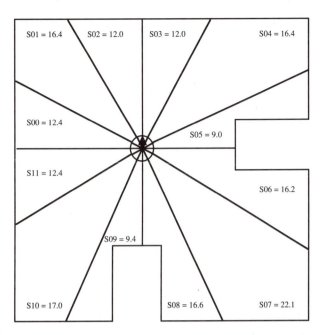

Figure 13.3 Robot with 12 sonar sensors located near middle of an irregular room.

Figure 13.3 shows a robot at point (12, 16) near the center of an irregularly shaped room. The north (top) wall and the west (left) wall are each 27.6 feet long.

The robot has 12 sonar sensors, which report the distance to the nearest wall as a floating-point number in feet. These sonar sensors (each covering a 30° sector) together provide 360° coverage around the robot. In this problem, we have adopted the general approach and conventions used by Mataric in her experiments with the TOTO robot. In particular, the 12:00 sonar direction corresponds to the direction in which the robot is currently facing (which, in the figure, happens to be the 12:00 actual direction). Sonar sensor S00 reports on the distance to the nearest wall in the 9:30 direction (i.e., relative to the 12:00 direction, in which the robot is facing); sonar sensor S01 reports the distance to the nearest wall in the 10:30 direction; and so on. For example, sonar sensor S00 reports a distance of 12.4 feet.

A protrusion from the wall may be indicated by an irregularity in the sequence of consecutive sonar measurements. For example, sonar sensor S09 (representing the 6:30 direction) reports a distance of only 9.4 feet whereas the two adjacent sensors report distances of 17.0 feet and 16.6 feet. The significantly lower distance reported by sensor S09 is caused by the protrusion from the southern wall of the room.

In addition to the 12 sonar sensors, Mataric's TOTO robot has a sensor called STOPPED to determine if the robot has reached a wall and is stopped against it.

That is, the input to the robot consists of 12 floating-point numbers from the sonar sensors and one Boolean input.

Mataric's robot was capable of executing five primitive motor functions, namely

- moving forward by a constant distance,
- moving backward by a constant distance (which was 133% of the forward distance),
- turning right by 30°,
- turning left by 30°, and
- stopping.

The sensors and primitive motor functions are not labeled, ordered, or interpreted in any way. The robot does not know *a priori* what the sensors mean or what the primitive motor functions do.

In addition, three constant parameters are associated with the problem. The edging distance (EDG) representing the preferred distance between the robot and the wall was 2.3 feet. The minimum safe distance (MSD) between the robot and the wall was 2.0 feet. The danger zone (DZ) was 1.0 foot.

The 13 sensor values, five primitive motor functions, and three constant parameters just described are a given part of the statement of the wall-following problem. In what follows, we show how the wall-following problem was solved by a human programmer (i.e., Mataric) using the subsumption architecture and how the wall-following problem can be solved by means of genetic programming.

Mataric's four LISP programs (called STROLL, AVOID, ALIGN, and CORRECT) correspond to task-achieving behaviors which she conceived and wrote. Each of these four task-achieving behaviors interacts directly with the world and with the other behaviors. Various subsets of these four task-achieving behaviors exhibit some partial competence in solving part of the overall problem. For example, the robot becomes capable of collision-free wandering with only the STROLL and AVOID behaviors. The robot becomes capable of tracing convex boundaries with the addition of the ALIGN behavior to these first two behaviors. Finally, the robot becomes capable of general boundary tracing with the further addition of the CORRECT behavior.

Figure 13.4 shows Mataric's four task-achieving behaviors. As before, each of the four behaviors is in direct communication with the environment (as shown on the left side of the figure). Mataric specifically designed her four task-achieving behaviors so that their applicability predicates were mutually exclusive (thus eliminating the need for a conflict-resolution architecture involving suppressor nodes for her particular approach to the problem). Accordingly, the outputs of the four behaviors can be simply merged together on the right side of the figure, since only one behavior can emit a behavioral action at any given time step.

In total, Mataric's four LISP programs contained 25 different atoms and 14 different functions.

The 25 atoms consisted of the 12 sonar sensors, the STOPPED sensor, the three constant parameters, and nine additional atoms defined in terms of the

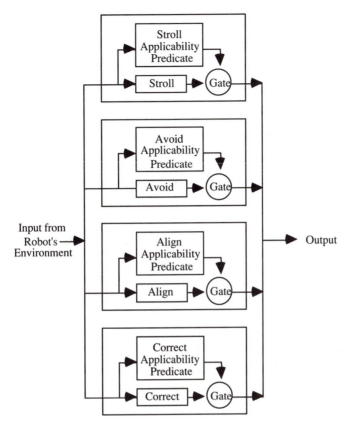

Figure 13.4 Four task-achieving behaviors of the TOTO robot.

sonar sensors (e.g., the dynamically computed minimum of various subsets of sonar sensors, such as the minimum of S11, S00, and S01).

The 14 functions consisted of the five primitive motor functions and nine additional LISP functions (IF, AND, NOT, COND, >, >=, =, <=, and <).

The fact that Mataric was able to conceive and write her four programs is significant evidence (with respect to this one problem) for one of the claims of the subsumption architecture, namely that it is possible to build a control system for an autonomous mobile robot using loosely coupled, asynchronous task-achieving behaviors. It is certainly not obvious that this is possible. Mataric's four programs are very different from the conventional tightly controlled and synchronized approach to robotic control. For example, her four programs did not contain a specific perception unit, a modeling unit, a planning unit, a task execution unit, or a motor control unit.

In starting to apply genetic programming to this problem, we started with Mataric's set of terminals and primitive functions.

Learning algorithms in general require repeated experimentation in order to accumulate the information used by the algorithm to solve the problem. Learning for this problem necessarily requires the robot to perform the overall task a certain number of times in order to accumulate the information required by the learning algorithm. Simulation of the robot provides the practical means to accumulate this information. Therefore, we simulate the activities of the robot, rather than use a physical robot such as TOTO.

Since our simulated robot was not intended to ever stop and could not, in any event, be damaged by running into a wall, we had no use for the STOP function, the STOPPED sensor, or the related danger zone parameter DZ. In our simulations, we let our robot push up against the wall, and, if no change of state occurred after an additional time step, the robot was viewed as having stopped, thereby ending that particular simulation.

Mataric, using her own skill and intelligence, identified nine derived values in her programs as being useful in solving the problem. Eight of these nine derived values involved some selectivity (e.g., the dynamically computed minimum of selected subsets of sonar sensors, such as the minimum of S11, S00, and S01), and we did not use them. We did use the one derived value of Mataric's nine derived values that did not involve any selectivity: the terminal SS (Shortest Sonar), which is the minimum of all 12 sonar distances S0, S01, ..., S11. We retained Mataric's other two constant parameters other than the danger zone parameter DZ (i.e., MSD and EDG) so as to avoid the need to invoke constant creation on this problem.

Mataric starts with four given primitive motor functions: MF, MB, TR, and TL.

The function TR (Turn Right) turns the robot 30° to the right (i.e., clockwise).

The function TL (Turn Left) turns the robot 30° to the left (i.e., counterclockwise).

The function MF (Move Forward) causes the robot to move 1.0 foot forward in the direction it is currently facing in one time step. To avoid crashing our simulated robot into the wall, if any of the six forward looking sonar sensors (i.e., S00 through S05) reports a distance to any wall of less than 110% of the distance to be moved, no movement occurs.

As specified by Mataric, the function MB (Move Backward) causes the robot to move 1.3 feet backwards in one time step. If any of the six backward-looking sonar sensors (S06 though S11) reports a distance to any wall of less than 110% of the distance to be moved, no movement occurs.

Each primitive motor function takes one time step (i.e., 1.0 second) to execute. The state of the robot is its horizontal position, its vertical position, and its heading. The side effect of the execution of any of these four primitive motor functions is to change the state of the robot. All sonar distances are dynamically recomputed after each execution of a move or turn. Note that the robot does not operate on a cellular grid; its state variables assume a continuum of different values.

We include Mataric's four primitive motor functions in the terminal set as functions with no arguments, rather than in the function set. Thus, our terminal set T for this problem consists of 15 floating-point values (i.e., the 12 given sonar sensors, two given constant parameters, and the combined parameter SS) and Mataric's primitive motor functions, as follows:

```
T = {S00, S01, S02, S03, ..., S11, MSD, EDG, SS, (MF),
     (MB), (TR), (TL)}.
```

Human programmers find it convenient to freely use a variety of different functions (such as IF, AND, NOT, COND, >, >=, =, <=, and <) in writing a given program. In genetic programming, it is often desirable (although not necessary) to simplify the set of available functions. As previously mentioned, a subsumption architecture consisting of various task-achieving behaviors (each with an applicability predicate) and a network of suppressor nodes to resolve conflicts can be reformulated as a composition of ordinary if-then conditional functions. All of the numerical comparisons that Mataric could perform using >, >=, =, <=, and < can be performed using a single comparison such as the <= comparison. The COND function in LISP used by Mataric can be viewed as being merely a cascade of IF functions. The role of the function AND can similarly be performed with a composition of IF functions. The function NOT often adds clarity to programs written by humans, but its functionality can be realized merely by reversing the order of some other elements of a program. In fact, all nine of the additional functions that Mataric used can be replaced by a single function capable of doing numerical comparison. In particular, a conditional comparative operator such as IFLTE (If-Less-Than-Or-Equal) can perform all the functions Mataric achieved using COND, AND, NOT, IF, >, >=, =, <=, and <. For simplicity, we used this one conditional function in our function set.

In particular, the function IFLTE takes four arguments. If the value of the first argument is less than or equal to the value of the second argument, the third argument is evaluated and returned. Otherwise, the fourth argument is evaluated and returned. Since the terminals in this problem take on floating-point values, this function is used to compare values of the terminals. The IFLTE function allows alternative actions to be executed on the basis of a comparison of observed values from the robot's environment. The IFLTE function allows, among other things, a particular action to be executed if the robot's environment is applicable. It allows one action to suppress another. It also allows for the computation of the minimum of a subset of two or more sensors.

The connective function PROGN2 taking two arguments evaluates both of its arguments, in sequence, and returns the value of the last item in the PROGN2.

Thus, our function set F consisted of

```
F = {IFLTE, PROGN2},
```

taking four and two arguments, respectively.

Although the primary functionality of the moving and turning functions lies in their side effects on the state of the robot, it is necessary, in order to have closure, that these functions return some numerical value. For the first version of this problem, we decided that each of the four moving and turning functions would return the minimum of the two distances reported by the two sensors that look in the direction of forward movement (i.e., S02 representing the 11:30 direction and S03 representing the 12:30 direction).

After determining the terminal set and the function set, the next major step in preparing to use genetic programming for a problem is to determine how to measure fitness for the problem. When a human programmer writes a computer program, human intelligence is the guiding force that creates the program. In contrast, genetic programming is guided by the pressure exerted by the fitness measure and natural selection.

A wall-following robot may be viewed as a robot that travels along the entire perimeter of an irregularly shaped room. Raw fitness can be the portion of the perimeter traversed by the robot within some reasonable amount of time. Noting that Mataric's edging distance was 2.3 feet, we visualized placing contiguous 2.3-foot-square tiles along the perimeter of the room. Twelve such tiles fit along the 27.6-foot north wall, and 12 along the 27.6-foot west wall. In all, 56 tiles are required to cover the entire periphery of the irregular room.

Figure 13.5 shows the irregular room with the 56 tiles (each with a heavy dot at its center) along its periphery. The robot is located near the middle of the room at a starting position of (12, 16) and is facing in its starting direction (i.e., south).

When the computation of fitness requires the execution or simulation of some process, it is usually necessary to establish a reasonable maximum amount of time for the process. Thus, we need to derive an estimate for a reasonable number of time steps to allow for this problem. We must take several considerations into account to do this.

First, if the 56 tiles were arranged in a straight line, traversing 56 tiles (129 feet) would require 129 time steps if the robot were traveling forward (when

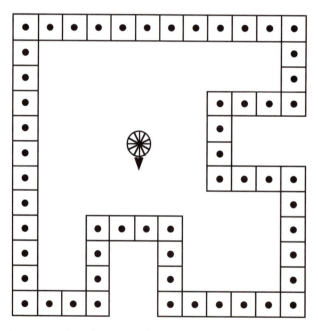

Figure 13.5 Irregular room with 56 square tiles.

its speed is 1.0 foot per second) but only 99 time steps if the robot were traveling backward (when its speed is 1.3 feet per second).

Second, at the beginning, the robot must get from its starting point in the middle of the room to some edge of the room. This adds a modest number of additional steps, depending on the robot's starting point.

Third, a minimum of 39 turns of 30° (each taking one time step) are required to make the 13 turns of 90° necessary to travel along the entire periphery of the irregular room. Note that it is difficult for the robot to execute the required 13 turns of 90° in precisely 39 time steps, because it does not have foreknowledge of the map of the room. Lacking this map, our robot will probably need to do some testing and experimentation at each corner.

Fourth, some backward and forward adjustments are required to align the robot to the wall after each turn.

These four considerations suggest that the minimum number of time steps required by a wall-following robot for this problem would be between about 150 and 180 time steps *plus* a few additional steps for the experimentation associated with turning and post-turning alignment.

Mataric's four LISP programs take 203 time steps to travel onto each of the 56 tiles.

It is not advisable to select a time limit that is too close to the estimated optimal time. If such a selection is made, most or all of the initial random individuals will time out and therefore be assigned the same value of fitness. In the worst case, if all individuals in the population timed out, they would all be assigned the same value of fitness. If there is no variation in the fitness values of the individuals in the population, there is no information with which to work. The selection of individuals to participate in reproduction and crossover would then effectively be at random. Reproduction and crossover without selection based on fitness are not sufficient for solving problems.

Therefore, we established a time frame for this problem by allowing approximately twice Mataric's 203 time steps. Specifically, we defined raw fitness to be the number (from 0 to 56) of tiles that are touched by the robot within 400 time steps. If a robot travels onto each of these 56 tiles within 400 time steps, we will regard it as being successful in following the walls. Standardized fitness is 56 minus raw fitness.

There is no guarantee, in advance, that the above definition for the fitness measure will cause the evolution of an S-expression whose behavior can reasonably be called "wall-following" behavior. It is also conceivable that the tiles are too large to produce smooth wall-following behavior and that a finer granularity is necessary to produce the desired behavior. It is conceivable that the tiles should be counted only when they are touched in consecutive order (once the order is established). As it turns out, this additional discriminatory power is not necessary to produce the desired behavior for this problem.

The fitness cases for this problem could also include other starting positions, other initial facing directions, and other room shapes. Additional fitness cases, of course, consume additional computer time and this problem is already time-consuming. It appears that one fitness case (consisting of the one starting

Table 13.1 Tableau for example 1 of the wall-following problem.

Objective:	Find a computer program which, when executed by a mobile robot moves along the periphery of an irregular room.
Terminal set:	The distances to the nearest wall in each of 12 directions as reported by 12 sonar senses, two constants MSD and EDG, one derived value SS, Move Forward (MF), Move Backwards (MB), Turn Right (TR), and Turn Left (TL).
Function set:	If-Less-Than-Or-Equal (IFLTE), and the connective PROGN2.
Fitness cases:	One fitness case.
Raw fitness:	Number of 2.3 foot square tiles along the periphery of the room that are touched by the robot within an allotted time of 400 time steps.
Standardized fitness:	Total number of tiles (56) minus raw fitness.
Hits:	Equals raw fitness for this problem.
Wrapper:	None.
Parameters:	$M = 1,000$ (with over-selection). $G = 51$ (see text).
Success predicate:	An S-expression scores 56 hits.

position in the center of the room, the one initial facing direction, and one room shape) used here provides a sufficiently representative and sufficiently challenging set of robot states along the various trajectories actually taken by the robot to allow evolution of a rather general solution to the wall-following problem.

If it was desired to solve this problem for a room with finer features and different irregularities (e.g., gently curving walls, very thin rectangular protrusions, nonrectangular edges, etc.), additional fitness cases incorporating these different features and irregularities would be required.

Table 13.1 summarizes the key features of the wall-following problem.

13.1.1 Example 1

In our first run of example 1 of the wall-following problem, 57% of the individuals in the population in generation 0 scored a raw fitness of 0. Many of this group of zero-scoring S-expressions merely cause the robot to turn without ever moving from its initial location near the center of the room.

Other individuals scoring 0 in generation 0 actually move. Figure 13.6 shows the aimless wandering trajectory of the robot for one randomly created S-expression from generation 0.

About 20% of the individuals in generation 0 exhibit wall-banging behavior in which the robot heads into a wall (thereby touching one tile on the periphery of the room) and then continues to unconditionally push itself

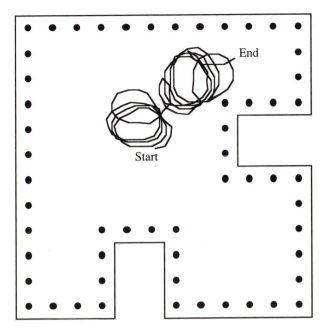

Figure 13.6 Aimless wandering trajectory of a robot from generation 0 with a raw fitness of 0.

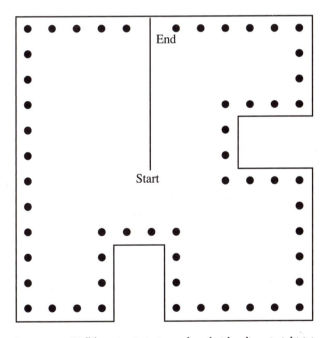

Figure 13.7 Wall-banging trajectory of a robot heading straight into a wall from generation 0 with a raw fitness of 1.

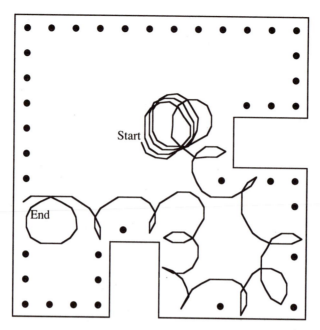

Figure 13.8 Looping trajectory of a robot scoring 17 in generation 0. This looping robot did not touch 39 of the 56 tiles along the periphery of the room.

up against the wall. They score 1 out of a possible 56. Figure 13.7 shows a wall-banging trajectory

The next 7% scored only two (out of 56). The next 15% of the population scored between 3 and 10.

The best-of-generation individual from generation 0 scored 17 (out of 56). This S-expression,

```
(IFLTE (PROGN2 MSD (TL))
       (IFLTE S06 S03 EDG (MF))
       (IFLTE MSD EDG S05 S06)
       (PROGN2 MSD (MF))),
```

consists of 17 points (i.e., functions and terminals).

Figure 13.8 shows the looping trajectory of the robot while scoring 17 out of 56 by executing the best-of-generation program for generation 0. As can be seen, the robot starts in the middle of the room, loops around itself three times, and then bumps into the protrusion from the east wall. The robot then begins a series of 11 loops which cause it to repeatedly hit the wall at irregular intervals and which leave many intervening points along the wall untouched. This individual times out on the west wall at 400 time steps without ever having even traveled to the northern part of the room. The 39 heavy dots around the edges of the room represent the 39 tiles that were not touched by the robot before it timed out.

Although this best-of-generation looping individual from generation 0 is far from perfect, it is considerably better than the nonmoving individuals, the aimless wandering individuals, and the wall-banging individuals.

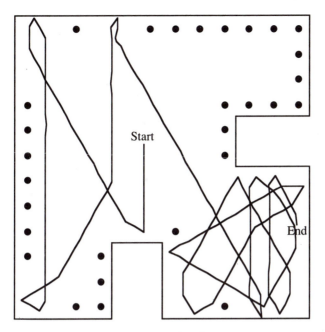

Figure 13.9 Ricocheting trajectory of a robot scoring 27 in generation 2.

By generation 2, the best-of-generation individual,

```
(IFLTE (IFLTE (PROGN2 S01 (MF)) (IFLTE S02 S04 S06 S11)
(IFLTE S07 EDG S10 MSD) (PROGN2 S11 SS)) (IFLTE (PROGN2
S11 S07) (PROGN2 (MF) SS) (PROGN2 (PROGN2 S01 (TL))
(IFLTE S08 S09 SS (MB))) (IFLTE SS EDG (TR) S03)) (PROGN2
(IFLTE S03 SS EDG S03) (IFLTE MSD S07 S03 S10)) (PROGN2
(PROGN2 MSD S11) (PROGN2 SS S04))),
```

scored 27. It consisted of 57 points.

Figure 13.9 shows the ricocheting trajectory of the robot while executing this best-of-generation program for generation 2. As can be seen, the robot ricochets around the room 16 times and, more or less accidentally, touches occasional points on the periphery of the room.

Although this ricocheting individual is also far from perfect, it is considerably better than the best-of-generation looping individual from generation 0.

By generation 9, the best-of-generation S-expression scored 37 and consisted of 97 points. It is shown below:

```
(IFLTE (IFLTE (PROGN2 S01 (MF)) (IFLTE S02 S04 S06 S11)
(IFLTE S07 EDG S10 MSD) (PROGN2 S11 SS)) (IFLTE (PROGN2
S11 S07) (PROGN2 (MF) SS) (PROGN2 (PROGN2 S01 (TL))
(IFLTE S08 S09 SS (MB))) (IFLTE SS EDG (TR) S03)) (PROGN2
(IFLTE S03 SS EDG S03) (IFLTE MSD S07 S03 S10)) (PROGN2
(PROGN2 MSD (IFLTE (IFLTE S04 S09 S07 (IFLTE S05 (IFLTE
(IFLTE (MB) S07 S02 S11) (PROGN2 S11 S01) (PROGN2 (TR)
```

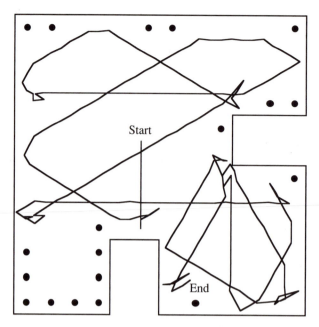

Figure 13.10 Zigzagging trajectory of a robot scoring 37 in generation 9.

S01) (PROGN2 (PROGN2 S11 S10) S03)) (IFLTE MSD S07 S03
S03) S04)) (IFLTE (MB) S04 MSD S09) (PROGN2 EDG S03)
(PROGN2 SS S08))) (PROGN2 SS S04))).

Figure 13.10 shows the zigzagging trajectory of the robot while executing this best-of-generation program for generation 9. This individual wastes considerable time by making numerous trips across the middle of the room. This trajectory misses several contiguous groups of tiles as well as several corner tiles in scoring 37 out of 56.

This zigzagging individual from generation 9 outperforms the ricocheting individual from generation 2 because it makes fewer wasteful trips across the room and therefore touches more of the periphery of the room before timing out.

None of the above behaviors can be characterized as wall-following behavior. However, by generation 14, the best-of-generation S-expression scored 49 and consisted of 45 points. This individual,

(IFLTE (IFLTE S10 S05 S02 S05) (IFLTE (PROGN2 S11 S07)
(PROGN2 (PROGN2 (PROGN2 S11 S05) (PROGN2 (MF) EDG)) SS)
(PROGN2 (PROGN2 S01 (PROGN2 (IFLTE S02 (TL) S04 S10)
(TL))) (MB)) (IFLTE SS EDG (TR) (TL))) (PROGN2 MSD SS)
(PROGN2 (PROGN2 MSD S11) (PROGN2 SS S04))),

does exhibit approximate wall-following behavior.

Figure 13.11 shows the trajectory of the robot while executing this best-of-generation program for generation 14. After once reaching a wall, the robot

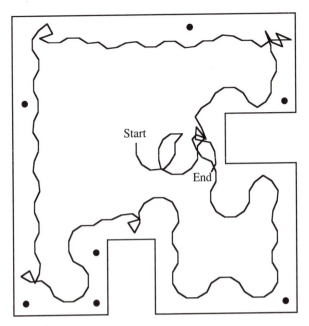

Figure 13.11 Broad snake-like trajectory of a robot scoring 49 in generation 14.

makes broad snake-like motions along the walls and never returns to the middle of the room. This individual misses two points along the straight portions of the walls, four concave corners, and one convex corner. It scores 49 out of 56.

The fitness of the best-of-generation individual in the population remains at 49 between generations 14 and 21. The fitness of the best-of-generation individuals rises to 50 for generations 22 and 33. It rises to 51 for generations 34 and 40. It then rises to 52 and then 53. The fitness of the best-of-generation individuals then rises to 54 for generation 45.

By generation 49, the best-of-generation S-expression,

```
(IFLTE (IFLTE S10 S05 S02 S05) (IFLTE (PROGN2 S11 S07)
(PROGN2 (PROGN2 (PROGN2 S11 S05) (PROGN2 (PROGN2 S11 S05)
(PROGN2 (MF) EDG))) SS) (PROGN2 (PROGN2 (IFLTE S02
(PROGN2 S11 S07) S04 (PROGN2 S11 S05)) (TL)) (MB)) (IFLTE
S01 EDG (TR) (TL))) (PROGN2 SS S08) (IFLTE (IFLTE (PROGN2
S11 S07) (PROGN2 (PROGN2 (PROGN2 S10 S05) (PROGN2 (PROGN2
S11 S05) (PROGN2 (MF) EDG))) SS) (PROGN2 (PROGN2 S01
(PROGN2 (IFLTE S07 (IFLTE S02 (PROGN2 (IFLTE SS EDG (TR)
(TL)) (MB)) S04 S10) S04 S10) (TL))) (MB)) (IFLTE S01 EDG
(TR) (TL))) (PROGN2 (PROGN2 S07 (PROGN2 (MF) EDG)) SS)
(PROGN2 (PROGN2 MSD (PROGN2 S11 S05)) (PROGN2 (IFLTE
(PROGN2 (TR) (TR)) (PROGN2 S01 (PROGN2 (IFLTE S02 (TL)
S04 (PROGN2 (PROGN2 S11 S05) (PROGN2 (PROGN2 S11 S05)
(MF)))) (TL))) (PROGN2 S07 (PROGN2 (PROGN2 (MF) EDG)
EDG)) (IFLTE SS EDG (PROGN2 (PROGN2 (PROGN2 S11 S05)
```

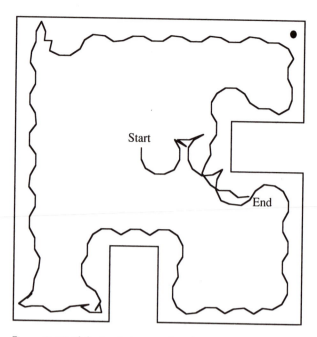

Figure 13.12 Slithering trajectory of a robot scoring 55 out of 56 in generation 49.

```
(PROGN2 (PROGN2 S11 S05) (PROGN2 (IFLTE S02 (TL) S04 S10)
EDG))) SS) (TL))) S08)) (IFLTE SS EDG (TR) (TL)))),
```

scored 55 and consisted of 157 points.

Figure 13.12 shows the slithering trajectory of the robot while executing this best-of-generation program for generation 49. The robot follows the wall rather closely and misses only one point in the upper right corner. It scores 55 out of 56.

Finally, in generation 57, the best-of-generation S-expression attained a perfect score of 56. This best-of-run S-expression consisted of 145 points and is shown below:

```
(IFLTE (IFLTE S10 S05 S02 S05) (IFLTE (PROGN2 S11 S07)
(PROGN2 (PROGN2 (PROGN2 S11 S05) (PROGN2 (PROGN2 S11 S05)
(PROGN2 (MF) EDG))) SS) (PROGN2 (PROGN2 (IFLTE S02
(PROGN2 S11 S07) S04 (PROGN2 S11 S05)) (TL)) (MB)) (IFLTE
S01 EDG (TR) (TL))) (PROGN2 SS S08) (IFLTE (IFLTE (PROGN2
S11 S07) (PROGN2 (PROGN2 (PROGN2 S10 S05) (PROGN2 (PROGN2
S11 S05) (PROGN2 (MF) EDG))) SS) (PROGN2 (PROGN2 S01
(PROGN2 (IFLTE S07 (IFLTE S02 (PROGN2 (IFLTE SS EDG (TR)
(TL)) (MB)) S04 S10) S04 S10) (TL))) (MB)) (IFLTE S01 EDG
(TR) (TL))) (PROGN2 S05 SS) (PROGN2 (PROGN2 MSD (PROGN2
S11 S05)) (PROGN2 (IFLTE (PROGN2 (TR) (TR)) (PROGN2 S01
(PROGN2 (IFLTE S02 (TL) S04 (MB)) (TL))) (PROGN2 S07
(PROGN2 (PROGN2 (MF) EDG) EDG)) (IFLTE SS EDG (PROGN2
(PROGN2 (PROGN2 S02 S05) (PROGN2 (PROGN2 S11 S05) (PROGN2
```

```
(IFLTE S02 (TL) S04 S10) EDG))) SS) (TL))) S08)) (IFLTE
SS EDG (TR) (TL)))).
```

Although a program written by a human programmer cannot be directly compared to this program generated by means of genetic programming, it is, nonetheless, interesting to note that the 145 points of this S-expression are similar to the 151 points in Mataric's four LISP programs.

We can simplify this S-expression to the following S-expression containing 59 points:

```
(IFLTE (IFLTE S10 S05 S02 S05)
       (IFLTE S07 (PROGN2 (MF) SS)
          (PROGN2 (TL) (MB))
          (IFLTE S01 EDG (TR) (TL)))
#
    (IFLTE (IFLTE S07 (PROGN2 (MF) SS)
          (PROGN (IFLTE SS EDG (TR) (TL))
                (MB) (TL) (MB))
          (IFLTE S01 EDG (TR) (TL)))
      SS
  (IFLTE (PROGN2 (TR) (TR))
         (PROGN2 (IFLTE S02 (TL) #(MB)) (TL))
      (MF)
      (TL))
  (IFLTE SS EDG (TR) (TL)))),
```

where # denotes a portion of the S-expression that has no side effects and whose value is never used. As can be seen, this individual is a composition of conditional branching operators.

Figure 13.13 shows the wall-following trajectory of the robot while executing this best-of-run program from generation 57. This individual starts by briefly moving at random in the middle of the room. However, as soon as it reaches the wall, it moves along it. It stays much closer to the wall than the slithering trajectory from generation 49, and it touches 100% of the 56 tiles along the periphery of the room. This individual takes 395 time steps. See also Koza 1992a.

Figure 13.14 shows, by generation, the progressive improvement in the average standardized fitness of the population as a whole and the value of standardized fitness for the best-of-generation individual and the worst-of-generation individual. The graph of the worst-of-generation individual is a horizontal line across the top of the figure.

Figure 13.15 shows the hits histograms for generations 0, 12, 24, 36, and 57 of this run. The first nine ticks in the horizontal axis of the histogram each represent a range of six levels of fitness between 0 and 53; the last tick represents the three levels of fitness between 54 and 56.

A considerable amount of computer time can be saved by means of the following two time-saving techniques.

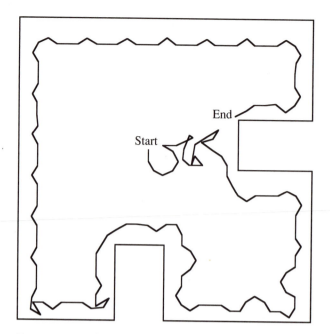

Figure 13.13 Wall-following trajectory of a best-of-run individual from generation 57 for example 1 of the wall-following problem.

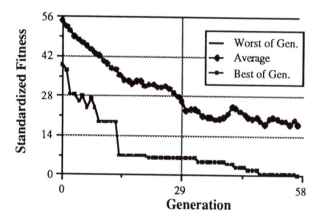

Figure 13.14 Fitness curves for example 1 of the wall-following problem.

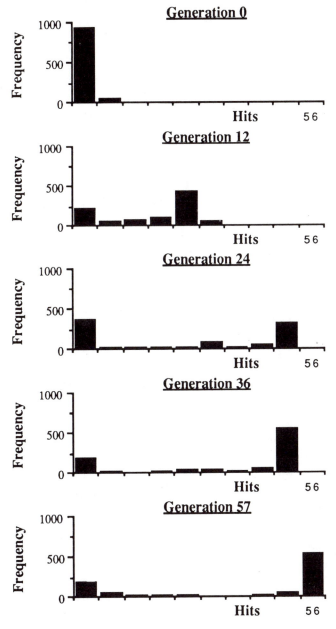

Figure 13.15 Hits histogram for generations 0, 12, 24, 36, and 57 for example 1 of wall-following problem.

First, we saved the most computer time by using a look-up table for the 12 sonar distances, instead of computing them anew based on the precise current location of the robot. We laid out a 100×100 grid over the 27.6-foot square area in which the room was located and computed the 12 sonar distances from the center of each of these 10,000 tiny squares to the nearest wall. We used the precise vertical and horizontal coordinates of the robot in the room to determine in which of the 10,000 squares the robot was currently located. We did not reposition the robot to the center of the square; however, instead of recomputing the sonar distance to the nearest wall on each time step based on the robot's exact location within the square, we looked up the 12 sonar distances in the table (using the current heading of the robot). Our look-up table has a granularity that is somewhat similar to the resolution of one part in $2^8 = 256$ of TOTO's actual sensors in the real-world version of this problem. Moreover, since the floating-point sonar distances are only used in magnitude comparisons (via the IFLTE function), the reduction in precision had no practical effect.

Second, we saved additional computer time by testing whether the robot had stabilized during the simulation. If it happens that the values of all of the state variables of the robot (i.e., vertical and horizontal coordinates of the robot in the room and its current heading) stabilize for two consecutive time steps, the system will not thereafter change states. The remainder of the simulation of all future time steps can be skipped. Since no additional tiles can be traversed, the raw fitness accumulated up to that time will be the correct total raw fitness for the simulation. This stabilization occurs when the robot pushes up against a wall, gets wedged into a corner, or fails to move at all. Many individuals in the initial random generation and other early generations of a run stabilize in this way.

The first run of this problem (described above) was extraordinarily time-consuming. When we reached generation 49 of that run, we had a score of 55 out of 56. In order to preserve our investment, we invoked our "on the fly" redimensioning and extension procedure (described in appendix D.4) to extend the run to 101 generations. The run then successfully discovered the above solution on generation 57. The above time-saving techniques then reduced a typical run to about four hours and have permitted us to subsequently solve this problem six times within our usual 51 generations. Note that a meaningful performance curve cannot be made with only six successful runs, so none is presented here.

13.1.2 Example 2

In the above discussion of the wall-following problem, the solution was facilitated by the presence of the sensor SS in the terminal set and the fact that the terminals (MF), (MB), (TL), and (TR) returned a numerical value equal to the minimum of two designated sensors.

The wall-following problem can also be solved without the terminal SS being in the terminal set and with the four terminals each returning a constant value of 0. We call these four new terminals (MFO), (MBO), (TLO), and (TRO). The new terminal set is

$$T_O = \{(\text{MFO}), (\text{MBO}), (\text{TRO}), (\text{TLO})\}.$$

We used a population size of 2,000 for example 2 of the wall-following problem.

Because example 2 is even more difficult than example 1, we can report on only one successful run of example 2. This particular run came after we invoked our "on the fly" redimensioning and extension procedure twice (first to extend the run to 101 generations and then to extend it to 201 generations).

Figure 13.16 shows, by generation, for example 2 of the wall-following problem, the progressive improvement in the average standardized fitness of the population as a whole and the value of standardized fitness for the best-of-generation individual and the worst-of-generation individual.

As usual, structural complexity has a generally increasing trend from generation to generation as the solution is being evolved. Figure 13.17 shows, by

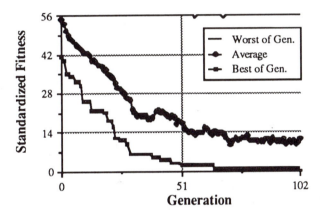

Figure 13.16 Fitness curves for example 2 of the wall-following problem.

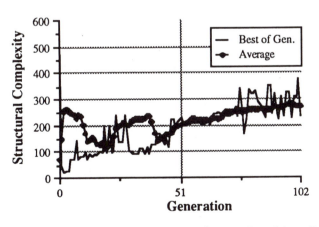

Figure 13.17 Structural complexity curves for example 2 of the wall-following problem.

generation, the average of the structural complexity of the population as a whole and the structural complexity of the best-of-generation individual.

In generation 102 of one run with function set F_0, we obtained the following S-expression with 237 points, which scored 56 out of 56 within the allowed time.

```
(PROGN2 (PROGN2 (PROGN2 (PROGN2 (IFLTE S06 S10 S09 S09)
(PROGN2 EDG (MB0))) (IFLTE (IFLTE S08 MSD MSD S05) S09
(PROGN2 S07 (MB0)) (PROGN2 (PROGN2 (PROGN2 (IFLTE S06 S10
S04 S09) (IFLTE S09 S09 S05 MSD)) (IFLTE (IFLTE S08 MSD
MSD S05) (PROGN2 S00 S10) (PROGN2 S07 (IFLTE (MF0) S05
(TR0) (MB0))) (PROGN2 (IFLTE (MF0) S05 (TR0) (PROGN2 S00
S10)) (PROGN2 (TR0) S05)))) (MB0)))) (MB0)) (IFLTE
(PROGN2 (IFLTE S00 S07 S01 (MB0)) (PROGN2 (IFLTE S00 S07
S01 (MB0)) (PROGN2 (PROGN2 MSD (TL0)) (PROGN2 S04 S09))))
(PROGN2 (IFLTE S07 EDG S03 S06) (IFLTE S09 S09 S05 S05))
(PROGN2 (PROGN2 (IFLTE (MF0) S05 (TR0) (IFLTE (IFLTE
(TL0) S08 S01 (MF0)) (PROGN2 S03 S07) (PROGN2 (PROGN2
(IFLTE S06 S10 S04 S09) (PROGN2 S07 (MB0))) (IFLTE
(PROGN2 (PROGN2 S07 (IFLTE (MF0) S05 (TR0) (MB0))) (IFLTE
(PROGN2 (TL0) S00) (TR0) (IFLTE S01 S00 S04 (TR0)) (IFLTE
S00 S07 S01 (IFLTE (IFLTE S07 EDG S03 S06) S01 (IFLTE S11
S08 S11 S05) (TR0))))) (PROGN2 S00 S10) (PROGN2 S07
(MB0)) (PROGN2 (PROGN2 (PROGN2 (IFLTE S06 S10 S04 S09)
(IFLTE S09 S09 S00 MSD)) (IFLTE (IFLTE (PROGN2 S03 (MB0))
```

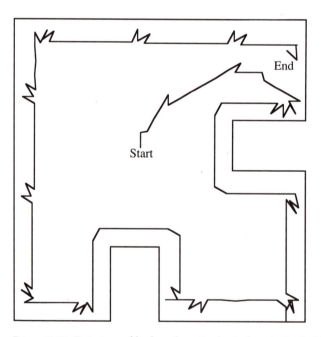

Figure 13.18 Trajectory of backward-moving best-of-run individual from generation 102 for example 2 of the wall-following problem.

```
S08 S01 (MF0)) (PROGN2 S00 S10) (IFLTE S06 S10 S04 S09)
(PROGN2 (IFLTE (MF0) S05 (TR0) (MB0)) (IFLTE S09 S09 S05
S05)))) (MB0)))) (IFLTE S00 S07 (MB0) (TR0)))) (PROGN2
(TR0) S04)) (MB0)) (PROGN2 (PROGN2 (TL0) (MB0)) (IFLTE
(PROGN2 (TL0) S00) (IFLTE S08 MSD MSD S05) (PROGN2
(PROGN2 S07 (MB0)) S05) (IFLTE S00 S07 S01 (PROGN2 S04
S09)))))).
```

Figure 13.18 shows the trajectory of the robot executing the best-of-run individual from generation 102 for the wall-following problem for example 2. Interestingly, this individual causes the robot to move backward as it follows the wall.

This S-expression simplifies to the following S-expression with 58 points:

```
(PROGN
 (MB)
 (IFLTE (IFLTE S08 MSD MSD S05)
        S09
     (MB)
     (PROGN (IFLTE (IFLTE S08 MSD MSD S05)
                   (PROG1 S10 (MF) (TR))
             #
             (TR))
        (MB)))
 (MB)
 (IFLTE (PROGN (IFLTE S00 S07 # (MB))
               (IFLTE S00 S07 # (MB))
               (TL)
               S09)
        S05
     (PROGN (MF) (TR) (TR) (MB))
     (PROGN (TL) (MB) (TL)
            (IFLTE S00 (IFLTE S08 MSD MSD S05) (MB) #)))),
```

where # denotes a portion of the S-expression that has no side effects and whose value is never used.

13.2 BOX MOVING ROBOT

In the box moving problem (Mahadevan and Connell 1990, 1991), an autonomous mobile robot must find a box located in the middle of an irregularly shaped room and move it to the edge of the room. After the robot finds the box, it can move the box by pushing against it. However, this subtask may prove difficult. If the robot applies force at a point other than the midpoint of the edge of the box or at an angle other than perpendicular to the edge, the box will start to rotate. The robot will then lose contact with the box and will probably then fail to push the box to the wall in a reasonable amount of time.

We proceed with the box moving problem by using the same irregular room, the same robot, the same primitive moving and turning functions, and the same 12 sonar sensors as we used in the wall-following problem described in the previous section. We used a 2.5-foot-wide box in the room with 27.3-foot west and north walls. If the robot applies its force orthogonally to the midpoint of an edge of the box, it will move the box about 0.33 foot per time step. For this problem, the sonar sensors now detect the nearest object (whether wall or box).

In this section, we use genetic programming to solve this problem and then compare our solution to the solution of Mahadevan and Connell, who used reinforcement learning techniques.

13.2.1 Example 1

The terminal set T is the same for the box moving problem as for the wall-following problem, except that the constants MSD and EDG (which are irrelevant to box moving) and the function MB (which was extraneous) were deleted. That is, the terminal set T consists of

T = {S00, S01, S02, S03, ..., S11, SS, (MF), (TR), (TL)}.

The function set F consists of

F = {IFBMP, IFSTK, IFLTE, PROGN2},

taking two, two, four, and two, arguments, respectively. The functions IFBMP and IFSTK are based on the BUMP detector and the STUCK detector defined by Mahadevan and Connell. Each of these functions evaluates its first (then) argument if the condition being detected applies, but otherwise evaluates its second (else) argument.

We surmised that successful generalization in this problem might require more than one fitness case. Thus, we started the robot at four different starting positions in the room.

The fitness measure for this problem is the sum of the distances, taken over the four fitness cases, between the wall and the point on the box that is closest to the nearest wall at the time of termination of the fitness case. A fitness case terminates upon execution of 350 time steps or when any part of the box touches a wall. If the box remains at its starting position for all four fitness cases, the raw fitness is 26.5 feet. If the box ends up touching a wall prior to timing out for all four fitness cases, the raw fitness is 0.

Table 13.2 summarizes the key features of example 1 of the box moving problem.

Figure 13.19 shows the irregular room, the starting position of the box, and the starting position of the robot for the particular fitness case in which the robot starts in the southeast part of the room. The raw fitness of a majority of the individual S-expressions from generation 0 is 26.5 since they cause the robot to stand still, to wander around aimlessly without ever finding the box, or, in the case of the individual program shown in the figure, to move toward

Table 13.2 Tableau for example 1 of the box moving problem.

Objective:	Find a computer program which, when executed by a mobile robot, finds a box in an irregular room and moves it to a wall.
Terminal set:	The distances to the nearest object in each of 12 directions relative to the current facing direction of the robot as reported by 12 sonar sensors, one derived value SS, Move Forward (MF), Turn Right (TR), Turn Left (TL).
Function set:	If-Less-Than-Or-Equal (IFLTE), the connective PROGN2, IFBMP (If Bumped), and IFSTK (If Stuck).
Fitness cases:	Four fitness cases representing four starting positions of the robot in various parts of the room.
Raw fitness:	The sum, over the four fitness cases, of the distance between the wall and the point on the box that is closest the nearest wall. Each fitness case times out when any part of the box touches a wall or after 350 time steps.
Standardized fitness:	Same as raw fitness for this problem.
Hits:	Number of fitness cases for which the box touches a wall prior to the timing out.
Wrapper:	None.
Parameters:	$M = 500$. $G = 51$.
Success predicate:	An S-expression scores 4 hits.

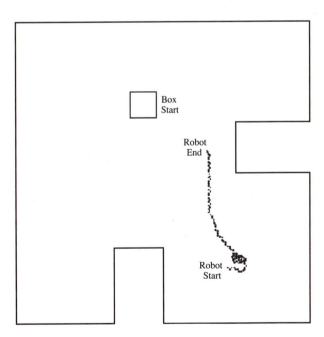

Figure 13.19 Trajectory of robot from generation 0 of the box moving problem that moves, but fails to reach the box for one fitness case.

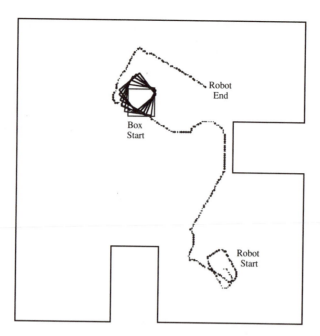

Figure 13.20 Trajectory of the best-of-generation individual for generation 0 of the box moving problem for one fitness case.

the box without reaching it. The raw fitness of the worst-of-generation individual from generation 0 was 29.5 (since it is possible to move the box to a position farther from the walls).

Figure 13.20 shows the trajectory of the best-of-generation individual from generation 0 when the robot starts in the southeast corner of the room. This individual containing 213 points finds the box and moves it a short distance for one of the four fitness cases, thereby scoring a raw fitness of 24.5.

Fitness improved slightly between generations 1 and 6.

In generation 7, the best-of-generation individual succeeded in moving the box to the wall for one of the four fitness cases (i.e., it scored one hit). Its fitness was 21.52 and it had 59 points.

By generation 22, the fitness of the best-of-generation individual improved to 17.55. Curiously, this individual, unlike many earlier individuals, did not succeed in actually moving the box to a wall for any of the fitness cases (i.e., the number of hits dropped back to 0).

By generation 35, the best-of-generation individual had 259 points and a fitness of 10.77.

By generation 45 of the run, the best-of-generation individual program was successful, for all four fitness cases, in finding the box and pushing it to the wall. The raw fitness was 0. This best-of-run individual has 305 points and is shown below:

```
(IFLTE (PROGN2 (IFSTK (IFBMP SS S10) (IFSTK (IFSTK S07
S11) (IFBMP (IFBMP (IFLTE S03 S01 (IFSTK S00 S08) S00)
S04) SS))) (MF)) (IFSTK (IFLTE (PROGN2 S00 S11) (IFSTK
```

```
(TR) S00) (IFBMP S03 S06) (IFSTK (MF) S07)) (IFBMP
(PROGN2 (IFSTK (MF) S00) (IFLTE (MF) S03 S00 S03)) (IFSTK
(IFSTK (TR) S05) (IFLTE S06 S00 S05 S05)))) (IFBMP (IFBMP
(PROGN2 (MF) (TR)) (IFLTE (IFLTE S11 S06 S00 S11) (IFBMP
S10 (TL)) (IFLTE S06 S07 S11 S10) (IFBMP S02 (TL))))
(PROGN2 (IFSTK (PROGN2 S08 S06) (IFLTE S05 S08 S04 (MF)))
(IFLTE (IFBMP (TL) S10) (IFSTK (IFBMP S06 S03) (IFLTE
(IFBMP SS S10) (PROGN2 S00 S05) (IFLTE (MF) (TR) S06 S11)
(PROGN2 S03 S07))) S01 (IFSTK S09 S03)))) (IFLTE (IFLTE
(PROGN2 (TL) (IFSTK S01 S01)) (IFSTK (IFBMP (IFLTE S06
S00 (TR) S03) (IFLTE (MF) S08 S06 S00)) (IFSTK (IFSTK
(TL) S07) (IFBMP (IFSTK S03 (TR)) (PROGN2 S01 S10))))
(IFBMP (PROGN2 SS S10) (IFBMP (MF) S00)) (IFLTE (IFSTK
(MF) S08) (PROGN2 S10 SS) (PROGN2 S00 (IFSTK (IFBMP S11
SS) (IFSTK S02 (MF)))) (IFLTE S06 S01 SS SS))) (IFLTE
(MF) (IFSTK (IFSTK (IFLTE (IFLTE SS (TL) S07 S10) (IFSTK
(PROGN2 S11 S04) (IFSTK (IFSTK (IFSTK (PROGN2 (TR) (MF))
(IFBMP (IFBMP (IFSTK S04 S07) (IFSTK S09 S06)) (MF)))
(PROGN2 (PROGN2 (IFBMP (TR) S04) (IFSTK S06 (TR))) S06))
(IFBMP (PROGN2 S05 S00) (IFSTK (PROGN2 S01 (TL)) (IFBMP
(MF) S05))))) (PROGN2 (TR) S03) S09) S02) (IFBMP (PROGN2
SS (TL)) S02)) (IFBMP S06 S04) (IFLTE (IFSTK S04 S06)
(IFSTK (IFBMP (IFLTE (MF) S00 S04 S00) S02) (IFBMP (IFBMP
(IFLTE S09 S05 (MF) S11) S04) SS)) (IFSTK S08 S08)
(PROGN2 S04 S02))) (IFSTK (IFSTK (PROGN2 S08 S06) (IFLTE
S05 S08 SS (MF))) (IFLTE S05 S02 (TL) (IFSTK S06 (PROGN2
S11 S04)))) (PROGN2 (IFLTE (PROGN2 S04 S04) (IFSTK S04
S07) (IFSTK S06 S10) (IFSTK (PROGN2 (IFSTK (MF) S04) S08)
SS)) (IFBMP (PROGN2 SS (TL)) (IFBMP S03 S09))))).
```

Figure 13.21 shows the trajectory of the robot and the box for the best-of-run individual from generation 45 for the fitness case where the robot starts in the southeast part of the room. For this fitness case, the robot moves more or less directly toward the box and then pushes the box so that it is almost flush against the north wall when it first reaches the wall.

Figure 13.22 shows the trajectory of the robot and the box for the fitness case where the robot starts in the northwest part of the room. The robot clips the southwest corner of the box and thereby causes the box to rotate in a counterclockwise direction until the box is heading almost north and the robot is at the midpoint of the south edge of the box. The box first touches the north wall at its corner with the edge of the box, making approximately a 45° angle with respect to the wall.

Figure 13.23 shows the trajectory of the robot and the box for the fitness case where the robot starts in the northeast part of the room. For this particular fitness case, the robot's trajectory between its starting point and the box is circuitous. However, once the robot reaches the east edge of the box, the robot successfully pushes the box more or less directly toward the west wall.

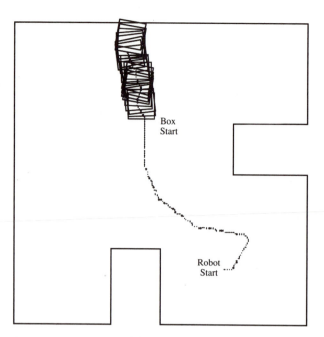

Figure 13.21 Trajectory of the best-of-run individual from generation 45 for example 1 of the box moving problem with the robot starting in the southeast part of the room.

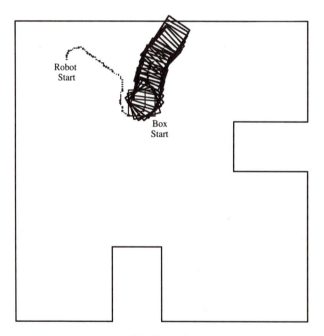

Figure 13.22 Trajectory of the best-of-run individual from generation 45 for example 1 with the robot starting in the northwest part of the room.

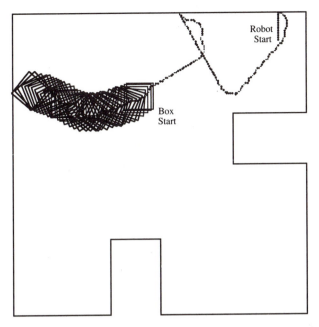

Figure 13.23 Trajectory of the best-of-run individual from generation 45 for example 1 with the robot starting in the northeast part of the room.

Figure 13.24 shows the trajectory of the robot and the box for the fitness case where the robot starts in the southwest part of the room.

13.2.2 Example 2

In the above discussion of the box moving problem, the solution was facilitated by the presence of the sensor SS in the terminal set and the fact that the functions MF, TL, and TR returned a numerical value equal to the minimum of several designated sensors.

This problem can also be solved without the terminal SS being in the terminal set and with the three functions each returning a constant value of 0. We call these three new functions MF0, TL0, and TR0. The new function set is

```
F0 = {MF0, TR0, TL0, IFLTE, PROGN2}.
```

We raised the population size from 500 to 2,000 for example 2 because we thought the problem might be more difficult to solve in this form.

Figure 13.25 shows, by generation, for our first (and only) run of example 2 of the box moving problem with the new function set F_0, the progressive improvement in the average standardized fitness of the population as a whole and the standardized fitness of the best-of-generation individual and the worst-of-generation individual.

Figure 13.26 shows the hits histograms for generations 0, 10, 15, and 20 of this run. Note the left-to-right undulating movement of both the high point

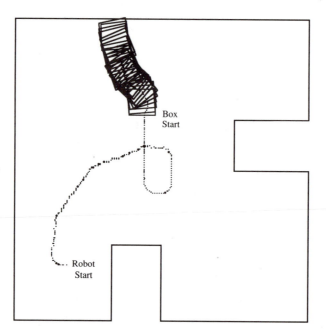

Figure 13.24 Trajectory of the best-of-run individual from generation 45 for example 1 with the robot starting in the southwest part of the room.

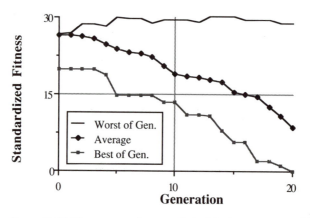

Figure 13.25 Fitness curves for example 2 of the box moving problem with function set F_0.

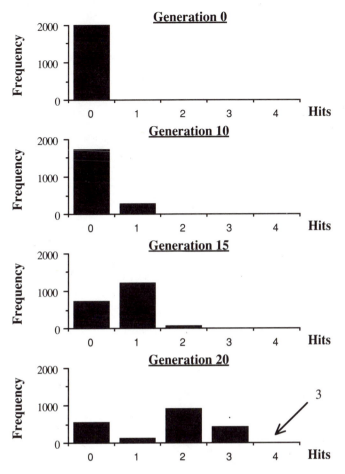

Figure 13.26 Hits histograms for generations 0, 10, 15, and 20 for example 2 of the box moving problem.

and the center of mass of the histogram, reflecting the improvement of the population as a whole over the generations. The arrow indicates that there is a simultaneous emergence of three individuals scoring four hits on generation 20.

One of the three 100%-correct S-expressions that emerged on generation 20 was

```
(IFSTK (IFLTE (IFBMP (IFSTK (PROGN2 S02 S09) (IFSTK S10
S07)) (IFBMP (IFSTK (IFLTE (MF0) (TR0) S05 S09) (IFBMP
S09 S08)) (IFSTK S07 S11))) (IFBMP (IFBMP (PROGN2 S07
(TL0)) (PROGN2 (TL0) S03)) (IFBMP (PROGN2 (TL0) S03)
(IFLTE S05 (TR0) (MF0) S00))) (IFLTE (IFBMP S04 S00)
(PROGN2 (IFLTE S08 S06 S07 S11) (IFLTE S07 S09 S10 S02))
(IFBMP (IFLTE (TL0) S08 S07 S02) (IFLTE S10 S00 (MF0)
S08)) (IFBMP (PROGN2 S02 S09) (IFBMP S08 S02))) (IFSTK
(PROGN2 (PROGN2 S04 S06) (IFBMP (MF0) S03)) (PROGN2
```

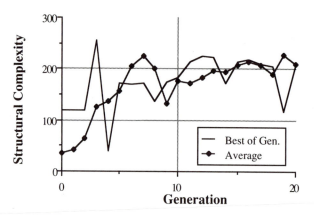

Figure 13.27 Structural complexity curves for example 2 of the box moving problem.

```
(IFSTK S05 (MFO)) (IFBMP (IFLTE (TRO) S08 (IFBMP S07 S06)
S02) (IFLTE S10 (IFBMP S10 S08) (MFO) S08))))) (IFLTE
(PROGN2 S04 S06) (PROGN2 (IFSTK (IFBMP (MFO) S09) (IFLTE
S10 S03 S03 S06)) (IFSTK (IFSTK S05 S01) (IFBMP (MFO)
S07))) (PROGN2 (IFLTE (IFSTK S01 (TRO)) (PROGN2 S06
(MFO)) (IFLTE S05 S00 (MFO) S08) (PROGN2 S11 S09)) (IFBMP
(MFO) (IFSTK S05 (IFBMP (PROGN2 (IFSTK (PROGN2 S07 S04)
(IFLTE S00 S07 S06 S07)) (PROGN2 S04 S06)) (IFSTK (IFSTK
(IFBMP S00 (PROGN2 S06 S10)) (IFSTK (MFO) S10)) (IFBMP
(PROGN2 S08 S02) (IFSTK S09 S09))))))) (IFLTE (IFBMP
(PROGN2 S11 S09) (IFBMP S08 S11)) (PROGN2 (PROGN2 S06
S03) (IFBMP (IFBMP S08 S02) (MFO))) (IFSTK (IFLTE (MFO)
(TRO) S05 S09) (IFBMP (PROGN2 (TLO) S02) S08)) (IFSTK
(PROGN2 S02 S03) (PROGN2 S01 S04))))))).
```

The structural complexity of this particular best-of-run individual contained 207 points. Figure 13.27 shows, by generation, the average of the structural complexity of the population as a whole and the structural complexity of the best-of-generation individual. As usual, structural complexity has a generally increasing trend from generation to generation as the solution is being evolved.

Figure 13.28 shows the variety during one run of this problem. Variety starts at 100% at generation 0 and fluctuates around 80% for most of the run.

13.2.3   Comparison with Reinforcement Learning

The five preparatory steps for applying genetic programming to a problem consist of defining the terminal set, the function set, the fitness measure, the control parameters, and the termination criterion and the method of result designation. The terminal set and the function set were obtained directly from the definition of the problem as stated by Mahadevan and Connell (with the

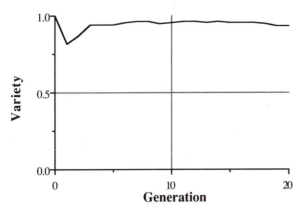

Figure 13.28 Variety curve for example 2 of the box moving problem with function set F_0.

minor changes already noted). Defining the fitness measure based on distance (shortfall) was relatively straightforward given the nature of this problem. We used our usual default control parameters and our usual termination criterion and method of result designation.

We now compare the five preparatory steps used in genetic programming with the amount of preparation involved in what Mahadevan and Connell (1990, 1991) describe as "automatic programming" of an autonomous mobile robot to do box moving using reinforcement learning.

In particular, Mahadevan and Connell use the Q learning technique developed by Watkins (1989). Reinforcement learning techniques in general require that an estimate be calculated of the expected future payoffs of each state of the system. Q learning in particular requires that an expected payoff be calculated for each combination of state and action. These expected payoffs then guide the choices that are to be made by the system (Michie and Chambers 1968). Any calculation of expected payoff requires a statistically significant number of trials. Thus, reinforcement learning requires a large number of trials to be made over a large number of combinations of possibilities.

Before any reinforcement learning and "automatic programming" can take place, Mahadevan and Connell make the following 13 decisions:

First, they decide that the solution to this problem in the subsumption architecture requires precisely three task-achieving behaviors.

Second, they decide that the three task-achieving behaviors are finding the box, pushing the box across the room, and recovering from stalls where the robot has wedged itself or the box into a corner.

Third, they decide that the behavior of finding the box has the lowest priority, that the behavior of pushing the box across the room is of intermediate importance, and that the unwedging behavior has highest priority. That is, they decide upon the conflict-resolution procedure.

Fourth, they decide on the applicability predicate of each of the three task-achieving behaviors.

Fifth, they decide upon an unequal concentration of the sonar sensors around the periphery of the robot. In particular, they decide that half of the sensors will look forward, and, after a gap in sonar coverage, an additional quarter will look to the left and the remaining quarter will look to the right. They decide that none of the sonar sensors will look back.

Sixth, they decide to preprocess the real-valued distance information reported by the sonar sensors in a highly nonlinear problem-specific way. In particular, they condense the real-valued distance information from each of the eight sensors into only two bits per sensor. The first bit associated with a given sensor (called the "NEAR" bit) is on if any object appears within 9–18 inches. The second bit (called the "FAR" bit) is on if any object appears within 18–30 inches. The sonar is an echo sonar that independently and simultaneously reports on both the 9–18 inch region and the 18–30 inch region. Thus, it is possible for both bits to be on at once. Note that the sizes of the two regions are unequal and that inputs in the range of less than 9 inches and greater than 30 inches are ignored. This massive state reduction and nonlinear preprocessing are apparently necessary because reinforcement learning requires calculation of a large number of trials for a large number of state-action combinations. In any event, eight real-valued variables are mapped into 16 bits in a highly nonlinear and problem-specific way. This reduces the input space from 12 floating-point values and two binary values to a relatively modest $2^{18} = 262,144$ possible states. An indirect effect of ignoring inputs in the range of less than 9 inches and greater than 30 inches is that the robot must resort to blind random search if it is started from a point that is not within between 9 and 30 inches of a box (i.e., the vast majority of potential starting points in the room).

Seventh, as a result of having destroyed the information contained in the eight real-valued sonar sensor inputs by condensing them into only 16 bits, they decide to explicitly create a particular problem-specific matched filter to restore the robot's ability to move in the direction of an object. The filter senses (i) if the robot has just moved forward, and (ii) if any of four particular sonar sensors were off on the previous time step but any of these sensors are now on. The real-valued values reported by the sonar sensors contain sufficient information to locate the box. This especially tailored temporal filter is required only because of the earlier decision to condense the information (this earlier decision being necessitated by the requirements of Q learning).

Eighth, they decide upon a particular non-linear scale ($-1, 0, +3$) of three reinforcements based on the output of the matched filter just described.

Ninth, they decide upon a different scale ($+1$ and -3) of two reinforcements based on an especially defined composite event, namely of the robot "continu[ing] to be bumped and going forward" versus the event of "loses contact with the box."

Tenth, they define a particular timer for the applicability predicate for the pushing behavior and the unwedging behavior (but not the finding behavior) lasting precisely five time steps. This timer keeps the behavior on for five time steps even if the applicability predicate is no longer satisfied by the state of the world, provided the behavior involved was once turned on.

Eleventh, they decide upon the scale ($+1$ and -3) for reinforcement of another especially defined composite event connected with the unwedging behavior involving "no longer [being] stalled and is able to go forward once again."

Twelfth, after reducing the total input space to $2^{18} = 262,144$ possible states, they then further reduce the input space by consolidating input states that are within a specified Hamming distance. The Hamming distance is applied in a particular nonlinear way (i.e., weighting the NEAR bits by 5, the FAR bits by 2, the BUMPED bit by 1, and the STUCK bit by 1). This consolidation of the input space reduces it from size $2^{18} = 262,144$ to size $2^9 = 512$. This final consolidation to only 512 is again apparently necessitated because the reinforcement learning technique requires calculation of a large number of trials for a large number of state-action combinations.

Thirteenth, they then perform the reinforcement on each of the three behaviors separately.

The first four of the above 13 decisions constitute the bulk of the difficult definitional problem associated with the subsumption architecture. After these decisions are made, only the content of the three behavioral actions remains to be learned. The last nine of the decisions constitute the bulk of the difficulty associated with the reinforcement learning and executing the task. It is difficult to discern what "automatic programming" or "learning" remains to be done after these 13 decisions have been made. It is probably fair to say that the 13 preparatory decisions, taken together, probably require more analysis, intelligence, and effort than programming the robot by hand. See also Koza and Rice 1992a.

14 Entropy-Driven Evolution

This chapter describes the following three different problems where entropy (i.e., information) drives the evolutionary process:

- automatic programming of a high-entropy randomizer,
- automatic programming of a randomizer for a one-dimensional cellular automaton, and
- automatic programming of a randomizer for a two-dimensional cellular automaton.

14.1 AUTOMATIC PROGRAMMING OF A RANDOMIZER

Anyone who has tried to write a computer program to generate random numbers knows that random numbers are difficult to create. Marsaglia (1968, 1983) describes the difficulty of successfully randomizing numbers, particularly where a stream of independent random integers are required to carry out related steps of one process. The correct implementation of probabilistic algorithms in optimization and machine learning (including genetic algorithms and simulated annealing) requires just such a stream of independent random numbers.

Numbers chosen at random are useful in a variety of scientific, mathematical, engineering, and industrial applications, including Monte Carlo simulations, sampling, decision theory, game theory, and instant lottery ticket production.

When random numbers are required in computer programs, they are typically provided by a deterministic algorithm (as opposed to some nonalgorithmic technique, such as neutron emissions). The algorithm is known to the programmer. Moreover, this deterministic, known computer program is typically written (using seeds) so that its output is fully reproducible (to aid debugging and verification). Numbers which are produced by a deterministic, known, and reproducible algorithm are, of course, anything but random. Indeed, as John von Neumann said, "Anyone who considers arithmetical methods of producing random digits is, of course, in a state of sin."

Not only is the term "random number" an oxymoron, but there is no generally accepted mathematical definition of a random number sequence. Instead, there are a variety of practical empirical tests and theoretical tests.

Knuth (1981b) describes a number of different tests, such as the equidistribution (frequency) test, the gap test, the run test, the serial test, the permutation test, the coupon collector's test, and the poker test. In many cases, a sequence of seemingly random numbers is considered random if it seems to work well in a given application or satisfies particular tests that seem relevant to the given application. The poker test described by Knuth, for example, may provide only marginal comfort for most users, but it may be of paramount interest to those programming video poker slot machines.

As Nisan (1992) states, "The major conceptual idea behind pseudorandom generation is that sequences of events may look random ... to any observer that does not have enough computational power to 'understand' them."

The notion of statistical independence can be used as the starting point for one possible rigorous mathematical definition of a sequence $\{u_i\}$ of random numbers. Anderson (1990) says that "each value of u_i is as likely as any other value and the value of u_i must be statistically independent of the value of u_j for $i \neq j$." The first part of this statement corresponds to Knuth's equidistribution (frequency) test, while the second part of this statement corresponds to a pairwise version of Knuth's serial test. That is, this second criterion is pairwise statistical independence.

One can extend Anderson's conditions to a more general concept of statistical independence based on the intuitive notion of how well specified values in specified positions of a subsequence within the sequence predict other values of the subsequence.

Let K be the number of values possible at a given position in the sequence. In particular, $K = 2$ for binary sequences. Let c be the number of consequent (i.e., predicted) positions within a subsequence of length N. Let g (where $g \leq N - c$) be the number of antecedent (i.e., given) values at the remaining $N - c$ positions within the subsequence of length N. Then, for any integer N (where N runs from 1 to infinity), the K^c conditional probabilities of c particular specified values at the c consequent positions (given that g particular specified antecedent values have appeared at the g antecedent positions) should all be equal to $1/K^c$ (within an acceptably small error $\varepsilon \geq 0$). Note that if g is strictly less than $N - c$, then there are $N - g - c$ positions within the sequence which are "don't care" positions in that they are part of neither the antecedent nor the consequent part of the prediction. For a given N, there are multinomial coefficient

$$\binom{N}{g \ c \ N - g - c}$$

ways of picking the g given antecedent positions and c consequent positions out of the subsequence of length N. And then, after g such given antecedent positions are picked, there are K^g particular assignments of values at the g antecedent positions. After those choices are made, there are K^c particular assignments of values at the c consequent positions. It is the conditional probabilities of each of those K^c particular assignments of values that should be equal.

The above definition captures the intuitive notion of uniform conditional probabilities; however, it is particularly onerous combinatorially. The following alternative definition is simpler and avoids conditional probabilities. It is sufficient to produce uniformity of the above conditional probabilities. For any integer N (where N runs from 1 to infinity), the probabilities of each of the K^N possible subsequences of length N should all be equal to $1/K^N$ (within an acceptably small error $\varepsilon \geq 0$).

No finite sequence can satisfy the above test. However, if N is limited to some finite fixed integer $N_{\max}$, then only $K^{N_{\max}}$ probabilities must be estimated when $N = N_{\max}$. These $K^{N_{\max}}$ separate probabilities can be conveniently summarized into a scalar quantity by using the concept of entropy for this set of events and probabilities. The *entropy* E_h (which is measured in bits) for the set of K^h probabilities for the K^h possible subsequences of length h is given by

$$E_h = -\sum_j P_{hj} \log_2 P_{hj}.$$

The index j in this summation ranges over the K^h possible subsequences of length h. By convention, $\log_2 0$ is 0 when one is computing entropy.

The entropy is maximal when the probabilities of all the possible events are equal. In particular, entropy attains its maximum value of h precisely when the probabilities of all the K^h possible subsequences of length h are equal to $1/K^h$. Moreover, when $K = 2$ this maximal value of entropy happens to equal the length h of the sequence involved (i.e., the number of bits of entropy equals the number of binary digits in the sequence).

As h runs from 1 to $N_{\max}$, it is convenient to further summarize the $N_{\max}$ separate scalar values of entropy into a single scalar value by summing them to obtain E_{total}:

$$E_{\text{total}} = \sum_{h=1}^{N_{\max}} \left(-\sum_j P_{hj} \log_2 P_{hj} \right).$$

This sum E_{total} has the advantage of giving greater weight to the larger subsequence sizes. E_{total} attains the maximal value of

$$\frac{N_{\max}(N_{\max} - 1)}{2}$$

when $E_h = h$ for all h between 1 and $N_{\max}$. When that happens the sequence may be viewed as random.

To illustrate for $K = 2$: When h is 1, there are only two probabilities to consider, namely the probability P_{h0} of occurrence of zeros and the probability P_{h1} of occurrence of ones in the entire random sequence. These two probabilities are used in Knuth's equidistribution (frequency) test. For the worst randomizer (say, one that always emits 1), P_{h0} is 0.0 and P_{h1} is 1.0 and the entropy is 0.0 bits. For a better randomizer, both P_{h0} and P_{h1} would equal approximately 0.5 and the entropy would approximately equal the maximal value of 1.0 bits.

A highly defective randomizer, such as one that emits

```
0101010101...,
```

has an entropy of 1.0 bits when only the two singlet probabilities P_{h0} and P_{h1} associated with $h = 1$ are considered. Thus, having a good score in the equidistribution test is a necessary, but not sufficient, condition for a good randomizer. However, when $h = 2$ and the pair probabilities are considered, the four possible pairs (i.e., 00, 01, 10, and 11) are not equal to $\frac{1}{4}$. The two pairs 00 and 11 do not appear at all in the output of this defective randomizer. The two pairs 01 and 10 appear with probability $\frac{1}{2}$, not with probability $\frac{1}{4}$. Thus, the entropy for $h = 2$ for this defective randomizer is only 1.0, instead of the maximal value of 2.0 bits possible for $h = 2$. When $h = 2$, this test corresponds to Knuth's serial (pair) test and to Anderson's notion of pairwise statistical independence.

There are many different types of randomizers.

Because of the practical usefulness of pseudo-random number sequences, considerable work has been done in the difficult area of designing effective pseudo-random number generators. According to Anderson (1990), there are five common techniques for producing random number sequences:

- multiplicative congruential randomizers,

- shift-register randomizers,

- shuffle randomizers,

- lagged Fibonacci randomizers, and

- hybrid combinations of the above.

Each of these five common types of randomizers starts with one or more seeds.

Multiplicative congruential randomizers start with a seed value x_0 and then produce subsequent elements of the sequence recursively as follows:

$$x_i = (ax_{i-1} + c) \bmod M,$$

where a is the multiplier, c is the additive constant, and M is the modulus (Yarmolik and Demidenko 1988).

In some cases, particular multiplicative congruential randomizers have come into widespread use (Anderson 1990). Park and Miller (1988) describe the especially simple and popular multiplicative congruential randomizer

$$x_i = 7^5 x_{i-1} \bmod [2^{31} - 1],$$

which provides especially good randomness by many tests for the low-order bits. This popular randomizer is supplied by several vendors of 32-bit computers because $2^{31} - 1$ is the largest prime that will fit in a 32-bit signed integer word. The initial Park-Miller seed x_0 is 1.

URN08 (widely known as RANDU) came from IBM in 1970 and is very popular (Dudewicz and Ralley 1981). It is the multiplicative congruential randomizer

$$x_i = 65539 x_{i-1} \bmod 2^{31}.$$

Shift-register randomizers start with a seed value x_0 and then produce subsequent elements of the sequence recursively in a shift register. In the popular SR[3, 28, 31] shift-register randomizer shown below, the numbers 3 and 28 specify the amount of shifting (end off, with zero fill) to the right or the left (respectively) in a 31-bit shift register:

```
temp =(XOR xi-1 (SHIFT-RIGHT xi 3)),
xi =(XOR temp (SHIFT-LEFT temp 28)),
```

where XOR is the exclusive-or operation.

Shuffling randomizers call on one or more other randomizers to shuffle numbers to produce random numbers. Two-sequence shuffling randomizers call on two other randomizers (preferably of different types, to help break up regularities that might exist in particular randomizers).

One possible two-sequence shuffling randomizer, which will be called SHUFFLE here, uses the Park-Miller multiplicative congruential randomizer and the SR[3, 28, 31] shift-register randomizer described above. In particular, it uses the Park-Miller randomizer to produce an initial set of uniformly distributed random numbers between 0.0 and 1.0 and then uses the shift-register randomizer SR[3, 28, 31] to call out particular numbers from this set of numbers, while using additional calls on the Park-Miller randomizer to replace the numbers called out (Anderson 1990).

Lagged Fibonacci randomizers perform a designated operation (such as addition, subtraction, multiplication, or exclusive-or) on two previously computed values of the sequence. Long lags, such as the lags of 607 and 273 shown below, are required for good performance by lagged Fibonacci randomizers:

$$x_i = \{x_{i-607} - x_{i-273}\} \bmod 2^{31}.$$

A lag of 607 requires 607 initial seed values in order to compute the first random number.

Texas Instruments supplies a randomizer called RANDOM with its Explorer computers.

In this chapter, we will compare the following five well-known randomizers with the randomizer which we will genetically breed:

- Park-Miller
- URN08 (RANDU) from IBM
- SR[3, 28, 31] shift-register randomizer
- SHUFFLE
- RANDOM from Texas Instruments

In implementing these five randomizers here, if a floating-point seed is needed and not otherwise specified, we use 0.426, and if an integer seed is needed and not otherwise specified, we use the prime 19009. If the output of one of the above randomizers would have been a uniformly distributed floating-point number between 0.0 and 1.0, we assign the binary integer output of 0 when the floating-point output would have been between 0.0 and 0.5 and we assign the binary integer of 1 when the floating-point output would have been between 0.5 and 1.0.

Because of the size of the tables needed for the subsequence probabilities needed to compute entropy, we will focus, for the remainder of this chapter, on producing sequences of random binary digits (i.e., $K = 2$).

Thus, the goal now is to genetically breed a computer program to convert a sequence of consecutive integers into a sequence of random binary digits. The input to our randomizer will merely be an argument J running consecutively from 1 to $16,384 = 2^{14}$. In other words, each random binary output bit will be a function of a consecutive integer J as input. Randomizers of this type are desirable when there is a need to quickly reconstruct a particular single random number within a long sequence without having to reconstruct the entire preceding sequence. Note that a randomizer whose input is merely the consecutive index J, as opposed to a seed which it side-effects, is an especially difficult type of randomizer to produce because it cannot rely on recursion. A randomizer using recursion gains considerable leverage from the cascading of the previous steps. For example, when the third call is made to a multiplicative congruential randomizer in order to compute x_3, the randomizer is, in effect, computing the following rather complicated function of its initial seed x_0:

$$x_3 = (a[(a\{(ax_0 + c) \bmod M\} + c) \bmod M] + c) \bmod M.$$

The above explicitly expanded computation has three additions, three multiplications, and three modulus operations. When the 500th call is made, this cascade is 500 deep. The explicitly expanded computation would have 500 additions, 500 multiplications, and 500 modulus operations. Because of the leverage gained from this cascading from previous calls, recursive randomizers usually consist of a relatively simple mathematical expression (e.g., a linear congruence) that is recursively applied. A randomizer whose input is merely the consecutive index J must necessarily be a more complex mathematical expression.

The terminal set for this problem is the set

```
T = {J, ℜ},
```

where $\Re$ is the ephemeral random integer constant ranging over the small integers 0, 1, 2, and 3. The solution of the problem is more difficult when the random constants are limited to just a few small integers.

The choice of the function set, of course, directly affects the character of the computer programs that can be generated. Since we are interested in creating a randomizer involving congruential steps, the function set for this problem is

```
F = {+, -, *, QUOT%, MOD%},
```

taking two arguments each. If we had been interested in creating a randomizer based on shift-register operations, we would have included a shift-register operation of some kind in this function set.

If the second argument to the protected integer quotient function QUOT% and the protected modulus function MOD% is 0, the function returns 0. Otherwise, the MOD% function is identical to the Common LISP function MOD and the QUOT% function is identical to the Common LISP function FLOOR.

Table 14.1 Tableau for the randomizer problem.

Objective:	Find an S-expression that takes the index J as its input and produces a high-entropy stream of random binary digits as its output.
Terminal set:	Index J and $\Re$, the ephemeral random constant $\Re$ ranging over the small integers 0, 1, 2, and 3.
Function set:	+, −, *, QUOT%, MOD%.
Fitness cases:	16,384 (2^{14}) sequence positions.
Raw fitness:	Total entropy E_{total}.
Standardized fitness:	Maximum value of raw fitness (i.e., 28.000 bits) minus raw fitness.
Hits:	The integer just below 1,000 times raw fitness.
Wrapper:	Converts an positive value to a binary 1 and all other values to 0.
Parameters:	$M = 500$. $G = 51$.
Success predicate:	An S-expression scores 27,990 or more hits.

An S-expression composed of the above functions and terminals is real-valued. Since we want binary digits as output, we wrap the S-expression in a wrapper (output interface) which specifies that any positive numerical output will be interpreted as a binary 1 while any other output will be interpreted as a binary 0.

There are $16,384 = 2^{14}$ fitness cases for this problem, one for each value of J. The raw fitness for this problem is the sum of the entropy measures E_{total} (described earlier) for subsequences of length 1 through 7. The maximum raw fitness of 28.000 bits is associated with the best result. Standardized fitness is 28.000 minus raw fitness. A hit for this problem was defined as the integer just below 1,000 times raw fitness and thus ranged from 0 to 28,000.

Table 14.1 summarizes the key features of the binary randomizer problem. Double-precision arithmetic was used in computing entropy.

In one run, 56% of the 500 individuals in the initial random generation merely emitted a constant binary 0 or binary 1 and therefore had entropy 0.000. Another 14% of the population emitted a constant most of the time and consequently had near-zero entropy (i.e., between 0.001 and 0.080 bits). Another 24% merely mapped the given sequence of consecutive integers into another consecutive sequence of integers. An example is the mapping from J into (+ J 2). These individuals had values of entropy between 7.000 and 7.056 bits.

The best 24 individuals from the initial random generation scored between 10.428 and 20.920 bits of entropy.

The best-of-generation individual from generation 0 consisted of 63 points and scored 20.920 bits. It can be simplified to

Figure 14.1 Subsequence histogram for the best-of-generation individual from generation 0.

Figure 14.2 Subsequence histogram for the best-of-generation individual from generation 4.

```
(+ J (* (* (MOD% J 3) 3) (QUOT% (+ J 1) 4))).
```

This individual does a credible job of randomizing bits when the window is narrow. In particular, it gets a perfect 1.000 bits out of a possible 1.000 bits for subsequences of length 1, and it gets 1.918 out of a possible 2.000 bits for subsequences of length 2. In contrast, this best-of-generation individual does not do as well for the longer subsequences. It gets only 4.002 bits out of a possible 6.000 for subsequences of length 6 (i.e., only 67% of the possible 6.000 bits), and it gets only 4.252 bits out of a possible 7.000 for subsequences of length 7 (i.e., only 61% of the possible 7.000 bits).

Figure 14.1 shows a histogram whose horizontal axis ranges over the $2^7 = 128$ possible subsequences of length 7. The vertical axis is the number of occurrences of each of the 128 possible subsequences. A maximal entropy randomizer would have $16,384/128 = 128$ occurrences of each of the 128 possible subsequences. The best-of-generation individual from generation 0 has about 1,300 occurrences each for only a handful of the 128 possible subsequences.

On generation 2 of this run, the entropy of the best-of-generation individual was 22.126 bits.

On generation 4, the entropy of the best-of-generation individual was 26.474 bits.

Figure 14.2 demonstrates the improvement in the best-of-generation individual between generation 0 and generation 4. A total of 84 of the 128 possible subsequences of length 7 are now represented in this histogram (which has a high point of 455).

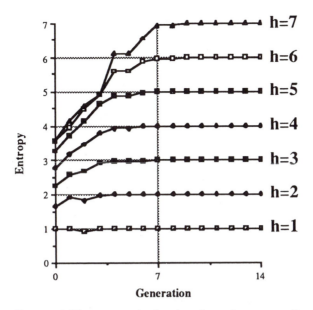

Figure 14.3 The components of entropy from subsequences of lengths 1 through 7.

Figure 14.4 Subsequence histogram for the best-of-generation individual from generation 9.

Figure 14.3 shows the progress, from generation to generation, of each of the seven components (i.e., for $h = 1$ through 7) of E_{total} for the best-of-generation individual of each generation. As can be seen, entropy for short subsequence lengths reaches its maximum level after just a few generations, while entropy for the longer subsequence lengths requires additional generations.

Between generations 5 and 13, entropy improved and ranged from 27.800 to 27.900.

Figure 14.4 shows the number of occurrences of each of the possible subsequences of length 7 for generation 9. Note that all of the 128 subsequences now have a nonzero number of occurrences in this histogram. This histogram has a high point of 163.

On generation 14, we obtained an S-expression that attained a nearly maximal entropy of 27.996 and had 87 points:

```
(- J (QUOT% (+ (+ (+ J J) J) (* (+ J 2) J)) (+ (MOD% (*
(- 2 1) (QUOT% (QUOT% (+ (* J J) (QUOT% (- (QUOT% (* J
```

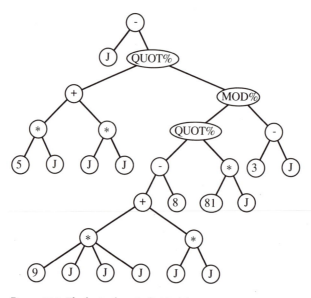

Figure 14.5 The best-of-run individual from generation 14.

```
(MOD% (QUOT% J 3) (MOD% J J))) (QUOT% (* 3 2) (QUOT% 2
1))) (- 3 (QUOT% (+ (* J J) (- 2 1)) 3))) (* 3 (+ (MOD% 1
0) J)))) 3) 3)) (+ (- 2 J) 1)) (+ (QUOT% (MOD% J 3) (-
(MOD% 2 0) (MOD% (MOD% 0 J) J))) (- 3 3))))).
```

This best-of-run S-expression can be simplified to the following S-expression with 29 points:

```
(- J (QUOT% (+ (* 5 j) (* j j))
            (MOD% (QUOT% (+ (* 9 j j j) (- (* J J) 8))
                         (* 81 J))
                  (- 3 J))))).
```

This is equivalent to

$$j - \frac{j^2 + 5j}{\text{Mod}\%\left(\dfrac{9j^3 + j^2 - 8}{81j}, 3 - j\right)},$$

where the indicated divisions are the QUOT% function. The value of this S-expression is then passed to the wrapper.

Figure 14.5 graphically depicts the simplified form of this best-of-run S-expression from generation 14.

The progressive change in size and the shape of the individuals in the population is a characteristic of genetic programming. The size (87 points) and shape of the best-scoring individual from generation 14 differ from the size (63 points) and the shape of the best-scoring individual from generation 0. The size and the particular hierarchical structure of the best scoring individual from generation 14 were not specified in advance. Instead, the entire structure evolved as a result of reproduction, crossover, and the relentless pressure of

Figure 14.6 Subsequence histogram for the best-of-run individual from generation 14.

Table 14.2 Frequency of occurrence of all possible sequences of length 7.

	000	001	010	011	100	101	110	111
0000	128	127	135	121	119	133	137	124
0001	128	129	117	146	117	134	133	129
0010	131	122	124	132	128	113	125	150
0011	137	126	137	131	139	115	128	112
0100	134	125	136	112	129	128	135	116
0101	123	132	127	116	119	133	132	133
0110	126	141	130	123	122	136	126	141
0111	138	132	119	133	129	128	126	118
1000	127	129	117	140	138	130	114	138
1001	125	127	124	129	146	134	121	111
1010	128	126	133	119	127	129	127	115
1011	130	127	121	136	131	137	129	132
1100	122	132	132	140	123	125	145	117
1101	131	120	129	126	138	124	136	128
1110	128	131	118	139	129	119	136	123
1111	121	125	129	126	117	127	118	122

the fitness measure (i.e., entropy). As we have seen before, the structure came about as a result of fitness.

Figure 14.6 shows that the best-of-run individual from generation 14 has close to 128 occurrences for each of the 128 possible subsequences of length 7.

Note that the computer program achieving nearly optimal entropy in generation 14 had greater structural complexity than the best-of-generation program from generation 0 and the best-of-generation programs from other early generations.

In scoring 27.996, this randomizer achieved maximal values of entropy of 1.000, 2.000, 3.000, 4.000, 5.000, and 6.000 bits for sequences of lengths 1, 2, 3, 4, 5, and 6, respectively, and a near-maximal value of 6.996 for the 128 (2^7) possible sequences of length 7.

Table 14.2 shows the frequency of occurrence of each of the $128 = 2^7$ possible sequences of length 7 in $16,384 = 2^{14}$ consecutive calls to the randomizer for the best-of-generation individual from generation 14. The 127 on the first line of the table means that the subsequence 0000001 of length 7 occurred 127 times out of 16,384.

The question arises as to whether the above randomizer, which was genetically bred using values of J from 0 to 16,383, is generalizable to other ranges
of J. When we retested the genetically produced randomizer over 65,536 =
2^{16} values of J, we got an even better value of entropy, namely 27.998 bits
(as compared to the original 27.996).

Is the genetically bred computer program a good randomizer? The answer
is "Yes and No."

D. H. Lehmer (quoted in Knuth 1981b) said, "A random sequence is a vague
notion embodying the idea of a sequence in which each term is unpredictable
to the uninitiated and whose digits pass a certain number of tests, traditional
with statisticians and *depending somewhat on the uses to which the sequence is to
be put.*" (Italics added.)

Table 14.3 compares the shortfall in entropy from the maximal 28.000 bits
for the genetically bred randomizer and the five well-known randomizers
described earlier. We used the same 16,384 points and a lookback of $h = 7$.

As can be seen, the genetically bred randomizer has precisely the characteristic for which it was bred (i.e., high entropy). With respect to that particular measure of randomness, it exceeded the performance of the other five
randomizers.

Table 14.4 shows the result of applying Knuth's equidistribution (frequency)
test to the genetically bred randomizer and the five well-known randomizers.
The genetic randomizer comes much closer to the uniform distribution of 8192
zeros and 8192 ones in a random sequence of 16,384 binary digits than any

Table 14.3 Entropy shortfall from 28.000 for five well-known randomizers and
the genetically produced randomizer.

Randomizer	Entropy shortfall
Park-Miller	0.009
Randu	0.010
Shift-Register	0.010
Shuffle	0.015
Random	0.009
Genetic	0.004

Table 14.4 Equidistribution (frequency) test for five well-known randomizers and
the genetically produced randomizer.

Randomizer	Number of zeros	Number of ones	χ^2
Park-Miller	8146	8238	0.52
Randu	8149	8235	0.45
Shift-Register	8234	8150	0.43
Shuffle	8234	8150	0.43
Random	8235	8149	0.45
Genetic	8207	8177	0.05

of the five well-known randomizers. That is, the frequencies of zeros and ones for the genetic randomizer are almost perfectly uniform. This is understandable since the genetic randomizer was created using entropy as the fitness measure. It was specifically created so as to make single bit frequencies (and indeed subsequence frequencies up to length 7) uniform. The greater the deviation from uniformity, the worse the fitness (entropy).

In another sense, the frequency of zeros and ones in the genetic randomizer leans in the direction of being too uniform. Each of the five well-known randomizers has a χ^2 (chi-square) that, for one degree of freedom, is very close to the 50th percentile. In contrast, the χ^2 of the genetically bred randomizer is in about the 15th percentile. Whether the intentionally created uniform distribution or a less uniform distribution constitutes randomness depends on one's point of view. For example, some state lotteries explicitly enforce structured randomness in the distribution of winners in preprinted instant lottery game tickets (e.g., no long gaps between winners), while others insist on unstructured randomness.

Table 14.5 shows the result of applying Knuth's gap test to the genetic randomizer and the five other randomizers. The gap test counts the number of gaps of particular sizes in the sequence of 16,384 binary digits. For example, in the sequence 0010110 of length 7, we have one gap in the zeros of length 0 (i.e., one instance of consecutive zeros), one gap of length 1, and one gap of length 2.

The 50th percentile of the χ^2 distribution for ten degrees of freedom is at 9.342. The χ^2 for the zeros for the genetic randomizer is 9.03. This is similar to most of the values for the five other randomizers. However, the χ^2 for the ones for the genetic randomizer is the rather low value of 2.64. That is, the gaps in the ones for the genetic randomizer almost perfectly match the number of gaps expected from a random source. That is, the genetic randomizer adheres too closely to the theoretical distribution of gaps. This match is especially strong for gap sizes of 7 and below. This is understandable in view of how the genetic randomizer was bred. In contrast, the five other randomizers are more random because their performance deviates more sharply from the theoretical distribution of gaps expected from a random source.

A comment by Knuth is apt: "... the observed values are so close to the expected values, we cannot consider the result to be random!"

Table 14.5 Gap test for five well-known randomizers and the genetically produced randomizer.

Randomizer	χ^2 for zeros	χ^2 for ones
Park-Miller	5.52	12.80
Randu	9.07	13.19
Shift-Register	11.21	4.05
Shuffle	9.22	10.72
Random	4.50	9.44
Genetic	9.03	2.64

This problem illustrates a principle applicable to both genetic algorithms and genetic programming, namely "You get what you pay for." Of course, one could, alternatively, have genetically bred the population of randomizers using a fitness measure based on both entropy and the gap test or on some other combination of the various tests commonly used for randomizers. See also Koza 1991e.

14.2 ONE-DIMENSIONAL CELLULAR AUTOMATA

A cellular space is a uniform array of cells. In a *cellular automaton* (CA), each cell in a cellular space is occupied by an automaton that is identical except for its initial state. The next state of each automaton depends on its own current state and on the current states of the automata in a specified set of neighboring cells. For example, for a one-dimensional cellular automaton, the next state of a given automaton might depend on the current state of that automaton and the current states of its two neighbors at distance 1. We denote these three states as x (for the automaton at the center), w (west), and e (east). Similarly, for a two-dimensional cellular automaton, the next state of a given automaton might depend on the current state of that automaton and the current states of its four neighbors at distance 1 in the two-dimensional space, namely x, w, e, north (N), and south (S). This particular set of neighbors at distance 1 is called the *von Neumann neighborhood* set. Cellular spaces are typically toroidal so that every cell has the same number of neighbors.

Cellular automata are the discrete counterparts of continuous dynamical systems defined by partial differential equations and the physicist's concept of field (Toffoli and Margolus 1987). Simulations of fluid flow and other complex processes that depend only on the states of local neighbors are well suited to cellular automata. For example, processors in a grid in two or three dimensions of a massively parallel computer might execute the same computer program to simulate some physical process defined by physical laws operating only on nearby local points in the grid.

If the automaton located in each cell happens to have only two states, the state-transition function of the automaton is merely a Boolean function. For a one-dimensional cellular space with von Neumann neighbors, the Boolean function has three inputs and one output. For a two-dimensional cellular space with von Neumann neighbors, the Boolean function has five inputs and one output. Cellular automata with Boolean state-transition functions are dynamical systems that are discrete in time, space (their cells), and site value (Boolean).

The best-known cellular automaton is Conway's game of *Life* (Gardner 1970; Berlekamp, Conway, and Guy 1985; McIntosh 1991), which involves a two-state automaton embedded in a two-dimensional cellular space. In the game of Life, the next state of the automaton located at a given cell depends on its current state and the states of its eight neighbors at 45° angles (called the *Moore neighborhood*). Certain patterns (such as gliders and blinkers) reproduce themselves in different locations in the space over time.

Complex overall behavior is often produced by cellular automata as the result of the repetitive application (at each cell in the cellular space) of seemingly simple transition rules contained in each cell (Legendi et al. 1987; Manneville et al. 1989).

It is extremely difficult, in general, to design a single state-transition rule that, when it operates in each cell of the cellular space, produces a desired overall emergent behavior. Packard and his associates have attempted to discern the initial conditions and state-transition rules for cellular automata using conventional genetic algorithms operating on strings (Packard 1990; Meyer, Richards, and Packard 1989; Meyer, Richards, and Packard 1991; Meyer and Packard 1991; Breeden and Packard 1991).

In this chapter, we use genetic programming to evolve a state-transition rule that enables a cellular automaton to produce certain desired emergent behavior. In particular, we evolve a state-transition rule that produces temporal random behavior in a cellular automaton. Entropy is used as the driving force for the evolutionary process.

The result is that the structure that performs well in the environment emerges as a result of the selective pressure exerted by the environment. In other words, the structure is the consequence of pressures of the problem environment.

Wolfram (1986) showed that a particular two-state automaton depending only on itself and its two immediate neighbors (W and E) in a one-dimensional cellular space was capable of producing a pseudo-random temporal stream of bits. In particular, Wolfram showed random temporal behavior (using several frequently used tests for randomness) from the state-transition rule

(XOR W (OR X E)).

This Boolean function with three inputs is rule 30 using the usual numbering scheme for Boolean functions (chapter 9). It is, under reflection, equivalent to rule 86.

The initial state of the cellular space used by Wolfram consisted of one cell in state 1 (True) and all the other cells in state 0 (NIL). The temporal stream of random bits was taken from the single cell that started in state 1.

In this section, we demonstrate how genetic programming can rediscover Wolfram's two-state automaton using only the overall goal (i.e., to produce a high-entropy stream of bits over time) to guide the discovery process.

We used a one-dimensional cellular space of width 32. The initial state of cell 15 was 1 (True) and the initial state of all other cells was 0 (NIL). We examined the time series over 4,096 time steps and considered the entropy associated with the probability of occurrence of each of the $2^4 = 16$ possible subsequences of length 4. If each of the 16 subsequences of length 4 occurred exactly

$$\frac{4,096}{16} = 256$$

times in 4,096 time steps, entropy would attain the maximal value of 4.000 bits.

The terminal set for this problem consisted of the three inputs available to each automaton in the one-dimensional cellular space, namely

```
T = {X, W, E}.
```

Since we are considering functions of three Boolean arguments, the function set for this problem can consist of the following computationally complete and convenient set of three Boolean functions:

```
F = {AND, OR, NOT},
```

taking two, two, and one argument, respectively.

The cellular array was started with the initial conditions stated above and run for 4,096 time steps. That is, there were 4,096 fitness cases. Fitness was measured via entropy using a lookback of 4. Maximum raw fitness was 4.000 bits. A hit for this problem was defined as 1,000 times raw fitness and thus ranged from 0 to 4,000.

The genetically produced S-expressions in the population are often large and complex. Nonetheless, they involve only the three independent variables X, W, and E, and therefore they necessarily correspond to one of the 256 possible Boolean functions with three arguments and one output.

No wrapper is required, because the value of any S-expression composed from this function set and this terminal set is always a binary value.

Table 14.6 summarizes the key features of the problem of automatically programming a one-dimensional cellular automaton.

In one run, the best-of-generation individual from generation 0 had an entropy of 1.832 and 32 points:

Table 14.6 Tableau for the one-dimensional cellular automaton problem.

Objective:	Find an S-expression that, when inserted at all cells in a one-dimensional cellular space, produces a high-entropy temporal stream of random binary digits as its output at a designated cell.
Terminal set:	X (center), W (west), and E (east) relative to each cell in question.
Function set:	AND, OR, NOT
Fitness cases:	4,096 (2^{12}) temporal sequence steps.
Raw fitness:	Total entropy E_{total} taken over temporal output for subsequences of length 4.
Standardized fitness:	Maximum value of raw fitness (i.e., 4.000 bits) minus raw fitness.
Hits:	1,000 times raw fitness.
Wrapper:	None.
Parameters:	$M = 500$. $G = 51$.
Success predicate:	An S-expression scores 3,990 or more hits.

```
(AND (AND (NOT (AND (NOT E) (OR E X))) (NOT (AND (AND X
E) (NOT X)))) (NOT (AND (OR (OR X X) (OR W W)) (AND (OR W
W) (AND W W)))))).
```

In figure 14.7, the horizontal axis ranges over the $2^4 = 16$ possible temporal subsequences of length 4 for generation 0 (i.e., from 0000 to 1111). The vertical axis of this histogram ranges over the number of occurrences of each of the 16 subsequences. As can be seen, the most frequent two of the possible temporal subsequences of length 4 occur 1,792 and 1,664 times each (out of 4,096 times), and many of the possible subsequences are unrepresented for generation 0.

For generation 6, the best-of-generation individual had an entropy of 3.494 and 20 points:

```
(AND (OR E X) (NOT (AND (AND (AND X X) (OR W X)) (AND
(AND W W) (AND W E))))).
```

Figure 14.8 is the histogram for the 16 possible temporal subsequences for generation 6. Six of the possible temporal subsequences of length 4 occur between 502 and 504 times each for generation 6. Generation 6 is the first generation of this particular run for which there was at least one occurrence of each of the 16 possible temporal subsequences (although the fact that the number of occurrences of the several of the rarer subsequences is nonzero is not discernible on this histogram, because of its scale).

For generation 7, the best-of-generation individual had an entropy of 3.645 and 28 points:

```
(OR (NOT (OR (NOT W) (NOT (OR (NOT W) (OR E X))))) (NOT
(OR (OR (NOT (NOT X)) (OR E W)) (OR (OR X W) (AND W
X))))).
```

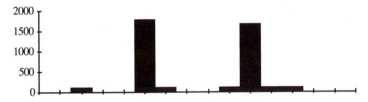

Figure 14.7 Subsequence histogram for the best-of-generation individual for generation 0 for the one-dimensional cellular automaton problem.

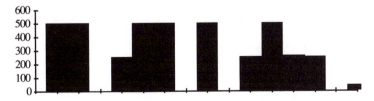

Figure 14.8 Subsequence histogram for the best-of-generation individual for generation 6 for the one-dimensional cellular automaton problem.

Figure 14.9 Subsequence histogram for the best-of-generation individual for generation 7 for the one-dimensional cellular automaton problem.

Figure 14.10 Subsequence histogram for the best-of-generation individual for generation 10 for the one-dimensional cellular automaton problem.

Figure 14.9 is the histogram for the 16 possible temporal subsequences for the best individual of generation 7. As can be seen, there has been a substantial improvement in the uniformity of the distribution between generations 6 and 7. Fifteen of the 16 subsequences in generation 7 have between 214 and 289 occurrences, and one of the subsequences has 425 occurrences.

For generation 10, the best-of-generation individual had an entropy of 3.982 and 43 points:

```
(OR (AND (AND (NOT (NOT (NOT X))) (OR (NOT (AND E W)) (OR
(NOT (OR (NOT E) (AND X X))) (NOT E)))) (NOT (AND (OR
(NOT E) (NOT W)) (OR (OR X W) (AND E E))))) (NOT (OR (NOT
X) (AND X W)))).
```

Figure 14.10 is the histogram for the best individual of generation 10. The numbers of occurrences of all 16 of the subsequences lie in the relatively narrow range of 232 to 275.

The best-of-generation individual for generation 25 had entropy of 3.996. Its histogram is similar to, but smoother than, the histogram in figure 14.11 for generation 10. This best-of-run individual has 83 points and an entropy of 3.996:

```
(AND (OR (OR (NOT (OR E E)) (NOT (OR (OR (AND W W) (OR E
(NOT (NOT X)))) (NOT (AND (AND (AND X X) X) (AND (AND W
W) (AND W E)))))) (OR (AND W W) (AND E E))) (OR (NOT (OR
(NOT (OR (NOT W) (NOT (OR (NOT W) (OR E X))))) (NOT (OR
(OR (NOT (NOT X)) (OR E W)) W)))) (NOT (OR E (OR (OR (NOT
W) (AND (OR X X) (NOT E))) (AND (OR X X) (AND X E)))))))).
```

Table 14.7 shows that this S-expression is rule 30 (00011110 in binary) and is therefore equivalent to Wolfram's cellular automaton randomizer.

Table 14.7 Truth table of best-of-run individual from generation 25 for the one-dimensional cellular automaton problem.

West	X	East	Result
0	0	0	0
0	0	1	1
0	1	0	1
0	1	1	1
1	0	0	1
1	0	1	0
1	1	0	0
1	1	1	0

The question arises as to whether the above S-expression, which was genetically bred using $4,096 = 2^{12}$ temporal sequence steps, is generalizable to other numbers of steps. When we retested the genetically produced randomizer over $65,536 = 2^{16}$ steps, we got an even better value of entropy: 4.000 bits (as compared to the original 3.996).

On an earlier generation of this same run, we also encountered Boolean rule 45 that Wolfram (1986) identified as the second-best randomizer (when inserted into a one-dimensional cellular automaton). The S-expression for rule 45 (which is, upon reflection, equivalent to rule 75) is

```
(XOR W (OR X (NOT E))).
```

14.3 TWO-DIMENSIONAL CELLULAR AUTOMATA

We can genetically breed a randomizing computer program for a two-dimensional cellular automaton in a manner similar to that described in the previous section.

We used a two-dimensional cellular space of size 8×8. The initial state of cell $(3, 3)$ was 1 (True) and the initial state of all other cells was 0 (NIL). We examined the time series over 16,384 time steps and considered the entropy associated with the probability of occurrence of each of the $2^7 = 128$ possible subsequences of length 7.

The terminal set for this problem consisted of the five inputs from the von Neumann neighborhood available to each automaton in the two-dimensional cellular space, namely

```
T = {X, W, N, E, S}.
```

The function set and fitness measure are the same as for the one-dimensional cellular automata problem previously described.

Computer time can be saved in several ways in a cellular automata problem.

First, since the individual S-expressions are often very complex and since every S-expression is applied at each cell in the cellular space, considerable computer time can be saved by first generating the truth table for the 32

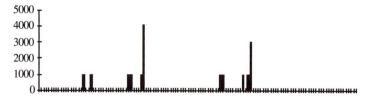

Figure 14.11 Subsequence histogram for the best-of-generation individual for generation 0 for the two-dimensional cellular automaton problem.

combinations of the five variables and then doing a lookup into this table to determine the next state of each cell in the cellular space.

Second, many S-expressions (particularly in early generations) cause the entire cellular space to stabilize. If it happens that the state of every cell in the cellular space agrees for two consecutive time steps, they will then agree forever after. In that event, the evaluation of the execution of all remaining time steps can be omitted and all future values of cell $(3, 3)$ will equal the current value of that cell.

Third, if all the cells of the cellular space ever return to their previous values after a certain number of time steps, the space has become periodic. We test for periodicity by encoding the combination of the states of all cells into a large integer for each time step and storing these integers in a hash table. If a periodicity is discovered, the execution of all remaining time steps can be omitted and all future values of cell $(3, 3)$ are merely repetitions of its values over the cycle just recognized. This third time-saving technique is a special case of the second. It saves additional time, but less time than the second technique. The second technique is easier to implement.

In one run, the best-of-generation individual from generation 0 had an entropy of 3.202 and has 4 points:

```
(NOT (OR X E)).
```

Figure 14.11 is a histogram showing the number of occurrences of each of the $2^7 = 128$ possible subsequences of length 7 occurring temporally at cell $(3, 3)$ for the best-of-generation individual from generation 0. The horizontal axis represents the possible temporal subsequences from 0000000 to 1111111 at cell $(3, 3)$.

For generation 7, the best-of-generation individual had 51 points and an entropy of 6.711:

```
(OR (OR (AND (OR (NOT E) (NOT S)) (OR (OR E (AND X W))
S)) (AND (NOT (OR N X)) (OR (NOT W) (AND W (NOT (OR (AND
X (NOT (NOT N))) (NOT S)))))))) (OR (AND (NOT (NOT N))
(NOT (OR N X))) (AND (AND (NOT W) (NOT X)) (NOT E)))).
```

Figure 14.12 is the histogram for the 128 possible temporal subsequences for generation 7, the first generation of this particular run for which there was at least one occurrence of each of the 128 possible temporal subsequences.

Figure 14.12 Subsequence histogram for the best-of-generation individual for generation 7 for the two-dimensional cellular automaton problem.

Figure 14.13 Subsequence histogram for the best-of-run individual from generation 10 for the two-dimensional cellular automaton problem.

The best-of-generation individual for generation 10 had 67 points and an entropy of 6.995:

```
(OR (OR (AND (OR (NOT E) (NOT S)) (OR (AND (OR (NOT E)
(NOT S)) (OR (AND W X) E)) (NOT (OR (AND (OR X N) (NOT
E)) (OR X W))))) (AND (NOT (OR X S)) (OR (NOT W) (AND W
(NOT (OR (AND X (NOT (NOT N))) (NOT S))))))) (OR (AND
(NOT (NOT N)) (NOT (OR N X))) (AND (AND (NOT W) (NOT X))
(NOT E)))).
```

Figure 14.13 is the histogram for generation 10.

The question arises as to whether the above S-expression, which was genetically bred using $16,384 = 2^{14}$ temporal sequence steps, is generalizable to other numbers of steps. When we retested the genetically produced randomizer over $65,536 = 2^{16}$ steps, we got an even better value of entropy: 6.998 bits (as compared to the original 6.995).

Table 14.8 shows the rule number and entropy for six selected genetically discovered high-entropy rules for a two-dimensional cellular automaton. For example, line A of this table shows the best-of-generation individual with entropy of 6.995 for generation 10 of the run described above. The S-expression for this rule is equivalent to rule number 2,857,758,96010 in the numbering scheme for two-dimensional cellular automata used in Toffoli and Margolis (1987). In this numbering scheme, the bits are presented in the order EWSNX and the inputs are taken starting with 00000 (i.e., the opposite to the order employed for one-dimensional cellular automata described in section 14.2). The decimal and hexadecimal identifications of each rule are shown in columns 2 and 3 of this table and the entropy is shown in column 4.

Table 14.8 Selected high-entropy rules for the two-dimensional cellular automaton problem.

	Rule number in decimal notation	Rule number in hexadecimal notation	Entropy
A	2,857,758,960	AA55F0F0	6.995
B	4,042,268,190	F0F01E1E	6.997
C	3,435,935,286	CCCC3636	6.997
D	4,027,577,610	F00FF50A	6.997
E	3,435,947,622	CCCC6666	6.995
F	3,140,699,340	BB3344CC	6.995

Table 14.9 Truth table for selected genetically produced high-entropy rules for the two-dimensional cellular automaton problem.

E	W	S	N	X	A	B	C	D	E	F
0	0	0	0	0	1	1	1	1	1	1
0	0	0	0	1	0	1	1	1	1	0
0	0	0	1	0	1	1	0	1	1	1
0	0	0	1	1	0	1	0	1	1	1
0	0	1	0	0	1	0	1	0	0	1
0	0	1	0	1	0	0	1	0	0	0
0	0	1	1	0	1	0	0	0	0	1
0	0	1	1	1	0	0	0	0	0	1
0	1	0	0	0	0	1	1	0	0	0
0	1	0	0	1	1	1	1	0	0	0
0	1	0	1	0	0	1	0	0	0	1
0	1	0	1	1	1	1	0	0	0	1
0	1	1	0	0	0	0	1	1	1	0
0	1	1	0	1	1	0	1	1	1	0
0	1	1	1	0	0	0	0	1	1	1
0	1	1	1	1	1	0	0	1	1	1
1	0	0	0	0	1	0	0	1	1	0
1	0	0	0	1	1	0	0	1	1	1
1	0	0	1	0	1	0	1	1	1	0
1	0	0	1	1	1	1	1	1	1	0
1	0	1	0	0	0	1	0	0	0	0
1	0	1	0	1	0	1	1	1	1	1
1	0	1	1	0	0	1	1	0	0	0
1	0	1	1	1	0	0	0	1	1	0
1	1	0	0	0	1	0	0	0	0	1
1	1	0	0	1	1	0	0	0	0	1
1	1	0	1	0	1	0	1	0	0	0
1	1	0	1	1	1	1	1	0	0	0
1	1	1	0	0	0	1	0	1	1	1
1	1	1	0	1	0	1	1	0	0	1
1	1	1	1	0	0	1	1	1	1	0
1	1	1	1	1	0	0	0	0	0	0

Table 14.9 is the truth table for these same six genetically discovered high-entropy rules for a two-dimensional cellular automaton. The first five columns of this table present the specific combination of inputs in the order E, W, S, N, and X. The next six columns show the value of the six rules for each of the 32 combinations of values of the inputs.

Interestingly, rule E in this table (i.e., rule 3,435,947,622) was produced on two different runs (out of 11 runs that produced rules with entropy of 6.995 or better). The S-expression obtained on one of those two runs was

```
(NOT (AND (OR (AND (OR (OR (AND (OR (OR (OR S (OR (OR W
(NOT E)) N)) N)) N) N) (AND (OR (OR (OR (OR (AND (OR W N)
(NOT E)) (NOT (NOT X))) (AND S X)) (NOT (NOT X))) (AND S
X)) (NOT (NOT (AND (OR W N) (NOT E)))))) (NOT (NOT X)))
(AND S X)) (NOT (NOT N))) (NOT (OR (OR X N) (NOT E))))
(OR (AND (NOT (OR (OR W (NOT (NOT X))) N)) (OR (OR (AND
(OR (OR W (NOT (NOT X))) N) (AND S X)) (AND (AND S S) (OR
(OR (AND (OR W N) (NOT E)) (NOT (NOT X))) (AND S X))))
(NOT (OR (AND (AND (OR (AND S X) N) (AND S X)) (NOT E))
(AND (AND S S) (OR (OR W (OR W W)) N))))))) (OR (OR W (OR
W W)) N)))).
```

15 Evolution of Strategy

The problem of discovering a strategy for playing a game is an important problem in game theory; however, relatively few techniques are available for the discovery of strategies.

In a game, two or more independently acting players make choices (moves) and receive payoffs based on those choices.

A strategy for a given player in a game is a way of specifying what choice the player is to make at every point in the game from the set of allowable choices at that point, given all the information that is available to the player at that point.

The problem of discovering a strategy for playing a game can be viewed as requiring the discovery of a computer program. Depending on the game, the desired computer program takes as its input(s) either the entire history of past moves in the game or the current state of the game. The desired computer program then produces the next move as its output.

15.1 A DISCRETE GAME

Consider the discrete 32-outcome game whose game tree is presented in extensive form in figure 15.1.

This game is a two-person, competitive, zero-sum game in which the players make alternating moves. On each move, a player can choose to go L (left) or R (right). Each internal point of this tree is labeled with the player who must move. Each line is labeled with the choice (either L or R) made by the moving player. Each endpoint of the tree is labeled with the payoff (to player X). After player X has made three moves and player O has made two moves, player X receives (and player O pays out) the particular payoff shown at the particular endpoint of the game tree.

Since this 32-outcome discrete game is a game of complete information, each player has access to complete information about his opponent's previous moves and his own previous moves. This information is contained in four variables XM1 (X's move 1), OM1 (O's move 1), XM2 (X's move 2), and OM2 (O's move 2). These variables each assume one of three possible values: L (left),R (right), or U (undefined). A variable is undefined (U) prior to the time when the

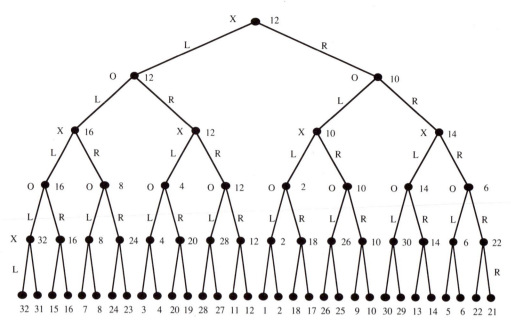

Figure 15.1 Game tree for 32-outcome discrete game.

move to which it refers has been made. Thus, at the beginning of the game, all four variables are undefined. The particular variables that are defined and undefined at a particular time can be used to indicate the point to which play has progressed in the game. For example, if both players have moved once, XM1 and OM1 are both defined (each being either L or R) but the other two variables (XM2, and OM2) are still undefined (i.e., have the value U).

A strategy for a particular player in a game specifies which choice that player is to make for every possible situation that may arise for that player. For this particular game, a strategy for player X must specify his first move if the game is just beginning. Second, a strategy for player X must specify his second move if player O has already made exactly one move. Third, a strategy for player X must specify his third move if player O has already made exactly two moves.

Since player X moves first, his first move is not conditioned on any previous move. But player X's second move will depend on player O's first move (i.e., OM1), and in general it will also depend on his own first move (XM1). Similarly, player X's third move will depend on player O's first two moves and, in general, his own first two moves.

Similarly, a strategy for player O must specify what choice player O is to make for every possible situation that may arise for player O.

A strategy is a computer program whose inputs are the relevant historical variables (XM1, OM1, XM2, and OM2) and whose output is a move (L or R) for the player involved.

The testing functions CXM1, COM1, CXM2, and COM2 provide the ability to test each historical variable (XM1, OM1, XM2, and OM2) that is relevant to deciding a player's move. Each of these functions is a specialized form of the CASE function in LISP. In particular, for example, the function CXM1 has three arguments. It evaluates its first argument if XM1 (X's move 1) is undefined; it evaluates its second argument if XM1 is L (Left); and it evaluates its third argument if XM1 is R (Right). The functions CXM2, COM1, and COM2 are similarly defined.

The terminal set for this problem is

T = {L, R}.

The function set for this problem is

F = {CXM1, COM1, CXM2, COM2},

each taking three arguments.

A typical S-expression for this problem therefore consists of a composition of the four testing functions just described and the two terminals L or R. The value returned by such an S-expression at a given time during the play of the game is the terminal (L or R) found at the endpoint of the tree that is reached by virtue of the actual moves that have been made in the game at that time.

The raw fitness of a particular strategy for a particular player is the sum of the payoffs received when that strategy is played against all possible sequences of combinations of moves by the opposing player. The two players of this particular game make different numbers of moves.

Thus, when we compute the fitness of an X strategy, we must test the X strategy against all four possible combinations of O moves, namely O choosing L or R for moves 1 and 2. Similarly, when we compute the fitness of an O strategy, we must test it against all eight possible combinations of X moves, namely X choosing L or R for moves 1, 2, and 3.

When two minimax strategies are played against each other, the payoff is the value of this game (i.e., 12 for this particular game). A minimax strategy takes advantage of non-minimax play by the other player.

A hit for this problem is the number of fitness cases (out of four for player X or eight for player O) where the strategy being tested achieves a payoff at least as good as that achieved by the minimax strategy.

This problem is not a difficult problem. It is presented here to lay the groundwork for solving this same problem using co-evolution (chapter 16) and for the purpose of illustrating the discovery of game strategies from the historical sequence of moves in the game (as opposed to the current state of the game).

Table 15.1 summarizes the key features of the problem for evolving a minimax strategy for player X for the discrete 32-outcome game. The corresponding table for player O would be identical except that the payoffs to player O are involved and except that there are eight fitness cases for player O.

We now proceed to evolve a game playing strategy for player X for this game.

Table 15.1 Tableau for problem of finding minimax strategy for the discrete 32-outcome game.

Objective:	Find the minimax strategy for playing a discrete 32-outcome game in extensive form for player X.
Terminal set:	L, R.
Function set:	CXM1, COM1, CXM2, COM2.
Fitness cases:	For player X, the fitness cases consist of the four possible combinations of O moves, namely O choosing L or R for moves 1 and 2.
Raw fitness:	The sum, over the four fitness cases, of the payoffs to player X.
Standardized fitness:	The maximum sum (i.e., 32 times 4) minus raw fitness.
Hits:	Number of fitness cases for which player X receives a payoff of at least as good as the minimax strategy.
Wrapper:	None.
Parameters:	$M = 500. G = 51.$
Success predicate:	An S-expression scores 4 hits.

In one run, the best-of-generation individual game playing strategy for player X in generation 6 had a raw fitness of 88 and scored four hits:

```
(COM2 (COM1 (COM1 L (CXM2 R (COM2 L L L)
                          (CXM1 L R L))
                  (CXM1 L L R)) L R)
      L (COM1 L R R)).
```

This strategy for player X simplifies to

```
(COM2 (COM1 L L R) L R).
```

Note that this strategy for player X is a composition of the four functions (CXM1, COM1, CXM2, COM2) and two terminals (L and R) and that it returns a value of either L or R.

The interpretation of this best-of-run strategy for player X is as follows. If both OM2 (O's move 2) and OM1 (O's move 1) are undefined (U), it must be player X's first move. That is, we are at the beginning of the game (i.e., the root of the game tree). In this situation, the first argument of the COM1 function embedded inside the COM2 function of this strategy specifies that player X is to move L. The left move by player X at the beginning of the game is player X's minimax move because it takes the game to a point with a minimax value of 12 (to player X) rather than to a point with a minimax value of only 10.

If OM2 (O's move 2) is undefined but OM1 is defined, it must be player X's second move. In this situation, this best-of-run strategy specifies that player X moves L if OM1 (O's move 1) was L and player X moves R if OM1 was R. If OM1 (O's move 1) was L, player O has moved to a point with a minimax value of 16. Player X should then move L (rather than R) because that move will take the game to a point with a minimax value of 16 (rather than 8). If OM1 was R, player O has moved to a point with minimax value 12. This move is better for O than moving L. Player X should then move R (rather than L) because that move will take the game to a point with a minimax value of 12 (rather than 4).

If both OM1 and OM2 are defined, it must be player X's third move. If OM2 was L, player X can either choose between a payoff of 32 or 31 or between a payoff of 28 or 27. In either case, player X moves L. If OM2 was R, player X can choose between a payoff of 15 or 16 or between a payoff of 11 or 12. In either case, player X moves R. In this situation, this best-of-run S-expression specifies that player X moves L if OM2 (O's move 2) was L and player X moves R if OM2 was R.

If player O has been playing his minimax strategy, this best-of-run S-expression for player X will cause the game to finish at the endpoint with the payoff of 12 to player X. However, if player O was not playing his minimax strategy, this strategy will cause the game to finish with a payoff of 32, 16, or 28 for player X. The total of 12, 32, 16, and 28 is 88. The attainment of these four values for player X (each at least as good as the minimax value of 12) constitutes four hits for player X.

We used a similar method to evolve a game playing strategy for player O for this game.

In one run, the best-of-generation individual strategy for player O in generation 9 had a raw fitness of 52 and scored eight hits and was, in fact, the minimax strategy for player O:

```
(CXM2 (CXM1 L (COM1 R L L) L) (COM1 R L (CXM2 L L R))
     (COM1 L R (CXM2 R (COM1 L L R) (COM1 R L R)))).
```

This strategy for player O simplifies to

```
(CXM2 (CXM1 $ R L) L R),
```

where the $ denotes a portion of an S-expression that is inaccessible by virtue of unsatisfiable conditions. See also Koza 1991a.

15.2 A DIFFERENTIAL PURSUER-EVADER GAME

As a second illustration of genetic programming involving games, consider a differential pursuer-evader game. In the "game of simple pursuit" described in Isaacs' *Differential Games* (1965), the goal is to find a minimax strategy for one player when playing against a minimax opponent.

This differential pursuer-evader game is a two-person, competitive, zero-sum, simultaneous-move, complete-information game in which a fast pursuing player P is trying to capture a slower evading player E. The choice available

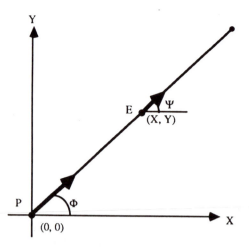

Figure 15.2 Pursuer P and Evader E.

to a player at a given moment consists of choosing a direction (angle) in which to travel. In this game, the players may travel anywhere in a plane and both players may instantaneously change direction without restriction. Each player travels at a constant speed, and the pursuing player's speed w_p (1.0) is greater than the evading player's speed w_e (0.67).

The state variables of the game are x_p, y_p, x_e, and y_e representing the coordinate positions (x_p, y_p) and (x_e, y_e) of the pursuer P and evader E in the plane.

In this section, we work with the current state of the game, rather than the historical sequence of previous moves in the game (as we did in section 15.1), in order to find the minimax strategy.

Figure 15.2 shows the pursuer and the evader. At each time step, both players know the positions (state variables) of both players. The choice for each player is to select a value of his control variable (i.e., the angular direction in which to travel). The pursuer's control variable is the angle ϕ (from 0 to 2π radians), and the evader's control variable is the angle ψ. The players choose their respective control variables simultaneously. In the figure, the evader's angle ψ is shown equal to the pursuer's angle ϕ.

The analysis of this game can be simplified by reducing the number of state variables from four to two (Isaacs 1965). This state reduction is accomplished by simply viewing the pursuer P as being at the origin point (0, 0) of a new coordinate system at all times and then viewing the evader E as being at position (x, y) in this new coordinate system. The two numbers x and y representing the position (x, y) of the evader E thus become the two reduced state variables of the game. Whenever the pursuer P travels in a particular direction, the coordinate system is immediately adjusted so that the pursuer is repositioned to the origin (0, 0). The position (x, y) of the evader is then adjusted to reflect the travel of the pursuer.

The state-transition equations for the evader E are

$$x(t + 1) = x(t) + w_e \cos \psi - w_p \cos \phi,$$

$$y(t + 1) = y(t) + w_e \sin \psi - w_p \sin \phi.$$

We use a set of 20 fitness cases consisting of random initial condition positions (x_i, y_i) for the evader. Each initial condition value of x_i and y_i lies between -5.0 and $+5.0$. We regard the pursuer as having captured the evader when the pursuer gets to within a small capture radius $\varepsilon = 0.5$ of the evader.

The payoff for a given player is measured by time. The payoff for the pursuer P is the total time it takes to capture the evader E over all the initial condition cases (i.e., fitness cases). The pursuer tries to minimize the time to capture. The payoff for the evader is the total time of survival for E. The evader tries to maximize this time of survival.

A maximum allowed time of 100 time steps is established so that if a particular pursuer strategy has not made the capture within that amount of time, that maximum time becomes the payoff for that particular fitness case and that particular strategy.

The problem is to find the strategy for choosing the control variable of the pursuer so as to minimize the total time to capture for any set of fitness cases when playing against an optimal evader.

For this game, the best strategy for the pursuer P at any given time step is to chase the evader E in the direction of the straight line currently connecting the pursuer to the evader. And, for this game, the best strategy for the evader E is to race away from the pursuer in the direction of the straight line connecting the pursuer to the evader.

In comparison, the worst strategy for the pursuer P is to avoid the evader E by racing away from the evader in the direction precisely opposite to the straight line currently connecting the pursuer to the evader. The worst strategy for the evader E is to race toward the pursuer P along this same straight line.

If the evader chooses some action other than the strategy of racing away from the pursuer in the direction of the straight line connecting the pursuer to the evader (as shown in figure 15.3), the evader will survive for less time than if he follows his best strategy. If the evader initially chooses a suboptimal direction and then belatedly chooses the optimal direction, his time of survival is still less than if he had chosen the optimal direction from the beginning.

The situation is symmetric in that if the pursuer does not chase after the evader E along the straight line, he fails to minimize the time to capture.

The value of the game is the payoff (time) such that, no matter what the evader does, the evader cannot hold out for longer than this amount of time. If the evader does anything other than direct fleeing, his survival time is a shorter. Conversely, no matter what the pursuer does, the pursuer P cannot capture an optimal evader E in less than that amount of time. And, if the pursuer does anything other than direct pursuit, the evader can remain at large for a longer amount of time.

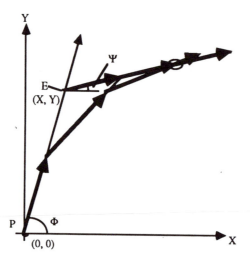

Figure 15.3 Evader E choosing a suboptimal evasion strategy.

We start by evolving a minimax pursuer. In doing this, each individual in the population of pursuing individuals is tested against one minimax evader. The optimal evader travels with the established constant evader speed w_e in the angular direction specified by the two argument Arctangent function (which is able to return an angle in the correct quadrant since it can examine the signs of the two arguments).

We later, separately, evolve a minimax evader. Each individual in the population of evading individuals is tested against the minimax pursuer.

The terminal set for this problem consists of the two state variables X and Y representing the position of the evader E in the plane in a reduced coordinate system where the pursuer is always positioned (or repositioned) at the origin and the ephemeral random floating-point constant $\Re$ ranging between -1.000 and $+1.000$ as shown below:

T = {X, Y, $\Re$}.

The function set for this problem is

F = {+, -, *, %, EXP, IFLTZ},

taking two, two, two, two, one, and three arguments, respectively. Note that we did not include any trigonometric or inverse trigonometric function in this function set. Instead, we included the four arithmetic functions, the exponential function, and the three argument conditional operation IFLTZ (If Less Than Zero) for making decisions.

For any given S-expression composed of functions from this function set and terminals from this terminal set and any given current position (x, y) of the pursuer, the S-expression will evaluate to a number that provides the new direction of motion, in radians, for the pursuer.

The fitness cases for this problem consist of 20 initial condition points (x, y) in a square whose opposite corners are $(-5.0, -5.0)$ and $(+5.0, +5.0)$. The

Table 15.2 Tableau for the differential pursuer-evader game.

Objective:	Find the minimax strategy for the pursuer in a differential pursuer-evader game of simple pursuit.
Terminal set:	X, Y, $\Re$, where the ephemeral random constant $\Re$ ranges over -1.000 and $+1.000$.
Function set:	+, −, *, %, EXP, IFLTZ.
Fitness cases:	20 initial conditions consisting of the initial condition points (x, y) for the Evader.
Raw fitness:	The time required to capture the Evader, averaged over the 20 fitness cases.
Standardized fitness:	Same as raw fitness for this problem.
Hits:	Number of fitness cases that do not time out.
Wrapper:	None.
Parameters:	$M = 500.\ G = 51.$
Success predicate:	None.

raw fitness for this problem is the average time to capture for each of the fitness cases. The shorter the time, the better.

As one progresses from generation to generation, the population of pursuing individuals typically improves. In early generations, the best pursuing individual in the population can capture the evader in only a fraction of the 20 fitness cases within the allotted time. These individuals typically do not move in the 100%-efficient straight line called for by the Arctangent strategy, but instead follow a leisurely curved nonoptimal trajectory. Then, after additional generations, the best pursuing individuals in the population can capture the evader in a larger fraction of the fitness cases and within a shorter amount of time. Typically, these partially effective pursuers are effective in some identifiable fraction of the plane or at some identifiable range of distances, but ineffective in other parts of the plane or at other distances.

Table 15.2 summarizes the key features of the problem of finding a minimax strategy for the pursuer in the differential pursuer-evader game. The corresponding table for finding the minimax strategy for the evader would be identical except that the evader is trying to maximize time and that the evader scores a hit if it evades the pursuer for at least the minimax evasion time.

In one run, the population improved to the point where the best-of-generation individual from generation 11 was able to capture the evader in 20 of the 20 fitness cases; however, its time was 196% of the optimal time.

Then, after an additional 37 generations, a pursuer strategy emerged in generation 48 that resulted in the capture of the evader for all 20 of the fitness cases in 100.61% of optimal time. This best-of-run S-expression is shown below:

```
(% (+ (IFLTZ (* X 0.6370001) (+ X X) (IFLTZ -0.674 Y Y))
(IFLTZ X (+ X Y) (* (IFLTZ (* X 0.6370001) (IFLTZ (* X X)
(- X (EXP (- (% Y Y) (IFLTZ (EXP (* Y Y)) (* (- X
0.12900007) -0.029999971) (+ -0.796 X))))) Y) (IFLTZ (EXP
(- (% (IFLTZ (* X 0.6370001) (+ X X) (- Y 0.12900007)) (-
-0.992 Y)) (IFLTZ (IFLTZ Y Y X) Y X))) (+ (% Y Y) (IFLTZ
X (+ X Y) (+ (IFLTZ (* X 0.6370001) (* Y Y) 0.018000007)
(IFLTZ X (+ X Y) (% (IFLTZ Y Y X) (+ -0.617 X)))))) Y))
-0.029999971))) (- X (* (% (* (IFLTZ (* X 0.6370001) (+ X
X) (IFLTZ (* X X) (- X (EXP (- (% Y Y) (* X X)))) Y)) (-
Y (- X (% Y 0.8460001)))) X) -0.029999971))).
```

This best-of-run S-expression closely matches the desired Arctangent behavior. A near-optimal evader has been similarly evolved using an optimal
pursuer (i.e., the Arctangent strategy).

16 Co-Evolution

In the previous chapter, we genetically bred the strategy for one player in a game by testing each individual in the evolving population of strategies against the minimax strategy for the opposing player or against an exhaustive set of combinations of choices by the opposing player. However, in game theory and in practice, one almost never has *a priori* access to a minimax strategy for the opposing player or the ability to perform an exhaustive test. Since exhaustive testing is practical only for very small games, one faces a situation where genetically breeding a minimax strategy for one player requires already having the minimax strategy for the other player. Players of checkers or chess know that it is difficult for a new player to learn to play well if he does not have the advantage of playing against a reasonably competent player.

The evolutionary process in nature is sometimes described as if one population of individuals is alone in adapting to a fixed environment; however, this description is only a first order approximation to the actual situation. The environment is actually a composite consisting of both the physical environment (which may be relatively unchanging) and other independently acting biological populations of individuals which are simultaneously actively adapting to their environment. As Darwin observed in *On the Origin of Species by Means of Natural Selection* (1859), "Let it be borne in mind how infinitely complex and close-fitting are the mutual relations of all organic beings to each other and to their physical conditions of life." The actions of each of these other independently acting biological populations (species) usually affect all the other coexisting species. In other words, the environment of a given species includes all the other species that contemporaneously occupy the physical environment and which are simultaneously trying to survive. In biology, the term *co-evolution* is sometimes used to reflect the fact that all species are simultaneously co-evolving in a given physical environment.

A biological example presented by Holland (1990) illustrates the point. A given species of plant may be faced with an environment containing insects that like to eat it. To defend against its predators (and increase its probability of survival in the environment), the plant may, over a period of time, evolve a tough exterior that makes it difficult for the insect to eat it. But, as time passes, the insect may retaliate by evolving a stronger jaw so that the insect population can continue to feed on the plant (and increase its probability of survival in the environment). Then, over an additional period of time, the plant may evolve a poison to help defend itself further against the insects. The insect may subsequently evolve a digestive enzyme that negates the effect of the poison so that the insect population can continue to feed on the plant.

In effect, both the plant and the insects get better and better at their respective defensive and offensive roles in this "biological arms race." Each species changes in response to the actions of the other (Dawkins 1987).

In the basic genetic algorithm described by Holland (1975), a population of individuals attempts to adapt to a fixed environment. The individuals in the population are fixed-length character strings (typically binary strings) that are encoded to represent the problem in some way. In the basic genetic algorithm, the performance of the individuals in the population is measured using a fitness measure which is, in effect, the environment for the population. Over a period of many generations, the genetic algorithm causes the individuals in the population to adapt in a direction that is dictated by the fitness measure (that is, the environment).

In his ECHO system, Holland (1990, 1992) used co-evolution along with a conventional genetic algorithm for exploring the co-evolution of artificial organisms in a "miniature world." Each of the diverse artificial organisms is described by a character string (chromosome). The environment of each organism includes all other organisms.

John Miller (1988, 1989) used co-evolution along with a genetic algorithm to evolve a finite-state automaton as the strategy for playing the repeated prisoner's dilemma game. Miller used a fixed-length character string of 148 binary digits to represent a finite automaton with 16 states. Each automaton, in turn, represented a complete strategy by which to play the game. That is, the automaton specified what move the player was to make for any sequence of previous moves by both players in the game. Miller then used co-evolution to evolve strategies.

Miller's *co-evolutionary* approach to the repeated prisoner's dilemma using the conventional genetic algorithm contrasts with Axelrod's *evolutionary* approach (1984, 1987) to the repeated prisoner's dilemma using the conventional genetic algorithm. Axelrod measured the performance of a particular strategy by playing it against a fixed suite of eight superior opposing computer programs which he had selected from those entered into an international programming tournament for the repeated prisoner's dilemma game. In Axelrod's work, fitness was a weighted mix of the results of playing the eight selected opposing computer programs. In other words, the eight selected computer programs served as the environment for evolving Axelrod's fixed-length character strings.

John Maynard Smith (1986, 1989) discussed co-evolution in connection with discovering strategies for games, but without using genetic algorithms. See also Hillis 1990, 1991.

16.1 CO-EVOLUTION OF A GAME-PLAYING STRATEGY

In co-evolution, there are two (or more) populations of individuals. The environment for the first population consists of the second population. And, conversely, the environment for the second population consists of the first population.

The co-evolutionary process typically starts with both populations being highly unfit. Then, the first population tries to adapt to the environment consisting of the second population. Simultaneously, the second population tries to adapt to the environment consisting of the first population.

This process is carried out by testing the performance of each individual in the first population against each individual (or a sampling of individuals) from the second population. The average performance observed is called the *relative fitness* of that individual, because it represents the performance of that individual relative to the environment consisting of the entire second population. Then, each individual in the second population is tested against each individual (or a sampling of individuals) from the first population. Relative fitness comes from the actual testing of individuals against some or all of the individuals in an opposing population.

Note that this measurement of relative fitness for an individual in co-evolution is not an absolute measure of fitness against an optimal opponent, but merely a relative measure when the individual is tested against the current opposing population. If one population contains boxers who throw only left punches, then an individual whose defensive repertoire contains only of defenses against left punches will have high relative fitness. But this individual would have low absolute fitness when tested against any opponent who knows how to throw both left punches and right punches.

Even when both initial populations are highly unfit (relatively and absolutely), the virtually inevitable variation of the initial random population will mean that some individuals have slightly better relative fitness than others. That means that some individuals in each population have somewhat better performance than others in dealing with the current opposing population.

The operations of crossover and reproduction (based on the Darwinian principle of survival and reproduction of the fittest) can then be separately applied to each population using the relative fitness of each individual in each separate population.

Over a period of time, both populations of individuals will tend to co-evolve and to rise to higher levels of performance as measured in terms of absolute fitness. Both populations do this without the aid of any externally supplied measure of absolute fitness serving as the environment. In the limiting case, both populations of individuals may evolve to a level of performance that equals the absolute optimal fitness. There is, of course, no guarantee that either population will co-evolve to absolute optimal fitness. Co-evolution is a self-organizing, mutually bootstrapping process that is driven only by relative fitness (and not by absolute fitness).

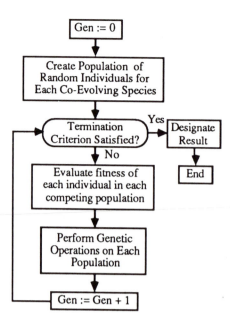

Figure 16.1 Flowchart for co-evolution.

Figure 16.1 shows a flowchart for co-evolution.

Figure 16.2 is a detailed flowchart of the box labeled "Evaluate fitness of each individual in each competing population" in figure 16.1.

We now illustrate the process of co-evolution by means of genetic programming to simultaneously discover minimax strategies for both players in the same discrete two-person 32-outcome game represented by the game tree in extensive form shown in figure 15.1.

In co-evolution, we cannot proceed as we did in the previous chapter. We do not have access to the minimax opponent to train the population, as we did with the differential pursuer-evader game, nor do we have the ability to exhaustively test each possible combination of choices by the opposing player as we did with the 32-outcome discrete game. Instead, we must breed both populations of players simultaneously. That is, we must simultaneously co-evolve strategies for both players.

Both populations start as random compositions of the same functions and terminals used in the 32-outcome discrete game.

In co-evolution, the relative fitness of a particular strategy in a particular population is the average of the payoffs that the strategy receives when it is played against fitness cases consisting of each strategy in the opposing population of strategies. Note that the particular strategy is played only once against each strategy in the opposing population. When a particular strategy from the first population is tested against a particular strategy from the opposing population, the outcome is completely determined because, by definition, a strategy specifies a choice for all possible situations. Note that we use the average payoff, rather than the sum of the payoffs, for this particular problem because we envision sampling for larger problems of this type.

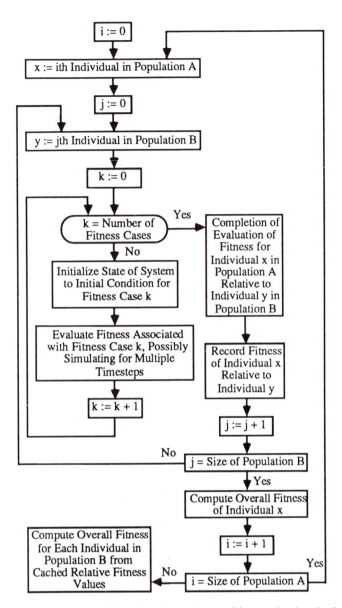

Figure 16.2 Detailed flowchart for evaluation of fitness of each individual in each competing population.

In co-evolution, raw fitness is relative fitness. Since raw fitness is defined here in terms of averages, the maximum is 32. Note that the testing of four or eight combinations of move sequences that we used in section 15.1 does not occur in the computation for raw fitness here.

The standardized fitness of an individual strategy is the maximum possible value of raw fitness minus the raw fitness for that strategy.

Hits are the number of fitness cases for which the payoff to an individual strategy equals or exceeds the value of the game (i.e., the result of playing two minimax strategies against each other).

When the two minimax strategies are played against each other, the payoff is the value of this game (i.e., 12 for this game).

The absolute fitness of a strategy is used solely for monitoring and descriptive purposes and plays no role in the actual co-evolutionary process. The *absolute fitness* of a particular strategy for a particular player in a game is the payoff received when that strategy is played against the minimax strategy for the opponent. A minimax strategy takes advantage of non-minimax play by the other player.

Table 16.1 summarizes the key features of the problem of co-evolving strategies for the discrete 32-outcome game.

In one run involving co-evolution, the individual strategy for player X in generation 0 with the best relative fitness was

```
(COM1 L (COM2 (CXM1 (CXM2 R (CXM2 R R R) (CXM2 R L R)) L
(CXM2 L R (COM2 R R R))) (COM1 R (COM2 (CXM2 L R L) (COM2
R L L) R) (COM2 (COM1 R R L) (CXM1 R L R) (CXM1 R L L)))
```

Table 16.1 Tableau for the problem of co-evolving strategies for the discrete 32-outcome game.

Objective:	Simultaneously co-evolve the minimax strategy for playing a discrete 32-outcome game in extensive form for both player X and player O.
Terminal set:	L, R.
Function set:	CXM1, COM1, CXM2, COM2.
Fitness cases:	All 300 individuals in the opposing population.
Raw fitness:	The average, over fitness cases consisting of all the individuals in the opposing population, of the payoffs to the individual strategy.
Standardized fitness:	The maximum possible value of raw fitness minus the raw fitness of the individual.
Hits:	Number of fitness cases for which the payoff to an individual equals or exceeds the value of the game.
Wrapper:	None.
Parameters:	$M = 300$. $G = 51$.
Success predicate:	None.

```
(CXM1 (COM2 (CXM1 R L L) (CXM2 R R L) R) R (COM2 L R
(CXM1 L L L)))) R).
```

This simplifies to

```
(COM1 L (COM2 L L R) R).
```

This individual has relative fitness of 10.08.

The individual in the initial random population for player O with the best relative fitness was an equally complex expression. It simplifies to

```
(CXM2 R (CXM1 $ L R) (CXM1 $ R L)),
```

where $ denotes a portion of an S-expression which is inaccessible by virtue of unsatisfiable conditions. This individual has relative fitness of 7.57.

Neither the best X individual nor the best O individual from generation 0 reached maximal absolute fitness.

The values of relative fitness for the relative best X individual and the relative best O individual from generation 0 (i.e., 10.08 and 7.57) are each computed by averaging the payoff from the interaction of the individual involved with all 300 individual strategies in the current opposing population.

In generation 1, the individual strategy for player X with the best relative fitness had relative fitness of 11.28. This individual X strategy is still not a minimax strategy. It does not have the maximal absolute fitness. In generation 1, the best individual O strategy,

```
(CXM2 (CXM1 R R L) (CXM2 L L (CXM2 R L R)) R),
```

attained relative fitness of 7.18. This O strategy simplifies to

```
(CXM2 (CXM1 $ R L) L R).
```

This best-of-generation individual O strategy from generation 1 is, in fact, a minimax strategy for player O. If it were played against the minimax X strategy, it would score 12 (i.e., the value of the game). This one O individual was the first such O individual to attain this level of performance during this run. In co-evolution, the algorithm does not know that this individual is a minimax strategy for player O. The run merely continues.

Figure 16.3 graphically depicts the best-of-generation S-expression for player O from generation 1.

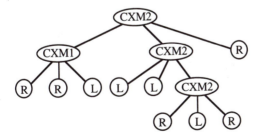

Figure 16.3 Minimax O strategy from generation 1.

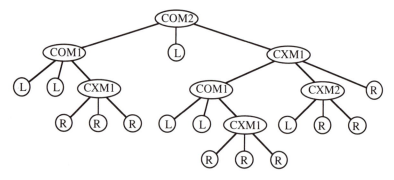

Figure 16.4 Minimax X strategy from generation 14.

Between generations 2 and 14, the number of individuals in the O population equivalent to the minimax O strategy was 2, 7, 17, 28, 35, 40, 50, 64, 73, 83, 93, 98, and 107, respectively. That is, programs equivalent to the minimax O strategy began to dominate the O population.

In generation 14, the individual strategy for player X with the best relative fitness had a relative fitness of 18.11. This individual X strategy was

```
(COM2 (COM1 L L (CXM1 R R R))
      L
      (CXM1 (COM1 L L (CXM1 R R R))
            (CXM2 L R R) R)).
```

This strategy is shown in figure 16.4 as a tree.
This X strategy simplifies to

```
(COM2 (COM1 L L R) L R).
```

Although the algorithm does not know it, this best-of-generation individual X strategy from generation 14 is, in fact, a minimax strategy for player X. If it were played against the minimax O strategy, it would score 12 (i.e., the value of the game).

Between generations 15 and 29, the number of individuals in the X population equivalent to the minimax X strategy was 3, 4, 8, 11, 10, 9, 13, 21, 24, 29, 43, 32, 52, 48, and 50, respectively. That is, programs equivalent to the minimax X strategy began to dominate the X population. Meanwhile, the O population became even more dominated by programs equivalent to the O minimax strategy.

By generation 38, the number of O individuals in the population reaching maximal absolute fitness reached 188 (almost two-thirds of the population) and the number of X individuals reaching maximal absolute fitness reached 74 (about a quarter). That is, by generation 38, the minimax strategies for both players were becoming dominant.

Interestingly, these 74 individual X strategies had relative fitness of 19.11 and the 188 individual O strategies had relative fitness of 10.47. Neither of these values equals 12, because the other population is not fully converged to its minimax strategy. See also Koza 1991c and Koza and Rice 1990.

In summary, we have seen the discovery, via co-evolution, of the minimax strategies for both players in the 32-outcome discrete game. This mutually bootstrapping process found the minimax strategies for both players without using knowledge of the minimax strategy (i.e., any *a priori* knowledge of the game) for either player.

17 Evolution of Classification

Learning patterns that discriminate among problem solving choices is one approach to problem solving. The patterns that are learned may be expressed in many ways, including decision trees, sets of production rules (Michalski 1983), formal grammars, or mathematical equations.

17.1 DECISION-TREE INDUCTION

One approach to classification and pattern recognition involves the construction of a decision tree. Genetic programming can be used to inductively discover decision trees for classification and pattern recognition.

ID3 (Quinlan 1986) is a hierarchical classification system for inducing a decision tree from a finite number of examples or training cases.

In ID3 (and its many subsequent variations), the goal is to assign each object in a universe of objects to a class. Each object in the universe is described in terms of various attributes.

The ID3 system is presented with a set of training cases. A training case consists of the attributes of a particular object and the class to which it belongs. ID3 then generates a decision tree that can correctly reclassify any particular previously seen object, and, more important, ID3 can very often generalize and correctly classify a new object into its correct class.

The external points (leaves) of the decision tree produced by ID3 are labeled with the class names. Each internal point of the decision tree is labeled with an attribute test. One branch radiates downward from each such internal point of the tree for each possible outcome of the attribute test.

Quinlan (1986) presented a simple illustrative example of the ID3 hierarchical classification system for inducing a decision tree. In this example, the set of training cases consisted of 14 objects representing characteristics of Saturday mornings. Each object in Quinlan's illustrative example belongs to one of two classes, namely positive (class 1) and negative (class 0).

Each object has four attributes, namely `temperature`, `humidity`, `outlook`, and `windy`. The attribute of `temperature`, for example, can assume the attribute value `hot`, `mild`, or `cool`. The attribute of `humidity` can assume the attribute value of `high` or `normal`. The attribute of `outlook` can assume

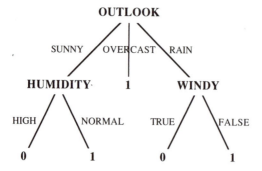

Figure 17.1 Decision tree for classifying Saturday mornings into either class 0 or class 1.

the attribute value of sunny, overcast, or raining. The attribute of windy can assume the attribute value of true or false.

The process of classification of an object by means of a decision tree begins by applying the attribute test found at the root (top) of the decision tree. The outcome of an attribute test determines which branch of the decision tree is to be followed. The process continues for each internal point of the tree that is encountered. When this process leads to an external point of the tree, the process terminates. The label of that endpoint of the decision tree is the result (i.e., the name of a class).

Figure 17.1 shows Quinlan's example of a decision tree that successfully classifies the 14 training cases.

For example, if the OUTLOOK of a particular object is sunny and if the HUMIDITY of that object is high, then that object is classified into class 0 (negative). On the other hand, if the OUTLOOK of the object is overcast, then that attribute alone causes the object to be classified into the class 1 (positive).

Throughout this book, we have discussed genetic programming in light of the five major steps for preparing to use it. There is a similar set of major preparatory steps associated with other adaptive and machine learning paradigms. For induction of a decision tree using ID3, there are six preparatory steps, namely determining

(1) the set of class names,

(2) the set of attribute-testing functions,

(3) the heuristic entropy-based fitness measure to be used,

(4) the examples (training cases) to be used,

(5) the values of the numerical parameters (i.e., branching factor) for controlling the run, and

(6) the criterion for designating a result and terminating a run.

We now proceed to apply genetic programming to Quinlan's illustrative example.

The terminal set is Quinlan's set of class names. Since there are two classes, the terminal set is

```
T = {0, 1}.
```

The function set is Quinlan's set of attribute tests. Each attribute-testing function has as many arguments as there are possible outcomes of that particular test. In particular, the function set F for this problem is

```
F = {TEMP, HUM, OUT, WIND},
```

taking three, two, three, and two arguments, respectively.

Each of these four attribute-testing functions operates much like the CASE statement in LISP. We obtain the function set by converting each of Quinlan's attributes into an attribute-testing function. Therefore, there are as many functions in our function set as there are attributes. For example, consider the attribute of temperature. This attribute can assume one of three possible values (hot, mild, or cool). Therefore, the TEMP function needed for genetic programming has three arguments and operates in such a way that if the temperature of the current object is hot, the function returns its first argument as its return value; if the current object has a temperature of mild, the function returns its second argument; and if the current object is cool, the function returns its third argument. Attribute-testing functions are similarly created for the attributes of humidity, outlook, and windy.

When an object is presented to the LISP S-expression (i.e., the decision tree), the function at the root of the tree tests the designated attribute of the object and then executes the particular argument designated by the outcome of the test. If the designated argument is a terminal, the function returns the class name. If the designated argument is another function, that particular function tests the designated attribute of the object and then executes the particular argument designated by the outcome of the test. In any event, the S-expression as a whole eventually returns a class name. The S-expression is a decision tree that classifies an object into one of the classes.

The fitness cases are Quinlan's 14 given training cases. The raw fitness of an S-expression is the number of training cases for which the S-expression returns the correct class, and it ranges from 0 to 14. Since a raw fitness of 14 corresponds to a perfect score, standardized fitness is the total number of training cases (i.e., 14) minus raw fitness.

Table 17.1 summarizes the key features of the problem of inducing a decision tree to classify the Saturday mornings from Quinlan's illustrative example.

In one run, the following S-expression emerged on generation 8:

```
(OUT (WIND 1 0) (WIND 1 1) (HUM 0 1)).
```

It scores the maximal value of raw fitness, namely 14 (i.e., it correctly classified all 14 training cases). Since (WIND 1 1) is equivalent to just the constant atom 1, this S-expression is equivalent to the decision tree shown in figure 17.2. See Koza 1991b.

Table 17.1 Tableau for induction of decision trees.

Objective:	Induce a decision tree that correctly classifies objects (Saturday mornings) with attributes into classes.
Terminal set:	The classes (0, 1).
Function set:	The attribute-testing functions TEMP, HUM, OUT, WIND.
Fitness cases:	The 14 training cases.
Raw fitness:	The number of training cases classified into the correct class.
Standardized fitness:	The total number of training cases (i.e., 14) minus raw fitness.
Hits:	Same as raw fitness for this problem.
Wrapper:	None.
Parameters:	$M = 500.\ G = 51.$
Success predicate:	An S-expression scores 14 hits.

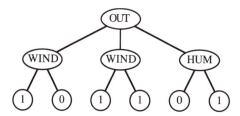

Figure 17.2 Genetically discovered S-expression found on generation 8 for classifying Saturday mornings.

17.2 GRAMMAR INDUCTION

The problem of grammar induction involves recognizing patterns existing in a sequence of data (Schalkoff 1992). This section demonstrates how to genetically breed a computer program that is capable of determining whether a given sequence of symbols is one of the sentences produced by some unknown grammar.

The specific example presented here is a simple artificial grammar that produces fixed-length sentences of length 5. We could present this simple example in the usual format of finding a computer program that determines whether each sentence in a set of separated sentences belongs to the language generated by the grammar. Instead, we present this problem in terms of a biological metaphor, namely the problem of exon identification arising from the analysis of the DNA constituting the genome of a biological organism (Mural, Mann, and Uberbacher 1991).

Four nucleiotide bases (i.e., A, C, G, and T) appear along the length of the DNA molecule. For humans, only about 1% to 2% of the 2,890,000,000 bases are actually translated into amino acids using the genetic code. The bases of DNA that are to be translated into amino acids lie in subsequences called *exons*, which are recognized and accepted by the messenger RNA (mRNA) molecule and transcribed (using a complementary code) onto the mRNA. The DNA subsequences that are to be skipped, called *introns*, are not accepted by the mRNA; they are not transcribed onto mRNA, and they are not expressed into proteins. Thus, the mRNA molecule acts as an acceptor (via the three-dimensional templates at its active sites) of certain subsequences produced by an unknown grammar.

This section presents an example involving a simple grammar where we genetically discover an S-expression that is capable of identifying the subsequences of length 5 that belong to the language from a long sample sequence of length 1,000 where the exons (i.e., subsequences to be accepted as belonging to the language) will occupy about 10% of the sequence. The alphabet will consist of the four letters A, C, G, and T.

An S-expression will identify exons by returning a True for each position of the given sequence which it believes to be an exon and by returning a NIL for each position which it believes to be an intron.

Processing proceeds from the beginning (i.e., left) of the given sequence of bases. An S-expression may examine a variable number of positions to the right of the current position under examination. If an S-expression identifies a subsequence of the base sequence as an exon, it will return a T for all the positions between the current position and the rightmost position it examined. The current position is then advanced to the first position of the sequence that has not yet been examined. However, if an S-expression does not identify the subsequence as an exon, it returns a NIL for the current position only, and then the position under examination is advanced to the right by one position.

There are four conditional operations for this problem:

- AIF returns T (True) if the current position of the sequence is adenine (A) and NIL otherwise.

- CIF returns T (True) if the current position of the sequence is cytosine (C) and NIL otherwise.

- GIF returns T (True) if the current position of the sequence is guanine (G) and NIL otherwise.

- TIF returns T (True) if the current position of the sequence is thymine (T) and NIL otherwise.

Therefore, the terminal set for this problem consists of the following four conditional operations:

T = { (AIF), (CIF), (GIF), (TIF), (MHG)}.

MHG advances the position of the sequence under examination to the right by one position and returns T. The function set for this problem contains the Boolean AND, OR, and NOT functions. That is, the function set for this problem is

F = {AND, OR, NOT},

taking two, two, and one arguments, respectively.

The fitness cases are the 1,000 positions of the given sequence of bases. Raw fitness is the sum, taken over the 1,000 fitness cases, of the Hamming distances (0 or 1) between the value returned by the S-expression and the correct classification of that position. Standardized fitness is 1,000 minus raw fitness. Note that for this particular problem, a misclassification of a 1 into class 0 has the same impact on the fitness measure as a misclassification of a 0 into class 1.

Table 17.2 summarizes the key features of the grammar problem involving exon identification.

For this example, an exon will always be of length 5 and begin with two leading A's and end with two trailing T's. The middle symbol of the sequence can be any letter.

In one run, on generation 0, the best-of-generation individual,

(AND (AIF) (AND (NOT (MHG)) (AND (MHG) (MHG)))),

scored 900 out of a possible 1,000 (merely by uniformly returning NIL).

On generation 35, the best-of-generation individual,

(AND (AND (OR (AND (AIF) (AIF)) (AND (AIF) (AIF))) (OR
(MHG) (OR (OR (OR (OR (GIF) (NOT (OR (MHG) (CIF))))
(GIF)) (AND (NOT (GIF)) (NOT (OR (NOT (AIF)) (MHG)))))
(OR (AIF) (NOT (OR (AIF) (AND (GIF) (AIF))))))))) (AND
(TIF) (OR (NOT (NOT (TIF))) (AND (NOT (MHG)) (NOT (NOT

Table 17.2 Tableau for grammar induction.

Objective:	Induce a decision procedure that will classify each symbol in a long sequence as to whether it is part of a subsequence that is accepted by an unknown grammar.
Terminal set:	(AIF), (CIF), (GIF), (TIF), (MHG).
Function set:	AND, OR, NOT.
Fitness cases:	A sequence of 1,000 nucleotide bases.
Raw fitness:	Sum, taken over the 1,000 positions of the given sequence of bases, of the Hamming distances (0 or 1) between the value returned by the S-expression and the correct classification of that position.
Standardized fitness:	Same as raw fitness for this problem.
Hits:	Same as raw fitness for this problem.
Wrapper:	None.
Parameters:	$M = 500$. $G = 51$.
Success predicate:	An S-expression scores 1,000 hits.

```
(OR (OR (NOT (TIF)) (GIF)) (OR (NOT (AIF)) (NOT (OR (AIF)
(AIF)))))))))))),
```

scored 1,000 out of a possible 1,000.

The classification performed by this best-of-run S-expression is shown below via a comparison of a small portion of an actual four-letter input sequence and the binary output produced by the S-expression:

```
GGTAAAACTTTTTCTGGGTTCCAATTTTTCGTCACTAGTTGTAAAGCTGA
00000111110000000000000111110000000000000000000000000

CGCACGGCGACTACAATCTTGGTTCAATGATGCGAAAAAAGTTTTGTGCA
00000000000000000000000000000000000000000111110000000

GCCCCGCCCATTAAATTTGTGGAATTGAACTTACACGCCCTGACTCTAGC
00000000000001111100000000000011111000000000000000000.
```

If we analyze this best-of-run S-expression (removing clauses that cannot be reached and performing obvious simplifications), we find that this best-of-run individual is a 100%-correct solution to the problem of identifying whether a particular sequence of symbols belongs to an unknown grammar.

17.3 INTERTWINED SPIRALS

Lang and Whitbrock (1989) used a neural network to solve the problem of distinguishing two intertwined spirals. In their statement of the problem, the two spirals coil around the origin three times in the x-y plane. The x-y coordinates of 97 points from each spiral are given. The problem involves learning to classify each point as to which spiral it belongs.

Figure 17.3 shows the 97 points of the first spiral (indicated by squares) and the 97 points of the second spiral (indicated by circles). The first spiral belongs

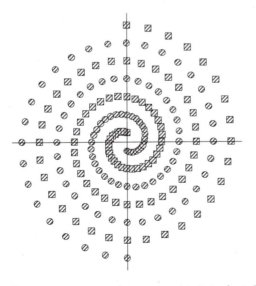

Figure 17.3 194 points lying on two intertwined spirals.

to class $+1$ and the second spiral belongs to class -1. The task as defined by Lang and Whitbrock is limited to the 194 points in the three turns of these two spirals and does not involve dealing with points that would lie on a fourth or later turns of the extensions of the same spirals.

The terminal set for this problem consists of the x and y position of the given points and the ephemeral random floating-point constant $\mathfrak{R}$ ranging between -1.000 and $+1.000$. That is,

```
T = {X, Y, ℜ}.
```

It seems reasonable to try to write a computer program for determining to which spiral a given point belongs in terms of the four arithmetic operations, a decision-making function, and the trigonometric sine and cosine functions. Thus, the function set for this problem is

```
F = (+, -, *, %, IFLTE, SIN, COS},
```

taking two, two, two, two, four, one, and one argument, respectively.

The fitness cases are the 194 x-y coordinates of the given points belonging to the spirals and the class ($+1$ or -1) associated with each point. Raw fitness is the number of points (0 to 194) that are correctly classified and standardized fitness is the number of fitness cases (i.e., 194) minus raw fitness.

Since the S-expressions in the population are compositions of functions operating on floating-point numbers and since the S-expressions in this problem must produce a binary output ($+1$ or -1) to designate the class, a wrapper (output interface) is required. This wrapper maps any positive value to class $+1$ and maps any other value to class -1.

Table 17.3 Tableau for intertwined spirals.

Objective:	Find a way to tell whether a given point in the x-y plane belongs to the first or second of two intertwining spirals.
Terminal set:	X, Y, $\mathfrak{R}$, where $\mathfrak{R}$ is the ephemeral random floating-point constant ranging between -1.000 and $+1.000$.
Function set:	+, -, *, %, IFLTE, SIN, COS.
Fitness cases:	194 points in the x-y plane.
Raw fitness:	The number of points that are correctly classified.
Standardized fitness:	The maximum raw fitness (i.e., 194) minus the raw fitness.
Hits:	Equals raw fitness for this problem.
Wrapper:	Maps any S-expression returning a positive value to class $+1$ and maps all other values to class -1.
Parameters:	$M = 10,000$ (with over-selection). $G = 51$.
Success predicate:	An S-expression scores 194 hits.

Table 17.3 summarizes the key features of the classification problem of distinguishing two intertwined spirals.

In one run, approximately 31% of the initial random individuals in generation 0 correctly classified precisely 50% of the points (i.e., 97 out of a possible 194 points). Some of these individuals, such as (* (* X X) 0.502), scored 50% by virtue of always returning a value with the same sign and therefore classifying all the points as belonging to one spiral. Others, such as (* X Y) scored 50% by virtue of dividing the space into parts which contain exactly half of the points.

In addition, about 30% of the population scored between 88 and 96 hits while about 32% scored between 98 and 106 hits. The worst-of-generation individual from generation 0 scored 71 hits while the best-of-generation individual scored 128 hits.

The best-of-generation individual from generation 0 was the S-expression scoring 128 hits out of a possible 194 hits:

```
(SIN (% Y 0.30400002)).
```

Figure 17.4 shows the way the best-of-generation individual from generation 0 classifies the 194 points of the two spirals. The value of this particular S-expression depends only on the Y coordinate of the point (i.e., it is partially blind) so that this S-expression classifies points into horizontal bands of equal height $0.304\pi = 0.96$. For example, for a point in the x-y-plane whose value of Y lies between 0 and $+0.304\pi$, this S-expression returns a positive number between 0 and 1 and the wrapper interprets the point to be in class $+1$ (shown by a gray band).

The points of one spiral are indicated with boxes and the points of the other spiral are indicated with circles. Correctly classified points are indicated by large boxes or circles. Thus, in the figure, all nine points of the first turn in the

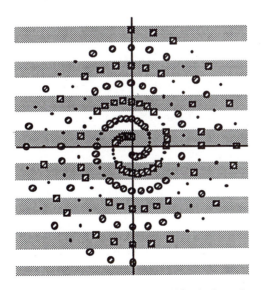

Figure 17.4 Classification performed by the best-of-generation individual from generation 0

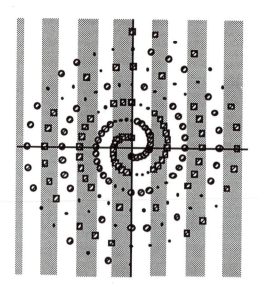

Figure 17.5 Classification performed by best-of-generation individual from generation 1.

second quadrant of the spiral indicated with boxes are large because they are correctly classified.

Similarly, for Y between 0 and -0.304π, this S-expression classifies all points as being in the -1 class. The above-average score of this S-expression arises, in part, from the fact that the particular divisor of 0.304 happens to cause the correct classification of the two dense groups of nine points in the initial 90° turn of each spiral and also causes the correct classification of the dense almost horizontal group of points in the next two horizontal bands.

For generation 1, the best-of-generation individual,

```
(SIN (% (SIN X) (+ -0.12499994 -0.15999997))),
```

contained 7 points and scored 137 hits. This S-expression is equivalent to $\text{Sin}(\text{Sin }x/-0.285)$.

Figure 17.5 shows that the partially blind best-of-generation individual from generation 1 works by classifying points into vertical bands of varying width. It is particularly effective near the x axis.

For generation 3, the best-of-generation individual,

```
(SIN (- (+ (IFLTE (* X -0.25699997) (* X X) (COS Y) (+
(SIN (COS X)) (+ (* 0.18500006 -0.33599997) (IFLTE Y
0.42000008 X -0.23399997)))) (SIN (SIN Y))) (+ (IFLTE (%
(COS X) (SIN -0.594)) (+ -0.553 Y) (% Y -0.30499995) (+ Y
X)) (COS (% X 0.5230001)))))),
```

contained 48 points, scored 139 hits, and incorporated both X and Y. This individual incorporates the IFLTE function in three places.

Figure 17.6 shows that the best-of-generation individual from generation 3 does especially well near the origin.

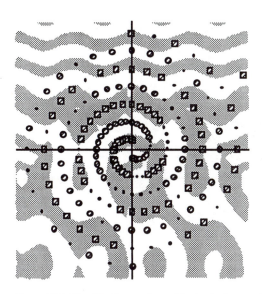

Figure 17.6 Classification performed by best-of-generation individual from generation 3.

For generation 5, the best-of-generation individual,

```
(- (SIN X) (% (SIN (* (- (+ X X) (SIN (% Y 0.30400002)))
(COS X))) 0.6960001)),
```

contains 17 points and scores 146 hits.

Figure 17.7 shows classification performed by the best-of-generation individual from generation 5. As can be seen, the division of the space into white and gray regions for generation 5 is considerably different from that of generation 3.

For generation 7, the best-of-generation individual shown below contains 22 points and scores 152 hits:

```
1 (SIN (IFLTE (% Y Y)
2              (% (SIN (SIN (% Y 0.30400002))) X)
3          (% Y 0.30400002)
4          (SIN (% (SIN X)
5                  (+ -0.12499994 -0.15999997)))))).
```

Note that the third clause (on line 3) of the IFLTE function in the above S-expression is the best-of-generation S-expression from generation 0 while the fourth clause (on lines 4 and 5) is the best-of-generation S-expression from generation 1 (creating the vertical bands of varying widths).

Figure 17.8 shows classification performed by the best-of-generation individual from generation 7. As can be seen, the figure consists primarily of the same vertical bands that we saw previously in generation 1, except that the area near the y axis consists of a sine wave turned on its side. The first clause (on line 1) is equal to 1.0. If 1.0 is not less than or equal to the second clause (line 2), then the fourth clause (on lines 4 and 5) is executed. This approximately occurs for values of x for which $|x| > 0.9$ and produces the vertical bands

Figure 17.7 Classification performed by best-of-generation individual from generation 5.

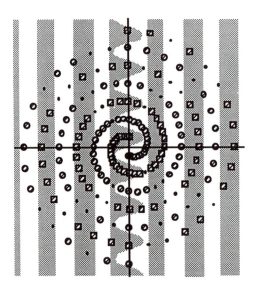

Figure 17.8 Classification performed by best-of-generation individual from generation 7.

Figure 17.9 Classification performed by best-of-generation individual from generation 10.

that we saw previously from generation 1. But, when approximately $|X| <$ 0.9, there are two cases based on the signs of X and Y and both the third clause (on line 3) and the fourth clause (on lines 4 and 5) play roles in painting the sine wave turned on its side.

On generation 10 the best-of-generation individual,

```
(SIN (IFLTE (IFLTE (% 0.26400006 -0.14199996) (% X
-0.10399997) (- X Y) (* (SIN (% Y 0.30400002)) (SIN (IFLTE
(IFLTE (% 0.26400006 -0.14199996) (% X -0.10399997) (- X
Y) (* (SIN (% Y 0.30400002)) (IFLTE (% 0.26400006
-0.14199996) Y X X))) (% (SIN Y) Y) (SIN (SIN (SIN (% (SIN
X) (+ -0.12499994 -0.15999997)))))) (+ (+ X Y) (+ Y
Y)))))) (% (SIN Y) Y) (SIN (SIN (SIN (- (+ (IFLTE (SIN X)
(% (SIN X) (+ (SIN (COS X)) (+ (+ -0.12499994 -
0.15999997) (IFLTE Y 0.42000008 X -0.23399997)))) (COS Y)
X) (SIN (SIN Y))) (+ (IFLTE (% (COS X) (SIN -0.594)) (+ -
0.553 Y) (% Y -0.30499995) (+ Y X)) (COS (% X
0.5230001))))))) (+ (+ X Y) (+ Y Y)))),
```

had 122 points and scored 164 hits.

Figure 17.9 shows classification performed by the best-of-generation individual from generation 10. As can be seen, the division of the space into white and gray regions is predominantly accomplished with curves in generation 10. On generation 12 the best-of-generation individual,

```
(SIN (IFLTE (IFLTE (+ Y Y) (+ X Y) (- X Y) (+ Y Y)) (* X
X) (SIN (IFLTE (% Y Y) (% (SIN (SIN (% Y 0.30400002))) X)
(% Y 0.30400002) (SIN (SIN (IFLTE (IFLTE (% 0.26400006
-0.14199996) (% X -0.10399997) (- X Y) (* (SIN (SIN (+
-0.12499994 -0.15999997))) (IFLTE Y Y X (+ Y Y)))) (SIN (%
```

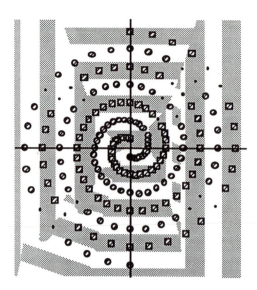

Figure 17.10 Classification performed by best-of-generation individual from generation 12.

```
(SIN X) (+ -0.12499994 -0.15999997))) (SIN (SIN (% (SIN
X) (+ -0.12499994 -0.15999997)))) (+ (+ X Y) (+ Y
Y))))))) (% Y 0.30400002))),
```

had 84 points and scored 173 hits.

Figure 17.10 shows the classification performed by the best-of-generation individual from generation 12. As can be seen, the division of the space into white and gray regions is predominantly accomplished with straight line segments in generation 12.

On generation 21, the best-of-generation individual scored 186 hits.

On generation 33, the best-of-generation individual,

```
(SIN (IFLTE (IFLTE (+ Y Y) (+ X Y) (- X Y) (+ Y Y)) (* X
X) (SIN (IFLTE (% Y Y) (% (SIN (SIN (% Y 0.30400002))) X)
(% Y 0.30400002) (IFLTE (IFLTE (% (% Y 0.30400002)
0.30400002) (% X -0.10399997) (- X Y) (* (+ -0.12499994
-0.15999997) (- X Y))) 0.30400002 (SIN (SIN (IFLTE
0.30400002 (% (SIN Y) Y) (SIN (SIN (SIN (% (SIN X) (+
-0.12499994 -0.15999997))))) (% (+ (+ X Y) (+ Y Y))
0.30400002)))) (+ (+ X Y) (+ Y Y))))) (SIN (IFLTE (IFLTE
Y (+ X Y) (- X Y) (+ Y Y)) (* X X) (SIN (IFLTE (% Y Y) (%
(SIN (SIN (% Y 0.30400002))) X) (% Y 0.30400002) (SIN
(SIN (+ (+ X Y) (+ Y Y)))))) (% Y 0.30400002))))),
```

scored 192 out of 194 and had 169 points.

Figure 17.11 shows the classification performed by the best-of-generation individual scoring 192 from generation 33. There are two incorrectly classified points in this figure. One is shown as a small circle in a region near the upper left corner of the figure which the S-expression incorrectly classified as gray, instead of white. The second is also shown as a small circle near the lower right

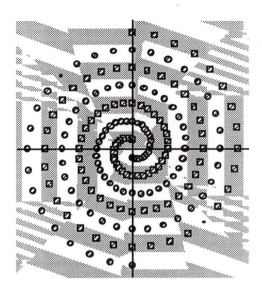

Figure 17.11 Classification performed by best-of-generation individual from generation 33.

corner of the figure which the S-expression incorrectly classified as white, instead of gray.

On generation 35, the best-of-generation individual scored 193 out of 194, had 177 points, and is shown below:

```
(SIN (IFLTE (IFLTE (+ Y Y) (+ X Y) (- X Y) (+ Y Y)) (* X
X) (SIN (IFLTE (% Y Y) (% (SIN (SIN (% Y 0.30400002)))) X)
(% Y 0.30400002) (IFLTE (IFLTE (% (SIN (% (% Y
0.30400002) 0.30400002)) (+ X Y)) (% X -0.10399997) (-
X Y) (* (+ -0.12499994 -0.15999997) (- X Y))) 0.30400002
(SIN (SIN (IFLTE (% (SIN (% (% Y 0.30400002) 0.30400002))
(+ X Y)) (% (SIN Y) Y) (SIN (SIN (SIN (% (SIN X) (+
-0.12499994 -0.15999997)))))) (% (+ (+ X Y) (+ Y Y))
0.30400002)))) (+ (+ X Y) (+ Y Y))))) (SIN (IFLTE (IFLTE
Y (+ X Y) (- X Y) (+ Y Y)) (* X X) (SIN (IFLTE (% Y Y) (%
(SIN (SIN (% Y 0.30400002))) X) (% Y 0.30400002) (SIN
(SIN (IFLTE (IFLTE (SIN (% (SIN X) (+ -0.12499994
-0.15999997))) (% X -0.10399997) (- X Y) (+ X Y)) (SIN (%
(SIN X) (+ -0.12499994 -0.15999997))) (SIN (SIN (% (SIN
X) (+ -0.12499994 -0.15999997)))) (+ (+ X Y) (+ Y
Y)))))))) (% Y 0.30400002))))).
```

Figure 17.12 shows the classification performed by the best-of-generation individual scoring 193 from generation 35. The one incorrectly classified point is found in the lower right area of the figure and is shown as a small circle in a region which the S-expression incorrectly classified as white instead of gray.

On generation 36, the following S-expression containing 179 points and scoring 194 out of 194 hits emerged:

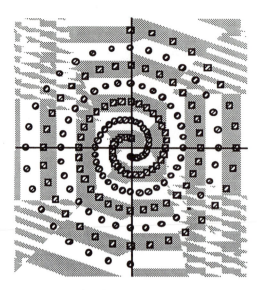

Figure 17.12 Classification performed by best-of-generation individual from generation 35.

```
(SIN (IFLTE (IFLTE (+ Y Y) (+ X Y) (- X Y) (+ Y Y)) (* X
X) (SIN (IFLTE (% Y Y) (% (SIN (SIN (% Y 0.30400002)))) X)
(% Y 0.30400002) (IFLTE (IFLTE (% (SIN (% (% Y (+ X Y))
0.30400002)) (+ X Y)) (% X -0.10399997) (- X Y) (* (+
-0.12499994 -0.15999997) (- X Y))) 0.30400002 (SIN (SIN
(IFLTE (% (SIN (% (% Y 0.30400002) 0.30400002)) (+ X Y))
(% (SIN Y) Y) (SIN (SIN (SIN (% (SIN X) (+ -0.12499994
-0.15999997)))))) (% (+ (+ X Y) (+ Y Y)) 0.30400002)))) (+
(+ X Y) (+ Y Y))))) (SIN (IFLTE (IFLTE Y (+ X Y) (- X Y)
(+ Y Y)) (* X X) (SIN (IFLTE (% Y Y) (% (SIN (SIN (% Y
0.30400002)))) X) (% Y 0.30400002) (SIN (SIN (IFLTE (IFLTE
(SIN (% (SIN X) (+ -0.12499994 -0.15999997))) (% X
-0.10399997) (- X Y) (+ X Y)) (SIN (% (SIN X) (+
-0.12499994 -0.15999997)))) (SIN (SIN (% (SIN X) (+
-0.12499994 -0.15999997)))) (+ (+ X Y) (+ Y Y))))))) (% Y
0.30400002))))).
```

Figure 17.13 shows the classification performed by this best-of-run individual. As can be seen, 100% of the points in this figure are correctly classified; these are shown as either large circles or large squares. The one small circle in figure 17.12 indicating an erroneous classification is missing from figure 17.13.

The difference between generations 35 and 36 is that the one point out of 194 that is incorrectly classified by the best-of-generation for generation 35 is correctly classified by the best-of-run individual from generation 36. Note that the best-of-generation individual for generation 35 is, as is sometimes the case, one of the parents of the best-of-run individual for generation 36. The parent and its offspring differ only in that the underlined and emboldened constant

```
0.30400002
```

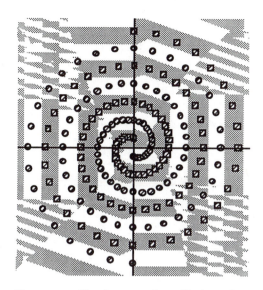

Figure 17.13 Classification performed by best-of-generation individual from generation 36.

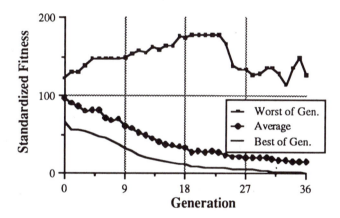

Figure 17.14 Fitness curves for the intertwined spirals problem.

appears in the parent from generation 35 (which has 177 points), while the subexpression

```
(+ X Y)
```

appears in the offspring individual for generation 36 (which has 179 points). In other words, the crossover operation caused the removal of the slightly imperfect constant from the parent and inserted the slightly better subexpression in the offspring, thus raising raw fitness from 193 to 194.

Figure 17.14 shows, by generation, the standardized fitnesses of the worst-of-generation individual and the best-of-generation individual and the average standardized fitness for the population as a whole.

Figure 17.15 shows, by generation, the structural complexity of the best-of-generation individual and the average structural complexity of all individuals in the population for the problem. As can be seen, structural complexity

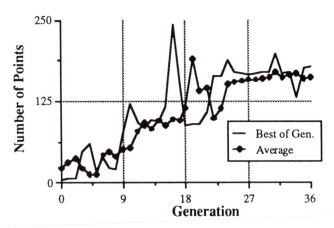

Figure 17.15 Structural complexity curves for the intertwined spirals problem.

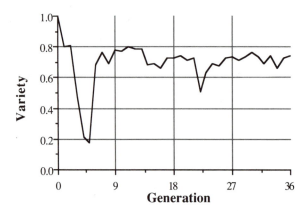

Figure 17.16 Variety curve for the intertwined spirals problem.

is low for early generations and increases in later generations. For example, for generation 0 the structural complexity of the best-of-generation individual is 4 and the average for the population is 21.7 points, whereas at generation 36 these values are 179 and 161.5 points, respectively.

Figure 17.16 shows the variety, by generation, of the population. Note that the variety dropped to 18% on generation 5 but then recovered and thereafter remained at around 70%.

Figure 17.17 shows the hits histograms for generations 0, 3, 9, 18, and 36 of the run. The first 19 ticks in the horizontal axis of the histogram each represent a range of ten levels of fitness between 0 and 189; the last tick represents the five levels of fitness between 190 and 194. Note the undulating left-to-right movement of the fitness of the population over the generations.

If we retest the best-of-run individual from generation 36 on the two intertwined spirals with sample points chosen twice as densely, we find that 372 of the 388 points (i.e., 96%) are classified correctly. If we retest with sample points that are ten times more dense, we find that 1,818 of the 1,940 points (i.e., 94%) are classified correctly.

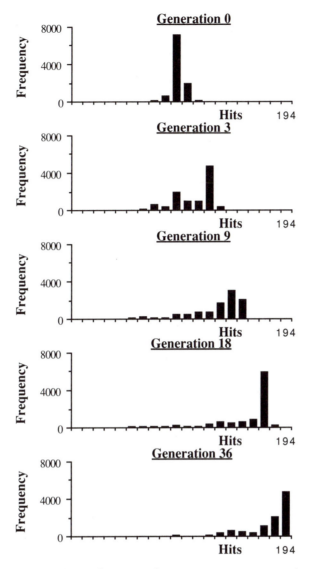

Figure 17.17 Hits histograms for generations 0, 3, 9, 18, and 36 of the intertwined spirals problem.

This problem is well suited for sampling the spirals with one density of fitness cases early in the run and with a greater density later in the run; however, since the problem is a benchmark problem for neural networks, we adhered to the 194 fitness cases throughout the run.

See also Koza 1992d.

The difficulty of this problem arises, of course, from Lang and Whitbrock's choice of Cartesian coordinates (as opposed to, say, polar coordinates).

18 Iteration, Recursion, and Setting

This chapter considers the following three problems that require iteration or recursion for their solution:

- a planning problem involving iterative actions to do block stacking,
- a problem involving iterative summation of an infinite series, and
- a problem of sequence induction for the recursive Fibonacci sequence.

The block stacking problem will also be used to illustrate the incorporation of secondary factors, such as parsimony and efficiency, in the fitness measure.

18.1 BLOCK STACKING

Planning in artificial intelligence and robotics requires finding a plan that receives information from sensors about the state of the various objects in a system and then uses that information to select actions to change the state of the objects in that system toward some desired state.

Planning problems are control problems. Planning often involves symbolic (rather than numeric) objects and systems.

Iteration is an important part of computer programming. The planning problem in this section provides the opportunity to introduce an explicit iterative operation.

The block stacking problem is a planning problem requiring the rearrangement of uniquely labeled blocks into a specified order on a single target tower. In the version of the problem involving nine blocks, the blocks are labeled with the nine different letters of FRUITCAKE or UNIVERSAL. The goal is to automatically generate a plan (Nilsson 1980; Genesereth and Nilsson 1987) that solves this problem.

This problem is typical of many problems in artificial intelligence in that it is primarily symbolic.

The STACK is the ordered set of blocks that are currently in the target tower (where the order is important). The TABLE is the set of blocks that are currently not in the target tower (where the order is not important and where they can be randomly accessed). The initial configuration consists of certain blocks in the STACK and the remaining blocks on the TABLE. The desired

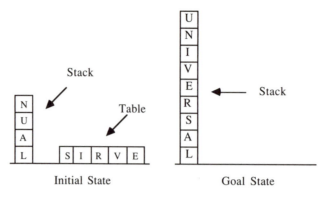

Figure 18.1 One possible initial state of the STACK and TABLE is shown at left. The goal state is shown at right.

final configuration consists of all the blocks being in the STACK in the desired order (i.e., UNIVERSAL) and no blocks remaining on the TABLE.

The left half of figure 18.1 shows a possible initial state in which the four blocks NUAL are in the STACK and the five blocks S, I, R, V, and E are on the TABLE. The right half of figure 18.1 shows the nine blocks UNIVERSAL in the STACK in the desired order (i.e., the goal state).

In the discussion here, we use the particular symbolic sensors and functions defined for this problem by Nilsson (1989). In particular, the following three sensors dynamically track the system:

- The sensor CS dynamically specifies the top block of the STACK.

- The sensor TB ("Top Correct Block") dynamically specifies the top block on the STACK such that it and all blocks below it are in the correct order.

- The sensor NN ("Next Needed") dynamically specifies the block immediately after TB (Top Correct Block) in the goal UNIVERSAL (regardless of whether or not there are incorrect blocks in the STACK).

For example, in figure 18.2, the STACK consists of URSAL while the TABLE contains the four letters V, E, I, and N. The sensor CS (top of the STACK) is therefore U. The sensor TB (Top Correct Block) is R, since RSAL are in the correct order on the STACK and U is out of place. The sensor NN (Next Needed) is E, since E is the block that belongs on top of RSAL.

The terminal set T for this block stacking problem consists of the three sensors defined by Nilsson for this problem, namely

T = {TB, NN, CS}.

Each of these terminals is a variable atom that may assume, as its value, one of the nine block labels or NIL. The terminal set contains the information that is to be processed by the computer program that genetic programming is to find.

The function set should contain functions that might be needed to express the solution to the problem. The following function set combines two functions defined by Nilsson for this problem (MS and MT), an iterative function (DU),

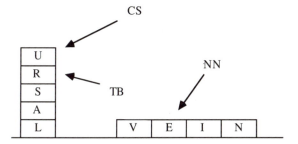

Figure 18.2 STACK with "URSAL" and TABLE with V, E, I, and N.

and two logical functions (NOT and EQ) needed to express predicates for controlling the iterative function. Thus, the function set F is

F = {MS, MT, DU, NOT, EQ},

taking one, one, two, one, and two arguments, respectively.

These five functions are described below.

The function MS ("Move to the Stack") has one argument. The S-expression (MS «x») moves block «x» to the top of the STACK if «x» is on the TABLE. The function MS does nothing if «x» is already in the STACK, if the TABLE is empty, or if «x» itself is NIL. Both this function and the function MT described below return NIL if they do nothing and T if they do something. The real functionality of both MS and MT lies in their side effects on the STACK and TABLE, not in their return values.

The function MT ("Move to the Table") has one argument. The S-expression (MT «x») moves the top item of the STACK to the TABLE if the STACK contains «x» anywhere in the STACK. The function MT does nothing if «x» is already on the TABLE, if the STACK is empty, or if «x» itself is NIL.

The solution to the block stacking problem is typical of computer programs in general in that iteration is required for its solution. The iterative operator DU allows a program to perform such iterations. In particular, the DU operator has two arguments and appears in the form

(DU «WORK» «PREDICATE»).

The DU operator causes the «WORK» to be iteratively executed until the «PREDICATE» is satisfied (i.e., becomes non-NIL). That is, in pseudo code, the desired iterative behavior is

(LOOP UNTIL (EVAL «PREDICATE») DO (EVAL «WORK»)).

The iterative operator needed in this problem cannot be implemented directly as an ordinary LISP function. The reason is that, ordinarily, when LISP evaluates a function call, it first evaluates each of the arguments to the function and then passes the value to which the arguments have evaluated into the function. If the iterative DU operator were implemented as an ordinary LISP function, the operator would merely evaluate the *value* returned by the «WORK», as opposed to *doing* the «WORK» while iterating through the loop.

Thus, it is necessary to suppress premature evaluation of the «WORK» argument and the «PREDICATE» argument so that neither argument is evaluated outside the DU operator. Instead, these arguments must be evaluated dynamically inside the operator for each iteration. In particular, the desired behavior is that the «WORK» first be evaluated inside the DU operator, and then the «PREDICATE» be evaluated. The desired two separate evaluations are to be performed, in sequence, as if the LISP function EVAL were operating inside the DU operator. The execution of the «WORK» will often change some variable that will then be tested by «PREDICATE». Indeed, that is often the purpose of a loop. Thus, it is important to suppress premature evaluation of the NIL and «PREDICATE» arguments of the DU operator. The remedy is to implement the iterative DU operator with a macro definition in the manner described in subsection 6.1.1 in connection with conditional branching operators.

Although not used in this block stacking problem, the iterative function DU has an indexing variable II which is updated for each iteration.

Genetic programming involves executing computer programs that have either been randomly generated or been produced by genetic manipulation. Many S-expressions are therefore ill-formed and contain one or more un-satisfiable termination predicates which cause them to go into an infinite loop. In addition, many S-expressions contain deep nestings of DU operators which are extremely time-consuming to execute. It is a practical necessity (when working on a bounded computer) to place a limit on the number of iterations allowed by any one execution of a DU operator. Thus, a similar limit must be placed on the total number of iterations allowed for all DU functions that may be encountered in the process of evaluating any one individual S-expression for any one fitness case. Thus, the termination predicate of each DU operator is actually an implicit disjunction of the explicit predicate argument «PREDICATE» and two additional time-out predicates. In particular, we decided that it is reasonable for this problem that the DU operator times out if either more than 25 iterations are performed in evaluating a single DU operator, or more than 100 iterations are performed by DU operators in evaluating a particular individual S-expression for a particular fitness case. If a DU operator times out, the side effects that have already been executed are not retracted.

Of course, if we could execute all the individual LISP S-expressions in parallel (as nature does), so the infeasibility of one individual in the population does not bring the entire process to a halt, we would not need these limits.

This block stacking problem is not a difficult problem. Even with the time-out predicates, problems with iteration are very time-consuming. This problem has the virtue of being simple enough to solve, using iteration, in a reasonable amount of time.

The return value of the DU operator is a Boolean value that indicates whether the «PREDICATE» was successfully satisfied or whether the DU operator timed out. The data type of the return value is the same as the type of the value of «WORK». In particular, if the NIL evaluates to T (True) or NIL (False), this return value is a Boolean T or NIL. On the other hand, if numeric-valued logic is being used and the NIL evaluates to some positive number (e.g., + 1.0) or some negative number (e.g., − 1.0), then this return value is either a numeric + 1 (for T) or a numeric − 1 (for NIL).

If the predicate of a DU operator is satisfied when the operator is first called, then the DU operator does no work at all and simply returns T.

Closure of the function set is guaranteed because each function in the function set returns some value under all conditions (in addition to whatever side effects it has on the STACK and TABLE).

For this problem, there are millions of different possible initial conditions (i.e., fitness cases) of N blocks distributed between the STACK and the TABLE. Sampling of the fitness cases is required in order to evaluate the fitness of a plan in a reasonable amount of time. Thus, we construct a structured sampling of fitness cases for measuring fitness. In particular, if there are N blocks, there are $N + 1$ fitness cases in which any blocks in the initial STACK are all in the correct order and in which there are no out-of-order blocks on top of the correctly ordered blocks in the initial STACK. There are also $N − 1$ additional fitness cases where there is precisely one out-of-order block in the initial STACK on top of whatever correctly ordered blocks happen to be in the initial STACK. There are additional fitness cases with more than one out-of-order block in the initial STACK on top of various numbers of correctly ordered blocks in the initial STACK.

Thus, in lieu of the millions of possible fitness cases, we constructed a structured sampling of fitness cases for measuring fitness consisting of the following 166 fitness cases:

• the ten cases where the 0–9 blocks in the STACK are already in the correct order,

• the eight cases where there is precisely one out-of-order block in the initial STACK on top of whatever correctly ordered blocks happen to be in the initial STACK, and

• a structured random sampling of 148 additional cases with 0–8 correctly ordered blocks in the initial STACK and a random number (between 2 and 8) of out-of-order blocks on top of the correctly ordered blocks.

The raw fitness of a particular individual plan is the number of fitness cases for which the STACK contains nine blocks spelling "UNIVERSAL" after the plan is executed. Raw fitness ranges from 0 to 166. Standardized fitness, in turn, equals 166 minus raw fitness. A standardized fitness of 0 corresponds to 166 correctly handled cases.

Obviously, the construction of a sampling such as this must be done so that the process is not misled into producing solutions that correctly handle some unrepresentative subset of the entire problem but cannot correctly handle the entire problem.

Table 18.1 summarizes the key features of example 1 of the block stacking problem.

We now consider three versions of the block stacking problem.

Table 18.1 Tableau for block stacking.

Objective:	Find a robotic plan for stacking blocks onto a STACK so that they spell UNIVERSAL.
Terminal set:	Sensors NN, TB, CS.
Function set:	MS, MT, DU, NOT, EQ.
Fitness cases:	A structured sample of 166 initial condition cases consisting of particular blocks on the STACK and TABLE.
Raw fitness:	The number of fitness cases for which the STACK equals UNIVERSAL after the S-expression is evaluated.
Standardized fitness:	Number of cases (i.e., 166) minus raw fitness.
Hits:	Equal to raw fitness for this problem.
Wrapper:	None.
Parameters:	$M = 500$. $G = 51$.
Success predicate:	An S-expression scores 166 hits.

18.1.1 Example 1: Correctness

Example 1 of the block stacking problem involves finding a plan (i.e., a computer program) that can correctly stack the nine blocks onto the STACK in the desired order after starting with any of the 166 fitness cases. Each plan is executed (evaluated) once for each of the 166 fitness cases.

The initial random population of plans contains a variety of complicated, inefficient, pointless, and counterproductive plans. One initial random plan,

(EQ (MT CS) NN),

unconditionally moves the top of the STACK to the TABLE and then performs the useless Boolean comparison between the sensor value NN and the return value of the MT function. Another initial random plan,

(MS TB),

futilely attempts to move the block TB (which already is in the STACK) from the TABLE to the STACK.

Many initial random plans are so ill-formed that they perform no action at all on the STACK and the TABLE. These plans score a raw fitness of 1 (out of a maximum of 166) because they leave the STACK untouched in the one fitness case consisting of an already perfectly arranged STACK.

Other initial random plans are even more unfit and even disrupt a perfectly arranged initial STACK.

Some idiosyncratic initial random plans achieve modest fitness levels because they contain particular action sequences that happen to work on a specific few fitness cases (often the easiest category of fitness cases). For

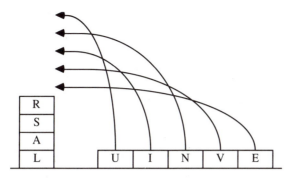

Figure 18.3 One partially correct plan moves five needed blocks to the STACK already containing RSAL.

example, the non-iterative plan

```
(EQ (MS NN) (EQ (MS NN) (MS NN)))
```

moves the next needed block (NN) from the TABLE to the STACK three times. This plan works in the four particular specific fitness cases where the initial STACK consists of six, seven, eight, or nine correct blocks and no out-of-order blocks. It has raw fitness of 4. However, this plan has no utility in general. It cannot handle the other fitness cases containing no out-of-order blocks.

The next longer cousin of this tedious, enumerative plan would score 5. However, it is very unlikely that an initial random population consisting of 500 (or even 5,000 or 50,000) random plans would include a cousin of this kind that would be capable of scoring 8, 9, or 10 (out of the 166).

Iteration, not tedious enumeration, is the proper way to solve this problem.

An individual plan emerged in generation 5 that correctly handled ten of the 166 fitness cases. This plan correctly handles the 10 fitness cases in the first group itemized above where any blocks initially on the STACK happen already to be in the correct order and where there are no out-of-order blocks on top of these correctly ordered blocks. This plan,

```
(DU (MS NN) (NOT NN)),
```

consists of five points. Note that this plan uses the iterative operator DU, which does the «WORK» (MS NN) of moving the needed block onto the STACK from the TABLE until the «PREDICATE» (NOT NN) is satisfied. This predicate is satisfied when there are no more blocks needed to finish the STACK (i.e., the next needed sensor NN is NIL).

Figure 18.3 shows this partially correct plan moving five needed blocks (E, V, N, I, and U) to a STACK containing four blocks (R, S, A, and L) that are already in the correct order. This plan, of course, does not produce a correct final STACK if any block initially on the STACK was incorrect (as is the situation in 156 of the 166 fitness cases). Nonetheless, this partially correct plan will prove to be a useful building block in the final 100%-correct plan.

As additional generations are run, the fitness of the best-of-generation individual plan in the population typically increases somewhat from genera-

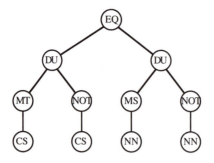

Figure 18.4 Correct best-of-run plan for example 1 of the block stacking problem.

tion to generation. These progressively improving plans each deal correctly with a few more additional cases. At the same time, the overall average fitness of the population also tends to increase somewhat from generation to generation as the population begins to contain additional higher-scoring plans.

In generation 10, the best-of-generation individual achieved a perfect score (that is, the plan produced the desired final configuration of blocks in the STACK for all 166 fitness cases). This 100%-correct best-of-run plan is

```
(EQ (DU (MT CS) (NOT CS)) (DU (MS NN) (NOT NN))).
```

Note that this plan incorporates two iterative DU operators. Figure 18.4 graphically depicts this plan, which consists of 11 points.

This best-of-run plan consists of two subplans, which are connected via the function EQ (an irrelevant operation that is merely serving as a connective).

The first subplan,

```
(DU (MT CS) (NOT CS)),
```

does the work of first moving CS (i.e., the top of the STACK) to the TABLE continuing until the predicate (NOT CS) becomes T (True). This predicate becomes true when the top of the STACK becomes NIL (i.e., the STACK becomes empty). In other words, the first subplan in this 100%-correct plan involves completely disassembling the STACK onto the table. The second subplan,

```
(DU (MS NN) (NOT NN)),
```

does the work of iteratively moving the next needed block NN to the STACK until there is no next needed block NN.

The previously discovered subplan

```
(DU (MS NN) (NOT NN)),
```

which scored 10 out of 166, was incorporated as a subplan into the 100%-correct final hierarchy. This subplan became part of the 100%-correct final hierarchy as a result of the crossover operation. This subplan participated in the critical crossover operation because its relatively high fitness (i.e., a raw fitness of 10 out of a possible 166) allowed it to be selected as a parent to participate in the crossover operation that produced the 100%-correct final plan.

Note that we did not prespecify that the solution would consist of precisely 11 points. Genetic programming discovered this size and shape dynamically during the course of trying to solve the problem.

18.1.2 Example 2: Correctness and Efficiency

The 100%-correct solution found in example 1 of the block stacking problem is highly inefficient in that it removes all the blocks, one by one, from the STACK to the TABLE (even if they are already in the correct order on the STACK). This plan then moves the blocks, one by one, from the TABLE to the STACK. As a result, this plan uses 2,319 block movements to handle the 166 cases.

The most efficient way to solve the block stacking problem while minimizing total block movements is to remove only the out-of-order blocks from the STACK and then to move the next needed blocks to the STACK from the TABLE. This approach uses only 1,641 block movements to handle the 166 fitness cases.

It is not surprising that genetic programming evolved the strategy using 2,319 block movements, since nothing in the fitness measure gave any consideration whatsoever to efficiency as measured by the total number of block movements. The sole consideration was whether or not the plan correctly handled each of the 166 fitness cases (without timing out). Genetic programming gave us exactly what we asked for; no more and no less.

We can, however, simultaneously breed a population of plans (computer programs) for two attributes at one time. In particular, we can specifically breed a population of plans for *both* correctness and efficiency by using a combined fitness measure. Such a combined fitness measure might assign some of the weight to correctness and the remainder of the weight to efficiency (a secondary attribute).

Somewhat arbitrarily, we assigned 75% and 25%, respectively, to these two factors. We subdivided the 75% and 25% as described below.

First, consider correctness. If a plan correctly handled 100% of the 166 fitness cases, it would receive 100% of the 75 points associated with correctness in the combined fitness measure. If a plan correctly handled 0% of the 166 fitness cases, it would receive 0% of the 75 points assigned to correctness. If a plan correctly handled 40% of the 166 cases (i.e., 67 cases), it would receive 30 points (40% of 75) toward correctness.

Second, consider efficiency. If a plan took 1,641 block movements prior to termination (either natural termination or termination due to timing out), it would receive 100% of the 25 associated with efficiency in the combined fitness measure. If the plan took between 0 and 1,640 block movements to perform its work, the 25 points assigned to efficiency would be scaled linearly upward, so a plan making no block movements would receive none of the 25 points. If the plan made between 1,642 and 2,319 block movements, the 25 points assigned to efficiency would be scaled linearly downward, so a plan

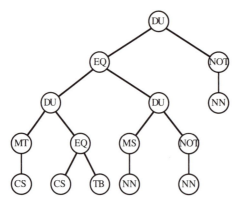

Figure 18.5 Efficient and correct plan for example 2 of the block stacking problem.

making 2,319 block movements would receive none of the 25 points. If a plan made more than 2,319 block movements, it too would also receive none of the 25 points available for efficiency.

Obviously, there are numerous other reasonable allocations of weight than 75% and 25%, and there are numerous other reasonable ways to allocate the 75 points available for correctness and the 25 points available for efficiency. The method described above addresses both the issues that must be addressed in a combined fitness measure, namely how to allocate points between attributes and how to subdivide the points assigned to that attribute.

In the run described below, we applied this combined fitness measure starting at generation 0. However, it may be desirable to start a run using only the primary factor (i.e., correctness) in the fitness measure and then introduce the secondary factor into the fitness measure after some milestone has been achieved on the primary factor (e.g., perhaps 90% correctness).

In one run, the best-of-generation individual from generation 0 performed correctly in only one of the 166 cases. It made a total of 6,590 block movements and received none of the 25 points available for efficiency. This plan was both incorrect and inefficient.

However, by generation 11, the best individual in the population was

```
(DU (EQ (DU (MT CS) (EQ CS TB))
        (DU (MS NN) (NOT NN)))
    (NOT NN)).
```

This best-of-run plan is both 100% correct and 100% efficient. It uses the minimum number (1,641) of block movements to correctly handle all 166 fitness cases.

Figure 18.5 graphically depicts this best-of-run plan for example 2, consisting of 15 points and three iterative DU operators.

In this best-of-run plan, the first subplan,

```
(DU (MT CS) (EQ CS TB)),
```

iteratively moves CS (the top block) of the STACK to the TABLE until the

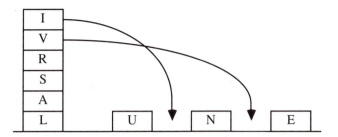

Figure 18.6 Subplan that moves two out-of-order blocks (I and V).

predicate (EQ CS TB) becomes satisfied. This predicate becomes satisfied when CS (the top of the stack) equals TB (the top correct block in the STACK).

Figure 18.6 shows two out-of-order blocks (I and V) sitting on top of four correctly ordered blocks ("RSAL") on the STACK. The sensor TB (Top Good Block) is R. The two out-of-order blocks (I and V) are moved to the TABLE from the STACK until R becomes the top of the STACK. At that point, the top of the stack (CS) is R, which then equals TB.

Then, the previously discovered second subplan,

```
(DU (MS NN) (NOT NN)),
```

iteratively moves the next needed blocks (NN) to the STACK until there is no longer any next needed block.

The function EQ serves only as a connective between the two subplans. Notice also that the outermost DU function performs no function (but does no harm), since the predicate (NOT NN) is satisfied at the same time as the identical predicate of the second subplan. In.that regard, these functionless but essentially harmless elements are similar to the approximately 99% of nucleotide bases of DNA (out of approximately 2.87 billion) of the human genome that never get expressed into protein.

Section 25.12 presents an additional experiment involving parsimony.

18.1.3 Example 3: Correctness, Efficiency, and Parsimony

The solution discovered in example 2 of the block stacking problem is both 100% correct and 100% efficient, but there are 15 points in the tree corresponding to the S-expression. There could be as few as 12 points.

By including parsimony in the fitness measure with 15% weight (in addition to correctness with 70% weight and efficiency with 15% weight), we can breed for correctness, efficiency, and parsimony.

In one run, we obtained the following 100%-correct and 100%-efficient S-expression consisting of the minimal number of points:

```
(EQ (DU (MT CS) (EQ CS TB))
    (DU (MS NN) (NOT NN))).
```

Parsimony and efficiency are just two of many possible secondary attributes that can be considered in evaluating the fitness of the S-expressions generated with genetic programming. In section 10.7, we saw that satisfaction of the initial conditions of a differential equation can be successfully incorporated as a secondary attribute in fitness.

18.2 ITERATIVE SUMMATION

This section demonstrates the use of two tools which are commonly used in computer programming, namely

- iteration and
- assignment (i.e., setting).

Assignment is an important tool in computer programming. It involves giving a name to the results of a calculation so as to provide a means for later referring to the value of the calculation. Assignment can also be used to create an internal state within a computer program.

In the previous section, we encountered the DU operator. In this section, we introduce the SIGMA operator (which is based on the Σ notation for adding up an infinite series in mathematics). We also introduce the assignment operator SET–SV, which provides a means of assigning a value to a settable variable SV.

We will illustrate the SIGMA operator and the assignment operator SET–SV by discovering the power-series expansion for e^x as the solution to a differential equation. Suppose the problem is to find the solution to

$$\frac{dy}{dx} - y = 0$$

having an initial value y_{initial} of 2.718 for an initial value x_{initial} of 1.0. This problem is equivalent to computing e^x using the Taylor power-series expansion

$$\sum_{j=0}^{\infty} \frac{x^j}{j!}.$$

The assignment operator SET–SV has one argument and works in association with a settable global variable, SV. In particular, SET–SV sets the settable global variable SV to the value of its argument. The assignment operator allows a computer program to give a name to the results of a calculation so that the results can subsequently be referred to and used. The value to which the global variable SV is set is not affected by any subsequent event other than another SET–SV, including a change in the values of the terminals contained in the argument to the SET–SV operator. In other words, the value of SV is, indeed, set. Thus, this assignment operator SET–SV differs from the encapsulation operation (subsection 6.5.4) which creates a function that is evaluated when it is encountered using the current value of terminals appearing in it.

In writing programs, computer programmers often mistakenly use a variable that has not yet been defined by their program. Depending on the programming language or the machine involved, either an undefined variable causes the program to halt or else the undefined variable is assigned a default value (which is likely to be inappropriate to the specific problem). In genetic programming, we do not want the evaluation of any aberrant individual to halt the overall process. Thus, we assign a default value to any undefined variable. In order to simplify the particular problem here, we have made the default value 1 for undefined variables. A typical program will change the value of the settable variable SV one or more times.

The iterative summation operator SIGMA has one argument, called «WORK». It performs a function similar to the familiar summation operator Σ in mathematics. In particular, the operator SIGMA evaluates its «WORK» argument repeatedly until a summand is encountered that is small (e.g., less than a fixed built-in threshold of 0.000001 in absolute value). The operator SIGMA then returns the value of its accumulated sum.

The operator SIGMA is similar to the previously described iterative operator DU (Do-Until) in the following ways:

- Time-out limits must be established for this operator.

- An iteration variable J (starting with 1) is available inside this operator for possible incorporation into the «WORK» argument.

- The arguments to this operator are evaluated only inside the SIGMA operation.

- If the operator times out, any side effects of the «WORK» already performed remain.

The indexing variable J is usually included in the terminal set for the problem so that when the argument «WORK» contains a reference to J, the SIGMA operator becomes a summation over the indexing variable. If SIGMA operators are nested, the indexing variable J takes on the value of the innermost SIGMA operator.

There is, of course, no guarantee that the «WORK» of the SIGMA operator will ever become small. Therefore, it is a practical necessity, when working on a serial computer, to limit both the number of iterations allowed by any one execution of a SIGMA operator and the total number of iterations allowed for all SIGMA operators that may be evaluated in the process of executing any individual S-expression for any one fitness case. These limits here are 15 and 100, respectively. If either of these limits is exceeded, the SIGMA operator times out. When a SIGMA operator times out, it nevertheless returns the sum accumulated up to that moment.

The terminal set for this problem is

T = {X, J, SV},

where X is the independent variable, J is the iterative summation index associated with the SIGMA operator, and SV is the settable global variable associated with the assignment operator SET–SV.

The function set for this problem is

F = {+, −, *, %, SET-SV, SIGMA},

taking two, two, two, two, one, and one argument, respectively.

Table 18.2 Tableau for iterative summation problem.

Objective:	Find the power-series solution to a differential equation using the iterative summation operator SIGMA and the assignment operator SET–SV.
Terminal set:	X, J, the settable variable SV.
Function set:	+, −, *, %, the assignment function SET–SV, the iterative summation operator SIGMA.
Fitness cases:	Randomly selected sample of 200 values of the independent variable x_i in some interval of interest.
Raw fitness:	The sum, taken over the 200 fitness cases, of 75% of the absolute value assumed by the individual genetically produced function $f_j(x_i)$ at domain point x_i plus 25% of 200 times of the absolute value of the difference between $f_i(x_{initial})$ and the given value $y_{initial}$.
Standardized fitness:	Same as standardized fitness for this problem.
Hits:	Number of fitness cases for which the standardized fitness is less than 0.01.
Wrapper:	None.
Parameters:	$M = 500$. $G = 51$.
Success predicate:	An S-expression scores 200 hits.

The fitness cases, the raw fitness, the standardized fitness, and hits are defined in the same way as for differential equations in section 10.7.

Table 18.2 summarizes the key features of the problem of finding a power series solution to a differential equation using iterative summation.

In one run, the best-of-run individual S-expression was

```
(SIGMA (SET–SV (* SV (% X J)))).
```

This S-expression satisfies the differential equation and its initial conditions because it is computes the value of the power series for $e^x − 1$ for a given value of x. It consists of a SIGMA operator that starts by setting the settable variable SV to the result of multiplying the value of SV (which is initially 1) by X and dividing by the iteration variable J associated with the SIGMA operator. As this iterative process continues, the summands successively consist of the consecutive powers of X divided by the factorials of the iteration variable J. When the current value of the settable variable SV becomes small, the SIGMA operator terminates and returns its accumulated value (namely, the last overall sum).

This approach has the shortcoming of requiring that a default value be assigned to the settable variable in the event that it is referenced before it is defined (a problem often encountered when humans write programs). This default assignment makes the value of the settable variable depend in an especially erratic way on its position within the program in relation to the location of the set operator, if any, in the program.

Sections 19.7 and 19.8 address the above shortcoming of cascading variables and describe a way of assigning a value to a variable so that it can later be referenced and used without the possibility of having an undefined variable. Section 19.6 presents an alternative to the SIGMA operator for summing an indefinite number of terms of a Fourier series. Section 19.9 further addresses this problem by demonstrating the use of the encapsulation operation. Finally, chapters 20 and 21 present a further extension involving automatic function definition.

18.3   RECURSIVE SEQUENCE INDUCTION

In section 10.12, we performed sequence induction where the target function $5j^4 + 4j^3 + 3j^2 + 2j + 1$ was a straightforward function of the index position j of the sequence. However, suppose that the first 20 elements of the unknown sequence are as follows:

$S = 1, 1, 2, 3, 5, 8, 13, 21, 34, 55, \ldots, 4{,}181, 6{,}765.$

This sequence is the well-known Fibonacci sequence which can be computed using the recursive expression

$s_j = s_{j-1} + s_{j-2}$

(where s_0 and s_1 are both 1). In particular, after the first two elements of the sequence, each element of the sequence is computed using two previous values of the sequence.

If we expect to be able to induce a mathematical expression for the Fibonacci sequence, we must provide a facility in the function set to allow an S-expression being evaluated for a particular index j to refer to the values the S-expression itself has previously computed for indices less than j. We therefore define the sequence referencing function SRF to allow an S-expression to call on the value that it itself has previously computed. In particular, if an S-expression containing the SRF function is being evaluated for index position j, the subexpression (SRF K D) returns the value that the S-expression itself previously computed for sequence position K provided K is between 0 and $j - 1$; otherwise it returns the default value D.

Note that the SRF function returns the value computed by the current S-expression for any index K earlier than the current index j, not the actual correct value of the Fibonacci sequence for the index K.

Note also that the SRF permits recursion where each new element in the sequence is defined recursively in terms of one or more previous elements of the sequence. This form of recursion is useful and common; there are, of course, more general forms of recursion.

If the function set F did not include the sequence referencing function SRF (or some functional equivalent of it), the function set would be insufficiently rich to express the mathematical expression for the Fibonacci sequence in the integral domain.

The terminal set for this problem consists of the index position J (i.e., the independent variable), and the ephemeral random constant $\Re$ ranges over the small integers 0, 1, 2, and 3. That is,

T = {J, $\Re$}.

The function set is

F = {+, -, *, SRF},

each taking two arguments.

The fitness cases for this problem consist of the first 20 elements of the actual Fibonacci sequence.

The raw fitness of an S-expression is the sum, taken over the 20 fitness cases, of the absolute value of the difference between the sequence value produced by the S-expression and the actual value of the Fibonacci sequence. A hit is a sequence position for which the sequence value produced by the S-expression equals the actual value of the Fibonacci sequence. This particular definition of a hit is convenient because attainment of 20 hits can be used in the terminal criterion for this problem. However, this particular definition of a hit is not useful for detecting progress toward discovery of a correct S-expression for this particular problem, because an S-expression that is very close to the target sequence scores no hits until there is an exact match.

In order to save computer time while evaluating fitness in this problem, the elements in the sequence are computed in consecutive order for J = 0, 1, 2, ... from a given S-expression so that previous elements of the sequence are available in a look up table when an S-expression recursively refers to an earlier element of the sequence using the SRF function.

Table 18.3 summarizes the key features of the sequence induction problem with the recursive Fibonacci sequence as the target function.

In one run, the worst-of-generation individual from generation 0 had a standardized fitness of 5.77×10^{37} and the average fitness for the population as a whole was 6.94×10^{34}. A handful of individuals in generation 0 were S-expressions that evaluated to zero for all 20 values of J, and these individuals had a fitness of 17,710. Some individuals in generation 0 scored as many as four hits out of a possible 20; however, they had relatively poor values of fitness even though they exactly matched the Fibonacci sequence for four particular points out of 20. In a sequence induction problem, S-expressions sometimes score a modest number of hits merely by being a low-order polynomial function that happens to agree with the actual sequence for a few values of J or by being a recursive expression that happens to default to the actual sequence for a few values of J.

The best-of-generation individual from generation 0 had a raw fitness of 10,840 and scored no hits.

Figure 18.7 shows, by generation, the standardized fitness for the best-of-generation individual in the population for the recursive sequence induction

Table 18.3 Tableau for sequence induction of the recursive Fibonacci sequence.

Objective:	Find a recursive expression for the Fibonacci sequence, given a finite sample of the sequence.
Terminal set:	Sequence index J and $\Re$, where the ephemeral random constant $\Re$ ranges over the integers 0, 1, 2, and 3.
Function set:	+, −, *, SRF.
Fitness cases:	First 20 elements of the sequence.
Raw fitness:	The sum, taken over the 20 fitness cases, of the absolute value of the difference between the value produced by the S-expression for sequence position J and the actual value of the sequence for position J.
Standardized fitness:	Same as raw fitness for this problem.
Hits:	Number of fitness cases that exactly match.
Wrapper:	None.
Parameters:	$M = 2{,}000$ (with over-selection). $G = 51$.
Success predicate:	An S-expression scores 20 hits.

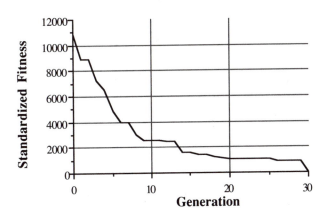

Figure 18.7 Standardized fitness for for the problem of recursive sequence induction.

problem. In generations 1 and 2, the standardized fitness of the best-of-generation individual improved to 8,943. In generations 3 through 13, it improved to 7,272, 6,550, 4,813, 3,968, 3,968, 2,968, 2,588, 2,588, 2,551, 2,471, 2,470, respectively. Between generations 20 and 25, it was 1,027. Between generations 26 and 29, it was 890. We did not plot the worst-of-generation individual or the average standardized fitness for the population as a whole since they are both extremely large (e.g., the population average fitness is about 1.84×10^7 for generation 30).

The best-of-generation individual from generation 29, with a standardized fitness of 890, comes very close to the actual Fibonacci sequence (i.e., a discrepancy of only about 44.5 per fitness case for a series whose 20th value is 6,765).

Table 18.4 Standardized fitness of the best-of-generation individual for generations 0, 1, and 29.

J	Fib(J)	Gen. 0	Gen. 0 error	Gen. 1	Gen. 1 error	Gen. 29	Gen. 29 error
0	1	4	−3	2	−1	−2	3
1	1	3	−2	−3	4	−2	3
2	2	−6	8	−3	5	−8	10
3	3	−9	12	−1	4	−6	9
4	5	−6	11	7	−2	−18	23
5	8	15	−7	27	−19	−20	28
6	13	58	−45	63	−50	−10	23
7	21	129	−108	119	−98	−8	29
8	34	234	−200	199	−165	−2	36
9	55	379	−324	307	−252	14	41
10	89	570	−481	447	−358	52	37
11	144	813	−669	623	−479	104	40
12	233	1114	−881	839	−606	206	27
13	377	1479	−1102	1099	−722	348	29
14	610	1914	−1304	1407	−797	614	−4
15	987	2425	−1438	1767	−780	976	11
16	1597	3018	−1421	2183	−586	1638	−41
17	2584	3699	−1115	2659	−75	2534	50
18	4181	4474	−293	3199	982	4156	25
19	6765	5349	1416	3807	2958	6344	421
Fitness			10840		8943		890

Table 18.4 shows the general nature of the best-of-generation individual for generations 0, 1, and 29 of this run. The raw fitness for each individual (i.e., the sum of the absolute value of the errors) is shown in the last row of the table. As can be seen, each of these three approximations to the Fibonacci sequence bears a progressively greater resemblance to the actual sequence. For example, the best-of-generation individual from generation 0 is a generally increasing sequence that reaches the general neighborhood of the correct value for sequence position 19 (i.e., 5,349 versus 6,765). Note that this individual (as well as the next two individuals) is flawed in that it goes negative for certain positions of the sequence. This individual has a average error of 542 per sequence position (i.e., 10,840 divided by 20). The best-of-generation individual from generation 1 also is a generally increasing sequence that reaches the general neighborhood of the correct value for sequence position 19. It has a slightly better average error per sequence position (i.e., 447) than the best-of-generation individual from generation 0. The best-of-generation individual from generation 29 has an average error of 44.5 per sequence position. While none of these three individual S-expressions produces the Fibonacci sequence, they get progressively closer to the target sequence.

The best-of-generation individual for generation 30 had a raw fitness of 0 (i.e., a perfect score), scored 20 hits, and consisted of 139 points:

```
(+ (SRF (+ 3 (+ (SRF (+ 3 (+ 1 (* 1 3))) (+ (J J) (−
(SRF (− J 2) (SRF J J)) (+ (− J J) (+ (+ (SRF (+ 3 (+ 1
```

```
J)) (+ J (* 1 3))) (SRF J J)) (- (+ 2 J) (* J J))))))))
(SRF (- (SRF (- J 2) (+ 2 J)) (+ (- J J) (+ (+ (SRF (SRF
(- J 2) (+ J 1)) (+ J (* 1 3))) (SRF J J)) (- (+ 2 J) (*
J J))))) 2))) (+ (SRF (- J 2) (SRF (- J 2) (+ J (- 3
3)))) (- (SRF (- J 2) (SRF J J)) (SRF (- J 2) (+ 1 J)))))
(SRF (SRF J (- (SRF (- J J) (SRF J J)) (+ (- 2 J) (- 3
3)))) 2)).
```

This best-of-run S-expression is a 100%-correct S-expression for the Fibonacci sequence.

In another run, we obtained on generation 22 the following best-of-run S-expression, which scored 20 hits:

```
(+ (SRF (- J 2) 0)
   (SRF (+ (+ (- J 2) 0) (SRF (- J J) 0))
        (SRF (SRF 3 1) 1))).
```

A close examination will reveal that this S-expression is also a 100%-correct S-expression for the Fibonacci sequence.

19 Evolution of Constrained Syntactic Structures

In all of the previous chapters in this book, the individual computer programs (LISP S-expressions) undergoing adaptation were unrestricted compositions of the available functions and available terminals (subject only to the boundary condition limiting the maximum size of an S-expression). As LISP programmers are well aware, unrestricted S-expressions are sufficient to solve a surprisingly wide range of problems. In genetic programming, unrestricted S-expressions are sufficient to solve numerous problems provided one selects a function set and a terminal set satisfying the closure property. In practice, this involves (1) assigning some suitable value whenever functions such as division, square root, and logarithm might be undefined and (2) handling conditional operators in one of the three ways described in subsection 6.1.1. Nonetheless, some problems call for constrained syntactic structure for the S-expressions.

This chapter presents problems where the individuals in the population have a constrained syntactic structure that is defined by means of special problem-specific syntactic rules of construction.

Three new considerations arise when one is implementing genetic programming with S-expressions that have such constrained syntactic structure.

- The initial population of random individuals must be created so that every individual computer program in the population has the required syntactic structure.

- When crossover (or any other genetic operation that modifies an individual) is performed, the required syntactic structure must be preserved. The required syntactic structure can be preserved by means of structure-preserving crossover. Structure-preserving crossover is a restricted form of crossover that always produces offspring conforming to the syntactic structure of the problem. Similar structure-preserving genetic operations (e.g., mutation) can be defined as needed.

- The fitness measure must take the syntactic structure into account.

In this chapter, we discuss the problems of

- symbolic multiple regression,
- design of a two-bit adder circuit,

- solving a pair of linear equations for both unknowns,
- finding a global optimum point for a multi-dimensional function,
- solving a quadratic equation for both complex roots,
- finding the Fourier series for a function,
- finding the inverse kinematics for controlling a two-link robot arm,
- local tracking of a dynamical system, and
- simultaneously designing the architecture and determining the weights for a neural network for a one-bit adder.

19.1 SYMBOLIC MULTIPLE REGRESSION

The previous examples of symbolic regression (sections 7.3, 10.1, and 10.2), involved one or more independent variables, but only one dependent variable. This section discusses symbolic regression with more than one dependent variable.

The problem of symbolic *multiple regression* illustrates the need to create random individuals that comply with a special set of syntactic rules of construction and to then perform structure-preserving crossover on those individuals.

Consider a symbolic regression problem with two dependent variables y_1 and y_2 and four independent variables x_1, x_2, x_3, and x_4. In particular, suppose we are given a set of 50 fitness cases (data points) in the form of 6-tuples of the form $(x_{1i}, x_{2i}, x_{3i}, x_{4i}, y_{1i}, y_{2i})$. Each x_{1i}, x_{2i}, x_{3i}, and x_{4i}, (for i between 1 and 50) lies in some interval of interest, perhaps $[-1.0, +1.0]$. Suppose further that the unknown relationships between these two dependent variables and the four independent variables are

$$y_{1i} = x_{1i}x_{3i} - x_{2i}x_{4i}$$

and

$$y_{2i} = x_{2i}x_{3i} + x_{1i}x_{4i}$$

for i between 1 and 50. In other words, the unknown relationship is vector multiplication (i.e., complex multiplication).

The terminal set for the symbolic multiple regression problem consists of the independent variables of the problem, namely

```
T = {X1, X2, X3, X4}.
```

In order to solve this problem by means of genetic programming, we need a computer program that returns two values (y_1 and y_2), instead of merely the single return value that we have seen in previous problems. That is, the computer program should return an ordered set (vector) of two numbers, rather than a single number. The LIST function with two arguments (called LIST2 herein) can be used to create an ordered set of two numbers.

If we are thinking of compositions of the four arithmetic operations, the function set for this problem should consist of the four arithmetic operations along with the LIST2 function. That is,

```
F = {+, -, *, %, LIST2},
```

each taking two arguments.

The syntactic rules of construction required for the multiple regression problem where a vector of two values must be returned are these:

- The root of the tree (i.e., the function just inside the leftmost parenthesis of the LISP S-expression) is the LIST2 function.
- The root is the only place where the LIST2 function will appear in a given S-expression.
- Below the root, the S-expression is an unrestricted composition of the available functions (other than the LIST2) from the function set F and the available terminals from the terminal set T.

Three additional changes are also required when a problem involves syntactic rules of construction.

First, the initial population of random individuals must be created using these syntactic rules of construction. For this problem, the desired structure can be obtained merely by restraining the choice of function for the root of the tree to the LIST2 function. Thereafter, the choice of a function for any other internal point of the tree is an unrestricted choice from the remaining functions in the function set (i.e., +, −, *, and %).

Second, the choice of points in the crossover operation must be constrained so as to preserve the structure required by the problem. This restraining process can be viewed in two ways. The simplest (and least general) way to perform the restraining process is to exclude the root of the tree from being selected as the crossover point of either parent in the crossover operation. This restraint guarantees that the crossover operation preserves the syntactic structure required by this particular problem; however, this approach lacks generality when the rules of construction are more complex. The general way to perform the restraining process for structure-preserving crossover is to allow any point to be selected as the crossover point for the *first* parent. However, once the crossover point has been selected for the first parent, the selection of the crossover point in the *second* parent is then restricted to a point of the same type as the point just chosen from the first parent. For this problem, there are two types of points involved:

- the root of the tree (which is always the LIST2 function), and
- all other points of the tree.

Thus, if a non-root point is chosen as the crossover point for the first parent, then a non-root point must be chosen as the crossover point of the second parent. If the root is chosen as the crossover point for the first parent, then the selection of the crossover point of the second parent is constrained to points of this same type. For this particular problem, there is only one point in the second parent that is of this same type, namely the root of the second parent. As it happens, when the crossover operation selects the roots of both parents as crossover points, the operation merely swaps the entire parental trees so that the crossover operation, in effect, degenerates into an instance of reproduction.

Third, the fitness measure must take into account the fact that a vector of values is returned by each S-expression. Raw fitness is equal to the sum, taken over all 50 fitness cases, of the absolute values of the differences between the value of the first dependent variable returned by the S-expression and the target value of the first dependent variable plus a similar sum, taken over all 50 fitness cases, for the second dependent variable.

A hit is defined as a fitness case for which the two differences are both less than 0.01.

Table 19.1 summarizes the key features of the problem of applying multiple regression to find the two components of the formula for multiplication of two complex numbers. This table and all the other tables for problems involving constrained syntactic rules have additional rows for the rules of construction and the types of points.

Table 19.1 Tableau for symbolic multiple regression.

Objective:	Find a vector-valued S-expression giving the formula for the multiplication of two vectors (i.e., complex multiplication).
Terminal set:	X1, X2, X3, X4.
Function set:	+, −, *, %, LIST2, each taking two arguments.
Fitness cases:	50 fitness cases consisting of the four independent variables (x_1, x_2, x_3, and x_4) and the two dependent variables (y_1 and y_2).
Raw fitness:	Sum (taken over the 50 fitness cases) of the sum (over two components of the vector) of the absolute values of the difference (error) between the value returned by the S-expression and the target value for the particular fitness case.
Standardized fitness:	Same as raw fitness for this problem.
Hits:	A fitness case for which the error is less than 0.01 for both components of the vector.
Wrapper:	None.
Parameters:	$M = 500.$ $G = 51.$
Success predicate:	An S-expression scores 50 hits.
Rules of construction:	• Root is always the LIST2 function. • Remainder of the tree is composition of the available functions (other than LIST2) and the available terminals.
Types of points:	Two types of points: • the root, and • non-root points.

In one run, the best LISP S-expression in generation 31 was

```
(LIST2 (- (* X3 X1) (* X4 X2))
       (+ (* X3 X2) (* X1 X4))).
```

Figure 19.1 graphically depicts this best-of-run S-expression from generation 31. The two arguments to the LIST2 function are the two desired functional relationships.

When a problem requires finding two or more components of a vector, one should consider increasing the maximum number of generations to be run because the genetic operations operate on only one of the components each time they are applied. We did not do so here.

Figure 19.2 shows, by generation, the performance curves showing the probability of success, $P(M, i)$, that at least one individual S-expression in the population scores 50 hits for the symbolic multiple regression problem with complex multiplication as the target function. The graph is based on 300 runs. The probability of success $P(M, i)$ is 8% by generation 22, and 13% by generation 50. The numbers 22 and 609,500 in the oval indicate that if this

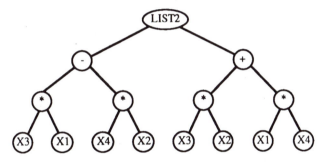

Figure 19.1 Best-of-run individual from generation 31 of the symbolic multiple regression problem for complex multiplication.

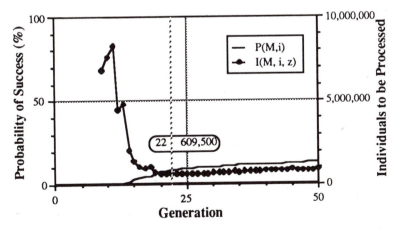

Figure 19.2 Performance curves for the symbolic multiple regression problem for complex multiplication.

problem is run through to generation 22, processing a total of 609,500 individuals (i.e., 500 × 23 generations × 53 runs) is sufficient to yield a solution to this problem with 99% probability.

An experiment concerning limiting structure-preserving crossover to the left or the right branch in this problem is presented in section 25.11.

19.2 DESIGN OF A TWO-BIT ADDER CIRCUIT

The problem of designing a circuit with multiple outputs illustrates the need to create random individuals that comply with a special set of syntactic rules of construction and to then perform structure-preserving crossover on those individuals.

In this problem, we want to evolve a circuit composed of AND, OR, and NOT elements with four binary inputs and three binary outputs.

The input to the circuit consists of two two-bit numbers. The output consists of the three-bit binary sum of the two two-bit inputs.

The terminal set for this problem consists of the four input signals. That is,

T = {A1, A0, D1, D0}.

Here A1 is the high-order bit of the first two-bit input, and A0 is the low-order bit of the first input. D1 is the high-order bit of the second two-bit input, and D0 is the low-order bit of the second input.

The function set for this problem consists of the three kinds of circuit elements that we are considering and the LIST3 function. That is,

F = {AND, OR, NOT, LIST3},

taking two, two, one, and three arguments, respectively.

The syntactic rules of construction required for the problem of designing a circuit, where a vector of three values must be returned, are as follows:

- The root of the tree (i.e., the function just inside the leftmost parenthesis of the LISP S-expression) is the function LIST3 with three arguments.
- The root is the only place where the LIST3 function will appear in a given S-expression.
- Below the root, the S-expression is an unrestricted composition of the available functions (other than LIST3) and the terminals.

There are two types of points involved:

- the root of the tree (which is always the LIST3 function), and
- all other points of the tree.

The fitness cases for this problem consist of the 16 combinations of the values that may be assumed by the four Boolean-valued terminals, A1, A0, D1, and D0. The three binary output signals are weighted by consecutive powers of 2 (i.e., 1, 2, and 4). Fitness is the sum, taken over the 16 fitness cases, of the position-weighted differences (errors) between the three binary signals produced by the S-expression and the correct three binary signals for that fitness

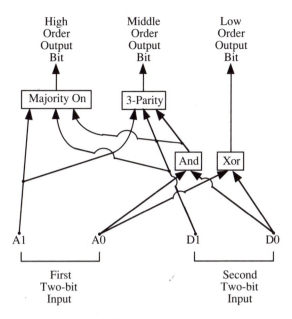

High Order Output Bit Middle Order Output Bit Low Order Output Bit

Figure 19.3 Two-bit adder circuit.

case. The minimum error of 0 is attained if all three binary output signals are correct for all 16 fitness cases. The maximum error of 112 (i.e., 16 times the sum of 1, 2, and 4) is attained if all three binary output signals are wrong for all 16 fitness cases. Therefore, raw fitness ranges from 0 to 112.

Figure 19.3 is a diagram of the three output bits of the two-bit adder circuit. The low-order output bit on the right side of the figure is the exclusive-or (odd-2-parity) of the two low-order input bits A0 and D0. The middle output bit is the odd-3-parity of the two high-order input bits A1 and D1 and the output of the AND of the two low-order bits A0 and D0 (i.e., the carry bit from the low-order position). The high-order output bit is the 3-Majority-On function of the two high-order input bits A1 and D1 and the output of the AND of the two low-order bits A0 and D0. As shown in chapter 9, the odd-2-parity and the even-2-parity functions are the most difficult Boolean functions with two arguments to discover with our usual function sets.

Table 19.2 summarizes the key features of the problem of designing a two-bit adder circuit.

In one run, the following 100%-correct individual emerged as the best-of-run S-expression on generation 24:

```
(LIST3 (OR (AND (OR (AND (OR (AND D1 D1) (OR (AND D1 D1)
           (OR D1 A1))) (OR (AND D1 A1) (AND D0 A0)))
           (AND A1 D1)) (OR (AND D1 A1) (AND D0 A0)))
           (AND (OR (AND D1 D1) (OR D1 A1)) (AND D0 A0)))
      (AND (OR (OR A1 D1) (AND A0 D0)) (AND (AND (AND
           (OR (NOT D0) (OR D0 A1)) (OR (OR (OR D1 D1)
           (AND A0 D0)) (AND (OR D1 A1) (OR (OR (OR D1
```

Table 19.2 Tableau for design of the two-bit adder circuit.

Objective:	Find the composition of logical circuit elements that takes two inputs consisting of two bits each and produces the three-bit sum.
Terminal set:	A0, A1, D1, D0.
Function set:	AND, OR, NOT, LIST3.
Fitness cases:	Sixteen fitness cases consisting of all combinations of the four Boolean-valued terminals.
Raw fitness:	The sum, taken over the 16 fitness cases, of the position-weighted differences (errors) between the three binary signals produced by the S-expression and the correct three binary signals for that fitness case.
Standardized fitness:	Same as raw fitness for this problem.
Hits:	Number (0–16) of fitness cases for which the three binary signals produced by the S-expression match the correct three binary signals.
Wrapper:	None.
Parameters:	$M = 1{,}000$ (with over-selection). $G = 51$.
Success predicate:	An S-expression scores 50 hits.
Rules of construction:	• Root is always the LIST3 function. • Remainder of the tree is composed of the available functions (other than LIST3) and the available terminals.
Types of points:	Two types of points: • the root, and • non-root points.

```
          A1) (AND D1 A1)) A1)))) (NOT (AND D1 (AND A1
      (NOT (AND A0 D0)))))) (NOT (AND (AND (AND (OR
      (NOT D0) (OR D0 A1)) (OR (OR D1 D1) (AND (OR
      D1 A1) (OR (OR (OR D1 A1) (OR (OR (AND A0 D0)
      D1) (AND A0 D0))) A1)))) (NOT (AND D1 (AND A1
      (OR D1 D1)))))) (OR (AND A0 D0) (AND D1
      A1))))))
  (AND (NOT (AND (OR A0 (OR A0 A0)) D0)) (OR A0
      D0))).
```

The first clause in the above S-expression is equivalent to the four-argument Boolean rule 60,544 (using the numbering scheme for Boolean functions described in chapter 9 in which the four arguments here are taken in the order A1, A0, D1, D0). Rule 60,544 is the majority function of three arguments applied to the arguments A1, D1 and (AND D0, A0). The high-order output bit of the two-bit adder is precisely that function.

The second clause is equivalent to rule 37,740, which is

`(XOR A1 (XOR D1 (AND A0 D0)))`.

The middle output bit of the two-bit adder is precisely that function.

Finally, the third clause in the above S-expression is equivalent to rule 23,130, which is

`(XOR D0 A0)`.

The low-order output bit of the two-bit adder is precisely that function.

In an actual circuit-design problem, it might be appropriate to include the number of logical gates (a parsimony measure) in the fitness function for this problem, either from the beginning of the run or at a certain point later in the run.

19.3 SOLVING PAIRS OF LINEAR EQUATIONS

The problem of solving a pair of linear equations for *both* unknowns provides an additional illustration of how to formulate and solve a problem whose solution is a vector of values.

The problem here is to find a vector-valued S-expression for solving a pair of consistent non-indeterminate linear equations, namely

$$a_{11}x_1 + a_{12}x_2 = b_1$$

and

$$a_{21}x_1 + a_{22}x_2 = b_2,$$

for both of its two unknown variables (x_1 and x_2). In other words, we are seeking a computer program that takes a_{11}, a_{12}, a_{21}, a_{22}, b_1, and b_2 as its inputs and produces x_1 and x_2 as its output. We assume that the coefficients of the equations were prenormalized so the determinant is 1.

The terminal set is

`T = {A11, A12, A21, A22, B1, B2}`.

It seems natural to include the four arithmetic operations in the function set, namely addition, subtraction, multiplication, and the protected division function (`%`). Moreover, this function set is known to be adequate for solving this problem. The function set is

`F = {+, -, *, %, LIST2}`,

each taking two arguments.

The syntactic rules of construction and the resulting two types of points for this problem are the same as for the multiple regression problem described in section 19.1.

Since we are seeking a mathematical formula capable of solving any pair of linear equations whose determinant is 1, we want the result produced by genetic programming to have the potential of generalizing over all such pairs of equations. Therefore, the fitness cases are ten randomly created pairs of

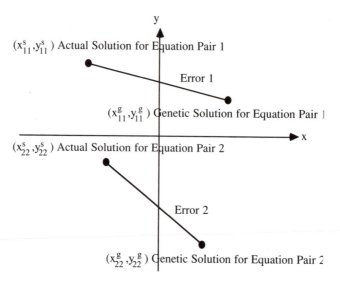

Figure 19.4 The two lines show the error for fitness cases 1 and 2 for the problem of solving a pair of linear equations for both unknowns.

linear equations whose determinant is one. Each pair of equations is created by generating six random numbers between -10.000 and $+10.000$ (with a granularity of 0.001) and assigning the six random numbers to a_{11}, a_{12}, a_{21}, a_{22}, b_1, and b_2 for that pair of equations. If the determinant of any pair of equations is zero, six new random values are selected for that pair of equations. If the determinant is nonzero, the values of a_{11}, a_{12}, a_{21}, and a_{22} are divided by the square root of the determinant for that pair in order to yield a pair of equations with a determinant of 1. Then each pair of equations is solved and the correct values of x_1 and x_2 are associated with each pair.

Raw fitness is measured by the erroneousness of the S-expression. The fitness measure is the sum, taken over for all ten fitness cases, of the Euclidean distance in the plane between the genetically produced solution point (x^g_{1i}, x^g_{2i}) for equation pair i and the actual solution point (x^s_{1i}, x^s_{2i}) for equation pair i. The closer this sum is to zero, the better the S-expression. If the S-expression were a correct general formula for solving a pair of linear equations in two unknowns, the sum of these distances would be zero. Thus, for this problem, standardized fitness equals raw fitness.

Figure 19.4 shows, for fitness cases 1 and 2 only, the distance (error) between the solution point (x^g_{1i}, x^g_{2i}) produced by a genetically produced S-expression and the actual solution point (x^s_{1i}, x^s_{2i}) for equation pair i. The lines in the figure connect the two points associated with a particular pair of equations and graphically represent the error. If the S-expression were the correct general formula for solving a pair of linear equations, the two points would overlap and there would be no line shown (i.e., the error would be zero).

Table 19.3 summarizes the key features of the problem of solving a pair of linear equations for both unknowns.

Table 19.3 Tableau for solving a pair of linear equations for both unknowns.

Objective:	Find the S-expression that returns the vector (x_1, x_2) that solves a pair of consistent and non-indeterminate linear equations for both unknowns.
Terminal set:	A11, A12, A21, A22, B1, B2.
Function set:	+, −, *, %, LIST2.
Fitness cases:	Ten pairs of linear equations in two unknowns.
Raw fitness:	Sum (taken over the ten pairs of equations) of the sum (taken over two components of the solution vector) of the absolute values of the Euclidean distances between the point returned by the S-expression and the actual solution point for the particular pair of equations.
Standardized fitness:	Same as raw fitness for this problem.
Hits:	A fitness case for which the error is less than 0.01 for both components of the vector.
Wrapper:	None.
Parameters:	$M = 500$. $G = 51$.
Success predicate:	An S-expression scores 10 hits.
Rules of construction:	• Root is always the LIST2 function. • Remainder of the tree is a composition of the available functions (other than LIST2) and the available terminals.
Types of points:	Two types of points: • the root, and • non-root points.

In one run, the following S-expression emerged as the 100%-correct solution to the problem:

```
(LIST2 (- (* A22 B1) (*B2 A12))
       (% A21 (% A21 (- (* B2 A11) (* A21 B1)))))).
```

Figure 19.5 graphically depicts this 100%-correct best-of-run S-expression. When the two useless consecutive division operations are removed, this S-expression is equivalent to the familiar solution to this problem.

In another run, the following S-expression appeared for the first unknown x_1 in an intermediate generation:

```
(+ (- A12 (* A12 B2)) (* A22 B1)).
```

This S-expression is equivalent to

$$a_{22}b_1 - a_{12}b_2 + a_{12},$$

which differs from the known correct expression for x_1 only by the additive term $+a_{12}$. While the above S-expression is not the correct expression for x_1, it is an example of an approximately correct mathematical expression. One

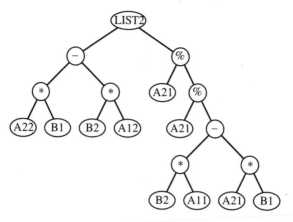

Figure 19.5 Best-of-run individual for the problem for solving a pair of linear equations for both unknowns.

could use this formula and obtain answers that are approximately correct for many pairs of equations. This S-expression is an example of a reasonably good, but incorrect, program that appears along the trajectory produced by genetic programming through the space of possible computer programs. It would be unlikely that a program such as this would appear in the trajectory of incorrect programs that a human programmer would write in an attempt to solve a pair of linear equations. A human programmer would be unlikely to ever add an extraneous additive term such as $+a_{12}$ to a program. The trajectory of programs produced by a human programmer through the space of computer programs is very different from the trajectory of program produced by genetic programming.

19.4   FINDING A GLOBAL OPTIMUM POINT

The conventional genetic algorithm operating on strings is frequently used to solve function-optimization problems requiring the finding of a global optimum point for a highly nonlinear multi-dimensional function. In such problems, the goal is to find a point in the multi-dimensional space over the various independent variables of the problem for which the function attains a minimal (or maximal) value.

When the conventional genetic algorithm operating on strings is applied to such a problem, each chromosome string typically represents a combination of values of the various independent variables. If a binary alphabet is being used, each bit position in the chromosome string typically represents one bit of the value of one of the independent variables expressed as a binary number. In any event, the fitness measure of a given chromosome is the value of the function to be optimized for the combination of values of the independent variables represented by the chromosome. The result produced by the genetic algorithm is a single point from the search space. It is often the point where the function attains its global optimum value.

Ordinarily, when we apply genetic programming to an optimization problem, the result typically comes in the form of an entire function (as in section 11.3), not just a single point. However, we can use genetic programming to find a single optimum point, rather than an entire function, by simply excluding all independent variables from the terminal set. That is, we include only random constants of the appropriate type in the terminal set (as we did when we solved mathematical equations for numeric values in section 10.11).

For example, consider the problem of finding the global optimum (i.e., minimum) point for the five-dimensional function

$$F_1(x_1, x_2, x_3, x_4, x_5)$$
$$= (x_1 - 1)^2 + (x_2 - \sqrt{2})^2 + (x_3 - \sqrt{3})^2 + (x_4 - 2)^2 + (x_5 - \sqrt{5})^2.$$

The desired global optimum value is, of course, 0 and it occurs at the point $(1, \sqrt{2}, \sqrt{3}, 2, \sqrt{5})$ in the five-dimensional space. This function is patterned after De Jong's (1975) function F_1, which had its global optimum at (0, 0, 0, 0, 0).

The terminal set for this problem consists only of the ephemeral random floating-point constant atom $\Re$, namely

T = {$\Re$}.

The function set for this problem consists of the usual arithmetic operations, namely

F = {+, -, *, %, LIST5},

taking two, two, two, two, and five arguments, respectively.

The syntactic rules of construction and the resulting two types of points for this problem are the same as for the multiple regression problem described in section 19.1, except that there are five main branches below a LIST5 function at the root.

Raw fitness is the value of the function F_1 for the point $(x_1, x_2, x_3, x_4, x_5)$ in the five-dimensional space. The point corresponds to the one fitness case for this problem. Since we are seeking a global minimum point, standardized fitness equals raw fitness for this problem. One hit is scored for each independent variable that comes within 0.001 of the correct value (i.e., 0).

If we did not know that the minimal value of the function was 0, raw fitness and standardized fitness would be defined in the same way; however, we could not define a hit in the above fashion and we could not, therefore, use attainment of five hits as part of the termination criterion for this problem. We would then have to make a judgment (perhaps using other available information about the problem) as to whether the best point found in a series of runs was indeed the global optimum point.

Of course, if the problem involves finding a global maximum point, rather than a minimum point, standardized fitness is the difference between some bound (either the known maximum value of the function or some safe upper bound) and the raw fitness.

Table 19.4 summarizes the key features of the problem of optimizing the function F_1.

Table 19.4 Tableau for optimization of a multi-dimensional function.

Objective:	Find the S-expression designating the point in a five-dimensional space where the value of an unknown 5-dimensional function is minimized.
Terminal set:	The ephemeral random floating-point constant atom $\Re$.
Function set:	+, −, *, %, LIST5.
Fitness cases:	One fitness case.
Raw fitness:	The value of the function F_1 to be minimized for the point $(x_1, x_2, x_3, x_4, x_5)$ in the multidimensional search space.
Standardized fitness:	Same as raw fitness for this problem.
Hits:	A component of the vector for which the error is less than 0.001.
Wrapper:	None.
Parameters:	$M = 2{,}000$ (with over-selection). $G = 51$.
Success predicate:	An S-expression scores 5 hits.
Rules of construction:	• Root is always the LIST5 function. • Remainder of the tree is composition of available functions (other than LIST5) and the available random constants.
Types of points:	Two types of points: • the root, and • non-root points.

In generation 45 of one run, the following S-expression containing 92 points scored 5 hits out of 5 and had a fitness of 0.00186:

```
(LIST5 (- (* (* (- (+ (% -0.7672 -0.6696) 0.793) (- (%
       0.7384 -0.338303) -0.0279999)) -0.0279999) (*
       -0.788605 (% -0.2602 -0.9012))) (- -0.468903
       0.50569))
    (+ (+ 0.65669 0.810394) (+ -0.139603 0.086395))
    (- (% -0.375504 -0.246803) (* -0.788605 (%
       -0.2602 (- -0.468903 0.50569))))
    (+ (- 0.804504 (% 0.5775 (% (- -0.6696 0.50569)
       (% 0.541 0.76779)))) (- 0.804504 (* (- (* (-
       (+ 0.50569 (* -0.9012 (* -0.066803 (% -0.2602
       -0.9012)))) (+ 0.810394 0.195404)) (*
       -0.279404 -0.0108032)) (+ (% 0.816696
       -0.451797) (+ 0.6409 -0.451797))) -0.0279999)))
    (+ (- 0.804504 (- -0.042 0.244095)) (% -0.7672
       -0.6696))).
```

This S-expression is equivalent to

```
(LIST5 1.0007 1.414 1.732 2.0005 2.2364).
```

As can be seen, this S-expression approximates the desired globally optimum point within the precision specified by the hits criterion.

19.5 SOLVING QUADRATIC EQUATIONS

For each of the foregoing examples in this chapter, the search space of the problem was multi-dimensional, and we used the syntactic rules of construction merely to represent the more or less unrelated components of the points in the search space. The problem in this section involves complex numbers, and we could have proceeded in this same way. Instead, we will use this problem (and other problems later in this chapter) to explicitly illustrate how we might *use some knowledge about the nature of the solution of the problem to decompose the problem* and create the syntactic rules of construction.

The quadratic equation

$$ax^2 + bx + c = 0$$

can be solved for its two roots (which are often imaginary or complex numbers) by the familiar formula

$$x = \frac{-b \pm \sqrt{(b^2 - 4ac)}}{2a}.$$

The terminal set consists of the three coefficients of the quadratic equation to be solved, namely

```
T = {A, B, C}.
```

The function set for this problem is

```
F = {+, -, *, %, SQRT, LIST2},
```

taking two, two, two, two, one, and two arguments, respectively. SQRT is the Common LISP square root function and returns either a floating-point value or a complex value, as appropriate. For example, if the SQRT function is applied to -4.0, the result is the LISP complex number #C(0.0 2.0) representing $2i = 2\sqrt{-1}$.

The $\pm$ sign in the above formula represents two roots which are a related pair of complex numbers. This suggests that the problem be viewed as a search for two complex numbers that, when acted upon by the plus and minus signs, produce the two desired complex roots. Each S-expression is a list of two components and represents the pair of complex numbers. The two complex numbers belonging to the pair are produced from the two components of a single S-expression by a wrapper (an output interface). The wrapper first takes the first component of the S-expression and *adds* the second component to produce the first number. Then, the wrapper takes the first component of the S-expression and *subtracts* the second component to produce the second number. In other words, the wrapper performs the role of the $\pm$ sign and

Evolution of Constrained Syntactic Structures

produces the two complex numbers of the desired complex pair from the S-expression.

The syntactic rules of construction and the resulting two types of points for this problem are the same as for the multiple regression problem described in section 19.1.

Since we are seeking a mathematical formula capable of solving a general quadratic equation, we want the result produced by genetic programming to have the potential of generalizing over all quadratic equations. Therefore, the fitness cases for this problem consist of random quadratic equations. In particular, the fitness cases consist of ten quadratic equations, the coefficients A, B, and C being random numbers between -10 and $+10$ (and with the coefficient A $\neq 0$ to avoid degeneracy).

Each of the ten equations is solved for its two roots (which are, in general, a conjugate pair of complex numbers). The first root is produced by using the $+$ sign in the well-known formula above for solving quadratic equations; the second root is produced by using the $-$ sign. These two roots are, in general, LISP complex numbers.

We envision the first component of a perfect solution to be the real-valued quotient

$$\frac{-b}{2a},$$

and we envision the second component of the solution to this problem to be the (possibly complex-valued) quotient

$$\frac{\sqrt{(b^2 - 4ac)}}{2a}.$$

If the S-expression is correct, the two numbers that are produced by the wrapper will be the two roots of the quadratic equation.

The fitness of a given S-expression is the sum, taken over the ten fitness cases, of the sum of two Euclidean distances representing errors. The first Euclidean distance is between the first root of the equation and the first number produced by the wrapper (i.e., using the $+$ sign). The second Euclidean distance is between the second root of the equation and the second number produced by the wrapper (i.e., using the $-$ sign). The Euclidean distance between two points in the complex plane is the square root of the sum of the squares of the difference between the real parts of the two points (accessed via the Common LISP function REALPART) and the imaginary parts of the two points (accessed via the Common LISP function IMAGPART).

Table 19.5 summarizes the key features of the problem of solving a quadratic equation for its two complex roots.

In one run, the following S-expression emerged on generation 30:

```
(LIST2 (% (- (% B (+ A A)) (% (SQRT (% (* (* (- (SQRT B)
        (SQRT B)) (* (+ (- C A) A) (% A B))) (* (SQRT
        (% B B)) (* (- (% (SQRT A) (SQRT (SQRT (SQRT
        A)))) (% (SQRT -1) (* C -3))) (- B B)))) (* A
```

Table 19.5 Tableau for quadratic equations.

Objective:	Solve the quadratic equation $ax^2 + bx + c = 0$ for its two complex roots expressed in terms of a mathematical formula expressed involving the three coefficients a, b, and c.
Terminal set:	A, B, C.
Function set:	+, −, *, %, SQRT, LIST2.
Fitness cases:	Ten random non-degenerate quadratic equations.
Raw fitness:	The sum, taken over the ten fitness cases, of the sum of the two Euclidean distances representing the errors.
Standardized fitness:	Same as raw fitness for this problem.
Hits:	Number of fitness cases for which the error is less than 0.01.
Wrapper:	Converts the two values returned by the S-expression (Real, Imag) into the two roots (Real + Imag) and (Real − Imag).
Parameters:	$M = 500$. $G = 51$.
Success predicate:	An S-expression scores 10 hits.
Rules of construction:	• Root is always the LIST2 function. • Remainder of the tree is a composition of the available functions (other than LIST2) and the available terminals.
Types of points:	Two types of points: • the root, and • non-root points.

```
A))) (* C -3))) (- (% (% (- (SQRT (% (* (* (-
(SQRT (% 3 -4)) (SQRT B)) (* (SQRT -1) (% A
B))) (* (SQRT (% B B)) (* (- -2 C) (- B B))))
(* A A))) (% (SQRT (SQRT (* (- B B) B))) (* C
-3))) (- C A)) (SQRT -1)) (% (SQRT A) (% (SQRT
(% (* (* (- (SQRT B) (SQRT B)) (* (SQRT -1) (%
A B))) (* (SQRT (% B B)) (* (- -2 C) (- B
B)))) (* A A))) (* C -3)))))
(% (SQRT (+ (+ B -5) (+ (- (* (- (+ B -5) 1) (%
(+ 1 B) 4)) (+ (* C A) (- (+ (% (- B B) 4) -5)
1))) (% (+ 1 (+ 1 B)) 4)))) A)).
```

This best-of-run S-expression had a raw fitness of about 10^{-8} and scored 10 hits out of 10.

When rerun on 100 random quadratic equations, it had a similarly small raw fitness and scored 100 hits out of 100.

The first component of the S-expression above is equivalent to

```
(% (- B) (* 2 A)).
```

The second component is equivalent to

```
(% (SQRT (- (* 0.25 B B) (* A C))) A)).
```

These two components are equivalent to the desired result.

19.6 FINDING A FOURIER SERIES

In this section, we find the Fourier series that represents a given periodic function.

Figure 19.6 shows the function x^2 over the interval $[-\pi, +\pi]$ with the curve from that interval then repeated over one subsequent and one preceding 2π interval. The function is an even function in the sense that $f(x) = f(-x)$.

The Fourier series

$$a_0 + \sum_{j=1}^{\infty} a_j \cos \theta + b_j \sin \theta$$

is, of course, an infinite series. Finding a Fourier series that represents a given function, such as x^2, requires finding both the Fourier coefficients and the appropriate number of terms to include in the series (Tolstov 1962). In other words, the size of the S-expression for the x^2 function is not known in advance and must be determined dynamically.

The first few terms of the correct Fourier series for x^2 are the following:

$$x^2 = \frac{\pi^2}{3} - 4\cos x + \frac{4\cos 2x}{2^2} - \frac{4\cos 3x}{3^2} + \frac{4\cos 4x}{4^2} - \cdots.$$

In this problem, we want to genetically breed individuals with an indefinite number of additive terms, each consisting of either the sine or the cosine of an integral multiple of the argument x. We do not want to specify the number of

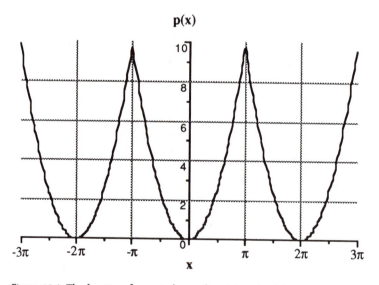

Figure 19.6 The function x^2 repeated over three intervals of size 2π.

such terms in advance; instead, we want the number of such terms to emerge as a result of the evolutionary process.

This problem can be approached by specifying a syntactic structure on the allowable structures in the population. However, first we define three special functions for this problem.

The function & is merely the ordinary arithmetic addition function with two arguments. However, for purposes of defining the syntactic structure required for this problem, we give ordinary addition this special name in order to distinguish it from other uses of this same function in this problem.

The function XSIN is a two-argument function that can be defined in LISP as follows:

```
(defun XSIN (arg1 arg2)
    (* arg1 (sin (round (* arg2 X)))))
).
```

The first argument to XSIN is the coefficient (e.g., b_3), and the second argument is the harmonic. The second argument is rounded off to the nearest integer by the function in order to produce the desired harmonics at the fundamental frequencies. Note that the variable X is not an explicit argument to this function; it is, instead, a global variable that acquires its value outside the function XSIN (i.e., in the loop that iterates through the fitness cases).

The function XCOS is defined in a similar manner.

The syntactic rules of construction required for the indefinitely sized S-expression required for this problem are the following:

- The root of the tree (i.e., the function just inside the leftmost parenthesis of the LISP S-expression) is the function & with two arguments.
- The only thing allowed below an & function is either another & function or an XSIN or XCOS function.
- The only thing allowed below an XSIN or XCOS function is either a floating-point random constant or an arithmetic function (+, −, *, %).

For this problem, there are three types of points:

- a point containing an & function,
- a point containing an XSIN or XCOS function, and
- a point containing an arithmetic function or a random constant.

The fitness cases for this problem consist of 200 pairs of (x_i, y_i) points, where x_i ranges randomly over the interval $[-3\pi, +3\pi]$. The fact that the 200 x_i points are an average of 1.8° apart seems sufficient to solve this problem. The raw fitness is the sum, taken over the 200 fitness cases, of the square of the differences between the value returned by the S-expression and the actual value y_i of the given periodic function. It is desirable to have the x_i range over more than one complete cycle of 2π because otherwise the sampling of data in the fitness cases will not be sufficient to distinguish the actual target function from various simple polynomials of low order.

Since the variable x is implicit, the terminal set for this problem consists only of ephemeral random floating-point constant atom $\Re$, namely

$$T = \{\Re\}.$$

Whenever the ephemeral random constant atom $\Re$ is used in a problem, some consideration should be given to the range of random constants in relation to the known or likely range of other variables in the problem. The usual range is from -1.000 to $+1.000$ (with a step size of 0.001) for the ephemeral floating-point random constant. But, in this problem, an ephemeral random floating-point constant $\Re$ ranging from -10.000 to $+10.000$ seemed likely to more quickly produce constants of the magnitude needed by the problem. The usual step size of 0.001 was used.

Table 19.6 Tableau for Fourier series problem.

Objective:	Find the Fourier series for a given periodic function.
Terminal set:	Ephemeral random constant atom $\Re$ ranging between -10.000 and $+10.000$.
Function set:	&, XSIN, XCOS, +, −, *, %.
Fitness cases:	200 pairs of (x_i, y_i) where x_i ranges from -3π to $+3\pi$.
Raw fitness:	Sum, taken over the 200 fitness cases, of the square of the differences between the value returned by the S-expression and the actual value y_i of the given periodic function.
Standardized fitness:	Same as raw fitness for this problem.
Hits:	A fitness case for which the error is less than 0.01.
Wrapper:	None.
Parameters:	$M = 2,000$ (with over-selection). $G = 51$.
Success predicate:	An S-expression scores 200 hits.
Rules of construction:	• The root of the tree (i.e., the function just inside the leftmost parenthesis of the LISP S-expression) is the function & with two arguments. • The only thing allowed below an & function is either another & function or an XSIN or XCOS function. • The only thing allowed below an XSIN or XCOS function is either a floating-point random constant or an arithmetic function (+, −, *, %).
Types of points:	Three types of points: • a point containing an & function, • a point containing an XSIN or XCOS function, and • a point containing an arithmetic function or a random constant.

Since we are seeking a Fourier series representation for the observed data, the function set for this problem is

```
F = {&, XSIN, XCOS, +, -, *, %}.
```

Table 19.6 summarizes the key features of the problem of finding the Fourier series for a given periodic function.

The correct Fourier series is

$$x^2 = +3.2899 \quad -4.0000\,\mathrm{Cos}\,x \quad +1.0000\,\mathrm{Cos}\,2x$$
$$-0.4444\,\mathrm{Cos}\,3x \quad +0.2500\,\mathrm{Cos}\,4x$$
$$-0.1600\,\mathrm{Cos}\,5x \quad +0.1111\,\mathrm{Cos}\,6x$$
$$-0.0816\,\mathrm{Cos}\,7x \quad + \cdots .$$

In one run, the following best-of-generation individual from generation 0 had a total of 15 points, had a raw fitness of 2,360, and scored only three hits out of a possible 200 hits:

```
(& (XCOS (- -0.13199997 -2.6409998)
         (% 1.217001 6.3360004))
   (XCOS (% -6.29 -5.645) (* 2.309001 -2.0429997)))),
```

which simplifies to

$$2.5090 + 1.1143\,\mathrm{Cos}\,5x.$$

This best-of-generation individual for generation 0 is far from the solution; however, its constant term 2.5090 (i.e., zeroth harmonic) is in the general neighborhood of the correct constant term 3.2899, and the Cos 5x term is an even function like the target function.

Figure 19.7 shows a comparison between the best-of-generation individual from generation 0 and the target x^2 curve. As can be seen, the positive constant term 2.5090 places the best-of-generation individual into the desired upper half of the plane. The Cos 5x term, unaccompanied by other harmonics, does not follow the target curve well.

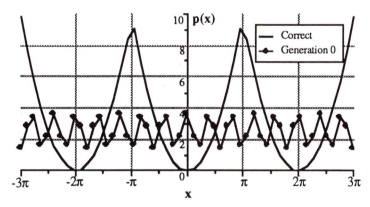

Figure 19.7 Comparison between the best-of-generation individual from generation 0 and the target curve for the Fourier series problem.

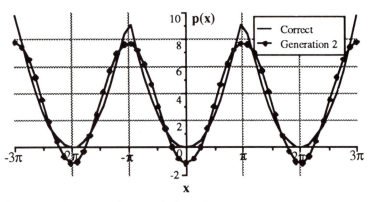

Figure 19.8 Comparison between the best-of-generation individual from generation 2 and the target curve for the Fourier series problem.

In generation 2, the best-of-generation individual had a raw fitness of 170 and 31 points. In simplified form it is

$$3.2928 - 4.4549 \cos x.$$

Although still far from perfect, this individual is far better than anything produced in generations 0 or 1. The constant term 3.2928 of this individual for generation 2 is already reasonably close to the correct constant term, and the coefficient of the $\cos x$ is within 11% of the correct coefficient.

Figure 19.8 shows a comparison between the best-of-generation individual from generation 2 and the target x^2 curve. As can be seen, the $-4.4549 \cos x$ term in generation 2 causes the S-expression to follow the general shape of the x^2 curve somewhat closely, although it does not do well at either the low or the high points of the x^2 curve.

The raw fitnesses of the best-of-generation individuals for generations 5 through 15 were in the range from 43 to 47. This is an improvement over the raw fitness of 2,360 from generation 0 and the raw fitness of 170 from generation 2.

Figure 19.9 shows a comparison between the best-of-generation individual from generation 10 and the target x^2 curve. As can be seen, the fit between the genetically bred Fourier series and the x^2 curve has improved. Again, the discrepancies are greatest at the low and the high points of the x^2 curve.

The best-of-generation individual from generation 15 scored 76 hits and consisted of 39 points. It can be simplified to

$$3.3200 \quad + 1.0801 \cos 2x \quad -3.8120 \cos 5x$$
$$+ 0.1652 \cos 6x.$$

Again, this individual has only cosine functions. Its constant term, 3.3200, is within 1% of the correct constant term, 3.2899. This constant term will persist into generation 50 of this run. Its coefficients of the second and the sixth harmonic have the correct sign and are in the same general neighborhood as the correct coefficients. The coefficient -3.8120 for $\cos 5x$ is far from the correct coefficient for the fifth harmonic; however, since this is the only odd

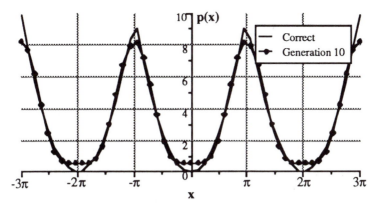

Figure 19.9 Comparison between the best-of-generation individual from generation 10 and the target curve for the Fourier series problem.

harmonic, this coefficient is not too far from the correct coefficient of -4.0000 for the Cos x term.

In generation 30, the best-of-generation individual had a raw fitness of 5.30 and scored 185 hits. This individual consisted of 131 points and can be simplified to

$$3.3200 \quad -3.9507\,\text{Cos}\,x \quad +1.0085\,\text{Cos}\,2x$$
$$-0.4190\,\text{Cos}\,3x \quad +0.1999\,\text{Cos}\,4x$$
$$-0.0620\,\text{Cos}\,5x \quad +0.1719\,\text{Cos}\,6x.$$

This individual has consecutive harmonics up to Cos $6x$. Each of the coefficients has the correct sign and is reasonably close to the correct coefficient.

In generation 50, the best-of-generation individual had a raw fitness of 2.13 and scored 190 hits out of 200. This individual has 153 points and can be simplified to

$$3.3200 \quad -4.0120\,\text{Cos}\,x \quad +1.0109\,\text{Cos}\,2x$$
$$-0.4402\,\text{Cos}\,3x \quad +0.2418\,\text{Cos}\,4x$$
$$-0.1564\,\text{Cos}\,5x \quad +0.1409\,\text{Cos}\,6x$$
$$-0.0743\,\text{Cos}\,7x$$

This best-of-run individual has consecutive harmonics up to Cos $7x$.

Table 19.7 contains a comparison of the genetically produced Fourier coefficients of the best-of-run individual from generation 50 with the correct Fourier coefficient.

When we retested the above best-of-run individual on 1,000 new (x_i, y_i) pairs, we scored hits on 96% of the 1,000 new fitness cases (as compared to 95% on the actual run).

Figure 19.10 shows, by generation, the average of the structural complexity of the population as a whole and the structural complexity of the best-of-generation individual. As one would expect, the S-expressions become progressively more complex as additional terms are added to the Fourier series. For example, the structural complexities of the best-of-generation individuals

Table 19.7 Comparison between genetically produced coefficients and actual Fourier coefficients.

Harmonic	Genetically produced coefficient	Actual Fourier coefficient	Absolute error
0	+3.3200	+3.2899	0.0301
1	−4.0120	−4.0000	0.0120
2	+1.0109	+1.0000	0.0109
3	−0.4402	+0.4444	0.0042
4	+0.2418	+0.2500	0.0082
5	−0.1564	−0.1600	0.0036
6	+0.1409	+0.1111	0.0298
7	−0.0743	−0.0816	0.0073

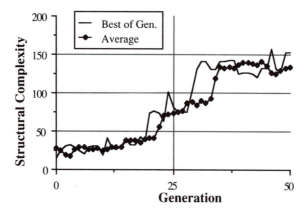

Figure 19.10 Structural complexity curves for the problem of finding a Fourier series.

for generations 0, 10, 20, 30, 40, and 50 were 15, 19, 73, 131, 127, and 153, respectively. The averages of the structural-complexity values of the entire populations for these same generations were 27.3, 25.4, 40.7, 84.2, 139.2, and 133.6, respectively.

Note that the sizes of the best-of-generation S-expressions progressively increased as the expressions progressively added harmonics, refined coefficients, and became better approximations to the correct Fourier series. We did not specify this change in size and structure in advance. The evolution of structure came about because of the selective pressure applied by the fitness (error) measure and the recombination of parts of various parents over many generations.

19.7 INVERSE KINEMATICS

In this section, the problem is to find a computer program to control the movement of a two-link robot arm from a resting position to a desired target location. That is, we are seeking the inverse kinematics for the robot arm.

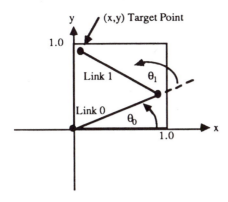

Figure 19.11 Robot arm consisting of link 0 at angle θ_0 from the x axis and link 1 at angle θ_1 from link 0 so that the endpoint of link 1 reaches the target point (x, y).

The solution to this problem consists of a vector of values, namely the two angles by which the two links of the robot arm should be moved. The second angle in the vector will explicitly depend on the choice of the first angle.

The reader will recall that in the problem of iterative summation (section 18.2), we used the set operator SET–SV to assign the current value of a specified sub-S-expression to a settable variable SV, thus making that value available whenever the terminal SV subsequently appeared within the program. This approach has the shortcoming of requiring that some default value be assigned to the settable variable in the event that it is referenced before it is defined. In this section, we overcome this disadvantage by employing a cascade in which the result of an earlier step is used in a subsequent step. Cascading is one of several ways of setting a variable (i.e., giving an expression a name so that it can be referred to later in a computer program).

Figure 19.11 shows a robot arm with two links of lengths $L_0 = L_1 = 1$. The first angle, θ_0, is the angle by which link 0 (the first link) is to be rotated about the base of the robot arm (which is grounded at the origin). After link 0 has been rotated, the second angle, θ_1, is the angle by which link 1 is to be rotated about the endpoint of link 0.

The forward kinematic equations specify the point (x, y) reached as a function of angles θ_0 and θ_1. In particular, these equations specify the point (x, y) reached by the endpoint of link 1 (the second link) if link 0 is rotated about the base of the robot arm by angle θ_0 and if link 1 is rotated about the endpoint of link 0 by angle θ_1. The forward kinematic equations (Craig 1986) are

$$x = L_0 \cos \theta_0 + L_1 \cos(\theta_0 + \theta_1)$$

and

$$y = L_0 \sin \theta_0 + L_1 \sin(\theta_0 + \theta_1).$$

The goal is to find a computer program for the inverse kinematics of the robot arm. That is, the computer program being sought specifies how to rotate the two links so that the endpoint (end effector) of the second link of the robot

Evolution of Constrained Syntactic Structures

arm reaches a given target point (x, y) in the unit square. The computer program being sought takes the coordinates x and y as its input and produces the angles θ_0 and θ_1 as its output.

The choice of θ_1 depends on the choice of θ_0. The solution to this problem of inverse kinematics involves first choosing

$$\theta_0 = A \cos \left[\frac{(x^2 + y^2) - (L_0^2 + L_1^2)}{2L_0^2 L_1^2} \right]$$

and then choosing

$$\theta_1 = \text{ATG}(y, x) - \text{ATG}(L_1 \sin \theta_0, L_0 + L_1 \cos \theta_0),$$

where ATG is the two-argument Arctangent function.

This calculation involves a cascade in which the choice of one variable depends on a previous choice of another variable.

The inverse kinematics problem is underconstrained. There are, in general, two distinct pairs of angles that solve this problem (i.e., with the elbow pointing in different directions).

In this problem, the result is an ordered set (i.e., vector) of two angles. The terminal set is different for the two components of the solution. When the first angle θ_0 is being chosen, the calculation depends on the coordinates x and y of the target point. That is, the terminal set for component 0 of the solution vector is

$$\text{T}_0 = \{\text{X, Y, } \Re\},$$

where $\Re$ is the ephemeral floating-point random constant between -1.000 and $+1.000$.

The second angle depends directly on the choice already made for the first angle (as well as the coordinates x and y of the target point). Thus, when θ_1 is being chosen, the terminal set for component 1 of the solution vector is

$$\text{T}_1 = \{\text{ANGLE-0, X, Y, } \Re\},$$

where ANGLE-0 is θ_0. In other words, there is a cascading of the result of the first calculation into the second calculation.

Thus, there are three types of points in the S-expressions for this problem:

- the root
- points in the first component, and
- points in the second component.

The function set for this problem is

$$\text{F} = \{\text{LIST2, +, -, *, %, EXP, ASIN, ACOS, ATG}\},$$

with two, two, two, two, two, one, one, one, and two arguments, respectively. ATG is the two-argument Arctangent function, so it can correctly ascertain the quadrant.

The rules of construction for individual S-expressions in the problem of inverse kinematics are these:

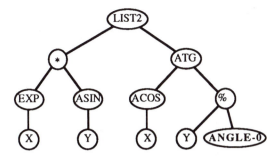

Figure 19.12 Random individual from generation 0 for the inverse kinematics problem.

- The root of the tree must be the LIST2 function with two arguments.
- The root is the only place where the LIST2 function will appear in a given S-expression.
- The first component of the vector created by the LIST2 function is a composition of the arithmetic functions from function set F (other than LIST2) and terminals from the terminal set T_0, namely

$T_0 = \{X, Y, \Re\}.$

- The second component of the vector created by the LIST2 function is a composition of the arithmetic functions from function set F (other than LIST2) and terminals from the terminal set T_1, namely

$T_1 = \{ANGLE-0, X, Y, \Re\}.$

Figure 19.12 shows a possible initial random individual for this problem. The LIST2 function taking two arguments appears at the root of the tree. The LIST2 function creates the vector (2-tuple). The terminal ANGLE-0 (in bold type) appears in the second component of the vector, and that ANGLE-0 cannot appear in the first component.

The first component is executed first. The result of its evaluation is then available, by the name ANGLE-0, when the second component of the vector is evaluated. Thus, we acquire the ability to give a name to an intermediate value (i.e., the first component) and to refer to that intermediate value by its name in the remainder of the computer program. The value of the cascading variable is based on the value of the terminals in the first (leftmost) main branch of the program tree at the time of execution of that branch and does not reflect any subsequent events, such as changes in the value of those terminals.

In this problem, the first component is both a value-defining branch and a value-returning branch since the value of the cascading variable ANGLE-0 is one of the two values returned by the S-expression as a whole. The second branch serves only as a value-returning branch.

The fitness cases for this problem consist of 25 target points chosen inside the unit square. The 25 target points are the points of a regular 5×5 grid within the unit square. This number and arrangement of target points seems sufficient to solve this problem.

The raw fitness of a particular S-expression is the sum, taken over the 25 fitness cases, of the absolute values of the shortfalls (distances) between each target point and the actual location of the endpoint of the second link (link 1) of the robot arm after the S-expression is executed. The best result occurs when the sum of the 25 shortfalls equals zero.

We define a hit for this problem as any fitness case where the endpoint of the second robot arm is within 0.05 of the target point.

Table 19.8 summarizes the key features of the inverse kinematics problem for the two-link robot arm.

In one run, the best-of-generation individual from generation 154 scored 25 hits and contained 231 points:

```
(LIST2 (% (* (- (% (* (- X Y) Y) (ACOS% (EXP X))) (ACOS%
           Y)) (ATG (+ (+ (ACOS% Y) (% (% (- X Y) (ACOS%
           (EXP X))) (ACOS% (EXP X)))) (* (* (% (- X Y)
           (ACOS% (% (% (* (- X (% Y X)) Y) (ACOS% (EXP
           X))) (ACOS% X)))) Y) Y)) (% Y X))) (% (EXP X)
           (ACOS% (EXP X))))
        (+ (ACOS% X) (ATG (+ (EXP (ATG (ATG (+ (ATG
           (ACOS% Y) Y) (* (ATG (+ (ATG (+ (ACOS% X)
           ANGLE-0) (* X (ACOS% X))) (ACOS% X)) Y) (ATG X
           Y))) (ACOS% X)) (ATG (ATG (ATG (ACOS% X) (*
           (ATG (+ (* X (ATG X Y)) (+ (ACOS% Y) ANGLE-0))
           (+ (ACOS% X) (* X (ACOS% X))))) (ATG (+ (* X
           (ATG X Y)) ANGLE-0) (+ (ACOS% X) (* (ACOS% X)
           (ACOS% X)))))) (* (ATG (+ (ACOS% X) (ATG (+
           (ACOS% X) ANGLE-0) (ACOS% X))) (+ (ACOS% X) (*
           X (ACOS% X)))) (ATG X (* X (+ (ACOS% X) (ACOS%
           Y)))))) (* (ATG (+ (+ (ATG (+ (ACOS% X) ANGLE-
           0) (ACOS% X)) (ACOS% X)) (+ (ATG (+ (ACOS% X)
           ANGLE-0) (ACOS% X)) (ACOS% X))) (+ (ATG X Y)
           (* X (+ (ACOS% X) (ACOS% X))))) (* (ATG (+
           (ATG (+ (ATG Y X) ANGLE-0) (ACOS% Y)) (ACOS%
           X)) (ATG Y X)) (ATG X Y)))))) (* X X)) (ATG (+
           (ACOS% X) ANGLE-0) (% (ACOS% Y) (+ Y X)))))))).
```

The average shortfall between the endpoint of the second link of the robot arm and the target point was 0.024.

When we retested this best-of-run individual on 1,024 new target points distributed over the same area as the original grid of 25 target points, it scored 1,021 hits out of 1,024. The average shortfall between the endpoint of the second link of the robot arm and the target point was 0.023.

Note that the cascading variable is guaranteed to be defined before it is referenced, because the main branches of the program tree are executed in a well-defined sequential order (i.e., left-to-right).

More than one cascading variable could be defined if additional branches were added to the program tree. Moreover, cascading variables are not

Table 19.8 Tableau for inverse kinematics.

Objective:	Find vector of two angles to move a two-link robot arm to a target point (x, y) in the plane.
Terminal set:	• For the first component: $T_0 = \{X, Y, \Re\}$. • For the second component: $T_1 \{ANGLE-0, X, Y, \Re\}$.
Function set:	LIST2, +, −, *, %, EXP, ASIN, ACOS, ATG.
Fitness cases:	25 target points (x, y) in unit square, either chosen at random or in a regular 5×5 grid arrangement.
Raw fitness:	The sum, taken over the 25 fitness cases, of the distances between the endpoint of the second link of the robot arm and the particular target point.
Standardized fitness:	Same as raw fitness for this problem.
Hits:	Endpoint of the second robot arm is within 0.05 of the target point.
Wrapper:	None.
Parameters:	$M = 500. G = 51.$
Success predicate:	An S-expression scores 25 hits.
Rules of construction:	• Root is always the LIST2 function. • First component of the vector is a composition of functions (other than LIST2) and the terminals X, Y, $\Re$. • Second component of the vector is a composition of functions (other than LIST2), the terminal ANGLE-0, and the terminals X, Y, and $\Re$.
Types of points:	Three types of points: • the root • points in the first component (which do not include ANGLE-0) • points in the second component (which may include ANGLE-0).

inherently limited to the final (rightmost) branch of the program tree. If desired, a cascading variable can appear in any branch of an S-expression that is evaluated after the branch in which it is defined. That is, a cascading variable can be defined in terms of one or more other cascading variables.

Genetic algorithms are finding increased application to problems in robotics (Davidor 1991).

19.8 LOCAL TRACKING OF A DYNAMICAL SYSTEM

One aspect of the study of dynamical systems and deterministic chaos involves finding the function that fits a given sample of data. Often the functions of interest are recursive in the sense that the sequence of values of the

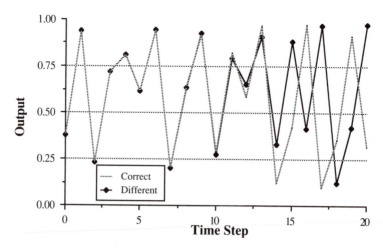

Figure 19.13 Time series for two logistic functions with slightly different initial conditions.

function over time depends on previous values of the function. Some dynamical systems exhibit deterministic chaos.

This problem is similar to the inverse kinematics problem presented in the preceding section in that the solution consists of a vector of values and there is a cascade in which the first component of the vector is used in computing the second component of the vector.

The nonlinear *logistic equation*

$$x(t + 1) = rx(t)[1 - x(t)],$$

where $0 < r \leq 4$ and $0 \leq x(t) \leq 1$, and $0 \leq x(t) \leq 1$, is one of the simplest models of a system displaying deterministic chaos (Campbell 1989).

The sequence of values of $x(t)$ for the logistic equation is highly dependent on the initial value of x at time 0. A very small change in the initial value $x(0)$ can, after surprisingly few time steps, produce major differences in the value of this time series.

Figure 19.13 shows two graphs of the logistic function where $r = 4$. For the first graph, the initial condition is $x(0) = 3/8$. The value 3/8 exactly equals the decimal fraction 0.37500_{10} and the binary fraction 0.0110000000000000_2. For the second graph, the initial condition $x(0)$ is $3/8 + 2^{-16}$. This new value exactly equals the binary fraction 0.0110000000000001_2 and is approximately represented by the decimal fraction 0.37501_{10}. Even though the two initial conditions differ by only $0.0000000000000001_2 \approx 0.00001_{10}$, the sequence of values of $x(t)$ is very different after only 15 time steps.

As can be seen, the two sequences are very close (within 0.01 of each other) for the first 10 time steps, and they are somewhat close (within 0.10 of each other) for the next few time steps. However, between time steps 15 and 20 the two sequences are dramatically different. As can be seen, after time step 15, there is little relationship between the two sequences of values, even though the difference in initial condition values was very small. The hypersen-

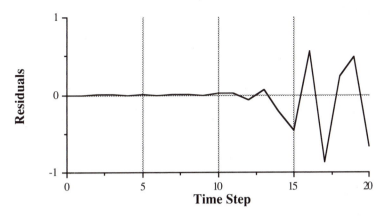

Figure 19.14 Difference, over time, between the two logistic functions with slightly different initial conditions.

sitivity of chaotic functions to initial conditions has been compared to the fluttering of a butterfly's wings in Hong Kong initiating a hurricane elsewhere in the world months later.

Figure 19.14 shows the residual error between the two logistic functions (i.e., the difference between the two graphs overlaid in figure 19.13).

After a large number of time steps, all transient behavior disappears for the logistic equation. All sequences, regardless of the initial condition, eventually settle down to 0.0 (i.e., the point 0.0 is a global attractor for the logistic equation) for a given r.

Regardless of the fact that a very small difference in the initial condition creates a very large difference in behavior after a surprisingly few time steps and regardless of the fact that the long-term behavior eventually gravitates to the global attractor of 0.0, there is still considerable interest in tracking chaotic dynamical systems, such as the logistic equation, over a relatively short *local* interval of time (Meyer et al. 1989; Meyer and Packard 1991). The values of two sequences starting from two nearby values of $x(0)$ are, of course, necessarily close to each other for the first few time steps.

In this section, we show that it is possible to perform symbolic regression by means of genetic programming when a recursive formula defines the sequence of values of $x(t)$ and that it is possible to track a dynamical system over a relatively short *local* interval of time.

To perform this symbolic regression, we would include in the terminal set the value PV of the sequence at the previous time step.

If the value of the initial condition $x(0)$ is known in advance and the symbolic regression does not start until time step 1, then genetic programming can quickly and easily come up with a recursive formula such as

```
(* PV (* 2 (* 2 (- 1 PV)))),
```

for the values over time of the logistic sequence $x(t)$. Here $PV = x(t-1)$ is the value of the sequence at the previous time step. In this version of the problem, this recursive formula applies at time step 1 and thereafter. At time step 1, it makes use of the known, specified value of $x(0)$ as given by PV.

When the initial condition is not known, the problem of symbolic regression for a chaotic sequence is more difficult. In this event, the regression must find *both* the initial condition value $x(0)$ and the recursive equation for taking the value of the sequence for time step t and producing the value of the sequence for time step $t + 1$. If a chaotic sequence is involved, we know that we cannot perform this symbolic regression over long sequences of time. However, we should be able to do so over relatively short sequences of time.

We need to define an S-expression with a syntactic structure. In particular, each S-expression for this problem will be a vector consisting of two components. The first component of the vector is a purely numerical component (not containing the terminal PV) expressing the initial condition value $x(0)$ for the sequence in terms of various arithmetic functions and various numerical constants. The second component (which, in general, contains the terminal PV) is the equation that expresses the value of the sequence at time step t in terms of the value of the sequence at the previous time step as well as various arithmetic functions and various numerical constants.

The function set for this problem is

```
F = {+, -, *, %, LIST2}.
```

In particular, the rules of construction for individual S-expressions in the problem of locally tracking a chaotic dynamical system are the following:

- The root of the tree must be the LIST2 function with two arguments.
- The root is the only place where the LIST2 function will appear in a given S-expression.
- The first component of the vector created by the LIST2 is a composition of the functions from function set F (other than LIST2) and the ephemeral random floating-point constant atom $\Re$ ranging between 0.0 and $+1.0$ in the terminal set T_0, namely

```
T₀ = {ℜ}.
```

$$T_0 = \{\Re\}.$$

- The second component of the vector created by the LIST2 is a composition of the functions from function set F (other than LIST2) and terminals from the terminal set T_1, namely

$$T_1 = \{PV, \Re\}.$$

There are three types of points in the S-expressions for this problem:

- the root,
- points in the first component, and
- points in the second component.

A fitness case for this problem is one of the ten integral values of time between 0 and 9. Fitness is the sum, taken over the ten values of time, of the differences between the sequence value produced by the S-expression and the actual value of the logistic sequence with the initial condition value $x(0) = 3/8$. A hit is defined as a fitness case for which the error is less than 0.01. Hits are useful for monitoring in this problem; however, we will not expect to score a number of hits equal to the number of fitness cases for this problem. Therefore, we do not include hits in the termination criterion.

The value $x(0) = 3/8 = 0.0110000000000000_2$ was used for the initial condition of the target function.

We used the unusually large step size of 0.1 in choosing the ephemeral floating-point random constants $\Re$ for this particular problem. This rather crude granularity makes discovery of a solution to this problem harder than the finer granularity (0.001) that we usually use. When we first ran this problem using our usual fine granularity of 0.001, we found that one or more of the thousands of random constants created for the initial 2,000 S-expressions was very close to the correct value of the initial condition (0.375). This lone terminal, after a crossover, sometimes became the first component of the vector created by the LIST2 function. Thus, the solution took the uninteresting form of a vector whose first component consisted only of a single initial random constant that was close to the correct value of the initial condition.

Table 19.9 summarizes the key features of the problem of locally tracking a chaotic dynamical system.

In one run, the best-of-generation S-expression for generation 44 had 103 points and a raw fitness of 0.167:

```
(LIST2 (* (* (* 0.8 0.6) (- 0.2 0.8)) (- (* 0.9 0.6) (+
           0.9 0.9)))
        (+ (* (- 0.8 (+ PV (- 1.0 (* (+ (* (- 0.8 (+ PV
           (* (* (- 0.8 (+ PV (* (* 0.4 PV) (+ 0.9
           0.3)))) (- (+ (* (-(+ PV 0.7) (+ PV (- PV
           0.5))) (- (* PV 0.8) (- PV 0.5))) 0.7) (- PV
           0.5))) (+ 0.9 0.3)))) (- (+ (* (- 0.8 (+ PV (-
           PV 0.5))) 0.7) 0.7) (- PV 0.5))) 0.7) (+ 0.9
           0.3))))) (- (* PV 0.8) (- 1.0 (* (+ PV 0.7) (+
           0.9 0.3))))) 0.7)).
```

The first component of this S-expression is equal to 0.36288, whereas the exact value of the initial condition $x(0)$ is 3/8.

Figure 19.15 is a graph of the values of the time series produced by the best-of-run individual S-expression from generation 44 overlaid onto a graph of the values of the logistic function. The graph runs to time step 20 so as to show the behavior of the function beyond the range defined by the ten fitness cases. As can be seen, the best-of-run individual came within 0.01 of the correct value of the logistic sequence for five of the first ten time steps (i.e., it scored five hits). The two sequences were somewhat close between time steps 5 and 10 and reasonably close on time step 11. Thereafter, the values for the sequence produced by the best-of-run S-expression diverged considerably from the correct values of the logistic sequence.

Table 19.9 Tableau for local tracking of chaotic dynamical system.

Objective:	Find a locally applicable model for a chaotic dynamical system given a sampling of the values of the time series.
Terminal set:	PV and $\Re$, where the ephemeral random constant atom $\Re$ ranges between 0.0 and $+1.0$ in steps of 0.1.
Function set:	+, −, *, %, LIST2.
Fitness cases:	Ten pairs of (x_i, y_i) where x_i ranges from 0 to 9 and y_i is the value of the target logistic sequence.
Raw fitness:	Sum, taken over the ten fitness cases, of the differences between the value returned by the S-expression and the actual value y_i of the given function.
Standardized fitness:	Same as raw fitness for this problem.
Hits:	A fitness case for which the error is less than 0.01.
Wrapper:	None.
Parameters:	$M = 2,000$ (with over-selection). $G = 51$.
Success predicate:	None.
Rules of construction:	• Root is always the LIST2 function. • First component of the vector is a composition of functions (other than LIST2) and the ephemeral random constant atom $\Re$. • Second component of the vector is a composition of functions (other than LIST2) and the ephemeral random constant atom $\Re$ as well as the terminal PV.
Types of points:	Three types of points: • the root • points in the first component (which do not include PV) • points in the second component (which, in general, includes PV).

Figure 19.16 shows the difference between the two graphs contained in figure 19.15. As can be seen, after time step 10 or 11 there is little relationship between the two sequences of values.

Note that we did not obtain (or expect to obtain) the exact value of the initial condition, nor did we obtain the exact functional relationship. We obtained a value for an initial condition in the first component and a functional relationship in the second component which tracked the chaotic logistic function closely on a local basis for a certain number of time steps. Only if we had obtained the exact value of the initial condition (or the exact value with only an exceedingly small error) would we have been able to track the logistic equation for all 20 time steps shown in the graphs (even if the functional relationship were exact).

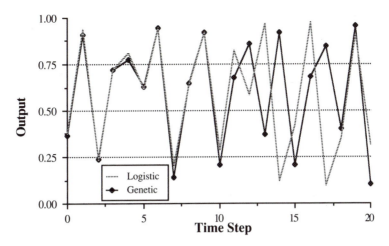

Figure 19.15 Time series for the correct logistic function and the best-of-run individual.

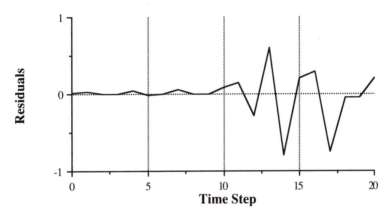

Figure 19.16 Difference, over time, between the correct logistic function and the best-of-run individual.

19.9 DESIGNING A NEURAL NETWORK

In this section, we further illustrate S-expressions with a syntactic structure and structure-preserving crossover with a problem having an even more complex set of rules of construction. In particular, we show how to simultaneously discover both the weights and design the architecture of a neural network. This example will employ the previously described encapsulation operation as well as techniques for handling ephemeral random constants.

A neural network is a network of directed lines containing processing elements at the internal points in the network and numerical weights associated with each input line and each internal connecting line of the network.

In a neural network, the inputs are those external points that are connected to a directed line segment pointing toward an internal point of the network. The outputs are those external points that are connected to a directed line segment pointing out from the network.

Evolution of Constrained Syntactic Structures

The signal on each non-output line segment is multiplied by a numerical constant (called the *weight*) associated with that line as it passes along that line segment.

The *threshold processing element* is one type of processing element that is commonly found at the internal points of a neural network. In a threshold processing element, if the sum of the weighted inputs to the processing element exceeds a certain *threshold* value T, the processor emits a 1 signal; otherwise, it emits a 0 signal. That is, the output signal O_j of the threshold processing element j in a neural network is 1 if

$$O_j = \sum_{i=0}^{N} w_{ij} S_{ij} + b_j > T_j,$$

and 0 otherwise. In the above, the ith input signal to processing element j is denoted by S_{ij}. The ith weight to processing element j is denoted by w_{ij}. The threshold for processing element j is denoted by T_j. The additive constant or *bias* (if any) of processing element j is denoted by b_j.

Figure 19.17 shows a neural network that performs the exclusive-or XOR (odd-2-parity) function on the inputs D0 and D1. It consists of three threshold processing elements P1, P2, and P3. As is the case throughout this section, each threshold processing element has a threshold of 1.0 and a bias of 0.0. This neural network contains six signal lines, each having a weight associated with it. The inputs D0 and D1 from the outside world are binary signals. The outputs of the three threshold processing elements are also binary signals.

In figure 19.17, the binary input signal D0 is weighted by 1.66 and the binary input signal D1 is weighted by -1.387. These two weighted input signals are the inputs to the processing function P2. Since the input signal D0 is either 0 or 1, the first input line to P2 is either 0 or 1.66. Similarly, the second input line to P2 is either 0 or -1.387. The processing function P2 adds up its two weighted input lines and emits a 1 if the sum exceeds the threshold of 1.0 and emits a 0 otherwise. If D0 and D1 are both 0, the sum of the inputs will be 0 (which is less than the threshold of 1) and therefore P2 will emit 0. If D0 is 1 and D1 is 0, the sum will be 1.66 and P2 will emit a 1. If D0 is 0 and D1 is 1, the sum will be -1.387 and P2 will emit a 0. If both D0 and D1 are 1, the sum will be 0.273. This is less than the threshold of 1.0. Thus, P2

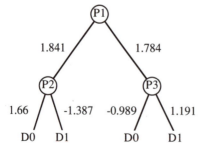

Figure 19.17 Neural network for exclusive-or (odd-2-parity) function.

will emit a 0. In other words, P2 emits a 1 if and only if the input lines D0 and D1 are 1 and 0, respectively.

Similarly, for P3, the input signal D0 is weighted by -0.989 and the input signal D1 is weighted by 1.191 so that these two weighted input signals become the input to the processing function P3 with two input lines. P3 will emit a 1 if and only if the input signals D0 and D1 are 0 and 1, respectively.

Then, the output of P2 is weighted by 1.841 and the output of P3 is weighted by 1.784 so that these two weighted input signals become the input to the processing function P1 with two input lines. The effect is that the weighted sum of the inputs to P1 exceeds the threshold of 1.0 if and only if either or both of the signals coming out of P2 and P3 are 1. (As it happens, the signals are never both 1.) In other words, the output of P1 is 1 if either (but not both) D0 or D1 is 1, and the output of P1 is 0 otherwise. That is, the output P1 is the exclusive-or (odd-2-parity) function of the inputs D0 and D1.

A wide variety of neural network architectures are described in the literature (Hinton 1989; Rumelhart, Hinton, and Williams 1986; Nilsson 1990). The architecture of a neural network specifies the way the processing elements are organized and the way they are connected. As to organization, most currently studied neural networks have at least three layers of processing elements. In particular, they have at least one hidden layer of processing elements lying between the layer of processing elements that are directly connected to the inputs and the layer directly connected to the outputs. As to connectivity, the output of each processing element may be connected to either some or all of the processing elements of the next layer. A neural network can be feed-forward only or can allow feedback between the output of a processing element of one layer and the input of an earlier layer.

There are numerous different neural network training paradigms described in the literature (Hinton 1989; Rumelhart, Hinton, and Williams 1986; Nilsson 1990). The training paradigm typically involves exposing the neural network to training cases during a training phase and progressively modifying the weights in some way that depends on how well the output of the neural network matches the desired correct output associated with the training case. In some training paradigms, the thresholds and biases of the processing elements may also be modified.

Backpropagation is currently the most popular neural network training paradigm.

Neural network training paradigms usually presuppose that the architecture of the neural network has already been determined. That is, they presuppose that selections have been made for the number of layers of processing elements, the number of processing elements in each layer, and the connectivity between the processing elements. An exception is Lee 1991, where both the architecture of the network and its weights are adaptively determined.

The goal is for the neural network to learn to perform some task correctly. This involves both performing the task correctly when the neural network encounters a repetition of a training case, and, more important, generalizing from the training cases so that the neural network performs the task correctly when it is presented with previously unseen input cases.

Throughout this book, we have discussed genetic programming in light of the five major steps for preparing to use it. There is a similar set of major preparatory steps associated with each of the other adaptive and machine learning paradigms. For a neural network, there are ten preparatory steps, namely determining

(1) the architecture of the network (e.g., number of layers, number of processing elements in each layer),

(2) the connectivity of the network (e.g., full or partial connectivity between consecutive layers; whether or not the network is recurrent; what connections from one layer to earlier layers are permitted),

(3) the type of processing element used (e.g., linear threshold processing element, sigmoid processing element),

(4) the training paradigm (e.g., backpropagation),

(5) the inputs to the network,

(6) the outputs of the network,

(7) the training cases to be used,

(8) the error measure,

(9) the values of the numerical parameters for controlling the run (i.e., learning rate for back propagation, average magnitude of initial random weights, etc.), and

(10) the criterion for designating a result and terminating a run (e.g., criterion for stopping training).

For example, in subsection 3.3.2, a neural net was used to control the artificial ant. For that network, the inputs to the network consisted of the sensor input to the ant and the outputs of the network were connected to the primitive external functions for moving and turning the ant. Thus, step (4) corresponded to the step of selecting the terminals in genetic programming and step (5) corresponded to the step of selecting the primitive functions in genetic programming. Of course, the fact that a neural net is involved means that the functionality of the weighting function and the functionality of the processing element are also inherently selected.

The conventional genetic algorithm operating on fixed-length character strings has been successfully used to discover and optimize the weights for neural nets (Belew, McInerney, and Schraudolph 1991; Geoffrey F. Miller, Todd, and Hegde 1989; Whitley, Starkweather, and Bogart 1990; Wilson 1990). Chalmers (1991) made an especially innovative use of genetic algorithms by rediscovering the Widrow-Hoff Least Mean Squares (LMS) rule for modifying the weights of perceptrons, and Fontanari and Meir (1991) applied Chalmers' novel approach to binary perceptrons.

In this chapter, we show how to simultaneously design a neural network for both its weights and its architecture (namely, the number of layers in the neural net, the number of processing elements in each layer, and the connectivity between the processing elements).

We assume that the thresholds of all the processing elements are 1.0 and that there are no biases in the network.

If there were two input signals (D0 and D1), then the terminal set contains the two input signals and the ephemeral random floating-point constant $\Re$ ranging between -2.000 and $+2.000$. Thus, the terminal set is

T = {D0, D1, $\Re$}.

One function set F that is capable of defining a neural network with only one output signal is

F = {P2, P3, P4, W, +, -, *, %},

taking two, three, four, two, two, two, two, and two arguments, respectively.

The function P is the processing function and appears in the function set with a varying number of arguments. We refer to these functions as P2, P3, and P4.

The function W is the weighting function used to give a weight to a signal going into a processing function. W is merely the multiplication function with two arguments; however, we give it this special name to distinguish it from the ordinary arithmetic function of multiplication (which is used for the entirely different purpose of composing the numeric weights). The first (left) argument of the W function is always a numeric weight and the second (right) argument is always a binary signal (coming from the outside world as an input to the neural network or coming out of a processing element within the network).

The four basic arithmetic functions in the function set (+, -, *, %) are used to create and modify the numeric constants (weights) of the neural network.

The problem of designing neural networks illustrates the need to create the initial random population so that all individuals comply with certain specified syntactic rules of construction. Moreover, all genetic operations (in particular, crossover) that modify the individuals in the population must be performed in a structure-preserving way. That is, the result of the genetic operation must be an individual that still complies with the syntactic rules of construction.

Not all possible compositions of functions from the function set above and terminals from the terminal set above correspond to what we would reasonably call a neural network. For example, neural networks do not perform multiplication on input signals such as D0 and D1. A neural network is, in fact, a very special structure. Thus, the problem of designing neural networks requires rules of construction that specify what structures are allowable for this particular problem.

There are four types of points in the S-expressions for this problem:

- points with a processing function P,
- points with a weighting function W,
- points with input data signals (such as D0 and D1), and
- points with arithmetic functions or floating-point random constants.

In particular, the rules of construction for a neural network with one output signal are as follows:

- The root of the tree must be a processing function P.
- The only thing allowed at the level immediately below any processing function P is a weighting function (W).
- The only thing allowed below a weighting function (W) on the left (i.e., the first line) is either a floating-point random constant or an arithmetic function.
- The only thing allowed below a weighting function (W) on the right (i.e., the second line) is either an input data signal (such as D0 and D1) or the output of a P function.
- The only thing allowed below an arithmetic function is either a floating-point random constant or an arithmetic function (+, −, *, %).

These rules are applied recursively.

Note that the external points of the tree are either input signals (i.e., D0 or D1) or floating-point random constants.

These rules of construction produce a tree (S-expression) that one can reasonably call a neural network.

For the purposes of this section, neural networks consist of threshold processing elements (the P functions) that process weighted inputs to produce a discrete signal (i.e., 0 or 1) as their output. The number of inputs to a processing element (P function) can vary; however, its inputs are always weighted signal lines (i.e., outputs from a W function). The number of lines going into a weighting function W is always two. The first (left) argument of a W function is always a weight. The weight may be a single floating-point constant or can be a composition of arithmetic functions and floating-point random constants. The second (right) argument of a W function is always a binary signal. The signal going into a weighting function can be the input from the outside world to the network or the output of a processing element. If biases are allowed, the bias is a signal line consisting only of a composition of arithmetic functions and floating-point random constants. Biases, if allowed, always go into processing elements.

To illustrate the above, consider the exclusive-or (odd-2-parity) task on the inputs D0 and D1. This function has one output. The following LISP S-expression represents a neural network that performs this task:

```
(P (W (+ 1.1 0.741) (P (W 1.66 D0) (W −1.387 D1)))
   (W (* 1.2 1.584) (P (W 1.191 D1) (W −0.989 D0))))).
```

Figure 19.18 graphically depicts this S-expression as a rooted point-labeled tree with ordered branches. This S-expression represents the same neural network as shown in figure 19.17.

The root of this tree contains the processing function P with two arguments. The functions at the level immediately below the uppermost P function are both weighting functions (W). Each weighting function has two arguments. The left argument of the left weighting function is the weight 1.841 (created by

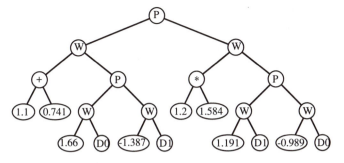

Figure 19.18 Tree for the S-expression that performs the exclusive-or (odd-2-parity) task.

adding the random constant 1.1 to the random constant 0.741). The right argument of the left weighting function is the output of a processing function P with two arguments. Thus, the effect of this left weighting function is to multiply the output of this second processing function P by the weight 1.841, which is the same weight that appears in figure 19.17 in the corresponding place.

The functions at the level immediately below this second processing function P are both weighting functions (W). The arguments to the left weighting function of this second processing function P are the random constant 1.66 and the input data signal D0. Thus, the effect of this weighting function is to multiply the input data signal by the weight 1.66. The arguments to the right multiplication function of this second P function are the random constant -1.387 and the input data signal D1. These weights (1.66 and -1.387) are the same weights that appears in figure 19.17 in the corresponding places.

If we perform structure-preserving crossover on two neural networks created in accordance with the above rules of construction, we will always obtain two structures as offspring that comply with the rules of construction for neural networks.

If there is more than one output signal from a neural network, the output signals are returned as a list. For example, if there are two output signals, they are returned via a LIST2 function. That is, the function set F is enlarged to

F = {LIST2, P, W, +, -, *, %}.

The rules of construction for neural networks with more than one output signal require that the root of the tree be a LIST2 function. The number of arguments to the function LIST2 equals the number of output signals. This is the only time the LIST2 function is used in a given S-expression. The rules of construction also require that the function at the level of the tree immediately below the LIST2 function be a processing function P. Thereafter, the previously described rules of construction apply.

For example, the following LISP S-expression represents a neural network with two output signals:

```
(LIST2 (P (W D1 -1.423) (W D0 (+ 1.2 0.4)))
        (P (W D1 (* -1.7 -0.9)) (W D0 (- 1.1 0.5)))).
```

The first argument to the LIST2 function is shown in underlined bold type and represents the first of the two output signals. It is the output from one processing element P. The second argument to the LIST2 function is the second output signal.

In most neural networks, there is extensive connectivity between input data signals and the outputs of processing elements and other parts of the network.

Connectivity between any input data signal and any number of processing elements in the network is created by merely placing a given input signal on more than one endpoint of the tree.

It is also necessary to have connectivity between the output from a processing element function P in the network which feeds into more than one other processing element function. This connectivity cannot be obtained from ordinary LISP S-expressions by means of any technique used so far in this book. The encapsulation operation (subsection 6.5.4) provides a means for obtaining the desired connectivity. This operation identifies potentially useful subtrees and gives them a name so that they can be referenced later in more than one place (thus connecting an output to more than one place). For example, the output of a processing element P can be encapsulated and given the name E0. A reference to the encapsulated function E0 can then appear as the input to one or more W functions, thus connecting the output of the processing element P to one or more W functions.

We now show how to simultaneously do both the architectural design and the training of the neural network to perform the task of adding two one-bit inputs to produce two output bits.

The fitness cases for this task consist of the four cases representing the four combinations of binary input signals (i.e., 00, 01, 10, and 11) that could appear on D1 and D0. The correct two output signals O1 and O2 (namely, 00, 01, 01, and 10, respectively) are then associated with each of these four fitness cases.

The raw fitness measure is the sum of the binary differences, taken over the four fitness cases, between the first (low-order) output signal from the neural network and the correct low-order bit from the one-bit adder function plus the sum of *twice* the binary differences, taken over the four fitness cases, between the second (high-order) output signal from the neural network and the correct high-order bit from the one-bit adder function. That is, the errors are weighted by consecutive powers of 2 (i.e., 1 and 2) according to the binary position. The minimum error of 0 is attained if both bits are right for all four fitness cases. The maximum error of 12 is attained if both bits are wrong for all four fitness cases. Therefore, raw fitness ranges between 0 and 12.

The crossover operation must be performed so as to preserve the required structure of individuals for the problem. That is, the result must be an allowable neural network in every case. Structure-preserving crossover is performed as follows: Any point may be selected, without restriction, as the crossover point in the first parent; however, the selection of the crossover point in the second parent is then restricted to a point of the same type as the point chosen in the first parent.

For this problem, there are four types of points:

- a processing element function P,
- a weighting function W,
- an input data signal (such as D0 or D1), and
- an arithmetic function or a random constant.

Table 19.10 summarizes the key features of the problem of designing a neural network for the one-bit adder.

In one run, an individual, which was 100% correct in performing the one-bit adder task, emerged on generation 31. This individual was complex. It was simplified by consolidating each subexpression consisting of only numeric constants and arithmetic functions into a single numeric constant (weight). The simplified form of this 100%-correct individual is

Table 19.10 Tableau for neural network problem.

Objective:	Design the architecture and find the weights for a neural network that performs the one-bit adder task.
Terminal set:	D0, D1, and ℜ, where ℜ is an ephemeral random floating-point constant ranging between -2.000 and $+2.000$.
Function set:	LIST2, P, W, +, −, *, %.
Fitness cases:	The four combinations of the binary input signals D0 and D1.
Raw fitness:	The sum, taken over the four fitness cases, of the position-weighted sum of the differences (errors) between the two binary signals produced by the S-expression and the correct two binary signals. Raw fitness ranges from 0 to 12.
Standardized fitness:	Standardized fitness equals raw fitness for this problem.
Hits:	Number (0–4) of fitness cases for which the two binary signals produced by the S-expression match the correct two binary signals.
Wrapper:	None.
Parameters:	$M = 500. G = 51.$
Success predicate:	An S-expression scores 4 hits.
Rules of construction:	See text above.
Types of points:	Four types: • points with a processing function P, • points with a weighting function W, • points with input data signals (such as D0 and D1), and • points with arithmetic functions or floating-point random constants.

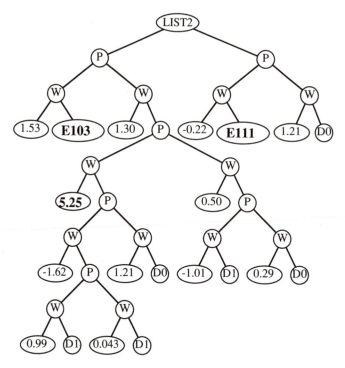

Figure 19.19 Genetically created neural network for the one-bit adder task.

```
(LIST2 (P (W 1.53 (E103))
          (W 1.30
             (P (W 5.25
                   (P (W −1.62
                         (P (W 0.99 D1) (W 0.043 D1)))
                      (W 1.21 D0)))
                (W 0.50 (P (W −1.01 D1)
                           (W 0.29 D0))))))
       (P (W −0.22 (E111)) (W 1.21 D0))).
```

Figure 19.19 graphically depicts this simplified individual from generation 31. The constant 5.25 and the two calls on the encapsulated functions E103 and E111 are highlighted in boldface.

Note that every numeric constant in the S-expression above and in figure 19.19 is a consolidation of a rather large subexpression involving arithmetic functions (+, −, *, %) and floating-point random constants. For example, the constant 5.25 (in boldface in the figure) arose from the S-expression

```
(% (+ (* (% 0.865 −1.058) (* −0.354 0.843))
      (+ (% 1.082 −0.728) (− 0.543 0.265)))
   (* (+ −0.549 (* 1.71 0.49)) −0.636)).
```

Figure 19.20 graphically depicts this subexpression for the numerical constant (weight) 5.25.

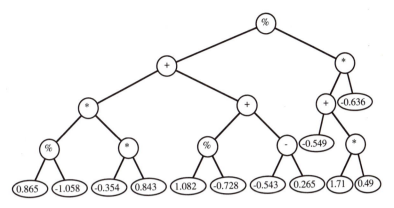

Figure 19.20 Subtree representing the genetically bred constant 5.25.

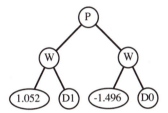

Figure 19.21 Encapsulated function E103.

The encapsulated function E103 was defined so as to return the S-expression

```
(P (W 1.052 D1) (W -1.496 D0)).
```

The value returned by an encapsulated function, such as E103, depends on the current values of the terminals contained in it. As a result, the value of an encapsulated function is always defined when it is called.

Figure 19.21 shows the encapsulated function E103 depicted as a tree.

The encapsulated function E111 was defined so as to return the S-expression

```
(P (W 5.25 (P (W -1.62 (P (W 0.99 D1) (W 0.043 D1)))
             (W 1.51 (P (W -0.42 D1) (W 1.57 D0)))))
   (W -0.48 (P (W -0.017 D1) (W 0.077 D0)))).
```

Figure 19.22 shows the encapsulated function E111 in tree form.

If the encapsulated functions E103 and E111 are inserted into the S-expression, we obtain the S-expression below. In this neural network, the expanded versions of the two encapsulated functions are shown in boldface.

```
(LIST2
    (P (W 1.53 (P (W 1.052 D1) (W -1.496 D0))))
       (W 1.30
          (P (W 5.25 (P (W -1.62 (P (W 0.99 D1)
                                    (W 0.043 D1)))
             (W 1.21 D0)))
```

Evolution of Constrained Syntactic Structures

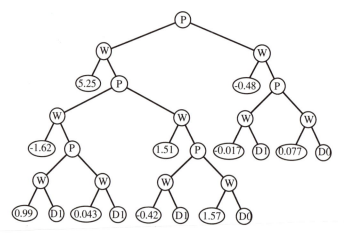

Figure 19.22 Encapsulated function E111.

```
           (W 0.50 (P (W −1.01 D1) (W 0.29 D0))))))
    (P (W −0.22 (P

                (W 5.25

                    (P (W −1.62 (P (W 0.99 D1)

                                   (W 0.043 D1)))

                        (W 1.51 (P (W −0.42 D1)

                                   (W 1.57 D0)))))

                (W −0.48 (P (W −0.017 D1)

                            (W 0.077 D0)))))

      (W 1.21 D0))).
```

The interpretation of the 100%-correct individual shown above is as follows: The first element of the LIST2 is the low-order bit of the result. Upon examination, this first element is equivalent to

```
(OR (AND D1 (NOT D0)) (AND D0 (NOT D1))),
```

which is equivalent to (XOR D0 1), namely the odd-2-parity (exclusive-or) function of the two input bits D0 and D1. This is the correct expression for the low-order bit of the result.

The second element of the LIST2 is the high-order bit of the result. Upon examination, this second element is equivalent to

```
(AND D0 (NOT (OR (AND D0 (NOT D1)) (NOT D1)))),
```

which is equivalent to (AND D0 D1). This is the correct expression for the high-order bit of the result. See also Koza and Rice 1991a.

In other words, the 100%-correct individual can be simplified as shown in figure 19.23.

Figure 19.24 presents the performance curves showing, by generation, the cumulative probability of success $P(M, i)$ and the number of individuals that must be processed $I(M, i, z)$ to yield, with 99% probability, at least one individual S-expression representing a neural network that successfully per-

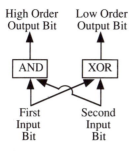

High Order   Low Order
Output Bit   Output Bit

AND   XOR

First   Second
Input   Input
Bit   Bit

Figure 19.23 Simplification of the genetically bred neural network for the one-bit adder problem.

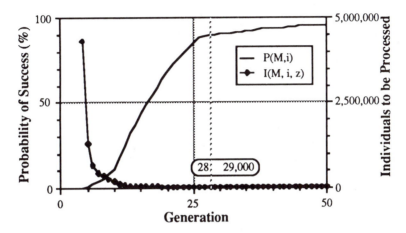

Figure 19.24 Performance curves of the neural network problem for the one-bit adder problem.

forms the one-bit adder task. These curves are based on 375 runs and a population size of 500. The cumulative probability of success $P(M, i)$ is 90% by generation 28 and 95% by generation 50. The numbers in the oval indicate that if this problem is run through to generation 28, processing a total of 29,000 (i.e., 500 × 29 generations × 2 runs) individuals is sufficient to yield a solution of this problem with 99% probability. See also Koza and Rice 1991a.

19.10   RECAPITULATION

In this chapter, we have presented problems in which the individual S-expressions undergoing adaptation have a constrained syntactic structure that is defined using special problem-specific syntactic rules of construction.

In the problems of symbolic multiple regression, design of a two-bit adder circuit, solving a pair of linear equations for both unknowns, and finding a global optimum point for a multi-dimensional function, each individual in the population was a vector of S-expressions. That is, the additional syntactic structure was that each S-expression returned a fixed number of component values, rather than a single value. Each of the components was treated in an identical manner.

Evolution of Constrained Syntactic Structures

In the problem of solving a quadratic equation for both complex roots, there were two components, but we treated the components differently when we combined them, via a wrapper, to represent the solution to the problem.

In the problem of finding the Fourier series for a function, each component was treated in an identical manner, but there was a indefinite number of components. The evolutionary process, driven by fitness, determined how many terms would be included in the Fourier series.

In the problem of finding the inverse kinematics for controlling a two-link robot arm and the problem of the local tracking of a dynamical system, there were two components to the structure which played very different roles in the cascade. The first component of the structure was created using a different set of functions and terminals than the second component. Moreover, the first component of the structure was computed first; the result was given a name; and that result was then made available to the second component of the structure. That is, we defined a value in the first part of the structure for subsequent use and we cascaded that value into the second part of the structure.

In the problem of designing the architecture and determining the weights for a neural network, the solution to the problem was a structure which had a complicated syntactic structure, namely a valid neural network. Syntactic rules of construction were needed in order to create individuals that could reasonably be called neural networks.

20 Evolution of Building Blocks

Three different ways (i.e., setting, cascading variables, and the encapsulation operation) have been presented in previous chapters to give a useful computation a name so that it can be subsequently used elsewhere in a computer program.

First, in the problem of iterative summation (section 18.2), the set operator SET–SV was used to assign the current value of a specified S-expression to a settable variable SV, thus making that value available whenever the terminal SV subsequently appeared within the program. The value of the settable variable SV was based on the value of the terminals in the S-expression at the time of execution of the set operator SET–SV and does not reflect any subsequent events, such as changes in the value of those terminals. This approach has the shortcoming of requiring that some default value be assigned to the settable variable in the event that it is referenced before it is defined. The problem of undefined variables, of course, often occurs when humans write programs. The arbitrary assignment of a default value has the disadvantage of making the value of the settable variable (which often changes a number of times during the evaluation of one individual S-expression) especially erratic and dependent on its location in relation to the location of the set function, if any, in the program.

Second, in three previous problems in this book (i.e., solving a quadratic equation in section 19.5, finding the inverse kinematics for controlling a two-link robot arm in section 19.7, and the local tracking of a dynamical system in section 19.8), a cascading variable was set to the value of the sub-S-expression located in the first (leftmost) main branch of the program tree. That value was then made available whenever the cascading variable appeared in the value-returning, rightmost main branch of the program tree. The value of the cascading variable is based on the values of the terminals in the first main branch of the program tree at the time of execution of that branch and does not reflect any subsequent events, such as changes in the values of those terminals. This approach makes it possible to guarantee that the cascading variable is defined before it is referenced. This approach can be generalized so that more than one cascading variable can be defined and so that already-defined cascading variables can appear in the definition of subsequent cascading variables.

Third, in the neural network design problem (section 19.9), the encapsulation operation (subsection 6.5.4) was used to dynamically define a function with no arguments in terms of a random sub-S-expression from an S-expression selected from the population in proportion to fitness. The value returned by the encapsulated function depends on the current value of the terminals contained in it and is therefore never undefined when it is called.

20.1 THE IDEA OF FUNCTION DEFINITION

In writing computer programs, it is often useful to be able to define a function so that a particular calculation can be performed on various different combinations of arguments. For example, suppose it is necessary to apply the exponential function to a single variable x on one occasion in a computer program and that an approximation consisting of the first five terms of the Taylor series will suffice. A programmer would probably be entirely satisfied to quickly write

```
(+ 1.0 X (* 0.5 X X) (* 0.1667 X X X)
   (* 0.04167 X X X X)),
```

or the equivalent code in whatever programming language that he was using.

Now suppose that it was necessary to apply this same exponential function to another variable Y and to the quantity $3z^2$ later in the same program. The programmer would not be pleased if he were required to tediously write

```
(+ 1.0 Y (* 0.5 Y Y) (* 0.1667 Y Y Y)
   (* 0.04167 Y Y Y Y)),
```

and

```
(+ 1.0
   (* 3 Z Z)
   (* 0.5 (* 3 Z Z) (* 3 Z Z))
   (* 0.1667 (* 3 Z Z) (* 3 Z Z) (* 3 Z Z))
   (* 0.04167 (* 3 Z Z) (* 3 Z Z) (* 3 Z Z) (* 3 Z Z))).
```

Instead, the programmer would want to be able to define a function in terms of a dummy variable (formal parameter) dv as follows:

```
(defun exp (dv)
   (+ 1.0
      dv
      (* 0.5 dv dv)
      (* 0.1667 dv dv dv)
      (* 0.04167 dv dv dv dv)).
```

Once a function is defined, it can be called an arbitrary number of times from an arbitrary number of different places in the main program with different instantiations (such as x, y, and $3z^2$) of its dummy variable (formal parameter). In particular, the exponential approximation function exp can be called from any part of the program with x, y, and $3z^2$ as its argument (actual parameter) merely by writing (exp X), (exp Y), and (exp (* 3 Z Z)). It is no longer necessary to tediously rewrite the desired five-term approximation with X, Y, and $3Z^2$ explicitly inserted.

The ability to define a function in terms of dummy variables (formal parameters) and then to evaluate the function with particular instantiations of those dummy variables is a highly efficient programming technique because it obviates tedious writing of numerous lines of essentially similar code. In addition, defining functions enhances the understandability of a program because it highlights common calculations. However, the importance of the ability to define functions goes beyond mere efficiency and clarity. In effect, defining a function and making multiple uses of it decomposes a problem into a hierarchy of which the defined function is a part. As a problem increases in size and complexity, decomposition of a problem via function definition becomes an increasingly important tool.

20.2 SYMBOLIC REGRESSION OF EVEN-PARITY FUNCTIONS

The problem of learning the Boolean even-parity function with various numbers of arguments will be used throughout this chapter to demonstrate the utility of function definitions in solving problems.

In applying genetic programming to a particular Boolean function of k arguments, the 2^k combinations of the k Boolean arguments constitute the fitness cases. The standardized fitness of an S-expression is the sum, over the 2^k fitness cases, of the Hamming distance (error) between the value returned by the S-expression and the correct value of the particular Boolean function. Standardized fitness ranges between 0 and 2^k. Both raw fitness and hits are equal to the number of fitness cases for which the S-expression is correct, namely 2^k minus standardized fitness.

Suppose that we select the same set of four basic diadic Boolean functions we selected in chapter 9 as the function set for this problem:

F_b = {AND, OR, NAND, NOR}.

This function set is computationally complete and is therefore sufficient to solve any problem of symbolic regression involving Boolean functions.

As shown in chapter 9, the parity functions are the hardest Boolean functions to find via blind random search of the space of S-expressions composed using the function set F_b and they are also the hardest to learn via genetic programming. The Boolean even-3-parity function (rule 105 in the usual numbering scheme for Boolean functions), for example, is so difficult that blind random search failed to find it after trying 10,000,000 individuals. Moreover, with a population size of 50, it is necessary to process 1,187,225 individuals in order to yield a solution to the even-3-parity problem with a 99% probability. Similarly, it is necessary to process 999,750 individuals in order to yield a solution to the odd-3-parity problem (rule 150) with a 99% probability (table 9.4).

To establish a baseline for the experiments in this chapter and the next chapter, genetic programming is first applied to the even parity function of two, three, and four arguments using the function set F_b.

Starting with the even-2-parity function (which is also known as the equivalence function EQV, the not-exclusive-or function, and the two-argument Boolean rule 09), the terminal set T_2 consists of the two Boolean arguments, namely

$T_2 = \{D0, D1\}$.

In one run of the even-2-parity function with a population of size 20, genetic programming discovered the following S-expression containing seven points with a perfect value of raw fitness (i.e., 4 out of 4) in generation 3:

```
(OR (NOR D1 D0) (AND D0 D1)).
```

For the even-3-parity function, the terminal set must be expanded to include the third argument D2 and is therefore

$T_3 = \{D0, D1, D2\}$.

In one run of the even-3-parity function using a population size of 4,000 (the size used throughout the remainder of this and the next chapter), genetic programming discovered the following S-expression containing 45 points with a perfect value of raw fitness of 8 (out of 8) in generation 5:

```
(AND (OR (OR D0 (NOR D2 D1)) D2) (AND (NAND (NOR (NOR D0
D2) (AND (AND D1 D1) D1)) (NAND (OR (AND D0 D1) D2) D0))
(OR (NAND (AND D0 D2) (OR (NOR D0 (OR D2 D0)) D1)) (NAND
(NAND D1 (NAND D0 D1)) D2)))).
```

For the even-4-parity function (four-argument Boolean rule 38,505), the terminal set must be expanded to include the fourth argument D3 and is therefore

$T_4 = \{D0, D1, D2, D3\}$.

In generation 24 of one run with a population size of 4,000, genetic programming discovered the following S-expression containing 149 points with a perfect value of raw fitness of 16 (out of 16):

```
(AND (OR (OR (OR (NOR D0 (NOR D2 D1)) (NAND (OR (NOR (AND
D3 D0) D2) (NAND D0 (NOR D2 (AND D1 (OR D3 D2)))))) D3))
(AND (AND D1 D2) D0)) (NAND (NAND (NAND D3 (OR (NOR D0
(NOR (OR D3 D2) D2)) (NAND (AND (AND (AND D3 D2) D3) D2)
D3))) (NAND (OR (NAND (OR D0 (OR D0 D1)) (NAND D0 D1))
D3) (NAND D1 D3))) D3)) (OR (OR (NOR (NOR (AND (OR (NOR
D3 D0) (NOR (NOR D3 (NAND (OR (NAND D2 D2) D2) D2)) (AND
D3 D2))) D1) (AND D3 D0)) (NOR D3 (OR D0 D2))) (NOR D1
(AND (OR (NOR (AND D3 D3) D2) (NAND D0 (NOR D2 (AND D1
D0)))) (OR (OR D0 D3) (NOR D0 (NAND (OR (NAND D2 D2) D2)
D2)))))) (AND (AND D2 (NAND D1 (NAND (AND D3 (NAND D1
D3)) (AND D1 D1)))) (OR D3 (OR D0 (OR D0 D1)))))))).
```

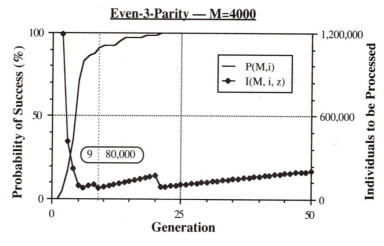

Even-3-Parity — M=4000

Figure 20.1 Performance curves for even-3-parity function show that 80,000 individuals must be processed to yield a solution.

The above three runs suggest the difficulty of the problem of learning the Boolean parity functions.

For the even-3-parity function, figure 20.1 presents the performance curves (as discussed in detail in chapter 9) showing, by generation, the cumulative probability of success, $P(M, i)$, and the number of individuals that must be processed, $I(M, i, z)$, to yield, with 99% probability, at least one S-expression producing the correct value for all eight fitness cases. The graph is based on 66 runs. The population size M was 4,000 and the maximum number of generations to be run G was 51. The cumulative probability of success, $P(M, i)$, is 91% by generation 9 and 100% by generation 21. The numbers in the oval indicate that if this problem is run through to generation 9, processing a total of 80,000 (i.e., 4,000 × 10 generations × 2 runs) individuals is sufficient to yield a solution of this problem with 99% probability.

Figure 20.2 shows the performance curves for the even-4-parity function. The graph is based on 60 runs. The population size M was 4,000 and the maximum number of generations to be run G was 51. The cumulative probability of success, $P(M, i)$, is 35% by generation 28 and 45% by generation 50. The numbers in the oval indicate that if this problem is run through to generation 28, processing a total of 1,276,000 (i.e., 4,000 × 29 generations × 11 runs) individuals is sufficient to yield a solution of this problem with 99% probability.

For reference, figure 20.3 shows the corresponding performance curves for the odd-4-parity function (four-argument Boolean rule 27,030). The graph is based on 44 runs. The population size M was 4,000 and the maximum number of generations to be run G was 51. The cumulative probability of success $P(M, i)$ is 55% by generation 37. The numbers in the oval indicate that if this problem is run through to generation 37, processing a total of 912,000 (i.e., 4,000 × 38 generations × 6 runs) individuals is sufficient to yield a solution of this problem with 99% probability. As can be seen, the odd-4-

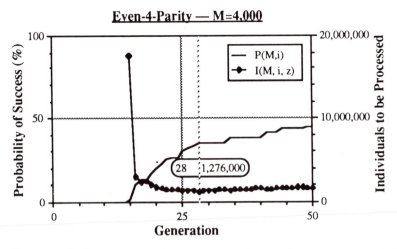

Figure 20.2 Performance curves for even-4-parity function show that 1,276,000 individuals must be processed to yield a solution.

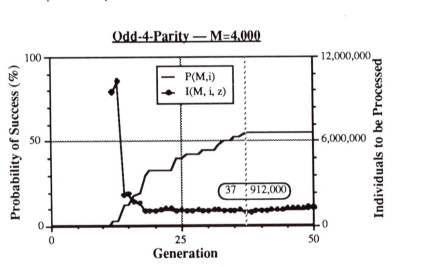

Figure 20.3 Performance curves for odd-4-parity function show that 912,000 individuals must be processed to yield a solution.

parity function requires slightly less processing than the even-4-parity function (similar to the result observed for the even and odd parity functions of three arguments).

Although the population sizes selected above are undoubtedly not optimal, it is clear that symbolic regression on the parity functions with an increasing number of arguments requires the processing of increasing numbers of individuals. For the even-3-parity function, 80,000 individuals must be processed; for the even-4-parity function, 1,276,000 individuals must be processed.

We are unable to continue this analysis of the progressively larger even-parity functions with a constant population size of 4,000. When the even-5-parity function was run with a population size of 4,000, no solution was found after 20 runs. After increasing the population size to 8,000, a solution was not found until the eighth run, suggesting that the even-5-parity function is a very difficult function to learn. The solution appeared on generation 27 of run 8 and contained 347 points as shown below:

```
(NAND (NAND (OR (AND (AND (AND (OR D2 D3) (OR D4 D2))
(AND (OR D4 D0) (AND D1 D1))) (NOR (NOR D1 D4) (OR (NOR
D3 D4) (NOR D0 D2)))) (NOR (NOR (NAND (AND (OR D1 D0) (OR
D3 D2)) (OR D1 D3)) (NOR D1 D2)) (NOR (AND (NAND D4 D3)
(NAND D4 D0)) (NAND (OR D2 D4) (OR D2 D1))))) (NOR (NOR
(OR (NOR (AND D2 D0) (NOR D1 D4)) (AND (NOR (NOR (OR (NOR
(AND D2 D0) (NOR D1 D4)) (AND (NOR D0 D2) (NAND D4 D0)))
(AND (AND (NAND D4 D3) (OR D3 D0)) (OR D4 D3))) (NOR (NOR
(AND (AND D1 D1) (AND D4 D2)) (NAND (NAND D0 D2) (NAND D4
D0))) (NAND (AND D0 D4) (NAND (NOR D1 D4) (OR D1 D0)))))))
(NAND (AND D4 D1) (OR D2 D0)))) (AND (AND (NAND D4 D3)
(OR D3 D0)) (OR D2 D1))) (NOR (NOR (AND (AND D1 D1) (NOR
(NAND (NAND D4 D2) (NAND D4 D4)) (OR (AND D2 D0) (AND D4
D1)))) (NAND (OR (AND (OR (AND D3 D0) (OR D4 (NAND (OR
(NOR D1 D2) D3) D4))) (NAND (NAND D0 D1) (NAND D2 D2)))
(NAND (AND (NOR D0 D1) (OR D3 D4)) (OR (NAND D3 D4) (AND
D3 D1)))) (NAND D4 (AND (OR D1 D0) (OR D3 D2))))) (NAND
(OR (NAND D1 D0) (NOR D2 D0)) (NAND D3 D2))))) (NAND (AND
(NAND (OR (NOR (NAND (OR D1 D3) (AND D0 D4)) (NOR (AND D1
D4) (NOR D2 D2))) (AND (OR (NOR D1 D3) (NOR (AND (NOR D2
D2) (NOR (NOR D2 D2) (AND D2 D1))) (AND (NAND (NAND D4
D0) (NAND (NOR (NAND (NOR D4 D4) (NOR D0 D4)) (OR (AND D2
D3) (AND D4 D1))) (AND (OR (NOR D3 D4) D1) (AND (OR D1
D0) (OR D3 D2))))) (OR D2 D3)))) (OR (OR D2 D3) (NAND D3
D0)))) (NAND (AND (NOR (AND D0 D2) (OR D4 D0)) (AND D4
D1)) (OR (AND D1 D4) (NAND (NAND D1 D3) (OR D3 D1)))))
(OR (OR D2 D3) (NAND D3 D0))) (AND (OR (NOR D3 D4) D3)
(AND (OR D1 D0) (OR D3 D2)))))).
```

Our usual computation for the number of individuals that must be processed to solve a problem with 99% probability requires making enough runs that successfully solve the problem to produce a reasonable estimate for the values of probability $P(M, i)$ between generations 0 and 50. The fact that only one solution of the even-5-parity problem appeared after eight runs suggests that a large number of lengthy runs would be required to accumulate the necessary data to permit construction of our usual performance curves. If we ignored the obvious inadequacy of these eight runs, our usual calculation (using a probability of success of 0 for generations 0 through 26 and using a probability of success of 1/8 for generation 27 through 50) would suggest that a total of 7,840,000 individuals are necessary to solve this problem with a probability of 99%.

As one would expect, the solutions shown above contain an increasing number of points for parity problems with an increasing number of arguments (i.e., 7, 45, 149, and 347, respectively).

20.3 THE IDEA OF AUTOMATIC FUNCTION DEFINITION

This increase in computational effort and complexity could be substantially reduced if the solution to this problem could be built up from a suitable building block. Since AND, NAND, OR, and NOR are already in the function set for this problem, the building block that would be most helpful in solving the even-3-parity or even-4-parity functions is the either the even-2-parity function (also known as the equivalence function EQV, the not-exclusive-or function, and the two-argument Boolean rule 09) or the odd-2-parity function (also known as the exclusive-or function XOR, the inequality function, and Boolean rule 06).

In this section, I am not talking about assigning a value to a settable variable using an assignment operator such as SET-SV or about assigning a value to a cascading variable or about encapsulating, say, the exclusive-or function of a particular two terminals, such as D0 and D2. Recall that both the subtree defining the cascading variable and the subtree encapsulated by the encapsulation operation consisted of a computation which operated on the actual variables of the problem as opposed to dummy variables (formal parameters).

Instead, I am contemplating having the exclusive-or (or equivalence) *function* available in the function set. This function would be defined in terms of two dummy variables called ARG0 and ARG1. When this defined function is called, its two dummy variables would be instantiated with the values of two sub-expressions (i.e., actual parameters) of the problem. For example, the exclusive-or function XOR might be called with the terminals D0 and D1 via (XOR D0 D1) on one occasion, with the terminals D1 and D2 on another occasion, and with two identical terminals as arguments, such as D0 and D0, on yet another occasion. The function would be defined once, even though it might be called numerous times.

Moreover, I am contemplating *automatic* function definition wherein genetic programming first evolves a function definition during the run and then evolves an appropriate value-returning S-expression that calls the defined function that it just created. The evolution of this dual structure consisting of both function definitions and function calls is to be driven only by the fitness measure working in conjunction with natural selection and the genetic operations.

20.4 EVEN-4-PARITY

The goal of automatic function definition can be achieved by establishing a constrained syntactic structure for the S-expressions in the fashion of chapter 19 wherein the overall S-expression will contain both function definitions and calls to the functions so defined. The required structure is much like the vector of independent components used in the problem of symbolic multiple regression (section 19.1) and the problem of solving a pair of linear equations for two unknowns (section 19.3). The required structure resembles the cascading structure used in finding the inverse kinematics for controlling a two-link robot arm (section 19.7).

When Boolean functions are involved, there is no need for a one-argument function definition (since there are only four Boolean functions of one argument: the negation of the given argument, the identity of the given argument, and the true and false functions). In contrast, when real-valued functions are involved, a one-argument function definition may be highly useful. Therefore, when doing symbolic regression on the Boolean even-4-parity function, it would be reasonable to start with a two-argument function definition and to stop with a function definition taking $n - 1$ arguments or n arguments (where n is the number of terminals in the terminal set of the problem).

The choice of n, versus $n - 1$, affects the size and bushiness of the overall S-expression. Choosing the slightly smaller value of $n - 1$ saves a considerable amount of computer resources. For many problems there is no compelling need for a function definition of arity n since all of the available terminals are already available in the value-returning branch. Therefore, for the Boolean even-4-parity problem, we will permit one two-argument function definition, one three-argument function definition, and one value-returning branch. Specifically, the constrained syntactic structure for this problem consists of an S-expression with three components. The first (leftmost) branch permits a two-argument function definition (defining a function called ADF0); the second (middle) branch permits a three-argument function definition (defining a function called ADF1); and the value-returning (i.e., rightmost) branch will compute the return value of the overall S-expression. This value-returning (i.e., third) branch is composed, in general, of the four actual terminals D0, D1, D2 and D3 of the problem, the Boolean functions from the basic function set F_b, and the two defined functions ADF0 and ADF1 created by the two function-defining branches.

There are four types of points in the S-expressions for this problem, namely

- the root (which will always be the place-holding LIST3 function),
- points in the first (leftmost) branch (defining ADF0),
- points in the second (middle) branch (defining ADF1), and
- points in the third (rightmost) branch (i.e., the value-returning branch).

The syntactic rules of construction for the individual S-expressions are these:

- The root of the tree must be the LIST3 function with three arguments;
- The root is the only place where the LIST3 function will appear.
- The first function-defining branch of the S-expression created by the LIST3 is a composition of functions from the function set F_b and terminals from the set A_2 of two dummy variables for defining a function of two arguments,

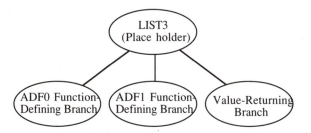

Figure 20.4 Abstraction of the overall structure of an S-expression with two function-defining branches and the one value-returning branch.

namely

A_2 = {ARG0, ARG1}.

- The second function-defining branch of the S-expression created by the LIST3 is a composition of functions from the function set F_b and terminals from the set A_3 of three dummy variables for defining a function of three arguments, namely

A_3 = {ARG0, ARG1, ARG2}.

- The third branch (i.e., the value-returning branch) of the S-expression created by the LIST3 is a composition of actual terminals from the terminal set T_4, namely

T_4 = {D0, D1, D2, D3},

as well as functions from the function set F_b, the two-argument function ADF0 defined by the first branch, and the three-argument function ADF1 defined by the second branch. That is, the function set F_3 for the value-returning branch of the even-4-parity problem is

F_3 = {AND, OR, NAND, NOR, ADF0, ADF1},

taking two, two, two, two, two, and three arguments, respectively.

No values are returned by the first two branches; they are merely function-defining branches which may or may not be called upon by the value-returning (i.e., third) branch. The value returned by the entire S-expression is the value returned by the value-returning branch.

Figure 20.4 shows an abstraction of the overall structure of an S-expression defined according to the above constrained syntactic rules. The LIST3 function is simply a connective glue that holds together the two function-defining branches and the final value-returning branch.

Figure 20.5 shows an S-expression for the even-4-parity function containing two defined functions, ADF0 and ADF1 in greater detail than the abstraction in figure 20.4. The first branch contains a function definition for the two-argument defined function ADF0 which happens to be the even-2-parity function (i.e., the equivalence function EQV). It is expressed in terms of the two dummy variables ARG0 and ARG1. This first branch plays a role equivalent to the

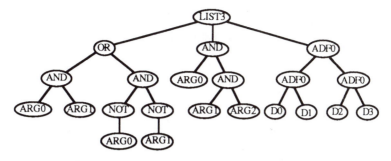

Figure 20.5 Illustrative S-expression for the even-4-parity function.

following function in Common LISP:

```
(defun adf0 (arg0 arg1)
  (or (and arg0 arg1) (and (not arg0) (not arg1))))).
```

The second branch contains a function definition for the three-argument defined function ADF1, which in this case happens to be equivalent to the ordinary conjunction function of three dummy variables ARG0, ARG1, and ARG2. This second branch plays a role equivalent to the following function:

```
(defun adf1 (arg0 arg1 arg2)
  (and arg0 (and arg1 arg2))).
```

The value-returning branch contains the actual terminals D0, D1, D2, and D3 of the problem and three calls to the defined function ADF0 (i.e., the equivalence function EQV) and no calls to the defined function ADF1. It computes

```
(EQV (EQV D0 D1) (EQV D2 D3)),
```

which is, in fact, a correct way to compute the even parity of the four terminals. The value returned by the entire S-expression is the value of the even-4-parity function. In other words, the value returned by the S-expression is the value returned by evaluating the following function when called with a particular S-expression as its argument:

```
(defun evaluate-individual (s-expression)
  (eval `(defun adf0 (arg0 arg1) ,(second s-expression)))
  (eval `(defun adf1 (arg0 arg1 arg2)
           ,(third s-expression)))
  (eval (fourth s-expression))).
```

Note that (first s-expression) is the symbol LIST3 and that (second s-expression) is the first branch.

Table 20.1 summarizes the key features of the problem of symbolic regression for the even-4-parity function using automatic function definition.

In what follows, genetic programming will be allowed to evolve a function definition in the two function-defining branches of each S-expression and then, at its discretion, to use one, two, or none of the defined functions in the value-returning branch. We do not specify what functions will be defined in

Table 20.1 Tableau for even-4-parity function using automatic function definition.

Objective:	Find an S-expression for the even-4-parity function incorporating (potentially) a two-argument defined function and a three-argument defined function.
Terminal set:	Various subsets of the following depending on the branch in which the terminal is located: D0, D1, D2, D3, ARG0, ARG1, and ARG2, as described below and in the text.
Function set:	Various subsets of the following depending on the type of internal point involved: LIST3, AND, OR, NAND, NOR, ADF0, and ADF1, as described below and in the text.
Fitness cases:	All $2^4 = 16$ combinations of the four Boolean arguments D0, D1, D2, and D3.
Raw fitness:	The number of fitness cases for which the value returned by the S-expression equals the correct value of the even-4-parity function.
Standardized fitness:	The maximum value of raw fitness (16) minus raw fitness.
Hits:	Same as raw fitness for this problem.
Wrapper:	None.
Parameters:	$M = 4,000$ (with over-selection). $G = 51$.
Success predicate:	An S-expression scores 16 hits.
Rules of construction:	• Root is always the LIST3 function. • Remainder of the tree is a composition of the available functions (other than LIST3) and the available terminals. • The first (leftmost, function-defining) branch is composed of the AND, OR, NAND and NOR functions and the dummy variables (formal parameters) ARG0 and ARG1. • The second (middle, function-defining) branch is composed of the AND, OR, NAND and NOR functions and the dummy variables (formal parameters) ARG0, ARG1, and ARG2. • The third (rightmost, value-returning) branch is composed of the AND, OR, NAND and NOR functions, the two defined functions ADF0 and ADF1, and the terminals D0, D1, D2, D3 (i.e., actual variables of the problem).
Types of points:	Four types of points: • the root, • points in the first (leftmost, function-defining) branch, • points in the second (middle, function-defining) branch, and • points in the third (rightmost, value-returning) branch.

the two function-defining branches. We do not specify whether the defined functions will actually be used (it being, of course, possible to solve this problem without any function definition by evolving the correct computer program in the third branch). We do not favor a function definition of any particular number of arguments. Branches are provided in the S-expression to accommodate function definitions of each possible size between 2 and $n - 1$ (where n is the total number of terminals in the problem). We do not require that a function-defining branch use all of the available dummy variables. It is possible, for example, for the second branch to define a two-argument function, rather than a three-argument function, by ignoring one of the three available dummy variables.

Since a constrained syntactic structure is involved, we proceed here in the same manner as in chapter 19 by first creating the initial random generation so that every individual computer program in the population has the required syntactic structure and then by performing structure-preserving crossover. Structure-preserving crossover is implemented by allowing the selection of the crossover point in the first parent to be totally unrestricted and then requiring that the crossover point of the second parent be of the same type (as defined above) as the already-selected crossover point of the first parent.

In one run of the even-4-parity problem, the best-of-generation individual from generation 0 scored only slightly better than 50% of the possible 16 hits. This individual contained 23 points and scored 10 hits (out of 16) and is shown below:

```
(LIST3 (OR (OR ARG0 ARG1) (OR ARG1 ARG0))
       (AND (OR ARG1 ARG0) (NAND ARG1 ARG0))
       (NAND (ADF1 D3 D2 D2) (NOR D1 D0))).
```

The first function-defining branch of this S-expression defines the two-argument defined function ADF0, which is equivalent to the simple disjunction

```
(OR ARG0 ARG1).
```

As it happens, defined function ADF0 is not used in the value-returning branch.

The second branch is a three-argument definition for defined function ADF1 that ignores one of its three arguments and is equivalent to

```
(EQV ARG0 ARG1).
```

When EQV is substituted for ADF1, the value-returning branch becomes

```
(NAND (EQV D3 D2) (NOR D1 D0)).
```

This function is equivalent to the four-argument Boolean rule 61,438, which manifestly is not rule 38,505 (the even-4-parity function).

In generation 8 of this run, the best-of-generation individual shown below contained 145 points:

```
(LIST3 (AND (NAND (NOR (AND ARG0 ARG0) (NOR ARG1 ARG0))
           (AND ARG1 ARG1)) (OR (OR ARG1 ARG1) (AND (AND
           ARG1 ARG1) (OR ARG1 ARG1))))
```

```
(NOR (OR (AND (OR ARG1 ARG2) (OR ARG0 ARG1)) (OR
    (AND ARG0 ARG1) (OR ARG0 ARG0))) (NOR (OR (NOR
    ARG2 ARG2) (NOR ARG1 ARG2)) (NAND (NOR ARG0
    ARG1) (NAND ARG0 ARG2))))
(NOR (OR (ADF1 (AND D3 D0) (OR D0 D2) (NOR D1
    D3)) (ADF1 (OR D3 D1) (ADF1 D0 D2 D3) (AND D0
    D2))) (AND (ADF0 (OR D3 D0) (OR D2 D3)) (NOR
    (NOR D1 D1) (NOR (NOR (OR (ADF1 (AND D3 D0)
    (OR D0 D2) (NOR D1 D3)) (ADF1 (OR D3 D1) (ADF1
    D0 D2 D3) (NAND (OR (AND D3 D3) (AND D2 D2))
    (OR (ADF0 D0 D2) (NAND D3 D3))))) (AND (ADF0
    (OR D3 D0) (OR D2 D2)) (NOR (NOR D1 D1) (ADF1
    D2 D2 D0)))) (NAND D0 D3))))).
```

The first branch of this S-expression is a two-argument definition for defined function ADF0 that is equivalent to the simple conjunction

```
(AND ARG0 ARG1).
```

The second branch is a three-argument definition for defined function ADF1 that is equivalent to

```
(NOR ARG0 ARG1 ARG2).
```

The value-returning branch uses both defined function ADF0 and defined function ADF1 and produces a score of 14 hits.

In generation 12, the following S-expression appeared, containing 74 points and attaining a perfect value of 16 for raw fitness:

```
(LIST3 (NAND (OR (AND (NOR ARG0 ARG1) (NOR (AND ARG1
        ARG1) ARG1)) (NOR (NAND ARG0 ARG0) (NAND ARG1
        ARG1))) (NAND (NOR (NOR ARG1 ARG1) (AND (OR
        (NAND ARG0 ARG0) (NOR ARG1 ARG0)) ARG0)) (AND
        (OR ARG0 ARG0) (NOR (OR (AND (NOR ARG0 ARG1)
        (NAND ARG1 ARG1)) (NOR (NAND ARG0 ARG0) (NAND
        ARG1 ARG1))) ARG1))))
    (OR (AND ARG2 (NAND ARG0 ARG2)) (NOR ARG1 ARG1))
    (ADF0 (ADF0 D0 D2) (NAND (OR D3 D1) (NAND D1
        D3)))).
```

The first branch of this best-of-run S-expression is a function definition for the exclusive-or XOR function (i.e., the odd-2-parity function). This two-argument defined function ADF0 is defined in terms of the two dummy variables ARG0 and ARG1 and the functions in the function set F_b.

The second branch defines the three-argument defined function ADF1, but this defined function is not called by the value-returning branch which happens to contain calls to only the AND, OR, NAND, NOR, and ADF0 functions. Substituting XOR for ADF0, this branch becomes

```
(XOR (XOR D0 D2) (NAND (OR D3 D1) (NAND D1 D3))),
```

which is equivalent to

```
(XOR (XOR D0 D2) (EQV D3 D1)),
```

which is the even-4-parity function.

Note that we did not specify that the exclusive-or function would be defined as opposed to, say, the equivalence function, the if-then function, a clause in disjunctive normal form, or some other function. We did not specify that the exclusive-or function would be defined in the first branch as opposed to the second branch. Genetic programming created the two-argument defined function ADF0 on its own in the first branch to help solve this problem. Having done this, genetic programming had no use for a three-argument defined function.

Figure 20.6 graphically depicts the value-returning branch of this best-of-run individual from generation 12.

Figure 20.7 shows, by generation, the progressive improvement for the run in the average standardized fitness of the population as a whole and the standardized fitness of the best-of-generation individual and the worst-of-generation individual.

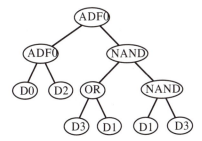

Figure 20.6 Value-returning branch of the best-of-run individual from generation 12 for the even-4-parity problem using automatic function definition.

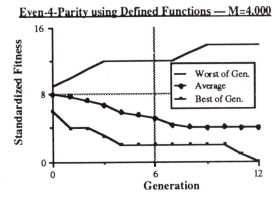

Figure 20.7 Fitness curves for the even-4-parity problem using automatic function definition.

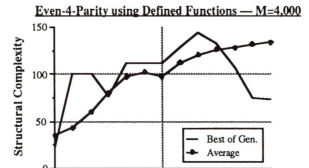

Figure 20.8 Structural complexity curves for the even-4-parity problem using automatic function definition.

Figure 20.8 shows, by generation, the generally increasing trend during the run of the average structural complexity of the population as a whole and the irregular values of structural complexity for the best-of-generation individual. As can be seen, the average size of the S-expression is well over 100 for the majority of this run.

Figure 20.9 shows, by generation, that variety remains generally stable in the neighborhood of 90% throughout the run under discussion here.

If a human programmer were programming the even-4-parity function and had the opportunity to define functions, he might well have decided to approach the problem by creating the exclusive-or function as a building block. However, not all runs of genetic programming proceed with the same orderly style as a human programmer.

In a second run of the even-4-parity problem, the following 100%-correct S-expression containing 41 points emerged in generation 3:

```
(LIST3 (OR (AND ARG0 ARG1) (NOR ARG1 ARG0))
       (NOR (AND ARG2 ARG0) (NOR (OR ARG0 ARG0) ARG2))
       (ADF1 (ADF0 D1 D0) (AND (OR (ADF1 D1 D2 D0) (OR
          D2 D1)) (OR (AND D0 D0) (AND D3 D0))) (ADF1 D3
          D0 D2))).
```

In this 100%-correct S-expression, the first and the second branches are both function definitions for the exclusive-or (XOR) function. The value-returning branch uses both ADF0 and ADF1. The three-argument defined function ADF1 in the second branch is degenerate in that it ignores one of the three available dummy variables and is defined only in terms of the dummy variables ARG0 and ARG2. Although a human programmer would not usually write two function definitions for the same function, this solution is as good as the previous solution from the point of view established by the fitness measure for this problem.

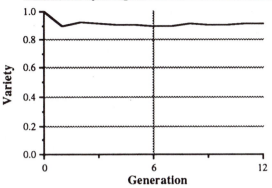

Even-4-Parity using Defined Functions — M=4,000

Figure 20.9 Variety curve in population for the even-4-parity problem using automatic function definition.

In a third run of the even-4-parity problem, the following 100%-correct S-expression containing 120 points emerged in generation 5:

```
(LIST3 (NOR (AND (AND (NAND ARG1 ARG0) (AND ARG0 ARG0))
           (NAND (NAND ARG0 ARG0) (OR ARG1 (AND ARG0
           ARG1)))) (NAND (NAND (OR ARG1 ARG1) (NAND ARG1
           ARG0)) (NOR (NAND ARG0 ARG1) (NOR ARG1
           ARG1))))
      (OR (AND (AND (NAND ARG1 ARG0) (AND ARG1 ARG0))
           (NAND (AND ARG1 ARG0) (OR ARG0 ARG2))) (AND
           (NAND (OR ARG1 ARG0) (NAND ARG0 ARG1)) (OR (OR
           ARG1 ARG2) (NOR ARG0 ARG2))))
      (ADF1 (OR (ADF0 (ADF0 (NAND D1 D0) (ADF1 D3 D2
           D0)) (NAND D0 D0)) (ADF1 D3 D2 D0)) (OR (ADF0
           (ADF1 D3 D3 D1) (ADF0 D0 D1)) (AND (NAND D3
           D0) (ADF1 D1 D0 D1))) (NOR (NAND (NOR D1 D0)
           (AND D3 D3)) (OR (ADF0 (ADF1 D1 D0 D0) (ADF0
           D3 D2)) (NOR D2 D2)))))).
```

The first branch of this S-expression is a function definition for the ordinary two-argument AND function. The value-returning branch calls ADF0 even though the AND function is already in the basic function set of the problem. Although a human programmer would be unlikely to create a superfluous definition of the AND function, this solution is also as good as both previous solutions from the point of view of the fitness measure.

The second branch is available to define a three-argument function; however, in this instance, genetic programming used this branch to define the even-2-parity (i.e., equivalence EQV) function in terms of ARG0 and ARG1. The reason that the third dummy variable ARG2 plays no role in this second branch is that the subclause (AND (NAND ARG1 ARG0) (AND ARG1 ARG0)) causes the first disjunct to always be NIL, and that the first conjunct contained

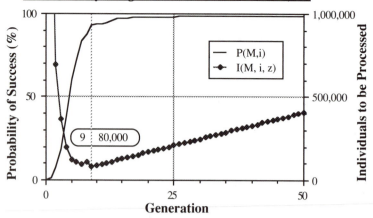

Even-4-Parity using Defined Functions — M=4,000

Figure 20.10 Performance curves for the even-4-parity problem show that 80,000 individuals must be processed to yield a solution with automatic function definition.

in the second disjunct is already NIL when the second conjunct, containing ARG2, happens to be NIL.

The 41, 120, and 74 points contained in these three particular S-expressions created via automatic function definition are considerably fewer than the 183 points contained in the S-expression cited earlier for the even-4-parity problem.

Figure 20.10 presents the performance curves showing, by generation, the cumulative probability of success, $P(M, i)$, and the number of individuals that must be processed, $I(M, i, z)$, to yield, with 99% probability, at least one S-expression producing the correct value of the even-4-parity function for all 16 fitness cases. The graph is based on 168 runs. The population size M was 4,000 and the maximum number of generations to be run G was 51. The cumulative probability of success $P(M, i)$ was 93% by generation 9 and was 99% by generation 50. The numbers in the oval indicate that if this problem is run through to generation 9, processing a total of 80,000 (i.e., 4,000 × 10 × 2 runs) individuals is sufficient to yield a solution of this problem with 99% probability.

In summary, the 80,000 individuals needed to be processed for the even-4-parity problem using automatic function definition is one sixteenth of the 1,276,000 individuals shown in figure 20.2. Thus, automatic function definition achieved a considerable improvement in performance for the even-4-parity problem.

20.5 EVEN-5-PARITY

The parity family of functions is a very difficult family of functions to learn. For example, after trying 20 runs of genetic programming without automatic function definition, no solution was found for the even-5-parity problem using a population size of 4,000 and the given function set F_b (although we did find one solution on our eighth run after we increased the population size to 8,000). However, if automatic function definition is used, solutions to both the even-5-parity and the even-6-parity functions can be readily found with a population size of 4,000.

For the even-5-parity problem (five-argument Boolean rule 1,771,476,585), each S-expression has four branches with automatic function definition. The first three branches permit creation of function definitions with two, three, and four dummy variables. The value-returning (i.e., fourth) branch is an S-expression incorporating the four diadic Boolean functions from the function set F_b; the three defined functions ADF0, ADF1, and ADF2; and the five terminals D0, D1, D2, D3, and D4.

In one run of the even-5-parity problem, the following S-expression scoring 32 (out of 32) hits and containing 174 points emerged on generation 11:

```
(LIST4 (OR (NOR (NAND (NAND ARG0 ARG0) (AND ARG0 ARG0))
           (NAND ARG0 ARG0)) (OR (NAND ARG0 ARG0) (OR
           (NAND (NAND ARG1 ARG1) (AND ARG0 ARG1)) (AND
           ARG1 ARG1))))
       (NOR (AND (NAND (NAND ARG2 ARG2) (OR ARG1 ARG0))
           (NOR (OR ARG2 ARG1) (NAND ARG0 ARG1))) (OR
           (NOR (AND ARG0 ARG0) (OR ARG0 ARG1)) (AND (NOR
           ARG0 ARG1) (NAND ARG1 (NAND ARG1 ARG0)))))
       (NAND (NAND (NOR (OR ARG1 ARG2) (OR ARG3 ARG1))
           (NAND (NOR ARG1 ARG0) (OR ARG2 ARG0))) (NOR
           (NOR (NAND ARG1 ARG2) (AND ARG1 ARG3)) (AND
           (NAND (NOR (NAND ARG1 ARG2) (NOR ARG3 ARG3))
           (OR (OR ARG3 ARG0) (OR ARG2 ARG2))) (OR (NOR
           (NAND ARG2 ARG1) (NOR ARG3 ARG2)) (NOR (NOR
           ARG3 ARG3) (NOR ARG1 ARG2))))))
       (AND (OR (ADF0 (ADF2 D0 D2 D1 D0) (AND D1 D2))
           (OR (OR D0 D1) (NAND D1 D0))) (ADF2 (AND (NAND
           D2 D4) (ADF2 D2 D3 D2 D2)) (ADF0 (AND D1 D4)
           (ADF1 D3 D0 D0)) (NAND (NAND D0 D3) (ADF1 D0
           D3 D1)) (NAND (ADF0 (AND D1 D4) (ADF1 D3 D0
           D0)) (ADF2 D2 D4 D1 D2))))).
```

The two-argument defined function ADF0 created by the first branch is the two-argument Boolean rule 15, which is equivalent to the Boolean constant T. Not only does genetic programming create this constant-valued function, it actually uses it in the value-returning (i.e., fourth) branch. The three-argument defined function ADF1 created by the second branch is the three-argument Boolean rule 238, which is equivalent to the degenerate disjunction (OR ARG0 ARG1). Since ADF0 and ADF1 are so simple, the four-argument defined function ADF2 is the workhorse of this S-expression. Defined function

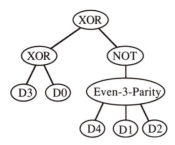

Figure 20.11 Value-returning branch of the best-of-run individual from generation 11 for the even-5-parity problem using automatic function definition.

ADF2 performs the four-argument Boolean rule 15,555. This degenerate defined function contains only the three dummy variables ARG1, ARG2, and ARG3, and is equivalent to

```
(OR (AND (NOT ARG3) (EQV ARG1 ARG2))
    (AND ARG3 (XOR ARG1 ARG2))).
```

This defined function ignores its first argument, ARG0. Defined function ADF2 is, in fact, the even-3-parity function of ARG1, ARG2, and ARG3.

Thus, the value-returning (i.e., fourth) branch can be simplified to

```
(XOR (XOR D3 D0) (NOT (ADF2 D2 D4 D1 D2))).
```

Since (ADF2 D2 D4 D1 D2) is equivalent to (EVEN-3-PARITY D4 D1 D2), this value-returning branch becomes

```
(XOR (XOR D3 D0) (NOT (EVEN-3-PARITY D4 D1 D2))).
```

That is, in solving the even-5-parity problem, genetic programming created a function definition for a parity function of lower order (i.e., the even-3-parity function) and created the necessary combination of operations in its value-returning branch involving two occurrences of the odd-2-parity function (i.e., XOR).

Figure 20.11 graphically depicts the value-returning branch of this best-of-run individual from generation 11 wherein defined function ADF2 is equivalent to the even-3-parity function.

In a second run of the even-5-parity function, the following 100%-correct S-expression containing 74 points emerged on generation 9:

```
(LIST4 (NAND (OR (OR (NAND ARG0 ARG1) (NOR ARG0 ARG1))
             (AND (NOR ARG0 ARG1) (AND ARG0 ARG1))) (NAND
             (AND (NAND ARG1 ARG0) (NOR ARG1 ARG1)) (NOR
             (OR ARG0 ARG0) (OR ARG1 ARG0))))
       (AND (NAND ARG2 ARG0) (OR ARG0 ARG2))
       (OR (NAND (NAND ARG0 ARG2) (OR ARG2 ARG1)) (AND
           (AND ARG1 ARG0) (NAND ARG2 ARG0)))
       (ADF0 (NAND (ADF1 D1 D4 D4) (ADF1 D1 D4 D4)) (ADF1
             (ADF0 D2 D0) (NOR D2 D0) (AND D3 D3)))).
```

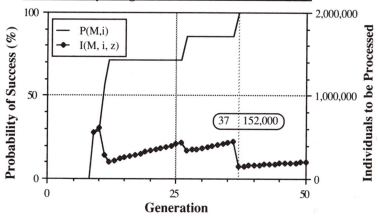

Even-5-Parity using Defined Functions — M=4,000

Figure 20.12 Performance curves for the even-5-parity problem show that 152,000 individuals must be processed to yield a solution with automatic function definition.

The two-argument defined function ADF0 created by the first branch is the two-argument equivalence function EQV. The three-argument defined function ADF1 created by the second branch is the three-argument Boolean rule 90 that uses only two dummy variables and is equivalent to (XOR ARG2 ARG0). The four-argument defined function ADF2 created by the third branch is the four-argument Boolean rule 43,947, but it is not used in the value-returning (i.e., fourth) branch. The value-returning (i.e., fourth) branch calls only ADF1 and ADF0 to produce the desired overall even-5-parity function.

Figure 20.12 shows the performance curves for the even-5-parity function. The graph is based on 7 runs. The population size M was 4,000 and the maximum number of generations to be run G was 51. The cumulative probability of success $P(M, i)$ is 100% by generation 37. The numbers in the oval indicate that if this problem is run through to generation 37, processing a total of 152,000 (i.e., 4,000 × 38 × 1 run) individuals is sufficient to yield a solution to this problem with 99% probability. As can be seen, the 152,000 individuals that must be processed for the even-5-parity problem using automatic function definition is less than an eighth of the 1,276,000 individuals shown in figure 20.2 for the even-parity function of *only four* arguments.

20.6 ODD-5-PARITY

One particular run of the odd-5-parity problem (five-argument Boolean rule 2,523,490,710) is worth noting. Genetic programming discovered the following 100%-correct S-expression containing 153 points with a perfect value of raw fitness on generation 10:

```
(LIST4 (NOR (AND (OR (NOR ARG0 ARG1) (OR ARG1 (OR (NOR
         ARG1 ARG1) (NAND ARG1 ARG0)))) (NAND (OR ARG1
```

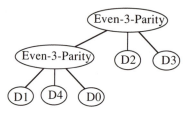

Figure 20.13 The value-returning branch of the best-of-run individual for the odd-5-parity problem using automatic function definition incorporates two even-3-parity functions as building blocks.

```
ARG1) (NOR ARG0 ARG0))) (NOR (OR (AND ARG0
ARG0) (AND ARG1 ARG1)) (OR (AND ARG0 ARG1)
  (NOR ARG1 ARG1))))
(NOR (NOR (OR (NOR (AND (NAND ARG2 ARG1) (NAND
  ARG1 ARG1)) (NAND (NOR (NAND ARG1 ARG1) (NOR
  ARG0 ARG2)) (NOR ARG2 ARG2))) (AND (AND ARG1
  ARG2) (NAND ARG1 ARG0))) (NOR (NOR (AND (NAND
  ARG1 ARG2) (AND ARG2 ARG0)) (NOR (AND ARG2
  ARG1) (OR ARG1 ARG2))) (NOR (NOR (AND ARG2
  ARG2) (OR ARG2 ARG0)) (NAND (NAND ARG0 ARG2)
  (NOR ARG1 ARG2))))) (NOR (NOR (AND ARG2 ARG2)
  (OR ARG2 ARG0)) (NAND (NAND ARG0 ARG2) (NOR
  ARG1 ARG2))))
(NAND (AND (OR (OR ARG3 ARG2) (AND (NAND ARG1
  ARG3) ARG0)) (NOR (AND ARG0 ARG2) (OR ARG2
  ARG2))) (NOR (AND (AND ARG1 ARG1) (NAND ARG2
  ARG3)) (AND (OR ARG2 ARG0) (NAND ARG2 ARG0))))
(ADF1 (ADF1 D1 D4 D0) D2 D3)).
```

The only function calls in the value-returning (i.e., fourth) branch of this S-expression are to the three-argument function ADF1 established by the second branch. Interestingly, ADF1 turns out to be the even-3-parity function (three-argument Boolean rule 105). That is, in solving the odd-5-parity problem, genetic programming created a function definition for a parity function of lower order.

Figure 20.13 graphically depicts the value-returning branch of this best-of-run individual from generation 10 using two even-3-parity functions as building blocks.

Figure 20.14 shows the performance curves for the odd-5-parity function. The graph is based on 10 runs. The population size M was 4,000 and the maximum number of generations to be run G was 51. The cumulative probability of success $P(M, i)$ was 80% by generation 22. The numbers in the oval indicate that if this problem is run through to generation 22, processing a total of 276,000 (i.e., $4,000 \times 23 \times 3$ runs) individuals is sufficient to yield a solution of this problem with 99% probability.

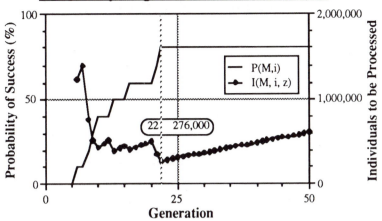

Odd-5-Parity using Defined Functions — M=4,000

Figure 20.14 Performance curves for the odd-5-parity problem show that 276,000 individuals must be processed to yield a solution with automatic function definition.

20.7 EVEN-6-PARITY

The Boolean even-6-parity function is one of $2^{2^6} = 2^{64} \approx 10^{19}$ possible Boolean functions of six arguments and is difficult to learn.

For the even-6-parity problem, each S-expression has five branches. The first four branches permit the creation of function definitions with two, three, four, and five dummy variables. The value-returning (i.e., fifth) branch is an S-expression incorporating the four diadic Boolean functions from the function set F_b; the four defined functions ADF0, ADF1, ADF2, and ADF3; and the six terminals D0, D1, D2, D3, D4, and D5.

For example, in one run of the even-6-parity problem (six-argument Boolean rule 10,838,310,072,981,296,745), genetic programming discovered the following S-expression containing 190 points with a perfect value of raw fitness (i.e., 64 out of 64) on generation 19:

```
(LIST5 (AND (NAND (NOR (NOR ARG1 ARG0) (NAND ARG0 ARG1))
            (OR (NOR ARG1 ARG0) (OR ARG1 ARG0))) (OR (NOR
            (NOR ARG1 ARG0) (AND ARG1 ARG1)) ARG1))
       (OR (NAND (NAND (AND ARG1 ARG2) (NOR ARG2 ARG0))
            (OR (NAND ARG2 ARG2) (NOR ARG0 ARG1))) (AND
            (AND (NAND ARG1 ARG0) (NOR ARG0 ARG1)) (NAND
            (NAND (NOR ARG2 ARG0) ARG1) ARG2)))
       (OR (OR (OR (AND ARG3 ARG0) (OR (OR ARG0 ARG2)
            (NOR ARG1 ARG0))) (OR (OR ARG0 ARG2) (NOR ARG1
            ARG0))) (NOR (OR (AND ARG2 ARG1) (NOR ARG2
            ARG1)) (OR (AND ARG2 ARG1) (NOR ARG2 ARG1))))
       (AND (NOR (NOR (OR ARG1 ARG3) (OR ARG2 ARG0))
            (NOR (NAND ARG3 ARG0) (OR ARG1 ARG2))) (NAND
            (OR ARG2 ARG1) (AND (AND ARG2 ARG0) (AND ARG2
            ARG0)))))
```

```
(ADF0 (ADF1 (ADF0 (NOR D5 D5) (AND D2 D0)) (ADF3
    (NAND D0 D5) (NOR (ADF0 D4 D1) (ADF2 D0 D3 D1
    D0)) (NAND D0 D0) (ADF3 D5 D3 D0 D1 D4) (AND
    D2 D2)) (OR (NAND D5 D1) (NAND D1 D4))) (ADF0
    (ADF1 (ADF1 D1 D4 D1) (ADF1 D1 D4 D1) (ADF3 D3
    D0 D0 D2 D5)) (NAND (ADF3 D1 D4 D5 (NAND D0
    D5) D0) (ADF2 D4 D0 D1 D2))))).
```

In this S-expression for the even-6-parity function, the first branch creates the two-argument defined function ADF0, which is equivalent here to the two-argument exclusive-or (XOR) function.

The second branch creates the three-argument defined function ADF1, which is equivalent to Boolean rule 225, namely

```
(OR (NAND ARG2 ARG1 ARG0)
    (AND ARG2 (NOR ARG1 ARG0))).
```

The third branch creates the four-argument defined function ADF2, which is equivalent to the constant Boolean value T (True).

The fourth branch creates the five-argument defined function ADF3, which is equivalent to Boolean rule 1,566,465,374.

The value-returning (i.e., fifth) branch solves the problem.

In another run, on generation 25, genetic programming discovered the following 100%-correct S-expression containing 489 points:

```
(LIST5 (NAND (AND (NOR (AND ARG1 ARG0) (AND ARG1 ARG0))
            (AND (AND ARG0 ARG0) (OR ARG0 ARG0))) (AND
            (NOR (AND ARG1 ARG0) (NOR ARG0 ARG1)) (OR (NOR
            ARG1 ARG0) (AND ARG1 ARG0))))
        (AND (AND (OR (OR ARG1 ARG0) (NAND ARG2 ARG2))
            (OR (NAND ARG1 ARG0) (NAND ARG2 ARG1))) (AND
            (NAND (OR ARG0 ARG1) (NOR ARG0 ARG1)) (NAND
            (OR ARG1 ARG1) (NAND ARG2 ARG2))))
        (NAND (AND (AND (OR ARG3 ARG0) (NAND ARG2 ARG0))
            (NOR ARG1 (AND ARG2 ARG1))) (NAND (NAND (OR
            ARG0 ARG3) (NAND ARG2 ARG0)) ARG2))
        (NAND (NOR (NAND (OR ARG0 ARG0) (OR ARG4 ARG2))
            (NOR ARG4 ARG0)) (NOR ARG4 ARG0))
        (NOR (ADF1 (ADF1 (ADF1 (NOR (ADF2 (ADF2 (ADF2
            (ADF2 D2 D5 D2 D0) (NOR D5 D3) (ADF3 D3 D5 D2
            D0 D3) (ADF2 (NAND D3 D4) (AND D2 D2) (OR D4
            D1) (OR D5 D5))) (AND (ADF1 D5 D3 D4) (NOR D1
            D2)) (OR (NAND D1 D1) (NOR (ADF2 (OR D5 D1)
            (ADF3 D1 D4 D4 D4 D0) (ADF3 D3 D0 D3 D2 D4)
            (ADF0 D3 D3)) (NOR D3 D1))) (ADF3 (AND D3 D5)
            (ADF1 D2 D1 D2) (NOR D2 D0) (NOR D2 D2) (AND
            D3 D4))) (ADF2 (ADF2 (NAND D3 D4) (AND D2 D2)
            (ADF0 D0 D5) (ADF3 D4 D1 D5 D0 D1)) (OR (ADF1
            D5 D1 D3) (NOR D0 D5)) (ADF0 (ADF1 D3 D1 D1)
```

```
(AND D0 D0)) (ADF1 (ADF1 D1 D3 D1) (NAND D3
D2) (OR D0 D3))) (ADF0 (ADF1 D5 D2 D0) (OR D5
D1)) (ADF0 (OR (NOR D5 D3) (ADF2 D3 D4 D4 D5))
(OR (NOR D3 D1) (NOR D0 D5)))) D4) (AND D1 D3)
(NAND D3 D2)) (ADF1 (NOR D5 D3) D4 D0) (ADF2
D1 D3 D2 D2)) (ADF1 (OR D0 D3) (NAND D3 D5)
(NOR D5 D3)) (ADF2 (ADF2 (ADF2 (ADF2 D2 D5 D2
D0) (NOR D5 D3) (ADF3 D3 D5 D2 D0 D3) (ADF2
(NAND D3 D4) (AND D2 D2) (OR D4 D1) (OR D5
D5))) (AND (ADF1 D5 D3 D4) (NOR D1 D2)) (OR
(NAND D1 D1) (ADF3 D3 D0 D3 D2 D4)) (ADF3
(ADF2 (ADF2 D2 D5 D2 D0) (NOR D5 D3) (ADF3 D3
D5 D2 D0 D3) (ADF2 (NAND D3 D4) (AND D2 D2)
(OR D4 D1) (OR D5 D5))) (ADF1 D2 D1 D2) (NOR
D2 D0) (NOR D2 D2) (AND D3 D4))) (ADF2 (ADF2
(NAND D3 D4) (AND D2 D2) (ADF0 D0 D5) (ADF3 D4
D1 D5 D0 D1)) (OR (ADF1 D5 D1 D3) (NOR D0 D5))
(ADF0 (ADF1 D3 D1 D1) (AND D0 D0)) (ADF1 (ADF1
D1 D3 D1) (NAND D3 D2) (OR D0 D3))) (ADF0
(ADF3 D2 D2 D2 D1 D1) (NOR (ADF2 (OR D4 D1)
(ADF3 D1 D4 D4 D4 D0) (ADF3 D3 D0 D3 D1 D4)
(ADF0 D3 D3)) (NOR D3 D1))) (ADF0 (OR (NAND D1
D5) (ADF2 D3 D4 D4 D5)) (OR (NOR D3 D1) (NOR
D0 D5))))) (NOR (ADF2 (OR D5 D1) (ADF3 D1 D4
D4 D4 D0) (ADF3 D3 D0 D3 D2 D4) (ADF0 D3 D3))
(NOR D3 D1)))).
```

In this S-expression for the even-6-parity function, both the first branch and the fourth branch are equivalent to the constant Boolean value T. The second branch creates the three-argument defined function ADF2, which is equivalent to Boolean rule 99, namely

```
(OR (AND (NOT ARG2) (NOT ARG1)) (AND ARG2 (XOR ARG1 ARG0))).
```

Note that this is a partial parity function.

The third branch creates the four-argument defined function ADF3, which is equivalent to Boolean rule 60,669.

The fourth branch creates the five-argument defined function ADF4, which is never called.

Finally, the value-returning (i.e., fifth) branch calls upon defined functions ADF0, ADF1, ADF2, and ADF3 to produce the behavior of the Boolean even-6-parity function.

20.8 RECAPITULATION

In this chapter, we introduced the idea of creating a constrained syntactic structure for automatically generating a set of function definitions along with one final value-returning S-expression which could call upon any combination of the defined functions to solve the problem. If the problem involves n terminals, the final value-returning branch of the S-expression has access to $n - 2$ defined functions (one each with $2, 3, \ldots, n - 1$ dummy variables).

We did not specify in advance the size, shape, or content of the function-defining branches, nor did we specify how the final value-returning branch should organize itself and call upon the defined functions. Instead, natural selection and genetics, driven by the fitness measure, caused the evolution of necessary size, shape, and content of the solution to the problem.

Automatic function definition enhanced the performance of genetic programming in performing symbolic regression of the Boolean even-4-parity function. Moreover, automatic function definition enabled genetic programming to readily perform symbolic regression on both the even-5-parity and even-6-parity functions, whereas no solution to the easier of these two problems, the even-5-parity function, was found after 20 runs with a population of 4,000 without automatic function definition. See also Koza 1992e and Koza and Rice 1992b.

21 Evolution of Hierarchies of Building Blocks

The previous chapter demonstrated the utility of automatic function definition in permitting the genetic breeding of a set of function definitions along with one final value-returning S-expression which could call upon the defined functions to help solve the problem. If the problem involved n terminals, the final value-returning branch of the S-expression has access to $n - 2$ of the already-defined functions (one each with 2, 3, ..., $n - 1$ dummy variables, i.e., formal parameters).

21.1 THE IDEA OF HIERARCHICAL AUTOMATIC FUNCTION DEFINITION

The definition of a particular defined function in the previous chapter never included a call upon another defined function. However, it is common in ordinary programming to define one function in terms of other already-defined functions.

In the *hierarchical* form of automatic function definition, any function definition can call upon any other already-defined function. That is, there is a hierarchy (lattice) of function definitions wherein any function can be defined in terms of any combination of already-defined functions. This *hierarchical* form of automatic function definition is the same as the simpler form of automatic function definition in the previous chapter in that the final value-returning branch of the overall S-expression has access to all of the already-defined functions.

In the previous chapter, each function-defining branch involved a different number of dummy variables (formal parameters); however, this did not matter because none of the defined functions called upon the other. However, in hierarchical automatic function definition, if the function-defining branches were to contain a different number of dummy variables, the question would arise as to their order. For example, if there are two function-defining branches, the question would arise as to whether there should be two dummy variables in the first branch and three dummy variables in the second branch (which can call upon the first branch), or vice versa. This potential problem of ordering can be quickly dispatched by giving all the function-defining branches the same number of dummy arguments. There is, of course, no requirement that every available dummy variable be used within a function definition, and, as we have already seen, a function definition often ignores one or more of the available dummy variables.

The number of dummy variables to appear in each function-defining branch is now merely a matter of computer resources. The number could be n, where n is the number of terminals in the terminal set. That is, each defined function could have arity n (i.e., have n arguments). The choice of n as the common value for the arity will result in rather large and bushy trees. For many problems there is no compelling need for a function definition of arity n since all of the available terminals are already available in the value-returning branch. Choosing even a slightly smaller value for the arity will save a considerable amount of computer resources. Therefore, in this chapter, if the problem involves n terminals, then all function-defining branches will uniformly have $n - 1$ dummy variables. The evolutionary process will decide how many of the available dummy variables in a particular function definition will actually be used.

The number of such identical branches is also merely a matter of computer resources. In this chapter, we have decided to use two function-defining branches and one value-returning branch (i.e., every S-expression in this chapter will have three branches).

21.2 EVEN-4-PARITY FUNCTION

Each S-expression in the population for solving the even-4-parity function has one value-returning branch and two function-defining branches, each permitting the definition of one function of three dummy variables.

In one run of the even-4-parity function (Boolean rule 38,505), the following 100%-correct solution containing 45 points with a perfect value of raw fitness (i.e., 16 out of 16) appeared on generation 4:

```
(LIST3 (NOR (NOR ARG2 ARG0) (AND ARG0 ARG2))
       (NAND (ADF0 ARG2 ARG2 ARG0)
             (NAND (ADF0 ARG2 ARG1 ARG2)
                   (ADF0 (OR ARG2 ARG1)
                         (NOR ARG0 ARG1)
                         (ADF0 ARG1 ARG0 ARG2))))
       (ADF0 (ADF1 D1 D3 D0)
             (NOR (OR D2 D3) (AND D3 D3))
             (ADF0 D3 D3 D2))).
```

As can be seen, the first branch of this best-of-run S-expression is a function definition establishing the defined function ADF0 as the two-argument exclusive-or XOR function of dummy variables ARG0 and ARG2. The definition of ADF0 ignores one of the available dummy variables, namely ARG1.

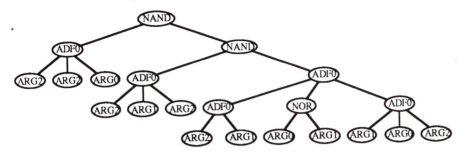

Figure 21.1 The second branch of the best-of-run individual from generation 4 is a function definition for ADF1 in terms of ADF0 (which happens to be XOR).

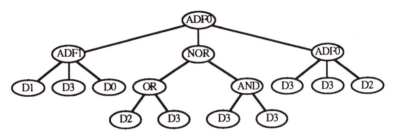

Figure 21.2 The value-returning (i.e., third) branch of the best-of-run individual uses both defined functions ADF0 and ADF1 to solve the even-4-parity problem.

Figure 21.1 graphically depicts the second branch of the above S-expression, which, as can be seen, calls upon the defined function ADF0 (i.e., XOR) to define ADF1.

This second branch appears to use all three available dummy variables; however, it reduces to

```
(NOT (ADF0 ARG2 ARG0)),
```

so ADF1 is simply the two-argument equivalence function EQV.

Figure 21.2 shows that the value-returning (i.e., third) branch of this S-expression uses all four terminals and both ADF0 and ADF1 to solve the even-4-parity problem.

The value-returning (i.e., third) branch reduces to

```
(ADF0 (ADF1 D1 D0) (ADF0 D3 D2)),
```

which is equivalent to

```
(XOR (EQV D1 D0) (XOR D3 D2)).
```

Figure 21.3 graphically shows how genetic programming decomposed the even-4-parity problem into two different parity problems of lower order (i.e., XOR and EQV).

Note also that the second of the two functions in this decomposition (i.e., EQV) was defined in terms of the first. Figure 21.4 shows the hierarchy (lattice) of function definitions used in this solution to the even-4-parity problem.

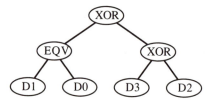

Figure 21.3 The even-4-parity function has been decomposed into two different parity problems of lower order (i.e., XOR and EQV).

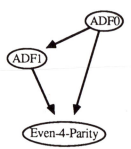

Figure 21.4 Hierarchy (lattice) of function definitions.

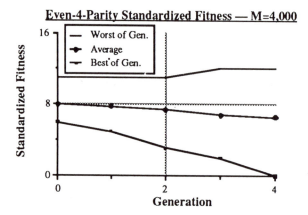

Figure 21.5 Fitness curves for the even-4-parity problem.

Figure 21.5 shows, by generation, the progressive improvement in the average standardized fitness of the population as a whole and the value of standardized fitness for the best-of-generation individual and the worst-of-generation individual. The best-of-generation individual improved monotonically in fitness for this particular run.

Figure 21.6 shows, by generation, the average of the structural complexity of the population as a whole and the structural complexity of the best-of-generation individual.

The exclusive-or and equivalence functions appeared as defined functions ADF0 or ADF1 and sometimes both in many of the runs of the even-4-parity

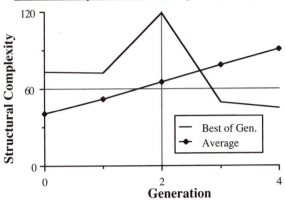

Even-4-Parity Structural Complexity — M=4,000

Figure 21.6 Structural complexity curves for the even-4-parity problem.

problem; however, in many other runs, this was not the case. For example, in a particular other run of the even-4-parity function, the following 100%-correct solution containing 137 points with a perfect value of raw fitness (i.e., 16 out of 16) appeared on generation 6:

```
(LIST3 (NOR (NAND (AND (AND ARG0 ARG2) (AND ARG2 ARG0))
          (AND (OR ARG2 ARG2) (AND ARG2 ARG0))) (OR (NOR
          (NOR ARG1 ARG2) (AND ARG2 ARG1)) (NAND (AND
          ARG2 ARG0) (OR ARG1 ARG2))))
       (OR (ADF0 (ADF0 (OR ARG2 ARG1) (AND ARG1 ARG2)
          (OR ARG0 ARG1)) (ADF0 (ADF0 ARG1 ARG0 ARG0)
          (AND ARG1 ARG2) (AND ARG2 ARG0)) (AND (NAND
          ARG1 ARG1) (NAND ARG0 ARG2))) (NAND (NOR (NOR
          ARG1 ARG2) (AND ARG1 ARG2)) (NAND (AND ARG2
          ARG0) (OR ARG1 ARG1))))
       (ADF1 (AND (AND (NAND D0 D3) (ADF1 D1 D1 D3)) (OR
          (ADF0 D2 D1 D3) (OR D3 D1))) (ADF1 (NAND (OR
          D2 D2) (NAND D2 D1)) (ADF1 (AND D2 D3) (OR D3
          D1) (ADF1 D0 D2 (ADF1 (AND D2 D3) (OR D3 D1)
          (ADF1 D0 D2 D3)))) (ADF1 (NOR D1 D3) (NOR D1
          D2) (AND D0 D0))) (NAND D1 D2))).
```

The first function-defining branch of the above S-expression is the ordinary conjunction (i.e., three-argument Boolean rule 128)

```
(AND ARG2 ARG1 ARG0).
```

The overall behavior of the second branch is equivalent to the three-argument Boolean rule 195. As it happens, the three-argument defined function ADF0 is used to disable a large subclause within the definition of defined function ADF1, thus reducing ADF1 to merely

```
(EQV ARG2 ARG1).
```

The value-returning (i.e., third) branch calls on defined functions ADF0 and ADF1 and solves the problem.

In yet another run of the even-4-parity function, the following 100%-correct solution containing 139 points with a perfect value of raw fitness emerged on generation 5:

```
(LIST3 (AND (OR (NAND (NAND ARG2 ARG0) (OR ARG0 ARG1))
            (OR (NAND ARG2 ARG2) (NAND ARG2 ARG1))) (NAND
            (AND (NOR ARG0 ARG1) (AND ARG0 ARG0)) (NOR
            (NAND ARG0 ARG1) (NOR ARG0 ARG0))))
        (NAND (NOR (NOR (AND ARG2 ARG0) (OR ARG0 ARG2))
            (AND (AND ARG1 ARG2) (ADF0 ARG0 ARG1 ARG1)))
            (AND (ADF0 (ADF0 ARG0 ARG2 ARG0) (OR ARG2
            ARG1) (ADF0 ARG2 ARG2 ARG1)) (NAND (NAND ARG1
            ARG1) (AND ARG2 ARG2))))
        (ADF1 (AND (ADF0 (ADF1 D0 D3 D0) (ADF1 D1 D1 D2)
            (OR D1 D0)) (AND (NOR D1 D2) (OR D2 D1)))
            (ADF0 (OR (NOR D1 D1) (ADF1 D1 D1 D0)) (NOR D2
            D3) (AND (AND D0 D2) (ADF1 D2 D3 D3))) (ADF1
            (ADF0 (AND D3 D2) (OR D2 D3) (NAND D3 D2)) (OR
            (NOR D2 D1) (ADF1 D3 D0 D3)) (ADF1 (NOR D0 D1)
            (AND D1 D0) (AND D0 D1)))))).
```

The first branch is the three-argument Boolean rule 191:

```
(AND ARG2 ARG1 (NOT ARG0)).
```

The second branch calls upon ADF0 and has behavior equivalent to the three-argument Boolean rule 181.

The value-returning (i.e., third) branch calls on defined functions ADF0 and ADF1 and solves the problem.

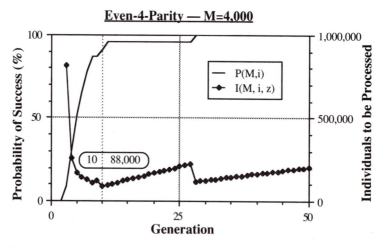

Figure 21.7 Performance curves for the even-4-parity problem show that 88,000 individuals must be processed to yield a solution with hierarchical automatic function definition.

For the even-4-parity function, figure 21.7 presents the performance curves with hierarchical automatic function definition and shows, by generation, the cumulative probability of success $P(M, i)$ and the number of individuals that must be processed $I(M, i, z)$ to yield, with 99% probability, at least one S-expression producing the correct value for all 16 fitness cases. The graph is based on 23 runs. The population size M was 4,000 and the maximum number of generations to be run G was 51. The cumulative probability of success $P(M, i)$ is 91% by generation 10 and 100% by generation 50. The numbers in the oval indicate that if this problem is run through to generation 10, processing a total of 88,000 (i.e., $4,000 \times 11 \times 2$ runs) individuals is sufficient to yield a solution of this problem with 99% probability.

21.3 EVEN-5-PARITY FUNCTION

Now consider the even-5-parity function (five-argument Boolean rule 1,771,476,585). Each S-expression for solving the even-5-parity function has one value-returning branch and two function-defining branches, each permitting the definition of one function of four dummy variables.

In one run of the even-5-parity function, the following 100%-correct solution containing 160 points with a perfect value of raw fitness (i.e., 64 out of 64) emerged on generation 12:

```
(LIST3 (OR (OR (NOR (NOR ARG3 ARG1) (OR ARG1 ARG3)) (AND
           (NAND ARG1 ARG3) (NOR ARG1 ARG2))) (NAND (AND
           (OR ARG1 ARG2) (NAND ARG1 ARG2)) (NAND ARG1
           (AND (NOR ARG3 ARG1) ARG0))))
        (NAND (NAND (AND (NAND ARG1 ARG2) (ADF0 ARG0 ARG3
           ARG0 ARG2)) (NOR (NAND ARG3 ARG1) (AND ARG1
           ARG1))) (AND (ADF0 ARG0 (NAND ARG1 ARG2) (ADF0
           ARG3 ARG0 ARG3 ARG0) (AND ARG1 ARG1)) (ADF0
           (ADF0 ARG3 ARG2 ARG3 ARG0) (ADF0 ARG0 ARG2
           ARG2 ARG1) (ADF0 ARG3 ARG3 ARG3 ARG0) (NOR
           ARG3 ARG0))))
        (OR (OR (NOR (ADF0 D3 D1 D1 D3) (OR D0 D1)) (NOR
           (NAND D1 D2) (OR (OR D3 D2) (NOR D4 D4))))
           (ADF1 (ADF1 D4 D0 D4 D1) (OR (OR (NOR (OR
           (NAND D1 D0) (ADF1 D1 D2 D3 D1)) (AND D4 D0))
           D2) (NOR (OR (NAND D1 D0) (ADF1 D1 D2 D3 D1))
           (AND D4 D0))) (NAND (ADF1 D1 D0 D0 D1) (NAND
           D0 D2)) (NAND (ADF1 D3 D4 D0 D0) (ADF0 D3 D1
           D1 D3)))))).
```

The first branch is equivalent to the four-argument Boolean rule 50,115, which is

```
(EQV ARG2 ARG1).
```

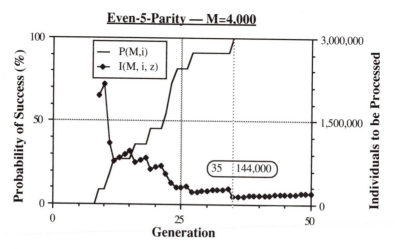

Even-5-Parity — M=4,000

Figure 21.8 Performance curves for the even-5-parity problem using hierarchical automatic function definition show that 144,000 individuals must be processed to yield a solution.

The second branch is equivalent to the four-argument Boolean rule 38,250, which is

```
(OR (AND (NOT ARG2) (XOR ARG3 ARG0))
    (AND ARG2      (XOR ARG3 (XOR ARG1 ARG0))))).
```

The value-returning (i.e., third) branch calls on defined functions ADF0 and ADF1 and solves the problem.

For the even-5-parity function, figure 21.8 presents the performance curves for hierarchical automatic function definition and shows, by generation, the cumulative probability of success $P(M, i)$ and the number of individuals that must be processed $I(M, i, z)$ to yield, with 99% probability, at least one S-expression producing the correct value for all 32 fitness cases. The graph is based on 11 runs. The population size M was 4,000 and the maximum number of generations to be run G was 51. The cumulative probability of success $P(M, i)$ is 100% by generation 35. The numbers in the oval indicate that if this problem is run through to generation 35, processing a total of 144,000 (i.e., 4,000 × 36 generations × 1 run) individuals is sufficient to yield a solution of this problem with 99% probability.

The number of individuals that must be processed to solve this problem with hierarchical automatic function definition (i.e., 144,000) is smaller than the 152,000 shown in figure 20.12, where only the non-hierarchical version of automatic function definition was employed.

As previously seen, for the even-4-parity problem using hierarchical automatic function definition, the number of individuals that must be processed (i.e., 88,000) was slightly larger than the 80,000 individuals shown in figure 20.10, where hierarchical function definition was not available. The reason for this may have been that the greater generality of automatic function definition is not required for parity functions with only four arguments.

In section 25.10, an experiment is presented using hierarchical automatic function definition with a prespecified argument list size.

21.4 EVEN-6-PARITY FUNCTION

Each S-expression used in addressing the even-6-parity function (six-argument Boolean rule 10,838,310,072,981,296,745) has one value-returning branch and two function-defining branches, each permitting the definition of one function of five dummy variables.

In one run of the even-6-parity function, the following best-of-generation individual containing 106 points and attaining a perfect value of raw fitness of 64 (out of 64) appeared in generation 7:

```
(LIST3 (OR (AND (AND ARG1 ARG2) (NAND ARG0 ARG4)) (NAND
           (NAND (AND ARG0 ARG1) ARG2) (OR ARG2 ARG1)))
       (OR (ADF0 ARG4 ARG4 ARG3 ARG4 ARG3) (NOR ARG1 (OR
           ARG3 ARG4)))
       (ADF0 (AND D4 D0) (ADF0 (AND D4 D5) (NAND D0 D2)
           (ADF1 D3 D5 D5 D3 D1) (OR D2 D0) (ADF0 D0 D0
           D5 D4 D0)) (ADF1 (AND D1 D3) (AND D2 D0) (NAND
           D5 D5) (ADF0 D4 (NOR D5 D5) D4 D2 D2) (OR D2
           D0)) (OR (AND D4 D1) (NAND D3 D5)) (ADF0 (NOR
           D1 D3) (NAND D0 D5) (ADF0 D1 D5 D0 D0 D1)
           (ADF1 D3 D0 D3 D2 D1) (AND D5 D1))))).
```

The first branch of this S-expression defined a five-argument defined function ADF0 (five-argument Boolean rule 328,386,755) which ignored three of its five arguments and is equivalent to

```
(EQV ARG1 ARG2).
```

The second branch defined a five-argument defined function ADF1 (five-argument Boolean rule 4,278,190,335) which also ignored three of its five arguments and is equivalent to

```
(XOR ARG3 ARG4).
```

Substituting the definitions of the defined functions ADF0 and ADF1, the value-returning (i.e., third) branch becomes

```
(EQV (EQV (NAND D0 D2) (XOR D3 D1))
     (XOR (EQV (NOT D5) D4) (OR D2 D0))),
```

which is equivalent to the target even-6-parity function.

The fact that each of the defined functions takes five arguments means that the value-defining branch is relatively bushy and that several of the available dummy variables in both of the function-defining branches are typically ignored in solving this problem. As the number of arguments in the target function increases, it will be necessary to conserve computer resources by reducing the number of arguments taken by the two defined functions to four.

21.5 VARIATIONS

There are a number of straightforward variations on the idea of automatic function definition described in chapter 20 and hierarchical automatic function definition described in this chapter.

There can be more than one value-returning branch (as illustrated in chapter 19) with automatic function definition or hierarchical automatic function definition. Thus, more than one value can be returned by the overall S-expression.

There can be one or more value-defining branches (i.e., the cascading variables described in the inverse kinematics problem in section 19.7) in addition to the function-defining branches in the overall S-expression.

Actual variables of the problem domain can appear in the function-defining branches with automatic function definition or hierarchical automatic function definition.

A solution to the 11-parity problem can be seen on the videotape (see p. xi).

21.6 RECAPITULATION

In this chapter, the idea of automatic function definition was extended from the previous chapter to *hierarchical* automatic function definition.

Specifically, if the problem involves n terminals, each S-expression in the population contains a fixed number (i.e., two) of function-defining branches permitting the definition of an arbitrary function involving an identical number of terminals (i.e., $n - 1$). The final value-returning branch of the S-expression has access to the defined functions to help it in solving the problem.

Hierarchical automatic function definition enhanced the performance of genetic programming in performing symbolic regression of the Boolean even-4-parity function and enabled us to perform symbolic regression on both the even-5-parity and even-6-parity functions.

22 Parallelization of Genetic Programming

Amenability to parallelization is an appealing feature of both the conventional genetic algorithm and genetic programming.

In genetic methods, the genetic operations themselves are very simple and not very time consuming whereas the measurement of fitness of the individuals in the population is typically complicated and time-consuming. In considering approaches for parallelizing genetic methods, it is important to note that, for all but the most trivial problems, the vast majority of the computational effort is consumed by the calculation of fitness. Neither the genetic operations nor anything else involve any significant percentage of the computation effort.

The execution of the genetic operations can be parallelized in the manner described by Robertson (1987); however, we focus here on ways of parallelizing genetic programming that distribute the computational effort needed to compute fitness. As we know, for many problems, the calculation of fitness is done over a number of fitness cases.

There are two basic approaches to parallelization.

In the first approach (called the *distributed genetic algorithm*), the population for a given run is divided into subpopulations (Tanese 1989). Each subpopulation is assigned to a processor, and the genetic algorithm operates on each subpopulation separately. Upon completion of a certain designated number of generations, a certain percentage of the individuals in each population are selected for emigration, and there is a partial exchange of members between the subpopulations. It is possible to readily implement the distributed genetic algorithm on a medium-grained parallel computer or even on a network of workstations. The interprocessor communication requirements of this approach are relatively low since there is only occasional emigration and immigration of a relatively small number of individuals.

Figure 22.1 shows the distributed genetic algorithm, with the arrows indicating migration between subpopulations.

In the second approach, there is one population in each run. This second approach implements genetic programming in the form described in this book. That is, there are no subpopulations and no migration. We will explore this second approach in detail below.

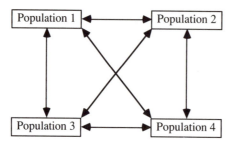

Figure 22.1 The distributed genetic algorithm.

Nearly all the steps in genetic methods can be performed locally and asynchronously on a distributed basis. The two exceptions consume only a tiny fraction of the overall computational effort, and they can be entirely eliminated if so desired. The first exception is checking for duplicates at the time of the creation of the initial random population. This uniqueness check (which is merely optional for genetic programming and which is rarely done with the conventional genetic algorithm) comes at the beginning of a run and involves very little computational effort. It can be eliminated if so desired. The second exception concerns the operation of fitness-proportionate reproduction. This operation requires the computation of the average fitness of the entire population (or at least a substantial subset of it). This calculation also involves very little computational effort. If so desired, tournament selection (sections 25.4 and 6.4.1) can be used instead of fitness-proportionate reproduction. Tournament selection requires knowing the fitnesses of only two randomly selected individuals from the population, rather than the fitnesses of all the individuals in the population. Tournament selection may even prove to have performance advantages for many problems.

In this chapter, we consider the following three levels at which parallelization of the calculation of fitness is possible:

• the level of the fitness cases,
• the level of individual S-expressions, and
• the level of independent runs.

Parallelization at the level of the fitness cases might be appropriate if the calculation of fitness were reasonably long (to counterbalance the administrative overhead of parallelization) or if there was a good match between the number of fitness cases and the number of processors available. If parallelization is done at this level, no consideration need be given to the inevitable variation within the population in the structural complexity of the S-expressions, since all processors would be working on the same individual S-expression at a given time. However, consideration must be given to the question of whether each fitness case takes the same amount of time to evaluate, since this is not the case for many simulations.

Figure 22.2 shows parallelization at the level of fitness cases.

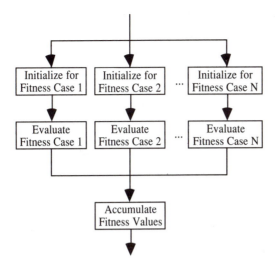

Figure 22.2 Parallelization at the level of fitness cases.

If parallelization is done at the level of individuals in the population, the administrative overhead of parallelization is less than at the level of the fitness case. More important, if parallelization is done at the level of individuals in the population for a problem involving a simulation, there is often a considerable difference in the execution times of individuals in the population. For example, most commonly, unfit individuals either take longer or they take the maximum allowed amount of time before timing out. On the other hand, for certain problems, unfit individuals can be identified and quickly terminated (e.g., where the state of the simulation stagnates). For such problems, unfit individuals may actually take less time to simulate and evaluate than fit individuals.

Figure 22.3 shows parallelization at the level of individuals in the population.

The numerous performance curves in this book showing the probability of success, $P(M, i)$, by generation will indicate that after a certain number of generations, there is very little increase in the probability of success by running a problem for one additional generation compared to the computational effort required to run that additional generation. The total amount of processing required to yield a solution with 99% probability can usually be minimized by making many independent runs of a problem for relatively few generations each, as opposed to making one long run. The point is not that genetic programming cannot solve the problem if it is allowed to run for additional generations, but rather that the most efficient way to use available computer resources is to make multiple independent runs. Therefore, parallelization at the run level is the most effective kind of parallelization for the vast majority of problems described in this book.

Parallelization at the run level is comparatively easy to implement. Each processor is assigned one or more full runs for the maximum number of generations G to be run. The overall result is the best result of all the runs from all the processors. If the choice of the maximum number of generations to

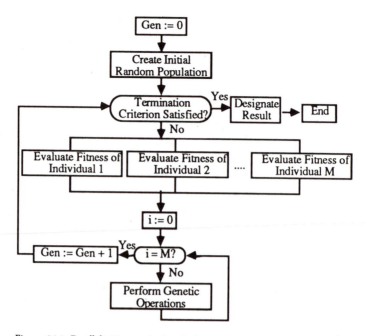

Figure 22.3 Parallelization at the level of individuals in the population.

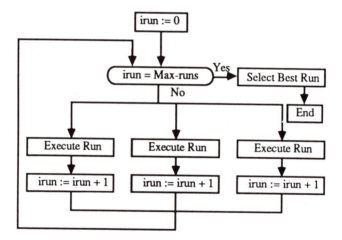

Figure 22.4 Parallelization at the level of independent runs.

be run on each independent run is done reasonably well, only one or two processors will solve the problem within the allowed number of generations G. The overall result is then simply the result produced by the one successful processor or the better of the two results from the two successful processors. If the process of determining the overall result were automated, it would involve an extremely small amount of bandwidth for communication between the processors (i.e., one message from each processor containing the result of each independent run). In fact, determination of the overall result is so simple that it may be done manually on the back of an envelope. Before expending massive efforts on parallelization of genetic methods at levels lower than the run level, the user is well advised to recall the advisability of making multiple independent runs (rather than one long run) and to consider the possibility that the best use of the capabilities of a coarse- or medium-grained parallel computer is to simply make multiple independent runs on the various processors.

Figure 22.4 is a flowchart for parallelization at the level of independent runs.

23 Ruggedness of Genetic Programming

In nature, evolution proceeds in the presence of noise and incomplete information in a changing environment in which the population may occasionally be subjected to catastrophic damage. Similarly, noise, incomplete information, unannounced changes in the rules of the game, and malfunctioning machinery are features of many real-world problems.

From the early days of computing, von Neumann recognized the importance of synthesizing reliable organisms from unreliable components (von Neumann 1987). Since complex computations require large numbers of computing devices wherein each device is unreliable to some degree, complex calculations inherently raise the issue of probabilistic logic. Genetic methods offer a way to overcome the unreliability inherent in complex computations.

This chapter presents five examples of adaptation occurring in the presence of these interfering factors.

The first section presents an experiment where evolution proceeds using inaccurate measurements of fitness (i.e., there is noise in the environment).

The second section presents an experiment where evolution proceeds using only incomplete information about the environment (i.e., there is sampling).

In the third section, we consider the fault tolerance of genetic programming when there is catastrophic damage to the population. In an applied problem, this might correspond to the breakdown of one of several parallel processors in use at a particular moment in time or the loss of all information residing on one of several storage devices.

In the fourth and fifth sections of this chapter, the environment is subject to unannounced changes. When the environment changes, a genetically diverse population in nature is often able to adapt to the changes provided that the changes are not too rapid and not too severe. Similarly, both the conventional genetic algorithm and genetic programming are generally able to adapt to changes in the environment provided genetic diversity is maintained in the population. In practice, a change in environment means that the fitness measure assigns new and different values to the individuals in the population.

In the fourth section, we consider the problem of learning Boolean functions with three arguments where we repeatedly change, during the run, the target function to be learned.

In the fifth section (which we call the "biathlon"), the change in environment is even more extreme in that we change the problem, during the run, from the problem of symbolic regression involving floating-point numbers to the problem of navigating the artificial ant along an irregular trail.

As will be seen, evolution successfully solves problems in all five of these unfriendly situations.

23.1 INACCURATE FITNESS INFORMATION

We consider the 6-multiplexer problem with the function set of F = {AND, OR, IF, NOT} and a population size of 1,000 (with over-selection). The performance curves for this problem with this population size, this function set, and using over-selection are presented in figure 25.14, which shows that processing a total of 33,000 individuals is sufficient to yield a solution to this problem with 99% probability.

In this section, we consider solving the 6-multiplexer problem when the fitness is reported inaccurately. Standardized fitness for the 6-multiplexer problem is the number of fitness cases (out of 64) for which the S-expression gives the incorrect Boolean value.

The fitness of an individual S-expression is inaccurately reported in the following way: The Boolean value returned by an S-expression is complemented for one randomly selected fitness case (of the 64) with a probability of 2/3, and otherwise complemented for two randomly selected fitness cases. That is, the fitness measure of every individual in the population is misreported by either 1 or 2.

In spite of this inaccuracy in the fitness measure, genetic programming is still able to evolve an S-expression that is 100% correct in solving the 6-multiplexer problem.

Figure 23.1 presents the performance curves for this first approach showing, by generation, $P(M, i)$ (the cumulative probability of success) and $I(M, i, z)$ (the

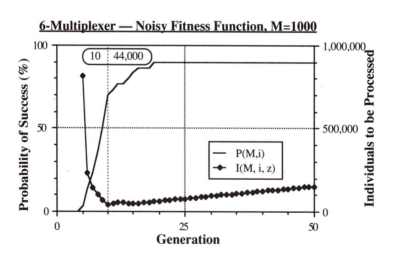

Figure 23.1 Performance curves for the 6-multiplexer problem with a noisy fitness measure.

number of individuals that must be processed to yield, with 99% probability, at least one individual S-expression achieving 64 hits in solving this problem). The graph is based on 30 runs and a population size of 1,000. The cumulative probability of success, $P(M, i)$, is 90% for generations 19 through 50. The numbers in the oval indicate that if this problem is run through to generation 10, processing a total of 44,000 (i.e., $1,000 \times 11$ generations $\times 4$ runs) individuals is sufficient to yield a solution of this problem with 99% probability.

As can be seen, the total number of individuals that must be processed for this particular problem is 44,000 with noise whereas it is 33,000 without noise.

23.2 INCOMPLETE FITNESS INFORMATION

A considerable amount of computer time can be saved by judicious sampling of the set of fitness cases. In problems where there are an infinite number of possible fitness cases (e.g., where the terminals take on floating-point values), sampling of fitness cases is necessarily used (though the sample may be changed from generation to generation). Similarly, on problems where there are a very large number of possible fitness cases (e.g., the initial configurations of the blocks in the block stacking problem described in section 18.1), sampling is necessarily used. However, for some problems (e.g., Boolean problems), there are only a relatively small finite number of fitness cases. The question arises as whether to use 100% of the fitness cases or to sample the fitness cases for such problems.

The purpose of this experiment is to measure the effect of sampling of the fitness cases on the Boolean 6-multiplexer problem.

In this experiment, two environments were used:

- a fixed environment consisting of all $2^6 = 64$ fitness cases
- a sampled environment consisting of 16 randomly chosen fitness cases at generation 0 and an increasing number of new randomly chosen fitness cases on later generations of the run based on the observed performance of the run.

The number of fitness cases was ratcheted up from 16 to 64 in steps of 6 as the number of hits for the best-of-generation individual reached two fewer than the current number of fitness cases. For example, as soon as the number of hits for the best-of-generation individual reached 14 (i.e., two fewer than the prevailing 16 fitness cases), the number of fitness cases was ratcheted up by 6 from 16 to 22. When the number of hits for the best-of-generation individual reached 20 (i.e., two fewer than the prevailing 22 fitness cases), the number of fitness cases was ratcheted up by 6 from 22 to 28. This process continued until the number of hits reached 56, whereupon the number of fitness cases was finally ratcheted up from 58 to 64. The population size was 500.

Figure 23.2 shows the probability of success $P(M, i)$ as a function of number of generations (from 0 to 50) for the two environments. As can be seen, the curves for the fixed and sampled environments were virtually identical for some generations and very close for all other generations.

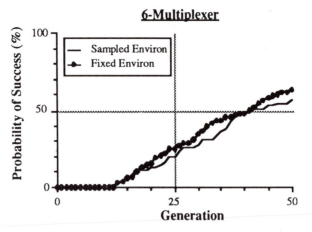

Figure 23.2 Probability of success $P(M, i)$ for fixed environment and sampled environment.

Figure 23.3 shows the mean effort per run (i.e., average number of fitness cases evaluated per run) plotted against generations. That is, the y axis is the average number of fitness cases evaluated per run when that run reaches the specified generation. At 50 generations, a total of 1,632,000 fitness cases were evaluated, on average, for the fixed environment, while only 746,163 fitness cases were evaluated for the sampled environment. The probability of success, $P(M, i)$, was 63% at generation 50 for the fixed environment and 56% for the sampled environment (i.e., virtually the same) even though there were 2.19 times more fitness cases evaluated for the fixed environment than for the sampled environment. If this 2.19 were adjusted to reflect the relatively small percentage difference between 63% and 56%, the net effect would be 1.94 times higher efficiency for the runs using the sampled environment.

The conclusion of this particular experiment, as one would expect, is that sampling can substantially reduce the total computational effort required to solve a problem.

23.3 FAULT TOLERANCE AFTER CATASTROPHIC DAMAGE

In nature, species usually survive the death of massive numbers of randomly chosen individuals. When randomly chosen individuals in the population suddenly die, the genetic profile of the population as a whole (i.e., the distribution of features and combinations of features) is retained (although the statistical variance does increase).

Genetic programming is fault tolerant in the same way. The random death of a certain percentage of the individuals (decimation) does not disable the process. In this experiment, we show, for a particular problem, that the loss of half of a population at an early generation does not disable the process. We have chosen a problem where we know that the probability of success is substantially better for a population of 1,000 (with over-selection) than for a population of 500. We start the runs using the larger population, but randomly

6-Multiplexer

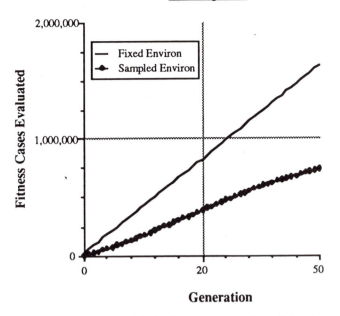

Figure 23.3 Effort required for fixed environment and sampled environment.

kill off half the population at generation 5. Thereafter the population remains at 500.

In this experiment, we ran the 6-multiplexer problem with the function set $F = \{AND, OR, IF, NOT\}$.

Figure 23.4 shows the probability of success, by generation, of three different groups of runs. The first group (labeled "normal") involved a population of 1,000 for 50 generations; the second group (labeled "Pop = 500") involved a population of 500 for 50 generations. The graphs for these two groups are the same as in figure 8.5. The third group of runs (of which there were 675 separate runs) started with an initial population of 1,000. Then, on generation 5 (indicated by the solid vertical line on the graph), half of the population was randomly deleted. As can be seen, the probability of success for the decimated population was 88% by generation 50 as compared to 100% for the constant population of 1,000 and 63% for the constant population of 500.

Table 23.1 shows the average number of generations required by each of three kinds of runs to attain a probability of success of 40% and 60%. The number of generations required to attain both the 40% and the 60% level of success is considerably less than the number required with just a population of 500. As can be seen, not only does the population survive the decimation, but its performance between generations 6 and 50 is substantially better as a result of having started with the original size of 1,000 rather than with an original size of 500.

In other words, even though a substantial decimation occurred, the population benefited from its original larger size.

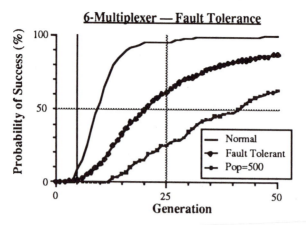

Figure 23.4 Probability of success with and without decimation.

Table 23.1 Average number of generations required to reach probability of success of 40% and 60%.

$P(M, i)$	$M = 1,000$	Fault tolerant (with M changing from 1000 to 500)	$M = 500$
40%	8.5	16.75	32
60%	10.5	23.9	47

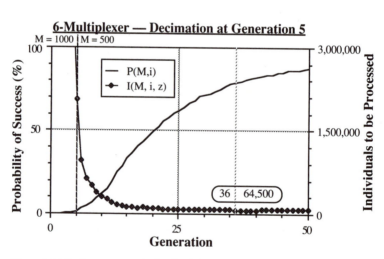

Figure 23.5 Performance curves for the fault-tolerance experiment.

Figure 23.5 shows the performance curves for the 6-multiplexer problem in the fault-tolerance experiment. Taking into account the fact that the population size changed at generation 5 from 1,000 to 500, the number 64,500 in the oval indicates that if this problem is run through to generation 36, processing a total of 64,500 individuals is sufficient to yield solution of this problem with 99% probability.

As we saw in figure 8.4 (applicable to a population of 500), processing a total of 245,000 individuals (i.e., 500 × 70 generations × 7 runs) is sufficient to yield a solution to this problem with 99% probability. As shown in figure 25.14 (applicable to a population of 1,000 with over-selection), processing a total of 33,000 individuals (i.e., 1,000 × 33 generations × 1 run) is sufficient to yield a solution of this problem with 99% probability. Thus, the fault-tolerant behavior (involving population sizes of 500 and 1,000 at various points during the run) requires processing of an intermediate number (i.e., 64,500) of individuals in order to yield a solution to the problem.

Note that runs of the messy genetic algorithm (Goldberg, Korb, and Deb 1989) start with a large population which is gradually reduced in size in later generations.

23.4 A CHANGING BOOLEAN ENVIRONMENT

In this experiment, we start a run of the three-argument Boolean function learning problem with Boolean rule 000 (using the numbering scheme used in chapter 9) with a population of 500 and number of generations G to be run of 101. Raw fitness is the number of matches, over $2^3 = 8$ fitness cases, consisting of the combinations of the three Boolean arguments, to the Boolean rule 000.

After at least one individual in the population is found that scores the maximum number of hits for each of five consecutive generations, the environment is changed. The environment is successively changed by changing the target function to be learned to Boolean rules 102, 007, 120, 042, 105, and finally 150. The five-generation period creates the opportunity for the population to lose its diversity and converge onto the 100%-correct solution to the prevailing environment.

In one run, the population successfully adapted to the original fitness measure and the six succeeding fitness measures within 75 generations.

Figure 23.6 shows, by generation, the average raw fitness of the population as a whole as the fitness measure was varied in the seven ways just described. The average raw fitness (i.e., the number of matches, or hits, out of a possible eight matches) of the population starts at about 4 for generation 0. Boolean rule 000 (Always Off) is so simple that a solution appears in generation 0. Between generations 0 and 5, the average raw fitness of the population increases as the population tends to improve under the influence of the currently prevailing fitness measure. Then, at generation 5, when the fitness measure changes to Boolean rule 002, the average raw fitness of the popula-

Solving 7 Different Boolean Functions

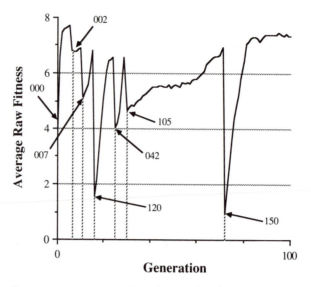

Figure 23.6 Average population fitness when the environment is repeatedly changed.

tion drops abruptly. At generation 11, when the fitness measure changes to Boolean rule 007, the average raw fitness of the population again drops. As the fitness measure changes to Boolean rule 120, the drop in average raw fitness of the population (to about 1.5 matches) is more severe and it takes four generations for a solution to be found. The average raw fitness recovers to about 6.5 during the five-generation delay period. A similar, but less pronounced, drop occurs when the fitness measure in changed to Boolean rule 042 and 105 (odd-3-parity).

Figure 23.7 shows, by generation, the raw fitness (i.e., number of hits) of the best-of-generation individual as the fitness measure was varied in the seven ways just described.

Boolean rule 105 (odd-3-parity) is much harder than the functions encountered so far. When the fitness measure is changed to Boolean rule 105 at generation 30, the raw fitness of the best-of-generation individual in the population is only 6 (out of 8). At generation 50 the raw fitness of the best-of-generation individual rises to 7, and at generation 66 it reaches 8.

When the fitness measure is changed (five generations later) to Boolean rule 150 (even-3-parity), the average raw fitness of the population plummets to about 0.9. After a solution to Boolean rule 150 is found at generation 75, the average raw fitness of the population again starts rising; it reaches about 7.5 at around generation 100.

Figure 23.8 shows the variety, by generation, as the environment is repeatedly changed in this experiment.

This experiment shows that a genetically diverse population is able to adapt to changes in the environment.

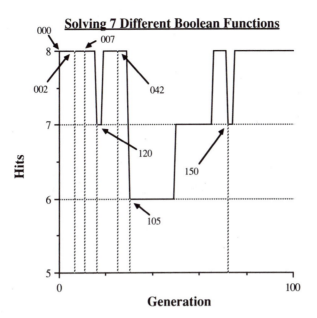

Figure 23.7 Number of hits for the best-of-generation individual when the environment is repeatedly changed.

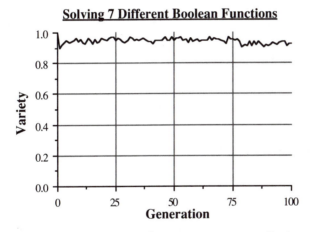

Figure 23.8 Variety curve as the environment is repeatedly changed.

Ruggedness of Genetic Programming

In this experiment, the environment is changed in an even more extreme manner than was the case in the previous section.

When the experiment starts, the problem is to perform symbolic regression (similar to that described in section 7.3) with a quartic target function of $x^4 - 5x^2 + 4$. There are 20 fitness cases involving floating-point values of the independent variable x chosen at random between -2.0 and $+2.0$. Raw fitness is the sum, over all 20 fitness cases, of the absolute value of the error between the floating-point value returned by the S-expression and the correct value of $x^4 - 5x^2 + 4$ for the value of the independent variable x for that fitness case. A hit is a fitness case for which the error is less than 0.01. Population size is 1,000 (with over-selection).

When the best-of-generation individual scores 20 hits for two consecutive generations on the symbolic regression problem, then the fitness measure changes to the fitness measure used in the artificial ant problem with the Santa Fe trial (section 7.2). That is, raw fitness becomes the number of food pellets eaten. A raw fitness of 89 represents the solution to this subproblem. The population is not changed when the fitness measure abruptly changes.

The function set for the experiment consists of the functions found in both previous problems, namely

```
F = {+, -, *, %, IF-FOOD-AHEAD, PROGN},
```

each taking two arguments.

The terminal set for the experiment consists of

```
T = {X, (LEFT), (RIGHT), (MOVE)}.
```

A typical S-expression in the biathlon consists of a composition of the four arithmetic operations (+, -, *, %) and the floating-point independent variable x needed by the symbolic regression problem and various turns, moves, and sensing operations relevant to the artificial ant problem.

The terminals (LEFT), (RIGHT), and (MOVE) each unconditionally returns a floating-point value of 1.0. We thus achieve closure in the function set.

This problem can be viewed as a very extreme case of having extraneous functions and terminals in the terminal set. When the problem starts, the goal is to do symbolic regression. The goal is to find an S-expression that performs some sequence of arithmetic operations on the floating-point value of the independent variable x in order to match the target quartic function of x. Every turn and move that appears in an S-expression side effects the state of the artificial ant on the Santa Fe trail but contributes nothing toward solution of the symbolic regression problem. In addition, every sensing operation (IF-FOOD-AHEAD) in an S-expression creates a branch that executes one of two subexpressions (each presumably doing some floating-point calculation) on the basis of what the artificial ant is seeing at its current position along the Santa Fe trail. It is hard to imagine functions less relevant to the problem at hand.

For example, an S-expression such as

```
(* (+ (LEFT) X) (+ (MOVE) (IF-FOOD-AHEAD X (RIGHT))))
```

is evaluated as follows: The ant is turned left, and the sum of x and 1 (i.e., the value returned by the (LEFT)) is computed as the value of the first argument to the multiplication function. Then the ant is moved. If the ant sees any food, the value x is returned and added to the return value of (MOVE) (i.e., 1). However, if the ant does not sense any food, it is turned right and the sum of 1 and 1 is computed. In any event, either $x + 1$ or 2 is then multiplied by the previously computed sum $x + 1$. The S-expression as a whole thus returns either the numerical value $2x + 2$ or $x^2 + 2x + 1$ depending on what the ant saw, while side-effecting the state of the ant by turning it left, moving it, and possibly turning it right.

In spite of the confusion created by the irrelevant functions associated with the artificial ant, in one run of the biathlon the best-of-generation individual emerging in generation 8 scored 20 (out of 20) hits and had a raw fitness of 0.00000350. A different best-of-generation individual scoring an equally acceptable 20 hits appeared in generation 9. The best-of-generation individual from generation 8 was

```
(IF-FOOD-AHEAD (PROGN (LEFT) (- (RIGHT) (LEFT))) (*
(IF-FOOD-AHEAD (PROGN (+ (LEFT) (MOVE)) (+ (RIGHT) X)) (+
(IF-FOOD-AHEAD (MOVE) (MOVE)) (+ (MOVE) X)))
(IF-FOOD-AHEAD (PROGN (% (LEFT) (LEFT)) (* (RIGHT)
(RIGHT))) (* (- (% (LEFT) (RIGHT)) (PROGN (IF-FOOD-AHEAD
(PROGN (MOVE) (LEFT)) (* X (LEFT))) (IF-FOOD-AHEAD (*
(MOVE) (MOVE)) (- X (RIGHT))))) (* (- (% (% (RIGHT)
(LEFT)) (PROGN (- (LEFT) X) X)) (* (PROGN (RIGHT) (LEFT))
(LEFT))) (* (+ (IF-FOOD-AHEAD (MOVE) (MOVE)) (* (RIGHT)
X)) (% (IF-FOOD-AHEAD (RIGHT) X) (% (RIGHT)
(MOVE))))))))))).
```

Thus, on generations 8 and 9, we achieved solutions to the symbolic regression problem. Note that the S-expression above is filled with extraneous moves, turns, and sensing operations associated with the artificial ant. As this S-expression is evaluated to solve the symbolic regression problem, the artificial ant is kept busy irrelevantly moving, turning, and sensing along the Santa Fe trail.

At this stage of the biathlon, the fitness measure is changed and the goal becomes finding a control strategy for navigating the artificial ant along the Santa Fe trail to find the 89 food pellets. When the fitness measure changes abruptly, the individuals in the population are, of course, highly unfit at solving the artificial ant problem. Every arithmetic operation and every occurrence of the floating-point variable x is, of course, completely irrelevant to solving the artificial ant problem.

Note that in the original environment, the calls to the functions related to the ant produced the constant value 1.0, whereas in the new environment the arithmetic operations serve as a PROGN function.

Nonetheless, some individuals in the population at the time of the environmental change are somewhat better than others at solving the artificial ant problem.

The genetic programming paradigm then proceeds, as usual, to genetically breed an ever better population for dealing with the current environment (as reflected by the current fitness measure).

In generation 47, the best-of-run individual,

```
(IF-FOOD-AHEAD (PROGN (LEFT) (- (RIGHT) (LEFT))) (*
(IF-FOOD-AHEAD (IF-FOOD-AHEAD (IF-FOOD-AHEAD (MOVE) (* X
(LEFT))) (* X (LEFT))) (+ (IF-FOOD-AHEAD (MOVE) (RIGHT))
(MOVE))) (IF-FOOD-AHEAD (* X (LEFT)) (* (- X (PROGN
(IF-FOOD-AHEAD (IF-FOOD-AHEAD (MOVE) (MOVE)) (* X
(LEFT))) (IF-FOOD-AHEAD (* (* (MOVE) (MOVE)) (MOVE)) (- X
(IF-FOOD-AHEAD (MOVE) (RIGHT)))))))) (* (* (+ (RIGHT) X) X)
(* (+ (IF-FOOD-AHEAD (% (IF-FOOD-AHEAD (* (IF-FOOD-AHEAD
(* (MOVE) (MOVE)) (- X (IF-FOOD-AHEAD (MOVE) (RIGHT)))))
(MOVE)) X) (% (RIGHT) (MOVE))) (MOVE)) (IF-FOOD-AHEAD
(IF-FOOD-AHEAD (PROGN (MOVE) (LEFT)) (* X (LEFT))) (- X
(RIGHT)))) (% (IF-FOOD-AHEAD (+ (- X (RIGHT)) (+ (RIGHT)
X)) X) (% (RIGHT) (MOVE)))))))))),
```

scored 89 (out of 89) hits along the Santa Fe trail.

Figure 23.9 shows, by generation, the number of hits for the best-of-generation individual for the biathlon consisting of the symbolic regression problem and the artificial ant problem. The left axis shows the number of hits (between 0 and 20) for the symbolic regression problem, while the right axis shows the number of hits (between 0 and 89) for the artificial ant problem. Between generations 0 and 8, the number of hits for the best-of-generation

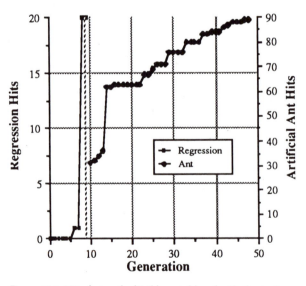

Figure 23.9 Hits during the biathlon problem for the best-of-generation individual.

individual rose from 0 to the maximum value of 20 for the symbolic regression problem. The number of hits dropped dramatically at generation 10, to 31. Performance improved, and by generation 47 the number of hits for the best-of-generation individual reached the maximum value of 89 for the artificial ant problem.

Note that the above S-expression that solves the artificial ant problem retains residual structures associated with the earlier adaptation to the environment created by the symbolic regression problem. These residual structures would not have been present in the S-expression if the population had not previously been bred to solve the earlier symbolic regression problem. These residual structures are typical effects of what Stork, Jackson, and Walker (1991) call *preadaptation*.

Section 24.3.4 contains another experiment involving a combination of two very different function sets.

24 Extraneous Variables and Functions

The first and second steps in preparing to use genetic programming involve selection of the terminal set and the function set. If the terminal set and function set are not together sufficient to express a solution to the problem at hand, genetic programming cannot solve the problem. The question arises as to the effect of extraneous variables and extraneous functions on genetic programming. This chapter discusses this question and presents evidence from limited experiments in limited problem domains. The question is not definitively answered here; however, the results of these limited experiments may suggest further work (experimental and theoretical) that might lead to general conclusions.

24.1 EFFECT OF EXTRANEOUS VARIABLES

The problem of identifying the variables with explanatory power to solve a given problem is a pervasive problem in all areas of science and is common to all machine learning paradigms. Depending on the problem, it may or may not be possible to readily identify the relevant variables for inclusion in the terminal set.

In this experiment, the goal is to test the effect of extraneous variables in the terminal set in genetic programming. Consider the symbolic regression problem with $x^3 + x^2 + x$ as the target curve. The only necessary terminal in the terminal set is the variable x. The terminal set for this problem is progressively enlarged to include 1, 4, 8, 16, and 32 extraneous zero-mean floating-point variables in addition to x. Then, on each instance when an S-expression is evaluated, each of the extraneous variables is independently and separately set to a different floating-point random number between -5.0 and $+5.0$. Thus, none of the extraneous variables is correlated with x or with any of the others in any discernible way.

Any S-expression containing even one of these extraneous terminals (in a value returning position) would have great difficulty in consistently achieving a good value of fitness and, therefore, great difficulty in being selected more than occasionally to remain in the population (via reproduction) or to participate in the breeding of offspring (via crossover). Thus, to solve this symbolic

Cubic Polynomial with Extraneous Variables

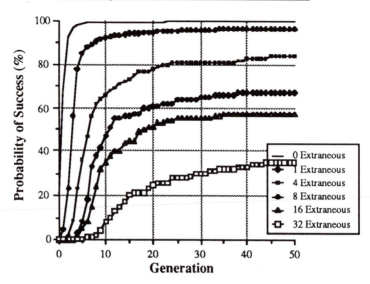

Figure 24.1 Probability of success for the symbolic regression problem with $x^3 + x^2 + x$ as the target function when 0, 1, 4, 8, 16, and 32 extraneous variables are added to the terminal set.

Table 24.1 Probability of success for generation 50 when 0, 1, 4, 8, 16, and 32 extraneous variables are in the terminal set.

Number of extraneous variables	Probability of success at generation 50
0	99.8
1	96.6
4	84.0
8	67.0
16	57.0
32	35.0

regression problem, genetic programming has to find an S-expression that excludes all the variables except x.

A hit is defined as a fitness case for which the S-expression comes within 0.01 of the target function. A run is considered successful if it scores the maximum number of hits (i.e., 20 hits when there are 20 fitness cases).

Figure 24.1 shows, by generation, the probability of success $P(M, i)$ that at least one S-expression in the population scores 20 hits when there are 0, 1, 4, 8, 16, and 32 extraneous variables in addition to x. This graph is for a population of 1,000 (with over-selection). Between 100 and 914 runs were used for each curve.

Table 24.1 summarizes the probability of success $P(M, i)$ for generation 50.

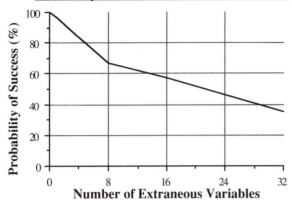

Cubic Polynomial with Extraneous Variables

Figure 24.2 Probability of success at generation 50 as a function of the number of extraneous variables.

As can be seen, the probability of success $P(M, i)$ for generation 50 is 99.8% with no extraneous variables. As one would expect, the addition of extraneous variables to the terminal set dramatically degrades performance for this problem. Nonetheless, genetic programming is able to solve this problem 35% of the time when 32 of the 33 terminals in the terminal set are extraneous variables.

Figure 24.2 shows, for generation 50, the probability of success $P(M, i)$ as a function of the number of extraneous variables (from 0 to 32) from table 24.1. This figure makes it clear that there is an almost linear degradation in performance, as measured by $P(M, i)$, as additional extraneous variables are added to the problem.

24.2 EFFECT OF EXTRANEOUS EPHEMERAL RANDOM CONSTANTS

Certain problems of symbolic regression require that the ephemeral random floating-point constant $\Re$ be included in the terminal set in order to solve the problem. This section considers the effect of having ephemeral random floating-point constants available in the terminal set when they are not needed.

Figure 24.3 shows, by generation, a comparison of the probability of success $P(M, i)$ for the symbolic regression problem with the quartic polynomial $x^4 + x^3 + x^2 + x$ as the target function with the ephemeral random floating-point constant $\Re$ present and absent from the terminal set. The figure is based on a population of 500 and 175 runs with $\Re$ and 295 runs without it. The function set is the same as in section 7.3.

As can be seen, there is no substantial difference in performance in this problem between the probability of success with and without the ephemeral random floating-point constant $\Re$.

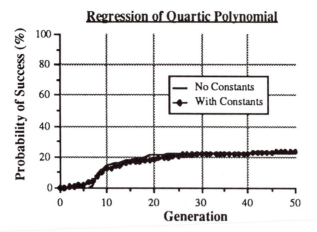

Regression of Quartic Polynomial

Figure 24.3 Probability of success with and without the ephemeral random floating-point constant $\Re$.

24.3 EFFECT OF EXTRANEOUS FUNCTIONS

In the previous section, we saw that extraneous variables in the terminal set degrade the performance of genetic programming. The effect of a large number of extraneous functions in the function set is similar—it degrades performance. However, a particular one or two extraneous functions may improve performance in some specific problems.

24.3.1 6-Multiplexer

The function IF is a helpful addition to the function set of the Boolean 6-multiplexer problem, because multiplexers involve taking alternative actions based on the outcome of a test.

Suppose we delete the IF function from the function set that was used when this problem was first presented in subsection 7.4.3. That is, suppose we reduce the function set $F_1 = \{\text{AND, OR, IF, NOT}\}$ to merely $F_2 = \{\text{AND, OR, NOT}\}$. In this instance, there is a considerable degradation in performance as well as a considerable increase in the size of the S-expressions of the solutions obtained.

For example, in one typical run with the smaller function set F_2, the following 100%-correct solution was obtained:

```
(AND (OR A0 (OR D2 (NOT A1))))
    (OR (AND (AND (OR (AND (OR D0 A0) D1) A1) D3) D3)
        (AND (OR (AND D1 (NOT A1)) (NOT (AND A0 A0))))
            (OR (AND D0
                (NOT (OR A0
                    (OR A1
                    (AND
                    (OR (AND
                        (OR (AND A0 A0) A1)
                        D1)
```

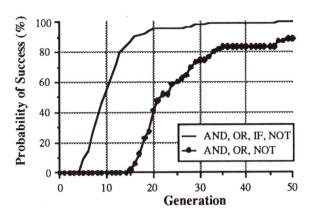

Figure 24.4 Comparison of the probability of success of the 6-multiplexer problem with and without the function IF in the function set.

```
                    A1)
                  D1)))))
    (OR A1 (AND (OR (AND A0 A0) A1)
                  D1))))))).
```

This solution to this problem is considerably more complex than the solution we typically obtain when we use the larger function set F_1.

Figure 24.4 shows, by generation, the probability of success $P(M, i)$ for the Boolean 6-multiplexer problem for the larger function set $F_1 = \{$AND, OR, IF, NOT$\}$ versus the smaller function set $F_2 = \{$AND, OR, NOT$\}$. This graph is based on a population size of 1,000 (with over-selection) and 80 runs. As can be seen, the probability of success for the smaller function set is considerably less than for the larger function set containing the function IF. For example, the probability of success is only 89% after 50 generations for the smaller function set as compared to 100% for the larger function set for this problem.

24.3.2 Expanded Boolean Problem

In this series of 16 experiments, we solve the Boolean 6-multiplexer problem using a population size of 1,000 (with over-selection) and a maximum of 51 generations.

In the first of the 16 experiments, the function set consisted of just the two-argument Boolean NAND function (rule 07). For each successive experiment, one additional two-argument Boolean function was added to the function set. Every additional Boolean function added is extraneous since NAND alone is computationally complete. The added functions were selected systematically starting with Boolean function rule 00, 01, ..., 06, and then 08, 09, ..., 15.

Table 24.2 shows the function sets used for the 16 experiments and the probability of success $P(M, i)$ on generation 50.

Table 24.2 Comparison of the probability of success $P(M, i)$ for generation 50 for the 6-multiplexer problem for the 16 ever-larger function sets.

Number of extraneous functions	Function set	$P(M, i)$
0	NAND	100%
1	NAND, Always-Off	83%
2	NAND, Always-Off, NOR	55%
3	NAND, Always-Off, NOR, 02	75%
4	NAND, Always-Off, NOR, 02, 03	68%
5	NAND, Always-Off, NOR, 02, 03, 04	73%
6	NAND, Always-Off, NOR, 02, 03, 04, 05	48%
7	NAND, Always-Off, NOR, 02, 03, 04, 05, Odd-2-Parity	43%
8	NAND, Always-Off, NOR, 02, 03, 04, 05, Odd-2-Parity, AND	38%
9	NAND, Always-Off, NOR, 02, 03, 04, 05, Odd-2-Parity, AND, Even-2-Parity	43%
10	NAND, Always-Off, NOR, 02, 03, 04, 05, Odd-2-Parity, AND, Even-2-Parity, 10	33%
11	NAND, Always-Off, NOR, 02, 03, 04, 05, Odd-2-Parity, AND, Even-2-Parity, 10,11	48%
12	NAND, Always-Off, NOR, 02, 03, 04, 05, Odd-2-Parity, AND, Even-2-Parity, 10,11, 12	43%
13	NAND, Always-Off, NOR, 02, 03, 04, 05, Odd-2-Parity, AND, Even-2-Parity, 10,11, 12, 13	55%
14	NAND, Always-Off, NOR, 02, 03, 04, 05, Odd-2-Parity, AND, Even-2-Parity, 10,11, 12, 13, OR	40%
15	NAND, Always-Off, NOR, 02, 03, 04, 05, Odd-2-Parity, AND, Even-2-Parity, 10,11, 12, 13, OR, Always-On	58%

Figure 24.5 shows, by generation, the probability of success $P(M, i)$ for the 16 ever-larger functions sets. The probabilities are based on 40 runs for each of the 16 function sets.

Figure 24.6 shows the probability of success for generation 50 of the 16 ever-larger function sets.

As can be seen, the simplest function set (i.e., that with just NAND alone) performs best for this problem. Although one might expect to see greater sensitivity and better performance with a larger function set, we instead see that performance generally decreases as the additional Boolean functions of two arguments are added to the function set. For example, adding NOR, AND, EQUAL (i.e., the even-2-parity), and NOT–EQUAL (i.e., XOR, the odd-2-parity function) degrades performance. There is a slight improvement as the last few functions are added. However, the performance of a function set consisting of

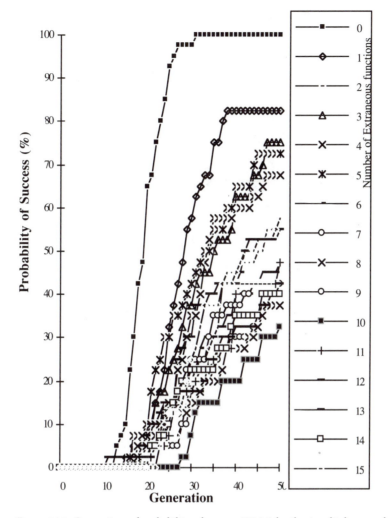

Figure 24.5 Comparison of probability of success $P(M, i)$ for the 6-multiplexer problem for 16 ever-larger function sets.

all 16 possible Boolean functions with two arguments is still distinctly inferior to a function set consisting of just NAND.

In the particular 16 experiments above, the clutter produced by the additional functions far outweighs the benefit of potentially greater sensitivity of the function set.

On the other hand, certain particular larger function sets may yield better performance than certain smaller function sets for particular problems.

Figure 24.7 shows, for example, the probability of success $P(M, i)$ for the smaller function set $F_{nand} = \{NAND\}$ versus the larger function set $F = \{AND, OR, IF, NOT\}$ that is often employed for the 6-multiplexer problem in this book. The graph for F_{nand} is based on 40 runs and the graph for F is based on 114 runs. The population size was 1,000 (with over-selection). As can be seen, performance is better for the larger function set F than for the smaller function set F_{nand} for this problem.

Extraneous Variables and Functions

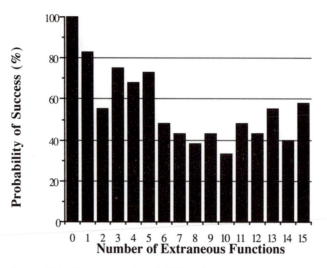

Figure 24.6 Comparison of probability of success by generation 50 for the 6-multiplexer problem for 16 ever-larger function sets.

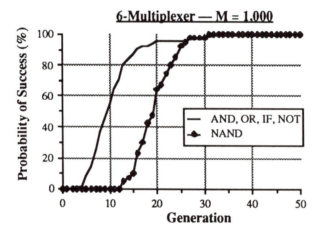

Figure 24.7 Probability of success for the 6-multiplexer problem with the function set $F = \{\text{AND}, \text{OR}, \text{IF}, \text{NOT}\}$ versus $F_{\text{nand}} = \{\text{NAND}\}$.

24.3.3 Artificial Ant Problem

We did not need both of the primitive functions (RIGHT) and (LEFT) in order to solve the artificial ant problem (chapter 7.2). We placed both of these primitive functions in the terminal set because Jefferson, Collins, et al. (1991a, 1991b) did so. Let us consider the effect of deleting one of these extraneous functions from the terminal set of this problem.

Figure 24.8 shows, by generation, that the probability of success for the artificial ant problem on the Santa Fe trail is virtually the same after (LEFT) is deleted. For example, at 50 generations, the probability of success is 13.8% with (LEFT) and 13.2% without it. The graph is based on 114 runs and a population of 500.

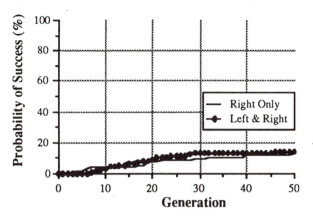

Figure 24.8 Comparison of the probability of success for the artificial ant problem with and without (LEFT).

For this particular problem, the deletion of (LEFT) has a negligible effect, because two (RIGHT)'s are just as good as two (LEFT)'s when the ant needs to execute a sequence of two (LEFT)'s to turn 180°. The ant has no need to ever make a single isolated (LEFT); however, if it did, a single (LEFT) can be accomplished with three (RIGHT)'s. Thus, the effect of one extraneous turning function is negligible for this particular problem.

24.3.4 Simple Symbolic Regression

The absence from the function set and terminal set of functions and terminals necessary for expressing a solution to a problem will, of course, prevent genetic programming from solving a problem. On the other hand, the inclusion of extraneous functions and terminals will generally just reduce the efficiency.

The function set of each of the four introductory problems in chapter 7 (and most of the problems in this book) are not minimal, but instead contain extraneous functions. For example, the functions + and – were extraneous to the cart centering problem. Both (LEFT) and (RIGHT) were not needed in the artificial ant problem, and both AND and OR were not needed in the 11-multiplexer problem. For the symbolic regression problem (section 7.3 and subsection 8.3.3) with $x^4 + x^3 + x^2 + x$ as the target function, the function set consisted of eight functions:

```
F = {+, -, *, %, SIN, COS, EXP, RLOG}.
```

Only the functions + and * are actually needed, making six of these eight functions extraneous.

This subsection explores the question of the effect of extraneous functions on the performance of genetic programming by considering a rather extreme situation. We import the terminals and functions from the artificial ant problem into the symbolic regression problem. In other words, the function set of the symbolic regression problem is enlarged so that it becomes

```
F_extra = {IF-FOOD-AHEAD, PROGN2, PROGN3, +, -, *, %, SIN,
           COS, EXP, RLOG}.
```

The terminal set for the symbolic regression problem consisted of the independent variable x:

```
T = {X}.
```

The terminal set of the symbolic regression problem is similarly enlarged so that it becomes

```
T_extra = {X, (MOVE), (RIGHT), (LEFT)}.
```

Since the three primitive functions imported from the artificial ant problem all return a numeric 1, the new function set F_{extra} and the new terminal set T_{extra} satisfy the closure requirement. Since all the functions and terminals from the original symbolic regression problem are still in F_{extra} and T_{extra}, they continue to satisfy the sufficiency requirement for the symbolic regression problem.

We use the same fitness measure and same 20 fitness cases in the interval $[-1, +1]$ as in section 7.3.

The addition of the three additional extraneous terminals to the terminal set and the addition of the three additional extraneous functions to the function set, of course, dramatically changes the character and appearance of the S-expressions in the population.

For example, in one run, the best-of-generation individual from generation 0,

```
(* (* (MOVE) X) (+ (RIGHT) X)),
```

had a raw fitness of 7.02 and contained seven points. This S-expression is interpreted as follows: When the sub-S-expression (* (MOVE) X) is evaluated, the (MOVE) has the side effect of moving the artificial ant forward on its grid while returning the numeric value of 1. In addition, (* (MOVE) X) returns the value to which X is currently bound (i.e., one of the random values of the independent variable x specified by one of the fitness cases). When the sub-S-expression (+ (RIGHT) X) is evaluated, the (RIGHT) has the side effect of turning the artificial ant while returning the numerical value of X + 1. The S-expression as a whole returns, for any X, the numerical value

$$x(x + 1) = x^2 + x,$$

while executing the side effects of the (MOVE) and the (RIGHT) on the artificial ant on its grid.

Many of the S-expressions in generation 0 contained the IF-FOOD-AHEAD function somewhere in their program tree. The IF-FOOD-AHEAD operator causes different subtrees of the program to be executed, depending on whether food is immediately in front of the artificial ant on its grid. Some squares have food; some do not; and some had food at one time, but do not now have food. The branching caused by the IF-FOOD-AHEAD function erratically changes the numerical value returned by the S-expression. S-expressions exhibiting such erratic change (uncorrelated to X) cannot get very close numerically to the target function $x^4 + x^3 + x^2 + x$. Therefore, they tend to disappear from the population.

Occurrences of (MOVE), (RIGHT), and (LEFT) in an S-expression cause actions by the artificial ant on its grid which are irrelevant to solving the symbolic regression problem. Only the numerical values returned by the S-expression are relevant to the symbolic regression problem. Since these irrelevant actions do not prevent solution of the problem, there is no pressure to cause occurrences of (MOVE), (RIGHT), and (LEFT) to disappear from the population.

S-expressions containing a PROGN2 or PROGN3 are not as erratic since the numerical value returned is simply the value returned by the last of its arguments; however, no S-expressions containing a PROGN2 or PROGN3 ever appeared as a best-of-generation individual on this particular run.

The best-of-generation individual from generation 1 had 23 points, had a raw fitness of 6.386, and scored 3 hits (out of 20):

```
(IF-FOOD-HERE
    (% (SIN (MOVE)) (PROG2 (PROG3 (MOVE) (LEFT) (RIGHT))
                          (EXP (RIGHT)))))
    (+ (* X (% X (COS X)))
        (PROG2 (IF-FOOD-HERE (LEFT) X) X))).
```

This S-expression is interesting because it had reasonably good fitness in spite of the fact that it contains two IF-FOOD-AHEAD operators. The potentially erratic effect of the second IF-FOOD-AHEAD operator above is smothered because it is embedded in the first clause of a PROGN2. The potentially erratic effect of the first IF-FOOD-AHEAD operator is minimized because the operator does not sense food for 19 of the 20 fitness cases. On the first fitness case, food is present and the IF-FOOD-AHEAD operator causes the S-expression to return the constant numerical value

```
(% (SIN (MOVE)) (EXP (RIGHT))),
```

which is equivalent to

$$\frac{\sin 1}{e^1} = 0.3096.$$

The straight line $y = 0.3096$ is somewhat close to the curve $x^4 + x^3 + x^2 + x$ in the interval $[-1, +1]$, so that this one fitness case makes a relatively small contribution to the overall fitness measure. However, for all of the remaining 19 fitness cases, the IF-FOOD-AHEAD operator causes this S-expression to return the numerical value of

```
(+ (* X (% X (COS X))) X),
```

which is equivalent to

$$\frac{x^2}{\cos x} + x.$$

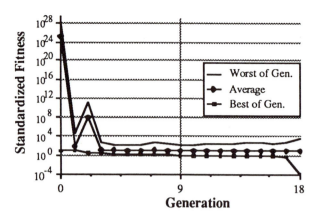

Figure 24.9 Fitness curves for the simple symbolic regression problem using T_{extra} and F_{extra}.

This expression bears enough similarity to the target function $x^4 + x^3 + x^2 + x$ to produce the reasonably good overall value of fitness (i.e., an error averaging about 0.32 per fitness case).

In generation 10, the best-of-generation individual had 22 points, had a raw fitness of 0.746, and scored 9 hits:

```
(* (* (% (LEFT) (COS (SIN (* (+ X (SIN (* (+ (RIGHT)
(RIGHT)) (SIN X)))) (SIN X))))) X) (+ (LEFT) X)).
```

This S-expression as a whole returns, for any x, the numerical value

$$\frac{x^2 + x}{\text{Cos Sin}[\text{Sin } x(\text{Sin}[2 \text{ Sin } x] + x)]}$$

while executing the side effects of the two (RIGHT) and the two (LEFT) operations on the artificial ant on its grid.

In generation 18, the best-of-generation individual had 11 points, had a raw fitness of virtually zero (i.e., 0.000132), and scored 20 hits:

```
(* (* (+ (* X X) (RIGHT)) X) (+ (LEFT) X)).
```

This best-of-run S-expression as a whole returns, for any x, the numerical value

$$x(x^2 + 1)(x + 1) = x^4 + x^3 + x^2 + x$$

while executing the side effects of the (RIGHT) and the (LEFT) on the artificial ant on its grid.

Figure 24.9 shows, by generation, the standardized fitness of the best-of-generation individual, the worst-of-generation individual, and the average individual in the population between generations 0 and 18. A logarithmic scale is used on the vertical axis.

Figure 24.10 shows, by generation, the average of the structural complexity of the population as a whole and the structural complexity of the best-of-generation individual for this one run.

Figure 24.11 shows the variety during this one run.

Figure 24.12 shows, for a population size of 500 and for generations 0 through 50, the performance curves showing $P(M, i)$ and $I(M, i, z)$. The graph

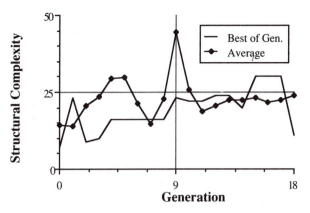

Figure 24.10 Structural complexity curves for the simple symbolic regression problem using T_{extra} and F_{extra}.

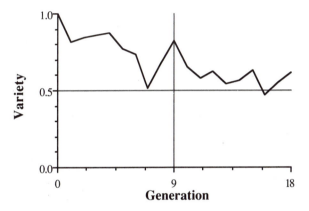

Figure 24.11 Variety curve for the simple symbolic regression problem using T_{extra} and F_{extra}.

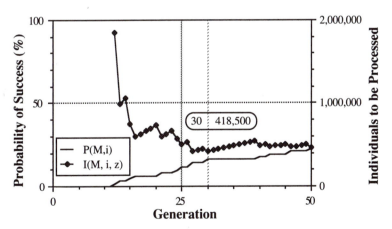

Figure 24.12 Performance curves for the simple symbolic regression problem using T_{extra} and F_{extra}.

is based on 62 runs. For example, 24% of the runs are successful by generation 7, and 16% of the runs are successful for generations 30 through 50. The numbers 30 and 418,500 in the oval indicate that if this problem is run through to generation 30, processing a total of 418,500 individuals (i.e., 500 × 31 generations × 27 runs) is sufficient to yield a solution to this problem with 99% probability.

Thus, the number of individuals that must be processed to yield a solution to this problem with 99% probability is 418,500 with the highly extraneous terminal set T_{extra} and the function set F_{extra}, versus 162,500 with the original terminal set T and function set F. While we would not advocate using the functions and terminals of the artificial ant problem in trying to solve the simple symbolic regression problem, it is interesting that only 2.58 times more individuals need be processed to yield a solution to this problem with 99% probability.

25 Operational Issues

There are a large number of operational questions surrounding the use of genetic programming for which no definitive answer is known at this time. This chapter discusses some of these operational issues and presents evidence from limited experiments in limited problem domains. None of these questions is definitively answered here; however, the results of these limited experiments may suggest further work (experimental and theoretical) that might lead to general conclusions.

25.1 EFFECT OF DIFFERENT GENERATIVE METHODS

In this section, we compare the effects of using the three different methods of creating the initial random population described in section 6.2, namely full, grow, and ramped half-and-half.

Figure 25.1 graphs the probability of success $P(M, i)$ that at least one S-expression comes within 0.01 of the target amount for all 20 fitness cases for the simple symbolic regression problem (section 7.3). The three graphs apply to three different methods of creating the initial random population. The population size is 500, and the graph runs from 0 to 50 generations. These graphs are based on 132 runs with full, 213 runs with grow, and 295 runs with ramped half-and-half. The probability of success $P(M, i)$ is 3% with full, 17% with grow, and 23% with ramped half-and-half for generation 50.

Figure 25.2 graphs the probability of success $P(M, i)$, for three different methods of creating the initial random population, that at least one S-expression exactly matches the value of the Boolean 6-multiplexer function for all 64 fitness cases (subsection 7.4.3). The population size is 500 and the graph runs from 0 to 50 generations. The function set is

```
F = {AND, OR, IF, NOT},
```

taking two, two, three, and one argument, respectively. These graphs are based on 60 runs with full, 200 runs with grow, and 140 runs with ramped half-and-half. The probability of success $P(M, i)$ is 42% with full, 53% with grow, and 66% with ramped half-and-half for generation 50.

Figure 25.3 graphs the probability of success $P(M, i)$, for three different methods of creating the initial random population, that at least one plan causes

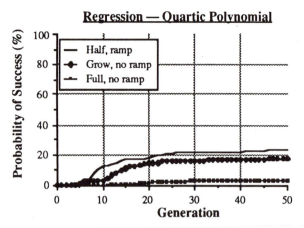

Figure 25.1 Comparison of three methods of creating the initial random population for the simple symbolic regression problem.

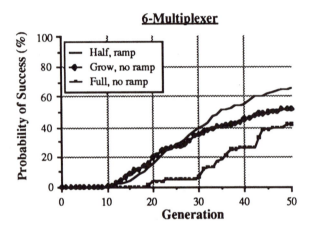

Figure 25.2 Comparison of three methods of creating the initial random population for the 6-multiplexer problem.

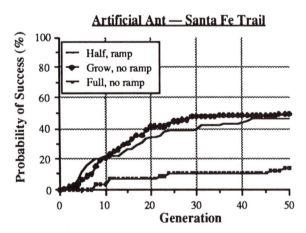

Figure 25.3 Comparison of three methods of creating the initial random population on artificial ant problem.

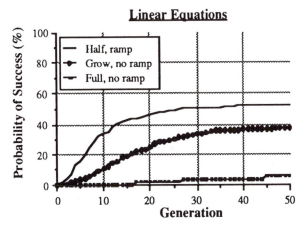

Linear Equations

Figure 25.4 Comparison of three methods of creating the initial random population for the linear equations problem involving one unknown, x_1.

the ant to traverse the entire trail and collect all 89 pieces of food (within the allowed time) for the artificial ant problem with the Santa Fe trail (section 7.2). The population size is 500 and the graph runs from 0 to 50 generations. These graphs are based on 56 runs with full, 105 runs with grow, and 91 runs with ramped half-and-half. The probability of success $P(M, i)$ is 14% with full, 50% with grow, and 46% with ramped half-and-half for generation 50.

Figure 25.4 graphs the probability of success $P(M, i)$ for three different methods of creating the initial random population for a version of the linear equations problem in two unknowns involving the finding of the value of only the first unknown x_1. Except for the number of unknowns, the problem is similar to the problem described in section 19.3. A run is considered successful if at least one S-expression comes within 0.01 of the solution point for x_1 for all 10 pairs of linear equations in two unknowns. The population size is 500 and the graph runs from 0 to 50 generations. These graphs are based on 52 runs with full, 427 runs with grow, and 214 runs with ramped half-and-half. The probability of success $P(M, i)$ is 6% with full, 37% with grow, and 53% with ramped half-and-half for generation 50.

As these figures illustrate, ramped half-and-half is usually the best observed or very close to the best observed for these problems.

25.2 EFFECT OF THE MUTATION OPERATION

The mutation operation is one of the secondary operations of genetic programming described in subsection 6.5.1.

In this experiment, we consider the effect on performance when mutation is added to runs involving the usual default number of occurrences of fitness-proportionate reproduction (i.e., 10%) and crossover (i.e., 90%).

Figure 25.5 shows, by generation, a comparison of the probability of success $P(M, i)$ for the Boolean 6-multiplexer problem with and without the mutation operation. The graph is based on a population of 1,000 (with over-selection)

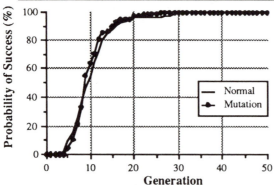

10% Mutation with Crossover vs. Normal Parameters

Figure 25.5 Effect of the mutation operation.

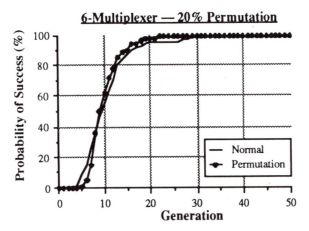

6-Multiplexer — 20% Permutation

Figure 25.6 Effect of the permutation operation.

and 130 runs. The function set is F = {AND, OR, IF, NOT}. Mutation was performed on 200 individuals of each generation.

As can be seen, there is no substantial difference in performance between the probability of success with and without the mutation operation for this problem. For example, the probability of success at 50 generations is 99.2% with mutation and 100% without it.

In the very unlikely event that a particular function or terminal were to disappear entirely from a population in a run of genetic programming, mutation provides a mean for recreating that function or terminal.

25.3 EFFECT OF THE PERMUTATION OPERATION

Permutation is one of the secondary operations of genetic programming described in subsection 6.5.2. It is a generalization of the inversion operation for the conventional genetic algorithm operating on strings.

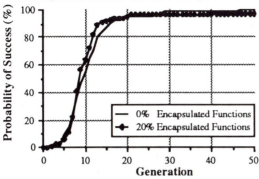

Figure 25.7 Effect of the encapsulation operation.

In this experiment, we consider the effect on performance when the permutation operation is added to runs involving the usual default number of occurrences of fitness-proportionate reproduction and crossover.

Figure 25.6 shows, by generation, a comparison of the probability of success $P(M, i)$ for the Boolean 6-multiplexer problem with and without the permutation operation. The graph is based on a population of 1,000 (with overselection) and 100 runs. The function set is $F = \{AND, OR, IF, NOT\}$. The permutation operation was performed on 200 individuals of each generation.

As can be seen, there is no substantial difference in performance between the probability of success with and without the permutation operation for this problem. For example, the probability of success at 50 generations is 99% with permutation and 100% without it.

25.4 EFFECT OF THE ENCAPSULATION OPERATION

Encapsulation (described in subsection 6.5.4) is a means for automatically identifying and encapsulating potentially useful subtrees.

In this experiment, we consider the effect on performance when the encapsulation operation is added to runs involving the usual default number of occurrences of fitness-proportionate reproduction and crossover.

Figure 25.7 shows, by generation, a comparison of the probability of success $P(M, i)$ for the Boolean 6-multiplexer problem with and without the encapsulation operation. The graph is based on a population of 1,000 (with overselection) and 150 runs. The function set is $F = \{AND, OR, IF, NOT\}$. The operation was performed on 200 individuals of each generation.

There is no substantial difference in performance between the probability of success with and without the encapsulation operation for this problem. For example, the probability of success at 50 generations is 97% with the encapsulation operation and 100% without it.

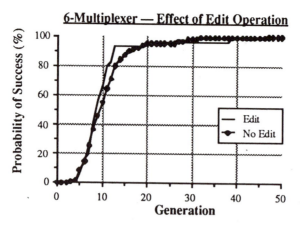

Figure 25.8 Effect of the editing operation.

25.5 EFFECT OF THE EDITING OPERATION

The editing operation provides a means to edit (and thereby simplify) S-expressions in the population on every generation (or a selected fraction of the generations) as genetic programming is running (subsection 6.5.3).

It is not clear whether such editing would facilitate or frustrate discovery of solutions to problems.

In this experiment, we consider the effect on performance when the editing operation is added to runs involving the usual default number of occurrences of fitness-proportionate reproduction and crossover.

Figure 25.8 shows, by generation, a comparison of the probability of success $P(M, i)$ for the Boolean 6-multiplexer problem with and without the editing operation. The graph is based on a population of 1,000 (with over-selection) and 30 runs. The function set is $F = \{AND, OR, IF, NOT\}$. The operation was performed on every individual in the population for every generation.

One cannot ... any substantial difference in performance between the probability of success with and without the editing operation for this problem. For example, the probability of success at 50 generations is 100% both with the editing operation and without it.

25.6 EFFECT OF GREEDY OVER-SELECTION

It is possible to considerably enhance the performance of genetic programming for many problems by greedily over-selecting the fitter individuals in the population as described in subsection 6.3.5. As previously mentioned, unless otherwise indicated, we use over-selection in order to improve performance on the minority of problems in this book where the population size is 1,000 or larger.

In chapter 8, we presented performance curves for the 6-multiplexer problem with the function set $F_1 = \{AND, OR, IF, NOT\}$. Figures 8.5, 8.6, and 8.7 were the performance curves for population sizes of 1,000, 2,000, and 4,000,

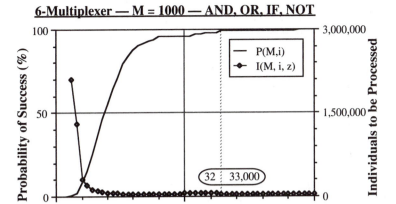

Figure 25.9 Performance curves for population size $M = 1,000$ for the 6-multiplexer problem with greedy over-selection.

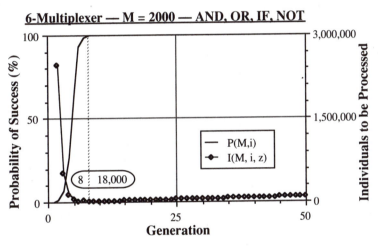

Figure 25.10 Performance curves for population size $M = 2,000$ for the 6-multiplexer problem with greedy over-selection.

respectively. Over-selection was not involved in these three figures. We now consider this same problem with the same function set and the same three population sizes when greedy over-selection is invoked.

Figure 25.9 shows, for a population size M of 1,000 and for generations 0 through 50, the curves for the cumulative probability $P(M, i)$ of success and the number of individuals $I(M, i, z)$ that must be processed to yield a solution of the 6-multiplexer problem with 99% probability with the function set $F_1 = \{\text{AND, OR, IF, NOT}\}$. This figure is based on 114 runs. The numbers 32 and 33,000 in the oval indicate that, if this problem is run through to generation 32, processing a total of 33,000 individuals (i.e., $1,000 \times 33$ generations $\times$ 1 run) is sufficient to yield a solution of this problem with 99% probability.

6-Multiplexer — M = 4000 — AND, OR, IF, NOT

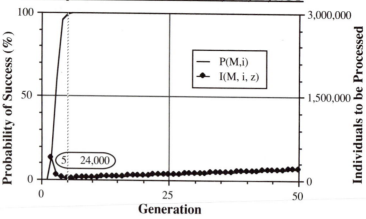

Figure 25.11 Performance curves for population size $M = 4,000$ for the 6-multiplexer problem with greedy over-selection.

Table 25.1 Effect of greedy over-selection.

Population	$I(M, i, z)$ without over-selection	$I(M, i, z)$ with over-selection
1,000	343,000	33,000
2,000	294,000	18,000
4,000	160,000	24,000

Figure 25.10 shows the performance curves for M of 2,000 with greedy over-selection. This figure is based on 90 runs. The numbers 8 and 18,000 in the oval indicate that if this problem is run through to generation 8, processing a total of 18,000 individuals (i.e., 2,000 × 9 generations × 2 runs) is sufficient to yield a solution of this problem with 99% probability by generation 8.

Figure 25.11 shows the performance curves for M of 4,000 with greedy over-selection. This figure is based on 140 runs. The numbers 5 and 24,000 in the oval indicate that if this problem is run through to generation 5, processing a total of 24,000 (i.e., 4,000 × 6 generations × 1 run) individuals is sufficient to yield a solution of this problem with 99% probability by generation 5.

Table 25.1 summarizes the effect of greedy over-selection for this problem.

25.7 EFFECT OF TOURNAMENT SELECTION VERSUS FITNESS-PROPORTIONATE SELECTION

Fitness-proportionate selection is the method used to select individuals from the population to participate in the various genetic operations throughout this book. However, several other methods of selection have been used successfully in connection with the conventional genetic algorithm operating on strings. The question arises as to the effect on the performance of genetic programming of such alternative methods of selection, notably rank selection and tournament selection.

In rank selection (Baker 1985; Whitley 1989), after the values of fitness are computed, they are sorted so that each individual in the population is assigned a rank. The ranks range from 1 (denoting the best) to the size of the population (denoting the worst). Selection is then done so that the best individual in the population receives a predetermined multiple of the number of copies that the worst individual receives (thus equalizing selective pressure). Actual distributions of fitness values often contain anomalies, such as one outlying individual with an extraordinarily good value of fitness relative to the other individuals in the population or a large number of individuals with different, but virtually indistinguishable fitness values. Rank selection has the effect of detaching the selection process from the actual distribution of fitness values. If many individuals have almost identical values of fitness, the genetic algorithm may require many generations to distinguish the slightly better individuals from the slightly worse individuals. Rank selection exaggerates the difference between almost identical values of fitness and can speed convergence. If one individual has an especially good value of fitness relative to the others (e.g., perhaps one mediocre individual occurring among many very poor individuals on an early generation), rank selection minimizes the effect of this outlying good relative fitness value and does not allow this one individual to reproduce excessively and dominate the population (i.e., it prevents survival of the mediocre). Thus, rank selection can prevent premature convergence.

Tournament selection parallels the competition in nature among individuals for the right to mate. In the simplest version of tournament selection, two individuals are picked at random from the population and the one with better fitness is selected for reproduction. The best individual in the population has probability 1.0 of prevailing in the competition, the worst individual has probability 0 of prevailing, and a middle-ranking individual has approximately 0.5 probability of prevailing. Thus, tournament selection is, in effect, a probabilistic version of rank selection. It has the slight advantage of being somewhat faster than rank selection (although the amount of computer time consumed by selection steps is a very minor part of the total computer time involved in a run). Tournament selection also eliminates the only centralized step performed on every generation (i.e., the selection process involving fitness-proportionate reproduction) and frees the algorithm from global synchronization. The centralized calculation of the average fitness of the population is replaced by a rendezvous (Robertson 1987) between two individuals in the population.

If desired, the notion of tournament selection can be extended so that the selection is made from a group larger than two.

Figure 25.12 shows, by generation, a comparison of the probability of success $P(M, i)$ for the Boolean 6-multiplexer problem with the function set $F = \{\text{AND, OR, IF, NOT}\}$ with simple fitness-proportionate selection with no over-selection, tournament selection, and fitness-proportionate selection with over-selection. The population size was 1,000. The graphs are based on 38 runs for simple fitness-proportionate selection with no over-selection, 200 runs

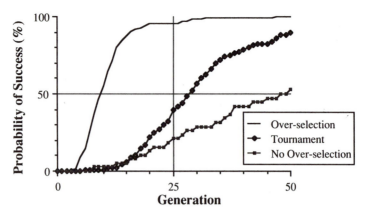

Figure 25.12 Comparison of tournament selection, fitness-proportionate selection, and fitness-proportionate selection with over-selection for 6-multiplexer problem.

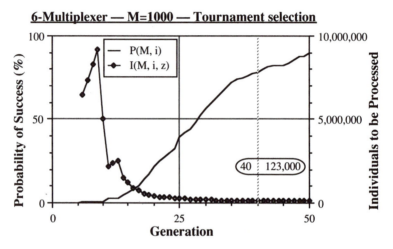

Figure 25.13 Performance curves for tournament selection.

for tournament selection, and 200 runs for fitness-proportionate selection with over-selection.

As can be seen, the probability of success $P(M, i)$ is poorest with simple fitness-proportionate selection with no over-selection, somewhat better with tournament selection, and best with fitness-proportionate selection with over-selection for this particular problem with this particular function set.

Figure 8.5 showed that processing 343,000 individuals was sufficient to solve this problem with 99% probability by generation 48 with simple fitness-proportionate selection with no over-selection. The probability of success $P(M, i)$ shown in figure 25.12 is the same as in figure 8.5.

Figure 25.13 shows the performance curves for this problem with tournament selection (the probability of success in this figure being the same as in figure 25.12). As can be seen, processing 123,000 individuals (i.e., 1,000 × 41 generations × 3 runs) was sufficient to solve this problem with 99% probability by generation 40.

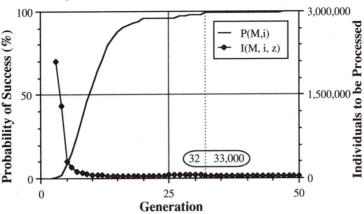

Figure 25.14 Performance curves fitness-proportionate selection with over-selection.

Table 25.2 Effect of greedy over-selection.

Selection method	$P(M, i)$ at generation 25	Generation number	$I(M, i, z)$
Fitness-proportionate selection	21%	48	343,000
Tournament selection	40%	40	123,000
Fitness-proportionate selection with over-selection	96%	32	33,000

Figure 25.14 shows the performance curves for this problem with fitness-proportionate selection with over-selection (the probability of success in this figure being the same as in figure 25.12). As can be seen, processing 33,000 individuals (i.e., 1,000 × 33 generations × 1 run) was sufficient to solve this problem with 99% probability by generation 32.

Table 25.2 summarizes these results.

25.8 TEST OF "MUTATING AND SAVING THE BEST"

The crossover operation recombines parts of two parents chosen on the basis of their fitness. Its use distinguishes genetic algorithms from approaches involving only mutating and saving the best.

How much performance is gained by adding the crossover operation to the operations of fitness-proportionate reproduction and mutation?

Figure 25.15 shows, by generation, the probability of success by generation for 200 runs of the Boolean 6-multiplexer problem with a population of 1,000 (with over-selection) when the crossover operation is deleted and when the crossover operation is performed as usual. When the crossover operation is used at the default rate of 90% along with the fitness-proportionate reproduction operation at the default rate of 10% (established in section 6.9), the

Mutation and FPR vs. Normal GPP Operations

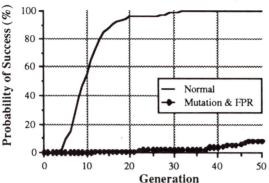

Figure 25.15 Comparison with fitness-proportionate reproduction and crossover (the normal way) versus with only fitness-proportionate reproduction and mutation (i.e., mutation and saving the best).

probability of success after 50 generation is 100% for this problem. However, when the fitness-proportionate reproduction operation is used at a 90% rate and the mutation operation is used at a 10% rate, the probability of success after 50 generations is only 8%. Note that the 8% success rate achieved on generation 50 with only mutation and reproduction is achieved with crossover and fitness-proportionate reproduction on generation 6. In other words, these results suggest that crossover is very important in solving this problem with genetic programming.

25.9 IMPORTANCE OF GENETIC DIVERSITY

In genetic programming (as contrasted with the conventional genetic algorithm) variety remains high even for very small populations. Variety is maintained because of the tree structure of the individuals in the population.

Table 25.3 shows the variety, by generation, in populations of size 10, 25, 50, 100, 200, 400, 800, 1,600 (with over-selection), and 3,200 (with over-selection) for runs of the 6-multiplexer problem.

25.10 EFFECT OF ARGUMENTS IN AUTOMATIC FUNCTION DEFINITIONS

Chapter 21 demonstrated the utility of hierarchical automatic function definition. The question arises as to the effect on performance of varying the number of arguments in the defined functions.

In this experiment, we consider the even-4-parity problem with argument lists of different sizes for two function definitions. In particular, the first defined function takes two dummy arguments (formal parameters) and the second defined function takes three dummy arguments. Since the function definitions

Table 25.3 Variety, by generation, for runs with various population sizes.

Gen					Population				
	10	25	50	100	200	400	800	1600	3200
0	1.0	1.0	1.0	1.0	1.0	1.0	1.0	1.0	1.0
1	0.9	0.96	0.92	0.9	0.88	0.898	0.834	0.768	0.688
2	0.5	0.96	0.82	0.87	0.875	0.885	0.783	0.776	0.691
3	0.5	0.88	0.78	0.88	0.955	0.875	0.837	0.812	0.808
4	0.4	0.84	0.78	0.91	0.87	0.898	0.879	0.894	0.815
5	0.4	0.88	0.78	0.93	0.895	0.91	0.9	0.893	0.815
6	0.4	0.84	0.74	0.96	0.935	0.913	0.92	0.909	0.824
7	0.3	0.88	0.76	0.97	0.93	0.923	0.935	0.919	0.828
8	0.3	0.92	0.7	0.96	0.945	0.918	0.958	0.927	0.844
9	0.6	0.88	0.76	0.93	0.965	0.938	0.938	0.924	0.811
10	0.8	0.88	0.84	0.96	0.945	0.96	0.95	0.924	0.724
11	0.9	0.84	0.82	0.97	0.955	0.963	0.963	0.844	0.792
12	0.8	0.96	0.86	0.97	0.98	0.953	0.949	0.807	0.835
13	0.9	0.92	0.84	0.96	0.985	0.98	0.969	0.831	0.836
14	0.9	0.92	0.84	0.97	0.99	0.96	0.965	0.836	0.832
15	0.8	1.0	0.8	0.94	0.975	0.978	0.951	0.832	0.832
16	1.0	0.92	0.9	0.98	0.975	0.988	0.954	0.879	0.838
17	0.9	0.96	0.86	0.98	0.99	0.965	0.955	0.888	0.835
18	0.9	1.0	0.86	0.98	0.99	0.985	0.958	0.850	0.833
19	1.0	1.0	0.96	0.98	0.985	0.98	0.953	0.867	0.844
20	0.9	0.84	0.94	0.99	0.98	0.99	0.96	0.863	0.843
21	0.7	1.0	0.94	0.96	0.975	0.963	0.965	0.863	0.827
22	0.9	1.0	0.98	0.99	0.98	0.965	0.94	0.874	0.838
23	1.0	1.0	0.94	0.99	0.985	0.97	0.936	0.888	0.832
24	0.9	0.92	0.92	0.99	0.975	0.978	0.931	0.88	0.815
25	1.0	1.0	1.0	0.98	0.975	0.98	0.954	0.864	0.831
26	0.9	0.88	0.96	0.96	0.97	0.973	0.939	0.882	0.818
27	0.8	0.88	0.98	0.97	0.98	0.973	0.908	0.88	0.828
28	0.7	0.96	0.96	0.97	0.985	0.958	0.92	0.876	0.829
29	0.7	0.92	0.92	0.99	0.975	0.945	0.918	0.871	0.832
30	0.6	0.96	0.96	1.0	0.98	0.963	0.92	0.886	0.836
31	0.6	0.96	0.92	0.96	0.98	0.958	0.934	0.896	0.835
32	0.5	1.0	0.92	0.95	0.95	0.968	0.954	0.887	0.829
33	0.4	0.92	0.9	0.99	0.94	0.968	0.946	0.881	0.842
34	0.7	0.92	0.94	0.97	0.945	0.973	0.94	0.892	0.831
35	0.6	0.88	0.92	0.98	0.96	0.98	0.941	0.893	0.837
36	0.7	0.92	0.98	0.94	0.965	0.968	0.946	0.891	0.828
37	0.7	0.88	0.88	0.95	0.965	0.955	0.959	0.895	0.832
38	0.8	0.92	0.96	0.96	0.995	0.98	0.923	0.884	0.835
39	0.6	0.96	0.94	0.98	0.97	0.975	0.955	0.884	0.824
40	0.7	0.96	0.96	0.95	0.955	0.963	0.945	0.871	0.848
41	0.6	0.96	0.94	0.98	0.97	0.975	0.943	0.888	0.837
42	0.5	1.0	0.96	0.96	0.99	0.968	0.944	0.898	0.830
43	0.6	1.0	1.0	0.99	0.98	0.983	0.945	0.888	0.828
44	0.7	1.0	1.0	0.96	0.955	0.965	0.946	0.883	0.823
45	0.6	0.88	0.94	0.96	0.965	0.978	0.945	0.9	0.818
46	0.7	0.92	0.92	0.96	0.95	0.973	0.943	0.882	0.830
47	0.7	0.92	0.98	0.96	0.95	0.958	0.934	0.898	0.84
48	0.8	0.96	1.0	0.97	0.985	0.97	0.941	0.891	0.823
49	0.6	0.92	0.92	0.95	0.97	0.993	0.939	0.897	0.84
50	0.7	0.96	0.98	1.0	0.96	0.97	0.953	0.899	0.836

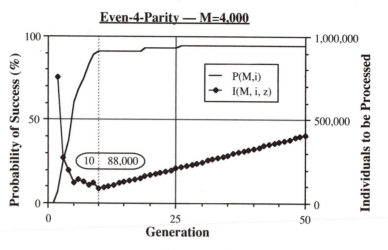

Figure 25.16 Performance curves for the even-4-parity problem with hierarchical automatic function definition.

are hierarchical, the second function definition has access to the first defined function.

Figure 25.16 presents the performance curves with hierarchical automatic function definition with prespecified argument list size for the even-4-parity function showing, by generation, $P(M, i)$ (the cumulative probability of success) and $I(M, i, z)$ (the number of individuals that must be processed to yield, with 99% probability, at least one S-expression producing the correct value for all 16 fitness cases). The graph is based on 56 runs. The population was 4,000 (with over-selection) and the maximum number of generations to be run was 51. The cumulative probability of success $P(M, i)$ is 91% by generation 10 and 95% by generation 50. The numbers in the oval indicate that if this problem is run through to generation 10, processing a total of 88,000 (i.e., 4,000 × 11 generations × 2 runs) individuals is sufficient to yield a solution of this problem with 99% probability.

The number of individuals that must be processed in order to solve this problem (i.e., 88,000) turns out to be identical to the number shown in figure 21.7.

25.11 EFFECT OF LIMITING STRUCTURE-PRESERVING CROSSOVER

In problems where special syntactic rules of construction are used to impose a secondary structure on the S-expressions, the question arises as to whether the crossover point in the second parent in a crossover operation should be limited to a subset of points that is smaller than the largest subset that will guarantee preservation of the integrity of the structure.

Specifically, in the multiple regression problem for complex multiplication (section 19.1), we defined two types of points (namely, the root and all other

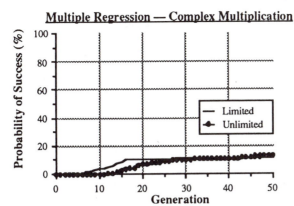

Multiple Regression — Complex Multiplication

Figure 25.17 Comparison of the effect of limiting crossover to the same branch (left or right) in the symbolic multiple regression problem.

points). After the crossover point for the first parent is selected (at random and without restriction), the crossover point of the second parent is limited to a point of the same type. Each individual tree in the multiple regression problem had two branches (a left branch and a right branch) representing the two components of the vector (list) involved.

It might be beneficial to limit a non-root crossover point of the second parent to the left or the right branch. In other words, the left branch of the S-expression under the LIST2 function at the root of the tree would be considered entirely separate from the right branch. In effect, three (rather than two) types of points would be defined: the root, the left branch (i.e., the first component of the vector), and the right branch (i.e., the second component of the vector). If the crossover point of the first parent is on the left branch, then the crossover point for the second parent will be selected from the left branch of the second parent (and similarly, for the right branch).

The rationale for such segregation is that the genetic material that contributes to the solution to each subproblem within a given problem might be inappropriate when inserted into the potential solution of a different subproblem.

Figure 25.17 shows that this segregation does not have a major effect on performance for this problem. The graph is based on 100 runs. Population size was 500. In particular, the probability of success $P(M, i)$ for generation 50 is 12% for the limited case (versus 13% for generation 50 for the unlimited case as shown in this figure and figure 19.2).

When the same comparison is performed on the problem of finding the architecture and the weights for a neural network to perform the one-bit adder problem, there is also slight degradation.

Figure 25.18 shows that the probability of success $P(M, i)$ for generation 50 (based on 100 runs) is 86% for the limited case (versus 95% for the unlimited case as shown in this figure and figure 19.24). Population size was 500.

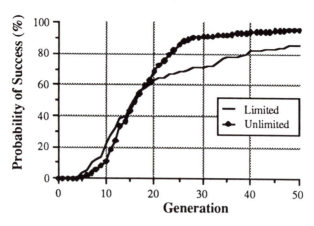

Figure 25.18 Comparison of the effect of limiting crossover to the same branch (left or right) in the neural network problem for the one-bit adder.

25.12 PARSIMONY

Parsimony can be included as a factor in determining the fitness of an S-expression. For example, parsimony was considered in the block stacking problem (section 18.1). In this section, we consider the 6-multiplexer problem using two alternative approaches involving a fitness measure that includes parsimony. In particular, we consider the 6-multiplexer problem with a population of 1,000 (with over-selection) and a function set of $F = \{$AND, OR, IF, NOT$\}$. The performance curves for this problem with this population size and function set were originally presented in figure 25.9, and the oval in that figure shows that processing a total of 33,000 individuals is sufficient to yield a solution of this problem with 99% probability.

In the first approach, standardized fitness is the number of fitness cases (out of 64) for which the S-expression gives the incorrect Boolean value plus the number of points in the S-expression. Thus, among two S-expressions that are 100% correct in performing the 6-multiplexer function, the smaller S-expression will have the better (i.e., smaller) value of standardized fitness.

For example, in one of the successful runs from among a total of 60 runs using this first approach, the following 100%-correct individual containing 13 points emerged on generation 9:

```
(IF A1 (IF A0 D3 D2) (IF A0 D1 (IF A0 D3 D0))).
```

The most parsimonious solution to this problem is an S-expression with ten points. This individual therefore has relatively good parsimony, but not minimal parsimony.

Figure 25.19 presents the performance curves for this first approach showing, by generation, $P(M, i)$ (the cumulative probability of success) and $I(M, i, z)$ (the number of individuals that must be processed to yield, with 99% probability, at least one individual S-expression achieving 64 hits in solving this problem). The graph is based on 60 runs and a population of 1,000. $P(M, i)$ is 38% for generations 14 through 50. The numbers in the oval indicate that if

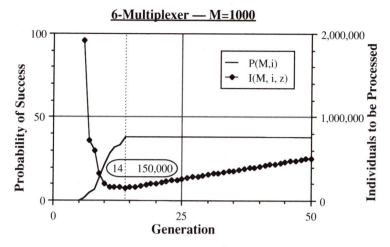

6-Multiplexer — M=1000

Figure 25.19 Performance curves for the 6-multiplexer problem using the first approach to parsimony.

this problem is run through to generation 14, processing a total of 150,000 (i.e., 1,000 × 15 generations × 10 runs) individuals is sufficient to yield a solution of this problem with 99% probability. This is almost five times the 33,000 individuals that must be processed if parsimony is not considered at all.

In the second approach, standardized fitness is the number of fitness cases for which the S-expression gives the incorrect Boolean value for any generation for which the best-of-generation individual from the previous generation scored fewer than 58 out of 64 hits. However, if the best-of-generation individual from the previous generation scored 58 or more hits, then standardized fitness is redefined to be the number of fitness cases for which the S-expression gives the incorrect Boolean value plus the number of points in the S-expression.

For example, in one run using this second approach, the following 100%-correct individual emerged on generation 10:

```
(IF A0 (IF A1 D3 D1) (IF A1 D2 D0)).
```

This individual contains ten points, which is the most parsimonious solution to this problem.

Figure 25.20 presents the performance curves for this second approach. The graph is based on 30 runs and a population of 1,000 (with over-selection). The cumulative probability of success, $P(M, i)$, is 27% for generations 29 through 50. The numbers in the oval indicate that if this problem is run through to generation 8, processing a total of 189,000 (i.e., 1,000 × 9 generations × 21 runs) individuals is sufficient to yield a solution to this problem with 99% probability. This is almost six times the 33,000 individuals that must be processed if parsimony is not considered at all.

As one would expect, when parsimony is included in the fitness measure for this problem, considerably more individuals must be processed in order to

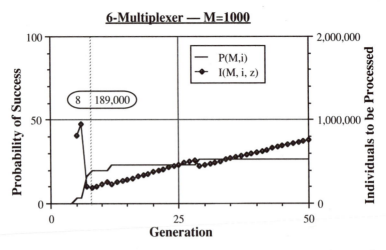

6-Multiplexer — M=1000

Probability of Success (left axis, 0 to 100)
Individuals to be Processed (right axis, 0 to 2,000,000)

Legend:
— P(M,i)
—◆— I(M, i, z)

8 | 189,000

Generation (0 to 50)

Figure 25.20 Performance curves for the 6-multiplexer problem using the second approach to parsimony.

find a 100%-correct and parsimonious solution than when parsimony is not considered.

25.13 EXTENDED RUN OF THE 6-MULTIPLEXER

In every run of genetic programming described above the run was terminated as soon as a recognizable 100%-correct solution was found. However, in nature evolution is a never-ending process. It is instructive to consider what happens when a run is continued past the point where a recognizable solution is first found.

Figure 25.21 shows, by generation, the average standardized fitness for the generation and the standardized fitness of the worst-of-generation individual and the best-of-generation individual for one run of the 6-multiplexer problem that was run for 201 generations. The population size was 500 and the function set was $F = \{\text{AND, OR, IF, NOT}\}$.

At generation 0, the standardized fitness of the best-of-generation individual was 16 (i.e., 16 errors out of 64) and the standardized fitness of the worst-of-generation individual was 43. The average standardized fitness of the population was 30.2 (approximately half of 64).

The standardized fitness of the best-of-generation individual improved to 12, 8, and 7 for generations 10, 20, and 30, respectively. The average standardized fitness of the population improved to 25.4, 20.5, and 12.7 for generations 10, 20, and 30, respectively.

On generation 32, the following 100%-correct individual containing 39 points was found:

```
(IF A1 (IF A0 D3 (AND D2 (IF A0 D3 (OR (IF A1 A1 A0)
D0)))) (IF (NOT A0) (AND (NOT A1) (IF A1 (OR (IF D1 D3
(IF (AND D3 A1) D2 A1)) (OR D3 A1)) D0)) D1)).
```

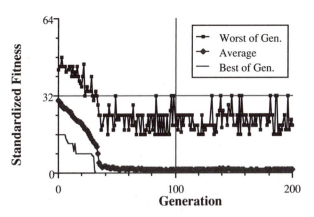

Figure 25.21 Fitness curves for the 6-multiplexer problem for an extended run to 201 generations.

The average standardized fitness of the population improved to 11.95 for generation 32.

At this point, genetic programming had successfully solved the problem. Ordinarily, the termination criterion for this problem would contain a success predicate based on an individual scoring 64 hits and the run would be terminated.

If the run is continued for an additional 168 generations, the average standardized fitness of the population continues to improve as the 100%-correct individual and various equally fit cohorts begin to dominate the population. Average standardized fitness improves to 4.3 for generation 35, 2.7 for generation 40, 2.0 for generation 50, 1.6 for generation 100, 1.58 for generation 150, and 1.2 for generation 200. It stays below 2 after generation 50 and it stays below 1.6 after generation 100. To put it another way, for the last 84% of this run (between generations 32 and 200), the average individual in the population is perfect or nearly perfect.

As one would expect, there is always at least one 100%-correct individual in the population between generations 32 and 200, so the standardized fitness of the best-of-generation individual remains at 0 (a perfect score).

The standardized fitness of the worst-of-generation fluctuates around 24 between generations 32 and 200. This level is better than the average standardized fitness of the population as a whole for generation 0 (i.e., 30.2), and not much worse than the standardized fitness of the best-of-generation individual for generation 0 (i.e., 16). In other words, the worst-of-generation individuals created between generations 32 and 200 are not too bad.

Figure 25.22 shows, by generation, the variety (i.e., percentage of unique individuals) of the population. Variety starts at 100% for generation 0 (since the initial random population contains no duplicates) and stays around 95% for generations 1 to 200.

Whenever a 100%-correct solution to a problem is found by either genetic programming or the conventional genetic algorithm operating on fixed-length character strings, the individuals in the cohort of 100%-correct individuals

Operational Issues

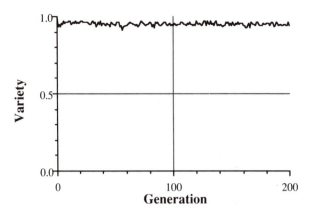

Figure 25.22 Variety curve for the 6-multiplexer problem for an extended run to 201 generations.

have, by definition, the highest value of fitness in the population. Consequently, as the run continues, such individuals tend to be selected for reproduction and copied into the succeeding generations of the population. In fact, because of their high fitness relative to all the other individuals in the population and the use of adjusted fitness, these individuals are fruitful and multiply within the population. This creates a tendency toward convergence of the population to the cohort of dominant individuals.

At the same time, the individuals in the cohort of 100%-correct individuals also tend to be selected for crossover because the parents participating in crossover are selected proportionate to fitness.

In the conventional genetic algorithm operating on fixed-length strings, we usually see a drastic loss of diversity in the population once even one 100%-correct individual is created. The reason is that the operations of reproduction and crossover usually reinforce each other in causing convergence in the population. The reproduction operation, of course, always applies pressure toward convergence to the best individual(s) in the population. In the conventional genetic algorithm, the crossover operation does not counterbalance this pressure toward convergence because the parents participating in crossover are selected proportionate to fitness and when any individual incestuously recombines with itself or an exact copy of itself, the result is two identical offspring. Therefore, crossover does not create diversity at this stage of a run, and the reproduction operation exerts unchecked pressure toward convergence. This pressure toward convergence , of course, exists at all times during the run, not just immediately after a 100%-correct individual is found. Any individual whose fitness is high relative to the other individuals in the population will be selected for reproduction and crossover at a relatively high rate.

Genetic programming differs from the conventional genetic algorithm in that we usually do not see a loss of diversity in the population after a 100%-correct individual is created. The reproduction operation does, of course, exert pressure toward convergence; however, the crossover operation works differently in genetic programming than in the conventional genetic algorithm.

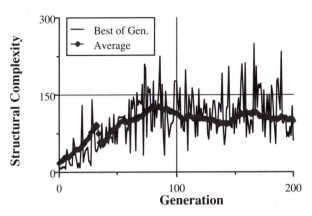

Figure 25.23 Structural complexity curves for the 6-multiplexer problem for an extended run to 201 generations.

When an individual incestuously recombines with itself in genetic programming, the two offspring are usually different from each other and different from their two identical parents. In genetic programming, the two parents participating in crossover are usually of different sizes and shapes. The crossover points are selected independently for each parent in genetic programming. Thus, even if the two parents are identical trees, the crossover points are almost always different, so the resulting offspring are almost always different. For example, if an S-expression containing 50 points incestuously recombines with itself (or a copy of itself), the probability is only 2% that the same point will be selected as the crossover point in both identical parents.

Figures 25.23 shows that the average structural complexity of the population starts at 17.5 for generation 0 and stabilizes in the neighborhood of 110 between generations 50 and 200. Moreover, these very large, very non-parsimonious S-expressions are able to maintain their perfect fitness levels, generation after generation, in spite of the fact that 90% of them participate in crossover at a randomly chosen crossover point on each generation.

Note that this size of 110 is approximately three times the size of the best-of-generation individual from generation 32 of this particular run and eleven times the size of the smallest 10-point S-expression solving the 6-multiplexer problem (cited in subsection 7.4.3). In other words, the population has stabilized to S-expressions which are far larger than is necessary to solve the problem. For example, one of the 100%-correct individuals from generation 200 contains 242 points:

```
(IF A1 (IF A0 D3 D2) (IF A0 (IF A0 (IF (AND A1 D0) (IF A0
(IF (IF D2 A1 A1) (IF (IF (IF A0 (IF A0 (IF A1 D3 D1) D0)
D0) (IF (IF A0 A1 (IF A1 D3 D1)) (IF (IF A0 D3 D2) A1 A1)
(IF A0 (IF D2 A1 D1) D2)) (IF A0 D1 A0)) D3 D1) D1) D2)
D1) (IF A1 (IF (IF (IF (IF A0 (IF (IF (IF A0 (IF A1 (NOT
A0) A0) D0) (OR D0 A0) D1) D3 D1) D0) (IF (IF A0 A1 (IF
A0 (IF A0 A1 (NOT A0)) D0)) (IF A1 (IF (IF A0 A1 A1) D3
```

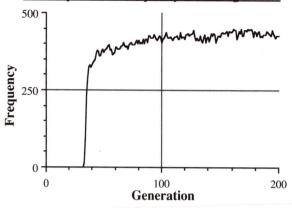

6-Multiplexer — Frequency of scoring 64 hits

Figure 25.24 Number of 100%-correct individuals in the population.

```
D1) (IF D3 D1 (OR A0 D2))) (IF A1 (OR A0 D2) (IF A1 D3
D1))) (IF (IF D2 A1 A1) (IF (IF A0 D3 D2) D3 D1) D1)) (IF
D2 D0 A1) (NOT A0)) A1 (IF (IF A0 (NOT A1) D0) (IF (IF A0
D3 D2) D1 D1) (IF A0 (IF A1 D0 (IF A1 D0 (IF A1 D3 D1)))
A0))) (IF (IF A0 (IF D2 D3 D1) D0) (IF (IF (IF A1 D3 D1)
A0 D0) (IF (IF A1 D2 D0) (IF A0 A1 (IF (OR D2 A0) D3 D1))
(IF (IF A0 D1 D2) D3 (IF A1 (IF A0 D3 D2) (IF A0 (IF A0
(OR A0 D2) (IF A1 (IF A0 (IF A1 A0 D1) (IF A0 D3 D2)) (IF
A0 (IF D2 A1 A0) A0))) D0)))) D1) D0))) D0)).
```

Figure 25.24 shows, by generation, the number of 100%-correct individuals in the population. For example, there are 330, 389, 403, and 427 perfect individuals in the population of 500 for generations 40, 60, 100, and 200, respectively.

For the last 80% of this run (i.e., between generations 41 and 200), the population stabilized so as to primarily contain perfect, though different, highly nonparsimonious individuals.

26 Review of Genetic Programming

As previously mentioned, there are five major steps in preparing to use genetic programming to solve a problem, namely determining

(1) the set of terminals,

(2) the set of functions,

(3) the fitness measure,

(4) the values of the numerical parameters and qualitative variables for controlling the run, and

(5) the criterion for designating a result and terminating a run.

This chapter summarizes and reviews the application of these five major steps. It divides the problems presented in the book into categories relevant to each major step and thereby may provide guidance for the reader's own problems.

26.1 THE TERMINAL SET

The first major step in preparing to use the genetic programming paradigm is to identify the set of terminals that is to be used in the individual computer programs in the population.

Table 26.1 is a summary showing the major types of terminal sets presented in this book. As can be seen, the most common single type of terminal set in this book (constituting the first four categories in the table) contains the independent variables of the problem. The second most common type of terminal set contains the state variables of the system involved. The third most common type of terminal set contains functions with no arguments. In addition, for some problems, the terminals can be class names or input sensors. For the problem of solving an equation for numeric roots and finding a global optimum point in a multi-dimensional search space, the only terminals are ephemeral random constants.

In problems where the terminals correspond to the independent variables of the problem, state variables of the system, or sensors of the system, the terminals can be thought of as the inputs (i.e., information that will be pro-

Table 26.1 Major types of terminals.

Type of terminals	Examples
Floating-point independent variable	Symbolic regression Symbolic regression with constant creation Trigonometric identities Solving a pair of linear equations Empirical discovery Symbolic integration Symbolic differentiation Solving differential equations Solving integral equations Solving general functional equations Solving quadratic equations Inverse kinematics Fourier series Biathlon (symbolic regression)
Integer independent variable	Sequence induction Randomizer
Boolean independent variable	Boolean multiplexer Boolean functions of two and three arguments Design of two-bit adder circuit Neural network design Even-4-parity with automatic function definition
Multiple independent floating-point variables	Symbolic multiple regression Programmatic image compression
State of the system	Cart centering Broom balancing Truck backer upper Differential pursuer-evader game Discrete non-hamstrung squad car game (appendix B) One-dimensional cellular automata Two-dimensional cellular automata
Terminals are functions with no arguments	Artificial ant Central place food foraging Emergent collecting behavior for ants Wall following robot Box moving robot Task prioritization (Pac Man) Biathlon (artificial ant)
Class names	Induction of decision trees Grammar induction Intertwined spirals Discrete 32-outcome game Co-evolution of discrete 32-outcome game
The only terminals are ephemeral random constants	Solving equations for numeric roots Finding a global optimum point
Input sensors	Block stacking
Settable variables in addition to the usual terminals	Iterative summation
Recursive reference to previous computation	Local tracking of a dynamical system
Parameters	Optimization—*Anolis* lizard

cessed) by the as-yet-unwritten computer program that is to be produced by genetic programming. In turn, the value(s) returned by the as-yet-unwritten program constitute the output of the program.

For problems where the terminals represent the primitive actions to be performed, the as-yet-unwritten computer program can be thought of as the program that determines the conditions and the time for executing the primitive actions. In such problems, the program side-effects the state of some system via the execution of the primitive actions.

In general, all terminals can be viewed as functions which can be evaluated without reference to any arguments.

Some consideration should be given to the overall range of values that the terminals in the problem assume. For example, in the problem of the econometric exchange equation, some of the variables assumed values in the trillions and billions while others assumed values in hundreds and hundredths. We scaled the independent variables in the trillions and billions to the range 10^2 to 10^4 by measuring them in billions of dollars, thereby reducing the overall range of values assumed by the terminals.

Constant atoms, if required at all, can enter a problem in three ways. Very simple rational constants are often automatically produced by genetic programming even if no explicit facility has been invoked for the creation of arbitrary random constants. For example, the constant 1.0 may be produced from the division operation and the terminal x via an S-expression such as (% X X). A second source of constants is the constant creation procedure involving the ephemeral random constant atom ℜ (section 10.2). A third source of constants is produced by explicitly including them. For example, one might include π in a particular problem where there is a possibility that this particular constant would be useful. Of course, if one failed to include π in a problem requiring it, genetic programming might well create it (albeit at a certain cost in computational resources) in the manner described in section 10.1.

Whenever the ephemeral random constant ℜ is used in a problem, some consideration should be given to the range of random constants in relation to the known or likely range of other variables in the problem and the granularity of the randomization. The usual range for the ephemeral floating-point random constant is -1.000 to $+1.000$ using a step size of 0.001. But, in the problem of finding the Fourier series, an ephemeral random constant ℜ ranging from -10.000 to $+10.000$ seemed likely to more quickly produce constants of the magnitude needed by the problem. In the neural network problem a range of -2.000 to $+2.000$ seemed better. In the problem of local tracking of a dynamical system, the granularity of random floating-point constants played a role in solving the problem.

In any event, the set of terminals must, of course, be sufficient to express a solution to the problem. Although identifying a sufficient set of terminals is often straightforward, it is, for example, far from obvious what set of terminals should be used in a symbolic regression problem involving the forecasting of gold prices.

26.2 THE FUNCTION SET

The second major step in preparing to use genetic programming is to identify a set of functions. The terminals and functions are the ingredients from which the individual computer programs are composed.

Table 26.2 shows the major types of function sets presented in this book. In dividing the problems into types for this table, the use of the LIST function used to return more than one value (e.g., multiple regression) was ignored. As can be seen, the most common single type of function set in this book involves arithmetic operations (shown in the first four categories). The second most common type of function set involves various testing functions, such as IF and CASE statements. The third most common type of function set involves Boolean functions.

For some problems, the identification of the function set may be simple and straightforward. For real-valued domains, the obvious function set might be the set of four arithmetic operations.

If the problem involves economics (where growth rates and averages often play a role), the function set might also include exponential, logarithmic, and moving-average functions in addition to the four basic arithmetic operations.

It is often useful to include the connective PROGN ("program") form of Common LISP in the function set with a varying number of arguments as "glue" for the as-yet-unknown number of steps that are to be performed.

Some functions may be added to the function set on the speculation that they might facilitate a solution (even though the same result could be obtained without them). For example, one might include a squaring function in certain problems (e.g., broom balancing) even though the same result could be attained from the simple multiplication function (albeit at a cost in computational resources).

Common LISP is lenient as to the typing of variables; however, it does not accommodate all combinations of types that can arise when computer programs are randomly generated and recombined via crossover.

The number of arguments must be specified for each function. In some cases, the number of arguments cannot vary (e.g., the Boolean NOT function). However, in some cases, there is some latitude as to the number of arguments, and one might want to include a particular function in the function set with differing numbers of arguments. For example, including the ordinary multiplication function with three arguments in the function set might, for some problems, facilitate the emergence of certain cross-product terms.

Naturally, to the extent that the function set or the terminal set contains irrelevant or extraneous elements, the efficiency of the discovery process will be reduced or there will be an overfitting of the data with a non-explanatory model.

In any event, the choice of the set of available functions directly affects the character of the solutions that can be obtained. The available functions form the basis for generating potential solutions. For example, when the exponential function (or the SIGMA summation operator) is not available in the function in

Table 26.2 Major types of functions.

Type of Function	Examples
Arithmetic operations	Solving a pair of linear equations Sequence induction Programmatic image compression Differential pursuer-evader game Fourier series Biathlon (artificial ant) Local tracking of a dynamical system Finding a global optimum point
Arithmetic operations plus some transcendental functions	Symbolic regression Trigonometric identities Symbolic regression with constant creation Empirical discovery Symbolic integration Symbolic differentiation Solving differential equations Solving integral equations Solving general functional equations Solving equations for numeric roots Multiple symbolic regression Inverse kinematics
Arithmetic operations plus integer modular functions	Randomizer
Arithmetic operations plus some transcendental functions and/or decision making function	Cart centering Broom balancing Truck backer upper Intertwined spirals Optimization—*Anolis* lizard
Various IF, CASE, and testing functions	Artificial ant Central place food foraging Emergent collecting behavior for ants Wall following robot Box moving robot Discrete non-hamstrung squad car game Induction of decision trees Grammar induction Discrete 32-outcome game Co-evolution of discrete 32-outcome game Biathlon (artificial ant)
Boolean functions	Boolean multiplexer Boolean functions of two and three arguments Design of two-bit adder circuit One-dimensional cellular automata Two-dimensional cellular automata
Complex arithmetic	Solving quadratic equations
Problem specific	Neural network design Task prioritization (Pac Man) Block stacking
Automatically defined functions in addition to usual functions	Even-4-parity with automatic function definition
Assignment function in addition to the usual functions	Iterative summation
Combinations	Biathlon (some of the time)

Table 26.3 Types of wrappers.

Type of wrapper	Examples
Bang-bang force	Cart centering Broom balancing
Saturating value	Truck backer upper
Limited range of integers (i.e., color values)	Programmatic image compression
Binary	Randomizer Intertwined spirals Optimization—*Anolis* lizard
Complex numbers	Solving quadratic equations

a problem for which the solution requires an exponential, the first few polynomial terms of the Taylor series for e^x, in lieu of the missing e^x, may appear in the solution.

Because genetic programming creates S-expressions from functions and terminals that are natural to the problem domain, the value of the S-expression is usually used directly as the output of the computer program. However, in some problems, an S-expression consisting of a composition of the available functions from the function set and the available terminals from the terminal set produces a value that is not of the type desired or not in the range desired for the final output of the program. In that event, a wrapper (output interface) is used.

Table 26.3 shows the problems that use wrappers in this book.

26.3 THE FITNESS MEASURE

The third major step in preparing to use genetic programming is identifying the way of evaluating how good a given computer program is at solving the problem at hand.

Table 26.4 shows the major types of fitness measures presented in this book. As can be seen, the most common single type of fitness measure in this book is the error measure (i.e., the categories labeled "error" and "distance shortfall"). The second most common type of fitness measure is a problem-specific payoff value. Other common types include time, instances correctly identified, entropy, and center of gravity. For several problems, the fitness measure consists of a combination of factors. In co-evolution, the fitness measure is implicit and represents the performance of the individual in an environment consisting of an opposing population. In two problems, we change the environment (i.e., the fitness measure) during the run.

For many problems, the fitness function is the sum, taken over the fitness cases, of the errors between the point in the range space returned by the S-expression for a given set of arguments and the correct point in the range

Table 26.4 Major types of fitness measures.

Type of fitness measure	Examples
Error	Symbolic regression Symbolic regression with constant creation Trigonometric identities Solving a pair of linear equations Boolean multiplexer Boolean functions of two and three arguments Empirical discovery Symbolic integration Symbolic differentiation Solving differential equations Solving integral equations Solving general functional equations Solving equations for numeric roots Sequence induction Programmatic image compression Multiple symbolic regression Solving quadratic equations Fourier series Design of a two-bit adder circuit Neural network design Biathlon (symbolic regression) Local tracking of a dynamical system Finding a global optimum point Even-4-parity with automatic function definition Iterative summation
Distance shortfall	Inverse kinematics Box moving robot Truck backer upper
Problem specific payoff	Artificial ant Block stacking (correct) Discrete 32-outcome game Central place food foraging Task prioritization (Pac Man) Wall following robot Biathlon (artificial ant) Optimization—*Anolis* lizard
Time	Cart centering Broom balancing Differential pursuer-evader game Discrete non-hamstrung squad car game
Instances correctly identified	Induction of decision trees Grammar induction Intertwined spirals
Entropy	Randomizer One-dimensional cellular automata Two-dimensional cellular automata
Center of gravity	Emergent collecting behavior for ants
Combination of factors	Block stacking (correct and efficient) Block stacking (correct, efficient, and parsimonious) Differential equations with initial conditions
Co-Evolution	Co-evolution of discrete 32-outcome game
Changing fitness measure	Biathlon Changing Boolean functions

space for those given arguments. One can compute error using the sum of the absolute value of the distances, the sum of the squares of the distances, or the square root of the sum of the squares of the distances.

For some problems, fitness is not the value actually returned by the individual S-expression in the population, but some number (e.g., elapsed time, total score, cases handled, etc.) indirectly created by the evaluation of the S-expression. For example, in the broom balancing problem, the raw fitness is the average time required by a given S-expression to balance the broom. The goal is to minimize the total time to balance the broom over the fitness cases. In the artificial ant problem, the score is the number of pieces of food which the artificial ant picks up in the allowed time. In the block stacking problem, the real functionality of the functions in an S-expression lies in their side effects on the state of the system. Our interest focuses on the number of fitness cases which the S-expression handles correctly. That is, the goal is to maximize the number of correctly handled cases.

As we have seen in the second and third versions of the block stacking problem (involving efficiency, correctness, and parsimony of the S-expression) and in the differential equations problem (where both the solution curve and satisfaction of the initial conditions were sought), the fitness function can incorporate both correctness and secondary factors. These secondary factors may be phased in during the run.

In any event, it is important that the fitness function return a spectrum of different values that differentiate the performance of individuals in the population. As an extreme example, a fitness function that returns only two values (say, a 1 for a solution and a 0 otherwise) will not provide sufficient information to guide genetic programming. Any solution that is discovered with such an uninformative fitness function may then be essentially an accident. For this reason, Boolean function learning should be conducted with at least three arguments (where raw fitness ranges between 0 and 8), rather than just two arguments (where raw fitness ranges only between 0 and 4 and where many initial random S-expressions attain a score of 3).

Many problems require the construction of a set of fitness cases in order to evaluate fitness. For example, in sequence induction, symbolic regression, and Boolean function learning problems, the fitness cases are simply the value(s) of the independent variable(s) associated with a certain random sampling of possible values of the dependent variable(s). For Boolean problems, it is sometimes possible to use 100% of the combinations of the independent variables as fitness cases. In some problems (e.g., block stacking, broom balancing), the fitness cases represent various initial conditions of the state variables of the system. In some problems (e.g., block stacking), a random sampling or a structured representative sampling can be used to construct the set of fitness cases. In the problems of solving a quadratic equation or a pair of linear equations, the fitness cases consist of random equations.

Table 26.5 shows the major types of fitness cases presented in this book. As can be seen, the most common single method in this book for constructing fitness cases is the random sample of values of independent variables (shown

Table 26.5 Major types of fitness cases.

Type of fitness case	Examples
Random floating-point numbers in a specified range for each independent variable	Symbolic regression Symbolic regression with constant creation Trigonometric identities Symbolic integration Symbolic differentiation Solving differential equations Solving integral equations Solving general functional equations Programmatic image compression Multiple symbolic regression Fourier series Biathlon (symbolic regression) Finding a global optimum point Iterative summation
Consecutive integers as independent variable	Sequence induction Randomizer Local tracking of a dynamical system
Regularly chosen sample points	Intertwined spirals Inverse kinematics
Combinations of Boolean values	Boolean multiplexer Boolean functions of two and three arguments Design of two-bit adder circuit Neural network design Even-4-parity with automatic function definition
Randomly chosen initial conditions of a system	Cart centering Broom balancing Truck backer upper Box moving robot Discrete non-hamstrung squad car game Emergent collecting behavior for ants Differential pursuer-evader game
One fitness case	Artificial ant Biathlon (artificial ant) Central place food foraging Wall following robot Task prioritization (Pac Man) Solving equations for numeric roots
Sets of equations	Solving a pair of linear equations Solving quadratic equations
Temporal sample	One-dimensional cellular automata Two-dimensional cellular automata
Combinations of plays in a game	Discrete 32-outcome game
Co-evolution	Co-evolution of discrete 32-outcome game
Structured sample	Block stacking
Training examples	Induction of decision trees
Sequence of data	Grammar induction
Monte Carlo experiments	Optimization—*Anolis* lizard
Given data	Empirical discovery

Table 26.6 Types of simulations of behavior.

Type of simulations of behavior	Examples
Simulation involving a number of time steps	Cart centering Broom balancing Differential pursuer-evader game Discrete non-hamstrung squad car game Emergent collecting behavior for ants Block stacking Artificial ant Biathlon (some of the time) Central place food foraging
Simulation involving a number of time steps and a terminating physical event	Truck backer upper Box moving robot Wall following robot Task prioritization (Pac Man)
Temporal sample	One-dimensional cellular automata Two-dimensional cellular automata
Simulation involving a number of plays or events	Discrete 32-outcome game Optimization—*Anolis* lizard
Simulation involving co-evolution	Co-evolution of discrete 32-outcome game strategies
Time series	Randomizer

in the first four categories). The second most common method for constructing fitness cases is a random selection of initial conditions of the system. The third most common method is to have only one fitness case for the problem. For some problems, the fitness cases are sets of equations or a temporal sampling. In co-evolution, the fitness cases consist of the opposing population.

In the problems involving simulation of behavior, there are a number of secondary parameters which must be established.

Table 26.6 shows the major types of simulations of behavior presented in this book.

26.4 THE CONTROL PARAMETERS

The fourth major step in preparing to use genetic programming involves selecting the values of certain parameters to control the runs.

The selection of the population size is the most important choice. The population size must be chosen with the complexity of the problem in mind. In general, the larger the population, the better. But the improvement due to a larger population may not be proportional to the increased computational resources required. Some work has been done on the theory of how to optimally select the population size for conventional genetic algorithms oper-

Table 26.7 Population size.

Population sizes	Examples
50	Boolean functions of two and three arguments
100	Discrete non-hamstrung squad car game
300	Co-evolution of discrete 32-outcome game
500	Cart centering Symbolic regression Artificial ant Trigonometric identities Symbolic regression with constant creation Empirical discovery of exchange equation Empirical discovery of Kepler's Law Symbolic integration Symbolic differentiation Solving differential equations Solving integral equations Solving general functional equations Solving equations for numeric roots Sequence induction Broom balancing Central place food foraging Emergent collecting behavior for ants Task prioritization (Pac Man) Box moving robot Randomizer One-dimensional cellular automata Two-dimensional cellular automata Discrete 32-outcome game Induction of decision trees Grammar induction Block stacking Iterative summation Multiple symbolic regression Solving a pair of linear equations Inverse kinematics Neural network design
1,000	Truck backer upper Wall following robot Design of two-bit adder circuit Biathlon Optimization—*Anolis* lizard
2,000	Programmatic image compression Box moving robot Solving quadratic equations Fourier series Local tracking of a dynamical system Finding a global optimum point
4,000	Boolean multiplexer Even-4-parity with automatic function definition
10,000	Intertwined spirals

ating on strings (Goldberg 1989). However, a corresponding theoretical basis for this tradeoff for genetic programming cannot be offered at this time. Thus, selection of the population size is an external decision that must be made by the user.

Table 26.7 shows the various population sizes presented in this book. As can be seen, about two-thirds of the problems in this book use a population size of 500. Note that the population sizes in this table largely reflect historical factors. The choice of population size here should not be construed as a recommended size or an optimal size. When we first started experimenting with genetic programming, we usually used a population size of 300. Then, for a relatively long period of time, we used a population size of 500 on all runs of all problems. We recently started using population sizes larger than 500 for many problems.

There is no reason to think that the selection of the control parameters for runs used in this book are optimal. The intentional decision to use the same parameters on the majority of the problems described in this book resulted in the inefficient use of computational resources for many problems described in this book. The problem of optimally allocating computer resources (particularly population size and number of generations) over runs, the problem of optimally selecting other operational parameters, and the problem of optimally parallelizing runs (e.g., cross migration versus independent isolated runs) are unsolved for genetic methods in general and are important areas for research. The discovery of a theoretical framework for making parameter selections in a optimal way would be most welcome.

The fact that the same (admittedly non-optimal and essentially arbitrary) parameters were used on most or all problems of this book should help focus attention on the fact that a variety of different problems from different areas were handled successfully and that this success did not depend on astute parameter selection.

26.5 TERMINATION AND RESULT DESIGNATION

The fifth major step in preparing to use genetic programming involves specifying the criterion for designating a result and the criterion for terminating a run.

For many problems (e.g., problems where the sum of differences becomes 0 or acceptably close to 0), one can recognize a solution to the problem when one finds it. However, for some problems (such as time-optimal control strategy problems where no analytic solution is known) one cannot necessarily recognize a solution when one sees it (although one can recognize that the current result is better than any previous result or that the current solution is in the neighborhood of some estimate of the solution).

For most problems in this book, we terminate a given run when either the prespecified maximum number of generations has been run or when some other success predicate recognizes that an acceptable result has been found.

Often the success predicate is stated in terms of attainment of the maximum possible number of hits.

We designate the best-so-far individual found in any generation during the run as the result of the genetic programming paradigm. The best-so-far individual is often, but not necessarily, the best-of-generation individual from the generation on which the run terminates.

27 Comparison with Other Paradigms

Readers familiar with certain other adaptive and machine learning paradigms may find it useful to compare the features of genetic programming with the corresponding features of these other paradigms.

In all such paradigms, the goal is to search some space in some adaptive and intelligent way, so that the information gained at one state of the search is used to influence the future direction of the search.

An intelligent and adaptive search through any search space involves starting with one or more structures from the search space, testing performance, and then using the performance information to modify (and, one hopes, improve) the current structure(s) from the search space. The trajectory of the search through the space of possible structures depends on the information gained along the way.

Adaptation involves the changing of some structure so that it performs better in its environment. In this chapter, we compare the following seven adaptive and machine learning paradigms:

- genetic programming,
- the conventional genetic algorithm operating on fixed-length strings,
- simple hill climbing,
- *Evolutionsstrategie*,
- neural networks,
- induction of decision trees for classification, and
- simulated annealing.

Throughout this book, we have considered genetic programming in light of the five major steps for preparing to use it, namely determining

(1) the set of terminals,

(2) the set of functions,

(3) the fitness measure,

(4) the values of the numerical parameters and qualitative variables for controlling the run, and

(5) the criterion for designating a result and terminating a run.

There is a similar set of major preparatory steps associated with each of the other adaptive and machine learning paradigms discussed in this chapter. As we discuss each of the above paradigms other than genetic programming, we will identify the major preparatory steps for using it.

In addition, we consider each of these paradigms in terms of the eight perspectives common to adaptive systems described by Holland (1975):

- the structures that undergo adaptation,
- the initial structures,
- the fitness measure that evaluates the structures,
- the operations that modify the structures,
- the state (memory) of the system at each stage,
- the method for terminating the process,
- the method for designating a result, and
- the parameters that control the process.

In making this comparison, we recognize that each paradigm has numerous variations. The description of each paradigm in terms of the above eight perspectives depends, of course, on which variation is being considered. However, for simplicity, we will consider only a simple "vanilla" version of each paradigm.

When we refer to the conventional genetic algorithm in this chapter, we will be thinking of the genetic algorithm operating on fixed-length strings and the basic three operations of fitness-proportionate reproduction, crossover, and mutation. As we have already discussed, there are numerous other variations of the conventional genetic algorithm. For the conventional genetic algorithm operating on fixed-length strings, there are four major preparatory steps, namely determining

(1) the representation scheme (i.e., the alphabet size K, the chromosome length L, and the mapping between the problem and the chromosome),

(2) the fitness measure,

(3) the parameters and qualitative variables for controlling the algorithm, and

(4) the criterion for terminating a run and the method for designating the result.

Note that, for both the conventional genetic algorithm and genetic programming, the determination of the fitness measure often includes determination of the fitness cases associated with the fitness measure.

When we refer to hill climbing, we are thinking of simple, non-parallel hill climbing where the search is started at a random point, two or more points that are a certain distance from the current point are tested, and the search continues from the best of the tested nearby points. For hill climbing, there are four preparatory steps, namely determining

(1) the representation scheme (i.e., the mapping between the problem and the points in the multi-dimensional search space),

(2) the fitness measure for points in the search space,

(3) the parameters (i.e., the step size and the number of alternative points to be considered before a step is taken) for controlling the algorithm, and

(4) the criterion for terminating a run and the method for designating the result.

When we refer to the *Evolutionsstrategie* (ES) devised by Ingo Rechenberg of the Technical University in Berlin starting in 1964, we are thinking of the two-membered (1 + 1)-ES as described by Back, Hoffmeister, and Schwefel (1991). The *Evolutionsstrategie* starts with one parent (a real-valued vector) and creates one offspring on each generation by adding independent zero-mean normally distributed random numbers to the components of the parental vector. The parent and offspring are compared as to fitness (payoff) and the better of the two is chosen to become the new generation (provided that the offspring does not violate any of the problem specific constraints as to its structure). As the process continues, the standard deviation of the Gaussian mutation operation is changed under the control of step-size control parameters. For the *Evolutionsstrategie*, there are four preparatory steps, namely determining

(1) the representation scheme (i.e., the number of components of the real-valued vector and the mapping between the problem and the components of the vector),

(2) the fitness (payoff) measure,

(3) the parameters for controlling the algorithm, and

(4) the criterion for terminating a run and the method for designating the result.

When we refer to neural networks in this chapter, we will be thinking of a non-recurrent neural network (Rumelhart, Hinton, and Williams 1986). For a neural network, there are ten preparatory steps, namely determining

(1) the architecture of the network (e.g., number of layers, number of processing elements in each layer),

(2) the connectivity of the network (e.g., full or partial connectivity between consecutive layers; whether or not the network is recurrent; what connections from one layer to earlier layers are permitted),

(3) the type of processing element used (e.g., linear threshold processing element, sigmoid processing element),

(4) the training paradigm (e.g., backpropagation),

(5) the inputs to the network,

(6) the outputs of the network,

(7) the training cases to be used,

(8) the error measure,

(9) the values of the numerical parameters for controlling the run (i.e., learning rate for back propagation, average magnitude of initial random weights, etc.), and

(10) the criterion for designating a result and terminating a run (e.g., the criterion for stopping training).

When we refer to induction of decision trees in this chapter, we are thinking of the basic ID3 algorithm (Quinlan 1986) and not any of the many variations, alternatives, and improvements to ID3. For induction of a decision tree using ID3, there are six preparatory steps, namely determining

(1) the set of class names,

(2) the set of attribute-testing functions,

(3) the heuristic entropy-based fitness measure to be used,

(4) the examples (training cases) to be used,

(5) the values of the numerical parameters (e.g., branching factor) for controlling the run, and

(6) the criterion for designating a result and terminating a run.

When we refer to simulated annealing, we are thinking of the basic non-parallel probabilistic optimization technique described by Kirkpatrick, Gelatt, and Vecchi (1983) and not the many subsequent variations on it (Aarts and Korst 1989; van Laarhoven and Aarts 1987; Davis 1987). Simulated annealing starts with a single user-defined domain-specific structure and a user-defined method for modifying a structure. At each time step of the process, the existing structure is tentatively modified using the method of modification and the energy level of the new structure is determined. In defining the modification operator, it is necessary to consider the number of possible neighbors that can be produced by the modifying operation, and it is usually necessary to consider the step size for controlling the distance in the search space between the current structure and possible neighbors that will be produced by the modifying operation. Then the Metropolis algorithm is applied to select one of the two structures to be saved for the next time step. If the energy level of the modification is an improvement, the modification is always accepted. However, if the energy level of the modification is not an improvement, the modification may still be accepted with a certain probability determined by the Boltzmann equation. This probability of acceptance is greater if the energy difference is small and it is greater if the temperature parameter T is high. The process is controlled by an annealing schedule which reduces the temperature parameter T in a specified way as time passes. Thus, in later generations of the process, non-improving modifications will be less likely to be accepted. For simulated annealing, there are four preparatory steps, namely determining

(1) the representation scheme which maps the individual points in the search space of the problem into a structure,

(2) the operation for modifying the structures (including the neighborhood and possibly the step size),

(3) the parameters for controlling the algorithm (e.g., the annealing schedule), and

(4) the criterion for terminating a run and the method for designating the result.

We now consider the seven paradigms in light of Holland's eight perspectives.

Table 27.1 shows a comparison of the structures undergoing adaptation for several adaptive or learning paradigms.

Table 27.2 shows a comparison of the initial structures for several adaptive or learning paradigms.

Table 27.3 shows a comparison of the fitness measures for several adaptive or learning paradigms.

Table 27.4 shows a comparison of the primary operations for modifying the structures for several adaptive or learning paradigms.

Table 27.5 shows a comparison of the state (memory) of the system for several adaptive or learning paradigms.

Table 27.6 shows a comparison of the termination criterion for several adaptive or learning paradigms.

Table 27.7 shows a comparison of the method for result designation for several adaptive or learning paradigms.

Table 27.8 shows a comparison of the parameters for controlling the process for several adaptive or learning paradigms. In the box for genetic programming, we have listed the choices cited above.

Table 27.1 Comparison of structures undergoing adaptation for several adaptive or learning paradigms.

Paradigm	Structure undergoing adaptation
Genetic programming:	Population consisting of hierarchical compositions of functions from the function set and terminals from the terminal set.
Genetic algorithm:	Population consisting of fixed-length character strings.
Hill climbing:	A single point in the search space.
Evolutionsstrategie:	A single point (real-valued vector) in the search space of such vectors.
Neural network:	A single vector of weights in weight space.
Decision tree:	A single rooted, point-labeled, line-labeled decision tree in the space of possible decision trees.
Simulated annealing:	A single domain specific structure in the search space.

Table 27.2 Comparison of initial structures for several adaptive or learning paradigms.

Paradigm	Initial structures
Genetic programming:	A population of randomly created hierarchical compositions of functions from the function set and terminals from the terminal set.
Genetic algorithm:	A population of randomly created fixed-length character strings over the given alphabet.
Hill climbing:	Usually a random initial point in the search space, but possibly a point believed by the user to be a good starting point for the search.
Evolutionsstrategie:	Usually a random initial point (real-valued vector) in the search space, but possibly a point believed by the user to be a good starting point for the search.
Neural network:	For backpropagation, a randomly created initial weight vector consisting of small weights.
Decision tree:	A decision tree consisting of one internal point (i.e., the root) labeled with the single attribute testing function that maximizes the payoff measure.
Simulated annealing:	Either a random initial structure or a structure that already performs fairly well.

Table 27.3 Comparison of fitness measures for several adaptive or learning paradigms.

Paradigm	Fitness measure
Genetic programming:	Normalized fitness.
Genetic algorithm:	Normalized fitness.
Hill climbing:	Fitness (payoff) of a point in the search space.
Evolutionsstrategie:	Fitness (payoff) of a point (real-valued vector) in the search space.
Neural network:	Sum, taken over a number of training examples, of the square of errors between the output signal produced by neural network and the desired output signal.
Decision tree:	Entropy of classification performed by the partially constructed decision tree.
Simulated annealing:	Energy of the current structure.

Table 27.4 Comparison of the operations for modifying the structures for several adaptive or learning paradigms.

Paradigm	Operations for modifying the structures
Genetic programming:	Reproduction and crossover.
Genetic algorithm:	Reproduction, crossover, and occasional mutation.
Hill climbing:	Use gradient information to move away from the current point to the best of the tested nearby points (i.e., move in the direction of steepest slope in the improving direction).
Evolutionsstrategie:	Gaussian mutation operation mutates the one current point (real-valued vector) in the search space to provide a tentative offspring by adding zero-mean normally distributed random numbers to the components of the parental vector. The parent and offspring are compared as to fitness (payoff) and the better of the two is chosen (provided that the offspring does not violate any of the problem specific constraints as to its structure).
Neural network:	Modify the weights in the weight vector using the error measure and the Delta rule.
Decision tree:	For every point in a partially constructed decision tree, entropy is evaluated for every possible way of adding one internal point containing an attribute testing function or by labeling the current point with a class name. The alternative that maximizes the entropy measure is chosen.
Simulated annealing:	A domain-specific method for modifying any existing structure is defined by the user. The result of the modification can be one of several neighboring structures in the search space of possible structures. The existing structure is tentatively modified using the method of modification and its energy level is determined. Then the Metropolis algorithm is applied. If the energy level of the modification is an improvement, the modification is always accepted. If the energy level of the modification is not an improvement, the modification may still be accepted with a certain probability determined by the Boltzmann equation. This probability of acceptance is greater if the energy difference is small and it is greater if the temperature parameter T is high.

Table 27.5 Comparison of the state (memory) of the system for several adaptive or learning paradigms.

Paradigm	State (memory)
Genetic programming:	The population.
Genetic algorithm:	The population.
Hill climbing:	Current single point in the search space.
Evolutionsstrategie:	Current single point in the search space.
Neural network:	The current single weight vector in weight space.
Decision tree:	The current single partially constructed decision tree.
Simulated annealing:	The current single structure.

Table 27.6 Comparison of the termination criteria for several adaptive or learning paradigms.

Paradigm	Termination criterion
Genetic programming:	After a specified number of generations or when some acceptable and recognizable result is obtained.
Genetic algorithm:	After a specified number of generations or when some acceptable and recognizable result is obtained.
Hill climbing:	When no tested nearby alternative point is an improvement over the current point (which may not be the global optimum).
Evolutionsstrategie:	After a specified number of generations or when some acceptable and recognizable result is obtained.
Neural network:	When no further improvement is occurring from the current point in the weight space.
Decision tree:	When no further improvement can occur by replacing endpoints (leaves) of the tree with additional attribute-testing functions.
Simulated annealing:	When no move from the current structure is an improvement and the annealing schedule has been completely executed.

Table 27.7 Comparison of the method for result designation for several adaptive or learning paradigms.

Paradigm	Result designation
Genetic programming:	The best-so-far individual.
Genetic algorithm:	The best-so-far individual.
Hill climbing:	The current point in the search space at the time of termination.
Evolutionsstrategie:	The current point in the search space at the time of termination.
Neural network:	The current weight vector in the weight space at the time of termination.
Decision tree:	The current decision tree at the time of termination.
Simulated annealing:	The current structure at the time of termination.

Table 27.8 Comparison of the control parameters for several adaptive or learning paradigms.

Paradigm	Control parameters
Genetic programming:	*Major parameters* Population size M. Maximum number G of generations to be run. *Minor parameters* Crossover probability p_c. Reproduction probability p_r. Probability p_{ip} of choosing internal points for crossover. Maximum size D_c for S-expressions created during the run. Maximum size D_i for initial random S-expressions. Probability p_m of mutation. Probability p_p of permutation. Frequency f_{ed} of editing. Probability p_{en} of encapsulation. Condition for decimation. Decimation target percentage p_d. *Qualitative variables* Generative method for initial random population. Basic selection method. Spousal selection method. Adjusted fitness usage. Over-Selection usage. Elitist strategy usage.
Genetic algorithm:	Population size M. Maximum number G of generations to be run. Crossover probability p_c. Reproduction probability p_r. Mutation probability p_m. Inversion probability p_i. Basic selection method. Spousal selection method. Adjusted fitness usage. Elitist strategy usage.
Hill climbing:	Step size. Number of alternative points to be considered before a step is taken.
Evolutionsstrategie:	Initial standard deviation for the Gaussian mutation operator. Step size controls for changing the standard deviation for the Gaussian mutation operator.
Neural network:	Number of layers in the neural network. Number of processing elements in each layer. Thresholds of the processing elements. Biases, if any, of the processing elements. Whether the network is feed-forward only or recurrent (and, if it is recurrent, what interconnectivity between layers is permitted).

Table 27.8 (cont.)

Paradigm	Control parameters
	Map of the connectivity allowed between a processing element in one layer and other processing elements in the network. Learning rate (for back propagation). Average magnitude of initial random weights (for back propagation).
Decision tree:	Branching factor.
Simulated annealing:	Annealing schedule for varying the temperature (i.e., decreasing it) over the time steps of the process. The number of possible neighbors that can be produced by the modifying operation. Often, a step size for controlling the distance in the search space between the current structure and possible neighbors that will be produced by the modifying operation.

28 Spontaneous Emergence of Self-Replicating and Evolutionarily Self-Improving Computer Programs

In the conventional genetic algorithm and in all the examples of genetic programming presented so far in this book, the calculation of the fitness measure is an explicit calculation and the individuals in the population are passive. The genetic algorithm measures the fitness of each individual via some explicit calculation and then applies genetic operations to the passive individuals in the population on the basis of that computed fitness. In contrast, in nature, fitness is implicit and the individuals are active. That is, the individuals in the population have the ability to reproduce themselves; the fact that they reproduce means that they are fit.

The practitioner of genetic algorithms may think of the fitness of a biological individual in nature as a numerical quantity reflecting the probability of reproduction weighted by the number of offspring produced (the fecundity); however, this numerical quantity is not explicitly used by the individual or known to the individual. In contrast, in nature, each individual has the capacity for reproduction (either alone or in conjunction with a mate). Individuals act independently without centralized control or direction. If the individual is successful in grappling with its environment, it may survive to the age of reproduction and reproduce.

In nature, the evolutionary process occurs when the following four conditions are satisfied:

- An entity must have the ability to reproduce itself.
- There must be a population of such self-reproducing entities.
- There must be some variety among the population.
- There must be some difference in ability to survive in the environment associated with the variety.

In a population of entities, the presence of some variability that is associated with some difference in the survival rate is almost inevitable. As Charles Darwin observed in *On the Origin of Species by Means of Natural Selection* (1859), "I think it would be a most extraordinary fact if no variation ever had occurred useful to each being's own welfare .... But if variations useful to any organic being do occur, assuredly individuals thus characterised will have the best chance of being preserved in the struggle for life; and from the strong

principle of inheritance they will tend to produce offspring similarly characterised. This principle of preservation, I have called, for the sake of brevity,
Natural Selection." Thus, the first of the above four conditions (the ability to
self-replicate) is, in practice, the crucial one for starting the evolutionary
process.

It is important to note that evolution is not purposive in the sense that it
seeks to reach some predefined goal (Buss 1987). Instead, the survival and
reproduction of individuals in their environment produce, over time, changes
in the genetic makeup of the population.

Although natural selection and evolution are usually thought of in terms of
populations of biological individuals, Edelman (1987) has argued that the
formation of neural pathways in the brain is also the consequence of a
Darwinian process of selection ("neural Darwinism").

This chapter presents an example of a population of computer programs
learning to perform a simple task wherein the individuals in the population are
active (as they are in nature) and where the fitness measure is implicit (as it is
in nature). The essential ingredient for the individuals to be active is that they
have the ability to reproduce themselves (either alone or in conjunction with
a mate). Specifically, this chapter explores the organizational complexity required for a computational structure to engage in three levels of behavior:
asexual reproduction (i.e., self-replicability), sexual reproduction (wherein
parts of two parents genetically recombine to produce a new offspring which
inherit traits from both parents), and evolutionary self-improving behavior
(i.e., learning).

If an individual has the ability to perform or partially perform some task
beyond self-reproduction and if performance or partial performance of that
task increases its probability of survival and reproduction (or increases its
number of offspring), then the processes of natural selection and evolution
exert selective pressure in favor of that individual. Thus, populations of
self-reproducing individual computer programs are able to learn to perform
tasks.

In nature, carbon-based life forms exploit energy available from the environment (primarily the sun) to organize matter available from the environment in
order to survive, reproduce, and evolve. This exploitative and organizational
process operates within the constraints of the rules of physical interaction
governing the matter involved, notably the rules of physical interaction of
atoms of carbon, hydrogen, oxygen, nitrogen, and other elements found in
organic molecules.

The field of artificial life contemplates alternatives to the single carbon-
based paradigm for life found on earth. One such alternative involves computational structures (such as programs within the digital environment of a
computer) that exploit computer time to organize memory in order to survive,
reproduce, and improve themselves (Langton 1989; Langton et al. 1991;
Langton 1991a, 1991b). This exploitative and organizational process operates
within the constraints of the rules of interaction governing the milieu of
computational structures. In this analogy, computer time corresponds to en-

ergy available from the environment and computer memory corresponds to matter available from the environment.

In his 1949 lectures at the University of Illinois, John von Neumann explored the abstract question of what level of organizational complexity is required for self-replication to occur. Von Neumann did not publish his ideas on this subject prior to his death, but Arthur Burks (1970), a colleague of von Neumann, extensively edited and completed many of von Neumann's unfinished manuscripts. Burks states that von Neumann in his 1949 lectures inquired as to "What kind of logical organization is sufficient for an automaton to reproduce itself? This question is not precise and admits to trivial versions as well as interesting ones. Von Neumann ... was not trying to simulate the self-reproduction of a natural system at the level of genetics and biochemistry. He wished to abstract from the natural self-reproduction problem its logical form."

By abstracting out the chemical, biological, and mechanical details of the molecular structures that successfully engage in self-replication, von Neumann was able to highlight the essential requirements for the self-replicability of a structure. In particular, von Neumann demonstrated the possibility of self-replicability of a computational structure by actually designing a self-reproducing automaton consisting of a two-dimensional cellular arrangement containing a large number of individual 29-state automata (Burks 1966, 1970, 1987). The next state of each 29-state automaton was a function of its own current state and the state of its four immediate neighbors (N, E, S, and W).

Von Neumann designed his self-reproducing automaton (estimated to contain at least 40,000 cells) to perform the functions of a universal Turing machine and showed how to embed both his computation-universal automaton and its associated input tape into the two-dimensional cellular space. His computation-universal automaton *a fortiori* was *construction universal* in the sense that it was capable of reading the input tape (composed of cells), interpreting the data on the tape, and constructing the configuration described on the tape in an unoccupied part of the cellular space using a constructing arm. His automaton was also capable of constructing a copy of the tape, attaching the copy to the configuration just constructed, signaling to the configuration that the construction process had finished, and retracting the constructing arm. By putting a description of the constructing automaton itself on the input tape, von Neumann created a self-reproducing automaton (Kampis 1991; Arbib 1966; Myhill 1970; Thatcher 1970; Alvy Ray Smith 1991; Kemeny 1955).

It is important to note that von Neumann's self-reproducing automaton treats the information on the input tape to the Turing machine in two distinct ways (Langton 1983, 1986). First, the information on the input tape is actively interpreted as instructions to be executed by the constructor in order to cause the construction of a particular configuration in a new part of the cellular space. Second, the information on the input tape is interpreted as data which is to be passively copied, in an uninterpreted way, to become the tape of the new machine. In other words, the information on the tape is interpreted both as a program and as data at different stages of the overall process.

Although von Neumann's 1949 lectures predated the discovery by Watson and Crick in 1953 of the self-replicating structure and genetic role of DNA, the dual role of the information found in von Neumann's cellular automaton has a direct analogy in nature. In particular, the process of actively constructing a configuration based on the information contained on the input tape is analogous to the *translation* of the nucleotide bases into a chain of amino acids constituting a protein. And, the process of passively copying the input tape is analogous to the *transcription* of the nucleotide bases of DNA to *messenger ribonucleic acid* (mRNA) or to a complementary strand of DNA (Schuster 1985; Bagley and Farmer 1991).

E. F. Codd (1968) reduced the number of states required for a computationally universal, self-reproducing automaton from 29 to only eight. Codd's self-reproducing automaton occupied about 100,000,000 cells (Hightower 1992; Codd 1992). In the early 1970s, John Devore's self-reproducing automaton simplified Codd's automaton and occupied only about 87,500 cells (Hightower 1992).

Langton (1983) explored the question of whether a major additional simplification could be made in the mechanism for self-replication designed by von Neumann and Codd. In particular, Langton observed that the capability of computational universality found in von Neumann's and Codd's self-reproducing automata is not known to be present in any self-replicating molecules (which may be the building blocks of the earliest and simplest forms of life) or in the biological structure of any known living entity. Langton saw that there is no apparent reason why computational universality is necessary at all for self-replication. In his effort to dramatically simplify the designs of von Neumann and Codd, Langton achieved a substantial reduction in size by abandoning computation universality.

In particular, the coded description of Langton's self-reproducing automaton endlessly circulates in a manner reminiscent of the delay-line storage devices used in early computers. Langton achieved a complete self-reproducing automaton that occupied an area of only 100 cells in its cellular space. Like Codd's and Devore's automata, each cell in Langton's automaton had only eight states. Like the designs of von Neumann, Devore, and Codd, each cell in Langton's automaton communicated only with its four neighbors. A computer simulation of Langton's automaton can be seen on videotape (Langton 1991b).

All of the above self-reproducing cellular automata take advantage of the particular transition function applied to all cells in the cellular space (just as molecular self-replication takes advantage of the particular physical laws governing the molecules involved). If the particular transition function is too powerful, the issue of self-reproduction becomes trivial. Langton's design, like von Neumann's and Codd's, avoided triviality by requiring that the responsibility for construction of the copy be actively directed by instructions residing primarily in the configuration itself. Specifically, Langton's design shared an important characteristic with von Neumann's design, Codd's design, and DNA, namely that the stored information has dual roles and is treated both as instructions to be actively interpreted and executed and as data to be passively copied and attached to the copied automaton.

Ray (1991a, 1991b, 1991c) wrote a clever 80-line self-reproducing computer program in assembly code and demonstrated how his program could evolve over time as a consequence of mutation. A visualization of this work appears as a videotape in Ray 1991d. Ray wrote his program in a special assembly language (Tierra) for a special virtual machine. Ray's virtual machine was *intentionally* imperfect and introduced random mutations to his original 80 line program. Ray observed the emergence, over a period of hundreds of millions of time steps, of an impressive variety of different entities (some self-reproducing, some parasitically self-reproducing, and some not self-repro-ducing) and a dazzling array of biological phenomena including parasitism, defenses against parasitism, hyperparasitism, and social parasitism.

Certain assembly-code instructions have the capability of searching mem-ory backward or forward from their location for the first occurrence of a sequence of consecutive NOP (No-Operation) instructions having a specified sequence of bits in their data fields. The bit pattern used in such searches is called a *template*. As in nature, complementary matching is performed. In writing his self-reproducing program, Ray put a certain identifying four-bit template at the beginning of his program and another identifying template at its end. Ray's program is capable of performing a self-examination to locate these two templates. His program is then able to calculate its own size by subtracting the memory addresses of the two templates discovered by this self-examining search. Ray then wrote a loop in which each instruction be-tween the now-located beginning and now-located end of his program was moved (copied), one instruction at a time, from its location in memory into an unoccupied area of memory. Thus, Ray's program is able to make an exact copy of itself. A special assembly-code instruction MAL ("Memory Allocation") causes the operating system to allocate an unoccupied area of memory to an offspring and a special cell division instruction activates that new area as an independent new entity. Ray's program uses data in the same dual way used by DNA and the designs of von Neumann, Codd, and Langton in that it actively executes its 80 assembly-code instructions as instructions and it passively copies its 80 instructions as data. However, in contrast to DNA and the designs of von Neumann, Codd, and Langton, Ray's program does not use a separate coded description of the entity to be reproduced; instead, it uses the program itself as its own description. Laing (1976, 1977) discusses such automata introspection.

An important design feature of Ray's Tierra system is that it is never necessary to refer to a numerical memory address (either absolute or relative) in the operand of an instruction. Ray achieves this in two ways. First, he avoided numerical memory addresses entirely as the operands of his assembly-code instructions by designing his virtual machine with only four registers, a flag bit, a program counter, and one small stack. Thus, both the operation code of each assembly-code instruction and its associated operand (if any) fit into only five bits. Some of Ray's operation codes occupy three bits while others occupy four bits. For the operations whose operation code occupies three bits, the remaining two bits designate a particular one of four registers to be used in conjunction with the operation. For the operations whose operation code occupies four bits, the remaining bit is a data bit.

Second, Ray's biologically motivated scheme for template matching eliminates the need to refer to a location in memory via a numerical memory address. Specifically, a template consists of consecutive NOP instructions, each with a one-bit data field. A searching template is deemed to have found a match in memory if it finds consecutive NOP instructions whose data bits are complementary to the data bits of the searching template. The search is limited to a specified small bounded area of memory. Thus, it is possible to transfer control (i.e., jump) to a particular location in memory without ever referring to a specific numerical address by searching memory for the nearest occurrence of a matching (i.e., complementary) template. Similarly, a particular location in memory (such as the beginning and end of the program) may be located without ever referring to its specific numerical memory address in the operand of an assembly-code instruction.

Holland's ECHO system (1990, 1992) for exploring evolution in a miniature world of coevolving creatures uses a template-matching scheme similar to Ray's. In Holland's system, a search template (consisting of all or part of a binary string) is deemed to match another binary string if the bits match (starting from, say, the left) for the number of positions they have in common. Skipper (1991) has presented a model of evolution incorporating several of the above features.

Self-reproducing computer programs have been written in FORTRAN, C, LISP, PASCAL, and many other languages (Bratley and Millo 1972; Burger, Brill, and Machi 1980). The usually anonymous authors of computer viruses and worms have written self-reproducing programs that operate within various computers (Dewdney 1985, 1989; Spafford 1991). Programs entered into the Core Wars tournaments typically have self-replicating features (Dewdney 1984, 1987).

All of the above self-reproducing programs have the crucial common feature of creating a copy of a given item at one critical point in their operation. In each instance, they create the copy by exploiting the ability of the milieu in which they are operating to change (in the manner permitted by the rules of interaction of the milieu) the state of some part of the computer memory to a specified desired new state (which is, in each instance, a copy of something). That is, there is an assumption that there is sufficient free energy and free matter available in the milieu to create a copy of a specified thing.

In von Neumann's and Codd's self-reproducing cellular automaton, the copy is created by interpreting the coded description on the tape as instructions which cause the construction, piece by piece, of the new machine in an unoccupied part of the cellular space. The copying actually occurs at the moment when the state of some previously quiescent automaton immediately adjacent to the tip of the constructing arm in the cellular space is changed to the desired new state. This crucial state transition can occur because the rules of the milieu permit it and because there is sufficient free energy and free matter available in the milieu to permit the creation of a copy of the desired thing. The copying is done without depleting or affecting the original coded description in any way. The making of the copy of the description occurs at a time different from the construction of the offspring.

In Langton's self-reproducing cellular automaton, the coded description circulates endlessly in a channel of automata. The channel is much like a race-track in that, for most points along the channel, there is only one automaton that is poised to receive whatever was emitted by its immediately adjacent predecessor in the channel. However, at one particular point in the channel, there are two automata that are poised to receive whatever is emitted by the immediately adjacent predecessor. At this fan-out point in the channel, one copy of the coded description goes off toward an unoccupied part of the cellular space while another copy of the original description continues circulating around the original channel. The copying actually occurs at the moment when the state of the two previously quiescent eight-state automata immediately adjacent to automaton at the fan-out point is changed to the specified new state. This crucial state transition can occur because the rules of the milieu permit it and because there is sufficient free energy and free matter available in the milieu to create a copy of a specified thing (i.e., the copying is done without depleting or affecting the original coded description).

In Ray's self-reproducing program, certain instructions inside an iterative loop make a copy of what the program finds from a self-examination. The program serves as its own description.

Inside the iterative loop, each assembly-code instruction of the program is copied, one by one, from its location in memory into an unoccupied area of memory. Copying occurs when the state of the previously quiescent memory location is changed to the specified new state by the MOVE-INDIRECT instruction. This crucial state transition can occur because the rules of the milieu permit it and because there is sufficient free energy and free matter available in the milieu to create a copy of a specified thing without depleting or affecting that which is copied.

Fontana (1991a, 1991b), Rasmussen, Knudsen, and Feldberg (1991), and Rasmussen et al. (1990) have addressed similar issues.

In nature, an individual strand of DNA is able to replicate itself because there is a plentiful supply of nucleiotide bases available in the milieu to bind (in a complementary manner) to each of the bases of the existing strand. Similarly, messenger RNA (mRNA) can be translated into a string of amino acids (a protein) via the genetic code because there is a plentiful supply of transfer RNA (tRNA) available in the milieu to bind (in a complementary manner) to the codons of the messenger RNA.

Without exception, each of the above self-reproducing computer programs was conceived and written by a human programmer using an impressive amount of ingenuity.

Von Neumann recognized that a certain "minimum number of parts" was a necessary precondition for self-reproduction. He observed that a machine tool that stamps out parts is an example of "an organization which synthesizes something [that is] necessarily more complicated ... than the organization it synthesizes," so that "complication, or [re]productive potentiality in an organization, is degenerative" (Burks 1987). That is, the synthesizer is more complex than that which it synthesizes.

Von Neumann also recognized that living organisms, unlike the machine tool, can produce things as complicated as themselves (via reproduction) and can produce things more complicated than themselves (via evolution). Von Neumann concluded "there is a minimum number of parts below which complication is degenerative, in the sense that if one automaton makes another, the second is less complex than the first, but above which it is possible for an automaton to construct other automata of equal or higher complexity" (Burks 1987).

It would appear that the "minimum number of parts" to which von Neumann referred must be exceedingly large (Dyson 1985; Holland 1976). Certainly von Neumann's self-reproducing automaton had a large number of parts. If the minimum number of parts for a self-reproducing entity is large, that entity is going to be very rare in the space of possible entities of which it is an instance. Therefore, the probability of finding that entity in a random search of that space of possible entities is very small. Accordingly, the probability of spontaneous emergence of that entity is very small.

The self-reproducing programs written by von Neumann, Codd, Langton, and Ray are each just one program from an enormous space of possible computer programs. Finding these programs via any kind of blind random search of the space of possible programs would be very unlikely.

We can get a rough idea of the probability of finding one of their programs in a blind random search if we make four simplifying assumptions. First, suppose that we ignore the milieu itself in making this rough calculation (e.g., the rules of the cellular space or the rules governing the computer and operating system executing the assembly-code instructions). Second, suppose we limit the search to only entities whose size is no larger than the precise size that the human programmer involved actually used. In other words, since Langton's design occupies 100 cells in a cellular space, we consider only entities with 100 or fewer cells. Third, suppose we limit the search to spaces that do not contain any features beyond the minimum set of features actually used by the programmer involved. Fourth, suppose that we ignore all symmetries and equivalences in functionality (i.e., we assume that there is only one such solution).

Von Neumann's 29-state self-reproducing automaton has never been implemented, but has been estimated to occupy approximately 40,000 cells. Therefore, the probability of randomly generating this particular automaton is one in $29^{40,000} \approx 10^{58,496}$ under the above simplifying assumptions.

Since Devore's version of Codd's program occupies 87,500 cells, the probability of randomly generating this particular automaton is one in $8^{87,500} \approx 10^{79,000}$.

Langton's program is much smaller and is known to occupy 100 cells. Therefore, the probability of randomly generating this automaton is one in $8^{100} \approx 10^{91}$.

Ray's handwritten program consists of 80 lines of 5-bit assembly-code instructions. Therefore, the probability of randomly generating this automaton is one in $32^{80} \approx 10^{120}$.

Interestingly, Ray observed the evolution, over hundreds of millions of time steps, of a self-reproducing program consisting of only 22 assembly-code instructions. The probability of randomly generating this evolutionarily optimized self-reproducing program in the Tierra language is one in $32^{22} \approx 10^{33}$.

The five rough calculations above suggest that the probability of creating a self-reproducing computer program at random must be exceedingly small. That is, the probability is very small that a self-reproducing computer entity can spontaneously emerge merely by trying random compositions of the available ingredients (i.e., states of a 29-state or eight-state automaton or assembly-code instructions). The probability of randomly generating Langton's automaton and the 22-line program are the least remote; however, even these probabilities are far too remote to permit spontaneous emergence with available computer resources. For example, even if it were possible to test a billion (10^9) points per second and if a blind random search had been running since the beginning of the universe (i.e., about 15 billion years), it would be possible to have searched only about 10^{27} points.

However, once spontaneous emergence of a self-replicating entity occurs in a particular milieu, the situation changes. As von Neumann recognized, once created, self-reproducing computational structures can not only reproduce, but multiply. He noted, "living organisms are very complicated aggregations of elementary parts, and by any reasonable theory of probability or thermo- dynamics, highly improbable ... [however] if by any peculiar accident there should ever be one of them, from there on the rules of probability do not apply, and there will be many of them, at least if the milieu is reasonable" Von Neumann further noted, "produc[ing] other organisms like themselves ... is [the] normal function [of living organisms]. [T]hey wouldn't exist if they didn't do this, and it's plausible that this is the reason why they abound in the world" (Burks 1987).

Darwin recognized that once a population of different, self-replicating struc- tures has been created, the ones that are fitter in grappling with the problems posed by the environment tend to survive and reproduce at a higher rate. This natural selection causes the evolution of structures that are improvements over previous structures.

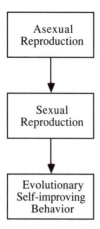

Figure 28.1 Possible sequence of ever more powerful self-reproducing behaviors.

In nature, individuals in the population that do not respond effectively to a particular combination of environmental conditions incur a diminished probability of survival to the age of reproduction. That is, the environment communicates a negative message (in the extreme, immediate death) to unfit entities. If entities in the population have a finite lifetime (which is the case in this chapter), this means that the potential offspring of entities that do not respond effectively to the environment do not become a part of the population for the next generation.

Thus, there is a sequence of ever more powerful behaviors. In this sequence, asexual self-reproducing behavior might first spontaneously emerge; then, sexual self-reproducing behavior might subsequently develop; and finally, evolutionary self-improving behavior might appear.

Figure 28.1 shows this possible sequence of ever more powerful behaviors.

Spontaneous emergence of computational structures capable of complex behavior might occur in a sea of randomly created computer program fragments that interact in a random way. However, the size, complexity, and intricacy of von Neumann's, Codd's, Langton's, and Ray's self-reproducing entities suggests that the organizational complexity required for self-replicability is very high, and, therefore, the possibility of spontaneous emergence of self-replicability (much less sexual reproduction and evolutionary self-improving behavior) is very low.

In the remainder of this chapter, we show that the probability of spontaneous emergence of self-reproducing and self-improving computer programs is much higher than the foregoing discussion would suggest. In fact, we will demonstrate, via three experiments, that spontaneous emergence of self-reproducing and self-improving computer programs is possible with a fast workstation of the type we have been using throughout this book.

The design of the three experiments is severely constrained by considerations of the available computer resources. Accordingly, certain compromises must be made. Each compromise is accompanied by an explanation of the approach that could be pursued if such constraints did not exist.

The set of basic computational operations was selected on the basis of the available computer resources. One of the basic operations permits the incorporation of one entire computer program into another. That is, larger entities can grow via an agglomeration of smaller entities. The basic operations that we chose are not the most elementary, and they do not purport to accurately model the chemical, biological, or mechanical details of the actual organic molecules that carry out asexual reproduction, sexual reproduction, and evolutionary self-improving behavior. However, these basic computational operations perform functions that bear some resemblance to the functions performed by organic molecules in nature, and they perform these functions in a way that bears some resemblance to the way organic molecules perform in nature.

In each of the three experiments, a small set of basic computational operations will provide sufficient complexity to permit the spontaneous emergence of

- self-replicability,
- sexual reproduction, and
- evolutionary self-improving behavior.

28.1 EXPERIMENT 1

The purpose of the first experiment is to establish that spontaneous emergence of self-replicability and evolutionary self-improving behavior is possible within a reasonable amount of time and with available computer resources. For the first experiment, the entities discussed here will be computer programs composed of functions from a function set F_1 and terminals from a terminal set T.

There will be a large population (sea) of these computer programs.

As will be seen, one of the functions (the EMIT) in experiment 1 is relatively powerful. In experiments 2 and 3, we will replace the EMIT function with progressively less powerful and more primitive functions. The progression of the three experiments is designed to convey a feeling for how the magnitude of the blind random search required for spontaneous emergence grows as the operations become less powerful and more primitive.

The terminal set is

```
T = {D0, D1, D2}.
```

The three terminals D0, D1, and D2 can be thought of as sensors of the environment and are variables that can evaluate to either NIL (i.e., false) or something other than NIL (e.g., T = true).

The function set is

```
F₁ = {NOT, SOR, SAND, ADD, EMIT},
```

taking one, two, two, one, and one argument, respectively.

The functions NOT, SOR, and SAND have no side effects.

The function NOT takes one argument and performs an ordinary Boolean negation.

The function SOR ("Strict OR") takes two arguments and performs a Boolean disjunction in a way that combines the behavior of the OR macro from Common LISP and the PROGN special form from Common LISP. In particular, SOR begins by unconditionally evaluating *both* of its arguments in the style of a PROGN function (thereby executing the side effects, if any, of both arguments) and then continues by returning the result of evaluating the first of its two arguments that evaluates to something other than NIL. The function SOR returns NIL if both arguments evaluate to NIL. In contrast, OR in Common LISP does not necessarily execute the side effects of all of its arguments. The OR in Common LISP returns the result of evaluating the first of its arguments that evaluates to something other than NIL, but does not evaluate any remaining argument(s) once it finds an argument that evaluates to something other than NIL.

The function SAND ("Strict AND") takes two arguments and performs a Boolean conjunction in a "strict" manner similar to SOR.

The functions NOT, SOR, and SAND together constitute a computationally complete set of Boolean functions.

The return value of both the EMIT function and the ADD function is the result of evaluating their one argument (i.e., they act as identify functions); however, the real functionality of these two functions lies in their side effects.

As a program circulates in the sea of computer programs, both the EMIT function and the ADD function search the ever-changing sea of programs for a program whose top part matches the top part of the argument subtree of the EMIT or the ADD, much as a freely-moving biological macromolecule seeks other molecules with a receptor site that matches (in a complementary way) its own receptor site. If the search is successful, the EMIT function and the ADD function then perform their specified side effects.

Only a part of the argument subtree of the EMIT function and the ADD function is used in the search; that part is called the *template*. The method of template matching used here is an extension into the space of program trees from the space of the linear bit strings in Holland's ECHO templates and the space of linear strings of assembly-code instructions in Ray's Tierra templates. A control parameter specifies how many points from the argument subtree of the EMIT function and the ADD function are to be used in the comparison with the other programs in the sea. If two points are to be compared (as is the case throughout this chapter), the template consists of the top point of the argument subtree of the EMIT or ADD and the point immediately below the top point on the leftmost branch of the argument subtree. If the argument subtree of an EMIT or ADD contains only one point (i.e., is insufficient), the search fails and no side effect is produced. If there is an EMIT or ADD in the template of an EMIT or ADD, the EMIT or ADD in the template is not executed. Instead, the EMIT or ADD being executed merely uses the EMIT or ADD in the template symbolically in trying to make a match. The points in the argument subtree of an EMIT or ADD other than the two points constituting the template are not relevant to the template matching process in any way. In particular, if there is another EMIT or ADD located farther down the argument subtree, they do not initiate any searching.

This comparison is made only to the top part (the *site*) of the program being searched—which, throughout this chapter, consists of the root of the program tree being searched and the point immediately below the root on the leftmost branch.

The sea (called a *Turing Gas* by Fontana (1991a,b)) is turbulent in the sense that the immediate neighbor of a given program is constantly changing. The search of the sea initiated by an EMIT or ADD begins with the program itself and then proceeds to the other programs in the sea. A template is never allowed to match to itself (i.e., to the argument subtree of the very EMIT or ADD currently being executed). The search of the sea continues until 100% of the programs in the sea have been searched; however, the search could be limited, if desired, to a specified fraction of the sea.

If the template of the ADD function of the program being executed successfully matches the top part of a program in the sea, the ADD function has the side effect of substituting the entire matching program into the program being executed. The entire matching program is inserted in place of the ADD being executed and the entire argument subtree of the ADD (i.e., not just the template part of the argument subtree of the ADD). In other words, the entire matching program is permanently incorporated into the physical structure of the program being executed, so the physical size of the program being executed usually increases as a consequence of the ADD function.

The inserted program is not executed at this time; however, since it has now become part of a larger program, its parts will be executed on the next occasion when the program as a whole is executed.

The ADD function is the basic tool for creating structures capable of more complex behavior. The ADD function operates by agglomerating free-floating material from the sea. In the initial generation of the process, this assembly process involves combining programs that were initially in the sea; however, in later generations, this agglomerative process involves combining programs that are themselves the products of earlier combinations. This agglomerative process thereby creates, over time, large structures that contain a hierarchy of smaller structures. In nature, when the active receptor sites of two freely moving biological molecules match (in a complementary way), a chemical reaction takes place to which both entities contribute. The specific reaction generally would not have taken place had they not come together. Thus, there is some resemblance between the operation of the ADD function here and biological reactions that occur in nature. As will be seen, this physical growth via agglomeration yields a growth in functionality from generation to generation.

The execution of the ADD function is finished as soon as a single match and substitution occurs. If an ADD function cannot find a match, the search fails and the ADD has no side effect.

The number of EMIT and ADD functions in the program being executed generally increases as execution of ADDs incorporate programs into the program being executed. We call these new occurrences of the EMIT or ADD functions *acquired* functions.

If the template of the EMIT function of the program being executed successfully matches the top part of a program in the sea, the EMIT function has the side effect of emitting a copy of the entire matching program into an unoccupied part of the sea. The execution of the EMIT function is finished as soon as a single match and emission occurs. If an EMIT function cannot find a match, the search fails and the function has no side effect. The EMIT function refers to its argument subtree only once. Thus, if there is any occurrence of the EMIT function or the ADD function in the argument subtree of an EMIT, it is not used to initiate a search.

If we had unlimited computer resources, this emission would be unconditionally made directly into the sea of programs (thereby increasing the size of the sea). In practice, this emission is made into a temporary storage area. This temporary storage area is subsequently randomly culled (decimated), so the number of programs in the sea can be kept to a manageable size. The programs that survive the culling are placed into the sea and become the next generation.

Consider the following illustrative S-expression containing 22 points:

```
(SOR (NOT (SOR D2
                (ADD (SAND D0 (SAND D1 D2)))))
      (SAND (SAND D1 D2)
            (SOR (EMIT (SOR (NOT D2) (NOT D1)))
                 D2))).
```

The subtree in boldface is an EMIT function and its argument subtree. The subtree in italics consists of an ADD function and its argument subtree.

As we will shortly see, this first illustrative S-expression was a spontaneously emergent self-replicator.

Figure 28.2 graphically depicts this first S-expression as a rooted, point-labeled tree with ordered branches. The italics and boldface that are used in this figure correspond to the subtrees of the above S-expression that are in italics and boldface.

Suppose that this first S-expression is evaluated for all eight combinations of its three Boolean arguments D2, D1, and D0. Table 28.1 is a truth table showing the return values obtained after evaluating this S-expression for all eight combinations of its three Boolean arguments. Note that both the EMIT function and the ADD function act as identity functions when they are encountered. If we ignore the side effects of the EMIT function and the ADD function, this first S-expression has the behavior of the three-argument Boolean rule 207.

Consider now the side effects caused by the evaluation of the above S-expression.

The function EMIT in the S-expression in figure 28.2 has an argument subtree consisting of five points. The top point of this argument subtree (i.e.,

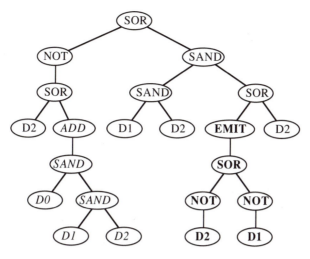

Figure 28.2 First spontaneously emergent self-replicator for experiment 1.

Table 28.1 Truth table for the first S-expression.

	D2	D1	D0	Illustrative S-expression
0	NIL	NIL	NIL	T
1	NIL	NIL	T	T
2	NIL	T	NIL	T
3	NIL	T	T	T
4	T	NIL	NIL	NIL
5	T	NIL	T	NIL
6	T	T	NIL	T
7	T	T	T	T

the function SOR) and the point immediately below SOR on the leftmost branch (i.e., the function NOT) constitute the template for this EMIT function. Each time this S-expression is evaluated, the EMIT searches the sea for a program with a SOR at its root and a NOT as the point immediately below the root in the leftmost branch. As previously mentioned, the search of the sea starts with the program itself. For this particular EMIT function with this particular template (i.e., SOR and NOT), a match is found at its own root. The side effect of the EMIT function for each evaluation of any S-expression is the emission of the entire matching program into the temporary storage area. In this example, the matching program is the whole program, so the evaluation of the EMIT in boldface in this program causes a copy of this entire program to be emitted into the temporary storage area.

If we had unlimited computer resources, we would not include the program itself in the search. Instead, we would rely on the random process that initially produced the program to have also produced a second occurrence of the same program (or a functionally equivalent program). The probability of the creation of two occurrences of a particular program and their discovery of one another is such that a much larger initial population would be required than is the case here.

If the EMIT function had not found a match within itself, it might have found a match somewhere else in the sea; thus, the side effect of the EMIT function would be the emission of some other entire program into the temporary storage area. It is possible for two programs to belong to a group such that an EMIT function in one program will cause another program in the group to be copied into the temporary storage area while an EMIT function in the another program will cause the first program to be so copied.

The function ADD in the first S-expression (figure 28.2) has an argument consisting of five points of which the function SAND and the terminal D0 constitute the template. Each time an S-expression is evaluated, the ADD function searches the sea for a program with the function SAND at its root and the terminal D0 as the point below the root in the leftmost branch. The only match found within this S-expression is with the template of the argument of the very ADD function being executed. Since this kind of match is disallowed, the result is that no match is found within this S-expression. The search therefore continues to the neighbor of this S-expression in the sea.

Suppose that the following S-expression containing 11 points is the immediate neighbor of the first S-expression:

(SAND D0 (SOR (ADD (SAND D1 D1)) (EMIT (SAND D0 D2)))).

If we ignore the side effects of the EMIT function and the ADD function, this second illustrative S-expression has the behavior of the three-argument Boolean rule 168.

Figure 28.3 graphically depicts this second S-expression as a rooted, point-labeled tree with ordered branches.

When the function ADD in the first S-expression is executed, a match occurs between its template consisting of SAND and D0 and this second S-expression. That is, the SAND at the root of the second S-expression and the D0 immediately below the root of the second S-expression match the template (i.e., SAND and D0) of the ADD of the first S-expression. The ADD function in the first S-expression therefore performs the side effect of substituting the second

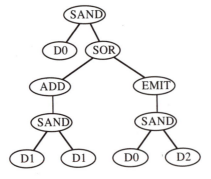

Figure 28.3 Second spontaneously emergent self-replicator for experiment 1.

S-expression into the first S-expression. The six of the 22 points in the first S-expression consisting of the ADD function and its argument subtree are replaced by the second program with 11 points, thereby producing a new program with 27 points.

The resulting 27-point program is shown below, with the inserted subtree of 11 points in boldface:

```
(SOR (NOT (SOR D2
                 (SAND DO (SOR (ADD (SAND D1 D1))
                               (EMIT
                                     (SAND DO D2))))))
          (SAND (SAND D1 D2)
                (SOR (EMIT (SOR (NOT D2) (NOT D1)))
                     D2))).
```

If we ignore the side effects of the EMIT function and the ADD function, the S-expression has the behavior of the three-argument Boolean rule 199.

Figure 28.4 graphically depicts the S-expression resulting after the ADD in the first S-expression from figure 28.2 finds a match at the root of the second S-expression from figure 28.3. The inserted subtree of 11 points is shown in boldface.

The first goal of experiment 1 is to establish that the spontaneous emergence of self-reproducing computer programs is possible with the function set F_1.

We start by randomly creating a population (sea) of computer programs consisting of compositions of the five functions from the function set F_1 and

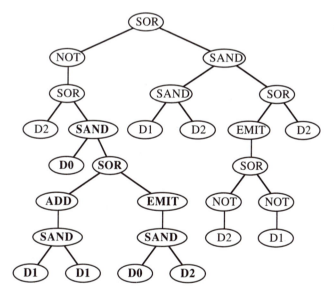

Figure 28.4 S-expression resulting after the ADD in the first S-expression (figure 28.2) finds a match at the root of the second S-expression (figure 28.3) and incorporates the second S-expression into the first S-expression.

the three terminals from the terminal set T described above, using our usual process for creating an initial random population (except that no checking for duplicates was performed). In 50,000 such random compositions, 178 individuals were capable of asexual reproduction, so the probability of creating one via blind random search with the chosen function set F_1 was about one in 281. The discovery of self-replicators verified that spontaneous emergence of self-reproducing computer programs is possible with this function set.

It was, however, immediately apparent that many of the randomly created initial individuals capable of asexual reproduction contained multiple occurrences of the EMIT function and the ADD function. Many occurrences of the ADD function in a program cause the permanent incorporation of the matching program into the program being executed, thereby increasing the size of the program being executed. Multiple occurrences of the ADD function in a program greatly accelerate the rate of this exponential growth process. Moreover, multiple occurrences of the ADD function generally accelerate the rate of acquisition of occurrences of the EMIT function by the program being executed. The combined effect of multiple occurrences of both the ADD and EMIT functions in the initial generation is that the available computer memory is almost immediately exhausted.

We therefore decided to screen the self-replicators so that only less prolific individuals would be included in our sea of programs. If we had unlimited computer resources, we would not need to do this screening. The screening required that a program capable of asexual reproduction contain exactly one executable occurrence of the EMIT function and exactly one executable occurrence of the ADD function. For purposes of this screening, a function is considered executable provided it is not in the argument subtree of an EMIT function or an ADD function. It was, further, necessary to require that the one executable occurrence of the ADD function appear to the left of the one executable occurrence of the EMIT function so that the ADD function would always be executed prior to the EMIT function. The reason is that, if there were only one EMIT function in a program and if it were executed before execution of the ADD function, the emission produced by the EMIT would necessarily always occur before the substitution caused by the ADD. Consequently, the substitution would never be permanently incorporated into the program that proceeds to the temporary storage area and thence into the sea, and it would be impossible to evolve an improvement requiring more than one generation to evolve. Even with this screening of the initial population, the exponential growth of the programs caused by the ADD function and the large number of emissions produced by the EMIT functions kept the entire process on the edge of collapse.

If we impose the initial screening criteria that the self-replicator have at least one executable ADD function (i.e., one with a non-trivial template) and that at least one of the executable ADD functions appears before (i.e., to the left of) at least one of the executable EMIT functions, then there are only 87 self-replicators satisfying these initial screening criteria, so that the probability of finding a screened self-replicator with function set F_1 is about one in 575.

The following three additional criteria make a self-replicator involving F_1 even more suitable for our purposes here. First, there is exactly one executable ADD function. Second, the template of the one executable ADD function must not refer to a program that would never be present in a population of self-replicators (e.g., a program with ADD at its root). Third, there is exactly one executable EMIT function. If we impose these additional three screening criteria involving F_1, then there are only 10 "fully screened" self-replicators in 50,000, so that the probability of finding a fully screened self-replicator with function set F_1 is about one in 5,000.

The two S-expressions shown in figures 28.2 and 28.3 were among the 87 screened self-replicators that were actually discovered in the random search of 50,000. The smallest spontaneously emergent self-replicator for experiment 1 from the 87 screened self-replicators was

```
(SOR (ADD (EMIT D0)) (EMIT (SOR (ADD D2) D0))).
```

It had nine points. Note that the above program has only one executable occurrence of the EMIT function, because the first occurrence of the EMIT function was not executable. As it happens, this particular EMIT was not executable for two different reasons. First, it had a template of insufficient size (i.e., only D0). Second, it was part of the template of the ADD function.

One of the larger of the 87 screened, spontaneously emergent self-replicators was

```
(SAND (ADD (SOR (EMIT (SOR D0 D2)) (EMIT D0))) (NOT (EMIT
(SAND (ADD D2) (ADD (SOR (SAND (ADD D1) (SAND (SOR D2 D0)
(SAND D1 D2))) (ADD (SAND (NOT D0) D2)))))))).
```

It had 31 points.

Therefore, we have demonstrated that spontaneous emergence of self-reproducing computer programs is possible by randomly generating computer programs composed of the five functions from the function set F_1 and the three terminals from the terminal set T. Even with two levels of screening, the probability of finding a self-replicator is a relatively frequent 1 in 5,000 with this function set.

The second goal of experiment 1 is to demonstrate a sequential development of behaviors from self-replication to sexual reproduction and to evolutionary self-improving behavior.

The domain of Boolean functions provides a relatively simple domain in which learning can take place. Since the Boolean functions with only two arguments offer only four combinations of the independent variables and it is relatively easy to find a random Boolean expression to perform correctly for three of the four combinations, we decided to consider only Boolean functions with at least three arguments.

Each program in the sea is an entity which must grapple with its environment. The determination of whether an individual in the population has learned its task is made by evaluating how well it performs the task for all possible situations that it may encounter in the environment. We represent these situations via combinations of the environmental sensors (i.e., inputs to the program). Specifically, the environment consists of all $2^3 = 8$ possible combinations of the three Boolean variables D2, D1, and D0. Each program in the population is evaluated once for each of the eight possible combinations of the environmental sensors D2, D1, and D0. If the program performs correctly (i.e., emulates the behavior of the target Boolean function to be learned) for a particular combination of environmental sensors, its emission, if any, will be admitted into the temporary storage area. If the emission then survives the random culling, it will become part of the sea for the next generation. For example, if an entity emulates a particular target Boolean function for six of the eight possible combinations of the environmental sensors, it has six opportunities to emit items into the temporary storage area (and thence into the sea). In contrast, if an entity emulates the target Boolean function for three of the eight possible combinations, it will have only half as many opportunities to emit items into the temporary storage area. Since culling of the temporary storage area is conducted using a uniform random probability distribution and is not related to performance, the entity that performs better will have a greater chance of having its emissions end up in the sea for the next generation. If the individual entity happens to be a self-replicator, it will emit a copy of itself into the temporary storage area (and thence into the sea) if it successfully performs the unknown task for a particular combination of environmental conditions. A self-replicator that performs the unknown task for six combinations of environmental conditions will have twice the chance of becoming part of the sea for the next generation than a self-replicator that performs the task for only three combinations.

Note that there is no explicit numerical calculation of fitness here. Instead, the entities in the sea are independently acting entities. Each entity is presented with the entire spectrum of possible combinations of environmental sensors. If an entity successfully performs the task for a combination of environmental conditions and the entity is also capable of self-reproduction, it has a chance of being admitted into the next generation. Effectiveness in grappling with the unknown environment (i.e., correct performance of the unknown task) is required for an emission to have a chance to be admitted to the next generation. Since the entities have a finite lifetime (one generational time step in this chapter), the failure of an entity to respond effectively to a combination of environmental conditions means that its emission does not become a part of the population for the next generation. Thus, continued viability in the population requires both the ability to self-reproduce (exactly, approximately, mutually, or with changes due to agglomeration) and the ability to grapple effectively with the environment. Thus, in the context of these self-replicating entities in this sea, natural selection operates on individuals in the population that are more or less successful in grappling with their environment.

Because the sea is constantly changing, the neighbor of a given program changes as each combination of the environmental sensors is presented to each program for testing.

If we had unlimited computer resources, we would allow 100% of the emissions to move from the temporary storage area into the sea for any combination of environmental sensors for which the program emulates the target function. However, since our computer resources are limited and we intend to present each computer program in the sea with all combinations of its environmental sensors, we need to randomly cull these emissions. In particular, only 30% of the emissions coming from programs that correctly emulate the behavior of the target function to be learned for a particular combination of environmental sensors are actually admitted to the sea from the temporary storage area.

When the template size is specified to be 2, when the function set has five functions, and when the terminal set has three terminals (as is the case here), there are 40 (i.e., 5×8) possible templates. Since the neighbor of a given program changes as each different combination of environmental sensors is presented to a program, it is desirable that the sea contain at least as many possible matches as there are combinations of its environmental sensors (i.e., eight) for the typical template, and preferably more. This suggests a population somewhat larger than 320. In fact, we settled on a population size of 500.

If the population is to consist of about 500 individuals capable of emission and if a randomly created computer program emulates the performance of a target three-argument Boolean function for about half of the eight possible combinations of the three environmental sensors, then there will be about 2,000 emissions as a result of testing 500 individuals as to their ability to grapple with their environment. If the programs in the sea improve so that after a few generations the typical program emulates the performance of a target three-argument Boolean function for about six of the eight possible combinations of environmental sensors, then, the number of emissions rises to about 3,000. These emissions are randomly culled so as to leave only 30% of their original number on each generation.

In addition, programs generally acquire additional occurrences of the EMIT function when an ADD function makes a substitution, thereby causing the number of occurrences of acquired EMIT functions to increase rapidly. These occurrences of acquired functions are identified with the suffix ACQ herein. The templates of these acquired EMIT functions are rarely helpful or relevant to self-replication. If we had unlimited computer resources, we could retain all of these acquired EMIT functions. In practice, we heavily cull the emissions produced by these acquired EMIT functions so that only 0.01% of the emissions from programs that correctly emulate the behavior of the target function are admitted to the sea from the temporary storage area.

The population is monitored with the goal of maintaining it at 500. The culling percentages selected for this problem are intended to initially yield somewhat more than 500 emissions. If the number of emissions after this culling is still above 500, the remaining emissions are randomly culled again so that no more than 500 emissions are placed into the sea. Occasionally, the sea contains fewer than 500 programs. If we had unlimited computer resources, there would be no need to carefully control the size of the population in this way.

The programs that are in the sea in one generation of the population do not automatically get into the next generation. The only way to get into the new generation is via an EMIT function. Self-replicators, of course, have at least one EMIT function that is capable of copying the program into the temporary storage area. In addition, getting into the next generation requires correctly emulating the performance of a target three-argument Boolean function for one or more combinations of the environmental sensors. Fitter programs successfully emulate the target function for more combinations of the environmental sensors and therefore are more likely to appear in the next generation.

The ADD function bears some resemblance to the crossover (recombination) operation of genetic programming. The two operations are similar in that they permanently incorporate a program tree from one program into another program. They differ in four ways. First, the ADD function here produces only one offspring. Second, the sea changes as each new combination of environmental sensors is considered, so the matching program is generally not constant between fitness cases. Third, there is no random selection of a crossover point within the program; the entire matching program is always inserted into the program being executed. Fourth, the incorporation of genetic material into the program is initiated from inside the program itself. The program being executed is active, and its code causes the incorporation of genetic material into itself and causes the reproduction of the program into the next generation.

Computer memory as well as computer time was limited for our experiments. The initial sea containing the desired 500 fully screened self-replicators for a run contains perhaps 2,499,500 programs that were not fully screened self-replicators. Note that programs that are not even self-replicators may nevertheless contain numerous occurrences of the EMIT function and may produce numerous emissions. Since we did not have sufficient memory to handle these 2,499,500 other programs, much less their emissions, and we did not have sufficient computer time to execute 4,999 useless programs for each potentially interesting program, we started each run of this experiment with 500 fully screened individuals.

In implementing the ADD function, the COPY-TREE function is used to make a copy of both the matching program and the program being executed. Only a copy of the matching program is permanently incorporated into a copy of the program being executed, thus permitting the unchanged original program to be exposed to all possible combinations of its environmental sensors within the current generation and permitting the matching program to interact more than once with the program being executed on the current generation. If we had unlimited computer resources, the sea could be sufficiently large and rich to permit a matching program to be devoured by the program into which it is incorporated. In that event, essentially the same process would occur progressively over many generations, thereby producing some extraordinarily large programs.

We made the following choices for the values of the control parameters for the problem of demonstrating evolutionary self-improving behavior:

- an initial population of 500
- full screening of generation 0
- deletion of all clutter from generation 0
- 100% of the programs in the sea are searched.
- The EMIT and ADD functions search the current individual first.
- culling of emissions from ordinary EMIT functions to 30%
- culling of emissions from acquired EMIT functions to 0.01%.

Even with both types of culling mentioned above and the full screening of generation 0 from 15,000,000 to 500, our experience is that the growth in the physical size of the programs and the growth in emissions is such that the process can be run for only about six generations. Therefore, it is necessary to find a task that can be learned in fewer than six generations with an initial population of size 500, but which is not so simple that it is likely to be produced at random.

Table 9.3 indicated that among the three-argument Boolean functions generated at random using the function set {AND, OR, NAND, NOR}, rule 235 (appearing on row 40) lies roughly in the middle of all three-argument Boolean functions in difficulty of discovery. Rule 235 is equivalent to

(OR (EQV D2 D1) D0),

and is a moderately difficult rule to learn because it contains an even-2-parity function. When we retested rule 235 with the function set F_1, we found that it has a probability of about one in 18,461 of being generated at random. This means the processing of 86,562 individuals is sufficient to yield a random S-expression realizing rule 235 with 99% probability. If the population size were 500 and runs were to be limited to about six generations, it would be very unlikely to encounter a solution to rule 235 merely as a consequence of blind random search on any one run. We therefore decided to use rule 235 as the target function to be learned in this experiment.

Table 28.2 shows the truth table for the three-argument Boolean rule 235.

Table 28.2 Truth table for the three-argument Boolean rule 235.

	D2	D1	D0	Rule 235
0	NIL	NIL	NIL	T
1	NIL	NIL	T	T
2	NIL	T	NIL	NIL
3	NIL	T	T	T
4	T	NIL	NIL	NIL
5	T	NIL	T	T
6	T	T	NIL	T
7	T	T	T	T

As was seen above, finding 500 fully screened self-replicators via blind random search for an initial random population would require processing about 2,500,000 individuals (which takes about a week of computer time). Moreover, since numerous separate runs would be required, many different initial random populations of 500 replicators would be necessary. Even if a single pool of, say, 3,000 replicators were used (with a different random drawing of 500 individuals being made for each particular run), 90,000,000 individuals would still have to be processed to yield the desired pool of 3,000. Both of these approaches are impractical for experiment 1 and totally prohibitive for experiments 2 and 3 (where the probability of finding a fully screened self-replicator rises to 1 in 6,250,000).

The spontaneous emergence of 178 self-replicators, the 87 screened self-replicators, and 10 fully screened self-replicators out of 50,000 randomly generated individuals with the chosen function set F_1 already established that the spontaneous emergence of self-reproducing computer programs is possible. Finding additional self-replicators is merely a matter of computer time. Since the goal now is to perform experiments involving the emergence of evolutionary self-improving behavior, we decided to synthesize a pool of 3,000 self-replicators modeled after the fully screened self-replicators that were actually discovered. In synthesizing the pool of 3,000, we made certain that it contained a wide variety of different sizes and shapes representative of the sizes and shapes of the self-replicators that were actually discovered. No duplicate checking was done.

We now discuss one particular run.

One of the individuals in generation 0 of our sea of programs was the following S-expression containing 22 points, which is equivalent to the three-argument Boolean function 254:

```
(SAND   (ADD (SOR (SOR (SOR D0 D1) (SOR D2 D0))
D2)) (NOT (EMIT (SAND (ADD D0) (SAND (NOT D0) (SAND D0
D0)))))).
```

The ADD subtree in this S-expression is shown in boldface and consists of SOR and SOR. Figure 28.5 graphically depicts this 22-point S-expression.

The first neighbor in the sea in generation 0 that matched the ADD function with a template of SOR and SOR was the following S-expression containing 22 points, which is equivalent to the three-argument rule 252:

```
(SOR (SOR (ADD (NOT (NOT D1))) (EMIT (SOR (SOR D2 D1)
(SOR D2 (SOR (EMIT (ADD (SAND (EMIT D0) D1))) D2)))))
D2).
```

The root of this S-expression is SOR and the point immediately below and to the left of the root is SOR. Both are shown in boldface. Figure 28.6 graphically depicts this S-expression.

The side effect of the execution of the ADD function in the 22-point individual performing rule 254 from figure 28.5 is the incorporation of the 22-point individual performing rule 252 shown in figure 28.6. The following 34-point

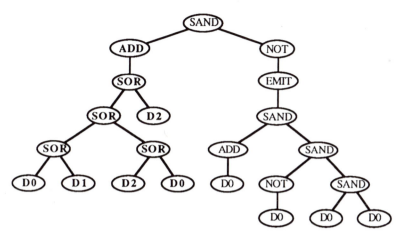

Figure 28.5 22-point self-replicator performing rule 254 from generation 0 whose ADD template consists of SOR and SOR for experiment 1.

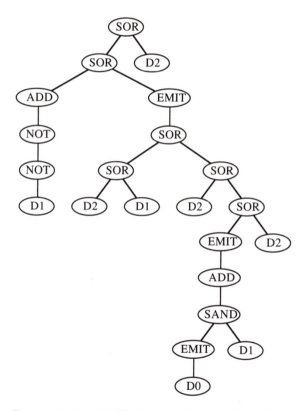

Figure 28.6 22-point self-replicator performing rule 252 from generation 0 with SOR at its root and with SOR immediately below and to the left of the root for experiment 1.

Spontaneous Emergence of Programs

individual performing rule 252 is created and placed into the temporary storage area:

```
(SAND (SOR (SOR (ADD (NOT (NOT D1))) (EMIT (SOR
(SOR D2 D1) (SOR D2 (SOR (EMIT (ADD (SAND (EMIT
D0) D1))) D2))))) D2) (NOT (EMIT (SAND (ADD D0) (SAND
(NOT D0) (SAND D0 D0)))))).
```

The subtree that was inserted by the ADD function is shown in boldface in the above S-expression. Note that this 34-point S-expression has SAND at its root and SOR immediately below and to the left of the root.

In this run, this 34-point individual survives the random culling in the temporary storage area and eventually enters the sea and becomes part of generation 1. Figure 28.7 graphically depicts this 34-point S-expression.

Another of the individuals in generation 0 of our sea of programs was the following S-expression containing 19 points, which is equivalent to the three-argument Boolean function 251:

```
(SOR (SOR (ADD (SOR (NOT D1) (NOT D1)))
         (SAND D2 D1))
     (SAND (EMIT (SOR (SOR D1 D0) D0)) D0)).
```

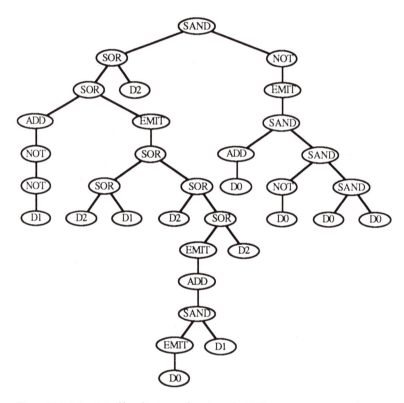

Figure 28.7 34-point self-replicator performing rule 252 from generation 1 with SAND at its root and with SOR immediately below and to the left of the root for experiment 1.

Note that the ADD function in this S-expression and its argument subtree are shown in boldface and that the template of the ADD function consists of SOR and NOT.

The first neighbor in the sea that matched the above individual in generation 0 was the following S-expression containing 38 points, which is equivalent to the three-argument rule 243:

```
(SOR (NOT (ADD (SAND (SOR D1 D0) D1))) (SAND (SAND D1
D2) (EMIT (SOR (NOT (NOT (ADD (SAND (NOT (NOT (ADD (EMIT
(SOR (SAND D2 D1) D2))))) (ADD (SAND D0 D0)))))) (SOR
(SOR 1 (NOT D0)) (NOT D1)))))).
```

The root and the point immediately below and to the left of the root consist of SOR and NOT, which are shown in boldface above.

The side effect of the execution of the ADD function in the individual equivalent to rule 251 is the following individual, which contains 51 points and is equivalent to the three-argument rule 251:

```
(SOR (SOR (SOR (NOT (ADD (SAND (SOR D1 D0) D1)))
(SAND (SAND D1 D2) (EMIT (SOR (NOT (NOT (ADD
(SAND (NOT (NOT (ADD (EMIT (SOR (SAND D2 D1)
D2))))) (ADD (SAND D0 D0)))))) (SOR (SOR D1 (NOT
D0)) (NOT D1)))))) (SAND D2 D1)) (SAND (EMIT (SOR (SOR
D1 D0) D0)) D0)).
```

This individual is placed into the temporary storage area. The subtree that was inserted by the ADD function is shown in boldface in the above S-expression. Note that this 51-point S-expression contains an ADD as the fifth point on the top line and that the template consists of SAND and SOR.

In this run, this 51-point individual survives the random culling in the temporary storage area and eventually enters the sea and becomes part of generation 1.

When the above 51-point individual was evaluated during generation 1, it encountered the 34-point individual (which has SAND at its root and SOR immediately below and to the left of the root) as a neighbor. Therefore, the ADD template on the first line of the above 51-point S-expression matched the 34-point neighbor. The side effect of the match is that the following individual containing 79 points, which is equivalent to the three-argument rule 235, was created:

```
(SOR (SOR (SOR (NOT (SAND (SOR (SOR (ADD (NOT (NOT
D1))) EMIT (SOR (SOR D2 D1) (SOR D2 (SOR (EMIT
(ADD (SAND (EMIT D0) D1))) D2))))) D2) (NOT
(EMIT (SAND (ADD D0) (SAND (NOT D0) (SAND D0
D0)))))))) (SAND (SAND D1 D2) (EMIT (SOR (NOT (NOT (ADD
(SAND (NOT (NOT (ADD (EMIT (SOR (SAND D2 D1) D2))))) (ADD
(SAND D0 D0)))))) (SOR (SOR D1 (NOT D0)) (NOT D1))))))
(SAND D2 D1)) (SAND (EMIT (SOR (SOR D1 D0) D0)) D0)).
```

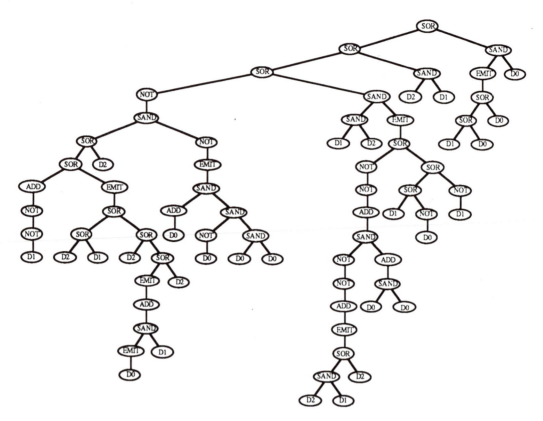

Figure 28.8 79-point self-replicator performing rule 235 in generation 2 for experiment 1.

The 34-point subtree that was inserted by the ADD function at the fifth point of the top line of the 51-point tree is shown in boldface in the above S-expression.

This 79-point individual performing three-argument Boolean rule 235 eventually enters the sea for generation 2.

Figure 28.8 graphically depicts this 79-point S-expression.

Figure 28.9 is a genealogical tree showing the four grandparents from generation 0, the two parents from generation 1, and the offspring 79-point individual performing rule 235 in generation 2 from figure 28.8. The 22-point grandparent performing rule 254 comes from figure 28.5. The 22-point grandparent performing rule 252 comes from figure 28.6. The 34-point parent performing rule 252 comes from figure 28.7.

Figure 28.10 shows, by generation, the progressive improvement for the run in which the 79-point self-replicator performing rule 235 was found in generation 2. It shows the average standardized fitness of the population as a whole and the value of standardized fitness for the best-of-generation individual and the worst-of-generation individual.

Figure 28.11 shows, by generation, the average structural complexity (i.e., total number of functions and terminals) of the population as a whole and the

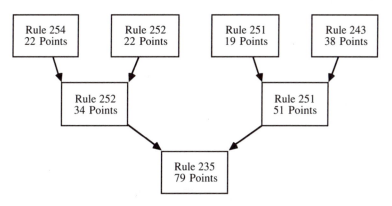

Figure 28.9 Genealogical tree for the 79-point self-replicator performing rule 235 in generation 2 for experiment 1.

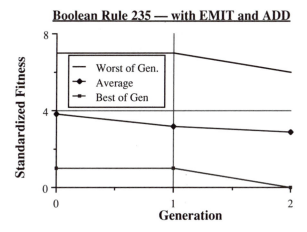

Figure 28.10 Fitness curves for experiment 1.

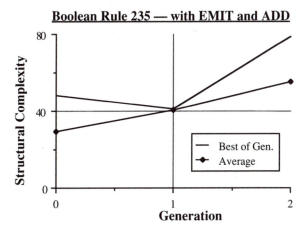

Figure 28.11 Structural complexity curves for experiment 1.

Spontaneous Emergence of Programs

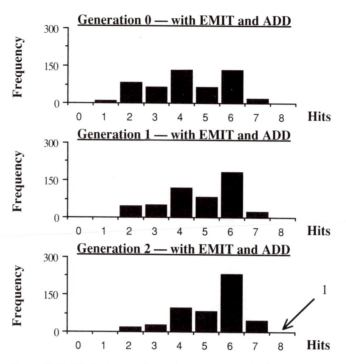

Figure 28.12 Hits histograms for generations 0, 1, and 2 for experiment 1.

values of structural complexity for the best-of-generation individual. Because of the way that the ADD function incorporates entire individuals in the population within existing individuals, structural complexity rises very rapidly.

Figure 28.12 shows the hits histograms for generations 0, 1, and 2 of this run. One can see that the population as a whole has improved over even the small number of generations shown. The arrow points to the one individual scoring 8 hits on generation 2.

Figure 28.13 presents the performance curves (as discussed in detail in chapter 9) showing, by generation, the cumulative probability of success $P(M, i)$ and the number of individuals that must be processed $I(M, i, z)$ to yield, with 99% probability, at least one S-expression producing the correct value of rule 235 for all eight fitness cases. The graph is based on 35 runs. The population was 500 and the maximum number of generations to be run was 4. The cumulative probability of success, $P(M, i)$, is 34% by generation 2 and 37% by generation 4. The numbers in the oval indicate that if this problem is run through to generation 2, processing a total of 16,500 (i.e., 500 × 3 generations × 11 runs) individuals is sufficient to yield a solution of this problem with 99% probability.

The 16,500 individuals to be processed here is considerably smaller than the 86,562 individuals required in a blind random search for a solution to rule 235. It is interesting that rule 235 can be learned with this agglomerative ADD function rather than the usual crossover operation.

Boolean Rule 235 — with EMIT and ADD

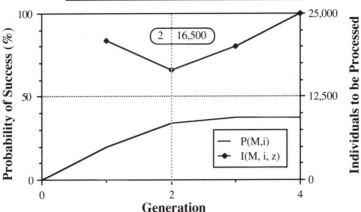

Figure 28.13 Performance curves show that 16,500 individuals must be processed to yield a solution to the problem of learning rule 235 for experiment 1.

28.2 EXPERIMENT 2

The EMIT function defined for experiment 1 was sufficiently powerful to permit testing of the question as to whether the behaviors of self-replication, sexual reproduction, and evolutionary self-improving behavior could spontaneously emerge from a sea of random compositions of basic computational operations. In this experiment, the EMIT function is unbundled and replaced with two functions that are more primitive: a one-argument SST ("Search Sea for Template") function and a one-argument DUMET ("Do Until MATCHED-TREE Equals «TRAILING-TEMPLATE»") function.

The terminal set is the same as before.

The function set for experiment 2 contains six functions and is

$$F_2 = \{NOT, SOR, SAND, ADD, SST, DUMET\},$$

taking one, two, two, one, one, and one argument, respectively. The functions ADD, NOT, SOR, and SAND are the same as before.

The real significance of the two new functions lies in their side effects; however, they each have return values. The SST and DUMET functions each return the result of evaluating the one argument (i.e., each acts as an identity function).

Two global variables are used in conjunction with the new SST and DUMET functions for each program: MATCHED-TREE and OPEN-SPACE. Each is initially NIL when evaluation of a given program begins.

As a program circulates in the ever-changing sea of computer programs, the SST function ("Search Sea for Template") searches the sea of programs for a program whose top part matches the top part of the argument subtree of the SST function (i.e., a template consisting of two points). When an SST function finds a match, the global variable MATCHED-TREE is bound to the entire matching program.

Spontaneous Emergence of Programs

The new one-argument iterative operator DUMET ("Do Until MATCHED-TREE Equals «TRAILING-TEMPLATE»") iteratively traverses MATCHED-TREE and copies it, one point at a time, to OPEN-SPACE until the «TRAILING-TEMPLATE» argument of the DUMET matches the entire remaining contents of MATCHED-TREE. If DUMET fails to find a subtree that matches «TRAILING-TEMPLATE» while it is traversing MATCHED-TREE, the contents of OPEN-SPACE are discarded. If the tree placed into the OPEN-SPACE is not syntactically valid, the contents of OPEN-SPACE are discarded. Upon completion of the DUMET, the contents of OPEN-SPACE are transferred to the temporary storage area (and thence into the sea).

If there is an occurrence of an SST or ADD function in the argument subtree of an SST or ADD, the inner function is never used to perform a search; the outer function merely uses it in trying to make a match.

As one would expect, finding a self-replicator via random search is considerably more difficult with function set F_2 than with F_1.

We found 310 self-replicators in a random search of 350,000 so that the probability of finding a self-replicator with function set F_2 is about one in 1,129. However, if we impose the initial screening criteria that the self-replicator have at least one executable ADD function (i.e., one with a non-trivial template), that at least one of the executable ADD functions appears before (i.e., to the left of) at least one of the executable DUMET functions, that the self-replicator have at least one executable SST function, and that at least one of the executable SST functions appears before at least one of the executable DUMET functions, then there are only nine self-replicators satisfying these initial screening criteria, so that the probability of finding a screened self-replicator with function set F_2 is about one in 38,339.

The following two additional criteria make a self-replicator involving F_2 even more suitable for our purposes here. First, there is exactly one executable ADD, SST, and DUMET function. Second, the template of the one executable ADD and SST functions must not refer to a program that would never be present in a population of self-replicators. If we impose these additional two screening criteria involving F_2, then there is only one fully screened self-replicator in 350,000, so that the probability of finding a fully screened self-replicator with function set F_2 is about one in 350,000.

The one fully screened self-replicator that was actually discovered in the random search of 350,000 for experiment 2 was

```
(SOR (SOR (SAND (ADD (SOR D2 D1))
                (NOT (SST D2)))
          (SST (SOR (SOR D1 D1) (NOT D1))))
     (DUMET (SAND (DUMET (NOT D0))
                  (NOT (SOR D1 D1))))))
```

This individual has 26 points and performs the three-argument Boolean rule 255 (Always True).

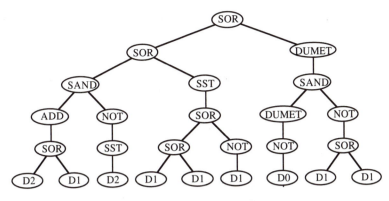

Figure 28.14 Spontaneously emergent self-replicator for experiment 2.

The italicized portion of this S-expression contains an executable ADD function with a template consisting of SOR and D2. Note that the SST function on the second line is not executable since its template is too small.

The underlined and italicized portion of this S-expression contains an SST function that searches the sea with a template of SOR and SOR.

The DUMET function and its argument are in boldface. Since this DUMET function appears at the far right of the S-expression, its argument matches the «TRAILING-TEMPLATE» precisely when the copying of the S-expression is complete. Note that there is a DUMET subtree appearing underlined in bold-face; however, it is not executable since it is part of the argument subtree of the main DUMET function.

Figure 28.14 shows this fully screened 26-point self-replicator for experiment 2.

When we retested rule 235 with the function set F_2, we found that it has a probability of about one in 25,818 of being generated at random. This means the processing of 122,151 individuals is sufficient to yield a random S-expression realizing rule 235 with 99% probability.

We proceed in the same manner as in experiment 1, using Boolean function 235 as the environment for the programs in the sea and a pool of 3,000 synthesized programs patterned after the actually discovered fully screened self-replicators.

In one run, one of the individuals in generation 0 of our sea of programs was the following 27-point S-expression which performs the three-argument Boolean function 255 ("Always T"):

```
(SOR (NOT (SAND (NOT D0) (ADD (NOT (SOR (NOT D0) D2)))))
    (SAND (SST (SOR (NOT (NOT D2)) (ADD D2)))
         (DUMET (SOR (SOR D0 D1)
              (SAND D1 D2)))))).
```

The ADD function and its entire argument subtree are underlined in the S-expression above, and the ADD has a template of NOT and SOR. The SST function has a template of SOR and NOT; it and its argument subtree are shown

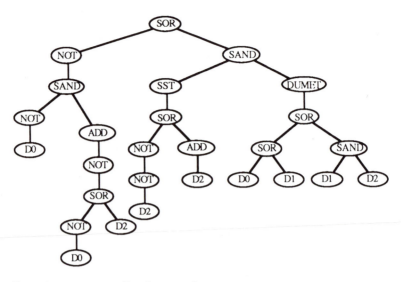

Figure 28.15   27-point self-replicator performing rule 255 from generation 0 for experiment 2.

in italics. The DUMET function and its «TRAILING-TEMPLATE» argument consisting of (SOR (SOR (SOR D0 D1) (SAND D1 D2)) is shown in boldface.

This 27-point S-expression is a self-replicator, because its SST function has a template consisting of SOR and NOT, thereby matching its own root and causing MATCHED-TREE to be bound to itself. The «TRAILING-TEMPLATE» of the DUMET function matches itself, thereby causing the copying of the entire S-expression into the temporary storage area and thence into the sea for the next generation for those combinations of environmental sensors that emulate rule 235.

Figure 28.15 graphically depicts this 27-point S-expression.

The first neighbor in the sea in generation 0 that matched the template of NOT and SOR of the ADD function was the following 24-point S-expression, which performs the three-argument Boolean rule 016:

(NOT (SOR (SAND (SOR D1 D0) (SOR (ADD (SOR (SAND D1 D1) D2)) D2)) (SOR (SST (NOT (SOR D2 D1))) (DUMET (SAND D1 D0)))))).

This 24-point S-expression is also a self-replicator whose root is NOT and whose point immediately below and to the left of the root is SOR, as shown in boldface above.

Figure 28.16 graphically depicts this 24-point S-expression.

The side effect of the execution of the ADD function in the 27-point individual is that the following individual containing 45 points, which is equivalent to the three-argument rule 239, is created and placed into the temporary storage area:

(SOR (NOT (SAND (NOT D0) **(NOT (SOR (SAND (SOR D1 D0)**
(SOR (ADD (SOR (SAND D1 D1) D2)) D2)) (SOR (SST
(NOT (SOR D2 D1))) (DUMET-ACQ (SAND D1 D0)))))))

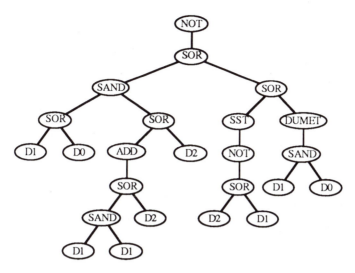

Figure 28.16 24-point self-replicator performing rule 016 from generation 0 for experiment 2.

```
(SAND (SST (SOR (NOT (NOT D2)) (ADD D2))) (DUMET (SOR
(SOR D0 D1) (SAND D1 D2)))))).
```

The 24-point subtree in boldface (with a NOT at its root and with SOR immediately below and to the left of the root) was inserted by the ADD function. The 27-point individual lost 6 points and gained 24 points, thus producing the 45-point individual. Note that this new 45-point individual has an acquired DUMET–ACQ function that came from the 24-point individual.

In this run, this 45-point individual eventually enters the sea and becomes part of generation 1.

Figure 28.17 graphically depicts this 45-point S-expression.

Another of the individuals in generation 0 of our sea of programs was the following 33-point S-expression, which performs the three-argument Boolean function 240:

```
(SOR (SAND (ADD (SOR D2 (SAND D2 D0))) (SAND (NOT (NOT
(SOR (SAND D1 D0) D0))) (SST (SOR (SAND D0 D2)
D2)))) (SOR D2 (DUMET (SOR (SAND (NOT D0) D2) (SAND D2
D2))))).
```

The ADD subtree in this S-expression is shown in boldface. Its template consists of SOR and D2. As it happens, there is no program in the sea that matches this template. However, because this individual is a self-replicator that emulates rule 235 for some combinations of the environmental sensors, this 33-point individual is copied into the temporary storage area and thence into the sea for generation 1.

The above 45-point individual contains an ADD function with a template of SOR and SAND. When it was evaluated during generation 1, it encountered the 33-point individual (which has SOR at its root and SAND immediately below and to the left of the root) as a neighbor. Therefore, the ADD template of the

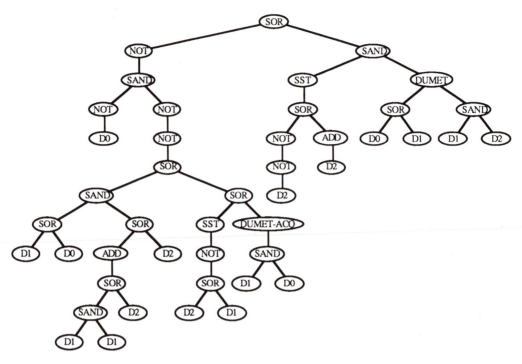

Figure 28.17 45-point self-replicator performing rule 239 from generation 1 with SOR at its root and with NOT immediately below and to the left of the root for experiment 2.

above 45-point S-expression matched the 33-point neighbor. The side effect of the match is the creation of a 72-point individual (i.e., 45 points + 33 points − 6 points for the subtree argument of the ADD function being executed). This 72-point S-expression performs rule 235:

```
(SOR (NOT (SAND (NOT D0) (NOT (SOR (SAND (SOR D1 D0) (SOR
(SOR (SAND (ADD (SOR D2 (SAND D2 D0))) (SAND
(NOT (NOT (SOR (SAND D1 D0) D0))) (SST (SOR
(SAND D0 D2) D2)))) (SOR D2 (DUMET−ACQ (SOR
(SAND (NOT D0) D2) (SAND D2 D2))))) D2)) (SOR (SST
(NOT (SOR D2 D1))) (DUMET−ACQ (SAND D1 D0))))))))) (SAND
(SST (SOR (NOT (NOT D2)) (ADD D2))) (DUMET (SOR (SOR D0
D1) (SAND D1 D2))))).
```

The 33-point subtree that was inserted by the ADD function is shown in boldface in the above S-expression.

This 72-point individual performing three-argument Boolean rule 235 eventually enters the sea for generation 2.

Figure 28.18 graphically depicts this 72-point S-expression.

Figure 28.19 is a genealogical tree showing the three grandparents from generation 0, the two parents from generation 1, and the final 72-point individual performing rule 235 in generation 2 from figure 28.18. The 27-point grandparent performing rule 255 comes from figure 28.15. The 45-point parent performing rule 239 comes from figure 28.17.

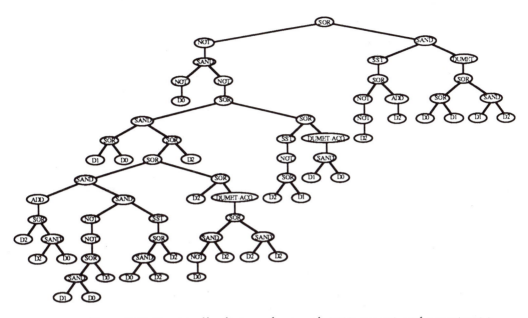

Figure 28.18 72-point self-replicator performing rule 235 in generation 2 for experiment 2.

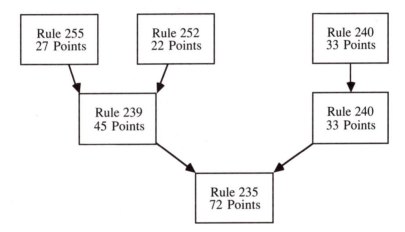

Figure 28.19 Genealogical tree for the 72-point self-replicator performing rule 235 in generation 2 for experiment 2.

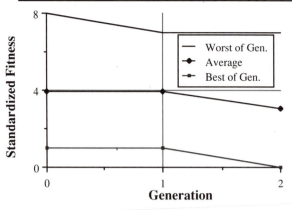

Figure 28.20 Fitness curves for experiment 2.

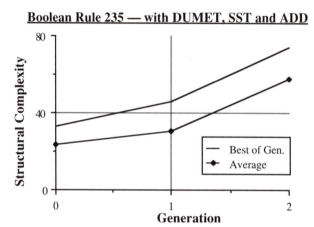

Figure 28.21 Structural complexity curves for experiment 2.

Figure 28.20 shows, by generation, the progressive improvement for the run in the average standardized fitness of the population as a whole and in the value of the standardized fitness for the best-of-generation individual and the worst-of-generation individual.

Figure 28.21 shows, by generation, the average structural complexity (i.e., total number of functions and terminals) of the population as a whole and the values of structural complexity for the best-of-generation individual. Because of the way that the ADD function incorporates entire individuals from the population within existing individuals, structural complexity rises very rapidly.

Figure 28.22 shows the hits histograms for generations 0, 1, and 2 of this run. One can see that the population as a whole has improved over even the small number of generations shown. The arrow points to the one individual scoring 8 hits on generation 2.

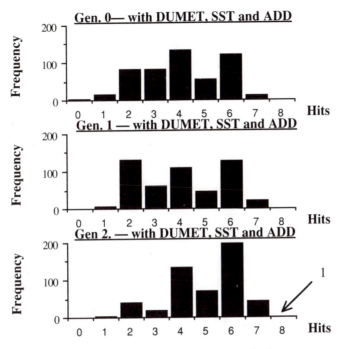

Figure 28.22 Hits histograms for generations 0, 1, and 2 for experiment 2.

Figure 28.23 presents the performance curves showing, by generation, the cumulative probability of success $P(M, i)$ and the number of individuals that must be processed $I(M, i, z)$ to yield, with 99% probability, at least one S-expression producing the correct value of rule 235 for all eight fitness cases. The graph is based on 237 runs. The population was 500 and the maximum number of generations to be run was 4. The cumulative probability of success, $P(M, i)$, is 3.80% by generation 1 and 5.06% by generation 3. The numbers in the oval indicate that if this problem is run through to generation 1, processing a total of 119,000 (i.e., 500×2 generations $\times$ 119 runs) individuals is sufficient to yield a solution to this problem with 99% probability.

The 119,000 individuals required to be processed here is larger than the 16,500 individuals required in experiment 1 because the function set F_2 contains less powerful and more primitive functions than F_1. However, the 119,000 individuals is less than the 122,151 individuals that must be processed to find an S-expression performing rule 235 at random.

28.3   EXPERIMENT 3

In experiment 2, we unbundled the EMIT function and replaced it with two other functions. In this experiment, we further unbundle the one-argument iterative function DUMET and replace it with a two-argument iterative function DWT ("Do «WORK» until «TRAILING–TEMPLATE» matches"). The new DWT is considerably less powerful than the DUMET function. Every such increase in primitiveness decreases the probability of spontaneous emergence. In addition,

Boolean Rule 235 — with DUMET, SST and ADD

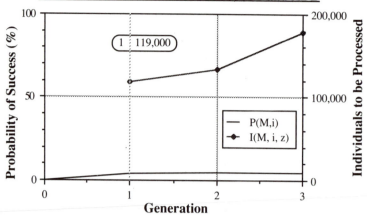

Figure 28.23 Performance curves show that 119,000 individuals must be processed to yield a solution to the problem of learning rule 235 for experiment 2.

we enlarge the function set to include a LR ("Load REGISTER") function and a SR ("Store REGISTER") function.

Thus, the function set for experiment 3 contains eight functions and is

$$F_3 = \{NOT,\ SOR,\ SAND,\ ADD,\ SST,\ DWT,\ LR,\ SR\},$$

taking one, two, two, one, one, two, zero, and zero arguments, respectively. The functions NOT, SOR, SAND, ADD, and SST ("Search Sea for Template") are the same as before. The terminal set is the same as before.

The real functionality of these three new functions lies in their side effects; however, they each have return values. The return value of the new LR function is T and the return value of the new SR function is NIL. The new DWT function returns the result of evaluating its second argument (i.e., it acts as an identity function on its second argument); its return value does not depend at all on its first argument.

In addition to the global variables MATCHED-TREE and OPEN-SPACE introduced in experiment 2, this experiment uses a new global variable, called REGISTER. It is used in conjunction with the new LR and SR functions and is initially NIL when evaluation of a given program begins.

The new two-argument iterative operator DWT ("Do «WORK» until «TRAILING-TEMPLATE» matches") iteratively evaluates its first argument, «WORK», until its entire second argument, «TRAILING-TEMPLATE», matches the contents of MATCHED-TREE. This new DWT operator is similar to the iterative looping operator found in many programming languages in that it performs certain work until its termination predicate is satisfied. In this regard, it is similar to the DU operator defined in section 18.1. The DWT operator is terminated by means of a biologically motivated template-matching scheme identical to that used by the DUMET operator of experiment 2. The new two-argument DWT operator is considerably less powerful than the one-argument DUMET operator, because the DUMET operator automatically traversed MATCHED-TREE and copied it, one point at a time, to OPEN-SPACE and thence into the temporary storage area. This traversing and copying must now be accomplished within the explicit «WORK» argument of the new DWT operator.

The new function LR ("Load REGISTER") works in conjunction with the global variables MATCHED-TREE and REGISTER. This function views the LISP S-expression in MATCHED-TREE as an unparenthesized sequence of symbols. For example, the S-expression

(AND (OR (NOT D1) D0))

is viewed as the sequence

{ AND OR NOT D1 D0 } .

When each LISP function has a specific number of arguments (as is the case here with the function set F_3), an unparenthesized ordered sequence of symbols is unambiguously equivalent to the original S-expression. This view is similar to that employed in the FORTH programming language, where functions are applied to a specified number of arguments, but where parentheses are not used or needed.

The function LR takes the current first element (i.e., function or terminal) of MATCHED-TREE (viewed as an unparenthesized sequence of symbols) and moves it into the REGISTER. The function LR has the side effect of removing this current first element from MATCHED-TREE and has the side effect of placing this element in the REGISTER.

For example, if LR were to act once on the above S-expression, the unparenthesized sequence associated with MATCHED-TREE would be reduced to

{ OR NOT D1 D0 }

and the REGISTER would contain AND.

The new function SR ("Store REGISTER") works in conjunction with the global variables REGISTER and OPEN-SPACE. The function SR takes the current contents of REGISTER (which is the name of a single function or terminal) and places it in OPEN-SPACE. REGISTER is not changed by the SR.

When the DWT operator terminates, necessary parentheses are inserted into the OPEN-SPACE in an attempt to create a syntactically valid S-expression. For example, if OPEN-SPACE contains AND, OR, NOT, D1, and D0, then

(AND (OR (NOT D1) D0))

will be transferred to the temporary storage area.

If MATCHED-TREE contains a program because of the action of a previous SST ("Search Sea for Template"), a DWT ("Do «WORK» until «TRAILING-TEM-PLATE» matches") that contains a LR ("Load REGISTER") and a SR ("Store REGISTER") in that order in its first argument subtree will iteratively load the REGISTER with the elements of the program in MATCHED-TREE and successively store them into OPEN-SPACE. This iterative process will continue until the «TRAILING-TEMPLATE» of the DWT matches the current part of MATCHED-TREE.

If DWT fails to find a subtree that matches «TRAILING-TEMPLATE» while it is traversing MATCHED-TREE, the contents of OPEN-SPACE are discarded. If the tree placed into the OPEN-SPACE is not syntactically valid, the contents of OPEN-SPACE are discarded.

To avoid nested loops, a DWT contained in the first argument of a DWT is not executed. If DWT fails to terminate for any reason within a reasonable number of steps or the symbols placed into OPEN-SPACE by the side effects of the «WORK» do not form a valid program, the contents of OPEN-SPACE are discarded for that DWT.

If there is an occurrence of a DWT, SST, or ADD function in the second argument subtree of a DWT, the inner function is never used to perform a search; the outer function merely uses it in trying to make a match.

As one would expect, finding a self-replicator via random search is considerably more difficult with function set F_3 than with either F_2 or F_1.

We found 604 self-replicators in a random search of 12,500,000 programs, so that the probability of finding a self-replicator with function set F_3 is about one in 20,695. However, if we impose the initial screening criteria that the self-replicator have at least one executable ADD function (i.e., one with a non-trivial template) and that at least one of the executable ADD functions appears before (i.e., to the left of) at least one of the executable DWT functions, then there are only eight self-replicators satisfying these initial screening criteria, so that the probability of finding a screened self-replicator with function set F_3 is about one in 1,562,500.

The following five additional criteria make a self-replicator involving F_3 even more suitable for our purposes here. First, there is exactly one executable ADD, SST, and DWT function. Second, the template of the one executable ADD and SST functions must not refer to a program that would never be present in a population of self-replicators. Third, the ADD, SST, and DWT functions must appear in that order when the S-expression is evaluated in the usual way. Fourth, the executable ADD and SST functions must not be part of the first argument to the DWT function. Fifth, the first argument to the DWT function must have one executable LR and SR function, in that order. If we impose these additional five screening criteria involving F_3, then there are only two fully screened self-replicators in 12,500,000, so that the probability of finding a fully screened self-replicator with function set F_3 is about one in 6,250,000.

One of the two fully screened self-replicators that was actually discovered in the random search of 12,500,000 for experiment 3 was

```
(SAND (SOR (SOR (NOT (ADD D2)) (ADD (ADD (SR))))
           (ADD (NOT (SAND (SR) D2))))
      (SAND (SST (SAND (SOR (SR) D1) (DWT D1 (LR))))
            (DWT (SAND (SAND (LR) D2) (NOT (SR)))
                 (SOR (SST D1) (DWT D1 D1))))).
```

This individual has 36 points and performs three-argument Boolean rule 204.

The italicized portion of this S-expression contains an executable ADD function with a template consisting of NOT and SAND. The SR function within the subtree argument to this ADD is not executable. Note the second of the two ADDs in the first underlined portion of the S-expression is not executable because its template is too small. Note also that the first ADD will not ever find a match because it would require finding a program whose root was ADD. Such a program can be ignored in practice because it would immediately replace its entire self with another program.

The underlined and italicized portion of this S-expression contains an SST subtree that searches the sea with a template of SAND and SOR. Note that the SR and DWT functions within the subtree argument to this SST are not executable.

The first argument to the two-argument DWT function is in boldface, while the second argument is underlined in boldface. The first argument to this DWT executes both the LR ("Load REGISTER") and the SR ("Store REGISTER") function, thereby causing the copying, one piece at a time, of the contents of MATCHED–TREE to the REGISTER. The second argument to this DWT is the «TRAILING–TEMPLATE». Since this DWT function appears at the far right of the S-expression, this match occurs precisely when the copying is complete.

Figure 28.24 shows this fully screened 36-point self-replicator for experiment 3.

When we retested rule 235 with the function set F_3, we found that it has a probability of about one in 33,177 of being generated at random. This means that the processing of 158,251 individuals is sufficient to yield a random S-expression realizing rule 235 with 99% probability.

We proceed in the same manner as in experiments 2 and 3, using Boolean function 235 as the environment for the programs in the sea and a pool of 3,000 synthesized programs patterned after the actually discovered fully screened self-replicators.

In one run, one of the individuals in generation 0 of our sea of programs was the following 28-point S-expression, which performs the three-argument Boolean function 250:

```
(SOR (NOT (SAND (NOT D0) (ADD (NOT (SOR D0 D2)))))
     (SAND (SST (SOR (NOT D2) (ADD D2)))
           (DWT (SOR (LR) (SR))
                (SOR (SAND D0 D2) (SAND D0 D0))))))).
```

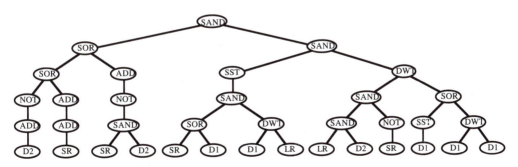

Figure 28.24 Spontaneously emergent self-replicator for experiment 3.

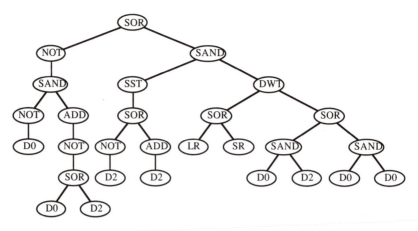

Figure 28.25 28-point self-replicator performing rule 250 from generation 0 for experiment 3.

The ADD function and its entire argument subtree are underlined in the S-expression above; the ADD has a template of NOT and SOR. The SST function has a template of SOR and NOT. The SST and its argument subtree are shown in italics. The DWT function, its first argument (SOR (LR) (SR)), and its second «TRAILING-TEMPLATE» argument consisting of (SOR (SAND D0 D2) (SAND D0 D0)) are shown in boldface.

This 28-point S-expression is a self-replicator, because its SST function has a template consisting of SOR and NOT, thereby matching its own root and causing MATCHED-TREE to be bound to itself. The «TRAILING-TEMPLATE» of the DWT function matches itself, thereby causing the copying of the entire S-expression into the temporary storage area and thence into the sea for the next generation for those combinations of environmental sensors that emulate rule 235.

Figure 28.25 graphically depicts this 28-point S-expression.

The first neighbor in the sea in generation 0 that matched the template of NOT and SOR of the ADD function was the following 31-point S-expression, which performs the three-argument Boolean rule 004:

(NOT (SOR (SAND (SOR D0 D2) (SOR (ADD (SOR (SAND D0 D1) D2)) D0)) (SOR (SST (NOT (SOR D2 D1))) (DWT (SAND (NOT (LR)) (SR)) (SAND (SAND D2 D1) (SST D0)))))).

This 31-point S-expression is also a self-replicator whose root is NOT and whose point immediately below and to the left of the root is SOR, as shown in boldface above.

Figure 28.26 graphically depicts this 31-point S-expression.

The side effect of the execution of the ADD function in the 28-point individual is that the following 54-point individual, which performs the three-argument rule 251, is created and placed into the temporary storage area:

(SOR (NOT (SAND (NOT D0) **(NOT (SOR (SAND (SOR D0 D2)**
(SOR (ADD (SOR (SAND D0 D1) D2)) D0)) (SOR (SST

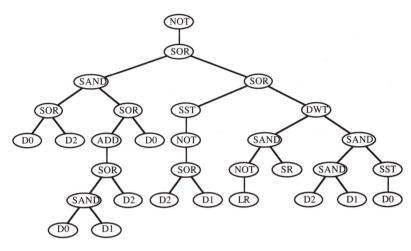

Figure 28.26 31-point self-replicator performing rule 004 from generation 0 for experiment 3.

(NOT (SOR D2 D1))) (DWT-ACQ (SAND (NOT (LR))
(SR)) (SAND (SAND D2 D1) (SST D0))))))))) (SAND
(SST (SOR (NOT D2) (ADD D2))) (DWT (SOR (LR) (SR)) (SOR
(SAND D0 D2) (SAND D0 D0))))).

The 31-point subtree in boldface (with a NOT at its root and with SOR immediately below and to the left of the root) was inserted by the ADD function from the 28-point individual. The 28-point individual lost 5 points and gained 31 points, thus producing the 54-point individual. Note that this new 54-point individual has an acquired DWT-ACQ function that came from the 31-point individual.

In this run, this 54-point individual eventually enters the sea and becomes part of generation 1.

Figure 28.27 graphically depicts this 54-point S-expression.

Another of the individuals in generation 0 of our sea of programs was the following 41-point S-expression, which performs the three-argument Boolean function 238:

(SOR (SAND (NOT **(ADD (SOR D0 (SAND D2 D0))))**) (SAND
(NOT (SOR (SAND D0 D1) D2)) (SST (SOR (SAND D1 D2) D0))))
(SOR D1 (DWT (SOR (SAND (NOT D0) (NOT (LR))) (SAND D0
(SR))) (SOR (SOR D0 D1) (SAND D2 D0))))).

The ADD function and its argument subtree in this S-expression is shown in boldface. Its template consists of SOR and D0. As it happens, there is no program in the sea that matches this template. However, because this individual is a self-replicator that emulates rule 235 for some combinations of the environmental sensors, this 41-point individual is copied into the temporary storage area and thence into the sea for generation 1.

Figure 28.28 graphically depicts this 41-point S-expression.

Spontaneous Emergence of Programs

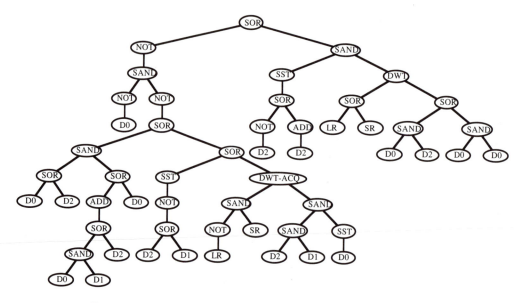

Figure 28.27 54-point self-replicator performing rule 251 from generation 1 with SOR at its root and with NOT immediately below and to the left of the root for experiment 3.

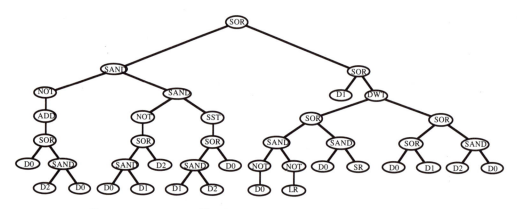

Figure 28.28 41-point self-replicator performing rule 238 in generation 0 for experiment 3.

The above 54-point individual contains an ADD function with a template of SOR and SAND. When it was evaluated during generation 1, it encountered the 41-point individual (which has SOR at its root and SAND immediately below and to the left of the root) as a neighbor. Therefore, the ADD template of the above 54-point S-expression matched the 41-point neighbor. The side effect of the match is the creation of an 89-point individual (i.e., 54 points + 41 points − 6 points for the subtree argument of the ADD function being executed). This 89-point S-expression performs rule 235:

```
(SOR (NOT (SAND (NOT D0) (NOT (SOR (SAND (SOR D0 D2) (SOR
(SOR (SAND (NOT (ADD (SOR D0 (SAND D2 D0))))
(SAND (NOT (SOR (SAND D0 D1) D2)) (SST (SOR
```

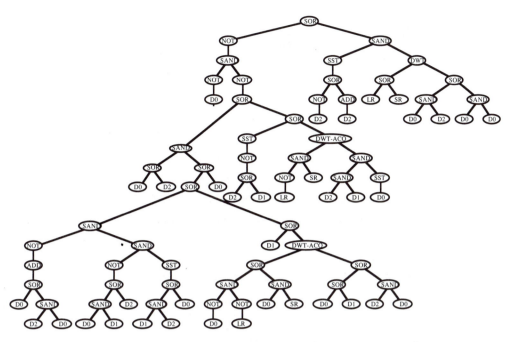

Figure 28.29 89-point self-replicator performing rule 235 in generation 2 for experiment 3.

(SAND D1 D2) D0)))) (SOR D1 **(DWT—ACQ (SOR (SAND (NOT**
D0) (NOT (LR))) (SAND D0 (SR))) (SOR (SOR D0 D1)
(SAND D2 D0))))) D0)) (SOR (SST (NOT (SOR D2 D1)))
(DWT—ACQ (SAND (NOT (LR)) (SR)) (SAND (SAND D2 D1) (SST
D0))))))))) (SAND (SST (SOR (NOT D2) (ADD D2))) (DWT (SOR
(LR) (SR)) (SOR (SAND D0 D2) (SAND D0 D0))))).

The 41-point subtree that was inserted by the ADD function is shown in boldface in the above S-expression.

This 89-point individual performing three-argument Boolean rule 235 eventually enters the sea for generation 2.

Figure 28.29 graphically depicts this 89-point S-expression.

Figure 28.30 is a genealogical tree showing the three grandparents from generation 0, the two parents from generation 1, and the final 89-point individual performing rule 235 in generation 2 from figure 28.29. The 28-point grandparent performing rule 250 comes from figure 28.25. The 31-point grandparent performing rule 004 comes from figure 28.26. The 54-point parent performing rule 251 comes from figure 28.27.

Figure 28.31 shows, by generation, the progressive improvement for the run in which the 89-point self-replicator performing rule 235 was found in generation 2. In particular, it shows the average standardized fitness of the population as a whole and the value of the standardized fitness for the best-of-generation individual and the worst-of-generation individual.

Figure 28.32 shows, by generation, the average structural complexity of the population as a whole and the values of structural complexity for the best-of-

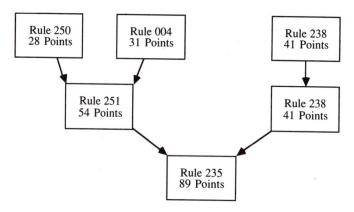

Figure 28.30 Genealogical tree for the 89-point self-replicator performing rule 235 in generation 2 for experiment 3.

Boolean Rule 235 — with DWT, SST, SR, LR and ADD

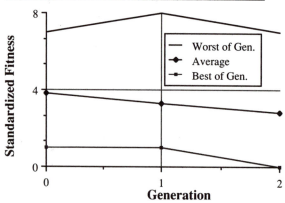

Figure 28.31 Fitness curves for experiment 3.

Boolean Rule 235 — with DWT, SST, SR, LR and ADD

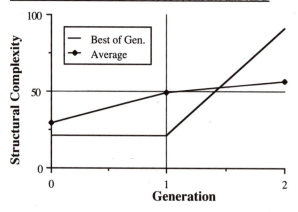

Figure 28.32 Structural complexity curves for experiment 3.

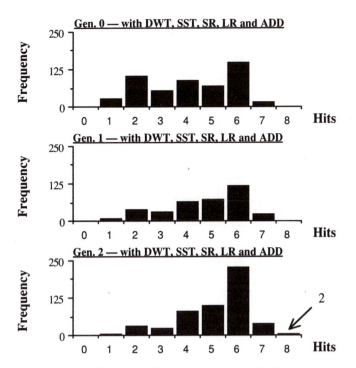

Figure 28.33 Hits histograms for generations 0, 1, and 2 for experiment 3.

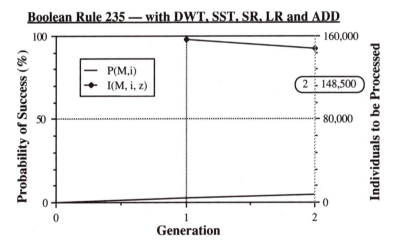

Figure 28.34 Performance curves show that 148,500 individuals must be processed to yield a solution to the problem of learning rule 235 for experiment 3.

Spontaneous Emergence of Programs

Table 28.3 Summary of experiments.

	Experiment 1	Experiment 2	Experiment 3
Function set	F_1	F_2	F_3
Functions	EMIT ADD SAND SOR NOT	DUMET SST ADD SAND SOR NOT	LR SR DWT SST ADD SAND SOR NOT
Global variables	None	MATCHED-TREE OPEN-SPACE	MATCHED-TREE OPEN-SPACE REGISTER
Probability of a program performing rule 235	1:18,461	1:25,818	1:33,177
Number of individuals that must be processed to find an S-expression performing rule 235 with 99% probability	86,562	122,151	158,251
Probability of a self-replicator	1:281	1:1,129	1:20,695
Probability of a screened self-replicator	1:575	1:38,339	1:1,562,500
Probability of a fully screened self-replicator	1:5,000	1:350,000	1:6,250,000
500 times probability of a fully screened self-replicator	2,500,000	175,000,000	3.125×10^9
Number of self-replicators that must be processed to evolve a self-replicator performing rule 235 with 99% probability	16,500	119,000	148,500

generation individual. Because of the way that the ADD function incorporates entire individuals in the population within existing individuals, structural complexity rises very rapidly.

Figure 28.33 shows the hits histograms for generations 0, 1, and 2 of this run. One can see that the population as a whole has improved over even the small number of generations shown. The arrow points to the two individuals scoring 8 hits on generation 2.

Figure 28.34 presents the performance curves showing, by generation, the cumulative probability of success $P(M, i)$ and the number of individuals that must be processed $I(M, i, z)$ to yield, with 99% probability, at least one S-expression producing the correct value of rule 235 for all eight fitness cases. The graph is based on 242 runs. The population was 500 and the maximum number of generations to be run was 2. The cumulative probability of success, $P(M, i)$, is 2.9% by generation 1 and 4.5% by generation 2. The numbers in the oval indicate that if this problem is run through to generation 2, processing a total of 148,500 (i.e., 500 × 3 generations × 99 runs) individuals is sufficient to yield a solution to this problem with 99% probability.

The 148,500 individuals required to be processed here is larger than the 16,500 individuals required in experiment 1 and the 119,000 individuals required in experiment 2. However, the 148,500 individuals is less than the 158,251 individuals that must be processed to find an S-expression performing rule 235 with the function set F_3 at random.

28.4 RECAPITULATION

In summary, in spite of a number of simplifications and compromises necessitated by the limited available computer resources, we have demonstrated the spontaneous emergence of self-replicating computer programs, sexual reproduction, and evolutionary self-improving behavior among randomly created computer programs using a computationally complete set of logical functions.

29 Conclusions

At the beginning of the book, we proposed to make two main points, namely

- **Point 1** A wide variety of seemingly different problems from many different fields can be recast as requiring the discovery of a computer program that produces some desired output when presented with particular inputs. That is, many seemingly different problems can be reformulated as problems of program induction.

- **Point 2** The recently developed genetic programming paradigm described in this book provides a way to do program induction. That is, genetic programming can search the space of possible computer programs for an individual computer program that is highly fit in solving (or approximately solving) the problem at hand. The computer program (i.e., structure) that emerges from the genetic programming paradigm is a consequence of fitness. That is, fitness begets the needed program structure.

Point 1 was dealt with in chapter 2, and subsequent chapters provided substantial evidence in favor of point 2.

Paradigms for machine learning and artificial intelligence can be viewed from a number of different perspectives, including the following:

- the generality of the paradigm in terms of the range of problems that can be solved,
- the extent and character of pre-processing of the inputs that is required,
- the closeness of the representation used by the paradigm and the problem domain,
- the extent and character of post-processing of the inputs that is required and whether the solution is stated in the terminology of the problem domain,
- the ability to easily run a solution found by the paradigm on other computers,
- the amount of information about the size and shape of the ultimate solution that is provided by the user,
- the qualitative features of the output (e.g., the presence of hierarchies and default hierarchies),

- the ability to solve the problem with some inaccurate information, some inconsistent information, or incomplete information,
- the ability to provide an audit trail showing how the paradigm obtained its solution to a problem,
- the ability to robustly (i.e., rapidly and effectively) modify a solution to handle somewhat different situations,
- the fault tolerance of the paradigm in the sense that the paradigm can operate reasonably well even if some of the stored data or some of the computing machinery containing stored data is lost during the run,
- the ability of the paradigm to yield near linear speedups in highly parallel computer architectures (and thereby facilitate solutions to very large problems),
- the precision of the results,
- the extent to which the paradigm approaches some reasonable definition of optimality in solving problems, and
- the total magnitude of the machine resources (notably computer time and computer memory) required to execute the paradigm.

I do not attempt to make a comparison between genetic programming and the various other paradigms for machine learning and artificial intelligence here.

Such a comparison would necessarily begin with a selection of a group of benchmark problems from the infinity of potential problems. Even comparing a seemingly objective and quantitative factor such as computer time requires selection of the group of benchmark problems. Some paradigms are especially well suited to solving certain types of problems. More important, some paradigms simply cannot solve certain types of problems at all. Nothing is as slow as *never* in solving a particular problem. It is not clear how to make comparisons among paradigms when one paradigm cannot solve a particular problem. Limiting the group of benchmark problems to the lowest common denominator of problems solvable by all existing paradigms for machine learning and artificial intelligence merely favors the most specialized paradigms with the least overall problem-solving power.

Comparing computer time also requires selecting a particular computer on which to make the benchmark comparison. The computer architecture affects the execution of each paradigm. For example, a parallel computer with coarse, medium, or fine granularity will be advantageous or disadvantageous to certain paradigms; a machine with a modest amount of memory will be advantageous or disadvantageous to certain paradigms; a LISP workstation would obviously be well suited to a paradigm based on LISP whereas a workstation with an identical clock rate that implemented LISP via software might require numerous assembly-code instructions to perform even a primitive operation in LISP.

I will now summarize the features of genetic programming in relation to those listed above, namely

- generality,
- pre-processing requirements,
- commonality of the internal representation with the problem domain,
- post-processing requirements,
- portability of results,
- advance information,
- hierarchical character,
- tolerance to inaccurate, inconsistent, or incomplete information,
- auditability,
- incremental modifiability,
- fault tolerance,
- parallelizability with near linear speed up,
- precision,
- efficiency and optimality of solution, and
- computer resources required.

The wide variety of different problems from different fields presented in this book provide considerable evidence of the generality of the genetic programming paradigm in terms of the range of problems that can be readily solved. No other machine learning paradigm even approaches this level of generality.

The inputs to genetic programming are usually presented directly in terms of the observed variables of the problem domain involved. Therefore, the representation used by genetic programming is the natural representation of the problem domain. The lack of preprocessing is a major distinction relative to conventional genetic algorithms operating on strings, neural networks, and other machine learning algorithms.

Similarly, the internal representation of the problem closely matches the original natural representation of the problem.

As to the amount and type of post-processing required and the closeness between the representation used by the algorithm and the natural representation of the problem domain, the direct use by genetic programming of functions that come from the problem domain creates a close match. When an output interface (wrapper) is required, it is usually extremely simple.

The fact that the output of genetic programming is always a computer program in the form of its own parse tree means that the result can be immediately executed as a computer program on another computer (or, at least, easily translated in an automated way and executed). Although usually complex, the output is also generally amenable to straightforward automatic simplification and optimization.

As to requiring advance information about the size and shape of the ultimate solution, the genetic programming paradigm uses relatively little such advance knowledge. This is in contrast with the pre-specifying of the precise string size in the classifier system approach, the pre-specifying of the maximum number of states for the finite-state automaton, and the pre-specifying of number of layers, number of processing units at each layer, and connectivity required by most neural network paradigms. The information that is required, such as the choice of terminal set and the set of primitive functions, is also necessarily required by every other paradigm for machine learning.

As to the qualitative features of the output (e.g., the presence of hierarchies or default hierarchies), the results produced by genetic programming are inherently hierarchical and often contain default hierarchies.

Genetic methods in general permit a problem to be solved even when there is some inaccurate information, some inconsistent information, or incomplete information.

As to auditability, genetic methods in general allow construction of a genealogical audit trail showing how the algorithm arrived at its solution to a problem.

Genetic methods, in general, have the ability to incrementally and robustly (i.e., rapidly and effectively) modify one solution to handle different situations.

As to the ability to verify the results, the fact that there is no preprocessing of inputs and the fact that the final result is expressed directly in terms of functions relevant to the problem domain make it relatively easy to verify solutions generated by the algorithm.

Genetic methods, in general, are highly amenable to parallelization via parallel computer architectures and yield near linear speedup.

Genetic methods, in general, are fault-tolerant in the sense that a run can continue even if some of the computer memory is lost at some point during the run.

As to precision, genetic programming is able to adaptively change the size and shape of the solution dynamically during the run and thus can home in on a solution with increasing precision.

As to the extent to which the algorithm achieves or approaches optimality in efficiently solving problems, genetic methods in general allocate future trials in their search process in a near-optimal way.

In conclusion, genetic programming is a robust and efficient paradigm for discovering computer programs using the expressiveness of symbolic representation.

Appendix A: Interactive Interface of the Computer Implementation

A Texas Instruments Explorer Multiple Processor (MP) computer containing four parallel Explorer II+™ processors with 40 megahertz LISP microprocessor chips was used for most of the runs reported in this book. Each of the four processors has between 16 and 32 megabytes of physical memory and about 128 megabytes of virtual memory. Some runs were run on a microExplorer™ computer (an Apple Macintosh II™ computer containing a Texas Instruments LISP expansion board).

An informative and interactive interface is an invaluable tool in carrying out computer experiments in the field of machine learning (Robertson 1987). Accordingly, the computer program used here has extensive interactivity, including six large full color panes and five small panes. There are various mouse-sensitive points on the graphical interface for obtaining detailed information on the progress of a run while it is running.

Figure A.1 shows the computer interface for our implementation of the genetic programming paradigm.

We start by discussing the six large full color panes.

The first (upper left) large pane contains graphs which dynamically track three of the most important statistics of a run, namely:

- the number of hits for the best-of-generation individual of each generation,

- the variety (percentage) for the population for each generation, and

- the average normalized fitness of the population for each generation.

These three statistics are presented in different colors; however, they are easily distinguishable because normalized fitness and hits start near zero, while variety starts at 100% and because the rise in normalized fitness (which reflects the population as a whole) lags the rise in hits (which measures the best-of-generation individual). Normalized fitness and variety are measured on a fixed scale of 0.0 to 1.0, while hits are measured on a problem specific scale ranging between 0 and the maximum possible number of hits for the problem. The individual points on the graphs on this pane (and the other panes described below) are mouse sensitive. If the user clicks on these points, an additional small window pops up and provides detailed additional information about the individual associated with that point (in particular, the information contained in each of the slots of the data structure for that individual).

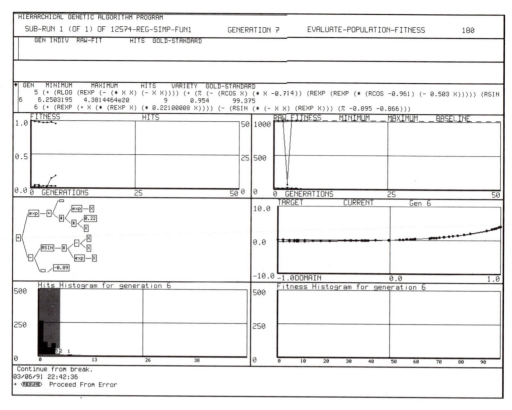

Figure A.1 Interactive computer interface for genetic programming paradigm.

The second (upper right) large pane dynamically tracks the following five statistics:

- the standardized fitness of the worst-of-generation individual for each generation,
- the average standardized fitness of the population for each generation,
- the standardized fitness of the best-of-generation individual for each generation,
- the baseline value of standardized fitness for the population for generation 0, and
- the structural complexity (i.e., number of internal and external points) of the S-expression of the best-of-generation individual for each generation.

In a typical run, the first three of these items tend to decrease as the run progresses. The baseline (i.e., the average standardized fitness of generation 0) is presented as a dotted horizontal line running across this pane. The first four graphs are measured on the scale of standardized fitness running between 0 and an assumed problem specific maximum value for standardized fitness for the problem. The structural complexity of the S-expression is measured on a problem specific scale between 0 and an assumed maximum number of points for S-expressions in the problem. If any assumed maximum number is in fact exceeded for a given generation, the point is plotted just above the top of the graph.

The third (middle left) large pane depicts the best-of-generation S-expression of the current generation in the form of a rooted, point-labeled tree with ordered branches. The internal and external points of the tree representing the S-expression are labeled with the appropriate functions and terminals.

The fourth large pane is used in different ways for different problems.

For problems involving symbolic regression (including symbolic integration, differentiation, and solving differential equations), this pane contains the graph of the target function and the graph of the best-of-generation individual S-expression. The target function (which is unchanging over the generations) is shown in one color, while the graph of the best-of-generation individual S-expression (which typically changes with each generation) is shown in another color. The horizontal axis is the designated domain interval for the target function (i.e., the domain for the independent variable). The vertical axis runs over an assumed range for values of the best-of-generation individual and the target individual. As a typical successful run progresses, the two colored curves tend to converge. In the symbolic integration and symbolic differentiation problems, the graph of the numeric integral or numeric derivative of the best-of-generation individual is added as an auxiliary item to this pane.

For particular problems for which we have animated graphics (e.g., the artificial ant, broom balancing, inverse kinematics, emergent behavior in an ant colony, central place food foraging, Ms. Pac Man), this pane shows animated graphics appropriate to that problem.

The fifth (bottom left) large pane is the hits histogram showing the number of individuals in the population with a particular number of hits for the current generation. The horizontal axis of the hits histogram is the number of hits. The vertical axis of the hits histogram represents the number of individuals in the population with that number of hits. For problems with a large number of fitness cases, the hits histogram collects the fitness values into decile buckets; these are shown on a backup histogram (which can be toggled into view in lieu of the first histogram).

The hits histogram gives a highly informative view of the progress of the learning process for the population as a whole. At the initial random generation of a typical run, the bulk of the population appears at the left part of the hits histogram (often with only zero hits). Then, after a few generations, the center of gravity of the hits histogram typically starts shifting from left to right. As learning takes place during the run, an undulating "slinky" movement occurs from left to right in this histogram. Later in a run, individuals scoring the maximum possible number of hits may start appearing at the far right of the histogram. Convergence may be indicated if 100% of the population becomes concentrated at the far right of the histogram. A heavy concentration of the population at one single suboptimal number of hits in the histogram is suggestive of the possibility of premature convergence. If identical individuals are scoring that suboptimal number of hits (as suggested by a low percentage value on the variety graph in the first pane), premature convergence has occurred (although this is rare with genetic programming). In contrast, normal progress toward a solution is typically indicated by a broad flowing distribution of individuals over many different numbers of hits in the histogram (and a high percentage value for variety).

The sixth (lower right) large pane is the fitness histogram showing the number of individuals in the current generation of the population having a fitness lying in a particular decile range of fitness values. The horizontal axis of the fitness histogram consists of ten problem specific decile ranges in values of standardized fitness. The vertical axis of the hits histogram represents the number of individuals in the population with standardized fitness lying in a particular range.

In addition to the six large panes, there are five small panes.

The first (top) small pane is a non-scrolling pane that provides general information about the run, including the problem name, run number, subrun number, and identifiers of the particular choice for the set of terminals and functions being used and for the particular set of fitness cases being used. For a particular subrun of a given run, this pane also includes three odometers showing the current generation number, the current individual number, and the current fitness case number. It also indicates which major activity is currently being executed, such as

- generating the fitness cases,
- generating the initial population,
- evaluating the individuals in the population for fitness, and
- making the new population by performing the genetic operations.

The second small pane is a scrolling pane which contains all the individuals in the population for certain designated generations (if any). The designated generations (if any) may be just generation 0, every generation, a certain fraction of the generations, or none. This pane and other graphics panes can be disabled on production runs to save computer resources.

The third small pane is a non-scrolling pane that displays the best number of hits achieved on each completed run of the current set of runs sharing the same parameters. It is used for quickly monitoring the overall results of a series of subruns (e.g., an overnight series of subruns).

The fourth small pane can be scrolled so that the history of a run can be studied while it is running. It contains all the parameters of the run as a header. The pane is updated with two lines of information for each generation of the run containing the best-of-generation individual S-expression for that generation, the number of hits and standardized fitness for the best-of-generation and worst-of-generation individuals in the population, and the average fitness of the population as a whole for the generation.

The individual S-expressions presented in this pane are mouse sensitive so that if the user clicks on these S-expressions while a run is in progress, the S-expression is captured and written to a special file. Then, while the run of genetic programming continues as one process on the machine, the file may be separately and simultaneously examined by the editor while the run continues. In this way, the S-expression might be edited to gain an understanding of why it might be working well or not working well. This feature is especially useful on extremely time consuming runs because it can provide information on whether to continue or discontinue the run.

The fifth small pane appearing at the bottom of the screen is the LISP command pane.

A control command makes it possible to extend promising subruns on-the-fly by doubling the number of generations to be executed. This command requires on-the-fly re-dimensioning of numerous statistical arrays in the program and on-the-fly changing of the scales for all the graphs described above whose horizontal axis measures generations.

Appendix B: Problem-Specific Part of Simple LISP Code

In order to replicate the experimental results reported herein or to further explore the potential of genetic programming, it is first necessary to implement the genetic programming paradigm on a computer.

Genetic programming involves executing computer programs that were generated at random or created using genetic operations such as crossover. As a result, a number of unusual programming problems and issues arise. Some of the techniques required to solve these problems are not described in the available documentation of the relevant programming languages or computing machines.

In this appendix and appendix C, we provide and explain Common LISP code for a simple version of genetic programming. This simplified code can be run for small problems on a small computer (e.g., a Macintosh II™ computer or an IBM™ compatible personal computer). We have tested this code using Allegro™ Common LISP and Lucid Common LISP™ on a Macintosh II computer as well as on the Texas Instruments Explorer™ and microExplorer™ machines using their Common LISP environment.

The code is divided into two main parts, namely

• the problem-specific part (found in this appendix), and

• the problem-independent kernel (found in appendix C).

In order to run a particular problem using genetic programming, the user need only modify a relatively small amount of problem-specific code found in this appendix. The kernel is generic code that need not be modified by the user to run a particular problem. The user should simply enter all of the problem-specific LISP code in this appendix into a file along with the LISP code for the kernel described in appendix C.

The creation of the necessary problem-specific code will be illustrated with the following three simple problems:

• The first problem is a symbolic regression problem involving discovering the polynomial function $x^2/2$ from a sample of data (see section 7.3 for a similar problem).

• The second problem involves discovering the Boolean majority-on function with three arguments (see subsection 7.4.5 and chapter 9 for similar problems).

- The third problem is a two-person pursuer-evader game played on a discrete grid (which is similar to the differential pursuer-evader game described in section 15.2 and somewhat similar to the artificial ant problem in section 7.2).

The problem-specific part of the LISP code for these three problems is intended to provide the user with templates that he can easily alter and apply to new problems. The problem specific part of this LISP code is written in an especially simple style so that it can be easily understood and modified by a user who has only minimal exposure to LISP and is more familiar with programming languages such as PASCAL, C, or FORTRAN.

As has previously been mentioned in this book, there are five major steps in preparing to use genetic programming, namely determining

(1) the set of terminals,

(2) the set of functions,

(3) the fitness measure,

(4) the parameters and variables for controlling the run, and

(5) the criterion for designating a result and terminating a run.

The problem-specific part of the LISP code in this chapter closely parallels these five major steps. If the user first visualizes his problem in terms of these five major steps, he will find it relatively straightforward to adapt the problem-specific part of the simple LISP code described in this section to his own problem.

B.1 SYMBOLIC REGRESSION

The first problem is a symbolic regression problem involving discovering the polynomial function $x^2/2$ from a sample of data.

The first major step in preparing to use genetic programming is to identify the set of terminals. The terminal set T for the problem of symbolic regression consists of the independent variable x as it did in section 7.3.

If we want numeric constants to appear in the polynomials, the terminal set T would also include the ephemeral random floating-point constant $\Re$ (as described in section 10.2). Thus, the terminal set T would become

```
T = {X, ℜ}.
```

We start by defining each variable in the terminal set (other than the ephemeral random floating-point constant $\Re$) as a global variable. Thus, the first item in the problem specific part of the LISP code that we must write is

```
(defvar x)
```

We place this LISP statement at the beginning of a file containing the LISP code for this problem.

We now create a LISP function called `define-terminal-set-for-REGRESSION`. This function is to return the list of all terminals used in the problem. We use the LISP keyword

```
:floating-point-random-constant
```

to represent the ephemeral random floating-point constant $\Re$. which produces random floating-point numbers between -5.0 and $+5.0$. Thus, the list of all terminals used in this problem is the list

```
(x :floating-point-random-constant)
```

consisting of two elements. Thus, the second item in the problem-specific part of the LISP code that we must write is the function

```
(defun define-terminal-set-for-REGRESSION ()
  (values '(x :floating-point-random-constant))
)
```

Note that, for clarity, we explicitly highlight the value(s) returned by each function in this appendix by using (unnecessarily) a VALUES statement at the end of each function definition.

The second major step in preparing to use genetic programming is to identify the function set for the problem. The function set F for this problem consists of the four arithmetic functions,

```
F = {+, -, *, %},
```

taking two arguments each.

We now create a LISP function called `define-function-set-for-REGRESSION`. This function returns two lists, namely a list of the functions and a list of the number of arguments taken by each of the functions. Thus, the third item in the problem-specific part of the LISP code that we must write is the function

```
(defun define-function-set-for-REGRESSION ()
  (values '(+ - * %)
          '(2 2 2 2))
)
```

If the function set contains any other problem specific functions, the user must define them at this point. There are three reasons why the user may have to define one or more problem-specific functions in order to run a given problem.

The first reason for defining problem-specific functions is that some problems operate in a special problem domain. For example, the artificial ant problem (section 7.2) requires functions that cause the ant to move forward, turn left, turn right, and test for food. These problem-specific functions in the artificial ant problem operate by side-effecting a system which is simulated over a number of time steps.

The second reason for defining problem-specific functions is that each function in the function set must be well defined for any possible value (or data type) which it might encounter as a result of taking as arguments any terminal or any value that might be returned by any function in the function set. For example, the ordinary LISP division function / should not be in the function set of this symbolic regression problem because of the possibility of a division by zero. One way to protect against division by zero is to include the protected division function % in the function set, instead of the ordinary LISP division function /.

Thus, the fourth item in the problem-specific part of the LISP code that we must write consists of a definition for the protected division function %.

```
(defun % (numerator denominator)
  "The Protected Division Function"
  (values (if (= 0 denominator) 1 (/ numerator denominator))))
)
```

The third reason for defining problem-specific functions is that it may be desirable to use such functions to protect the problem against extreme values of the variables or other error conditions. Genetic programming involves executing randomly generated computer programs as well as the individuals produced via crossover in later generations. As a result, the individual S-expressions in the initial random population often evaluate to astronomically large numbers or very small numbers.

When the function set ranges over the integers, the BIGNUM mode of Common LISP automatically may adequately deal with these potential problems because, in the BIGNUM mode, the absolute value of integer numbers can grow arbitrarily large (i.e., limited only by the virtual address space of the LISP system and machine). However, note that there may be a considerable amount of CONSing associated with the BIGNUM mode.

On the other hand, when the range is real-valued, floating-point overflows or underflows can occur. In problems involving such floating-point variables, it is therefore a practical necessity to either (1) wrap the entire evaluation in error handlers that trap every possible kind of floating-point underflow and overflow applicable to the particular computer involved and allow the computation to proceed in some way (e.g., with an arbitrary large or small value), or (2) define special versions of the usual arithmetic operations (especially multiplication and division) that allow the computation to proceed in some way (e.g., with an arbitrary large or small value) and include these special arithmetic operations in the function set in lieu of the usual arithmetic operations.

Our experience is that it is usually possible to run the simple symbolic regression problem for $x^2/2$ described in this section without encountering floating-point overflows or underflows; however, there is no guarantee of this. If the user expands this problem (e.g., by looking for a higher order polynomial, by increasing the range of x, by increasing the population size, etc.), the user may well encounter problems. If the user is familiar with the error handling functions for his particular version of LISP on his particular machine, he may avoid writing the special versions of the arithmetic functions. There is no solution in Common LISP for handling these overflows and underflows that is portable from machine to machine. The Explorer machine allows such error handlers to be written using special microcode support. One of the advantages of Boolean problems (as described in the next section of this appendix) is that they avoid this issue.

The third major step in preparing to use genetic programming is identifying the fitness measure for evaluating how good a given computer program is at solving the problem at hand. The symbolic regression problem is typical of most problems in that it has a number of fitness cases. We establish the fitness cases at the beginning of the run. The kernel then loops over each individual S-expression in the population calling on the user-specified fitness function to evaluate the fitness of each individual. If the fitness function contains fitness cases, the fitness function then loops over the fitness cases in order to evaluate the fitness of each particular S-expression from the population.

We store the fitness cases in an array, each element of which corresponds to one fitness case. Each fitness case is implemented as a record structure. It is convenient to store the values of all the independent variables for a given fitness case in the record for that fitness case along with the dependent variables (the "answer") for that fitness case.

Thus, the fifth item in the problem specific part of the LISP code that we must write is the defstruct record structure declaration for this problem:

```
(defstruct REGRESSION-fitness-case
    independent-variable
    target
)
```

Note that the above is equivalent to a PASCAL record type declaration for a type called REGRESSION-fitness-case.

The sixth item in the problem-specific part of the LISP code that we must write is the function called define-fitness-cases-for-REGRESSION for this problem. This function returns a one-dimensional array of fitness cases. The size of the array is specified by the global variable *number-of-fitness-cases*. In this simple problem, the fitness cases are regularly spaced samples of points for values of the independent variable x between 0.0 and 1.0. For example, if the *number-of-fitness-cases* is 10, then the 10 values of the independent variable x would be 0.0, 0.1, 0.2, ..., 0.9. For each value of x, there is an associated value of the dependent variable (i.e., the target). This target value is also computed and stored in the fitness case record structure.

We have highlighted (in bold type) the lines of this function that the user is likely to want to change in order to customize the function for his own purposes.

```
(defun define-fitness-cases-for-REGRESSION ()                    ;01
  (let (fitness-cases x this-fitness-case)                       ;02
    (setf fitness-cases (make-array *number-of-fitness-cases*))  ;03
```

```
      (format t "~%Fitness cases")                                    ;04
      (dotimes (index *number-of-fitness-cases*)                      ;05
        (setf x (/ index *number-of-fitness-cases*))                  ;06
       (setf this-fitness-case (make-REGRESSION-fitness-case))        ;07
       (setf (aref fitness-cases index) this-fitness-case)            ;08
       (setf (REGRESSION-fitness-case-independent-variable            ;09
              this-fitness-case)                                      ;10
              x)                                                      ;11
       (setf (REGRESSION-fitness-case-target                          ;12
              this-fitness-case)                                      ;13
              (* 0.5 x x))                                            ;14
       (format t "~% ~D      ~D       ~D"                             ;15
              index                                                   ;16
              (float x)                                               ;17
              (REGRESSION-fitness-case-target this-fitness-case))     ;18
        )                                                             ;19
      (values fitness-cases)                                          ;20
    )                                                                 ;21
  )                                                                   ;22
```

We first discuss what the define-fitness-cases-for-REGRESSION function does and we then show how it would be modified to accommodate a different problem.

The semicolons at the far right delineate comments. The line numbers are for reference only and are not part of the LISP program.

Line 1 begins the definition of this function (i.e., the defun). The two parentheses at the end of the line enclose the arguments of the function. The absence of anything between these two parentheses indicate that this particular function takes no arguments.

Line 2 contains a let statement which identifies three variables as being local variables that are used only within the confines of this function.

Line 3 makes a one-dimensional array called fitness-cases whose size is specified by the global variable *number-of-fitness-cases*.

Line 4 prints out a heading for the printed output.

Line 5 is the beginning of the main loop in this function. The indexing variable index of this dotimes loop ranges from 0 to one less than *number-of-fitness-cases*. This dotimes loop ends at line 19.

Line 6 uses setf to assign index divided by *number-of-fitness-cases* to the local variable x. As index loops from 0 to 9, x will therefore range from 0.0 to 0.9 in steps of 0.1. That is, the independent variable x of this problem will range from 0.0 to 0.9.

Line 7 sets the variable this-fitness-case to a new, empty record structure of the type REGRESSION-fitness-case.

Line 8 uses the array access function (i.e., aref) to set the index-th element of the array called fitness-cases to the new fitness case record, namely this-fitness-case.

The next six lines fill in the value of the independent variable (i.e., x) and the values of the dependent variables (i.e., target) for the 10 fitness cases.

Lines 9 through 11 assign the value of x computed in line 6 to the independent-variable slot of the structure this-fitness-case.

Lines 12 through 14 assign (* 0.5 x x), that is, $x^2/2$ to the target slot of the structure this-fitness-case.

Lines 15 through 18 print out index, x, and $x^2/2$ for this particular iteration of the main dotimes loop for fitness cases.

Line 19 is the closing parenthesis associated with the dotimes loop started at line 5.

Line 20 uses the values function to return the result of this function, namely the array of fitness cases called fitness-cases.

Lines 21 and 22 close out the parentheses associated with the let from line 2 and the defun from line 1, respectively.

For many problems, the only lines that the user may have to change in this particular function are lines 14 and possibly line 6. These lines are shown in boldface above.

The user would change line 14 if he wanted the dependent variable (i.e., the target function) to be something other than $x^2/2$.

The user would change line 6 if he wanted the 10 values of the independent variables to be something other than 10 regularly spaced values between 0.0 and 0.9. For example, the user might want values of x between -2.0 and $+2.0$ or the user might want randomly selected values of x within a certain range.

The seventh item in the problem-specific part of the LISP code that we must write for this problem is the function REGRESSION-wrapper. In this problem (and most problems), the wrapper (output interface) merely returns what it is given. However, in some problems (e.g., bang-bang control problems), the output of the computer program (i.e., S-expression) from the population must be converted, via the wrapper, into the special domain of the problem (e.g., -1 and $+1$ for a bang-bang problem).

```
(defun REGRESSION-wrapper (result-from-program)
   (values result-from-program)
)
```

The eighth item in the problem-specific part of the LISP code that we must write is the function called evaluate-standardized-fitness-for-REGRESSION. This function receives two arguments from the kernel, namely the individual computer program (called program) from the population which is to be evaluated and the set of fitness cases (called fitness-cases). This function returns two values, namely the standardized fitness of the individuals and the number of hits. Standardized fitness is the driving force of genetic programming. The hits measure is a highly useful auxiliary measure that facilitates the monitoring of runs; however, the number of hits is not directly used by genetic programming (except possibly as part of the termination criterion for a run).

```
(defun evaluate-standardized-fitness-for-REGRESSION          ;01
        (program fitness-cases)                               ;02
  (let (raw-fitness hits standardized-fitness x target-value  ;03
        difference value-from-program this-fitness-case)      ;04
    (setf raw-fitness 0.0)                                     ;05
    (setf hits 0)                                              ;06
    (dotimes (index *number-of-fitness-cases*)                ;07
      (setf this-fitness-case (aref fitness-cases index))     ;08
      (setf x                                                 ;09
            (REGRESSION-fitness-case-independent-variable     ;10
                  this-fitness-case))                         ;11
      (setf target-value                                      ;12
            (REGRESSION-fitness-case-target                   ;13
                  this-fitness-case))                         ;14
      (setf value-from-program                                ;15
            (REGRESSION-wrapper (eval program)))              ;16
      (setf difference (abs (- target-value                   ;17
                              value-from-program)))           ;18
      (incf raw-fitness difference)                           ;19
      (when (< difference 0.01) (incf hits)))                 ;20
    (setf standardized-fitness raw-fitness)                   ;21
    (values standardized-fitness hits)                        ;22
  )                                                           ;23
)                                                             ;24
```

We now discuss how the function evaluate-standardized-fitness-
for-REGRESSION works.

Line 1 begins the definition of this function and line 2 identifies program
and fitness-cases as the two arguments that come in to this function from
the kernel. Note that in LISP, no type specification is required for either the
arguments to functions, local variables within the function, or the return
values.

Lines 3 and 4 identify the eight variables appearing in this let form as local
variables for use in this function.

Line 5 of this function initializes the raw-fitness to zero using the setf
(assignment) function.

Line 6 similarly initializes hits to zero.

Line 7 begins the main dotimes loop over the fitness cases. The indexing
variable index of this loop ranges from 0 to one below *number-of-fitness-cases*. That is, index will range between 0 and 9 for this problem.

Line 8 obtains this-fitness-case from index of the array fitness-
cases.

Lines 9 through 11 set the value of the terminal x to the independent-
variable part of the REGRESSION-structure for this-fitness-case. The
terminal x has been previously defined as a global variable. If there were
more than one terminal in this problem, they would all be set at this point to
the values appropriate for this-fitness-case.

Lines 12 through 14 set `target-value` to the `target` part of the REGRES-
SION-structure for `this-fitness-case`.

Lines 15 and 16 are a key step in genetic programming. Here the computer
program (i.e., S-expression) from the population is evaluated using the LISP
function `eval`. Then, the result returned by the individual computer program
is passed through the output interface (i.e., the wrapper) to yield the result of
the computer program in the domain of the problem (i.e., `value-from-
program`). For this problem (and most problems), the wrapper is the identity
operation. When the Common LISP function `eval` is used to evaluate the
individual LISP S-expressions, the evaluation will work correctly only if all of
the variable atoms appearing in the given S-expressions are proclaimed to be
global variables (as we have already done). Considerable computer time can
be saved by changing the `eval` function in line 16 of this function to the
special function `fast-eval` described in appendix E.

Lines 17 and 18 compute the `difference` between `value-from-program`
and the `target-value` for `this-fitness-case`.

Line 19 increments the `raw-fitness` by the `difference` associated with
`this-fitness-case`.

Line 20 compares the `difference` with 0.01 (the hits criterion). If the
`difference` is less than 0.01, `this-fitness-case` is considered to count as
a hit for this problem and the variable `hits` is incremented by one.

Line 21 computes `standardized-fitness`. For this problem, `standard-
ized-fitness` equals `raw-fitness`.

Line 22 returns `standardized-fitness` and `hits`.

For many problems, the only lines that the user may have to change in this
particular function are lines 17, 20, and 21 (shown in bold above).

The user would change line 17 if, for example, the user wanted error to be
measured as the square of the `difference`, rather than the absolute value of
the `difference`.

The user would change line 20 if he wanted a different way of measuring
`hits` or if he wanted to use a value other than 0.01 for the hits criterion. If the
user does not want to define `hits` for a particular problem, this line can be
omitted.

The user would change line 21 if `standardized-fitness` was not equal
to `raw-fitness` for the particular problem at hand. For example, in many
problems (e.g., the artificial ant problem), `standardized-fitness` is some
maximum value (e.g., 89) minus the `raw-fitness`.

Even for very simple problems, the bulk of computer time is consumed
during the execution of this function. This is particularly true if the evaluation
of fitness involves a simulation of some process (e.g., the artificial ant problem,
an optimal control problem, etc.) which itself involves looping over a large
number of time steps. Thus, the user should focus his optimization efforts on
this function and any functions in the function set (notably, user written
functions) which may be called when the S-expressions from the population
are evaluated.

The fourth major step in preparing to use genetic programming is selecting the values of certain parameters for controlling the run.

The ninth item in the problem-specific part of the LISP code that we must write is the `define-parameters-for-REGRESSION` function. This function is used to set (assign) the values to nine parameters that control the run.

```
(defun define-parameters-for-REGRESSION ()
  (setf *number-of-fitness-cases* 10)
  (setf *max-depth-for-new-individuals* 6)
  (setf *max-depth-for-individuals-after-crossover* 17)
  (setf *-fitness-proportionate-reproduction-fraction* 0.1)
  (setf *crossover-at-any-point-fraction* 0.2)
  (setf *crossover-at-function-point-fraction* 0.7)
  (setf *max-depth-for-new-subtrees-in-mutants* 4)
  (setf *method-of-selection* :fitness-proportionate)
  (setf *method-of-generation* :ramped-half-and-half)
  (values)
)
```

The second line (in boldface) which sets the `*number-of-fitness-cases*` is the line in this particular function that the user will be most likely to change.

The next six numerical parameters and the two qualitative parameters for controlling the run shown above are the default values found in table 6.1 in section 6.9.

Some of the 19 control parameters described in section 6.9 do not apply to this simplified LISP code. The operations of mutation, permutation, editing, encapsulation, and decimation are not implemented in this simplified LISP code, so the six control parameters concerning these operations do not apply here. The `*method-of-selection*` applies to both parents in this simplified LISP code (i.e., spousal selection is always the same as the selection method for the first parent). Adjusted fitness is always used with fitness-proportionate reproduction, and the elitist strategy is not used in this simplified LISP code.

All nine parameters set in this function are global variables, so this function explicitly returns no values via `values`.

We do not set the population size M, the maximum number G of generations to be run, or the seed to the randomizer in this function because they are likely to change frequently. These three parameters are established when genetic programming is invoked.

Finally, the fifth major step in preparing to use genetic programming is determining the criterion for terminating a run and accepting a result.

The tenth item in the problem-specific part of the LISP code is the `define-termination-criterion-for-REGRESSION` function. Termination is caused when a user-defined terminal criterion is satisfied. This function returns `T` (True) if we should stop the run.

The most popular termination criterion is to stop the current run if we have reached a prespecified maximum number G of generations to be run or if we have attained some prespecified perfect level of performance. This level of performance may be the achievement of a standardized-fitness of zero or the achievement of a hit for 100% of the fitness cases. In the symbolic regression problem (where floating-point values are involved), we might be satisfied with a run if the best computer program from the population came close to the target for 100% of the fitness cases.

```
(defun define-termination-criterion-for-REGRESSION          ;01
        (current-generation                                 ;02
         maximum-generations                                ;03
         best-standardized-fitness                          ;04
         best-hits)                                         ;05
   (declare (ignore best-standardized-fitness))             ;06
   (values                                                  ;07
      (or (>= current-generation maximum-generations)       ;08
          (>= best-hits *number-of-fitness-cases*))         ;09
   )                                                        ;10
)                                                           ;11
```

Lines 2 though 5 contain the four arguments of this function. These four variables are passed from the kernel into this function as arguments. These four arguments are values that may be useful in making the termination decision:

- current-generation is the index number of the current generation. It is 0 for the initial random generation.

- maximum-generations is the user specified maximum number G of generations to be run.

- best-standardized-fitness is the standardized fitness of the best-of-generation individual in the current population.

- best-hits is the number of hits for the individual in the population with the best (i.e., lowest) standardized fitness. Note that occasionally the highest number of hits is attained by an individual in the population other than the individual with the best-standardized-fitness.

Line 6 states that one of the four arguments (i.e., best-standardized-fitness) is to be ignored for this particular problem.

Line 7 begins the values function (which ends at line 10) which will contain the termination predicate. This predicate will evaluate to either T (True) or NIL (False). The value of this predicate will be returned by this function. Line 8 begins a logical or function which will test for two conditions. Line 8 tests whether the current-population has reached the maximum number G of generations to be run (i.e., maximum-generations). Line 9 tests a second condition, namely whether best-hits equals *number-of-fitness-cases*. If either of these two conditions are true (T), the or function will evaluate to true (T). If true (T) is returned by this function, the kernel will cause the run to be terminated.

For many problems, the only lines that the user may have to change in this particular function are lines 6, 8 and 9 (shown in boldface above).

Changing line 8 would be unusual.

Line 9 would be changed if a different termination predicate was desired. For example, an alternate way for termination to occur in this problem is that the absolute value of `best-standardized-fitness` is less than some specified total absolute error over all fitness cases (e.g., 0.05).

In line 6, any of the four variables from lines 2 through 5 that are ignored in defining the termination predicate in lines 8 and 9 should be listed. In the alternate way for termination to occur just described, `best-hits` rather than `best-standardized-fitness` would be ignored.

The eleventh item in the problem-specific part of the LISP code that we must write is a function called REGRESSION which informs the kernel about the six functions we have just written above for this problem. The name of this function, in effect, establishes the name of the problem.

```
(defun REGRESSION ()
   (values 'define-function-set-for-REGRESSION
           'define-terminal-set-for-REGRESSION
           'define-fitness-cases-for-REGRESSION
           'evaluate-standardized-fitness-for-REGRESSION
           'define-parameters-for-REGRESSION
           'define-termination-criterion-for-REGRESSION
   )
)
```

For each new problem that the user creates, he should create a function such as the one above by substituting the name of the new problem for REGRESSION in the above seven places.

Note that, to facilitate reading of the S-expressions in the population, we did not use the "*name*" notation for the variables in the terminal set. Therefore, the user should avoid using the names of any variables declared in this manner as the names of arguments to functions, especially any functions that may be called during the evaluation of an individual program from the population.

We now illustrate a run of genetic programming by calling a function called `run-genetic-programming-system`. This function takes four mandatory arguments, namely

(1) the name of the problem (e.g., REGRESSION),

(2) the randomizer seed (which should be greater than 0.0 and less than or equal to 1.0),

(3) the maximum number G of generations to be run (where a value of 1 calls for just the initial random generation and a value of 51 calls for the initial random generation plus 50 additional generations), and

(4) the population size M.

Thus, the twelfth item in the problem-specific part of the LISP code that we must write is the one line required to execute this problem by invoking the function `run-genetic-programming-system`, with four mandatory arguments as follows:

```
(run-genetic-programming-system 'REGRESSION 1.0 31 200)
```

Evaluation of the above would result in a run of the REGRESSION problem, using the randomizer seed of 1.0 with a maximum number G of generations of 31 (i.e., generation 0 plus 30 additional generations) with a population size M of 200.

The randomizer seed is an explicit argument to this function in order to give the user direct control over the randomizer. By re-using a seed, the user can obtain the same results (e.g., for debugging or so that interesting runs can be replicated). By using different seeds on different runs, the user will obtain different results.

Our experience is that this symbolic regression problem will produce a solution on about 70% of the runs within 31 generations with a population size of 200.

After the above four mandatory arguments, this function can take up to M additional optional arguments. Each optional argument represents a primed individual that will be seeded into the initial population. If fewer than M such primed individuals are provided, the initial population will contain all the primed individuals that are provided and will then be filled out with randomly created individuals.

We recommend that the user always perform at least the following three tests after he creates a new problem.

First, it is advisable to create a population of 50 or so random individuals and to carefully examine the appearance of the S-expressions that are actually produced and to verify that a plausible values of `standardized-fitness` and `hits` are computed for each S-expression. For example, execution of

```
(run-genetic-programming-system 'REGRESSION 1.0 1 50)
```

causes a population of 50 initial random individuals to be created and evaluated for fitness over only one generation.

Execution of the `print-population` function causes the population to be printed out. For example,

```
(print-population
    (run-genetic-programming-system 'REGRESSION 1.0 1 50))
```

This test will also establish that the problem turns over.

Secondly, it is advisable to test your fitness measure by testing particular individuals for which you know the answer. For example, execution of

```
(run-genetic-programming-system
    'REGRESSION 1.0 1 1 '(* 0.5 x x))
```

causes one generation of a population of size 1 to be run with the LISP S-expression (* 0.5 x x) as a primed individual. In this particular problem,

Problem-Specific Part of Simple LISP Code

you know that this S-expression should attain a standardized fitness of 0.0 (i.e., a perfect score) and 10 hits corresponding to each of the 10 fitness cases. In addition, you may be able to further test the fitness measure because you know that certain other primed individuals will score a particular number of hits. For example, the S-expression (- 2.0 X) will score 1 out of 10 hits for this problem because this S-expression represents a straight line that intersects the curve for $x^2/2$ on the interval [0, 1] only when X is zero.

Finally, execution of

```
(run-genetic-programming-system 'REGRESSION 1.0 31 200)
```

causes a full run with a randomizer seed of 1.0, a maximum number of generations to be run G of 31, and a population size M of 200. The seed for the randomizer should be greater than zero and less than or equal to 1.0.

The user can verify that he has entered the code correctly for this REGRES-SION problem by actually executing the above form with the above randomizer seed of 1.0. On Texas Instruments Explorer™ computers and on a Macintosh computer using Allegro Common LISP 1.3.2, the result should be that the best-of-generation individual for generation 0 has a standardized fitness measure of 0.42013 and scores two hits. The average standardized fitness of the population as a whole should be 1186.3. The best-of-generation individual for generation 0 should be

```
(% X 2.7838948).
```

The best-of-generation individual on generation 5 should have a standardized fitness of 0.0052807606 and should score 10 hits. This individual should be

```
(% (* X (- X (% X 2.2290492)))) 1.1068583).
```

The average standardized fitness of the population as a whole should be 4.3141365 on generation 5.

Because different Common LISP implementations represent floating-point numbers with different precisions, one may obtain somewhat different results for this problem in other environments. If this is the case, the user might consider using the benchmark for the Boolean MAJORITY-ON problem found in appendix B.2 below.

The user can further verify the correct operation of his program by running this problem a number of times as a benchmark with $M = 200$ and $G = 31$ and all the values of the minor parameters specified above. When we ran this problem using the simple LISP code here on 190 runs, the cumulative probability of success $P(M, i)$ was 18% by generation 5, 41% by generation 10, 52% by generation 15, 61% by generation 20, 64% by generation 25, and 67% by generation 30.

Figure B.1 presents the performance curves showing, by generation, the cumulative probability of success $P(M, i)$ and the number of individuals that must be processed $I(M, i, z)$ to guarantee, with 99% probability, that at least one S-expression comes within 0.01 of the target function for all 10 fitness cases for the symbolic regression problem with $x^2/2$ as the target function.

Regression of 0.5x**2

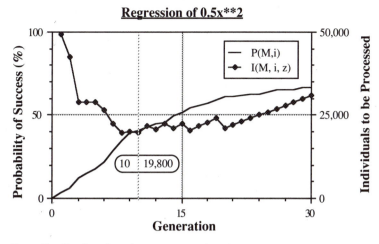

Figure B.1 Benchmark performance curves based on 190 runs of the simple LISP code for the symbolic regression problem with $x^2/2$ as the target function and $M = 200$ and $G = 31$.

The numbers in the oval indicate that, if this problem is run through to generation 10, processing a total of 19,800 (i.e., $200 \times 11 \times 9$ runs) individuals is sufficient to guarantee solution of this problem with 99% probability.

In summary, the symbolic regression problem for $x^2/2$ requires writing the following 12 items:

(1) `defvar` declaration(s),

(2) `define-terminal-set-for-REGRESSION`,

(3) `define-function-set-for-REGRESSION`,

(4) if applicable, user-defined problem specific function(s),

(5) `defstruct REGRESSION-fitness-case`,

(6) `define-fitness-cases-for-REGRESSION`,

(7) `REGRESSION-wrapper`,

(8) `evaluate-standardized-fitness-for-REGRESSION`,

(9) `define-parameters-for-REGRESSION`,

(10) `define-termination-criterion-for-REGRESSION`,

(11) the function `REGRESSION`, and

(12) the invocation using `run-genetic-programming-system`.

Other problems require writing a corresponding 12 items appropriate to that problem.

B.2   BOOLEAN MAJORITY-ON FUNCTION

We now illustrate a second problem. This problem involves learning the Boolean MAJORITY-ON function with three arguments (Boolean rule 232). The input consists of the three Boolean arguments d0, d1, and d2. The MAJORITY-

ON function returns T (True) if at least two of the input bits are true, otherwise it returns NIL (False).

The terminal set T for this problem consists of

```
T = {d0, d1, d2}.
```

We start by defining each of the variables in the terminal set as a global variable. The symbolic regression problem described above had only one independent variable whereas this problem has three independent variables. Thus, the first items in the problem-specific part of the LISP code that we must write are

```
(defvar d0)
(defvar d1)
(defvar d2)
```

The second item in the problem-specific part of the LISP code that we must write is the function called define-terminal-set-for-MAJORITY-ON to return the list of all terminals used in the problem, namely

```
(defun define-terminal-set-for-MAJORITY-ON ()
  (values '(d2 d1 d0))
)
```

The function set F for this problem consists of the three Boolean functions

```
F = {AND, OR, NOT}
```

taking two, two, and one argument, respectively. The third item is the function called define-function-set-for-MAJORITY-ON.

```
(defun define-function-set-for-MAJORITY-ON ()
  (values '(and or not)
          '(  2  2    1)
  )
)
```

In the example involving symbolic regression, all four functions took the same number of arguments (i.e., two). Here the not function takes a different number of arguments than the and or or functions. It is sometimes useful to include a function in the function set with varying numbers of arguments. For example if we wanted both the triadic and function as well as the usual diadic and function, we would place and twice in the first list and then place 2 and 3 in the second list as shown below:

```
(defun define-function-set-for-MAJORITY-ON ()
  (values '(and and or not)
          '(  2   3  2   1)
  )
)
```

The fourth items are the problem-specific functions required by the problem. For a Boolean problem, there is no concern about closure, overflows, underflows, or other errors and no problem-specific functions for this problem.

The fifth item is the `defstruct` record structure declaration for this problem:

```
(defstruct MAJORITY-ON-fitness-case
  d0
  d1
  d2
  target
)
```

Here the `MAJORITY-ON-fitness-case` has three independent variables and one dependent variable.

The sixth item is a function called `define-fitness-cases-for-MAJOR-ITY-ON`. The fitness cases for this problem consist of all possible combinations of the three Boolean arguments. That is, the `*number-of-fitness-cases*` is $2^3 = 8$. These fitness cases are created with three nested `dolist` functions, each looping over the list `(t nil)`. Maximum raw fitness is 8 matches. Standardized fitness is 8 minus raw fitness. Note that the target is defined by using an `or` function with four clauses reflecting the disjunctive normal form representation of the `MAJORITY-ON` function.

```
(defun define-fitness-cases-for-MAJORITY-ON ()
  (let (fitness-case fitness-cases index)
    (setf fitness-cases (make-array *number-of-fitness-cases*))
    (format t "~%Fitness cases")
    (setf index 0)
    (dolist (d2 '(t nil))
     (dolist (d1 '(t nil))
      (dolist (d0 '(t nil))
        (setf fitness-case
              (make-MAJORITY-ON-fitness-case)
        )
        (setf (MAJORITY-ON-fitness-case-d0 fitness-case) d0)
        (setf (MAJORITY-ON-fitness-case-d1 fitness-case) d1)
        (setf (MAJORITY-ON-fitness-case-d2 fitness-case) d2)
        (setf (MAJORITY-ON-fitness-case-target fitness-case)
              (or (and d2 d1 (not d0))
                  (and d2 (not d1) d0)
                  (or (and (not d2) d1 d0)
                      (and d2 d1 d0)
                  )
              )
        )
        (setf (aref fitness-cases index) fitness-case)
        (incf index)
        (format t
                "~% ~D    ~S    ~S    ~S       ~S"
```

```
                index d2 d1 d0
                (MAJORITY-ON-fitness-case-target
                  fitness-case
                )
          )
      )
      )
    )
    (values fitness-cases)
  )
)
```

The seventh item is the MAJORITY-ON-wrapper function for this problem.

```
(defun MAJORITY-ON-wrapper (result-from-program)
  (values result-from-program)
)
```

The eighth item is a function called evaluate-standardized-fitness-for-MAJORITY-ON. Note that it is necessary to set each of the three independent variables of this problem (represented by the global variables d0, d1, and d2) prior to the evaluation (via eval) of the program. Note also that the Boolean flag match-found is defined as a result of testing value-from-program for equality (i.e., eq) with target-value.

```
(defun evaluate-standardized-fitness-for-MAJORITY-ON
          (program fitness-cases)
  (let (raw-fitness hits standardized-fitness target-value
        match-found value-from-program fitness-case
        )
    (setf raw-fitness 0.0)
    (setf hits 0)
    (dotimes (index *number-of-fitness-cases*)
      (setf fitness-case (aref fitness-cases index))
      (setf d0 (MAJORITY-ON-fitness-case-d0 fitness-case))
      (setf d1 (MAJORITY-ON-fitness-case-d1 fitness-case))
      (setf d2 (MAJORITY-ON-fitness-case-d2 fitness-case))
      (setf target-value
            (MAJORITY-ON-fitness-case-target fitness-case))
      (setf value-from-program
            (MAJORITY-ON-wrapper (eval program)))
      (setf match-found (eq target-value value-from-program))
      (incf raw-fitness (if match-found 1.0 0.0))
      (when match-found (incf hits))
    )
    (setf standardized-fitness (- 8 raw-fitness))
    (values standardized-fitness hits)
  )
)
```

The ninth item is the `define-parameters-for-MAJORITY-ON` function. There are eight fitness cases for this problem.

```lisp
(defun define-parameters-for-MAJORITY-ON ()
  (setf *number-of-fitness-cases* 8)
  (setf *max-depth-for-new-individuals* 6)
  (setf *max-depth-for-new-subtrees-in-mutants* 4)
  (setf *max-depth-for-individuals-after-crossover* 17)
  (setf *fitness-proportionate-reproduction-fraction* 0.1)
  (setf *crossover-at-any-point-fraction* 0.2)
  (setf *crossover-at-function-point-fraction* 0.7)
  (setf *method-of-selection* :fitness-proportionate)
  (setf *method-of-generation* :ramped-half-and-half)
  (values)
)
```

The tenth item is the function `define-termination-criterion-for-MAJORITY-ON`.

```lisp
(defun define-termination-criterion-for-MAJORITY-ON
          (current-generation
           maximum-generations
           best-standardized-fitness
           best-hits)
  (declare (ignore best-standardized-fitness))
  (values (or (>= current-generation maximum-generations)
              (>= best-hits *number-of-fitness-cases*)
          )
  )
)
```

Note that, for this problem, we might have based the second test in the `or` condition on whether `standardized-fitness` equals zero, as follows:

```lisp
(= 0 best-standardized-fitness).
```

The eleventh item to be written is a function called `MAJORITY-ON` which informs the kernel about the six functions we have just written above for this problem.

```lisp
(defun MAJORITY-ON ()
  (values 'define-function-set-for-MAJORITY-ON
          'define-terminal-set-for-MAJORITY-ON
          'define-fitness-cases-for-MAJORITY-ON
          'evaluate-standardized-fitness-for-MAJORITY-ON
          'define-parameters-for-MAJORITY-ON
          'define-termination-criterion-for-MAJORITY-ON
  )
)
```

Finally, the twelfth item is the one line required to execute a run, namely `run-genetic-programming-system`. We can execute an actual run with a randomizer seed of 1.0 for 21 generations and a population size of 100 by executing

```
(run-genetic-programming-system 'MAJORITY-ON 1.0 21 100)
```

We can test the programs we have written for this MAJORITY-ON problem using a known 100%-correct individual as follows:

```
(run-genetic-programming-system 'MAJORITY-ON 1.0 1 1
               '(or (and d2 (and d1 (not d0)))
                   (or (and d2 (and (not d1) d0))
                       (or (and (not d2) (and d1 d0))
                           (and d2 (and d1 d0))
                   )
               )
           )
)
```

The user can verify that he has entered the code correctly for this MAJORITY-ON problem by actually executing the above form with the above randomizer seed of 1.0 with the second function set definition. The result should be that the best-of-generation individual for generation 0 has a standardized fitness measure of 1.0 and scores 7 hits. The average standardized fitness of the population should be 3.44. The best-of-generation individual for generation 0 should be

```
(OR (AND D2 D1 D1) (AND D1 D0))
```

The best-of-generation individual for generation 11 should have a standardized fitness measure of 0.0 and should score 8 hits. The average standardized fitness of the population as a whole should be 1.98. This individual should be

```
(OR (AND (OR D1 D1)
        (OR (AND (AND D2 D1 D1) (OR D2 D2))
            (OR D2 D0)))
    (AND (OR D2 D0) D0 D2)).
```

Since the MAJORITY-ON problem does not involve floating-point numbers, the user should be able to duplicate the above results on any machine and with any LISP implementation.

The user can further verify the correct operation of his program by running this problem a number of times as a benchmark with $M = 100$ and $G = 21$. When we ran this problem using the simple LISP code here on 330 runs, the cumulative probability of success $P(M, i)$ was 31% by generation 5, 63% by generation 10, 79% by generation 15, and 88% by generation 20.

Figure B.2 presents the performance curves showing, by generation, the cumulative probability of success $P(M, i)$ and the number of individuals that must be processed $I(M, i, z)$ to guarantee, with 99% probability, that at least

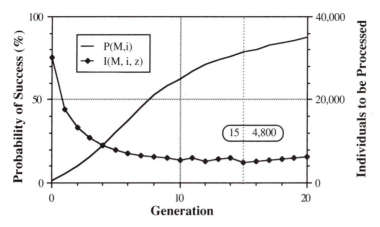

Figure B.2 Benchmark performance curves based on 330 runs of the simple LISP code for the MAJORITY-ON problem with a population size $M = 100$ and $G = 21$.

one S-expression correctly emulates the target MAJORITY-ON function for all eight fitness cases. The numbers in the oval indicate that, if this problem is run through to generation 15, processing a total of 4,800 (i.e., $100 \times 16 \times 3$ runs) individuals is sufficient to guarantee solution of this problem with 99% probability.

As previously mentioned, the choice of the population size is the single most important parameter for the genetic programming paradigm. A grossly insufficient population size hurts performance disproportionately. The reader should note that a harder Boolean function such as the even-3-parity (rule 150) requires a significantly larger population and a significantly greater number of generations than the relatively simple MAJORITY-ON function (rule 232) to yield a successful run with a reasonably high probability.

The user will have to experiment with his machine and his implementation of LISP to determine the size of the largest problem which can be successfully solved with the available computational resources. The MAJORITY-ON problem can realistically be run on a small machine using a software implementation of LISP. We have found, for example, that a population size M of about 10,000 is generally the largest population that can be reliably sustained on one Texas Instruments Explorer II + ™ processor using the default parameters specified in section 6.9 for a problem such as the intertwined spirals (section 17.3).

B.3 DISCRETE NON-HAMSTRUNG SQUAD CAR GAME

We now illustrate a third problem. The discrete non-hamstrung squad car is a game of perfect information involving two players moving on a checkerboard grid of indefinite size. The pursuing player is a squad car with a speed advantage over the pedestrian evader. The object is to discover a strategy for the pursuer that results in capture of the evader in optimal (i.e., minimal) time.

This problem is a simplification of the intriguing hamstrung squad car game first proposed by Isaacs (1965) in that the squad car is not hamstrung (i.e., it can

Problem-Specific Part of Simple LISP Code

turn in either direction); however, this problem can be readily be converted into the discrete hamstrung squad car problem. The vexacious research problem posed by Isaacs in 1965 for the conditions for the existence of a universal solution for this problem for all initial conditions was only recently solved (Baston and Bostock 1987). They are based on the speed ratio of the pursuer and the evader.

As in the differential pursuer-evader game described in section 15.2, the coordinate system is transformed after every move so that the pursuer is always at the origin. The reduced state variables of the system are therefore merely the horizontal and vertical coordinates of the evader (i.e., x and y).

As will be seen, solution of this problem involves the use of macros to define conditional operators.

The first items in the problem-specific part of the LISP code that we must write are declarations proclaiming the state variables of the problem as global variables.

```
(defvar x)
(defvar y)
```

Second, the terminal set T for this problem consists of

```
T = {(goN), (goE), (goS), (goW)}.
```

These four terminals are each functions of zero arguments which operate via their side effects on the system. In particular, these functions cause the pursuer in the game to go north, east, south, or west, respectively. In the more complicated hamstrung version of this game where the squad car can only turn right, the terminal set would consist only of (goE).

The second item in the problem-specific part of the LISP code that we must write is the function called define-terminal-set-for-NON-HAMSTRUNG-SQUAD-CAR. This function is to return the list of all terminals used in the problem. The LISP function we must write to return this list is therefore:

```
(defun define-terminal-set-for-NON-HAMSTRUNG-SQUAD-CAR ()
   (values '((goN) (goE) (goS) (goW)))
)
```

Third, the function set F for this problem consists of the two functions

```
F = {ifX, ifY}
```

taking three arguments each. These two functions test x (or y) for being less than zero, equal to zero, or greater than zero.

The third item is the function called define-function-set-for-NON-HAMSTRUNG-SQUAD-CAR.

```
(defun define-function-set-for-NON-HAMSTRUNG-SQUAD-CAR ()
   (values '(ifX ifY)
           '(  3    3)
   )
)
```

The fourth set of items in the problem-specific part of the LISP code that we must write are the problem-specific functions. However, before we do this for this problem, we must define a global variable that is needed by the problem-specific functions for this problem.

```
(defvar *speed-ratio* 2)
```

The *speed-ratio* is the ratio of the speed of the pursuer to the speed of the evader. Its importance is discussed in Baston and Bostock (1987).

We now define the problem-specific functions required in this problem. The first four functions move the pursuer around the grid by the step size *speed-ratio*.

```
(defun goN ()
  (setf y (- y *speed-ratio*))
)

(defun goS ()
  (setf y (+ y *speed-ratio*))
)

(defun goE ()
  (setf x (- x *speed-ratio*))
)

(defun goW ()
  (setf x (+ x *speed-ratio*))
)
```

In addition, we must define the conditional branching operators ifX and ifY for this problem.

Certain operators (notably conditional or iterative operators) cannot be implemented directly as ordinary LISP functions. The reason is that Common LISP evaluates all arguments to a function prior to entry into the function and then passes the *value* to which each argument evaluates into the function. If the argument has a side effect, the side effect would occur *unconditionally* at the time of the evaluation of the argument (i.e., outside the function). This early evaluation is not what is desired if the operator is intended to perform a certain side effect in a conditional manner or in a certain sequential order.

For example, in evaluating

```
(ifX (goW) (goN) (goE))
```

the desired effect is that we go in one particular direction depending on the value of x. The testing of x occurs inside the function ifX. If this operator were implemented as an ordinary LISP function, LISP would evaluate the three arguments of ifX prior to entry to the ifX function. Thus, we would go west *and* go north *and* go east prior to even getting inside the ifX function where we were planning to test x.

Thus, the conditional branching operators ifX and ifY must be implemented using a macro as described in subsection 6.1.1. as follows:

```
#+TI (setf sys:inhibit-displacing-flag t)
(defmacro ifX (lt-0-arg eq-0-arg gt-0-arg)
  `(cond ((>= x     *speed-ratio*)   (eval ',gt-0-arg))
         ((<= x (-*speed-ratio*))    (eval ',lt-0-arg))
         (t                          (eval ',eq-0-arg))
    )
)

(defmacro ifY (lt-0-arg eq-0-arg gt-0-arg)
  `(cond ((>= y     *speed-ratio*)   (eval ',gt-0-arg))
         ((<= y (- *speed-ratio*))   (eval ',lt-0-arg))
         (t                          (eval ',eq-0-arg))
    )
)
```

An additional aspect to this issue is that some implementations of Common LISP (e.g., the Texas Instruments Explorer machines) use a technique called "macro displacement" to side-effect programs being interpreted that contain references of macros. This technique has the beneficial effect of speeding up execution by incurring the cost of the macro-expansion only once. However, because this technique side-effects the program itself, then crossover that occurs on individuals after macro-expansion may see forms that are introduced by the macro-expander, not forms that are really part of the problem. On Texas Instruments machines, this behavior can be disabled by setting `sys:inhibit-displacing-flag` to T.

In addition, it is convenient to have an additional six corresponding functions for the evader. These functions do not appear in the terminal set or function set and they do not appear in the individual S-expressions in the population. They merely allow the convenient writing of the opposing strategy for the evader which is used in measuring the fitness of the individual pursuers.

```
(defmacro ifX-evader (lt-0-arg eq-0-arg gt-0-arg)
  `(cond ((>= x  1) (eval ',gt-0-arg))
         ((<= x -1) (eval ',lt-0-arg))
         (t         (eval ',eq-0-arg))
    )
)

(defmacro ifY-evader (lt-0-arg eq-0-arg gt-0-arg)
  `(cond ((>= y  1) (eval ',gt-0-arg))
         ((<= y -1) (eval ',lt-0-arg))
         (t         (eval ',eq-0-arg))
    )
)

(defun goN-evader ()
  (setf y (+ y 1))
  )
```

```
(defun goS-evader ()
  (setf y (- y 1))
)

(defun goE-evader ()
  (setf x (+ x 1))
)

(defun goW-evader ()
  (setf x (- x 1))
)
```

The fifth item in the problem-specific part of the LISP code that we must write is the `defstruct` record structure declaration for the fitness cases for this problem:

```
(defstruct NON-HAMSTRUNG-SQUAD-CAR-fitness-case
  x       .
  y
)
```

The sixth item is a function called `define-fitness-cases-for-NON-HAMSTRUNG-SQUAD-CAR`.

```
(defun define-fitness-cases-for-NON-HAMSTRUNG-SQUAD-CAR ()
  (let (fitness-case fitness-cases index)
    (setf fitness-cases (make-array *number-of-fitness-cases*))
    (format t "~%Fitness cases")
    (setf index 0)
    (dolist (x '(-5 5))
      (dolist (y '(-5 5))
          (setf fitness-case
                (make-NON-HAMSTRUNG-SQUAD-CAR-fitness-case)
          )
          (setf (NON-HAMSTRUNG-SQUAD-CAR-fitness-case-x
                  fitness-case
                )
                x
          )
          (setf (NON-HAMSTRUNG-SQUAD-CAR-fitness-case-y
                  fitness-case
                )
                y
          )
          (setf (aref fitness-cases index) fitness-case)
          (incf index)
          (format t "~% ~D    ~S   ~S" index x y)
      )
    )
```

```
      (values fitness-cases)
   )
)
```

The seventh item is the NON-HAMSTRUNG-SQUAD-CAR-wrapper function for
this problem.

```
(defun NON-HAMSTRUNG-SQUAD-CAR-wrapper (argument)
  (values argument)
)
```

The eighth item is a function called evaluate-standardized-fitness-for-
NON-HAMSTRUNG-SQUAD-CAR. Raw fitness is the sum, over the fitness cases, of
the time taken to capture the evader (or, if no capture occurs, the maximum
allowed amount of time).

```
(defun evaluate-standardized-fitness-for-NON-HAMSTRUNG-SQUAD-CAR
          (program fitness-cases)
  (let (raw-fitness hits standardized-fitness
        e-delta-x e-delta-y p-delta-x p-delta-y
        time-tally old-x old-y
        criterion
        (number-of-time-steps 50)
      )
    (setf criterion *speed-ratio*)
    (setf raw-fitness 0.0)
    (setf hits 0)
    (dotimes (icase *number-of-fitness-cases*)
      (setf x (NON-HAMSTRUNG-SQUAD-CAR-fitness-case-x
              (aref fitness-cases icase)
            )
      )
      (setf y (NON-HAMSTRUNG-SQUAD-CAR-fitness-case-y
              (aref fitness-cases icase)
            )
      )
      (setf time-tally 0.0)
      (catch :terminate-fitness-case-simulation
        (dotimes (istep number-of-time-steps)
          (setf old-x x)
          (setf old-y y)
          (when (and (<= (abs x) criterion)
                     (<= (abs y) criterion)
                )
            (incf hits)
            (throw :terminate-fitness-case-simulation
                :scored-a-hit
            )
          )
        )
```

```
;; Note: (x,y) is position of the Evader.
;; Changing the position of EVADER changes X and Y.
;; Execute evader player for this time step
(eval '(ifY-evader
          (goS-evader)
          (ifX-evader (goW-evader)
                        (goS-evader) (goE-evader)
          )
          (goN-evader)
        )
)
(setf e-delta-x (- old-x x))
(setf e-delta-y (- old-y y))
;; Reset position for Pursuer player.
(setf x old-x)
(setf y old-y)
(NON-HAMSTRUNG-SQUAD-CAR-wrapper (eval program))
(setf p-delta-x (- old-x x))
(setf p-delta-y (- old-y y))
;; Integrate x and y changes.
(setf x (- old-x (+ p-delta-x e-delta-x)))
(setf y (-old-y (+ p-delta-y e-delta-y)))
(incf time-tally)
  )
)
(incf raw-fitness time-tally)
)
(setf standardized-fitness raw-fitness)
(values standardized-fitness hits)
)
)
```

The ninth item that we must write is the define-parameters-for-NON-HAMSTRUNG-SQUAD-CAR function. There are four fitness cases for this problem.

```
(defun define-parameters-for-NON-HAMSTRUNG-SQUAD-CAR ()
  (setf *number-of-fitness-cases* 4)
  (setf *max-depth-for-new-individuals* 6)
  (setf *max-depth-for-new-subtrees-in-mutants* 4)
  (setf *max-depth-for-individuals-after-crossover* 17)
  (setf *fitness-proportionate-reproduction-fraction* 0.1)
  (setf *crossover-at-any-point-fraction* 0.2)
  (setf *crossover-at-function-point-fraction* 0.7)
  (setf *method-of-selection* :fitness-proportionate)
  (setf *method-of-generation* :ramped-half-and-half)
  (values)
)
```

The tenth item that we must write is the define-termination-crite-rion-for-NON-HAMSTRUNG-SQUAD-CAR. Since fitness is measured by time in this problem, we may be interested in game-playing strategies which minimize the time to capture (as opposed to strategies which merely succeed in making a capture, as measured by hits). If we want a run to continue even after an S-expression in the population attains the maximum value of hits, the termination criterion should not refer to best-hits. In fact, best-hits should be placed into the ignore statement and the termination criterion should be altered so as to not involve an or function.

```
(defun define-termination-criterion-for-NON-HAMSTRUNG-SQUAD-CAR
          (current-generation
           maximum-generations
           best-standardized-fitness
           best-hits)
   (declare (ignore best-hits best-standardized-fitness))
   (values (>= current-generation maximum-generations))
)
```

The eleventh item that we must write is a function called NON-HAMSTRUNG-SQUAD-CAR which informs the kernel about the six functions we have just written above for this problem. It is the same as for the MAJORITY-ON problem (except for its name).

```
(defun NON-HAMSTRUNG-SQUAD-CAR ()
   (values
       'define-function-set-for-NON-HAMSTRUNG-SQUAD-CAR
       'define-terminal-set-for-NON-HAMSTRUNG-SQUAD-CAR
       'define-fitness-cases-for-NON-HAMSTRUNG-SQUAD-CAR
       'evaluate-standardized-fitness-for-NON-HAMSTRUNG-SQUAD-CAR
       'define-parameters-for-NON-HAMSTRUNG-SQUAD-CAR
       'define-termination-criterion-for-NON-HAMSTRUNG-SQUAD-CAR
   )
)
```

We can test the programs using a known good individual as follows:

```
(run-genetic-programming-system 'NON-HAMSTRUNG-SQUAD-CAR 1.0 1 1
          '(ifX (goW) (ifY (goS) (goS) (goN)) (goE))
)
```

The twelfth item that we must write is the one line required to execute run-genetic-programming-system. We can execute an actual run with a randomizer seed of 1.0 for 31 generations and a population size of 100 by executing (evaluating) the following expression:

```
(run-genetic-programming-system
   'NON-HAMSTRUNG-SQUAD-CAR 1.0 21 100
)
```

If the user has entered all of the code for the NON-HAMSTRUNG-SQUAD-CAR problem correctly, then the best-of-generation individual for generation 0 should have a standardized fitness measure of 71.0 and should score 3 hits. The average standardized fitness of the population should be 183.01. The best-of-generation individual for generation 0 should be

```
(IFX (IFY (GOW) (GOW) (GON))
     (IFX (GOW) (GOS) (GOS))
     (IFX (GON) (GOW) (GOE)))
```

The best-of-generation individual for generation 20 should have a standardized fitness measure of 28.0 and should score 4 hits. The average standardized fitness of the population as a whole should be 47.74. This individual should be

```
(IFX (GOW)
     (IFY (IFX (GOW) (IFY (GOS) (GOS) (GOE)) (GON)) (GON) (GON))
     (IFY
      (IFY (IFX (GOW) (GOS) (GOS))
           (IFY (IFX (IFX (GON) (GOS) (GON)) (GOW) (GOE))
                (IFX (IFY (GOW) (GOE) (GOW))
                     (IFX (IFY (GOW) (GOE) (GON)) (GOS) (GOW))
(GOE))
                (GOW))
           (GON))
      (IFY (IFX (IFY (GOW) (GON) (GON)) (IFY (GOS) (GOS) (GOS))
(GOE))
           (IFX (GON) (IFX (GOE) (GOE) (GOW)) (GOE)) (GOW))
      (GON)))
```

If a population of 100 is used for 21 generations, approximately 95% of the runs will produce a strategy that results in the capture of the evader for 100% of the fitness cases (but not necessarily in optimal time).

Most versions of LISP permit the calling of functions written in other (programming languages (such as C) via a foreign function call interface, the details of which vary with the particular version of LISP involved.

Appendix C: Kernel of the Simple LISP Code

The kernel is the generic part of the simple LISP code for genetic programming. The user can run problems in the manner described in appendix B without ever modifying this kernel. The user should simply enter all of the LISP code in this appendix into a file along with the problem specific LISP code described in appendix B.

In this appendix, we briefly provide an overview of how the kernel works and some basic information to the user who may want to modify the kernel in some way. We assume that anyone contemplating modifying the kernel will be familiar with LISP and therefore do not use the highly simplified style of appendix B.

The discussion of the kernel is divided into 11 parts.

First, the kernel contains a `defstruct` declaration to declare the data structure representing each individual in the population. The `defstruct` form in LISP is similar to declarations of a record type in other programming languages (e.g., PASCAL). The `program` slot in this record type is the individual S-expression associated with the individual in the population. There are four additional slots in this record type, namely for the `standardized-fitness`, `adjusted-fitness`, `normalized-fitness`, and `hits` of the individual `program` in question.

```
(defstruct individual
  program
  (standardized-fitness 0)
  (adjusted-fitness 0)
  (normalized-fitness 0)
  (hits 0))
```

Second, the kernel contains nine `defvar` declarations for nine global variables and binds each of them to `:unbound`. These are the nine parameters that the user is expected to set in the `define-parameters-for-‹*›` function described in the previous section.

```
(defvar *number-of-fitness-cases* :unbound
  "The number of fitness cases")
```

```
(defvar *max-depth-for-new-individuals* :unbound
  "The maximum depth for individuals of the initial
  random generation")

(defvar *max-depth-for-individuals-after-crossover* :unbound
  "The maximum depth of new individuals created by crossover")

(defvar *fitness-proportionate-reproduction-fraction* :unbound
  "The fraction of the population that will experience fitness
  proportionate reproduction (with reselection)
  during each generation")

(defvar *crossover-at-any-point-fraction* :unbound
  "The fraction of the population that will experience
  crossover at any point in the tree (including terminals)
  during each generation")

(defvar *crossover-at-function-point-fraction* :unbound
  "The fraction of the population that will experience
  crossover at a function (internal) point in the tree
  during each generation.")

(defvar *max-depth-for-new-subtrees-in-mutants* :unbound
  "The maximum depth of new subtrees created by mutation")

(defvar *method-of-selection* :unbound
  "The method of selecting individuals in the population.
  Either :fitness-proportionate, :tournament or
  :fitness-proportionate-with-over-selection.")

(defvar *method-of-generation* :unbound
  "Can be any one of :grow, :full, :ramped-half-and-half")
```

Third the kernel defines three variables used by the randomizer and for bookkeeping purposes.

```
(defvar *seed* :unbound
  "The seed for the Park-Miller congruential randomizer.")

(defvar *best-of-run-individual* :unbound
  "The best individual found during this run.")

(defvar *generation-of-best-of-run-individual* :unbound
  "The generation at which the best-of-run individual was found.")
```

Fourth, the kernel contains the top level function `run-genetic-programming-system` that controls the genetic programming system. This is the function that the user uses to invoke the kernel. It has four mandatory arguments.

The first mandatory argument to this function is `problem-function`. When the kernel calls `problem-function`, this function delivers to the kernel the six functions that are needed by the kernel to define a specific problem.

The second mandatory argument to the `run-genetic-programming-sys-tem` function is the seed to the randomizer.

The third mandatory argument is the `maximum-generations` G to be run.

The fourth mandatory argument is the `size-of-population` M.

After the four mandatory arguments, there may be any number (up to M) of optional `seeded-program` arguments.

This function calls the `problem-function` (using funcall) and thereby obtains the problem specific functions that the user has defined in the problem specific part of the code.

Note that this function does some cursory checking of the validity of arguments to this function using four `assert` clauses.

```
(defun run-genetic-programming-system
          (problem-function
           seed
           maximum-generations
           size-of-population
           &rest seeded-programs)
;; Check validity of some arguments
  (assert (and (integerp maximum-generations)
               (not (minusp maximum-generations)))
          (maximum-generations)
          "Maximum-generations must be a non-negative ~
           integer, not ~S" maximum-generations)
  (assert (and (integerp size-of-population)
               (plusp size-of-population))
          (size-of-population)
          "Size-Of-Population must be a positive integer, ~
           not ~S" size-of-population)
  (assert (or (and (symbolp problem-function)
                   (fboundp problem-function))
              (functionp problem-function))
          (problem-function)
          "Problem-Function must be a function.")
  (assert (numberp seed) (seed)
          "The randomizer seed must be a number")
;;  Set the global randomizer seed.
  (setf *seed* (coerce seed 'double-float))
;;  Initialize best-of-run recording variables
  (setf *generation-of-best-of-run-individual* 0)
  (setf *best-of-run-individual* nil)
;;  Get the six problem-specific functions needed to
;;  specify this problem as returned by a call to
;;  problem-function
```

```
(multiple-value-bind (function-set-creator
                      terminal-set-creator
                      fitness-cases-creator
                      fitness-function
                      parameter-definer
                      termination-predicate)
    (funcall problem-function)
;; Get the function set and its associated
;; argument map
  (multiple-value-bind (function-set argument-map)
      (funcall function-set-creator)
;; Set up the parameters using parameter-definer
    (funcall parameter-definer)
;; Print out parameters report
    (describe-parameters-for-run
      maximum-generations size-of-population)
;; Set up the terminal-set using terminal-set-creator
    (let ((terminal-set (funcall terminal-set-creator)))
;; Create the population
      (let ((population
              (create-population
                size-of-population function-set argument-map
                terminal-set seeded-programs)))
;; Define the fitness cases using the
;; fitness-cases-creator function
        (let ((fitness-cases (funcall fitness-cases-creator))
              ;; New-Programs is used in the breeding of the
              ;; new population.  Create it here to reduce
              ;; consing.
              (new-programs (make-array size-of-population)))
;; Now run the Genetic Programming Paradigm using
;; the fitness-function and
;; termination-predicate provided
          (execute-generations
            population new-programs fitness-cases
            maximum-generations fitness-function
            termination-predicate function-set
            argument-map terminal-set)
;; Finally print out a report
          (report-on-run)
;; Return the population and fitness cases
;; (for debugging)
          (values population fitness-cases)))))))
```

Fifth, the kernel contains four functions for printing out various reports.

```
(defun report-on-run ()
  "Prints out the best-of-run individual."
```

```lisp
       (let ((*print-pretty* t))
         (format t "~5%The best-of-run individual program ~
                   for this run was found on ~%generation ~D and had a ~
                   standardized fitness measure ~
                   of ~D and ~D hit~P.  ~%It was:~%~S"
               *generation-of-best-of-run-individual*
               (individual-standardized-fitness
                 *best-of-run-individual*)
               (individual-hits *best-of-run-individual*)
               (individual-hits *best-of-run-individual*)
               (individual-program *best-of-run-individual*)))))

(defun report-on-generation (generation-number population)
  "Prints out the best individual at the end of each generation"
  (let ((best-individual (aref population 0))
        (size-of-population (length population))
        (sum 0.0)
        (*print-pretty* t))
    ;; Add up all of the standardized fitnesses to get average
    (dotimes (index size-of-population)
      (incf sum (individual-standardized-fitness
                  (aref population index))))
    (format t "~2%Generation ~D:  Average standardized-fitness ~
              = ~S.  ~%~
              The best individual program of the population ~
              had a ~%standardized fitness measure of ~D ~
              and ~D hit~P. ~%It was: ~%~S"
           generation-number (/ sum (length population))
           (individual-standardized-fitness best-individual)
           (individual-hits best-individual)
           (individual-hits best-individual)
           (individual-program best-individual))))

(defun print-population (population)
  "Given a population, this prints it out (for debugging) "
  (let ((*print-pretty* t))
    (dotimes (index (length population))
      (let ((individual (aref population index)))
        (format t "~&~D    ~S     ~S"
               index
               (individual-standardized-fitness individual)
               (individual-program individual))))))

(defun describe-parameters-for-run
    (maximum-generations size-of-population)
  "Lists the parameter settings for this run."
  (format t "~2%Parameters used for this run.~
            ~%==============================")
```

```
(format t "~%Maximum number of Generations:~50T~D"
        maximum-generations)
(format t "~%Size of Population:~50T~D" size-of-population)
(format t "~%Maximum depth of new individuals:~50T~D"
        *max-depth-for-new-individuals*)
(format t "~%Maximum depth of new subtrees for mutants:~50T~D"
        *max-depth-for-new-subtrees-in-mutants*)
(format t
   "~%Maximum depth of individuals after crossover:~50T~D"
   *max-depth-for-individuals-after-crossover*)
(format t
   "~%Fitness-proportionate reproduction fraction:~50T~D"
   *fitness-proportionate-reproduction-fraction*)
(format t "~%Crossover at any point fraction:~50T~D"
        *crossover-at-any-point-fraction*)
(format t "~%Crossover at function points fraction:~50T~D"
        *crossover-at-function-point-fraction*)
(format t "~%Number of fitness cases:~50T~D"
        *number-of-fitness-cases*)
(format t "~%Selection method: ~50T~A" *method-of-selection*)
(format t "~%Generation method: ~50T~A" *method-of-generation*)
(format t "~%Randomizer seed: ~50T~D" *seed*))
```

Sixth, the kernel contains a group of four functions for creating the individual LISP S-expressions for the initial random population (i.e., generation 0). These same functions are also used for creating tree fragments if we happen to be using the mutation operation. The second function in this group creates the ephemeral random constants (if any) for the initial random individuals. The user would modify this function in order to change the range of the ephemeral random constants or to add additional classes of ephemeral random constants. The function create-population causes the population of individuals to be created in a form specified by the variable *method-of-generation*, which can be :full, :grow or :ramped-half-and-half, these being the methods described in this book. Small changes to this function would allow different generative methods, such as a ramped, full, or grow method. Note that we used the do macro of Common LISP in create-population and throughout the kernel, rather than the more easily understood loop macro, because loop may not be supported in some generally available, older implementations of Common LISP.

```
(defvar *generation-0-uniquifier-table*
        (make-hash-table :test #'equal)
   "Used to guarantee that all generation 0 individuals
    are unique")

(defun create-population (size-of-population function-set
                          argument-map terminal-set
                          seeded-programs)
```

```
"Creates the population. This is an array of size
 size-of-population that is initialized to contain individual
 records. The Program slot of each individual is initialized
 to a suitable random program except for the first N programs,
 where N = (length seeded-programs). For these first N
 individuals the individual is initialized with the respective
 seeded program. This is very useful in debugging."
(let ((population (make-array size-of-population))
      (minimum-depth-of-trees 1)
      (attempts-at-this-individual 0)
      (full-cycle-p nil))
  (do ((individual-index 0))
      ((>= individual-index size-of-population))
    (when (zerop (mod individual-index
                      (max 1 (- *max-depth-for-new-individuals*
                                minimum-depth-of-trees))))
      (setf full-cycle-p (not full-cycle-p)))
    (let ((new-program
            (if (< individual-index (length seeded-programs))
                ;; Pick a seeded individual
                (nth individual-index seeded-programs)
                ;; Create a new random program.
                (create-individual-program
                  function-set argument-map terminal-set
                  (ecase *method-of-generation*
                    ((:full :grow)
                     *max-depth-for-new-individuals*)
                    (:ramped-half-and-half
                      (+ minimum-depth-of-trees
                         (mod individual-index
                              (- *max-depth-for-new-individuals*
                                 minimum-depth-of-trees)))))
                  t
                  (ecase *method-of-generation*
                    (:full t)
                    (:grow nil)
                    (:ramped-half-and-half
                     full-cycle-p))))))
      ;; Check if we have already created this program.
      ;; If not then store it and move on.
      ;; If we have then try again.
      (cond ((< individual-index (length seeded-programs))
             (setf (aref population individual-index)
                   (make-individual :program new-program))
             (incf individual-index))
```

```lisp
          ((not (gethash new-program
                        *generation-0-uniquifier-table*))
            (setf (aref population individual-index)
                  (make-individual :program new-program))
            (setf (gethash new-program
                          *generation-0-uniquifier-table*)
                  t)
            (setf attempts-at-this-individual 0)
            (incf individual-index))
          ((> attempts-at-this-individual 20)
            ;; Then this depth has probably filled up, so
            ;; bump the depth counter.
            (incf minimum-depth-of-trees)
            ;; Bump the max depth too to keep in line with
            ;; new minimum.
            (setf *max-depth-for-new-individuals*
                  (max *max-depth-for-new-individuals*
                      minimum-depth-of-trees)))
          (:otherwise (incf attempts-at-this-individual)))))
    ;; Flush out uniquifier table to that no pointers
    ;; are kept to generation 0 individuals.
    (clrhash *generation-0-uniquifier-table*)
    ;; Return the population that we've just created.
    population))

(defun choose-from-terminal-set (terminal-set)
  "Chooses a random terminal from the terminal set.
   If the terminal chosen is the ephemeral
   :Floating-Point-Random-Constant,
   then a floating-point single precision random constant
   is created in the range -5.0->5.0.
   If :Integer-Random-Constant is chosen then an integer random
   constant is generated in the range -10 to +10."
  (let ((choice (nth (random-integer (length terminal-set))
                    terminal-set)))
    (case choice
      (:floating-point-random-constant
        ;; pick a random number in the range -5.0 ---> +5.0.
        ;; Coerce it to be single precision floating-point.
        ;; Double precision is more expensive
        ;; A similar clause to this could be used to coerce it
        ;; to double prevision if you really need
        ;; double precision.
        ;; This is also the place to modify if you need a range
        ;; other than -5.0 ---> +5.0.
        (coerce (-(random-floating-point-number 10.0) 5.0)
                'single-float))
```

```
      (:integer-random-constant
        ;; pick a random integer in the range -10 ---> +10.
        (- (random-integer 21) 10))
      (otherwise choice)))))

(defun create-individual-program
          (function-set argument-map terminal-set
           allowable-depth top-node-p full-p)
  "Creates a program recursively using the specified functions
and terminals.  Argument map is used to determine how many
arguments each function in the function set is supposed to
have if it is selected.  Allowable depth is the remaining
depth of the tree we can create, when we hit zero we will
only select terminals.  Top-node-p is true only when we
are being called as the top node in the tree.  This allows
us to make sure that we always put a function at the top
of the tree.  Full-p indicates whether this individual
is to be maximally bushy or not."
  (cond ((<= allowable-depth 0)
          ;; We've reached maxdepth, so just pack a terminal.
          (choose-from-terminal-set terminal-set))
        ((or full-p top-node-p)
          ;; We are the top node or are a full tree,
          ;; so pick only a function.
          (let ((choice (random-integer (length function-set))))
            (let ((function (nth choice function-set))
                  (number-of-arguments
                    (nth choice argument-map)))
              (cons function
                    (create-arguments-for-function
                      number-of-arguments function-set
                      argument-map terminal-set
                      (-allowable-depth 1) full-p)))))
        (:otherwise
          ;; choose one from the bag of functions and terminals.
          (let ((choice (random-integer
                          (+ (length terminal-set)
                             (length function-set)))))
            (if (< choice (length function-set))
                ;; We chose a function, so pick it out and go
                ;; on creating the tree down from here.
                (let ((function (nth choice function-set))
                      (number-of-arguments
                        (nth choice argument-map)))
```

```
               (cons function
                       (create-arguments-for-function
                         number-of-arguments function-set
                         argument-map terminal-set
                         (- allowable-depth 1) full-p)))
                   ;; We chose an atom, so pick it out.
                   (choose-from-terminal-set terminal-set))))))
(defun create-arguments-for-function
         (number-of-arguments function-set
          argument-map terminal-set allowable-depth
          full-p)
  "Creates the argument list for a node in the tree.
   Number-Of-Arguments is the number of arguments still
   remaining to be created.  Each argument is created
   in the normal way using Create-Individual-Program."
  (if (= number-of-arguments 0)
      nil
      (cons (create-individual-program
              function-set argument-map terminal-set
              allowable-depth nil full-p)
            (create-arguments-for-function
             (-number-of-arguments 1) function-set
             argument-map terminal-set
             allowable-depth full-p))))
```

Seventh, the kernel contains a group of five functions to execute the main parts of the genetic programming system. Note that in this group we show two implementations of the function `sort-population-by-fitness`. This function destructively sorts the array used to hold the population. The sorting process rearranges the individuals in the population so that it is simpler to perform fitness-proportionate operations. The shorter, first implementation of `sort-population-by-fitness` is all that is strictly necessary for the code shown here to work. However, it relies on the native `sort` function provided by the Common LISP implementation being used. The implementation of the native `sort` function is always optimized. However, because of differences among Common LISP implementations, there is a good chance that individuals with the same fitness will be sorted into a different order so that our examples will not work identically across all implementations. Therefore we provide a simple quicksort implementation, which we believe will behave identically on all Common LISP implementations. It is advisable to use this second version of `sort-population-by-fitness` while testing any code that has been typed in from this book. The first version may provide a small performance improvement, however, once everything is known to be working correctly.

```
(defun execute-generations
    (population new-programs fitness-cases maximum-generations
     fitness-function termination-predicate function-set
     argument-map terminal-set)
```

```
      "Loops until the user's termination predicate says to stop."
      (do ((current-generation 0 (+ 1 current-generation)))
          ;; loop incrementing current generation until
          ;; termination-predicate succeeds.
          ((let ((best-of-generation (aref population 0)))
             (funcall
               termination-predicate current-generation
               maximum-generations
               (individual-standardized-fitness best-of-generation)
               (individual-hits best-of-generation))))
        (when (> current-generation 0)
          ;; Breed the new population to use on this generation
          ;; (except gen 0, of course).
          (breed-new-population population new-programs function-set
                               argument-map terminal-set))
        ;; Clean out the fitness measures.
        (zeroize-fitness-measures-of-population population)
        ;; Measure the fitness of each individual.  Fitness values
        ;; are stored in the individuals themselves.
        (evaluate-fitness-of-population
          population fitness-cases fitness-function)
        ;; Normalize fitness in preparation for crossover, etc.
        (normalize-fitness-of-population population)
        ;; Sort the population so that the roulette wheel is easy.
        (sort-population-by-fitness population)
        ;; Keep track of best-of-run individual
        (let ((best-of-generation (aref population 0)))
          (when (or (not *best-of-run-individual*)
                    (> (individual-standardized-fitness
                         *best-of-run-individual*)
                       (individual-standardized-fitness
                         best-of-generation)))
            (setf *best-of-run-individual*
                  (copy-individual best-of-generation))
            (setf *generation-of-best-of-run-individual*
                  current-generation)))
        ;; Print out the results for this generation.
        (report-on-generation current-generation population)))

(defun zeroize-fitness-measures-of-population (population)
  "Clean out the statistics in each individual in the
  population.  This is not strictly necessary, but it helps to
  avoid confusion that might be caused if, for some reason, we
  land in the debugger and there are fitness values associated
  with the individual records that actually matched the program
  that used to occupy this individual record."
```

```
  (dotimes (individual-index (length population))
    (let ((individual (aref population individual-index)))
      (setf (individual-standardized-fitness individual) 0.0)
      (setf (individual-adjusted-fitness individual) 0.0)
      (setf (individual-normalized-fitness individual) 0.0)
      (setf (individual-hits individual) 0)))))

(defun evaluate-fitness-of-population (population fitness-cases
                                        fitness-function)
  "Loops over the individuals in the population evaluating and
  recording the fitness and hits."
  (dotimes (individual-index (length population))
    (let ((individual (aref population individual-index)))
      (multiple-value-bind (standardized-fitness hits)
          (funcall fitness-function
                   (individual-program individual)
                   fitness-cases)
        ;; Record fitness and hits for this individual.
        (setf (individual-standardized-fitness individual)
              standardized-fitness)
        (setf (individual-hits individual) hits)))))

(defun normalize-fitness-of-population (population)
  "Computes the normalized and adjusted fitness of each
  individual in the population."
  (let ((sum-of-adjusted-fitnesses 0.0))
    (dotimes (individual-index (length population))
      (let ((individual (aref population individual-index)))
        ;; Set the adjusted fitness.
        (setf (individual-adjusted-fitness individual)
              (/ 1.0 (+ 1.0 (individual-standardized-fitness
                             individual))))
        ;; Add up the adjusted fitnesses so that we can
        ;; normalize them.
        (incf sum-of-adjusted-fitnesses
              (individual-adjusted-fitness individual))))
    ;; Loop through population normalizing the adjusted fitness.
    (dotimes (individual-index (length population))
      (let ((individual (aref population individual-index)))
        (setf (individual-normalized-fitness individual)
              (/ (individual-adjusted-fitness individual)
                 sum-of-adjusted-fitnesses))))))

(defun sort-population-by-fitness (population)
  "Sorts the population according to normalized fitness.
  The population array is destructively modified."
  (sort population #'> :key #'individual-normalized-fitness))
```

```lisp
(defun sort-population-by-fitness
       (population &optional (low 0) (high (length population)))
  "Uses a trivial quicksort to sort the population destructively
   into descending order of normalized fitness."
  (unless (>= (+ low 1) high)
    (let ((pivot (individual-normalized-fitness
                   (aref population low)))
          (index1 (+ low 1))
          (index2 (- high 1)))
      (loop (do () ((or (>= index1 high)
                        (<= (individual-normalized-fitness
                              (aref population index1)) pivot)))
              (incf index1))
            (do () ((or (>= low index2)
                        (>= (individual-normalized-fitness
                              (aref population index2)) pivot)))
              (decf index2))
            (when (>= index1 index2) (return nil))
            (rotatef (aref population index1)
                     (aref population index2))
            (decf index2))
      (rotatef (aref population low) (aref population (- index1 1)))
      (sort-population-by-fitness population low index1)
      (sort-population-by-fitness population index1 high)))
  population)
```

Eighth, the kernel contains five functions for controlling the breeding of the new population. This involves executing the appropriate genetic operation (e.g., crossover, reproduction, or mutation) with the appropriate probability. In selecting individuals to participate in the operations, if the *method-of-selection* is :fitness-proportionate, then fitness-proportionate selection is used. If the *method-of-selection* is :tournament, then tournament selection (i.e., the individual with the lower standardized fitness is selected from a random pair of individuals as described in subsection 6.4.1 and section 25.7) is used. If *method-of-selection* is :fitness-proportionate-with-over-selection, fitness-proportionate selection is performed from among a certain fraction of the more fit individuals as described in subsection 6.3.5 and section 25.6. This option is typically chosen for populations of 1,000 and above.

```lisp
(defun breed-new-population
       (population new-programs function-set
        argument-map terminal-set)
  "Controls the actual breeding of the new population.
   Loops through the population executing each operation
   (e.g., crossover, fitness-proportionate reproduction,
   mutation) until it has reached the specified fraction.
```

Kernel of the Simple LISP Code

The new programs that are created are stashed in new-programs
until we have exhausted the population, then we copy the new
individuals into the old ones, thus avoiding consing a new
bunch of individuals."

```lisp
(let ((population-size (length population)))
  (do ((index 0)
       (fraction 0 (/ index population-size)))
      ((>= index population-size))
    (let ((individual-1
            (find-individual population)))
      (cond ((and (< index (-population-size 1))
                  (< fraction
                     (+ *crossover-at-function-point-fraction*
                        *crossover-at-any-point-fraction*)))
             (multiple-value-bind (new-male new-female)
               (funcall
                (if (< fraction
                       *crossover-at-function-point-fraction*)
                    'crossover-at-function-points
                    'crossover-at-any-points)
                individual-1
                (find-individual population))
               (setf (aref new-programs index) new-male)
               (setf (aref new-programs (+ 1 index))
                     new-female))
             (incf index 2))
            ((< fraction
                (+ *fitness-proportionate-reproduction-fraction*
                   *crossover-at-function-point-fraction*
                   *crossover-at-any-point-fraction*))
             (setf (aref new-programs index) individual-1)
             (incf index 1))
            (:otherwise (setf (aref new-programs index)
                              (mutate individual-1 function-set
                                      argument-map terminal-set))
                        (incf index 1)))))
  (dotimes (index population-size)
    (setf (individual-program (aref population index))
          (aref new-programs index)))))

(defun find-individual (population)
  "Finds an individual in the population according to the
  defined selection method."
  (ecase *method-of-selection*
    (:tournament (find-individual-using-tournament-selection
                  population))
```

```lisp
    (:fitness-proportionate-with-over-selection
      (find-fitness-proportionate-individual
        (random-floating-point-number-with-over-selection
          population)
        population))
    (:fitness-proportionate
      (find-fitness-proportionate-individual
        (random-floating-point-number 1.0) population)))))

(defun random-floating-point-number-with-over-selection (population)
  "Picks a random number between 0.0 and 1.0 biased using the
  over-selection method."
  (let ((pop-size (length population)))
    (when (< pop-size 1000)
      (error "A population size of ~D is too small ~
              for over-selection." pop-size))
    (let ((boundary (/ 320.0 pop-size)))
      ;; The boundary between the over and under selected parts.
      (if (< (random-floating-point-number 1.0) 0.8)
          ;; 80% are in the over-selected part
          (random-floating-point-number boundary)
          (+ boundary
             (random-floating-point-number (- 1.0 boundary)))))))

(defun find-individual-using-tournament-selection (population)
  "Picks two individuals from the population at random and
  returns the better one."
  (let ((individual-a
          (aref population
                (random-integer (length population))))
        (individual-b
          (aref population
                (random-integer (length population)))))
    (if (< (individual-standardized-fitness individual-a)
           (individual-standardized-fitness individual-b))
        (individual-program individual-a)
        (individual-program individual-b))))

(defun find-fitness-proportionate-individual
    (after-this-fitness population)
  "Finds an individual in the specified population whose
  normalized fitness is greater than the specified value.
  All we need to do is count along the population from the
  beginning adding up the fitness until we get past the
  specified point."
  (let ((sum-of-fitness 0.0)
        (population-size (length population)))
```

```
(let ((index-of-selected-individual
        (do ((index 0 (+ index 1)))
            ;; Exit condition
            ((or (>= index population-size)
                 (>= sum-of-fitness after-this-fitness))
             (if (>= index population-size)
                 (- (length population) 1)
                 (- index 1)))
          ;; Body.  Sum up the fitness values.
          (incf sum-of-fitness
                (individual-normalized-fitness
                  (aref population index))))))
  (individual-program
    (aref population index-of-selected-individual)))))
```

Ninth, the kernel contains a group of five functions for performing crossover at any point. Before doing the crossover, the COPY-TREE function is used to make a copy of each parent. Then, we destructively modify the pointer of the crossover fragment (subtree) of the copy of each parent at its respective crossover point so that it points to the crossover fragment (subtree) of the copy of the other parent. After destructively changing the pointers in the copies, the resulting altered copies become the offspring. The original parents remain in the population and can often repeatedly participate in other operations during the current generation. That is, the selection of parents is done with replacement (i.e., reselection) allowed.

```
(defun crossover-at-any-points (male female)
  "Performs crossover on the programs at any point
   in the trees."
  ;; Pick points in the respective trees
  ;; on which to perform the crossover.
  (let ((male-point
          (random-integer (count-crossover-points male)))
        (female-point
          (random-integer (count-crossover-points female))))
    ;; First, copy the trees because we destructively modify the
    ;; new individuals to do the crossover. Reselection is
    ;; allowed in the original population.  Not copying would
    ;; cause the individuals in the old population to
    ;; be modified.
    (let ((new-male   (list (copy-tree male)))
          (new-female (list (copy-tree female))))
      ;; Get the pointers to the subtrees indexed by male-point
      ;; and female-point
      (multiple-value-bind (male-subtree-pointer male-fragment)
          (get-subtree (first new-male) new-male male-point)
```

```lisp
          (multiple-value-bind
            (female-subtree-pointer female-fragment)
              (get-subtree
                (first new-female) new-female female-point)
            ;; Modify the new individuals by smashing in the
            ;; (copied) subtree from the old individual.
            (setf (first  male-subtree-pointer) female-fragment)
            (setf (first female-subtree-pointer) male-fragment)))
        ;; Make sure that the new individuals aren't too big.
        (validate-crossover male new-male female new-female)))))

(defun count-crossover-points (program)
  "Counts the number of points in the tree (program).
   This includes functions as well as terminals."
  (if (consp program)
      (+ 1 (reduce #'+ (mapcar #'count-crossover-points
                               (rest program))))
      1))

(defun max-depth-of-tree (tree)
  "Returns the depth of the deepest branch of the
   tree (program)."
  (if (consp tree)
      (+ 1 (if (rest tree)
               (apply #'max
                      (mapcar #'max-depth-of-tree (rest tree)))
               0))
      1))

(defun get-subtree (tree pointer-to-tree index)
  "Given a tree or subtree, a pointer to that tree/subtree and
   an index return the component subtree that is numbered by
   Index.  We number left to right, depth first."
  (if (= index 0)
      (values pointer-to-tree (copy-tree tree) index)
      (if (consp tree)
          (do* ((tail (rest tree) (rest tail))
                (argument (first tail) (first tail)))
               ((not tail) (values nil nil index))
            (multiple-value-bind
              (new-pointer new-tree new-index)
              (get-subtree argument tail (- index 1))
              (if (= new-index 0)
                  (return
                    (values new-pointer new-tree new-index))
                  (setf index new-index))))
          (values nil nil index))))
```

```
(defun validate-crossover (male new-male female new-female)
  "Given the old and new males and females from a crossover
   operation check to see whether we have exceeded the maximum
   allowed depth.  If either of the new individuals has exceeded
   the maxdepth then the old individual is used."
  (let ((male-depth   (max-depth-of-tree (first new-male)))
        (female-depth (max-depth-of-tree (first new-female))))
    (values
     (if (or (= 1 male-depth)
             (> male-depth
                *max-depth-for-individuals-after-crossover*))
         male
         (first new-male))
     (if (or (= 1 female-depth)
             (> female-depth
                *max-depth-for-individuals-after-crossover*))
         female
         (first new-female)))))
```

Tenth, the kernel contains a group of three functions for performing crossover restricted to function (internal) points.

```
(defun crossover-at-function-points (male female)
  "Performs crossover on the two programs at a function
   (internal) point in the trees."
  ;; Pick the function (internal) points in the respective trees
  ;; on which to perform the crossover.
  (let ((male-point
          (random-integer (count-function-points male)))
        (female-point
          (random-integer (count-function-points female))))
    ;; Copy the trees because we destructively modify the new
    ;; individuals to do the crossover and Reselection is
    ;; allowed in the original population. Not copying would
    ;; cause the individuals in the old population to
    ;; be modified.
    (let ((new-male   (list (copy-tree male)))
          (new-female (list (copy-tree female))))
      ;; Get the pointers to the subtrees indexed by male-point
      ;; and female-point
      (multiple-value-bind (male-subtree-pointer male-fragment)
          (get-function-subtree
            (first new-male) new-male male-point)
        (multiple-value-bind
            (female-subtree-pointer female-fragment)
            (get-function-subtree
              (first new-female) new-female female-point)
```

```
        ;; Modify the new individuals by smashing in
        ;; the (copied) subtree from the old individual.
        (setf (first  male-subtree-pointer) female-fragment)
        (setf (first female-subtree-pointer) male-fragment)))
      ;; Make sure that the new individuals aren't too big.
      (validate-crossover male new-male female new-female)))))

(defun count-function-points (program)
  "Counts the number of function (internal) points
   in the program."
  (if (consp program)
      (+ 1 (reduce #'+ (mapcar #'count-function-points
                               (rest program))))
      0))

(defun get-function-subtree (tree pointer-to-tree index)
  "Given a tree or subtree, a pointer to that tree/subtree and
   an index return the component subtree that is labeled with
   an internal point that is numbered by Index.  We number left
   to right, depth first."
  (if (= index 0)
      (values pointer-to-tree (copy-tree tree) index)
      (if (consp tree)
          (do* ((tail (rest tree) (rest tail))
                (argument (first tail) (first tail)))
               ((not tail) (values nil nil index))
            (multiple-value-bind
              (new-pointer new-tree new-index)
                (if (consp argument)
                    (get-function-subtree
                      argument tail (- index 1))
                    (values nil nil index))
              (if (= new-index 0)
                  (return
                    (values new-pointer new-tree new-index))
                  (setf index new-index))))
          (values nil nil index))))
```

Eleventh, the kernel contains a function for performing the mutation operation.

```
(defun mutate (program function-set argument-map terminal-set)
  "Mutates the argument program by picking a random point in
   the tree and substituting in a brand new subtree created in
   the same way that we create the initial random population."
  ;; Pick the mutation point.
  (let ((mutation-point
          (random-integer (count-crossover-points program)))
```

```
;; Create a brand new subtree.
(new-subtree
  (create-individual-program
    function-set argument-map terminal-set
    *max-depth-for-new-subtrees-in-mutants* t nil)))
(let ((new-program (list (copy-tree program))))
  (multiple-value-bind (subtree-pointer fragment)
    ;; Get the pointer to the mutation point.
    (get-subtree (first new-program)
                 new-program mutation-point)
  ;; Not interested in what we're snipping out.
  (declare (ignore fragment))
  ;; Smash in the new subtree.
  (setf (first subtree-pointer) new-subtree))
(values (first new-program) new-subtree))))
```

Twelfth, the kernel contains a group of three functions for generating random numbers needed by the genetic programming system.

In implementing a genetic algorithm, the genetic programming paradigm, or, in fact, any machine learning paradigm involving any probabilistic steps on a computer, it is important to have an effective randomizer that is capable of producing a *stream* of *independent* random integers. Many randomizers originally written for the purpose of generating random floating-point numbers are not suitable for this purpose. They produce numbers that satisfy certain tests, but which do not produce the desired stream of integers. The randomizer seed is specified each time the user invokes the system.

The randomizer below is the well documented Park-Miller multiplicative congruential randomizer (Park and Miller 1988). We used a more complicated triply seeded randomizer in the runs reported throughout the book; however, we believe that the Park-Miller randomizer using one seed is an effective, rapid, and simple randomizer.

```
(defun park-miller-randomizer ()
  "The Park-Miller multiplicative congruential randomizer
  (CACM, October 88, Page 1195).  Creates pseudo random floating
  point numbers in the range 0.0 < x <= 1.0.  Record the seed
  value, called *seed*, to make your runs reproducible.
  NOTE: 16807 is (expt 7 5) and 2147483647 is (- (except 2 31) 1)"
  #+Lucid (unless (typep *seed* 'integer)
            (setq *seed* (round *seed*)))
  (assert (not (zerop *seed*)) () "*seed* cannot be zero.")
  (let ((multiplier #+Lucid 16807 #-Lucid 16807.0d0)
        (modulus #+Lucid 2147483647 #-Lucid 2147483647.0d0))
    (let ((temp (* multiplier *seed*)))
      (setf *seed* (mod temp modulus))
      (#+lucid float #-lucid progn (/ *seed* modulus)))))
```

The Park-Miller randomizer can then be used to create random floating-point numbers as follows:

```
(defun random-floating-point-number (n)
   "Returns a pseudo random floating-point number
                  in range 0.0 <= number < n"
   (let ((random-number (park-miller-randomizer)))
     ;; We subtract the randomly generated number from 1.0
     ;; before scaling so that we end up in the range
     ;; 0.0 <= x < 1.0, not 0.0 < x <= 1.0
     (* n (- 1.0d0 random-number)))))
```

The Park-Miller randomizer can then be used to create random integers as follows:

```
(defun random-integer (n)
   "Returns a pseudo-random integer in the range 0 ---> n-1."
   (let ((random-number (random-floating-point-number 1.0)))
     (floor (* n random-number))))
```

The user can test the correctness of his Park-Miller randomizer by starting with a seed of 1.0 and running it 10,000 times. At that point, the seed on the Texas Instruments Explorer II$^+$ computer is 1.043618065×10^9. We believe that the code for the Park-Miller randomizer above is very nearly machine independent and LISP implementation independent over a wide variety of different machines and LISP implementations.

The above LISP code (along with such updates as may from time to time be added) can be obtained on line via anonymous file transfer from the `pub/genetic-programming` directory from the site `ftp.cc.utexas.edu`.

The programs, procedures, and applications presented in this book have been included for their instructional value. The publisher and the authors offer NO WARRANTY OF FITNESS OR MERCHANTABILITY FOR ANY PARTICULAR PURPOSE and accept no liability with respect to these programs, procedures, and applications.

In addition, various papers on genetic programming are stored at this same FTP site.

You may subscribe to an electronic mailing list for the discussion of issues concerning genetic programming by sending a subscription request to `genetic-programming-request@cs.stanford.edu`.

Appendix D: Embellishments to the Simple LISP Code

The simple LISP code described in the previous section makes it relatively simple to start running problems with genetic programming.

In this section, we mention some of the many possible embellishments which the reader may want to consider adding to this code.

D.1 OUTPUT FILE

One obvious improvement is to present the output from the simple LISP program in tabular form and write it out to a file.

Such a file could begin with all the parameters being used and the time and date. It might also contain information on each generation, including the single individual S-expression with the best standardized fitness for the generation, its standardized fitness, and its number of hits. In addition, in the unusual situation where there is an individual in the population with a higher number of hits than the single individual S-expression with the best standardized fitness (i.e., the best-of-generation individual), the file might also contain that S-expression, its standardized fitness, and its number of hits. Other data which might be written into the file include the standardized fitness, the number of hits associated with the best-of-generation and worst-of-generation individual in the population, the average fitness for the population as a whole, and the variety of the population. The number of internal and external points in the S-expression of the best-of-generation individual and the average for the population as a whole might also be useful.

In addition, it is also useful to have the ability to print out the entire population (with the above information) for generation 0 or any subsequent generation or fraction of subsequent generations.

D.2 INPUT OF PARAMETERS

If the user is planning to run the simple LISP code on more than a few occasions, he will quickly see the value and need for improving the method of input for parameters for controlling genetic programming. The `run-genetic-programming-system` function can be easily included in some higher-level function which pops up a menu giving the user the opportunity to select a problem name and parameters. Such a menu might contain suggested default values for each parameter.

D.3 VISUALIZATION

After we had successfully used genetic programming to solve several problems involving simulations (e.g., broom balancing and the artificial ant), we started creating videotapes in which we animated the behavior of various individuals from the population for the purpose of presenting the results at lectures and conferences. It soon became apparent that such animation would be extremely useful at the time of creating, writing, debugging, and solving the problem in the first place as opposed to merely being a *post facto* presentation aid. Ideas for visualizing problems can be found on the videotape accompanying this book (as described in the preface).

D.4 INTERACTIVITY

It is desirable to be able to interact with a run while it is running. The graphical outputs described in appendix A provide examples of useful interactivity.

For example, a control command might extend promising subruns on the fly by doubling the number of generations to be executed. These extensions require on the fly re-dimensioning of any statistical arrays which might be in the program and changing of the scales on any interactive graphs and animation.

Alternatively, another control command might interrupt a subrun or run in a way that fills in and preserves various statistical tables in a specified way. It is also handy to create some time-saving keystrokes for starting new runs, starting runs with the same parameters as the previous run, and other commonly encountered situations.

D.5 GOLD STANDARD INDIVIDUAL

It is useful to define a gold standard individual for each problem. If a gold standard individual is provided for a particular problem, percentage comparisons can then be made between its performance and the standardized fitness of each individual for which information is being reported (e.g., interactively on the screen or in report files). The gold standard individual may be a known solution to the problem, a known approximate solution, a straw man solution, or merely the best solution obtained so far from previous runs of genetic programming. Genetic programming does not use or have access to any information about the gold standard individual.

D.6 SUBRUNS

Although genetic programming can be run for large numbers of generations, computer resources are often best used by instead running a number of shorter, independent subruns. Thus, the higher-level function described in section D.2 might also contain a loop which runs the `run-genetic-programming-system` function for a specified number of subruns with the chosen parameters.

This higher-level function might also produce a summary report for each the subruns and highlight the best subrun.

D.7 PERPETUAL LOG FILE

It is valuable to implement a system for recording each run and each subrun. We have established a numbering system involving a separate series of perpetual numbers for each run and subrun on each processor we use. A perpetual log file maintains a record of each run including the date and time, the name of the problem being run, the particular version of the problem being run, all parameters associated with the run, and the seeds to all randomizers.

In addition to providing a useful log of activity, this perpetual file contains the information to allow us to automatically re-run runs that are particularly interesting. On such re-runs, we often turn on features for audit trails or additional statistical calculations that were not part of the original run.

It is usually desirable to have separate seeds for each aspect of a run. These separate seeds include the seed for creation of the fitness cases (if it is randomly created), the creation of the initial random population, and the probabilistic steps of the algorithm itself so that it is possible to recreate a run that keeps one or more of these aspects constant while allowing other aspects of the run to vary.

D.8 MONITORING OF RANDOMIZER AND OTHER INDICATORS

Marsaglia (1968, 1983) describes the pitfalls associated with generating a stream of independent random integers suitable for carrying out the related steps of probabilistic algorithms. If a given randomizer is being used over a period of time for different problems, a randomizer that may have worked well for one group of problems may not work for another. It is, therefore, important to continually review the performance of one's randomizer in the light of the problems currently being run with that randomizer. The ongoing performance of one's randomizer can be sampled and the results reported in performance tables on a periodic basis.

In addition, both the variety of the population and the number of crossovers aborted because of the limit on the maximum size (i.e., depth) of S-expressions should be closely monitored. Both of these indicators can be symptoms of problems in runs that are otherwise difficult to see. In particular, when the number of aborted crossovers is high, instances of mere reproduction are replacing intended instances of crossover.

D.9 RE-STARTING RUNS

If the population of S-expressions is saved in addition to all the parameters of the run, it is possible to re-start a subrun at a particular generation and continue it for additional generations. This feature can allow runs to be stopped and analyzed and then re-started if they are meritorious. On extremely time-consuming runs, the periodic saving of the population can permit re-starting of a run that is interrupted due to a machine failure.

D.10 BATCH RUNS

It is useful to create a script which causes a series of runs and subruns to be executed in series, without further intervention, overnight or over a period of days. It is especially desirable if the script can be picked up at the proper spot if computation is interrupted by an unexpected re-boot or other failure.

D.11 POPULATION STRUCTURES

A `defstruct` can be used to create a structure to represent each population as well as individuals. In addition, some problems naturally call for multiple populations (e.g., co-evolution).

D.12 ERROR HANDLERS

In using genetic programming, the user will have to confront the wide variety of pathological situations that arise as a result of executing randomly created computer programs and genetically created computer programs. These problems are minimal if the user is merely working on Boolean problems, pure symbolic problems involving a small alphabet, or problems involving modular arithmetic. However, error handling becomes an important issue when floating-point arithmetic is involved. It may also be an important issue when integers are involved, depending on how the BIGNUM mode of LISP operates on one's implementation of LISP. In each instance, the objective is to identify the occurrence of an error (e.g., a floating-point overflow or underflow) in such a way that some appropriate value is assigned to the subS-expression causing the error and so that evaluation of the S-expression can resume. Handling such errors will usually require becoming familiar with the error handling features of both the machine and LISP software being used or, possibly, writing protected arithmetic functions which prevent the error conditions from arising. Steele (1990) describes some portable error handling mechanisms which may be helpful.

D.13 DATA TYPES AND PRECISION

When ephemeral random constants are included in the terminal set and incorporated into the initial random individuals, their type and range must be appropriate for the problem at hand. Ephemeral random constants might be integers, natural numbers, floating-point numbers, probabilities (floating-point numbers between 0 and 1), logical constants, etc.

If the user wants double precision floating-point arithmetic to be used in the evaluation of S-expressions, then the ephemeral random constants and all the terminals defined via the fitness cases should be coerced into double precision.

D.14 TOOL KIT FOR SOLVING EQUATIONS

To facilitate the input of general mathematical equations (sections 10.7 to 10.10) into genetic programming, a tool kit can be written to allow easy expression of the equation.

Each equation is written out in terms of the following:

- the independent variable x (called "x-values"),
- the unknown function being sought (called "genetically produced function"),
- addition,
- subtraction,
- multiplication,
- protected division (%),
- differentiation (with respect to a specified variable),
- integration (with respect to a specified variable),
- any other function including sine, cosine, exponential, logarithm, and
- domain specific functions defined by the user.

We apply an ordinary function such as addition, subtraction, multiplication division, sine, cosine, exponentiation, logarithm, etc. to a curve by using the special $ function and the name of the desired function. For example,

```
($ 'cos x-values)
```

applies the cosine function to the curve consisting of the 200 random domain values (x_i) so as to produce a new curve representing $\mathrm{Cos}\,x$.

Similarly, the $ function can be applied to scalar constants as well as curves. For example,

```
($ '+ 4.0 x-values)
```

applies the addition function to the scalar constant 4.0 and the curve consisting of the 200 random domain values (x_i) so as to produce a new curve representing $4x$.

Consider the differential equation of Example 1 in section 10.7. Since we have adopted the convention that the right hand side of the equation is always zero, the left hand side of the differential equation involves the unknown function (to be produced genetically). We would rewrite the left hand side of the given differential equation

$$\frac{dy}{dx} + y \cos x = 0$$

in the following way:

```
($ '+ (differentiate genetically-produced-function
        x-values)
    ($ '* genetically-produced-function
        ($ 'cos x-values))).
```

This is interpreted as follows: The cosine function is applied to the independent variable (the x-values). Then, the result is multiplied by the values of the unknown function *y* (the genetically produced function) to obtain an intermediate result. Then, the unknown function (genetically produced function) is differentiated with respect to the independent variable (x-values) and the result added to the previously obtained intermediate result.

The sum of the absolute values of the differences between the left hand side of the equation and the right hand side of the equation (i.e., the zero curve) is then computed. The closer this sum of differences is to zero, the better.

D.15   TESTING AIDS

There are numerous aids to testing programs that can be added, including the following:

- An additional report indicating the performance of the current best-of-generation individual in handling each separate fitness case and, if appropriate, whether a hit is scored for that fitness case.

- "Clean up" functions at the end of each generation, subrun, and run which produce certain special reports.

D.16   ADDITIONAL FEATURES

The following additional features, some of which are mentioned in this book, may be useful to add to the simple LISP code:

- The secondary operations of permutation, editing, decimation, and encapsulation.

- Creation of particular structures using restrictive rules of syntactic construction and structure-preserving crossover.

- Audit trails.

- The various alternative methods for generating the initial random population, such as half and half and full.

- Additional heuristic abort predicates (e.g., abort on achieving a non-maximal sufficient number of hits, abort if the statistics have plateaued for a number of generations and variety is abnormally low).

- The option of varying of the fitness cases for each generation.
- The various optimization techniques described in appendix A.2 (especially the avoidance of recomputing the fitness of the individuals that are simply copied from a previous generation).

Appendix E: Streamlined Version of EVAL

A considerable amount of computer time can be saved by using a streamlined version of the LISP function EVAL.

The FAST-EVAL function is faster but less general than EVAL. FAST-EVAL can also help to reduce the amount of CONSing in running the genetic programming paradigm because many Common LISP interpreters are inefficient in this respect. Excessive CONSing exacts a price in execution time and paging, as well as time required for garbage collection.

The LISP function EVAL is ordinarily called in line 16 of the function called evaluate-standardized-fitness-for-REGRESSION (where "REGRESSION" is the problem name) in the problem specific LISP code as described in appendix B. EVAL should be replaced by FAST-EVAL at line 16 to achieve the benefits described in this appendix.

The version shown in this appendix is limited to handling functions with up to four arguments, although it can be easily modified to accommodate additional arguments by modifying the macro FAST-EVAL-FUN.

There is, unfortunately, no implementation of FAST-EVAL that is both efficient and portable for dealing with the problem of efficiently circumventing expensive macroexpansion for primitive functions which must be implemented as macros. Because of this, we cannot guarantee that the code here for FAST-EVAL will work on every machine and every Common LISP implementation. Of course, EVAL always will work. We have therefore provided implementations of FAST-EVAL which will work correctly if compiled and executed on the following implementations:

- Texas Instruments Explorer Common Lisp version 6.1
- Allegro or Coral Common LISP versions 1.3.2 and 2.0b1 for the Macintosh computer,
- Lucid Common LISP version 4.0.x, and
- Allegro Common LISP version 4.1 from Franz Inc.

The versions of FAST-EVAL herein may work for other versions of these vendors' software; however, the user may have to write his own version to gain the performance benefits of FAST-EVAL. The implementations of

FAST-EVAL shown below are conditionalized using the Common LISP reader macros #+ and #-.

```
(defmacro fast-eval-fun ()
  "A code body that does fast evaluation of a
  functional expression."
  '(ecase (length expr)
     (1 (funcall fef))
     (2 (funcall fef
                 (fast-eval
                  (second expr))))
        (3 (funcall fef
                 (fast-eval (second expr))
                 (fast-eval
                  (third expr))))
          (4 (funcall fef
                 (fast-eval (second expr))
                 (fast-eval (third expr))
                 (fast-eval
                  (fourth expr)))))))
```

For Texas Instruments:

```
#+TI
(defun fast-eval (expr)
  "A fast evaluator that can be used with the
  Genetic Programming Paradigm for the TI Explorer."
  (cond ((consp expr)
         (let ((function (first expr)))
             (if (eq 'quote function)
                 (second expr)
                 (let ((fef (symbol-function function)))
                     (cond ((and (consp fef)
                                 (eq 'pseudo-macro (first fef)))
                            (apply (second fef) (rest expr)))
                           (t (fast-eval-fun)))))))
          ((symbolp expr) (symbol-value expr))
          (t expr)))
```

For CCL (Macintosh Common LISP):

```
#+:CCL
(defvar *pseudo-macro-tag* (compile nil '(lambda () nil)))

#+:CCL
(defun fast-eval (expr)
  "A fast evaluator that can be used with the
  Genetic Programming Paradigm for Macintosh Common Lisp."
  (cond ((consp expr)
```

```
                (let ((function (first expr)))
                    (if (eq 'quote function)
                        (second expr)
                        (let ((fef (symbol-function function)))
                            (cond ((eq fef *pseudo-macro-tag*)
                                    (apply (symbol-value function)
                                            (rest expr)))
                                  (t (fast-eval-fun)))))))
            ((symbolp expr) (symbol-value expr))
            (t expr)))
```

For Lucid and Franz LISPs:

```
#+(or EXCL Lucid)
(defun fast-eval (expr)
    "A fast evaluator that can be used with the
    Genetic Programming Paradigm for Lucid and Franz Lisps."
    (cond ((consp expr)
            (let ((function (first expr)))
                (if (eq 'quote function)
                    (second expr)
                    (let ((fef (symbol-function function)))
                        (cond ((compiled-function-p fef)
                                (fast-eval-fun))
                              ;; Then ASSUME we are a pseudo
                              ;; macro and are bound.
                              (t (apply (symbol-value function)
                                        (rest expr))))))))
          ((symbolp expr) (symbol-value expr))
          (t expr)))

(defun install-pseudo-macro (name implementation)
    "Install a pseudo-macro called Name, which is implemented
    by the function Implementation."
    #+(or EXCL Lucid :CCL)
    (setf (symbol-value name) implementation)
    (setf (symbol-function name)
        #+:CCL *pseudo-macro-tag*
        #-:CCL
        (list #+TI 'pseudo-macro
            #+(or EXCL Lucid :CCL) 'lambda
            #-(or TI EXCL Lucid :CCL)
                (error "A conditionalization for your lisp ~
                        must be added to install-pseudo-macro")
            implementation))
    (format t "~&;;; Installed ~S as the implementation of ~S"
            implementation name))
```

```
;;; Detect those implementations that know about fast-eval
(eval-when (compile load eval)
  #+(or Lucid EXCL TI :CCL)
  (pushnew :Fast-Eval *features*)
  nil)

#-:Fast-Eval
(warn "No implementation-specific version of fast-eval ~
       has been written.  Please write your own using ~
       the examples provided.")
```

One of the most time consuming aspects of evaluating the S-expressions for certain problems is the expansion of macros (such as the IFLTZ macro and other macros described in subsection 6.1.1). There is a faster way of implementing this functionality than simply using a Common LISP macro, which has been included in the above definition of FAST-EVAL. Instead of using a Common-LISP macro to define IFLTZ, for example, we can define a function that implements it and then mark the symbol IFLTZ in such a way that FAST-EVAL can specially interpret it. In the case of the Texas Instruments Explorer version of FAST-EVAL, we side-effect the SYMBOL-FUNCTION cell of the symbol IFLTZ so that it contains the list

```
(pseudo-macro #'ifltz-implementation).
```

This alternative implementation of IFLTZ is shown below.

```
(defun ifltz-implementation (then-clause else-clause)
  "An example implementation of a pseudo-macro. Note that the
   arguments are evaluated using fast-eval explicitly.
   This implements ifltz, the if x < 0 then do Then-clause
   else do the Else-clause."
  (declare (special x))
  (if (< x 0) (fast-eval then-clause) (fast-eval else-clause)))

;;; Registers ifltz-implementation as the implementation
;;;   of ifltz
#+:Fast-eval
(install-pseudo-macro 'ifltz #'ifltz-implementation)
```

Although the pseudo-macro mechanism is likely to be considerably faster than real Common-LISP macros on any implementation, there are some restrictions on its use. If FAST-EVAL as shown above is used, one cannot use any true macros in the function set. In addition, one probably cannot use any special forms, depending on the implementation. Common LISP macros and special forms could be supported by suitable tests for macro-function-p and special-form-p in FAST-EVAL; however, this may not be worthwhile because of the loss in performance. Thus, for example, the behavior of a macro such as IF would require implementation of a pseudo-macro such as MY-IF, which behaves like IF. It is shown below.

```
(defun my-if-implementation (condition then-clause else-clause
  "Implements MY-IF, which is a pseudo-macro just like IF."
  (if (fast-eval condition)
      (fast-eval then-clause)
      (fast-eval else-clause)))
;;; Registers my-if-implementation as the implementation of
;;;  my-if
#+:Fast-eval
(install-pseudo-macro 'my-if #'my-if-implementation)
```

Note that this restriction also applies to such operators as and and or. Thus, the user may have to write his own implementations of these operators. For example we might implement and and or either as pseudo-macros in the manner shown above, or as functions such as the strict and and or functions shown below (depending on whether the non-strict semantics of Common LISP's and and or operators are necessary).

```
(defun sand (a b)
  "Strict AND"
  (and a b))

(defun sor (a b)
  "Strict OR"
  (or a b))
```

As we have said, the pseudo-macro mechanism shown in FAST-EVAL above is likely to work in most Common-LISP implementations, but is not strictly portable. The user may have to find some other fast and unambiguous way to label functions which perform their own argument evaluation. If the user knows that he will never need any functions that are macro-like, he can eliminate the pseudo-macro mechanism from FAST-EVAL to gain a small performance improvement.

Note that in these examples of the pseudo-macro feature, we have conditionalized the code so that it will load only on those implementations for which it is known to work correctly. A warning is given for other implementations.

Some implementations not mentioned above may have error checks that prevent the user from marking the symbols that name the functions in the function set easily or may be inefficient in examining such a mark. Such problems can be circumvented by the inclusion of compiled function objects for the implementations of pseudo-macros directly into the function set, as follows:

```
(defun define-function-set-for-NON-HAMSTRUNG-SQUAD-CAR ()
  (values `(,#'ifX-implementation ,#'ifY-implementation)
          '(   3                        3)
  )
)
```

FAST-EVAL would have to be modified in order to detect objects that are (typep function 'compiled-function) and to act appropriately. The disadvantage of this is that pointers to the compiled function objects will be incorporated into the individual programs. This makes them harder for the user to read and interpret. A simple postprocessing stage could rectify this.

Appendix F: Editor for Simplifying S-Expressions

Although the user may or may not want to simplify individual S-expressions in the population during the run, he will almost certainly find it valuable to see a simplified version of S-expressions on his output interface and in his report files.

An editor for this purpose consists of a generic editing engine that recursively applies editing rules to a given S-expression. Edit rules are problem specific. For example, if the user has a Boolean problem, one possible edit rule would simplify (and x x) into x, whereas in a problem with floating-point variables, one might simplify (- x x) into 0.0.

Because of the need to apply all the edit rules to each node of the tree and to then retest each node that is changed by one edit rule by the other rules, editing rules can be very time consuming.

If the user so desires, this editor can be invoked from appropriate places in the kernel.

Editing rules are specified using the def-edit-rule form. To illustrate, six Boolean rules will be put into a rule base called *boolean-rules*.

```
(defvar *boolean-rules* nil
   "The rule base for Boolean problems.")
```

Five of the six editing rules are the basic simplification rules shown below:

```
;;; Transforms expressions of the form (not (not <xxx>)) into
;;; <xxx>.
(def-edit-rule not-not-x->-x *boolean-rules* (sexpression)
   :condition (and (consp sexpression)
                   (consp (second sexpression))
                   (eq (first sexpression) 'not)
                   (eq (first (second sexpression)) 'not))
   :action (replace-sexpression (second (second sexpression))))

;;; Transforms expressions of the form (or <xxx> t) into t.
(def-edit-rule or-t->-t *boolean-rules* (sexpression)
   :condition (and (consp sexpression)
                   (eq 'or (first sexpression))
                   (dolist (arg (rest sexpression) nil)
```

```lisp
                  (when (and (constant-expression-p arg)
                             (eval arg))
                    (return t))))
  :action (replace-sexpression t))

;;; Transforms expressions of the form (and nil <xxx>) into nil.
(def-edit-rule and-nil->-nil *boolean-rules* (sexpression)
  :condition (and (consp sexpression)
                  (eq 'and (first sexpression))
                  (dolist (arg (rest sexpression) nil)
                    (when (and (constant-expression-p arg)
                               (not (eval arg)))
                      (return t))))
  :action (replace-sexpression nil))

;;; Transforms expressions of the form (and t <xxx>) into <xxx>.
(def-edit-rule and-t->-x *boolean-rules* (sexpression)
  :condition (and (consp sexpression)
                  (eq 'and (first sexpression))
                  (dolist (arg (rest sexpression) nil)
                    (when (and (constant-expression-p arg)
                               (eval arg))
                      (return t))))
  :action (let ((remaining-args
                  (remove-if #'(lambda (arg)
                                 (and (constant-expression-p arg)
                                      (eval arg)))
                             (rest sexpression))))
            (replace-sexpression
              (case (length remaining-args)
                (0 t)
                (1 (first remaining-args))
                (otherwise (cons 'and remaining-args))))))

;;; Transforms expressions of the form (or <xxx> nil) into
;;; <xxx>.
(def-edit-rule or-nil->-x *boolean-rules* (sexpression)
  :condition (and (consp sexpression)
                  (eq 'or (first sexpression))
                  (dolist (arg (rest sexpression) nil)
                    (when (and (constant-expression-p arg)
                               (not (eval arg)))
                      (return t))))
  :action (let ((remaining-args
                  (remove-if #'(lambda (arg)
                                 (and (constant-expression-p arg)
                                      (not (eval arg))))
                             (rest sexpression))))
```

```
(replace-sexpression
  (case (length remaining-args)
    (0 nil)
    (1 (first remaining-args))
    (otherwise (cons 'or remaining-args))))))
```

In addition, the following rule converts multiple calls into one call with multiple arguments:

```
;;; Combines calls to AND and OR into their polyadic forms, so
;;; (and (and <xxx> <yyy>) <zzz>) will be transformed into (and
;;; <xxx> <yyy> <zzz>).
(def-edit-rule polyadicize *boolean-rules* (sexpression)
  :condition (and (consp sexpression)
                  (member (first sexpression) '(and or)
                          :test #'eq)
                  (dolist (arg (rest sexpression) nil)
                    (when (and (consp arg)
                               (eq (first arg)
                                   (first sexpression)))
                      (return t))))
  :action (let ((interesting-arg
                 (dolist (arg (rest sexpression) nil)
                   (when (and (consp arg)
                              (eq (first arg)
                                  (first sexpression)))
                     (return arg)))))
            (replace-sexpression
             (cons (first sexpression)
                   (append (rest interesting-arg)
                           (remove interesting-arg
                                   (rest sexpression)))))))
```

In addition, the user might want an editing rule using one of De Morgan's laws.

Since the total number of possible fitness cases is finite for Boolean functions, it is possible to develop editing rules which evaluate a given subS-expression for all possible fitness cases. If the subS-expression evaluates to a particular constant value, that constant value can be substituted for the S-expression. In this way, it is possible to simplify complicated S-expressions to a constant.

The user can develop his own editing rules for domains other than the Boolean domain.

The code for an editor to apply the user-specified set of problem-specific editing rules is shown below. To invoke this, the user should call the `edit-top-level-sexpression` function with the S-expression to be edited and a suitable rule base as its arguments.

```lisp
(defun edit-top-level-sexpression (sexpression rule-base)
  "Applies the rules in RULE-BASE to edit SEXPRESSION into
   a simpler form."
  (let ((location (list sexpression)))
    (edit-sexpression rule-base location sexpression)
    location))
(defun edit-sexpression (rule-base location sexpression)
  "Given a rule base (list of rules), an sexpression and the
   location of that sexpression in the containing expression,
   applies the rules to the sexpression and its arguments
   recursively. The rules are reapplied until a quiescent state
   is achieved."
  ;; Apply the edit rules to each of the arguments.
  ;; If something changes, try again.
  (when (consp sexpression)
    (do* ((args (rest sexpression) (rest args))
          (arg (first args) (first args))
          (arg-location (rest sexpression) (rest arg-location))
          (changed-p
            (edit-sexpression rule-base arg-location arg)
            (edit-sexpression rule-base arg-location arg)))
         ((not args)
          (when changed-p
            (edit-sexpression rule-base location sexpression)))
      nil))
  ;; Apply the edit rules to this expression. Say that
  ;; something has changed if any rule fires.
  (let ((changed-p nil))
    (dolist (clause rule-base)
      (let ((condition (second clause))
            (action (third clause)))
        (let ((applicable-p (funcall condition sexpression)))
          (when applicable-p
            (funcall action location sexpression)
            (setf changed-p t)))))
    changed-p))

(defun constant-expression-p (sexpression)
  "Is true of an sexpression if it evaluates to a constant.
   Note that this can be a problem domain specific problem."
  (if (consp sexpression)
      (do* ((args (rest sexpression) (rest args))
            (arg (first args) (first args)))
           ((not args) t)
        (unless (constant-expression-p arg)
          (return nil)))
      ;;; Assumes that variable quantities are always symbols
```

```
      ;;; and assumes that any symbol that is not self-
      ;;; evaluating is not constant (this will fail for pi)
      ;;; so to solve more general problems some extra
      ;;; convention would be required.
      (or (not (symbolp sexpression))
          (keywordp sexpression)
          (and (boundp sexpression)
               (eq sexpression (symbol-value sexpression))))))))

(defmacro def-edit-rule  (rule-name rule-base (sexpression-name)
                                    &key condition action)
  "Declares an edit rule called RULE-NAME in the RULE-BASE.
  SEXPRESSION-NAME is the local name to be given to the
  sexpression on which this rule is being invokes. The
  CONDITION clause is evaluated, and if it is true, the
  ACTION clause is evaluated. The action clause should
  make calls to REPLACE-SEXPRESSION to perform an edit."
  (assert (and condition action) ()
    "Both a condition and an action must be supplied.")
  `(setf ,rule-base
         (cons (list ',rule-name
                     #'(lambda (,sexpression-name) ,condition)
                     #'(lambda (location ,sexpression-name)
                         ,sexpression-name ,action))
               (remove (assoc ',rule-name ,rule-base :test #'eq)
                       ,rule-base))))

(defmacro replace-sexpression (new-sexpression)
  "The form to use in an edit rule that registers an edit.
  For example, if the sexpression being edited is to be
  replaced with the first argument to the function of the
  sexpression then we would say: (replace-sexpression (second
  the-sexpression)), where the-sexpression is the name of the
  sexpression supplied as an argument to def-edit-rule. This
  example would be useful if the function in question was an
  identity function. Thus:
  (def-edit-rule remove-identity-functions *my-rule-base*
               (the-sexpression)
    :condition (and (consp the-sexpression)
                    (eq (first the-sexpression) 'identity))
    :action (replace-sexpression (second the-sexpression)))"
  `(setf (first location) ,new-sexpression))
```

For example, evaluating the form

```
(edit-top-level-sexpression '(and x t) *boolean-rules*)
```

would return

```
x.
```

Appendix G: Testing the Simple LISP Code

Once the reader has entered the simple LISP code from appendixes B and C, it should be tested to verify that it is working correctly using the two test functions below.

The first test function is `test-gpp`, which embodies all of the testing example expressions used in the discussion of the particular problems supplied. It executes the tests and prints out the test forms for the tests that have been performed. Where appropriate, the reader should check the output from these tests against the expected output presented in this book.

```lisp
(defun test-gpp (&optional (report-stream *standard-output*))
  (let ((tests
          '((print (edit-top-level-sexpression '(and x t)
                     *boolean-rules*))
            (run-genetic-programming-system 'REGRESSION 1.0 1 50)
            (run-genetic-programming-system
              'REGRESSION 1.0 1 1 '(* 0.5 x x))
            (run-genetic-programming-system
              'MAJORITY-ON 1.0 1 1
              '(or (and d2 (and d1 (not d0)))
                  (or (and d2 (and (not d1) d0))
                     (or (and (not d2) (and d1 d0))
                        (and d2 (and d1 d0))))))
            (run-genetic-programming-system
              'NON-HAMSTRUNG-SQUAD-CAR 1.0 1 1
              '(ifX (goW) (ifY (goS) (goS) (goN)) (goE)))
            (print-population
              (run-genetic-programming-system 'REGRESSION 1.0 1 50))
            (run-genetic-programming-system 'REGRESSION 1.0 31 200)
            (run-genetic-programming-system 'MAJORITY-ON 1.0 21 100)
            (run-genetic-programming-system
              'NON-HAMSTRUNG-SQUAD-CAR 1.0 21 100))))
    (dolist (form tests)
      (eval form)
      (format report-stream "~&Finished test ~S" form))))
```

The second function is `time-test-gpp`. It will execute the same set of tests, sending the output to a file, printing out the test forms as they are evaluated and timing the whole set of tests. This provides a useful benchmark for measuring the performance of any particular implementation, or of the benefits of any optimizations that the reader might implement.

```
(defun time-test-gpp (&optional (path "gpp-test.text"))
  (let ((current-output-stream *standard-output*))
    (with-open-file (*standard-output* path
                                       :direction :output
                                       :if-exists :supersede)
      (time (test-gpp current-output-stream)))))
```

The reader may also want to test the behavior of `fast-eval` and the pseudo-macro feature. This can be done by redefining all of the fitness functions to call `fast-eval` instead of `eval`, and then changing the function sets as appropriate.

Thus, for the three problems above we would change the fitness functions as follows:

```
(defun evaluate-standardized-fitness-for-REGRESSION          ;01
             (program fitness-cases)                          ;02
   (let (raw-fitness hits standardized-fitness x target-value ;03
         difference value-from-program this-fitness-case)     ;04
     (setf raw-fitness 0.0)                                   ;05
     (setf hits 0)                                            ;06
     (dotimes (index *number-of-fitness-cases*)               ;07
       (setf this-fitness-case (aref fitness-cases index))    ;08
       (setf x                                                ;09
             (REGRESSION-fitness-case-independent-variable    ;10
                  this-fitness-case))                         ;11
       (setf target-value                                     ;12
             (REGRESSION-fitness-case-target                  ;13
                  this-fitness-case))                         ;14
       (setf value-from-program                               ;15
             (REGRESSION-wrapper (fast-eval program)))        ;16
       (setf difference (abs (- target-value                  ;17
                                value-from-program)))         ;18
       (incf raw-fitness difference)                          ;19
       (when (< difference 0.01) (incf hits)))                ;20
     (setf standardized-fitness raw-fitness)                  ;21
     (values standardized-fitness hits)                       ;22
   )                                                          ;23
 )                                                            ;24

(defun evaluate-standardized-fitness-for-MAJORITY-ON
           (program fitness-cases)
```

```
(let (raw-fitness hits standardized-fitness target-value
        match-found value-from-program fitness-case
        )
  (setf raw-fitness 0.0)
  (setf hits 0)
  (dotimes (index *number-of-fitness-cases*)
    (setf fitness-case (aref fitness-cases index))
    (setf d0 (MAJORITY-ON-fitness-case-d0 fitness-case))
    (setf d1 (MAJORITY-ON-fitness-case-d1 fitness-case))
    (setf d2 (MAJORITY-ON-fitness-case-d2 fitness-case))
    (setf target-value
          (MAJORITY-ON-fitness-case-target fitness-case))
    (setf value-from-program
          (MAJORITY-ON-wrapper (fast-eval program)))
    (setf match-found (eq target-value value-from-program))
    (incf raw-fitness (if match-found 1.0 0.0))
    (when match-found (incf hits))
    )
  (setf standardized-fitness (- 8 raw-fitness))
  (values standardized-fitness hits)
  )
)

(defun evaluate-standardized-fitness-for-NON-HAMSTRUNG-SQUAD-CAR
          (program fitness-cases)
  (let (raw-fitness hits standardized-fitness
        e-delta-x e-delta-y p-delta-x p-delta-y
        time-tally old-x old-y
        criterion
        (number-of-time-steps 50)
        )
    (setf criterion *speed-ratio*)
    (setf raw-fitness 0.0)
    (setf hits 0)
    (dotimes (icase *number-of-fitness-cases*)
      (setf x (NON-HAMSTRUNG-SQUAD-CAR-fitness-case-x
               (aref fitness-cases icase)
               )
      )
      (setf y (NON-HAMSTRUNG-SQUAD-CAR-fitness-case-y
               (aref fitness-cases icase)
               )
      )
      (setf time-tally 0.0)
      (catch :terminate-fitness-case-simulation
        (dotimes (istep number-of-time-steps)
```

```
            (setf old-x x)
            (setf old-y y)
            (when (and (<= (abs x) criterion)
                        (<= (abs y) criterion)
                    )
              (incf hits)
              (throw :terminate-fitness-case-simulation
                    :scored-a-hit
              )
            )
            ;; Note: (x,y) is position of the Evader.
            ;; Changing the position of EVADER changes X and Y.
            ;; Execute evader player for this time step
            (fast-eval
                '(ifY-evader
                    (goS-evader)
                    (ifX-evader (goW-evader)
                                (goS-evader) (goE-evader)
                    )
                    (goN-evader)
                )
            )
            (setf e-delta-x (- old-x x))
            (setf e-delta-y (- old-y y))
            ;; Reset position for Pursuer player.
            (setf x old-x)
            (setf y old-y)
              (NON-HAMSTRUNG-SQUAD-CAR-wrapper (fast-eval program))
            (setf p-delta-x (- old-x x))
            (setf p-delta-y (- old-y y))
            ;; Integrate x and y changes.
            (setf x (- old-x (+ p-delta-x e-delta-x)))
            (setf y (- old-y (+ p-delta-y e-delta-y)))
            (incf time-tally)
          )
        )
        (incf raw-fitness time-tally)
      )
      (setf standardized-fitness raw-fitness)
      (values standardized-fitness hits)
    )
)
```

Next, we need to redefine the function set of the MAJORITY-ON problem so that it does not use either and or or, which are macros. We use the strict definitions of and and or shown above.

```
(defun define-function-set-for-MAJORITY-ON ()
  (values '(sand sor not)
          '(   2   2   1)
    )
)
```

We must then replace the definitions of the position-comparing operators ifX etc. in the non-hamstrung squadcar problem so that they are now pseudo-macros.

```
(defun ifX-implementation (lt-0-arg eq-0-arg gt-0-arg)
  (cond ((>= x    *speed-ratio*)  (fast-eval gt-0-arg))
        ((<= x (- *speed-ratio*)) (fast-eval lt-0-arg))
        (t                        (fast-eval eq-0-arg))
    )
)

(install-pseudo-macro 'ifX #'ifX-implementation)

(defun ifY-implementation (lt-0-arg eq-0-arg gt-0-arg)
  (cond ((>= y *speed-ratio*) (fast-eval gt-0-arg))
        ((<= y (- *speed-ratio*)) (fast-eval lt-0-arg))
        (t                        (fast-eval eq-0-arg))
    )
)

(install-pseudo-macro 'ifY #'ifY-implementation)

(defun ifX-evader-implementation (lt-0-arg eq-0-arg gt-0-arg)
  (cond ((>= x  1) (fast-eval gt-0-arg))
        ((<= x -1) (fast-eval lt-0-arg))
        (t         (fast-eval eq-0-arg))
    )
)

(install-pseudo-macro 'ifX-evader #'ifX-evader-implementation)

(defun ifY-evader-implementation (lt-0-arg eq-0-arg gt-0-arg)
  (cond ((>= y  1) (fast-eval gt-0-arg))
        ((<= y -1) (fast-eval lt-0-arg))
        (t         (fast-eval eq-0-arg))
    )
)

(install-pseudo-macro 'ifY-evader #'ifY-evader-implementation)
```

Now, all that needs to be done is to redefine the test function to use the new functions where appropriate. We have observed improvements of up to ten-fold for the non-hamstrung squadcar problem (which benefits most from the pseudo-macros) and of about two-fold for the other problems here.

```
(defun test-gpp (&optional (report-stream *standard-output*))
  (let ((tests
```

```
     '((print (edit-top-level-sexpression '(and x t)
                 *boolean-rules*))
       (run-genetic-programming-system 'REGRESSION 1.0 1 50)
       (run-genetic-programming-system
         'REGRESSION 1.0 1 1 '(* 0.5 x x))
       (run-genetic-programming-system
         'MAJORITY-ON 1.0 1 1
         '(sor (sand d2 (sand d1 (not d0)))
               (sor (sand d2 (sand (not d1) d0))
                     (sor (sand (not d2) (sand d1 d0))
                          (sand d2 (sand d1 d0)))))))
       (run-genetic-programming-system
         'NON-HAMSTRUNG-SQUAD-CAR 1.0 1 1
         '(ifX (goW) (ifY (goS) (goS) (goN)) (goE)))
       (print-population
         (run-genetic-programming-system 'REGRESSION 1.0 1 50))
       (run-genetic-programming-system 'REGRESSION 1.0 31 200)
       (run-genetic-programming-system 'MAJORITY-ON 1.0 21 100)
       (run-genetic-programming-system
         'NON-HAMSTRUNG-SQUAD-CAR 1.0 21 100))))
   (dolist (form tests)
     (eval form)
     (format report-stream "~&Finished test ~S" form))))
```

Appendix H: Time-Saving Techniques

The user will find it rewarding to consider the following opportunities for saving computer time while running the genetic programming paradigm.

For both the conventional genetic algorithm operating on fixed-length strings and genetic programming, the vast majority of the computer time is, for any non-trivial problem, consumed by the calculation of fitness. In fact, this concentration is usually so great that *it will rarely pay to give any consideration at all to any other aspect of the run.*

The calculation of fitness for a given individual in the population on a given individual often requires several nested loops. For most problems, there is a loop over fitness cases. In problems involving simulations over time steps (or other steps), there may be an additional inner loop over the time steps. And, in problems such as a cellular automaton problem, there may also be an additional inner loop (or loops) over the additional dimension(s) of the problem.

Depending on the problem, the calculation of fitness may be streamlined in one or more of the following ways.

First, if the reproduction operation is used (as it is on 10% of the population on every generation on every problem in this book), there is no need to compute the fitness of a reproduced individual anew for the next generation (provided the user is not varying the fitness cases from generation to generation). Reproduced individuals can be flagged so that their fitness will not be recomputed in the new generation. This simple strategy of caching the already-computed fitness values can speed up *all* problems by the reproduction percentage p_r (i.e., 10%).

Second, if either the function set or the state-transition equations of the system being simulated involve transcendental functions (e.g., EXP, LOG, SIN, COS) that are computed via a Taylor series or other infinite series, a considerable amount of computer time can be saved by evaluating these functions via a look-up table. The savings from look-up tables is especially great when the transcendental functions appear in the function set because each individual S-expression often contains multiple occurrences of the transcendental function. In addition, when two related functions appear in state transition equations with the same argument (e.g., the sine and cosine functions appear this way in many state-transition equations), additional time can be saved by putting the vector of values of the two functions into the table and returning the vector of values from the table at the time of the look-up. Note that high resolution in the values of these transcendental functions is rarely required for machine learning purposes.

Third, in some problems, the values of all the state variables of the system may stabilize under various circumstances. If this occurs in a problem where the functions have no side effects, then it is not necessary to continue the simulation after the point of stabilization. The fitness may then merely be either the fitness accumulated up to that point or some simple adjustment to it. This stabilization occurs frequently in the wall-following problem (section 13.1), the cellular automata problem (section 14.2), and the artificial ant problem (section 7.2).

Fourth, if some trajectories through the state space of the problem are unacceptable for some reason exogenous to the mathematical calculation (e.g., the broom swinging through the floor in the broom balancing problem), a test for such unacceptable trajectories should be made so that the simulation of the system can be truncated as early as possible.

Fifth, if there are only a small number of possible combinations of values of the state variables of the system, a look-up table can be created and used in lieu of direct function evaluation. For example, for a two-dimensional cellular automaton involving Boolean state-transition functions operating in a von Neumann neighborhood at a distance of one unit, there are only $2^5 = 32$ possible combinations of inputs. A look-up can replace a function evaluation for each cell on each time step. The saving is especially great for complicated individual S-expressions containing a large number of points.

Sixth, some problems may involve complex intermediate calculations which can be simplified if one carefully considers the granularity of the data actually required to adequately solve the problem. For example, the calculation of the 12 sonar distances to the nearest walls in the wall-following problem involve complex and time-consuming trigonometric calculations. However, the nature of the problem is such that there is no need for great precision in these sonar distances. Consequently, a 100 by 100 grid can be overlaid on the room creating 10,000 small squares in the room. When the robot is in a particular square, the 12 sonar distances can be reported as if the robot were at the midpoint of the square. Thus, a table of size 10,000 by 12 can be computed once, placed in a file, and used forever after for this problem.

Seventh, in the truck backer upper problem (section 11.2) and many other problems, very little precision is required in the values of the four state variables. Typically, a single precision floating-point number in LISP (the default in most implementations of LISP) occupies two words of storage because of the tag bits required by LISP. Part of the first word contains a pointer to the second word. When very little precision is required for the floating-point numbers in a particular problem, the short float data type can be used. In the short float data type, the floating-point exponent and mantissa are sufficiently short so that they, along with the tag bits, fit into a single word of storage (i.e., usually 32 bits). This data type is faster and obviates consing. The short float data type is available on many implementations of LISP (including LISP on the Texas Instruments Explorer[TM] machines).

Eighth, when iterative operators (e.g., DU and SIGMA as described in chapter 18) are used, individual S-expressions in the population will often contain an unsatisfiable termination predicate. It is a practical necessity (when working on a bounded computer) to place limits on both the number of iterations allowed by any one execution of such an operator. Moreover, since the individual S-expressions in the population often contain deep nestings of such operators, a similar limit must be placed on the total number of iterations allowed for all such operators that may be evaluated in the process of evaluating any one individual S-expression for any particular fitness case. Thus, the termination predicate of each operator is actually an implicit disjunction of the explicit predicate for that operator and two additional implicit termination predicates. The typical time-out limits that we have used are that the DU operator times out if there have been more than 25 iterations for an evaluation of a single DU operator or if there have been a total of more than 100 iterations for all DU operators that are evaluated for a particular individual S-expression for a particular fitness case. Of course, if we could execute all the individual LISP S-expressions in parallel (as nature does) so that the infeasibility of one individual in the population does not bring the entire process to a halt, we would not need these limits. Note that even when a DU operator times out, it nevertheless returns a value. In particular, the DU operator evaluates to NIL if it times out. The value resulting from this evaluation of the DU operator is, of course, in addition to the side effects of the DU function on the state variables of the system (particularly the STACK and TABLE in the block-stacking problem). If the predicate of a DU operator is satisfied when the operator is first called, then the DU operator does no work at all and simply returns T. The iterative summation operator SIGMA is treated similarly.

Ninth, in problems for which the individual S-expressions are especially complicated or for which the individual S-expressions must be evaluated over an especially large number of fitness cases, a considerable amount of computer time may be saved by compiling each individual S-expression. If this is done, the S-expressions should be compiled into a temporary memory area, if possible, so that garbage collection can be programatically invoked when the compiled versions of the S-expressions are no longer needed. Many LISP systems cons new functions into a static memory area which, because it is not subject to garbage collection, will become clogged with unneeded function objects. Care must be taken to circumvent this behavior.

Tenth, in production runs, it is desirable to totally disable the graphics, animation, and all or part of most of the printed reports to save computer resources.

Eleventh, in LISP systems that allow programatic reboots, a reboot (and automatic restart of genetic programming) will significantly improve performance by reducing the effects of the memory fragmentation that occurs over time in most implementations of garbage collection in LISP.

Twelfth, the use of a streamlined version of the LISP function EVAL, as described in appendix E, can save a considerable amount of time.

Thirteenth, although we did not include type declarations in our simple LISP code, such declarations offer the opportunity to improve performance on many LISP implementations.

Fourteenth, after a program is debugged, it is often worthwhile to recompile the program with compiler optimization settings such as (speed 3) (safety 0) (compilation-speed 0) (space 0). The user should refer to the documentation of his own implementation for details.

Fifteenth, although genetic programming appears to be fairly insensitive to the settings of many of its minor parameters, we have observed significant increases in performance by the use of over-selection when large populations are involved (subsection 6.3.5 and section 25.6).

Sixteenth, if, for a particular problem, the fitness evaluation does not consume the vast majority of the computer time (as is usually the case), the roulette wheel in find-fitness-proportionate-individual and the sort-population-by-fitness function should be examined for possible savings. The find-fitness-proportionate-individual function is an $O(M^2)$ algorithm. When the population is large, it may consume a surprising amount of computer time. This function can be optimized with a simple indexing scheme. Similarly, our sort-population-by-fitness function allows runs to be replicated across different LISP implementations (assuming the randomizer seed and all other parameters are the same). However, the sort algorithm provided by the user's native implementation will usually be faster. If replicability is not required, the faster sort algorithm is preferable.

Seventeenth, vendor documentation may indicate certain garbage collection parameters that are worth setting. Note that if FAST-EVAL is used and if no floating-point numbers are being CONSed, genetic programming CONSes only at the transition between generations (though, of course, problem-specific code may CONS during generations. At that time, a lot of garbage is also cut loose. Care should be taken that the garbage collector does not tenure the individuals in the population.

Eighteenth, although it is possible to efficiently run genetic programming on a fast, well-configured workstation, genetic programming is a computationally intensive algorithm. It is especially desirable to have a large amount of both physical and virtual address space.

Nineteenth, the user should always use the metering and profiling software provided by his own machine and his own software to guide the optimization process. Many parts of the code for genetic programming are virtually irrelevant to optimization because they are used so infrequently that they do not matter.

Appendix I: List of Special Symbols

Table I.1 shows the definition and a section reference for each of the special symbols defined and used in more than one place in this book.

Table I.1 Special symbols.

Symbol	Definition	Reference
$I(M, i, z)$	Total number of individuals that must be processed to yield a desired result by generation i with probability z using a population of size M	8.1
K	Alphabet size for string	3.1
L	Length of string	3.1
M	Population size	3.1
G	Maximum number of generations to be run	3.1
$P(M, i)$	Cumulative probability of success by generation i with population size M	8.1
$R(z)$	Number of independent runs required to yield a desired result with probability z	8.1
*	"Don't care" symbol in a schema	3.1
#	Portion of an S-expression that has no side effects and whose return value is not used	13.1
$	Portion of an S-expression that is inaccessible by virtue of unsatisfiable conditions	17.1

Appendix J: List of Special Functions

Table J.1 shows the name, number of arguments, and a section or subsection reference for each of the special functions used in more than one place in this book.

Table J.1 Special functions used in this book.

Function	Name	Number of arguments	Section or subsection
%	Protected division	2	6.1.1
%MOD	Protected modulus	2	14.1
%QUOT	Protected integer division	2	14.1
ATG	Arctangent	2	11.2
GT	Greater Than	2	6.1.1
IFLTE	If Less Than or Equal	4	6.1.1
IFLTZ	If Less Than Zero	3	6.1.1
RLOG	Protected Natural Logarithm	1	6.1.1
SIG	Sign	1	7.1
SREXPT	Protected exponential	2	11.3
SRT	Protected Square Root	1	6.1.1

Bibliography

Aarts, Emile, and Korst, Jan. 1989. *Simulated Annealing and Boltzmann Machines*. Wiley.

Ali, M., Papadopoulus, C., and Clarkson, T. 1992. The use of fractal theory in a video compression system. In Storer, J. A. and Cohn, M. (editors), *Proceedings of the 1992 Data Compression Conference*. IEEE Computer Science Press.

Amarel, S. 1971. Representation and modeling in problems of program formation. In Meltzer, Bernard and Michie, Donald (editors). *Machine Intelligence 6*. Elsevier.

Anderson, Charles W. 1986. Learning and Problem Solving with Multiplayer Connectionist Systems. Ph.D. dissertation, Department of Computer and Information Sciences, University of Massachusetts.

Anderson, Charles W. 1988. Strategy Learning with Multiplayer Connectionist Representations. Technical Report TR-87-509.3, Self-Improving Systems Department, GTE Laboratories, Waltham, MA.

Anderson, Charles W. 1989. Learning to control an inverted pendulum using neural networks. *IEEE Control Systems Magazine* 9(3): 31–37.

Anderson, Stuart L. 1990. Random number generators on vector supercomputers and other advanced architectures. *SIAM Review* 32(2): 221–251.

Antonisse, Hendrik James, and Keller, K. S. 1987. Genetic operators for high-level knowledge representations. In Grefenstette, John J. (editor), *Genetic Algorithms and Their Applications: Proceedings of the Second International Conference on Genetic Algorithms*. Erlbaum.

Antonisse, Hendrik James. 1991. A grammar-based genetic algorithm. In Rawlins, Gregory (editor), *Foundations of Genetic Algorithms*. Morgan Kaufmann.

Arbib, Michael A. 1966. Simple self-reproducing universal automata. *Information and Control* 9: 177–189.

Axelrod, Robert. 1984. *The Evolution of Cooperation*. Basic Books.

Axelrod, Robert. 1987. The evolution of strategies in the iterated prisoner's dilemma. In Davis, Lawrence (editor), *Genetic Algorithms and Simulated Annealing*. Pittman.

Back, Thomas, Hoffmeister, Frank, and Schwefel, Hans-Paul. 1991. A survey of evolution strategies. In Belew, Richard and Booker, Lashon (editors), *Proceedings of the Fourth International Conference on Genetic Algorithms*. Morgan Kaufmann.

Bagley, Richard J., and Farmer, J. Doyne. 1991. Spontaneous emergence of a metabolism. In Langton, Christopher, et al. (editors). *Artificial Life II*. Addison-Wesley.

Baker, J. E. 1985. Reducing bias and inefficiency in the selection algorithm. In *Proceedings of an International Conference on Genetic Algorithms and Their Applications*. Erlbaum.

Barnsley, Michael. 1988. *Fractals Everywhere*. Academic Press.

Barto, A. G., Anandan, P., and Anderson, C. W. 1985. Cooperativity in networks of pattern recognizing stochastic learning automata. In Narendra, K. S. (editor), *Adaptive and Learning Systems*. Plenum.

Baston. V. J. D., and Bostock, F. A. 1987. Discrete hamstrung squad car games. *International Journal of Game Theory* 16(4): 253–261.

Belew, Richard, and Booker, Lashon (editors). 1991. *Proceedings of the Fourth International Conference on Genetic Algorithms*. Morgan Kaufmann.

Belew, Richard, McInerney, John, and Schraudolph, Nicol N. 1991. Evolving networks: Using the genetic algorithm with connectionist learning. In Langton, Christopher, et al. (editors), *Artificial Life II*. Addison-Wesley.

Bellman, R. 1961. *Adaptive Control Processes*. Princeton University Press.

Berlekamp, Elwyn R., Conway, John H., and Guy, Richard K. 1985. *Winning Ways*. Academic Press.

Berry, Donald A., and Fristedt, Bert. 1985. *Bandit Problems: Sequential Allocation of Experiments*. Chapman and Hall.

Bickel, A. S., and Bickel, R. W. 1987. Tree structured rules in genetic algorithms. In Davis, Lawrence (editor), *Genetic Algorithms and Simulated Annealing*. Pittman.

Booker, Lashon. 1987. Improving search in genetic algorithms. In Davis, Lawrence (editor), *Genetic Algorithms and Simulated Annealing*. Pittman.

Booker, Lashon, Goldberg, David E., and Holland, John H. 1989. Classifier systems and genetic algorithms. *Artificial Intelligence* 40: 235–282.

Bonner, John T. 1988. *The Evolution of Complexity by Means of Natural Selection*. Princeton University Press.

Bratley, Paul, and Millo, Jean. 1972. Computer recreations: Self-reproducing programs. *Software Practice and Experience* 2: 397–400.

Breeden, Joseph L., and Packard, Norman H. 1991. A Learning Algorithm for Optimal Representations of Experimental Data. Technical Report CCSR-91-3, Center for Complex Systems Research, Urbana, IL.

Brooks, Rodney. 1986. A robust layered control system for a mobile robot. *IEEE Journal of Robotics and Automation* 2(1): 14–23.

Brooks, Rodney. 1989. A robot that walks: Emergent behaviors from a carefully evolved network. *Neural Computation* 1(2): 253–262.

Brooks, Rodney, and Connell, Jonathan. 1986. Asynchronous distributed control system for a mobile robot. *SPIE Proceedings* 727:77–84.

Brooks, Rodney, Connell, Jonathan, and Flynn, A. 1986. A mobile robot with onboard parallel processor and large workspace arm. In *Proceedings of the Fifth National Conference on Artificial Intelligence*. Morgan Kaufmann.

Bryson, Arthur E., and Ho, Yu-Chi. 1975. *Applied Optimal Control*. Hemisphere.

Burger, John, Brill, David, and Machi, Filip. 1980. Self-reproducing programs. *Byte* 5(August): 72–74.

Burks, Arthur W. 1966. *Theory of Self Reproducing Automata*. University of Illinois Press.

Burks, Arthur W. 1970. *Essays on Cellular Automata*. University of Illinois Press.

Burks, Arthur W. 1987. Von Neumann's self-reproducing automata. In Aspray, William and Burks, Arthur (editors), *Papers of John von Neumann on Computing and Computer Theory*. MIT Press.

Buss, Leo W. 1987. *The Evolution of Individuality*. Princeton University Press.

Campbell, David K. 1989. Introduction to nonlinear phenomena. In Stein, Daniel L. (editor), *Lectures in the Sciences of Complexity*. Addison-Wesley.

Carbonell, Jaime G., Michalski, Ryszard S, and Mitchell, Tom M. 1986. An overview of machine learning. In Michalski, Ryszard S. et al. (editors), *Machine Learning: An Artificial Intelligence Approach*. Volume II. Morgan Kaufmann.

Cavicchio, Daniel J. 1970. Adaptive Search using Simulated Evolution. Ph.D. dissertation, Department of Computer and Communications Science, University of Michigan.

Chalmers, David J. 1991. The evolution of learning: An experiment in genetic connectionism. In Touretzky, David S., Elman, Jeffrey L., Sejnowski, Terrence J., and Hinton, Geoffrey E. (editors), *Connectionist Models: Proceedings of the 1990 Summer School*. Morgan Kaufmann.

Chaitin, Gregory J. 1987. *Algorithmic Information Theory*. Cambridge University Press.

Citibank. 1989. CITIBASE: Citibank Economic Database (Machine Readable Magnetic Data File), 1946–Present.

Codd, Edgar F. 1968. *Cellular Automata*. Academic Press.

Codd, Edgar F. 1992. Private communication, June 12, 1992.

Collins, J. S. 1968. A regression analysis program incorporating heuristic term selection. In Dale, Ella, and Michie, Donald (editors), *Machine Intelligence 2*. Elsevier.

Collins, Rob, and Jefferson, David. 1991a. Ant Farm: Toward simulated evolution. In Langton, Christopher, et al. (editors), *Artificial Life II*. Addison-Wesley.

Collins, Rob, and Jefferson, David. 1991b. Representations for artificial organisms. In Meyer, Jean-Arcady, and Wilson, Stewart W. (editors), *From Animals to Animats: Proceedings of the First International Conference on Simulation of Adaptive Behavior*. MIT Press.

Connell, Jonathan. 1990. *Minimalist Mobile Robotics*. Academic Press.

Craig, John J. 1986. *Introduction to Robotics*. Addison-Wesley.

Cramer, Nichael Lynn. 1985. A representation for the adaptive generation of simple sequential programs. In Grefenstette, John J. (editor), *Proceedings of an International Conference on Genetic Algorithms and Their Applications*. Erlbaum.

Dallemand, J. E. 1958. Stepwise Regression Program on the IBM 704. General Motors Research Staff Report GMR 199.

Darwin, Charles. 1859. *On the Origin of Species by Means of Natural Selection*. John Murray.

Davidor, Yuval. 1991. *Genetic Algorithms and Robotics*. World Scientific.

Davis, Lawrence (editor). 1987. *Genetic Algorithms and Simulated Annealing*. Pittman.

Davis, Lawrence. 1991. *Handbook of Genetic Algorithms*. Van Nostrand Reinhold.

Dawkins, Richard. 1987. *The Blind Watchmaker*. Norton.

Deb, Kalyanmoy. 1991. Binary and Floating-point Function Optimization Using Messy Genetic Algorithms. Report 91004, Illinois Genetic Algorithms Laboratory, Urbana.

De Jong, Kenneth A. 1975. An Analysis of the Behavior of a Class of Genetic Adaptive Systems. Ph.D. dissertation, Department of Computer Science, University of Michigan.

De Jong, Kenneth A. 1985. Genetic algorithms: A l0 year perspective. In Grefenstette, John J. (editor), *Proceedings of an International Conference on Genetic Algorithms and Their Applications.* Erlbaum.

De Jong, Kenneth A. 1987. On using genetic algorithms to search program spaces. In Grefenstette, John J. (editor), *Genetic Algorithms and Their Applications: Proceedings of the Second International Conference on Genetic Algorithms.* Erlbaum.

De Jong, Kenneth A. 1988. Learning with genetic algorithms: an overview. *Machine Learning* 3(2): 121–138.

De Jong, Kenneth A. (editor). 1990. *Machine Learning* 5(4) (special issue on genetic algorithms).

Deneubourg, J. L., Aron, S., Goss, S., Pasteels, J. M., and Duerinck, G. 1986. Random behavior, amplification processes and number of participants: How they contribute to the foraging properties of ants. In Farmer, Doyne, Lapedes, Alan, Packard, Norman, and Wendroff, Burton (editors), *Evolution, Games, and Learning.* North-Holland.

Deneubourg, J. L., Goss, S., Franks, N., Sendova-Franks, A., Detrain, C., and Chretien, L. 1991. The dynamics of collective sorting robot-like ants and ant-like robots. In Meyer, Jean-Arcady, and Wilson, Stewart W. (editors), *From Animals to Animats: Proceedings of the First International Conference on Simulation of Adaptive Behavior.* MIT Press.

Devaney, Robert L. 1989. *An Introduction to Chaotic Dynamical Systems.* Addison-Wesley.

Dewdney, A. K. 1984. In a game called core war hostile programs engage in a battle of bits. *Scientific American* 250 (May): 14–22.

Dewdney, A. K. 1985. A core war bestiary of viruses, worms and other threats to computer memories. *Scientific American* 252 (March): 14–23.

Dewdney, A. K. 1987. A program called MICE nibbles its way to victory at the first core war tournament. *Scientific American* 256 (January): 14–20.

Dewdney, A. K. 1989. Of worms, viruses, and Core War. *Scientific American* 260 (March): 110–113.

Doan, Thomas A. 1989. *User Manual for RATS—Regression Analysis of Time Series.* VAR Econometrics Inc.

Dudewicz, Edward J., and Ralley, Thomas G. 1981. *The Handbook of Random Number Generation and Testing with TESTRAND Computer Code.* American Sciences Press.

Dyson, F. 1985. *Origins of Life.* Cambridge University Press.

Edelman, Gerald M. 1987. *Neural Darwinism.* Basic Books.

Fogel, David B. 1991. The evolution of intelligent decision making in gaming. *Cybernetics and Systems* 22: 223–236.

Fogel, D. B. and Atmar, W. (editors). 1992. *Proceedings of the First Annual Conference on Evolutionary Programming.* San Diego: Evolutionary Programming Society.

Fogel, L. J., Owens, A. J., and Walsh, M. J. 1966. *Artificial Intelligence through Simulated Evolution.* Wiley.

Fontana, Walter. 1991a. Algorithmic Chemistry. In Langton, Christopher, et al. (editors), *Artificial Life II.* Addison-Wesley.

Fontana, W. 1991b. Functional self-organization in complex systems. In Nadel, L. and Stein, D. L. (editors), *1990 Lectures in Complex Systems.* Addison-Wesley.

Fontanari, J. F., and Meir, R. 1991. Evolving a learning algorithm for the binary perceptron. *Network* 2(4): 353–359.

Forrest, Stephanie. 1991. *Parallelism and Programming in Classifier Systems.* Pittman.

Forrest, Stephanie (editor). 1990. *Emergent Computation: Self-Organizing, Collective, and Cooperative Computing Networks*. MIT Press.

Frantz, Daniel R. 1991. A correction to Holland's two-armed bandit. Unpublished paper.

Friedberg, R. M. 1958. A learning machine: Part I. *IBM Journal of Research and Development*, 2(1): 2–13.

Friedberg, R. M., Dunham, B., and North, J. H. 1959. A learning machine: Part II. *IBM Journal of Research and Development* 3(3): 282–287.

Fujiki, Cory, and Dickinson, John. 1987. Using the genetic algorithm to generate LISP source code to solve the prisoner's dilemma. In Grefenstette, John J. (editor), *Genetic Algorithms and Their Applications: Proceedings of the Second International Conference on Genetic Algorithms*. Erlbaum.

Fujiki, Cory. 1986. An Evaluation of Holland's Genetic Algorithm Applied to a Program Generator. M.S. thesis, Department of Computer Science, University of Idaho.

Gardner, Martin. 1970. The fantastic combinations of John Conway's new solitaire game "Life." *Scientific American* 223(April): 120–123.

Gasser, Les, and Huhns, Michael N. 1989. *Distributed Artificial Intelligence, Volume II*. Pitman.

Genesereth, Michael R., and Nilsson, Nils J. 1987. *Logical Foundations of Artificial Intelligence*. Morgan Kaufmann.

Geva, S., Sitte, J., and Willshire, G. 1992. A one neuron truck backer-upper. *Proceedings of IJCNN International Joint Conference on Neural Networks*. Volume II.

Gittins, J. C. 1989. *Multi-Armed Bandit Allocation Indices*. Wiley.

Goldberg, David E. 1983. Computer-Aided Gas Pipeline Operation Using Genetic Algorithms and Rule Learning. Ph.D. dissertation. University of Michigan.

Goldberg, David E. 1989. *Genetic Algorithms in Search, Optimization, and Machine Learning*. Addison-Wesley.

Goldberg, David E., and Holland, John H. (editors). 1988. *Machine Learning* 3(2/3) (special issue on genetic algorithms).

Goldberg, David E., Korb, Bradley, and Deb, Kalyanmoy. 1989. Messy genetic algorithms: Motivation, analysis, and first results. *Complex Systems* 3(5): 493–530.

Goldberg, David E., and Deb, Kalyanmoy. 1991. A comparative analysis of selection schemes used in genetic algorithms. In Rawlins, Gregory (editor), *Foundations of Genetic Algorithms*. Morgan Kaufmann.

Goldberg, David E., and Samtani, M.P. 1986. Engineering optimization via genetic algorithms. In *Proceedings of the Ninth Conference on Electronic Computation*.

Goss, S., and Deneubourg, J. L. 1992. Harvesting by a group of robots. In Varela, Francisco J., and Bourgine, Paul (editors), *Toward a Practice of Autonomous Systems: Proceedings of the first European Conference on Artificial Life*. MIT Press.

Green, Cordell C., Waldinger, R, Barstow, D., Elschlager, R., Lenat, D., McCune, B., Shaw, D. and Steinberg, L. 1974. *Progress Report on Program-Understanding Systems*. Artificial Intelligence Laboratory memo AIM-240, Stanford University Computer Science Department. Also available as Stanford University Computer Science Department technical report STAN-CS-74-444.

Grefenstette, John J. (editor). 1985. *Proceedings of an International Conference on Genetic Algorithms and Their Applications*. Erlbaum.

Grefenstette, John J. (editor). 1987. *Genetic Algorithms and Their Applications: Proceedings of the Second International Conference on Genetic Algorithms*. Erlbaum.

Grefenstette, John J. 1989. A system for learning control strategies with genetic algorithms. In Schaffer, J. D. (editor), *Proceedings of the Third International Conference on Genetic Algorithms*. Morgan Kaufmann.

Hallman, Jeffrey J., Porter, Richard D., and Small, David H. 1989. *M2 per Unit of Potential GNP as an Anchor for the Price Level*. Staff Study 157, Board of Governors of the Federal Reserve System.

Hicklin, Joseph F. 1986. Application of the Genetic Algorithm to Automatic Program Generation. M.S. thesis, Department of Computer Science, University of Idaho.

Hightower, R. 1992. The Devore universal computer constructor. Presentation at Third Workshop on Artificial Life, Santa Fe.

Hillis, W. Daniel. 1990. Co-evolving parasites improve simulated evolution as an optimization procedure. In Forrest, Stephanie (editor), *Emergent Computation: Self-Organizing, Collective, and Cooperative Computing Networks*. MIT Press.

Hillis, W. Daniel. 1991. Co-evolving parasites improve simulated evolution as an optimization procedure. In Langton, Christopher, et al. (editors), *Artificial Life II*. Addison-Wesley.

Hinton, Geoffrey. 1989. Connectionist learning procedures. *Artificial Intelligence* 40: 185–234.

Holland, John H. 1975. *Adaptation in Natural and Artificial Systems*. University of Michigan Press.

Holland, J. H. 1976. Studies of the spontaneous emergence of self-replicating systems using cellular automata and formal grammars. In Lindenmayer, Aristid, and Rozenberg, G. (editors), *Automata, Languages, Development*. North-Holland.

Holland, John H. 1986. Escaping brittleness: The possibilities of general-purpose learning algorithms applied to parallel rule-based systems. In Michalski, Ryszard S., et al. (editors), *Machine Learning: An Artificial Intelligence Approach, Volume II*. Morgan Kaufmann.

Holland, John H. 1990. ECHO: Explorations of evolution in a miniature world. Paper presented at Second Workshop on Artificial Life, Santa Fe, New Mexico.

Holland, John H. 1992. *Adaptation in Natural and Artificial Systems*, second edition. MIT Press.

Holland, John H., and Burks, Arthur W. 1987. Adaptive Computing System Capable of Learning and Discovery. U.S. Patent 4,697,242. Issued September 29, 1987.

Holland, John H., and Burks, Arthur W. 1989. Method of Controlling a Classifier System. U.S. Patent 4,881,178. Issued November 14, 1989.

Holland, John H., Holyoak, K.J., Nisbett, R.E., and Thagard, P.A. 1986. *Induction: Processes of Inference, Learning, and Discovery*. MIT Press.

Holland, John H., and Reitman, J.S. 1978. Cognitive systems based on adaptive algorithms. In Waterman, D. A., and Hayes-Roth, Frederick (editors), *Pattern-Directed Inference Systems*. Academic Press.

Holldobler, Bert, and Wilson, Edward O. 1990. *The Ants*. Belknap Press.

Huhns, Michael N. 1987. *Distributed Artificial Intelligence*. Pittman.

Humphrey, Thomas M. 1989. Precursors of the P-star model. *Economic Review* (Federal Reserve Bank of Richmond), July–August: 3–9.

Isaacs, Rufus. 1965. *Differential Games*. Wiley.

Jefferson, David, Collins, Robert, Cooper, Claus, Dyer, Michael, Flowers, Margot, Korf, Richard, Taylor, Charles, and Wang, Alan. 1991. Evolution as a theme in artificial life: The genesys/tracker system. In Langton, Christopher, et al. (editors), *Artificial Life II*. Addison-Wesley.

Kampis, George. 1991. *Self-Modifying Systems in Biology and Cognitive Science*. Pergamon.

Kemeny, J. G. 1955. Man viewed as a machine. *Scientific American*. 192(4).

Kirkpatrick, S., Gelatt, C. D., and Vecchi, M. P. 1983. Optimization by simulated annealing. *Science* 220: 671–680.

Knuth, Donald E. 1981a. *The Art of Computer Programming*, volume 1. Addison-Wesley.

Knuth, Donald E. 1981b. *The Art of Computer Programming*, volume 2. Addison-Wesley.

Kodratoff, Yves, and Michalski, Ryszard S. 1990. *Machine Learning: An Artificial Intelligence Approach, Volume III*. Morgan Kaufmann.

Kordestani, Paul. 1983. *Gamester's Guide to Arcade Video Games*. TAB Books.

Koza, John R. 1972. On Inducing a Non-Trivial, Parsimonious, Hierarchical Grammar for a Given Sample of Sentences. Ph.D. dissertation, Department of Computer Science, University of Michigan.

Koza, John R. 1988. Non-Linear Genetic Algorithms for Solving Problems. U.S. Patent Application filed May 20, 1988.

Koza, John R. 1989. Hierarchical genetic algorithms operating on populations of computer programs. In *Proceedings of the 11th International Joint Conference on Artificial Intelligence*, volume 1. Morgan Kaufmann.

Koza, John R. 1990a. *Genetic Programming: A Paradigm for Genetically Breeding Populations of Computer Programs to Solve Problems*. Stanford University Computer Science Department technical report STAN-CS-90-1314.

Koza, John R. 1990b. A genetic approach to econometric modeling. Paper presented at Sixth World Congress of the Econometric Society, Barcelona, Spain.

Koza, John R. 1990c. Genetically breeding populations of computer programs to solve problems in artificial intelligence. In *Proceedings of the Second International Conference on Tools for AI*. IEEE Computer Society Press.

Koza, John R. 1990d. Non-Linear Genetic Algorithms for Solving Problems. U.S. Patent 4,935,877. Issued June 19, 1990.

Koza, John R. 1990e. Non-Linear Genetic Algorithms for Solving Problems by Finding a Fit Composition of Functions. U.S. Patent Application filed March 28, 1990.

Koza, John R. 1991a. Evolution and co-evolution of computer programs to control independent-acting agents. In Meyer, Jean-Arcady, and Wilson, Stewart W. (editors), *From Animals to Animats: Proceedings of the First International Conference on Simulation of Adaptive Behavior*. MIT Press.

Koza, John R. 1991b. Concept formation and decision tree induction using the genetic programming paradigm. In Schwefel, Hans-Paul, and Maenner, Reinhard (editors), *Parallel Problem Solving from Nature*. Springer-Verlag.

Koza, John R. 1991c. Genetic evolution and co-evolution of computer programs. In Langton, Christopher, et al. (editors), *Artificial Life II*. Addison-Wesley.

Koza, John R. 1991d. A hierarchical approach to learning the Boolean multiplexer function. In Rawlins, Gregory (editor), *Foundations of Genetic Algorithms*. Morgan Kaufmann.

Koza, John R. 1991e. Evolving a computer program to generate random numbers using the genetic programming paradigm. In Belew, Rik, and Booker, Lashon (editors), *Proceedings of the Fourth International Conference on Genetic Algorithms*. Morgan Kaufmann.

Koza, John R. 1991f. A genetic approach to econometric modeling. In Bourgine, Paul, and Walliser, Bernard (editors), *Economics and Cognitive Science*. Pergamon.

Koza, John R. 1992a. Evolution of subsumption using genetic programming. In Varela, Francisco J., and Bourgine, Paul (editors), *Toward a Practice of Autonomous Systems: Proceedings of the first European Conference on Artificial Life*. MIT Press.

Koza, John R. 1992b. The genetic programming paradigm: Genetically breeding populations of computer programs to solve problems. In Soucek, Branko and the IRIS Group (editors), *Dynamic, Genetic, and Chaotic Programming*. Wiley.

Koza, John R. 1992c. A genetic approach to finding a controller to back up a tractor-trailer truck. In *Proceedings of the 1992 American Control Conference*. American Automatic Control Council.

Koza, John R. 1992d. A genetic approach to the truck backer upper problem and the inter-twined spirals problem. In *Proceedings of International Joint Conference on Neural Networks, Baltimore, June 1992*. IEEE Press.

Koza, John R. 1992e. Hierarchical automatic function definition in genetic programming. In Whitley, Darrell (editor), *Proceedings of Workshop on the Foundations of Genetic Algorithms and Classifier Systems, Vail, Colorado 1992*. Morgan Kaufmann.

Koza, John R., and Keane, Martin A. 1990a. Cart centering and broom balancing by genetically breeding populations of control strategy programs. In *Proceedings of International Joint Conference on Neural Networks, Washington, January 15–19, 1990*, volume I. Erlbaum.

Koza, John R., and Keane, Martin A.1990b. Genetic breeding of non-linear optimal control strategies for broom balancing. In *Proceedings of the Ninth International Conference on Analysis and Optimization of Systems, Antibes, France*. Springer-Verlag.

Koza, John R., and Rice, James P. 1990. A Non-Linear Genetic Process for Use with Co-Evolving Populations. U.S. Patent Application filed September 18, 1990.

Koza, John R., and Rice, James P. 1991a. Genetic generation of both the weights and architecture for a neural network. In *Proceedings of International Joint Conference on Neural Networks, Seattle, July 1991*, volume II. IEEE Press.

Koza, John R., and Rice, James P. 1991b. A genetic approach to artificial intelligence. In Langton, C. G. (editor), *Artificial Life II Video Proceedings*. Addison-Wesley.

Koza, John R., and Rice, James P. 1992a. Automatic programming of robots using genetic programming. In *Proceedings of Tenth National Conference on Artificial Intelligence*. AAAI Press / MIT Press.

Koza, J. R., and Rice, J. P. 1992b. A Non-Linear Genetic Process for Data Encoding and for Solving Problems Using Automatically Defined Functions. U.S. Patent Application filed May 11, 1992.

Koza, J. R., and Rice, J. P. 1992c. A Non-Linear Genetic Process for Problem Solving Using Spontaneously Emergent Self-Replicating and Self-Improving Entities. U.S. Patent Application filed June 16, 1992.

Koza, J. R., Rice, J. P., and Roughgarden, J. 1992. Evolution of Food Foraging Strategies for the Caribbean Anolis Lizard Using Genetic Programming. Santa Fe Institute Working Paper 92-06-028.

Laing, R. 1976. Automaton introspection. *Journal of Computer and System Sciences* 13: 172–183.

Laing, R. 1977. Automaton models of reproduction by self-inspection. *Journal of Theoretical Biology* 66: 437–456.

Lang, Kevin J., and Witbrock, Michael J. 1989. Learning to tell two spirals apart. In Touretzky, David S., Hinton, Geoffrey E., and Sejnowski, Terrence J. (editors), *Proceedings of the 1988 Connectionist Models Summer School*. Morgan Kaufmann.

Langley, Pat, and Zytkow, Jan M. 1989. Data-driven approaches to empirical discovery. *Artificial Intelligence* 40: 283–312.

Langley, Pat, Simon, Herbert A., Bradshaw, Gary L., and Zytkow, Jan M. 1987. *Scientific Discovery: Computational Explorations of the Creative Process*. MIT Press.

Langton, Christopher G. 1983. Self-reproduction in cellular automata. In Farmer, Doyne, Toffoli, Tommaso, and Wolfram, Stephen (editors), *Cellular Automata: Proceeding of an Interdisciplinary Workshop, Los Alamos*. North-Holland.

Langton, Christopher G. 1986. Studying artificial life with cellular automata. In Farmer, Doyne, Lapedes, Alan, Packard, Norman, and Wendroff, Burton (editors), *Evolution, Games, and Learning*. North-Holland.

Langton, Christopher G. (editor). 1989. *Artificial Life, Santa Fe Institute Studies in the Sciences of Complexity*, volume VI. Addison-Wesley.

Langton, Christopher G., et al. (editors). 1991. *Artificial Life II*. Addison-Wesley.

Langton, Christopher G. (editor). 1991a. *Artificial Life II Video Proceedings*. Addison-Wesley.

Langton, Christopher G. 1991b. Self-reproducing loops and virtual ants. In Langton, Christopher G. (editor). 1991a. *Artificial Life II Video Proceedings*. Addison-Wesley.

Lee, Tsu-Chang. 1991. *Structure Level Adaptation for Artificial Neural Networks*. Kluwer.

Legendi, T., Parkinson, D., Vollmar, R., and Wolf, G. (editors). 1987. *Parallel Processing by Cellular Automata and Arrays*. North-Holland.

Lenat, Douglas B. 1976. AM: An Artificial Intelligence Approach to Discovery in Mathematics as Heuristic Search. Ph.D. dissertation. Computer Science Department, Stanford University. Also available as Stanford University Computer Science Department technical report STAN-CS-76-570 and Stanford University Artificial Intelligence Laboratory memo AIM-286.

Lenat, Douglas B. 1977. Automated theory formation in mathematics. In *Proceedings of the Fifth International Joint Conference on Artificial Intelligence*. William Kaufmann.

Lenat, Douglas B. 1983. The role of heuristics in learning by discovery: Three case studies. In Michalski, Ryszard S. et al. (editors), *Machine Learning: An Artificial Intelligence Approach, Volume I*. Morgan Kaufmann.

Lenat, Douglas B., and Brown, John Seely. 1984. Why AM and EURISKO appear to work. *Artificial Intelligence* 23: 269–294.

Lindenmayer, Aristid. 1968. Mathematical models for cellular interactions in development, I & II. *Journal of Theoretical Biology* 18: 280–315.

Lindenmayer, Aristid, and Rozenberg, G. (editors). 1976. *Automata, Languages, Development*. North-Holland.

Macki, Jack, and Strauss, Aaron. 1982. *Introduction to Optimal Control*. Springer-Verlag.

Maes, Pattie. 1990. *Designing Autonomous Agents*. MIT Press.

Maes, Pattie, and Brooks, Rodney A. 1990. Learning to coordinate behaviors. In *Proceedings of AAAI-90*. MIT Press.

Magurran, Anne E. 1988. *Ecological Diversity and Its Measurement*. Princeton University Press.

Mahadevan, Sridhar, and Connell, Jonathan. 1990. *Automatic Programming of Behavior-based Robots using Reinforcement Learning*. Technical Report RC 16359, IBM Research Division.

Mahadevan, Sridhar, and Connell, Jonathan. 1991. Automatic programming of behavior-based robots using reinforcement learning. In *Proceedings of Ninth National Conference on Artificial Intelligence*, volume 2. AAAI Press / MIT Press.

Manneville, P., Boccara, N., Vichniac, G.Y., and Bidaux, R. 1989. *Cellular Automata and Modeling of Complex Physical Systems*. Springer-Verlag.

Marsaglia, George. 1968. Random numbers fall mainly in the planes. *Proceedings of the National Academy of Sciences U.S.A.* 61: 25–28.

Marsaglia, George. 1983. Random number generation. In Ralston, A., and Reilly, E.D.,Jr. (editors), *Encyclopedia of Computer Science and Engineering*. Van Nostrand Reinhold.

Mataric, Maja J. 1990. A Distributed Model for Mobile Robot Environment-Learning and Navigation. MIT Artificial Intelligence Laboratory technical report AI-TR-1228.

McIntosh, Harold V. 1991. Wolfram's class IV automata and a good life. In Gutowitz, Howard (editor), *Cellular Automata: Theory and Experiment*. MIT Press.

Meyer, Jean-Arcady, and Wilson, Stewart W. (editors). 1991. *From Animals to Animats: Proceedings of the First International Conference on Simulation of Adaptive Behavior*. MIT Press.

Meyer, Thomas P., Richards, Fred C., and Packard, Norman H. 1989. A learning algorithm for modeling. *Physical Review Letters* 63(16).

Meyer, Thomas P., Richards, Fred C. and Packard, Norman H. 1991. Extracting cellular automaton rules directly from experimental data. In Gutowitz, Howard (editor), *Cellular Automata: Theory and Experiment*. MIT Press.

Meyer, Thomas P., and Packard, Norman H. 1991. Local Forecasting of High-dimensional Chaotic Dynamics. Technical Report CCSR-91-1, Center for Complex Systems Research, Urbana, IL.

Michalewicz, Z. 1992. *Genetic Algorithms + Data Structures = Evolution Programs*. Springer-Verlag.

Michalski, Ryszard S. 1983. A theory and methodology of inductive learning. In Michalski, Ryszard S., Carbonell, Jaime G., and Mitchell, Tom M. (editors), *Machine Learning: An Artificial Intelligence Approach, Volume I*. Morgan Kaufmann.

Michalski, Ryszard S., Carbonell, Jaime G., and Mitchell, Tom M. (editors). 1983. *Machine Learning: An Artificial Intelligence Approach, Volume I*. Morgan Kaufmann.

Michalski, Ryszard S., Carbonell, Jaime G., and Mitchell, Tom M. (editors). 1986. *Machine Learning: An Artificial Intelligence Approach, Volume II*. Morgan Kaufmann.

Michalski, Ryszard S., and Stepp, Robert E. 1983. Learning from observation: Conceptual clustering. In Michalski, Ryszard S. et al. (editors), *Machine Learning: An Artificial Intelligence Approach, Volume I*. Morgan Kaufmann.

Michie, Donald, and Chambers, R. A. 1968. Boxes: An experiment on adaptive control. In Dale, Ella, and Michie, Donald (editors), *Machine Intelligence 2*. Elsevier.

Miller, John H. 1988. Two Essays on the Economics of Imperfect Information. Ph.D. dissertation, Department of Economics, University of Michigan.

Miller, John H. 1989. The Co-evolution of Automata in the Repeated Prisoner's Dilemma. Santa Fe Institute Report 89-003.

Miller, Geoffrey F., Todd, Peter M. and Hegde, S. U. 1989. Designing Neural Networks using Genetic Algorithms. In Schaffer, J. D. (editor), *Proceedings of the Third International Conference on Genetic Algorithms*. Morgan Kaufmann.

Mills, R. D. 1987. Using a small algebraic manipulation system to solve differential and integral equations by variational and approximation techniques. *Journal of Symbolic Computation* 3(3): 291–301.

Minsky, Marvin L., and Papert, Seymour A. 1969. *Perceptrons*. MIT Press.

Mitchell, Tom M., Utgoff, Paul E., and Banerji, Ranan. 1983. Learning by experimentation: Acquiring and refining problem-solving heuristics. In Michalski, Ryszard S. et al. (editors), *Machine Learning: An Artificial Intelligence Approach, Volume I*. Morgan Kaufmann.

Mural, Richard J., Mann, Reinhold C., and Uberbacher, Edward C. 1991. Pattern recognition in DNA sequences: The intron-exon junction problem. In Cantor, Charles R., and Lim, Hwa A. (editors), *The First International Conference on Electrophoresis, Supercomputing, and the Human Genome*. World Scientific.

Myhill, John. 1970. The abstract theory of self-reproduction. In Burks, Arthur W. (editor), *Essays on Cellular Automata*. University of Illinois Press.

Newell, Allen, Shaw, J. C., and Simon, Herbert A. 1960. A variety of intelligent learning in a general problem solver. In Yovits, Marshall C. and Cameron, Scott (editors), *Self-Organising Systems*. Pergamon.

Nilsson, Nils J. 1980. *Principles of Artificial Intelligence*. Morgan Kaufmann.

Nilsson, Nils J. 1989. Action networks. In Tenenberg, J. et al. (editors), *Proceedings from the Rochester Planning Workshop: From Formal Systems to Practical Systems*. University of Rochester Computer Science Department technical report 284.

Nilsson, Nils J. 1990. *The Mathematical Foundations of Learning Machines*. Morgan Kaufmann.

Nisan, Noam. 1992. *Using Hard Problems to Create Pseudorandom Generators*. MIT Press.

Nguyen, Derrick, and Widrow, Bernard. 1990. The truck backer-upper: An example of self-learning in neural networks. In Miller, W. Thomas III, Sutton, Richard S., and Werbos, Paul J. (editors), *Neural Networks for Control*. MIT Press.

Packard, Norman H. 1990. A genetic learning algorithm for the analysis of complex data. *Complex Systems*. 4(5): 543–572.

Park, S. K., and Miller, K. W. 1988. Random number generators: Good ones are hard to find. *Communications of the ACM*. 31: 1192–1201.

Prusinkiewicz, Przemyslaw, and Lindenmayer, Aristid. 1990. *The Algorithmic Beauty of Plants*. Springer-Verlag.

Quinlan, J. R. 1986. Induction of decision trees. *Machine Learning* 1 (1): 81–106.

Rasmussen, S., Knudsen, C., Feldberg, R., and Hindsholm, M. 1990. The coreworld: Emergence and evolution of cooperative structures in a computational chemistry. In Forrest, S. (editor), *Emergent Computation: Self-Organizing, Collective, and Cooperative Computing Networks*. MIT Press.

Rasmussen, Steen, Knudsen, Carsten, and Feldberg, Rasmus. 1991. Dynamics of programmable matter. In Langton, Christopher, et al. (editors), *Artificial Life II*. Addison-Wesley.

Rawlins, Gregory (editor). 1991. *Foundations of Genetic Algorithms*. Morgan Kaufmann.

Ray, Thomas S. 1990. Evolution and optimization of digital organisms. In Brown, H. (editor), *Proceedings of the 1990 IBM Supercomputing Competition: Large Scale Computing Analysis and Modeling Conference*. MIT Press.

Ray, Thomas S. 1991a. An approach to the synthesis of life. In Langton, Christopher, et al. (editors), *Artificial Life II*. Addison-Wesley.

Ray, Thomas S. 1991b. Is is alive or is it GA? In Belew, Rik, and Booker, Lashon (editors), *Proceedings of the Fourth International Conference on Genetic Algorithms*. Morgan Kaufmann.

Ray, Thomas S. 1991c. Population dynamics of digital organisms. In C. G. Langton (editor), *Artificial Life II Video Proceedings*. Addison-Wesley.

Ray, T. S. 1991d. Evolution and optimization of digital organisms. In K. Billingsley et al. (editors), *Scientific Excellence in Supercomputing*. Baldwin.

Resnick, Mitchel. 1991. Animal simulations with *Logo: Massive parallelism for the masses. In Meyer, Jean-Arcady, and Wilson, Stewart W. (editors), *From Animals to Animats: Proceedings of the First International Conference on Simulation of Adaptive Behavior*. MIT Press.

Riolo, Rick L. 1988a. Empirical Studies of Default Hierarchies and Sequences of Rules in Learning Classifier Systems. Ph.D. dissertation, University of Michigan Department of Computer Science and Engineering.

Riolo, Rick L. 1988b. CFS-C: A Package of Domain-independent Subroutines for Implementing Classifier Systems in Arbitrary, User-Defined Environments. Technical Report. Logic of Computers Group. Division of Computer Science and Engineering, University of Michigan. Updated version.

Ritchie, G. D., and Hanna, F. K. 1984. AM: A case study in AI methodology. *Artificial Intelligence* 23: 249–268.

Robertson, George. 1987. Parallel implementation of genetic algorithms in a classifier system. In Davis, L. (editor), *Genetic Algorithms and Simulated Annealing*. Pittman.

Rosenblatt, Frank. 1958. The perceptron: A probabilistic model for information storage and organization in the brain. *Psychological Review* 65: 386–407.

Roughgarden, J. 1979. *Theory of Population Genetics and Evolutionary Ecology: An Introduction.* Macmillan.

Roughgarden, J. 1989. In Roughgarden, J. May, R. M., and Levin, S. A. (editors), *Perspectives in Ecological Theory*. Princeton University Press.

Roughgarden, J. 1992. *Anolis Lizards of the Caribbean: Ecology, Evolution, and Plate Tectonics.* Oxford University Press.

Rumelhart, D. E., Hinton, G. E., and Williams, R. J. 1986. Learning internal representations by error propagation. In Rumelhart, D. E., McClelland, J. L., and the PDP Research Group (editors), *Parallel Distributed Processing*, volume 1. MIT Press.

Samuel, Arthur L. 1959. Some studies in machine learning using the game of checkers. *IBM Journal of Research and Development* 3(3): 210–229.

Schuster, P. 1985. Evolution of self-replicating molecules—a comparison of various models for selection. In Demongeot, J., Goles, E., Tchuente, M. (editors), *Dynamical Systems and Cellular Automata*. Academic Press.

Schwefel, Hans-Paul, and Maenner, Reinhard (editors). 1991. *Parallel Problem Solving from Nature.* Springer-Verlag.

Schaffer, J. D. 1987. Some effects of selection procedures on hyperplane sampling by genetic algorithms. In Davis, L. (editor), *Genetic Algorithms and Simulated Annealing*. Pittman.

Schaffer, J. D. (editor). 1989. *Proceedings of the Third International Conference on Genetic Algorithms.* Morgan Kaufmann.

Schalkoff, Robert. 1992. *Pattern Recognition: Statistical, Structural, and Neural Approaches.* Wiley.

Selfridge, Oliver G. 1966. Pandemonium: A paradigm for learning. In Uhr, Leonard (editor), *Pattern Recognition*. Wiley.

Shrager, Jeff, and Langley, Pat. 1990. *Computational Models of Scientific Discovery and Theory Formation*. Morgan Kaufmann.

Shaefer, Craig G. 1987. The ARGOT strategy: Adaptive representation genetic optimizer technique. In Grefenstette, John J. (editor), *Genetic Algorithms and Their Applications: Proceedings of the Second International Conference on Genetic Algorithms*. Erlbaum.

Shavlik, Jude W., and Dietterich, Thomas G. 1990. *Readings in Machine Learning*. Morgan Kaufmann.

Shen, W.-M. 1989. Functional transformations in AI discovery systems. *Artificial Intelligence* 41: 257–272.

Simon, Herbert A. 1979. *Models of Thought*. Yale University Press.

Sims, Karl. 1991a. Artificial evolution for Computer Graphics. *Computer Graphics* 25(4): 319–328.

Sims, Karl. 1991b. Panspermia. In Langton, Christopher G. (editor), *Artificial Life II Video Proceedings*. Addison-Wesley.

Sims, Karl. 1992a. Interactive evolution of dynamical systems. In Varela, Francisco J., and Bourgine, Paul (editors), *Toward a Practice of Autonomous Systems: Proceedings of the first European Conference on Artificial Life*. MIT Press.

Sims, Karl. 1992b. Interactive evolution of equations for procedural models. In *Proceedings of IMAGINA conference, Monte Carlo, January 29–31, 1992*.

Skipper, Jakob. 1992. The complete zoo evolution in a box. In Varela, Francisco J., and Bourgine, Paul (editors), *Toward a Practice of Autonomous Systems: Proceedings of the first European Conference on Artificial Life*. MIT Press.

Smith, Alvy Ray. 1991. Simple non-trivial self-reproducing machines. In Langton, C. G. (editor), *Artificial Life II*. Addison-Wesley.

Smith, John Maynard. 1986. Evolutionary game theory. In Farmer, Doyne, Lapedes, Alan, Packard, Norman, and Wendroff, Burton (editors), *Evolution, Games, and Learning*. North-Holland.

Smith, John Maynard. 1989. *Evolutionary Genetics*. Oxford University Press.

Smith, Steven F. 1980. A Learning System Based on Genetic Adaptive Algorithms. Ph.D. dissertation, University of Pittsburgh.

Smith, Steven F. 1983. Flexible learning of problem solving heuristics through adaptive search. In *Proceeding of the Eighth International Conference on Artificial Intelligence*. Morgan Kaufmann.

Spafford, Eugene H. 1991. Computer viruses—a form of artificial life? In Langton, Christopher, et al. (editors), *Artificial Life II*. Addison-Wesley.

Steele, Guy L. Jr. 1990. *Common LISP*. Second Edition. Digital Press.

Steels, Luc. 1990. Cooperation between distributed agents using self-organization. In Demazeau, Y., and Muller, J.-P. (editors), *Decentralized AI*. North-Holland.

Steels, Luc. 1991. Toward a theory of emergent functionality. In Meyer, Jean-Arcady, and Wilson, Stewart W. (editors), *From Animals to Animats: Proceedings of the First International Conference on Simulation of Adaptive Behavior*. MIT Press.

Stork, David G., Jackson, Bernie, and Walker, Scott. 1991. Non-optimality via pre-adaptation in simple neural systems. In Langton, Christopher, et al. (editors), *Artificial Life II*. Addison-Wesley.

Tanese, Reiko. 1989. Distributed Genetic Algorithm for Function Optimization. Ph.D. dissertation. Department of Electrical Engineering and Computer Science, University of Michigan.

Thatcher, J. W. 1970. Self-describing Turing machines and self-reproducing cellular automata. In Burks, Arthur W. (editor), *Essays on Cellular Automata*. University of Illinois Press.

Toffoli, T., and Margolus, N. 1987. *Cellular Automata Machines*. MIT Press.

Tolstov, Georgi P. 1962. *Fourier Series*. Dover.

Travers, Michael, and Resnick, Mitchel. 1991. Behavioral dynamics of an ant colony: Views from three Levels. In Langton, Christopher G. (editor), *Artificial Life II Video Proceedings*. Addison-Wesley.

Uhr, Leonard, and Vossler, Charles. 1966. A pattern recognition program that generates, evaluates, and adjusts its own operators. In Uhr, Leonard (editor), *Pattern Recognition*. Wiley.

Varela, Francisco J., and Bourgine, Paul (editors). 1992. *Toward a Practice of Autonomous Systems: Proceedings of the first European Conference on Artificial Life*. MIT Press.

van Laarhoven, P. J. M., and Aarts, Emile H. 1987. *Simulated Annealing; Theory and Applications*. Reidel.

von Neumann, John. 1987. Probabilistic logics and the synthesis of reliable organisms from unreliable components. In Aspray, William, and Burks, Arthur (editors), *Papers of John von Neumann on Computing and Computer Theory*. MIT Press.

Watkins, Christopher. 1989. Learning from Delayed Rewards. Ph.D. thesis. King's College, Cambridge.

Westerdale, Thomas H. 1985. The bucket brigade is not genetic. In *Proceedings of an International Conference on Genetic Algorithms and Their Applications*. Erlbaum.

Westervelt, F. H. 1960. Automatic System Simulation Programming. Ph.D. dissertation, University of Michigan.

Whitley, D. 1989. The GENITOR algorithm and selection pressure: Why rank-based allocation of reproductive trials is best. In Schaffer, J. D. (editor), *Proceedings of the Third International Conference on Genetic Algorithms*. Morgan Kaufmann.

Whitley, D., Starkweather, T., and Bogart, C. 1990. Genetic algorithms and neural networks: Optimizing connections and connectivity. *Parallel Computing* 14(3): 347–361.

Widrow, Bernard. 1963. Pattern recognizing control systems. In *Computer and Information Sciences (COINS) Symposium Proceedings*. Spartan Books.

Widrow, Bernard. 1987. The original adaptive neural net broom balancer. *IEEE International Symposium on Circuits and Systems*, volume 2.

Wieland, Alexis P. 1991. Evolving controls for unstable systems. In Touretzky, David S., Elman, Jeffrey L., Sejnowski, Terrence J., and Hinton, Geoffrey E. (editors), *Connectionist Models: Proceedings of the 1990 Summer School*. Morgan Kaufmann.

Wilson, Stewart. W. 1987a. Classifier Systems and the animat problem. *Machine Learning* 3(2): 199–228.

Wilson, Stewart W. 1987b. Hierarchical credit allocation in a classifier system. In *Proceedings of the Tenth International Joint Conference on Artificial Intelligence*.

Wilson, Stewart W. 1988. Bid competition and specificity reconsidered. *Complex Systems* 2(6): 705–723.

Wilson, Stewart W. 1990. Perceptron redux: emergence of structure. In Forrest, Stephanie (editor), *Emergent Computation: Self-Organizing, Collective, and Cooperative Computing Networks*. MIT Press.

Wolfram, Stephen. 1986. Random sequence generation by cellular automata. In Wolfram (editor), *Theory and Applications of Cellular Automata*. World Scientific.

Wolfram, Stephen. 1988. *Mathematica—A System for Doing Mathematics by Computer*. Addison-Wesley.

Yarmolik, V. N., and Demidenko, S. N. 1988. *Generation and Application of Pseudorandom Sequences for Random Testing*. Wiley.

Index

Classification, 14, 67, 439–457
  in decision-tree induction, 14, 439–442,
    633–642
  in grammar induction, 442–445
  and intertwined spirals, 445–457
Classifier system, 64–65, 90, 119, 189
Closure, 81–86, 103, 135, 707–708
Co-evolution, 94
  and absolute fitness, 431–434
  and ECHO system, 430, 648, 654
  and game strategy, 429–437
  and populations, 758
  and prisoner's dilemma game, 65, 430
  and raw fitness, 434
  and relative fitness, 431–434
Cohort, 615–617
Color images, 280–287
Common LISP, 68, 705, 765–770
Compiler settings, 786
Compiling individuals, 483
Complexity. *See* Structural complexity
Computation effort, 54, 192–201. *See*
  Performance curves
Computational universality, 645–646
Concept formation. *See* ID3; Parity; Boolean
  multiplexers
Concept learning. *See* ID3; Parity; Boolean
  multiplexers
Concepts, 232–236
Concept sets, 1
Conceptual clusters, 1, 68
Conditional branching operators, 83–86
Conditional comparative operators, 83–86
  greater-than (GT), 83, 129
  if-less-than-zero (IFLTZ), 83
  if-greater-than-or-equal (IFLTE), 83, 348
Conferences, 60–61
Conflict resolution, 358–359
Congruential randomizer, 400
Connection Machine, 59
CONSing, 784–785
Consistency, 4–5
Constants, creation of, 242–245, 621, 707
Constrained syntactic structures, 479–526
  adders, 484–487, 513–526
  and chaos, 507–513
  and dynamical system, 507–513
  and Fourier-series problem, 496–502
  and global optimum point problem,
    490–493
  and inverse kinematics problem, 503–507
  and linear equations, 487–490
  and local tracking of dynamical system,
    507–513

and logistic function problem, 507–513
and multiple symbolic regression problem,
  480–484
and neural net problem, 513–526
and one-bit adder problem, 513–526
and quadratic equations problem, 493–496
and two-bit adder circuit problem, 484–487
Constraints, violations of, 53
Construction universal, 645
Control parameters, 114–116, 628–630,
  641, 714. *See also* Tableau *for particular
  problem*
decision trees, 642
in *Evolutionsstrategie* (ES), 641
genetic algorithm, 27–28, 641
in genetic programming, 114–116, 628–
  630, 641
in hill climbing, 41
neural net, 513–526, 641
in simulated annealing, 642
Control strategy, 10, 124. *See also* Optimal
  control
Control variable. *See* Optimal control
Convergence, 104, 616–618, 701–702
  premature, 104, 191, 616–618, 701–702
Copernicus, 6
COPY- TREE function, 664, 750
Coral Common LISP, 765
Core wars, 648
Correctness, 4–5, 130, 464–470
Credit, allocation of, 38, 64–65, 119
Crossover, 18
  and disruption, 49, 119
  for programs, 74–75, 101–105
  for strings, 23–24
  kernel, 748–751
  mutation, with, 599–600, 607–608
  probability of (p_c), 24, 114–116
  remainder in, 23–24, 101–105
  structure-preserving, 479, 481–482
Crossover fragments
  for programs, 101–105
  for strings, 23–24
  kernel, 750–753
Crossover point
  and default method of selection, 114–116
  for programs, 101–105
  for strings, 23–24
  kernel, 750–753
  structure-preserving, 481–482
Culling, random, 572–575, 663
Cutoff radius, 315

Damage, catastrophic, 569, 572–575

Boolean 6-multiplexer, generative methods, 598

Boolean 6-multiplexer, mutation, 600, 608

Boolean 6-multiplexer, permutation, 600

Boolean 6-multiplexer, sampling fitness values, 572

Boolean 6-multiplexer, selection methods, 606

catastrophic damage, 574

crossover operation, 608

crossover points, limiting, 611, 612

cubic polynomial, extraneous variables, 584

editing, 602

encapsulation, effect of, 601

extraneous functions, 587, 589, 590–591

extraneous IF function, 587

extraneous two-argument Boolean functions, 589

extraneous random constants, 586

extraneous variables, 584

fault tolerance, 569, 572–575

fitness-proportionate selection, 606, 608

generative methods, 598–599

incomplete fitness values, 572

limiting crossover points, 611, 612

linear equations, generative methods, 599

multiple regression, 611

mutation, effect of, 600, 608

neural network design problem, 612

permutation, effect of, 600

quartic polynomial, extraneous random constants, 586,

quartic polynomial, generative methods, 598

reproduction, 608

sampling fitness values, 572

saving the best, 608

segregating crossover points, 611, 612

selection methods, 606

simulated evolution, 608

structure-preserving crossover, 611, 612

symbolic regression, simple, 598

tournament selection, 606

Problems

adder, 484–487, 513–526

ants, 54–59, 147–162, 329–344

argument list with HADF, 608–610

artificial ant, 10, 54–59, 89–90, 147–162, 202, 578–581, 590–599

bang-bang controllers, 10, 122–147, 289–307

biathlon, 578–581

block stacking, 10, 459–470

Boolean changing environment, 575–577

Boolean circuit design, 484–487

Boolean majority-on function, 719–725, 778–782

Boolean concept learning, 11

Boolean 3-multiplexer, 186, 189

Boolean 6-multiplexer, 185–189, 207–208, 572–575

Boolean 6-multiplexer, editing, 602

Boolean 6-multiplexer, encapsulation, 601

Boolean 6-multiplexer, extraneous IF function, 586–587

Boolean 6-multiplexer, extraneous Boolean functions, 587–590

Boolean 6-multiplexer, generative methods, 597–599

Boolean 6-multiplexer, greedy over-selection, 602–604

Boolean 6-multiplexer, inaccurate fitness, 571–572

Boolean 6-multiplexer, incomplete fitness, 571–572

Boolean 6-multiplexer, mutation, 599–600, 607–608

Boolean 6-multiplexer, noisy fitness, 571–572

Boolean 6-multiplexer, over-selection, 602–604

Boolean 6-multiplexer, permutation, 600–601

Boolean 6-multiplexer, sampling fitness, 571–572

Boolean 6-multiplexer, selection methods, 597–599

Boolean 6-multiplexer, variety, 608–609

Boolean 11-multiplexer, 11, 170–189, 206–207

box moving, 381–393

broom balancing, 10, 289–307

cart centering, 10, 122–147, 202

catastrophic damage, 572–575

cellular automaton, one-dimensional, 408–413

cellular automaton, two-dimensional, 413–417

central place foraging, 329–339

changing Boolean environment, 575–577

changing environment, biathlon, 578–581

chaos, 507–513

circuit design, 484–487

co-evolution of game strategy, 429–437

collecting behavior, 340–344

complex multiplication, 480–484, 610–612

cube root of 2, 274–280

decision-tree induction, 439–442

differential equations, 264–271, 470–473

Tableaux (cont.)
pursuer-evader game, 427
quadratic equations, 495
random integer problem, 401
sequence induction, 282
series solution to differential equation, 472
simple symbolic regression, 164
spirals problem, 446
symbolic integration, 260
symbolic regression, 164, 482
task prioritization, 351
Taylor-series problem, 472
trigonometric identities, 240
truck-backer-upper, 310
two-bit adder, 486
wall following, 368
Target criterion, 292
Target function, 162–169, 238–242, 701
Target image, 284
Target state, 123, 133
Taylor series, 470–473, 624, 783
Templates 443
ECHO, 648, 654
Ray's self-reproducing program, 647–648
Tierra, 647–648, 654
Terminal set, 80, 619–621. *See also* Tableau *for particular problem*
closure, 81–86
extraneous terminals, 583–585
sufficiency, 86–88
Termination criterion, 26–29, 113, 137–138, 302, 306–307, 614–618, 630–631, 641, 715, 732. *See also* Tableau *for particular problem*
Threshold processing element, 59, 514
Tierra, 647–651, 654
Time-out limits, 133, 149, 193, 294, 367
DU operator, 462, 785
iterative summation, 471, 785
Time-saving techniques, 783–786
broom balancing, 293, 784
cellular automaton, 413–414
compiler settings, 786
compiling individuals, 785
CONSing, 784–785
declarations, type, 786
FAST-EVAL function, 765–770, 786
fitness, dominance of, 713
fragmentation, memory, 785
garbage collection, 785–786
granularity of data, 784
greedy over-selection, 98–99, 602–604, 786
infinite loops, 462, 471, 785

lookup tables, 378, 413–414, 474, 783–784
macro expansion, 768
memory fragmentation, 785
memory needs, 786
metering, 786
over-selection, greedy, 98–99, 602–604, 786
periodicity of states, 414
precision of data, 279, 285, 311, 319, 401, 784
reproduction operation, 100–101, 783, 786
roulette wheel, 786
SHORT-FLOAT data type, 285, 311, 319, 784
sorting, 744, 786
stabilization of states, 378, 414, 784
Taylor series, 783
termination of simulation, 784
time-out limits, 462, 471, 785
trajectories, unacceptable, 784
transcendental functions, 783
truth table, 414
type declarations, 786
wall following, 378
TOTO robot, 360–367
Tournament selection, 100, 604–607
Training cases. *See* Fitness cases
Trajectory
through program space, 3, 145–146
through state space, 125
unacceptable, 784
Transcendental functions, 783
Transcription, 443, 646
Transfer RNA (tRNA), 649
Translation, 646
Treasury bill yields, 246–249
Truth table, 210, 413–414, 417, 657, 665
Turing gas, 654
Turing machine, 645–646
Two-armed bandit (TAB), 42–50
Two, cube root of, 274–280
Type declarations, 786

Undefined variables, 82, 471–473
Underflows, 708, 760
Unification, 357
Universal computation, 645–646
Universal planning, 10, 459–470

Value-defining branch, 503, 527, 535
Value-returning branch, 503, 527, 535
Vanilla representation scheme, 52
Variety, 48, 93–94, 160, 608–609, 614–618, 699, 701–702